Lafeu: They say miracles are past: and we have our philosophical persons, to make modern and familiar things supernatural and causeless. Hence it is that we make trifles of terrors, esconcing ourselves into seeming knowledge when we should submit ourselves to an unknown fear.

William Shakespeare, All's Well that Ends Well.

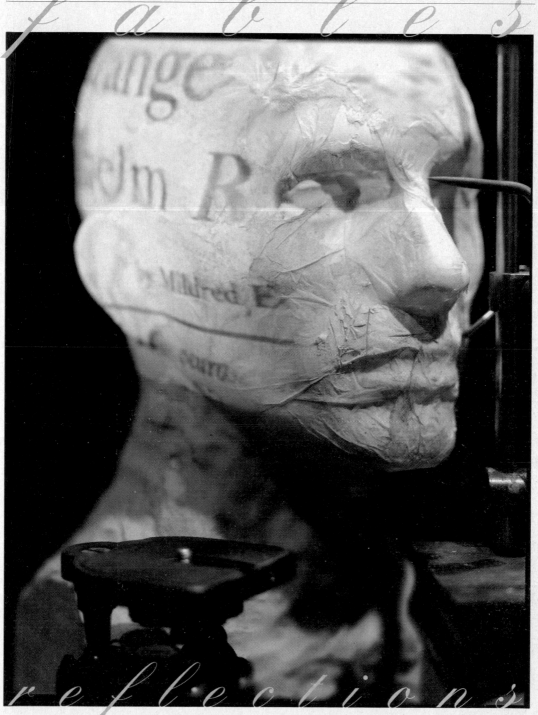

I know the story, you see. I'm writing it all down for you. So it'll be remembered.

Rustichello of Pisa.

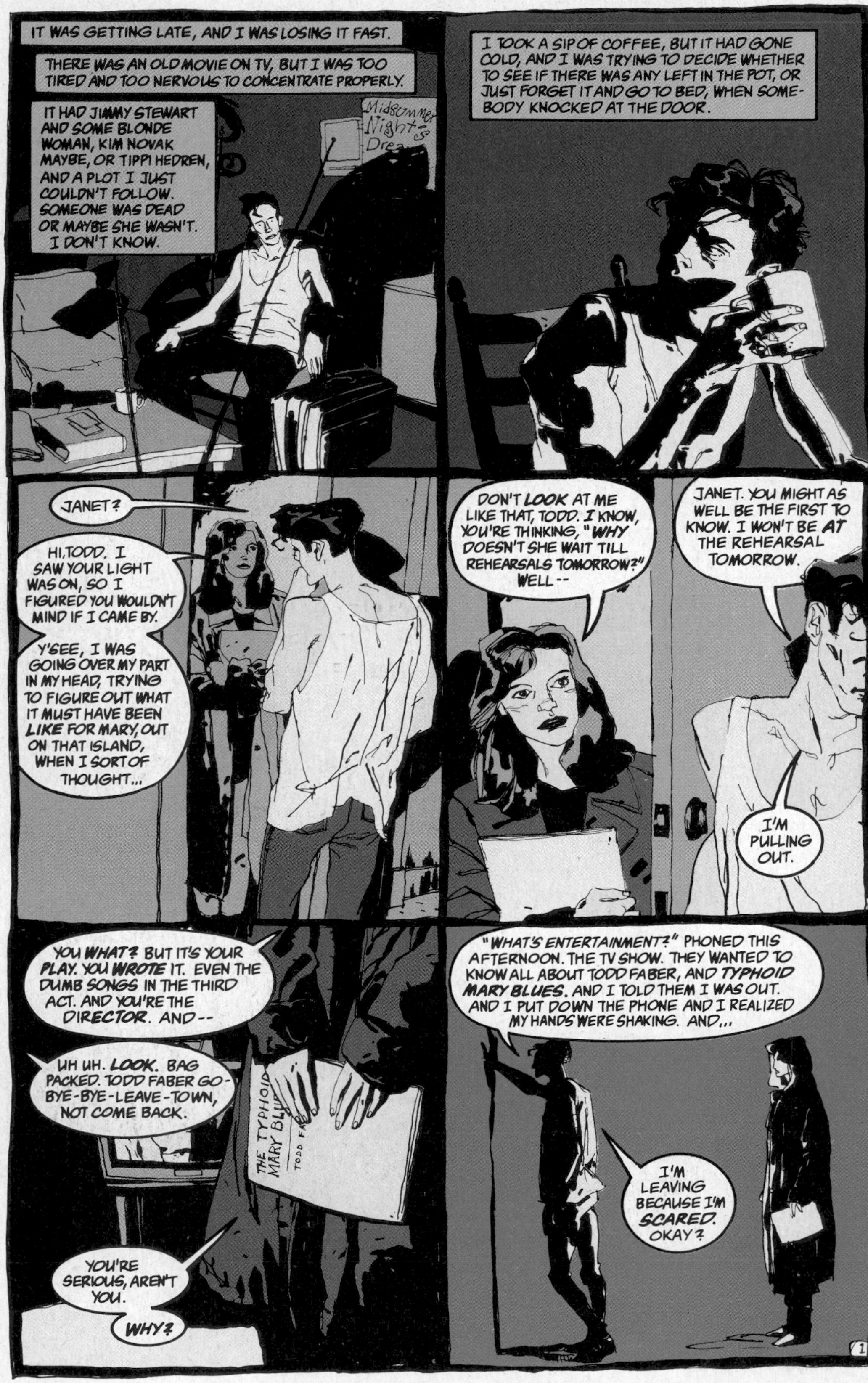
IT WAS GETTING LATE, AND I WAS LOSING IT FAST.
THERE WAS AN OLD MOVIE ON TV, BUT I WAS TOO TIRED AND TOO NERVOUS TO CONCENTRATE PROPERLY.
IT HAD JIMMY STEWART AND SOME BLONDE WOMAN, KIM NOVAK MAYBE, OR TIPPI HEDREN, AND A PLOT I JUST COULDN'T FOLLOW. SOMEONE WAS DEAD OR MAYBE SHE WASN'T. I DON'T KNOW.
I TOOK A SIP OF COFFEE, BUT IT HAD GONE COLD, AND I WAS TRYING TO DECIDE WHETHER TO SEE IF THERE WAS ANY LEFT IN THE POT, OR JUST FORGET IT AND GO TO BED, WHEN SOMEBODY KNOCKED AT THE DOOR.
JANET?
HI, TODD. I SAW YOUR LIGHT WAS ON, SO I FIGURED YOU WOULDN'T MIND IF I CAME BY.
Y'SEE, I WAS GOING OVER MY PART IN MY HEAD, TRYING TO FIGURE OUT WHAT IT MUST HAVE BEEN LIKE FOR MARY, OUT ON THAT ISLAND, WHEN I SORT OF THOUGHT...
DON'T LOOK AT ME LIKE THAT, TODD. I KNOW, YOU'RE THINKING, "WHY DOESN'T SHE WAIT TILL REHEARSALS TOMORROW?" WELL --
JANET. YOU MIGHT AS WELL BE THE FIRST TO KNOW. I WON'T BE AT THE REHEARSAL TOMORROW.
I'M PULLING OUT.
YOU WHAT? BUT IT'S YOUR PLAY. YOU WROTE IT. EVEN THE DUMB SONGS IN THE THIRD ACT. AND YOU'RE THE DIRECTOR. AND --
UH UH. LOOK. BAG PACKED. TODD FABER GO-BYE-BYE-LEAVE-TOWN, NOT COME BACK.
THE TYPHOID MARY BLU
YOU'RE SERIOUS, AREN'T YOU.
WHY?
"WHAT'S ENTERTAINMENT?" PHONED THIS AFTERNOON. THE TV SHOW. THEY WANTED TO KNOW ALL ABOUT TODD FABER, AND TYPHOID MARY BLUES. AND I TOLD THEM I WAS OUT. AND I PUT DOWN THE PHONE AND I REALIZED MY HANDS WERE SHAKING. AND...
I'M LEAVING BECAUSE I'M SCARED. OKAY?
1

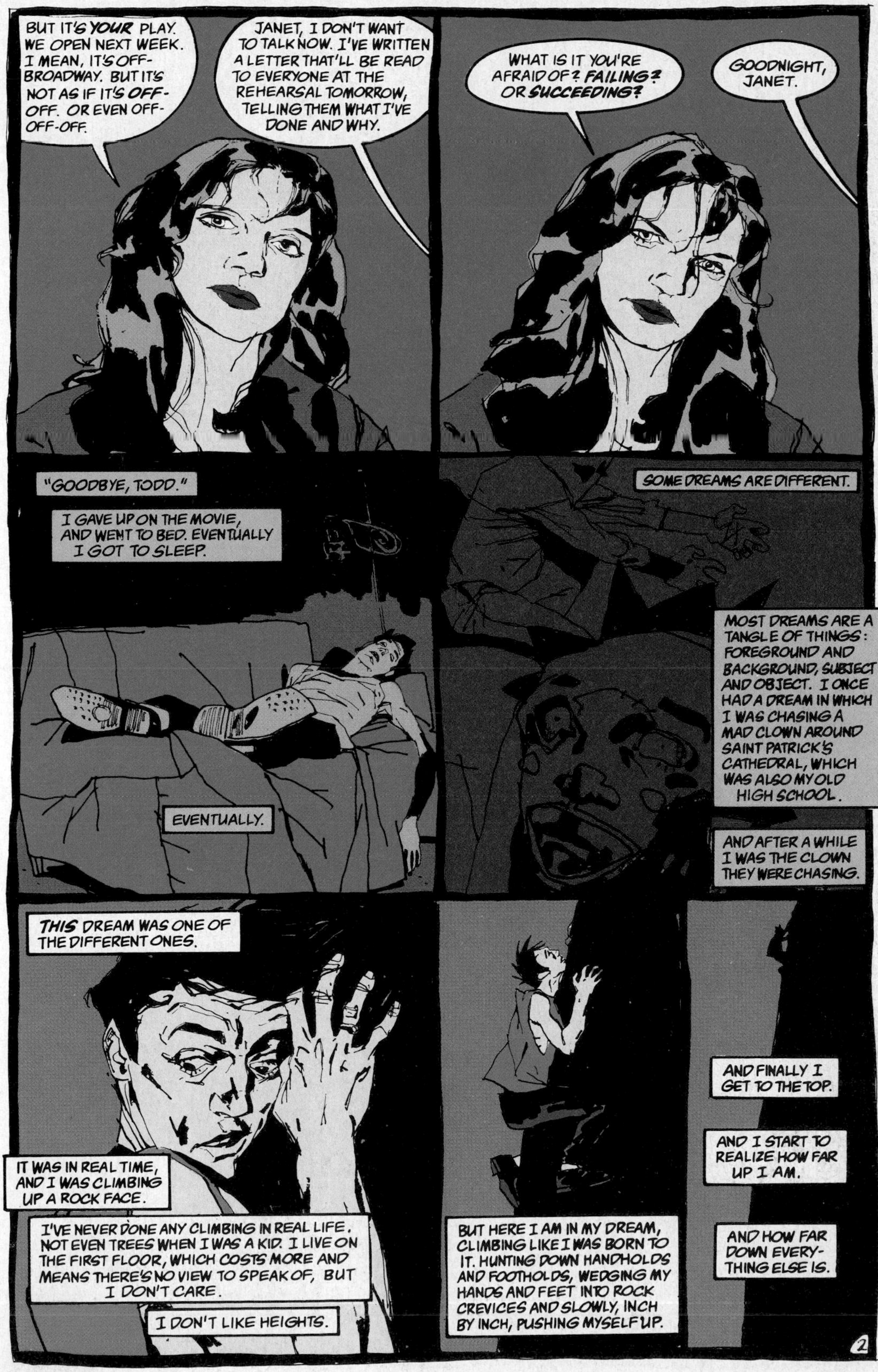
BUT IT'S YOUR PLAY. WE OPEN NEXT WEEK. I MEAN, IT'S OFF-BROADWAY. BUT IT'S NOT AS IF IT'S OFF-OFF. OR EVEN OFF-OFF-OFF.
JANET, I DON'T WANT TO TALK NOW. I'VE WRITTEN A LETTER THAT'LL BE READ TO EVERYONE AT THE REHEARSAL TOMORROW, TELLING THEM WHAT I'VE DONE AND WHY.
WHAT IS IT YOU'RE AFRAID OF? FAILING? OR SUCCEEDING?
GOODNIGHT, JANET.
"GOODBYE, TODD."
I GAVE UP ON THE MOVIE, AND WENT TO BED. EVENTUALLY I GOT TO SLEEP.
EVENTUALLY.
SOME DREAMS ARE DIFFERENT.
MOST DREAMS ARE A TANGLE OF THINGS: FOREGROUND AND BACKGROUND, SUBJECT AND OBJECT. I ONCE HAD A DREAM IN WHICH I WAS CHASING A MAD CLOWN AROUND SAINT PATRICK'S CATHEDRAL, WHICH WAS ALSO MY OLD HIGH SCHOOL.
AND AFTER A WHILE I WAS THE CLOWN THEY WERE CHASING.
THIS DREAM WAS ONE OF THE DIFFERENT ONES.
IT WAS IN REAL TIME, AND I WAS CLIMBING UP A ROCK FACE.
I'VE NEVER DONE ANY CLIMBING IN REAL LIFE. NOT EVEN TREES WHEN I WAS A KID. I LIVE ON THE FIRST FLOOR, WHICH COSTS MORE AND MEANS THERE'S NO VIEW TO SPEAK OF, BUT I DON'T CARE.
I DON'T LIKE HEIGHTS.
BUT HERE I AM IN MY DREAM, CLIMBING LIKE I WAS BORN TO IT. HUNTING DOWN HANDHOLDS AND FOOTHOLDS, WEDGING MY HANDS AND FEET INTO ROCK CREVICES AND SLOWLY, INCH BY INCH, PUSHING MYSELF UP.
AND FINALLY I GET TO THE TOP.
AND I START TO REALIZE HOW FAR UP I AM.
AND HOW FAR DOWN EVERY-THING ELSE IS.
2

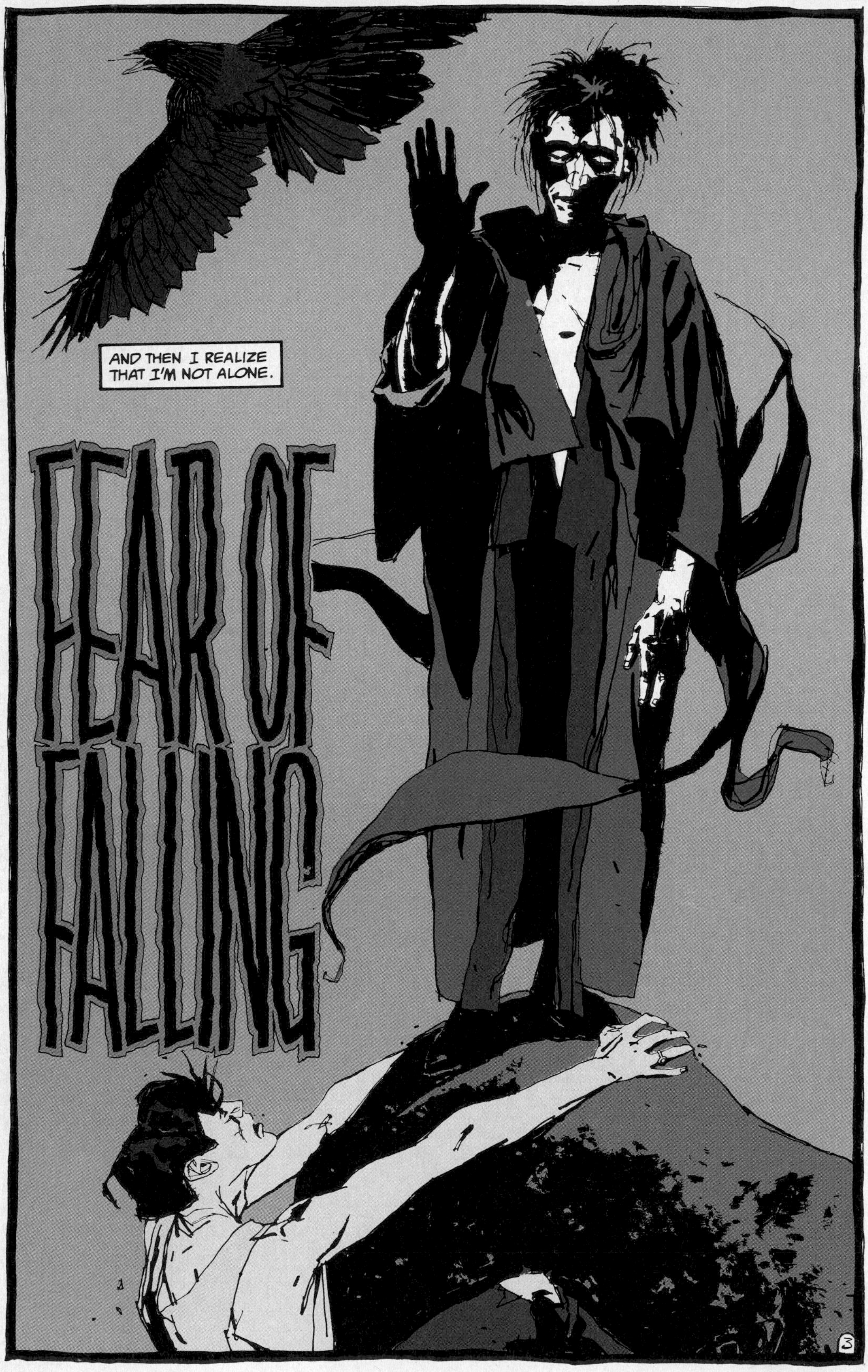
AND THEN I REALIZE THAT I'M NOT ALONE.
FEAR OF FALLING
3

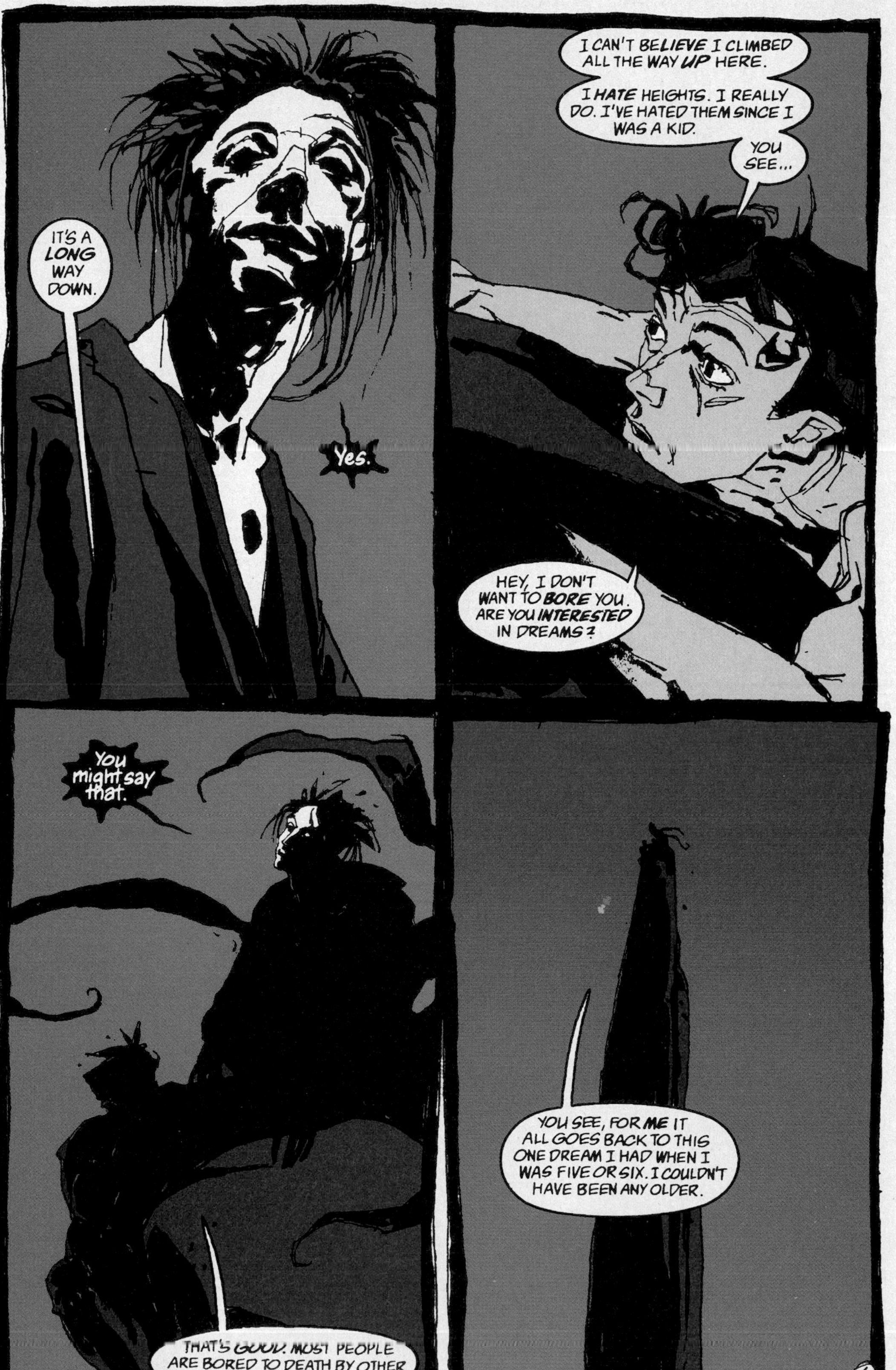

IT'S A LONG WAY DOWN.
Yes.
I CAN'T BELIEVE I CLIMBED ALL THE WAY UP HERE.
I HATE HEIGHTS. I REALLY DO. I'VE HATED THEM SINCE I WAS A KID.
YOU SEE...
HEY, I DON'T WANT TO BORE YOU. ARE YOU INTERESTED IN DREAMS?
You might say that.
THAT'S GOOD. MOST PEOPLE ARE BORED TO DEATH BY OTHER PEOPLE'S DREAMS.
YOU SEE, FOR ME IT ALL GOES BACK TO THIS ONE DREAM I HAD WHEN I WAS FIVE OR SIX. I COULDN'T HAVE BEEN ANY OLDER.
4

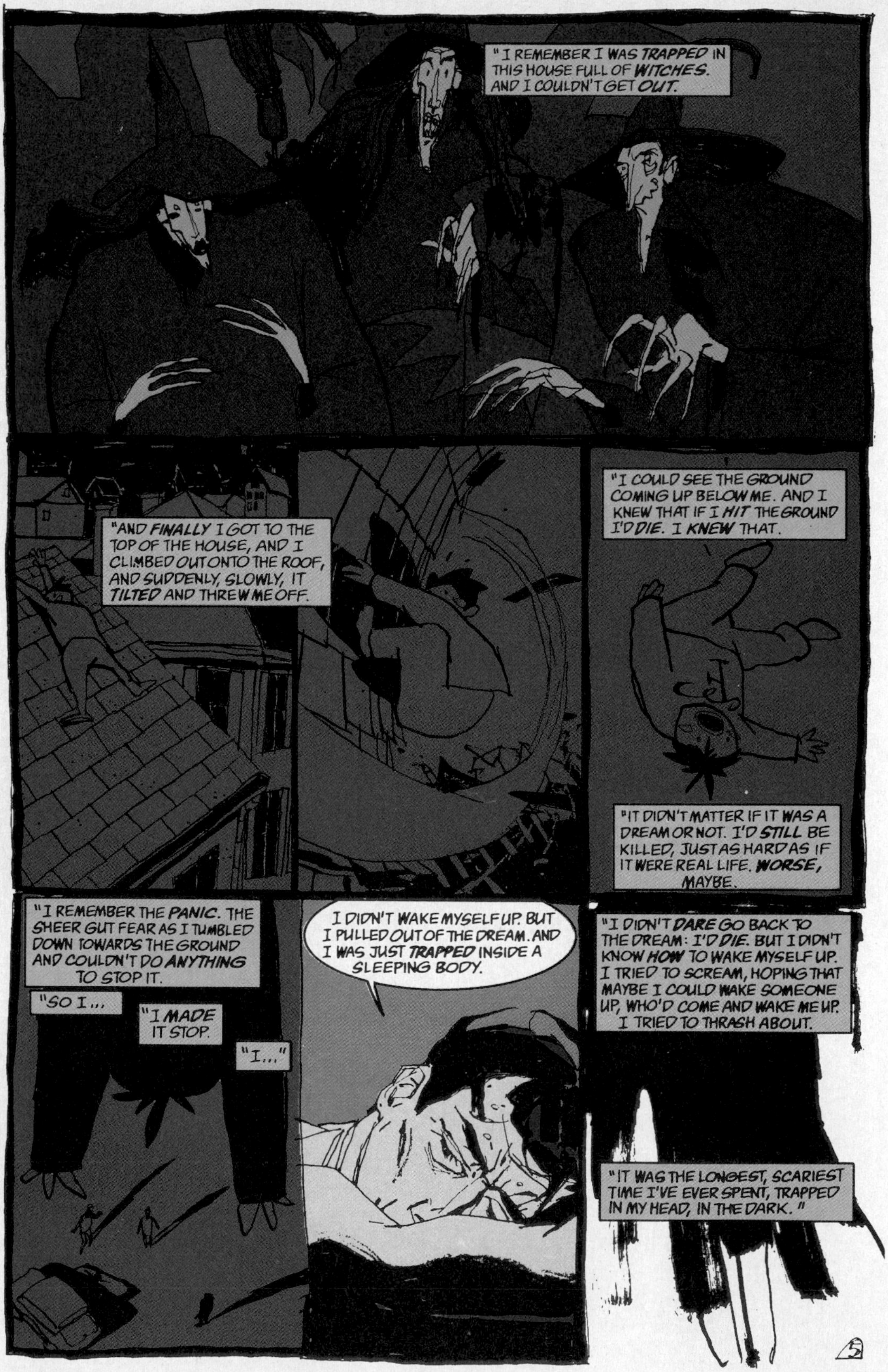
"I REMEMBER I WAS TRAPPED IN THIS HOUSE FULL OF WITCHES. AND I COULDN'T GET OUT.
"AND FINALLY I GOT TO THE TOP OF THE HOUSE, AND I CLIMBED OUT ONTO THE ROOF, AND SUDDENLY, SLOWLY, IT TILTED AND THREW ME OFF.
"I COULD SEE THE GROUND COMING UP BELOW ME. AND I KNEW THAT IF I HIT THE GROUND I'D DIE. I KNEW THAT.
"IT DIDN'T MATTER IF IT WAS A DREAM OR NOT. I'D STILL BE KILLED, JUST AS HARD AS IF IT WERE REAL LIFE. WORSE, MAYBE.
"I REMEMBER THE PANIC. THE SHEER GUT FEAR AS I TUMBLED DOWN TOWARDS THE GROUND AND COULDN'T DO ANYTHING TO STOP IT.
"SO I...
"I MADE IT STOP.
"I..."
I DIDN'T WAKE MYSELF UP. BUT I PULLED OUT OF THE DREAM. AND I WAS JUST TRAPPED INSIDE A SLEEPING BODY.
"I DIDN'T DARE GO BACK TO THE DREAM: I'D DIE. BUT I DIDN'T KNOW HOW TO WAKE MYSELF UP. I TRIED TO SCREAM, HOPING THAT MAYBE I COULD WAKE SOMEONE UP, WHO'D COME AND WAKE ME UP. I TRIED TO THRASH ABOUT.
"IT WAS THE LONGEST, SCARIEST TIME I'VE EVER SPENT, TRAPPED IN MY HEAD, IN THE DARK."
5

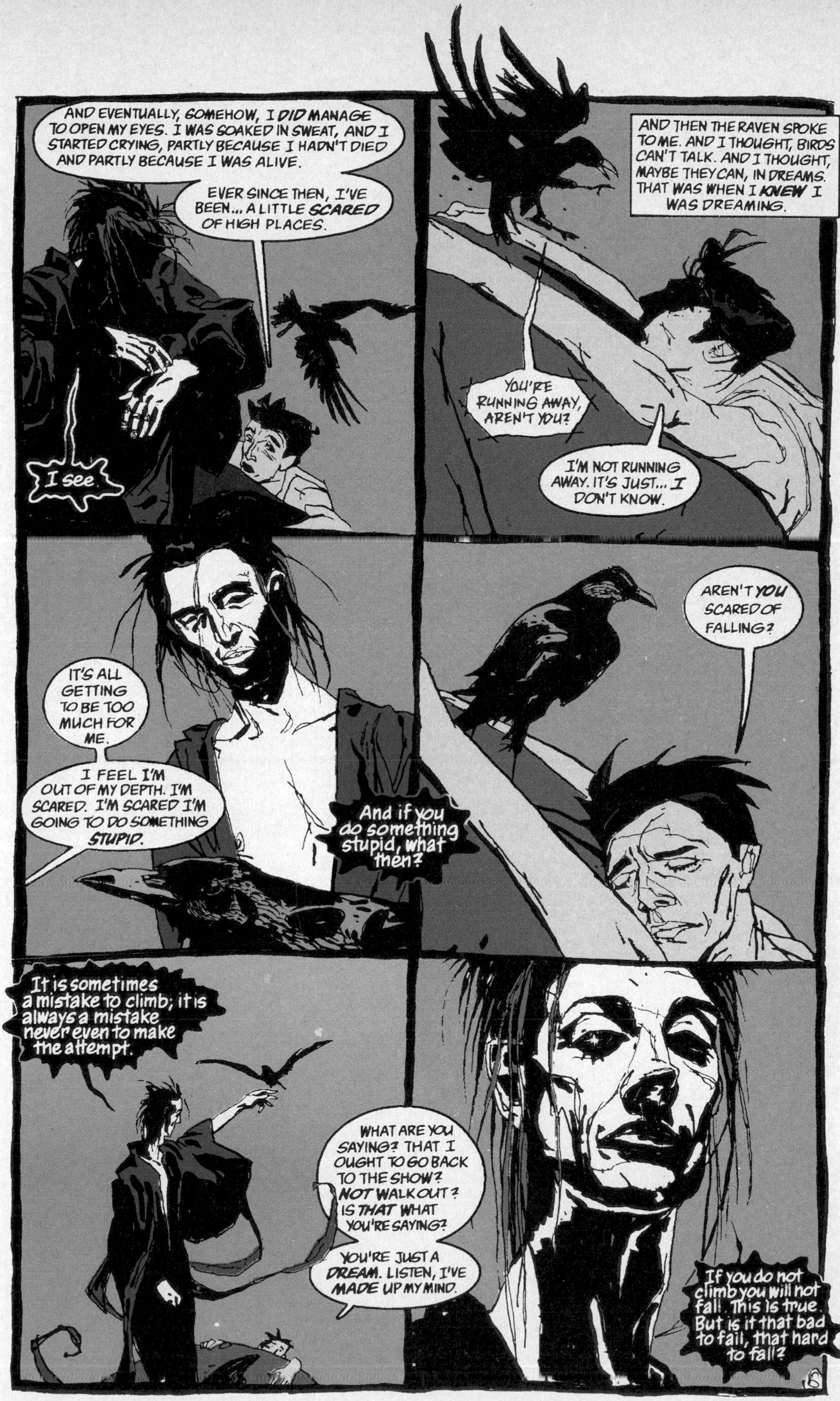
AND EVENTUALLY, SOMEHOW, I DID MANAGE TO OPEN MY EYES. I WAS SOAKED IN SWEAT, AND I STARTED CRYING, PARTLY BECAUSE I HADN'T DIED AND PARTLY BECAUSE I WAS ALIVE.
EVER SINCE THEN, I'VE BEEN... A LITTLE SCARED OF HIGH PLACES.
I see.
AND THEN THE RAVEN SPOKE TO ME. AND I THOUGHT, BIRDS CAN'T TALK. AND I THOUGHT, MAYBE THEY CAN, IN DREAMS. THAT WAS WHEN I KNEW I WAS DREAMING.
YOU'RE RUNNING AWAY, AREN'T YOU?
I'M NOT RUNNING AWAY. IT'S JUST... I DON'T KNOW.
IT'S ALL GETTING TO BE TOO MUCH FOR ME.
I FEEL I'M OUT OF MY DEPTH. I'M SCARED. I'M SCARED I'M GOING TO DO SOMETHING STUPID.
And if you do something stupid, what then?
AREN'T YOU SCARED OF FALLING?
It is sometimes a mistake to climb; it is always a mistake never even to make the attempt.
WHAT ARE YOU SAYING? THAT I OUGHT TO GO BACK TO THE SHOW? NOT WALK OUT? IS THAT WHAT YOU'RE SAYING?
YOU'RE JUST A DREAM. LISTEN, I'VE MADE UP MY MIND.
If you do not climb you will not fall. This is true. But is it that bad to fail, that hard to fall?
18

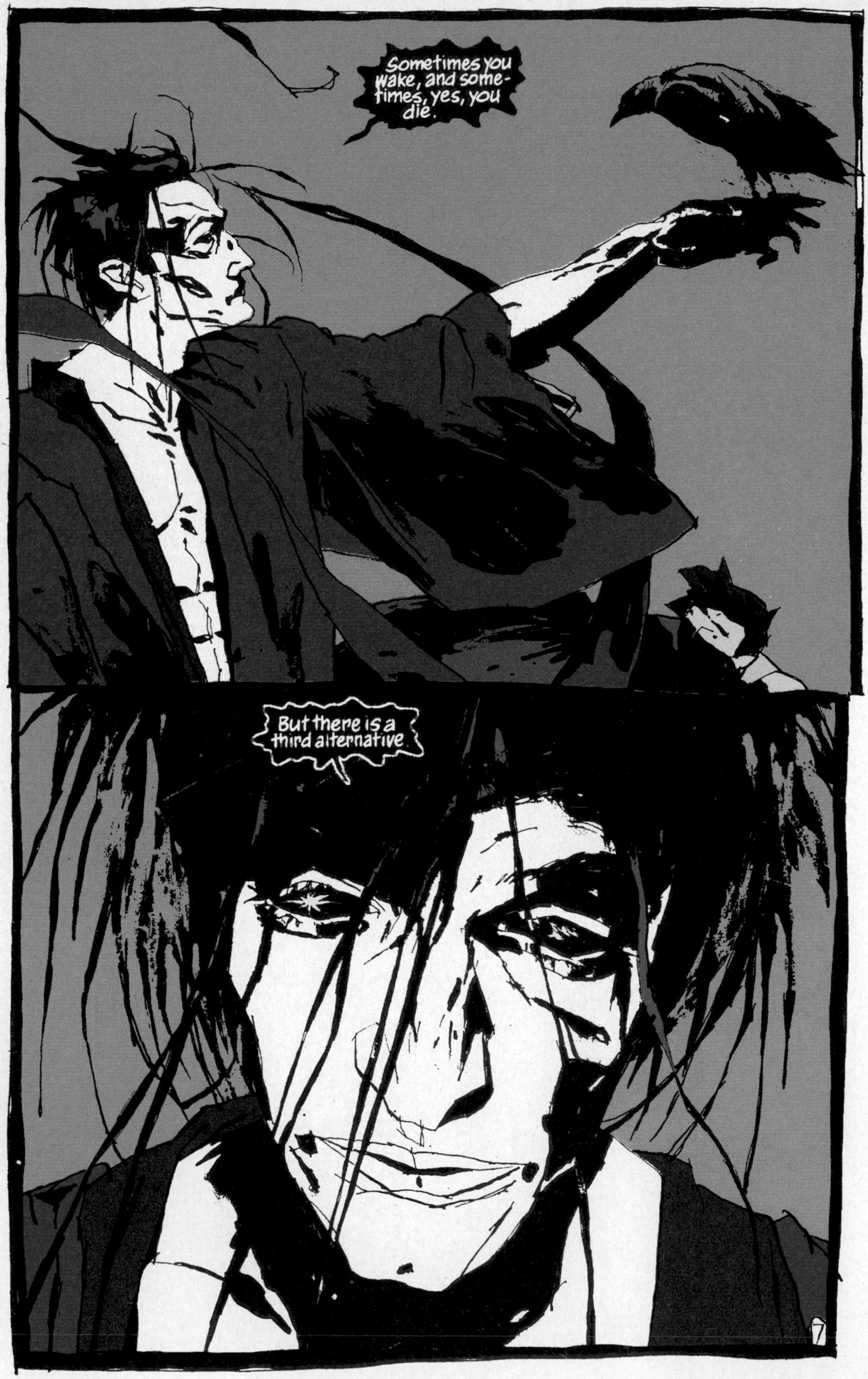
Sometimes you wake, and sometimes, yes, you die.
But there is a third alternative.
7

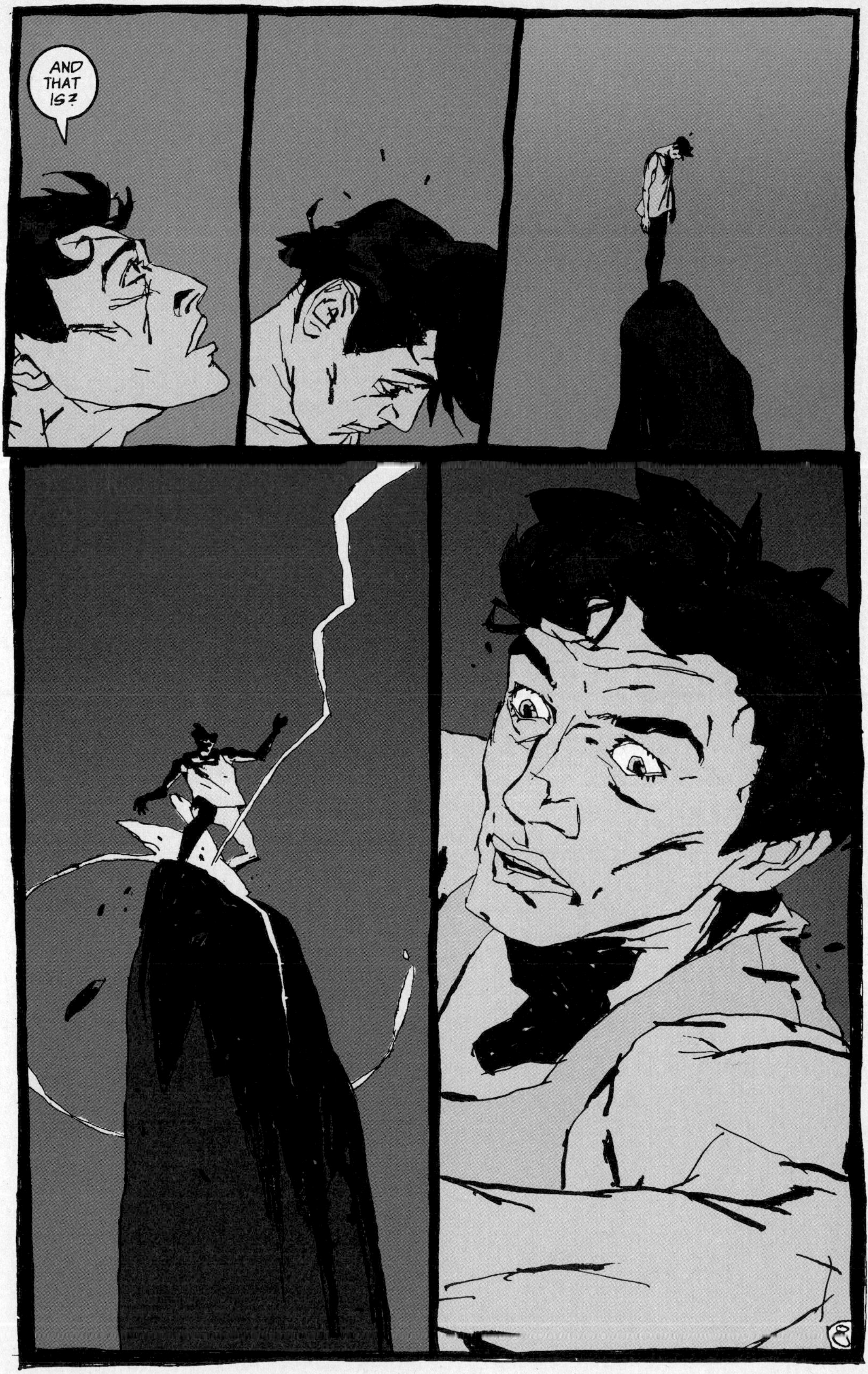
AND THAT IS?

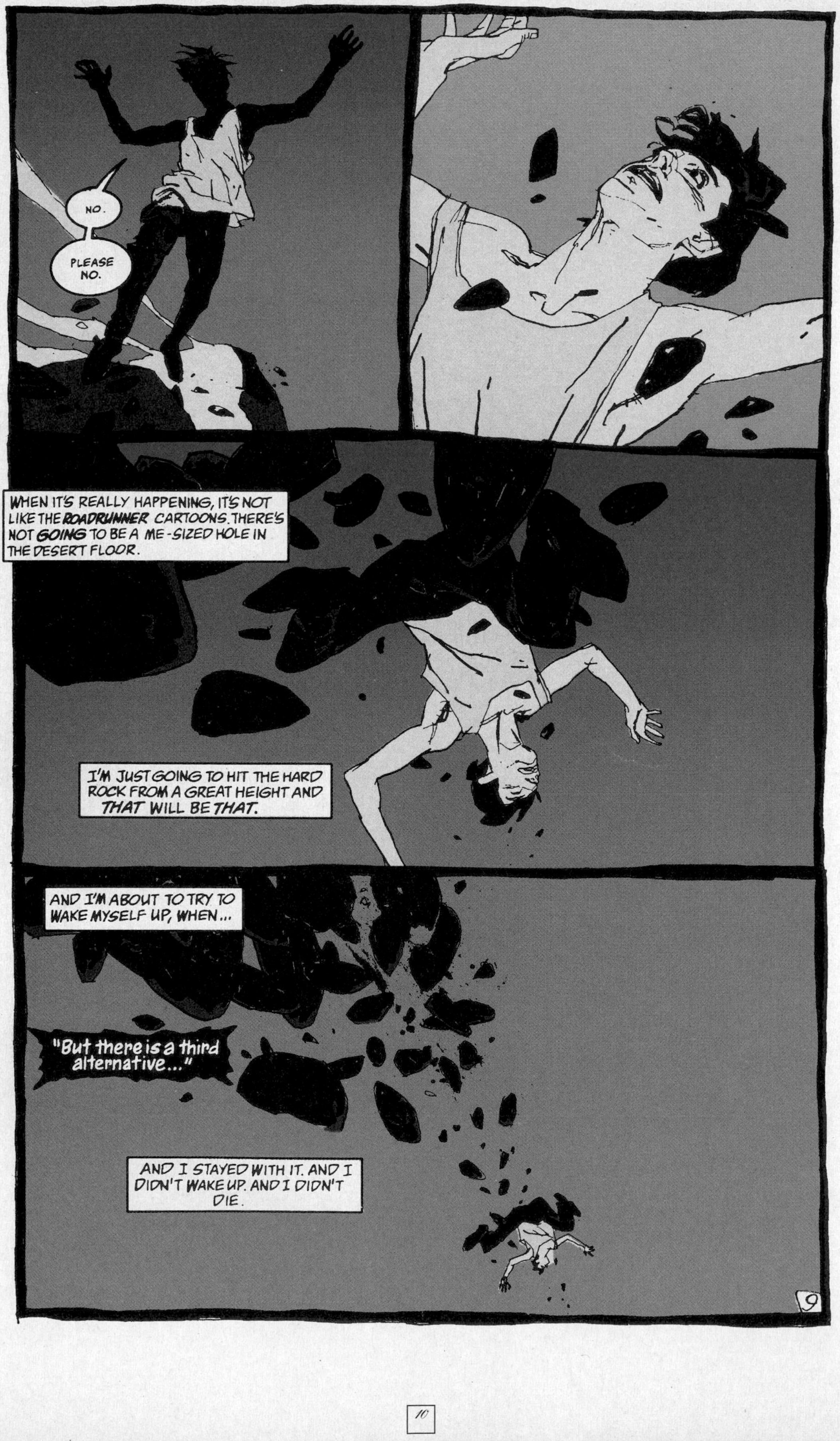
NO.
PLEASE NO.
WHEN IT'S REALLY HAPPENING, IT'S NOT LIKE THE ROADRUNNER CARTOONS. THERE'S NOT GOING TO BE A ME-SIZED HOLE IN THE DESERT FLOOR.
I'M JUST GOING TO HIT THE HARD ROCK FROM A GREAT HEIGHT AND THAT WILL BE THAT.
AND I'M ABOUT TO TRY TO WAKE MYSELF UP, WHEN...
"But there is a third alternative..."
AND I STAYED WITH IT. AND I DIDN'T WAKE UP. AND I DIDN'T DIE.
9

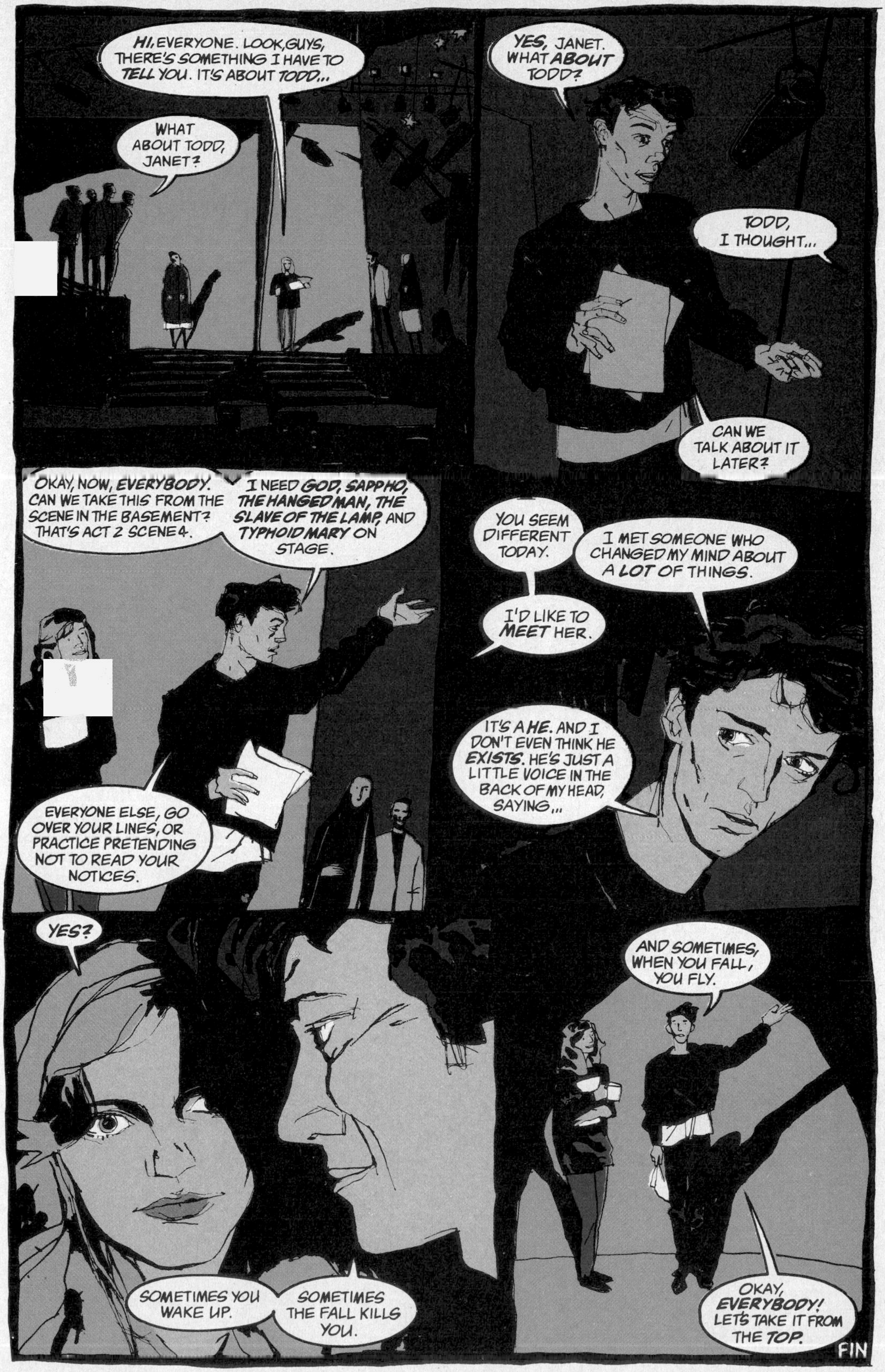
HI, EVERYONE. LOOK, GUYS, THERE'S SOMETHING I HAVE TO TELL YOU. IT'S ABOUT TODD...
WHAT ABOUT TODD, JANET?
YES, JANET. WHAT ABOUT TODD?
TODD, I THOUGHT...
CAN WE TALK ABOUT IT LATER?
OKAY, NOW, EVERYBODY. CAN WE TAKE THIS FROM THE SCENE IN THE BASEMENT? THAT'S ACT 2 SCENE 4.
I NEED GOD, SAPPHO, THE HANGED MAN, THE SLAVE OF THE LAMP, AND TYPHOID MARY ON STAGE.
EVERYONE ELSE, GO OVER YOUR LINES, OR PRACTICE PRETENDING NOT TO READ YOUR NOTICES.
YOU SEEM DIFFERENT TODAY.
I MET SOMEONE WHO CHANGED MY MIND ABOUT A LOT OF THINGS.
I'D LIKE TO MEET HER.
IT'S A HE. AND I DON'T EVEN THINK HE EXISTS. HE'S JUST A LITTLE VOICE IN THE BACK OF MY HEAD, SAYING...
YES?
SOMETIMES YOU WAKE UP.
SOMETIMES THE FALL KILLS YOU.
AND SOMETIMES, WHEN YOU FALL, YOU FLY.
OKAY, EVERYBODY! LET'S TAKE IT FROM THE TOP.
FIN

THE SANDMAN

fables and reflections

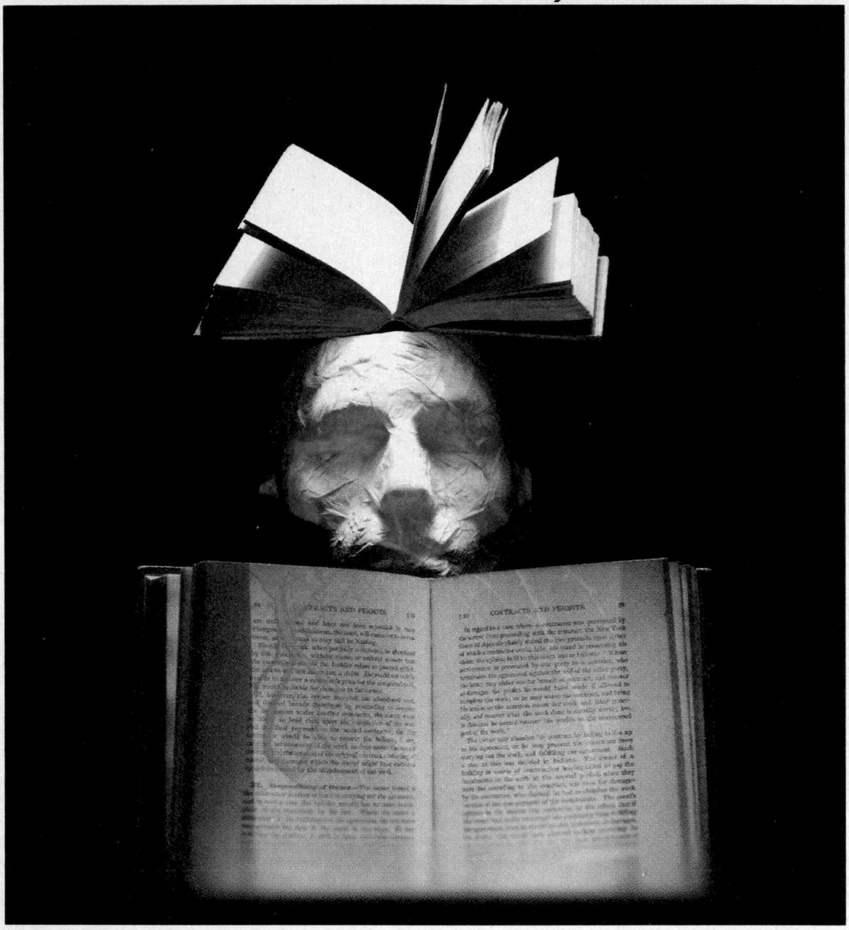

WRITTEN BY neil gaiman

ILLUSTRATED BY bryan talbot + stan woch + p. craig russell + shawn mcmanus + john watkiss + jill thompson + duncan eagleson + kent williams + mark buckingham + vince locke + dick giordano

LETTERED BY todd klein

COLORED BY daniel vozzo + digital chameleon + sherilyn van valkenburgh

Featuring characters created by neil gaiman, sam kieth & mike dringenberg

Table of Contents

FABLES & REFLECTIONS

ALL STORIES WRITTEN BY

neil gaiman

LETTERED BY *todd klein*

COLORED BY *daniel vozzo* (unless otherwise stated)

COVERS AND DESIGN BY *dave mckean*

READER, MEET THE SANDMAN

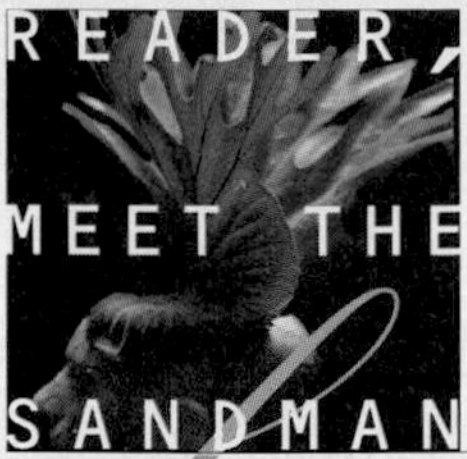

fables

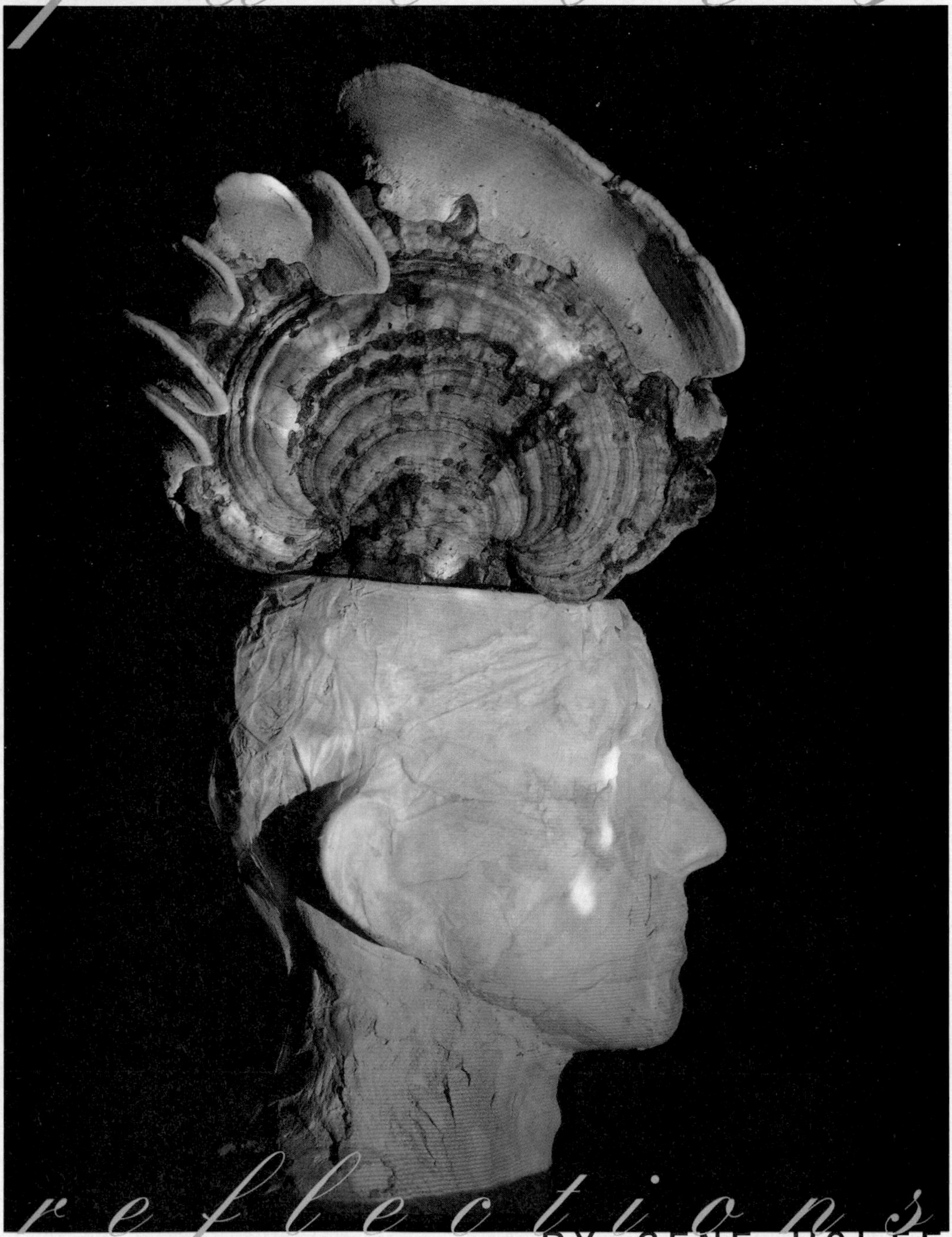

reflections

BY GENE WOLFE

$\mathcal{D}$o you read introductions? I do, and after having read a good many of them, I am sadly aware that most of us who write them do not know what they are supposed to accomplish, which is to enable you to start the stories without embarrassment. Like a social introduction — some friend says, "This is Nina. She likes mint juleps and breeds ferrets," and you're off.

So here. I am not to introduce you to Neil Gaiman or the artists (though I would like that), or solely to His Darkness Dream of the Endless (that is to say to the Sandman, about whom more later) but to his stories, the most extraordinary ever in this graphic form, and among the most extraordinary of all time in *any* form.

What makes them so extraordinary? For that matter, why should they require an introduction, when most stories do not? Well, let's suppose that after you'd chatted awhile with Nina, the friend who had introduced you to her were to say, "This is Pythia. She lives in a cave — it's haunted by the ghost of a giant snake and she answers questions in cryptic verse. Her answers are always true, and generally a little truer than we like." You'd feel that you'd met somebody extraordinary then, wouldn't you? And you'd want all the introduction you could get.

So here. I'm tempted to say that because these are all, in their various ways, about the Lord of Dream — and dreams are forever telling us truths so large that we can assimilate them only with difficulty — naturally these stories do, too.

Which would be a lie. *Non sequitur*; it does not follow. In the hands of almost any other writer, the characters in these remarkable stories would talk nonsense. If that other writer were good, it would be spectacular and even plausible nonsense, but nonsense nevertheless.

When I was much smaller, it seemed to me that the best way to achieve the spectacular effects I loved in the movies would be for the people making the movie actually to do them.

If (a random example) Imperial Scouts were to chase Luke on antigravity speeder bikes, the best way to photograph it would be for Lucasfilm to build some speeder bikes and put Imperial Scouts on them. Why not? If Commander Skywalker and Han Solo were going to visit the Ewoks' arboreal village, why, round up some Ewoks and have them build one. After furious lectures by a dozen or so of my contemporaries, I realized that I had been wrong; it was far better, far more *adult*, to fake everything, which is what the studios did.

But now that I am an adult myself, a grown-up depicter of things that don't exist, I realize that the child I used to be was right. It would be better, really, to build the speeder bikes. Lucasfilm doesn't do it because it can't.

Not so Neil Gaiman. Let him conceive an entity who is to speak large and cryptic truths, and he makes that entity speak large and cryptic truths like, "His madness kept him sane."

You must consider this, as Miyamoto Musashi the samurai is always telling us. Then read the story about Sam the newspaperman and the Emperor of America, and think about it again.

"'You look terrible. White as the man in the moon. Are you always so pale?' 'That depends on who's watching.'"

Hidden in a string of throwaway lines: "Any view of things that is not strange is false..."

These one-liners, these minor aphorisms or whatever you want to call them, are merely the little stuff, of course; I quoted them just to give you the idea and because it was easy. What is important and central is that, time after time, the stories themselves are true. I don't mean simply that Neil Gaiman's history is good history and that his myth is good myth — although they are. I mean that you will understand yourself and the world better for having read them, and that you will have been both ennobled and troubled by the experience; that this is not just art — all sorts of ugly and foolish things are art — but great art.

When Harlan Ellison introduced <u>The Sandman: Season of Mists,</u> he described the dismay of "all those artsy-fartsy writers and artists and critics" at Neil Gaiman's winning the World Fantasy Award with a "comic book," thus (it seems to me) dulling the real point he should have made. Which is simply that it's almost incredible that a "comic book" should be good enough to win — to force itself upon the judges. That the wildly improbable has occurred, and some of the best writing of our time is appearing in a graphic medium in which writing traditionally comes second — and a long way second at that. "Any view of the universe that is not strange is false."

So here. Now let's get to the people, because that's what I've led you to expect. I'll try to sneak in a little stuff about the stories, too. And if you and one story or another decide to leave the party for awhile, that's great. It'll be good for both of you, and you'll be back.

Some People You'll Meet

"Darling, let me introduce you to my uncles and aunts," says the groom in "The Song of Orpheus." They are Teleute, Aponia, Mania, Epithumia, Olethros, and Potmos; their names mean End, Inaction, Madness, Desire, Destruction, and Destiny. All are Greek. We meet some of these relatives in the other stories, too.

Orpheus is Dream's son, a shaman — wizard — of Thrace. The temple at the end of "Thermidor" is Apollo's on Lesbos. Robespierre has been called an idealist by some and a dictator by others — neither side realizing that it's possible to be both at the same time. Idealistic dictators, of whom there have been many, are the most dangerous kind.

Haroun al Raschid (Aaron the Upright) in "Ramadan" was the caliph of Baghdad when Islamic culture was at its height. He appears in many of the Arabian Nights as a wise and just ruler. The month-long religious fast of Ramadan falls in the ninth month of the Muslim lunar year.

Matthew, whom you'll meet in "The Parliament of Rooks," is Dream's pet raven. Eve (Life) is, of course, the first woman, Adam's wife and the mother of Cain (Spear) and Abel (Breath).

Caius, in "August," is Caius Octavius, better known as the emperor Augustus, the best and greatest of the early Roman Emperors, and the patron of Vergil, Ovid, Livy, and Horace; he reigned from 27 B.C. to A.D. 14.

Speaking of emperors, Norton I is a historical figure; when you've read "Three Septembers and a January" you'll know his story rather better than most historians. Sam (as I hardly need tell you) is Samuel Clemens, better known as Mark Twain, the author of "The Celebrated Jumping Frog of Calaveras County."

The People — werewolves — are entirely legendary. All evidence to the contrary results from superstition, mass hysteria, or outright falsehood. Pay no attention to Neil Gaiman on this, we weren't within miles of the place and he can't prove a thing. "The Hunt" is pure fiction from beginning to end.

Marco Polo of Venice was the first European to write a factual account of China. He was a prisoner of war when he wrote his book; you'll meet him as a much younger man in "Soft Places." The mysterious, hospitable fat man in the big hat is G.K. Chesterton, sometimes known as Gideon Fell and various other things; he wrote "The Angry Street: A Bad Dream" which no doubt endeared him to...

The Sandman, the Lord of Dream, a slender and pale figure remarkably like Neil Gaiman himself, whom you are about to meet in every one of these stories. He is perhaps not quite as bad as he looks. Good night. Sleep tight. Don't let the bedbugs bite. Sorry about the nightlight, I'll get a new one in the morning. Turn the page.

teleute

(Gene Wolfe is the author of the four-volume Book of the New Sun, The Fifth Head of Cerberus, Peace, The Devil in a Forest, Free Live Free, Soldier of the Mist, The Urth of the New Sun, There Are Doors, Soldier of Arete, Castleview, and other books. Some of his short stories have been collected in The Island of Doctor Death and Other Stories and Other Stories, Storeys from the Old Hotel, and Endangered Species. His most recent novel is Pandora by Holly Hollander, a mystery. A new science-fiction novel, Nightside the Long Sun, was published in April, 1993 and Lake of the Long Sun is forthcoming.

Mr. Wolfe has won the John W. Campbell Memorial Award, the Prix Apollo, the British Fantasy Award, the British Science Fiction Award, the Chicago Foundation for Literature Award, two Nebulas, and two World Fantasy Awards.)

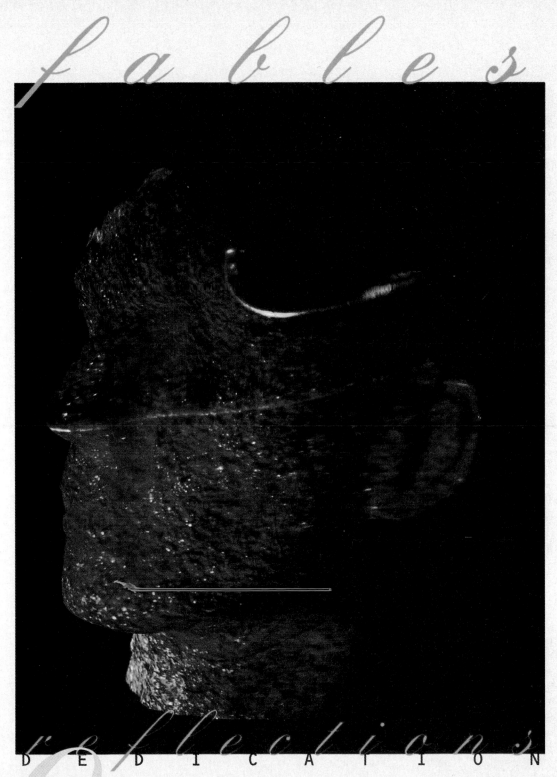

fables

reflections

DEDICATION

Nine short stories for nine people, with affection and respect:
For Steve Jones, James Herbert, Mary Gentle, Geoff Ryman, Colin Greenland,
Ramsey Campbell, Roz Kaveney, John Clute and Lisa Tuttle.

Neil Gaiman

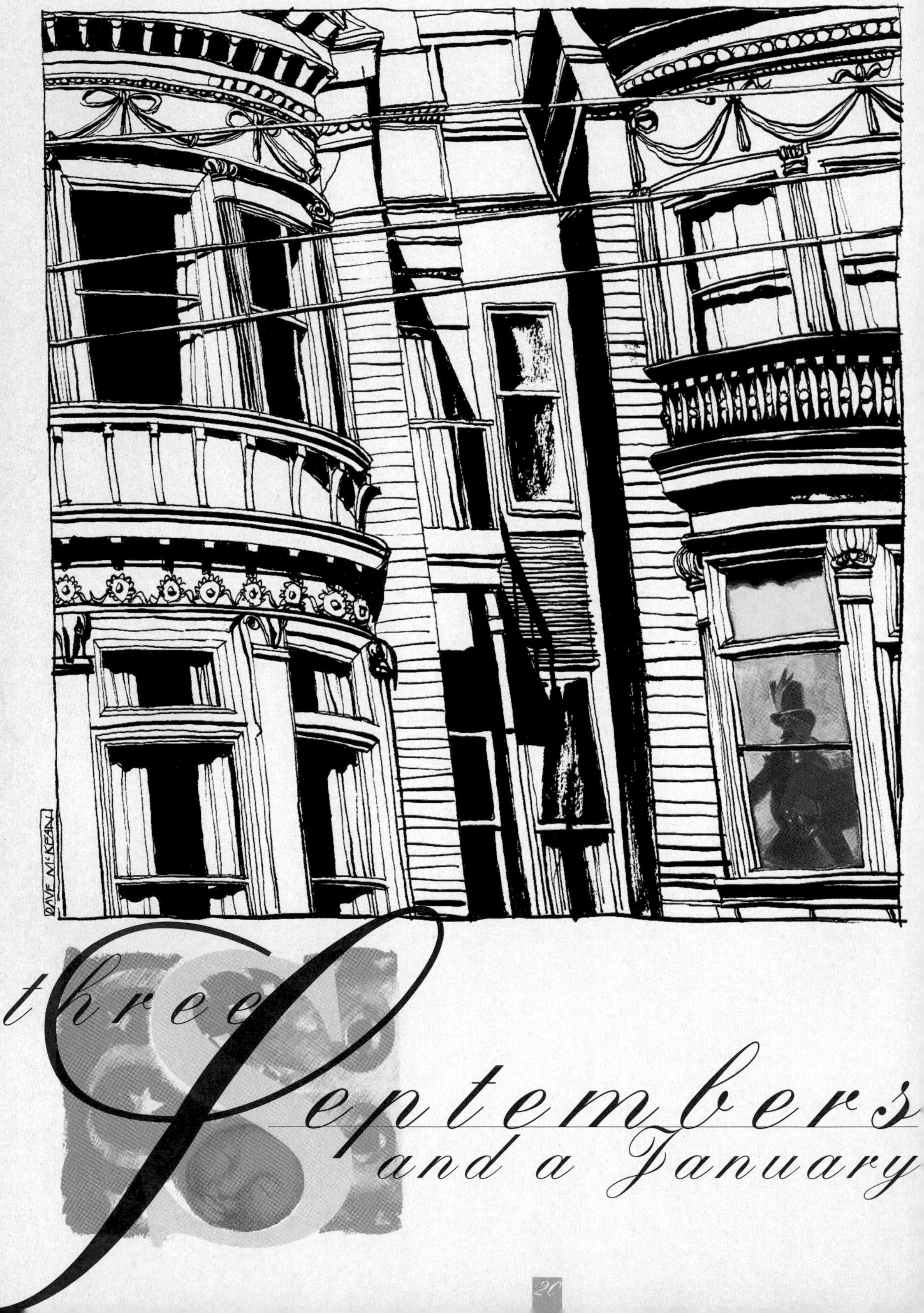
DAVE McKEAN

three Septembers and a January

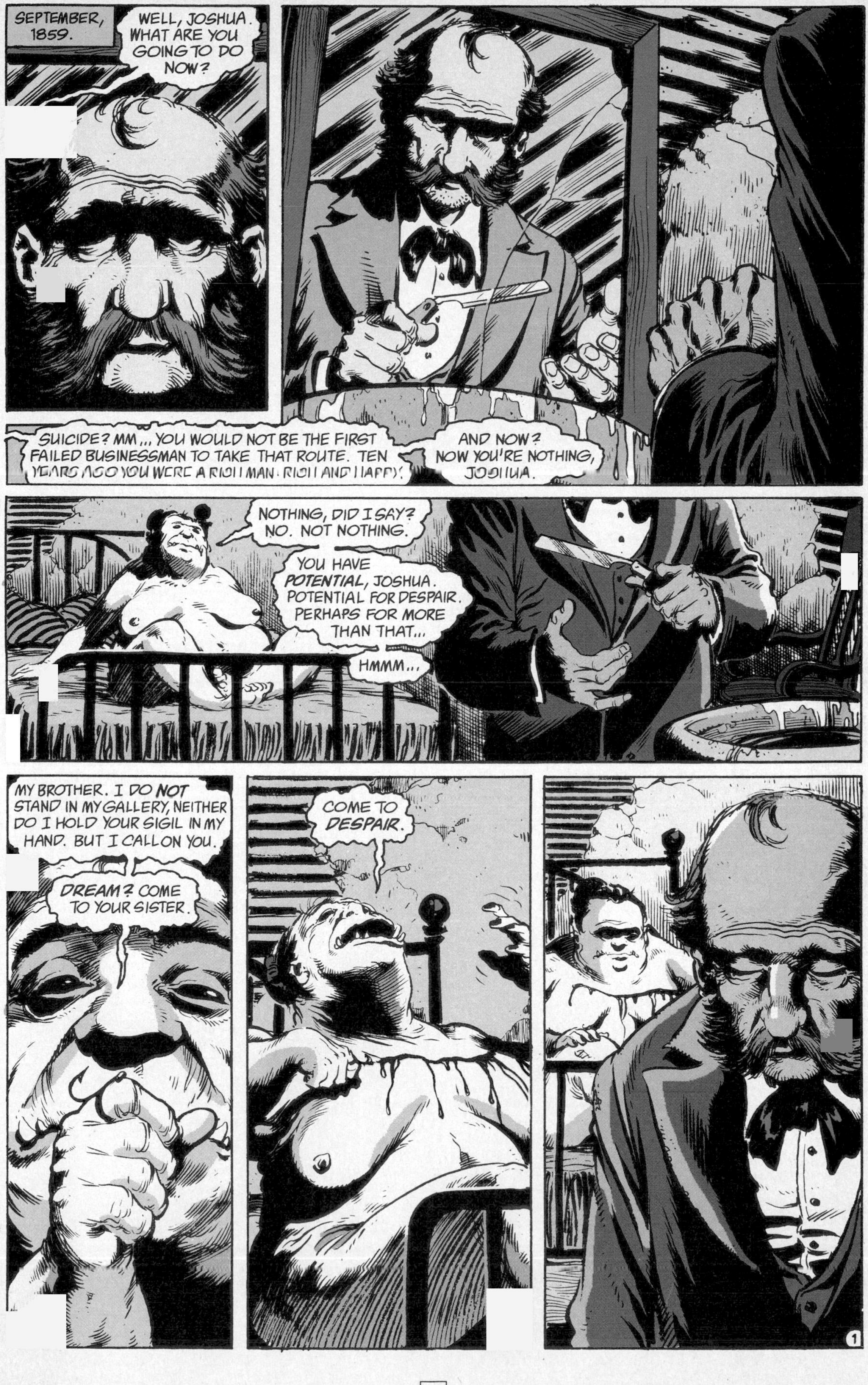
SEPTEMBER, 1859.
WELL, JOSHUA. WHAT ARE YOU GOING TO DO NOW?
SUICIDE? MM... YOU WOULD NOT BE THE FIRST FAILED BUSINESSMAN TO TAKE THAT ROUTE. TEN YEARS AGO YOU WERE A RICH MAN. RICH AND HAPPY.
AND NOW? NOW YOU'RE NOTHING, JOSHUA.
NOTHING, DID I SAY? NO. NOT NOTHING.
YOU HAVE POTENTIAL, JOSHUA. POTENTIAL FOR DESPAIR. PERHAPS FOR MORE THAN THAT...
HMMM...
MY BROTHER. I DO NOT STAND IN MY GALLERY, NEITHER DO I HOLD YOUR SIGIL IN MY HAND. BUT I CALL ON YOU.
DREAM? COME TO YOUR SISTER.
COME TO DESPAIR.

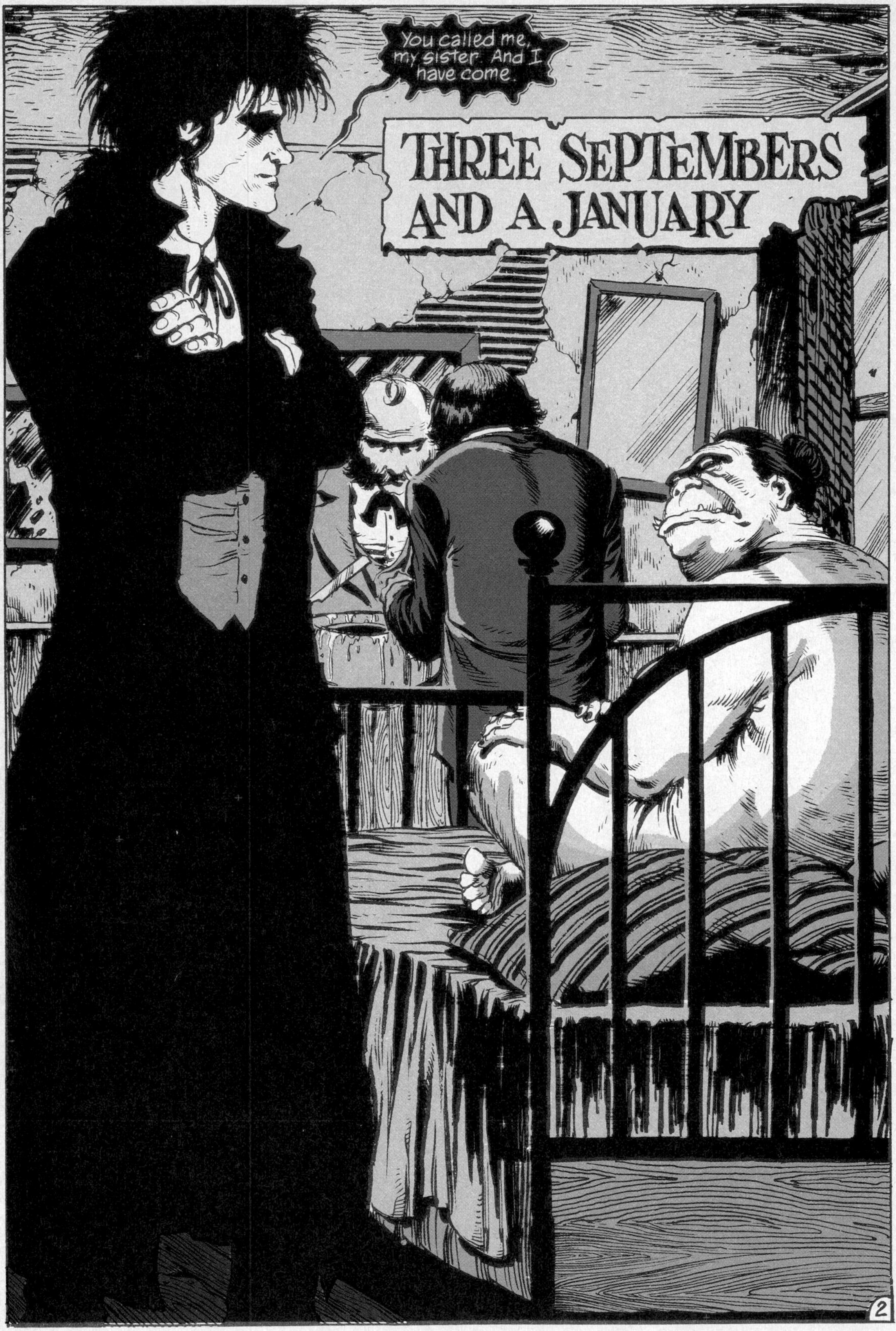
You called me, my sister. And I have come.
THREE SEPTEMBERS AND A JANUARY
2

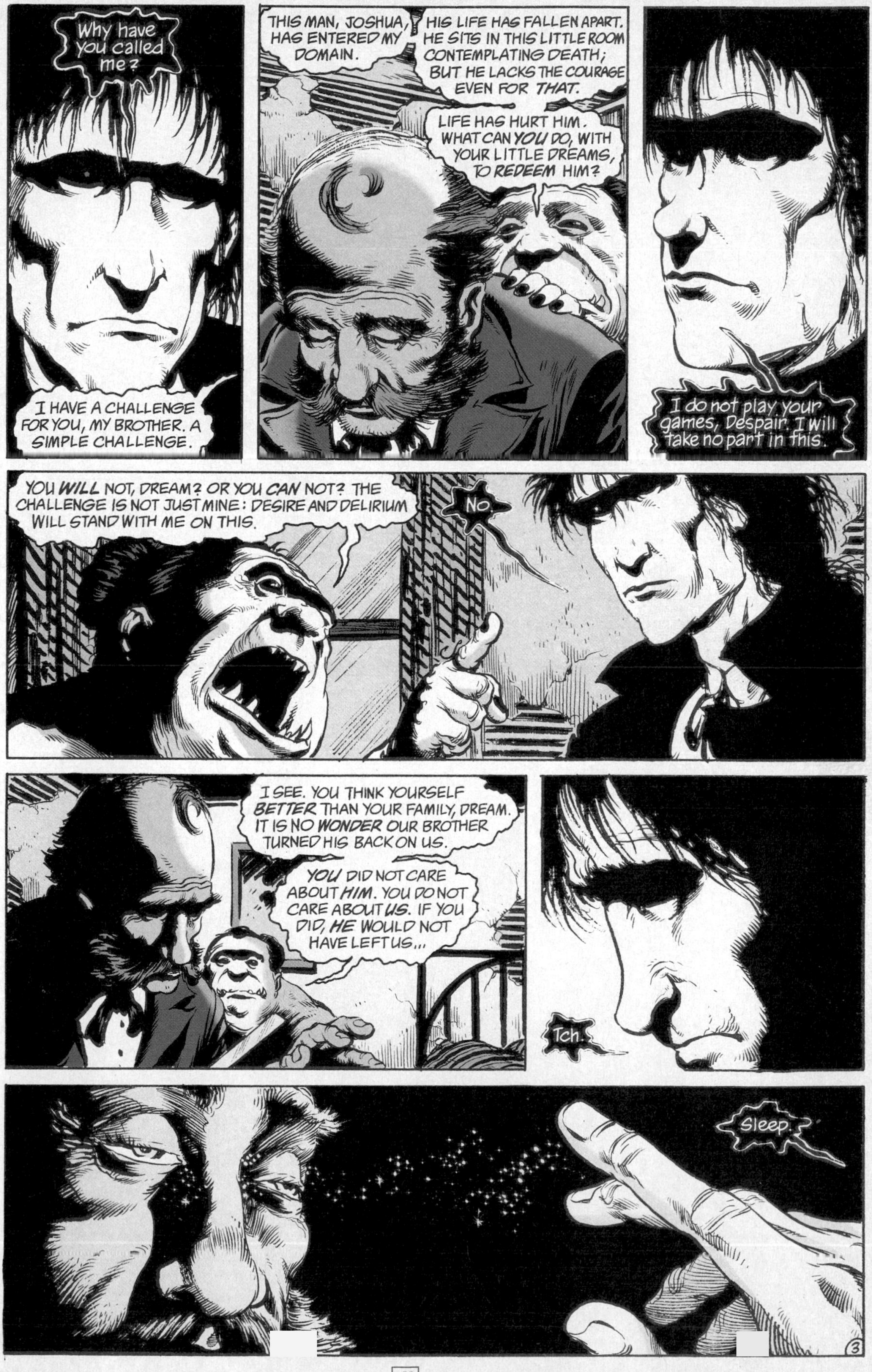
Why have you called me?
I HAVE A CHALLENGE FOR YOU, MY BROTHER. A SIMPLE CHALLENGE.
THIS MAN, JOSHUA, HAS ENTERED MY DOMAIN.
HIS LIFE HAS FALLEN APART. HE SITS IN THIS LITTLE ROOM CONTEMPLATING DEATH; BUT HE LACKS THE COURAGE EVEN FOR THAT.
LIFE HAS HURT HIM. WHAT CAN YOU DO, WITH YOUR LITTLE DREAMS, TO REDEEM HIM?
I do not play your games, Despair. I will take no part in this.
YOU WILL NOT, DREAM? OR YOU CAN NOT? THE CHALLENGE IS NOT JUST MINE: DESIRE AND DELIRIUM WILL STAND WITH ME ON THIS.
No.
I SEE. YOU THINK YOURSELF BETTER THAN YOUR FAMILY, DREAM. IT IS NO WONDER OUR BROTHER TURNED HIS BACK ON US.
YOU DID NOT CARE ABOUT HIM. YOU DO NOT CARE ABOUT US. IF YOU DID, HE WOULD NOT HAVE LEFT US...
Tch.
Sleep.
3

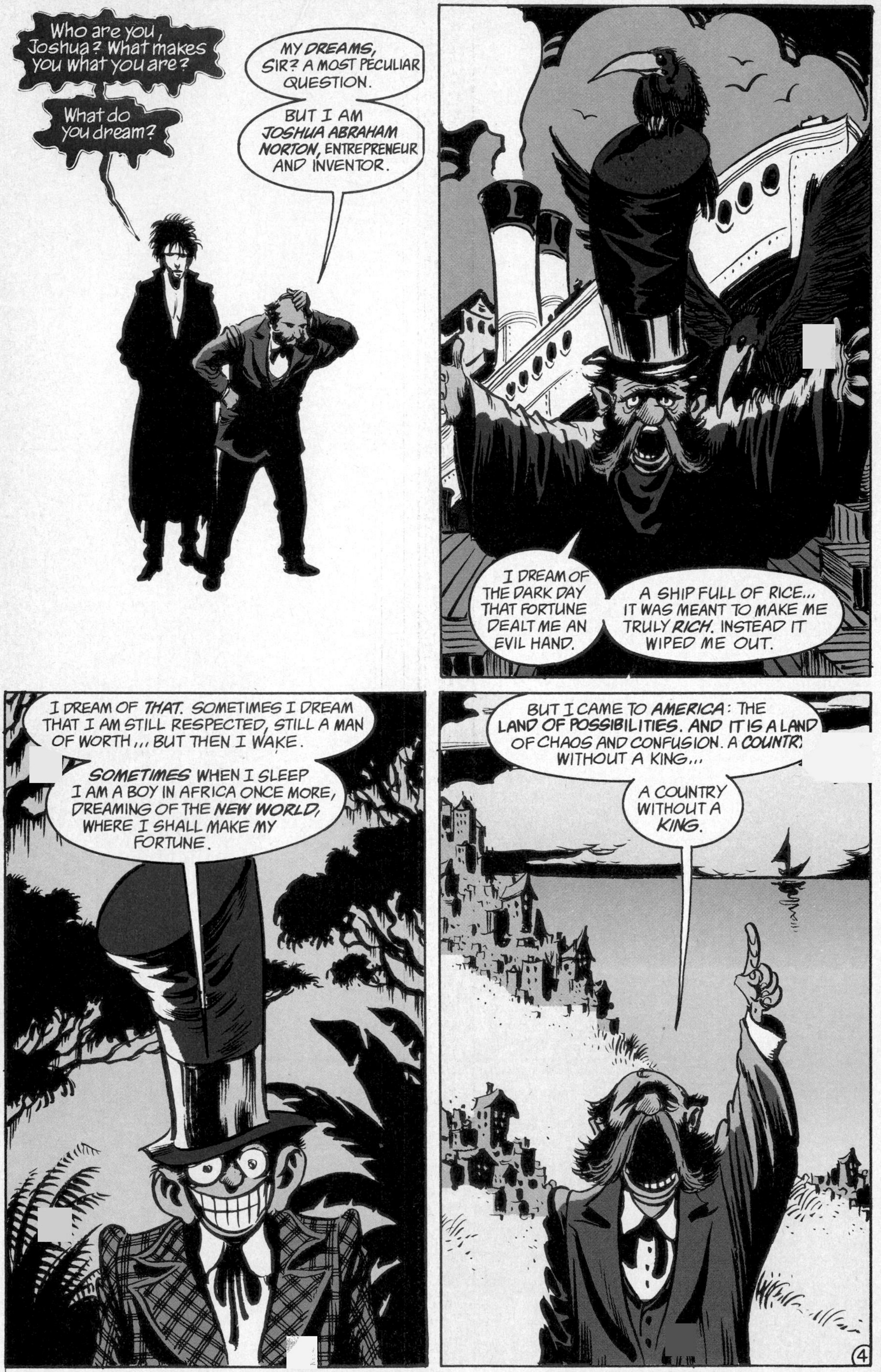

Who are you, Joshua? What makes you what you are?
What do you dream?
MY DREAMS, SIR? A MOST PECULIAR QUESTION.
BUT I AM JOSHUA ABRAHAM NORTON, ENTREPRENEUR AND INVENTOR.
I DREAM OF THE DARK DAY THAT FORTUNE DEALT ME AN EVIL HAND.
A SHIP FULL OF RICE... IT WAS MEANT TO MAKE ME TRULY RICH. INSTEAD IT WIPED ME OUT.
I DREAM OF THAT. SOMETIMES I DREAM THAT I AM STILL RESPECTED, STILL A MAN OF WORTH... BUT THEN I WAKE.
SOMETIMES WHEN I SLEEP I AM A BOY IN AFRICA ONCE MORE, DREAMING OF THE NEW WORLD, WHERE I SHALL MAKE MY FORTUNE.
BUT I CAME TO AMERICA: THE LAND OF POSSIBILITIES. AND IT IS A LAND OF CHAOS AND CONFUSION. A COUNTR WITHOUT A KING...
A COUNTRY WITHOUT A KING.
4

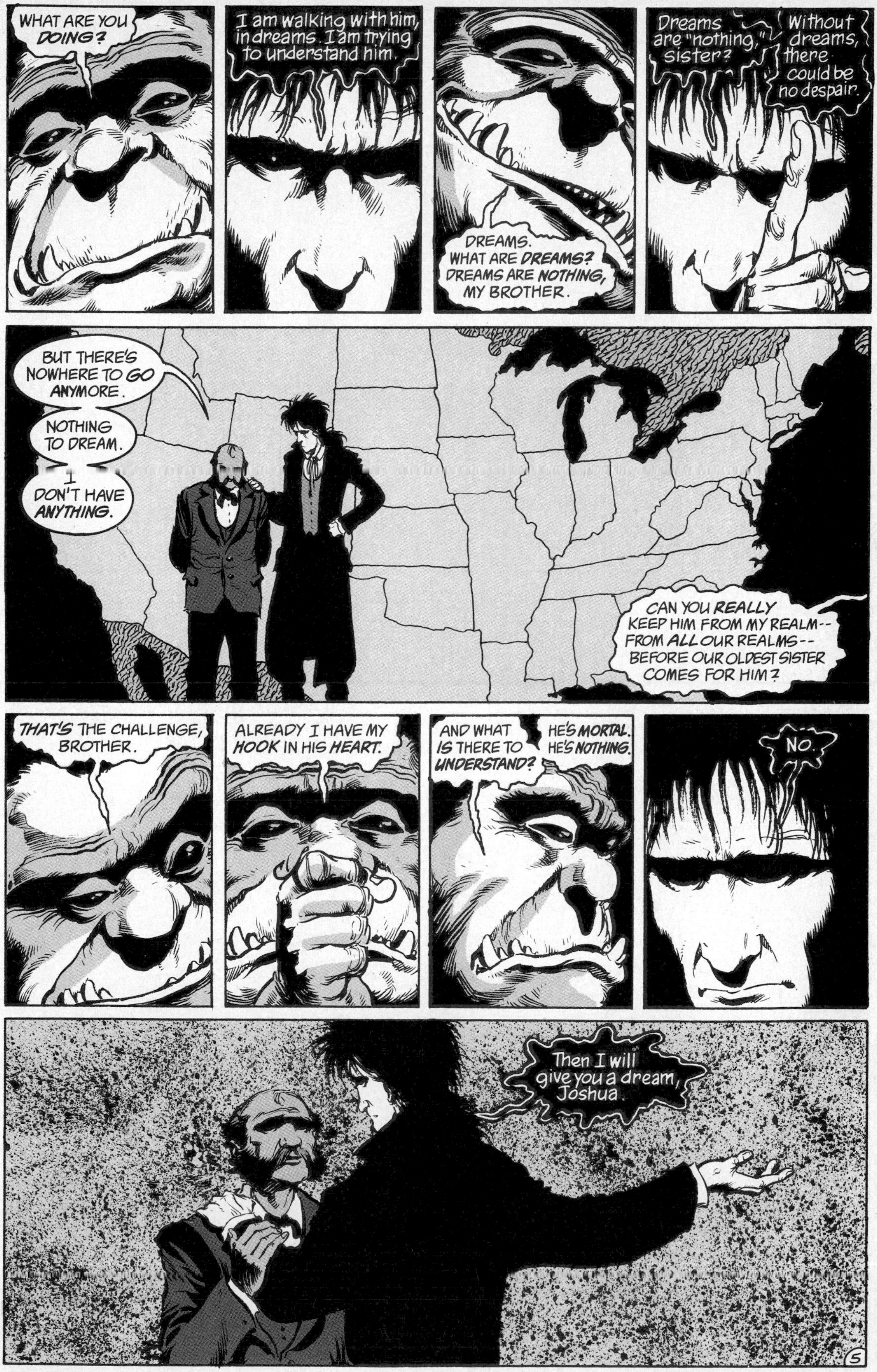
WHAT ARE YOU DOING?
I am walking with him, in dreams. I am trying to understand him.
DREAMS. WHAT ARE DREAMS? DREAMS ARE NOTHING, MY BROTHER.
Dreams are "nothing," sister?
Without dreams, there could be no despair.
BUT THERE'S NOWHERE TO GO ANYMORE.
NOTHING TO DREAM.
I DON'T HAVE ANYTHING.
CAN YOU REALLY KEEP HIM FROM MY REALM-- FROM ALL OUR REALMS-- BEFORE OUR OLDEST SISTER COMES FOR HIM?
THAT'S THE CHALLENGE, BROTHER.
ALREADY I HAVE MY HOOK IN HIS HEART.
AND WHAT IS THERE TO UNDERSTAND?
HE'S MORTAL. HE'S NOTHING.
NO.
Then I will give you a dream, Joshua.
5

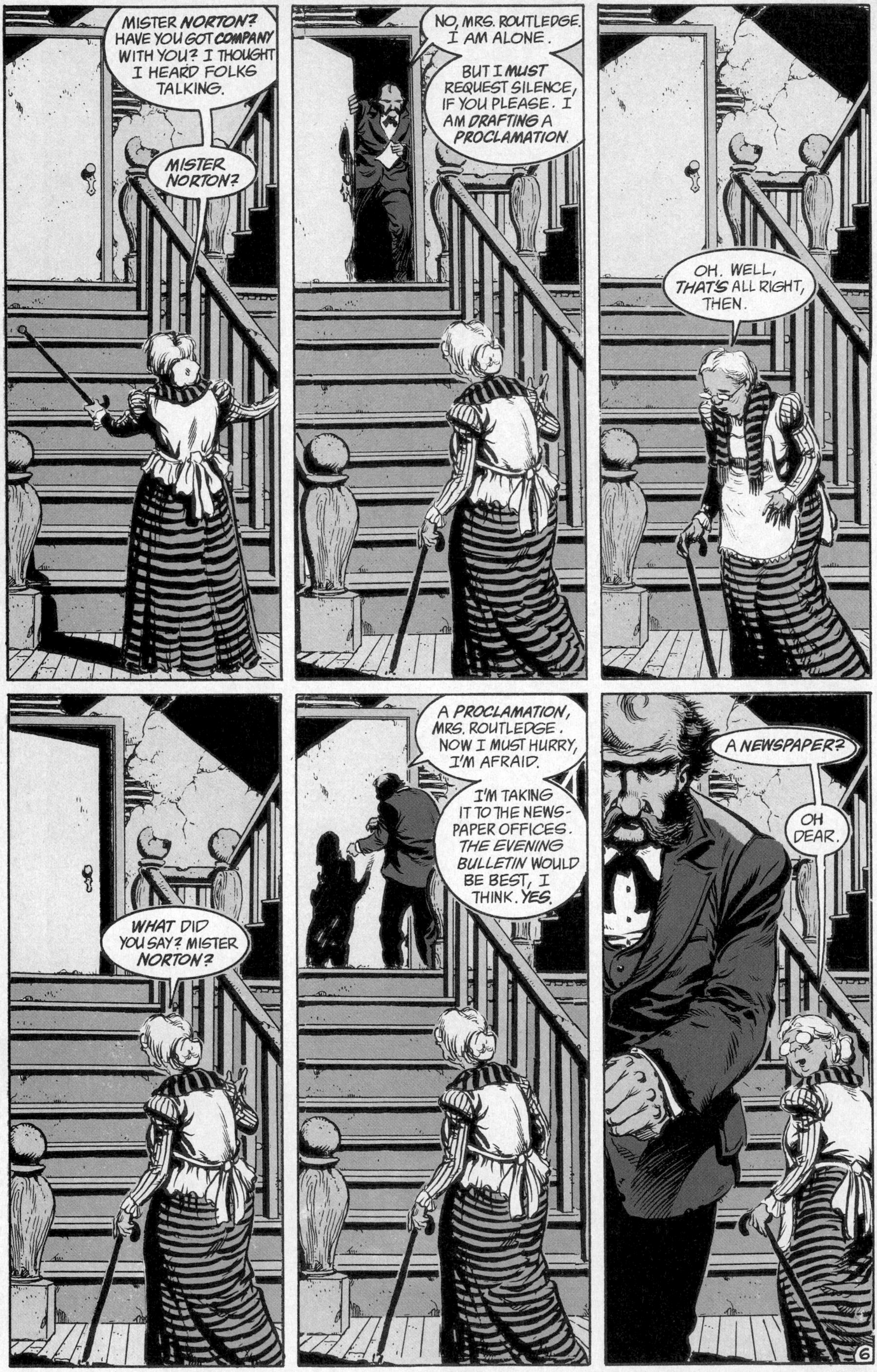

MISTER NORTON? HAVE YOU GOT COMPANY WITH YOU? I THOUGHT I HEARD FOLKS TALKING.
MISTER NORTON?
NO, MRS. ROUTLEDGE. I AM ALONE.
BUT I MUST REQUEST SILENCE, IF YOU PLEASE. I AM DRAFTING A PROCLAMATION.
OH. WELL, THAT'S ALL RIGHT, THEN.
WHAT DID YOU SAY? MISTER NORTON?
A PROCLAMATION, MRS. ROUTLEDGE. NOW I MUST HURRY, I'M AFRAID.
I'M TAKING IT TO THE NEWS-PAPER OFFICES. THE EVENING BULLETIN WOULD BE BEST, I THINK. YES.
A NEWSPAPER?
OH DEAR.
6

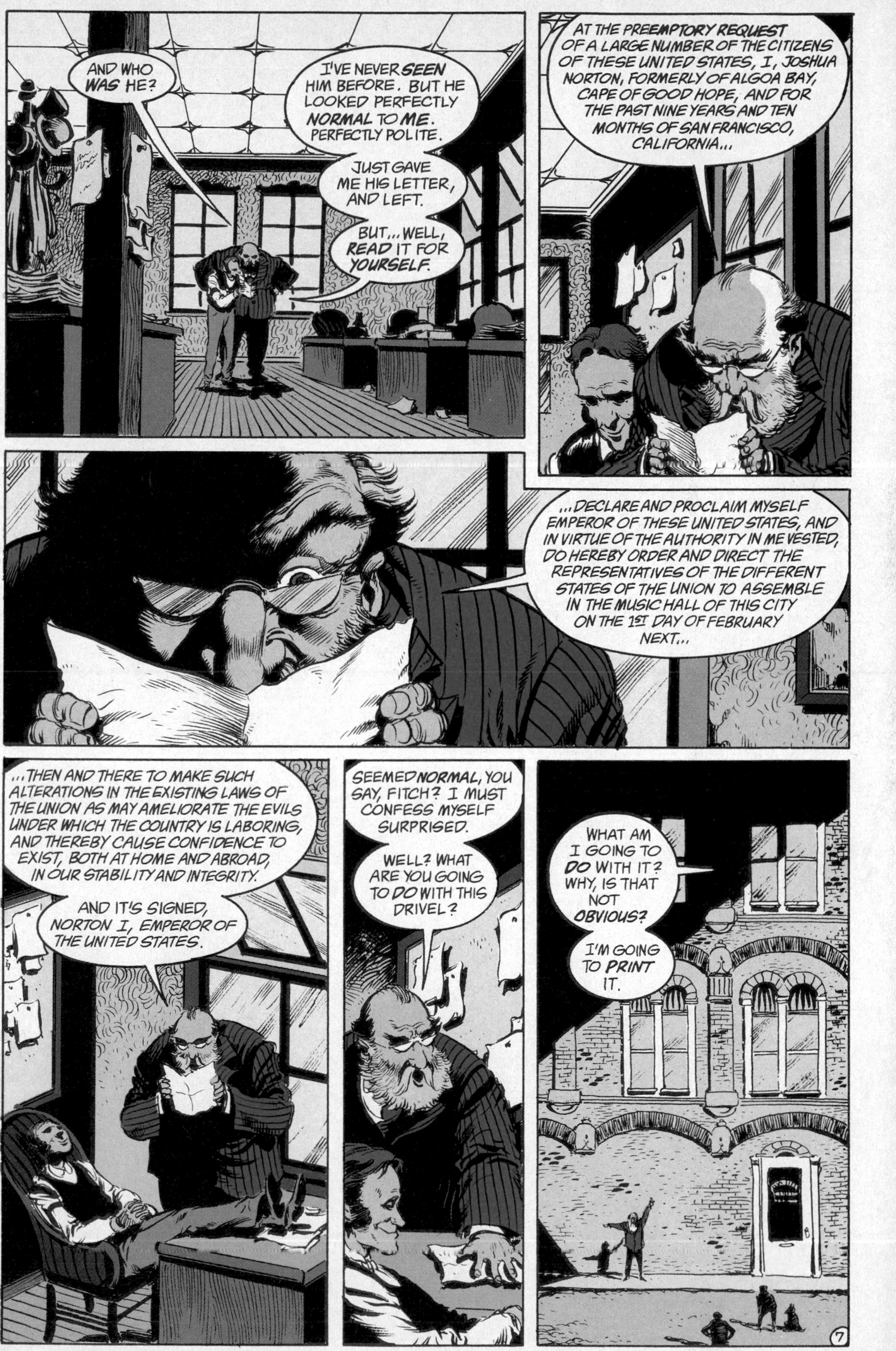
AND WHO WAS HE?
I'VE NEVER SEEN HIM BEFORE. BUT HE LOOKED PERFECTLY NORMAL TO ME. PERFECTLY POLITE.
JUST GAVE ME HIS LETTER, AND LEFT.
BUT... WELL, READ IT FOR YOURSELF.
AT THE PREEMPTORY REQUEST OF A LARGE NUMBER OF THE CITIZENS OF THESE UNITED STATES, I, JOSHUA NORTON, FORMERLY OF ALGOA BAY, CAPE OF GOOD HOPE, AND FOR THE PAST NINE YEARS AND TEN MONTHS OF SAN FRANCISCO, CALIFORNIA...
...DECLARE AND PROCLAIM MYSELF EMPEROR OF THESE UNITED STATES, AND IN VIRTUE OF THE AUTHORITY IN ME VESTED, DO HEREBY ORDER AND DIRECT THE REPRESENTATIVES OF THE DIFFERENT STATES OF THE UNION TO ASSEMBLE IN THE MUSIC HALL OF THIS CITY ON THE 1ST DAY OF FEBRUARY NEXT...
...THEN AND THERE TO MAKE SUCH ALTERATIONS IN THE EXISTING LAWS OF THE UNION AS MAY AMELIORATE THE EVILS UNDER WHICH THE COUNTRY IS LABORING, AND THEREBY CAUSE CONFIDENCE TO EXIST, BOTH AT HOME AND ABROAD, IN OUR STABILITY AND INTEGRITY.
AND IT'S SIGNED, NORTON I, EMPEROR OF THE UNITED STATES.
SEEMED NORMAL, YOU SAY, FITCH? I MUST CONFESS MYSELF SURPRISED.
WELL? WHAT ARE YOU GOING TO DO WITH THIS DRIVEL?
WHAT AM I GOING TO DO WITH IT? WHY, IS THAT NOT OBVIOUS?
I'M GOING TO PRINT IT.
7

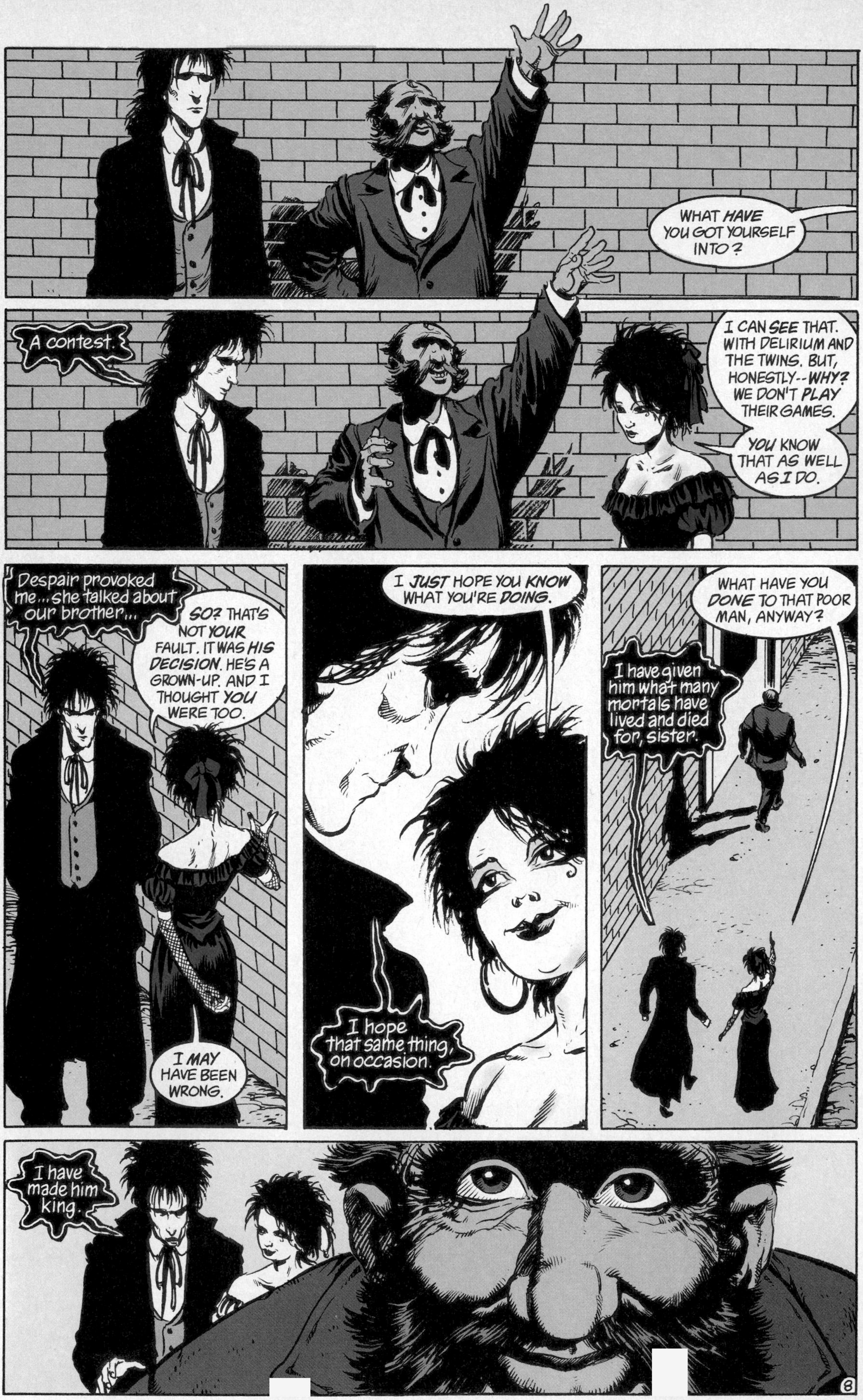
WHAT HAVE YOU GOT YOURSELF INTO?
A contest.
I CAN SEE THAT. WITH DELIRIUM AND THE TWINS. BUT, HONESTLY--WHY? WE DON'T PLAY THEIR GAMES.
YOU KNOW THAT AS WELL AS I DO.
Despair provoked me...she talked about our brother...
SO? THAT'S NOT YOUR FAULT. IT WAS HIS DECISION. HE'S A GROWN-UP. AND I THOUGHT YOU WERE TOO.
I MAY HAVE BEEN WRONG.
I JUST HOPE YOU KNOW WHAT YOU'RE DOING.
I hope that same thing, on occasion.
WHAT HAVE YOU DONE TO THAT POOR MAN, ANYWAY?
I have given him what many mortals have lived and died for, sister.
I have made him king.
8

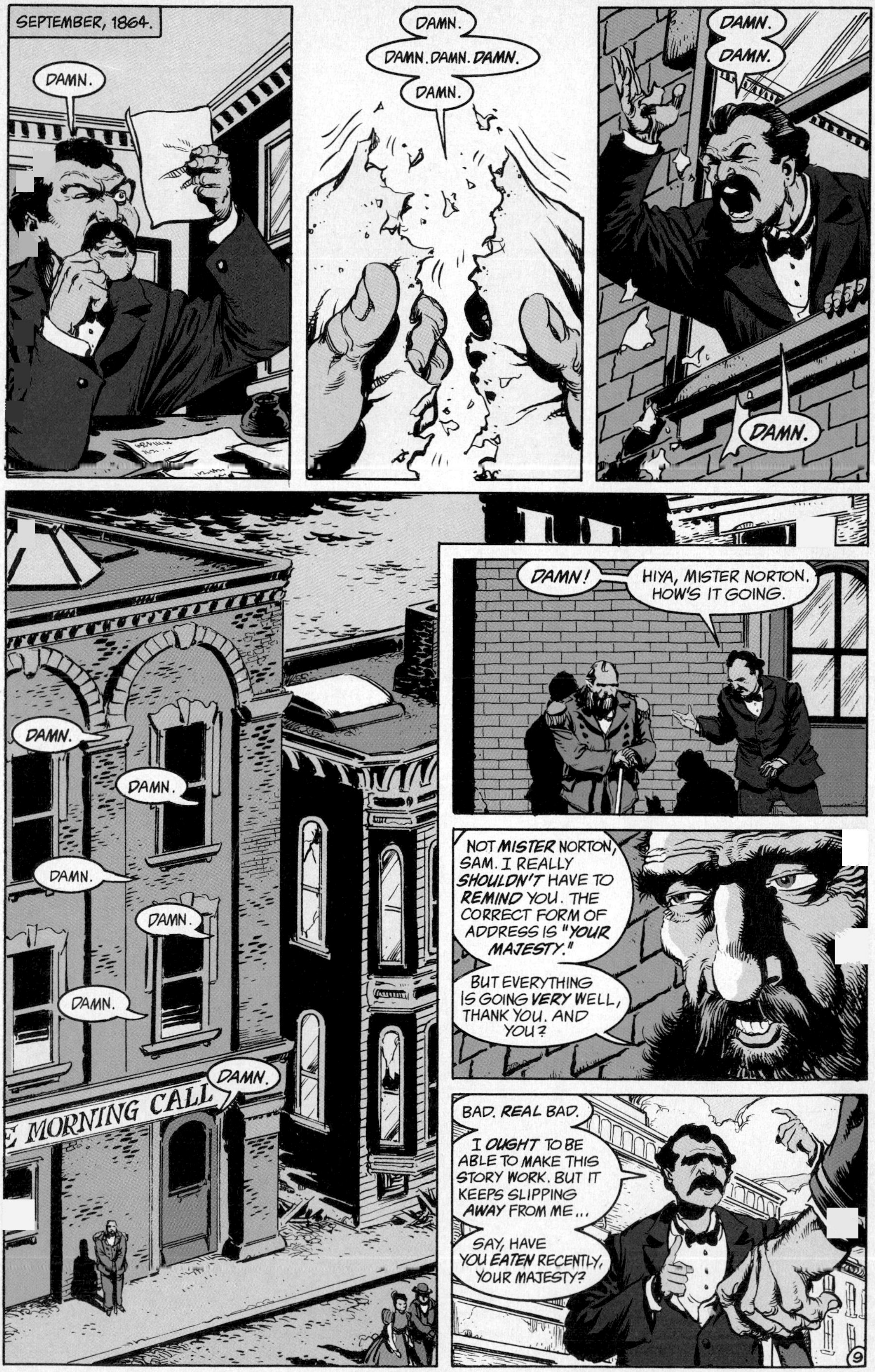
SEPTEMBER, 1864.
DAMN.
DAMN.
DAMN. DAMN. DAMN.
DAMN.
DAMN.
DAMN.
DAMN.
DAMN.
DAMN.
DAMN.
DAMN.
DAMN.
DAMN.
THE MORNING CALL
DAMN!
HIYA, MISTER NORTON. HOW'S IT GOING.
NOT MISTER NORTON, SAM. I REALLY SHOULDN'T HAVE TO REMIND YOU. THE CORRECT FORM OF ADDRESS IS "YOUR MAJESTY."
BUT EVERYTHING IS GOING VERY WELL, THANK YOU. AND YOU?
BAD. REAL BAD.
I OUGHT TO BE ABLE TO MAKE THIS STORY WORK. BUT IT KEEPS SLIPPING AWAY FROM ME...
SAY, HAVE YOU EATEN RECENTLY, YOUR MAJESTY?
9

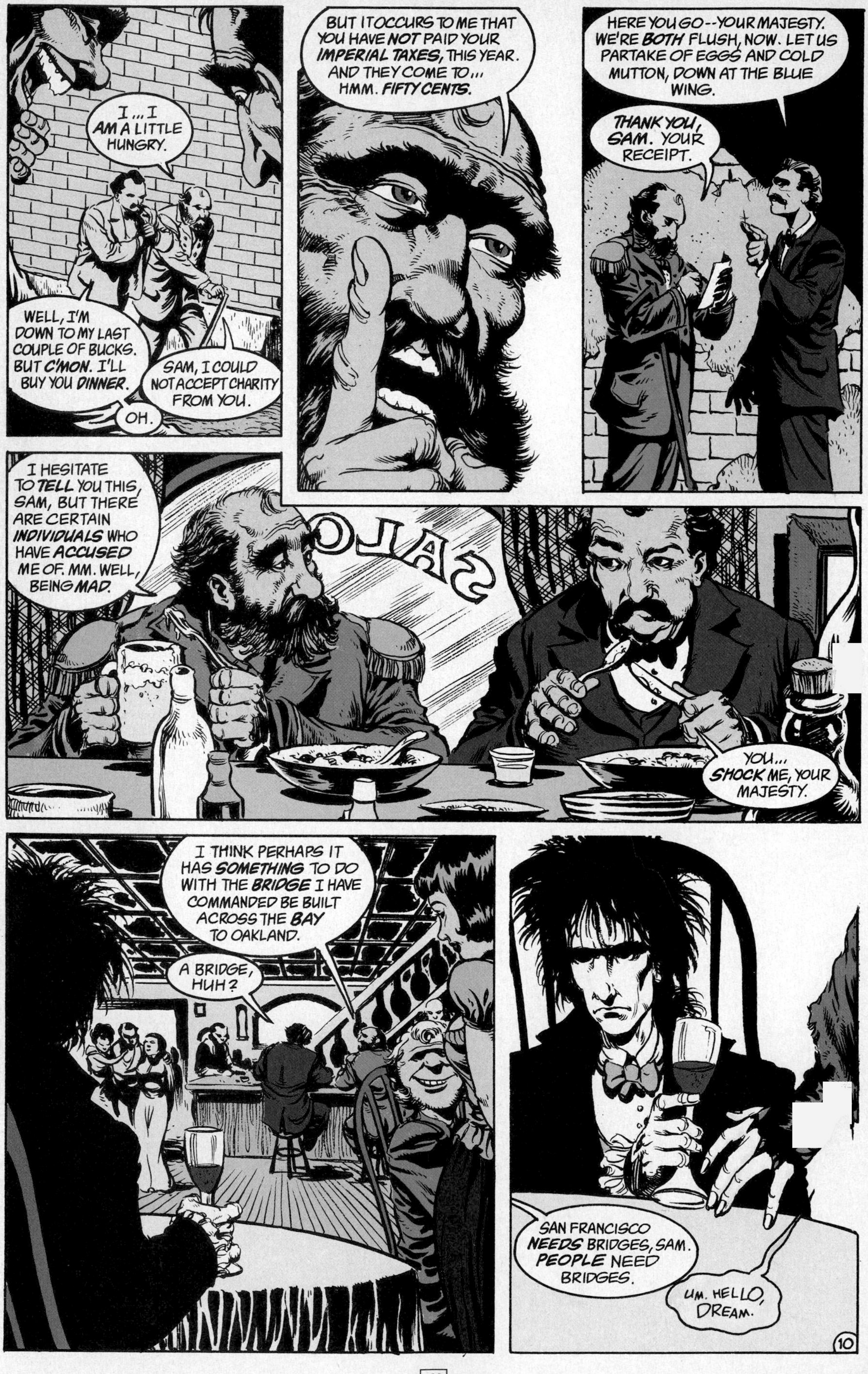
I... I AM A LITTLE HUNGRY.
WELL, I'M DOWN TO MY LAST COUPLE OF BUCKS. BUT C'MON. I'LL BUY YOU DINNER.
SAM, I COULD NOT ACCEPT CHARITY FROM YOU.
OH.
BUT IT OCCURS TO ME THAT YOU HAVE NOT PAID YOUR IMPERIAL TAXES, THIS YEAR. AND THEY COME TO... HMM. FIFTY CENTS.
HERE YOU GO--YOUR MAJESTY. WE'RE BOTH FLUSH, NOW. LET US PARTAKE OF EGGS AND COLD MUTTON, DOWN AT THE BLUE WING.
THANK YOU, SAM. YOUR RECEIPT.
I HESITATE TO TELL YOU THIS, SAM, BUT THERE ARE CERTAIN INDIVIDUALS WHO HAVE ACCUSED ME OF. MM. WELL, BEING MAD.
SALO
YOU... SHOCK ME, YOUR MAJESTY.
I THINK PERHAPS IT HAS SOMETHING TO DO WITH THE BRIDGE I HAVE COMMANDED BE BUILT ACROSS THE BAY TO OAKLAND.
A BRIDGE, HUH?
SAN FRANCISCO NEEDS BRIDGES, SAM. PEOPLE NEED BRIDGES.
UM. HELLO, DREAM.
10

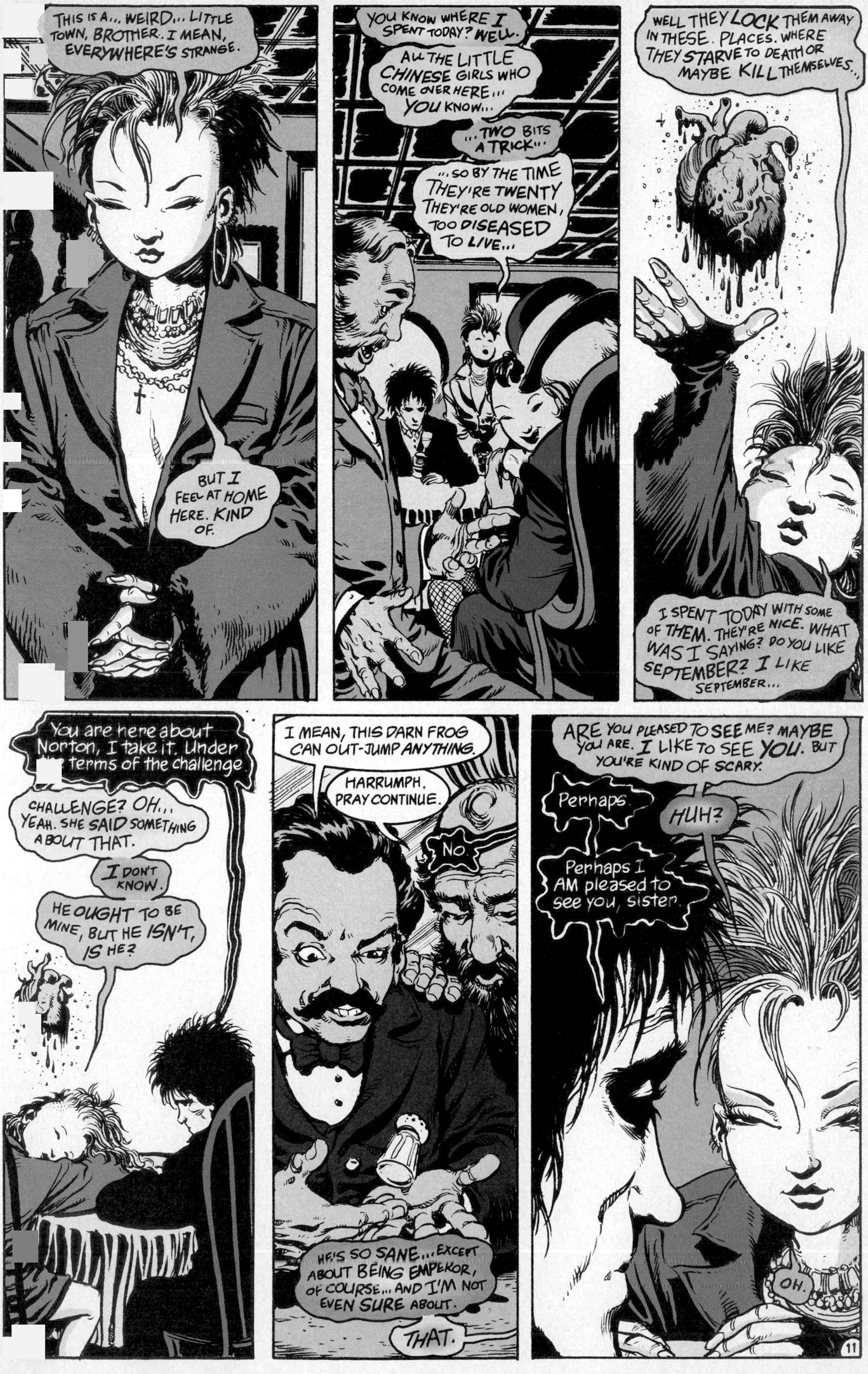

THIS IS A... WEIRD... LITTLE TOWN, BROTHER. I MEAN, EVERYWHERE'S STRANGE.
BUT I FEEL AT HOME HERE. KIND OF.
YOU KNOW WHERE I SPENT TODAY? WELL.
ALL THE LITTLE CHINESE GIRLS WHO COME OVER HERE... YOU KNOW...
...TWO BITS A TRICK...
...SO BY THE TIME THEY'RE TWENTY THEY'RE OLD WOMEN, TOO DISEASED TO LIVE...
WELL THEY LOCK THEM AWAY IN THESE. PLACES. WHERE THEY STARVE TO DEATH OR MAYBE KILL THEMSELVES...
I SPENT TODAY WITH SOME OF THEM. THEY'RE NICE. WHAT WAS I SAYING? DO YOU LIKE SEPTEMBER? I LIKE SEPTEMBER...
You are here about Norton, I take it. Under the terms of the challenge
CHALLENGE? OH... YEAH. SHE SAID SOMETHING ABOUT THAT.
I DON'T KNOW.
HE OUGHT TO BE MINE, BUT HE ISN'T, IS HE?
I MEAN, THIS DARN FROG CAN OUT-JUMP ANYTHING.
HARRUMPH. PRAY CONTINUE.
No
HE'S SO SANE... EXCEPT ABOUT BEING EMPEROR, OF COURSE... AND I'M NOT EVEN SURE ABOUT.
THAT.
ARE YOU PLEASED TO SEE ME? MAYBE YOU ARE. I LIKE TO SEE YOU. BUT YOU'RE KIND OF SCARY.
Perhaps.
HUH?
Perhaps I AM pleased to see you, sister.
OH.
11

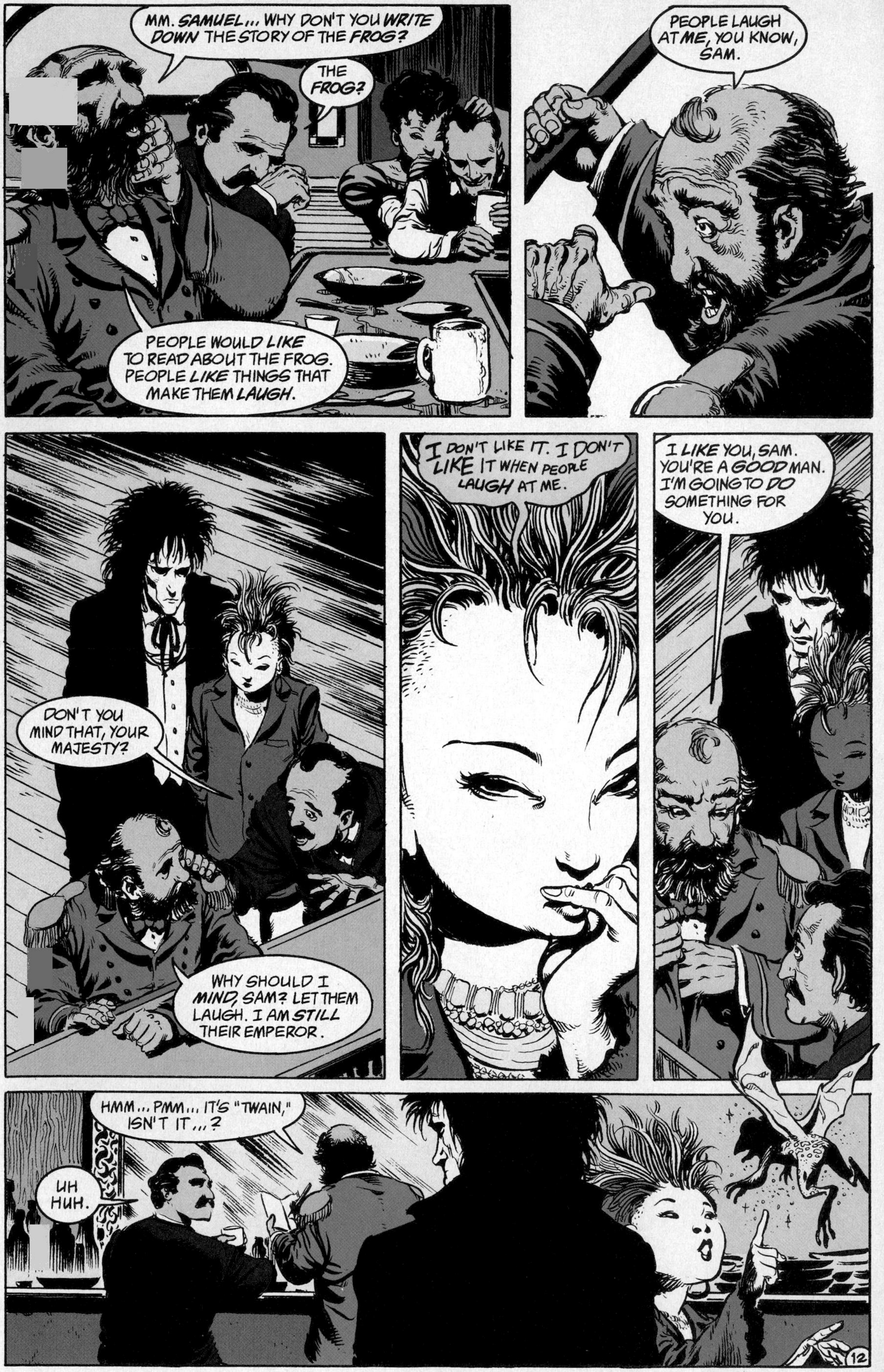
MM. SAMUEL... WHY DON'T YOU WRITE DOWN THE STORY OF THE FROG?
THE FROG?
PEOPLE WOULD LIKE TO READ ABOUT THE FROG. PEOPLE LIKE THINGS THAT MAKE THEM LAUGH.
PEOPLE LAUGH AT ME, YOU KNOW, SAM.
DON'T YOU MIND THAT, YOUR MAJESTY?
WHY SHOULD I MIND, SAM? LET THEM LAUGH. I AM STILL THEIR EMPEROR.
I DON'T LIKE IT. I DON'T LIKE IT WHEN PEOPLE LAUGH AT ME.
I LIKE YOU, SAM. YOU'RE A GOOD MAN. I'M GOING TO DO SOMETHING FOR YOU.
HMM... PMM... IT'S "TWAIN," ISN'T IT...?
UH HUH.
12

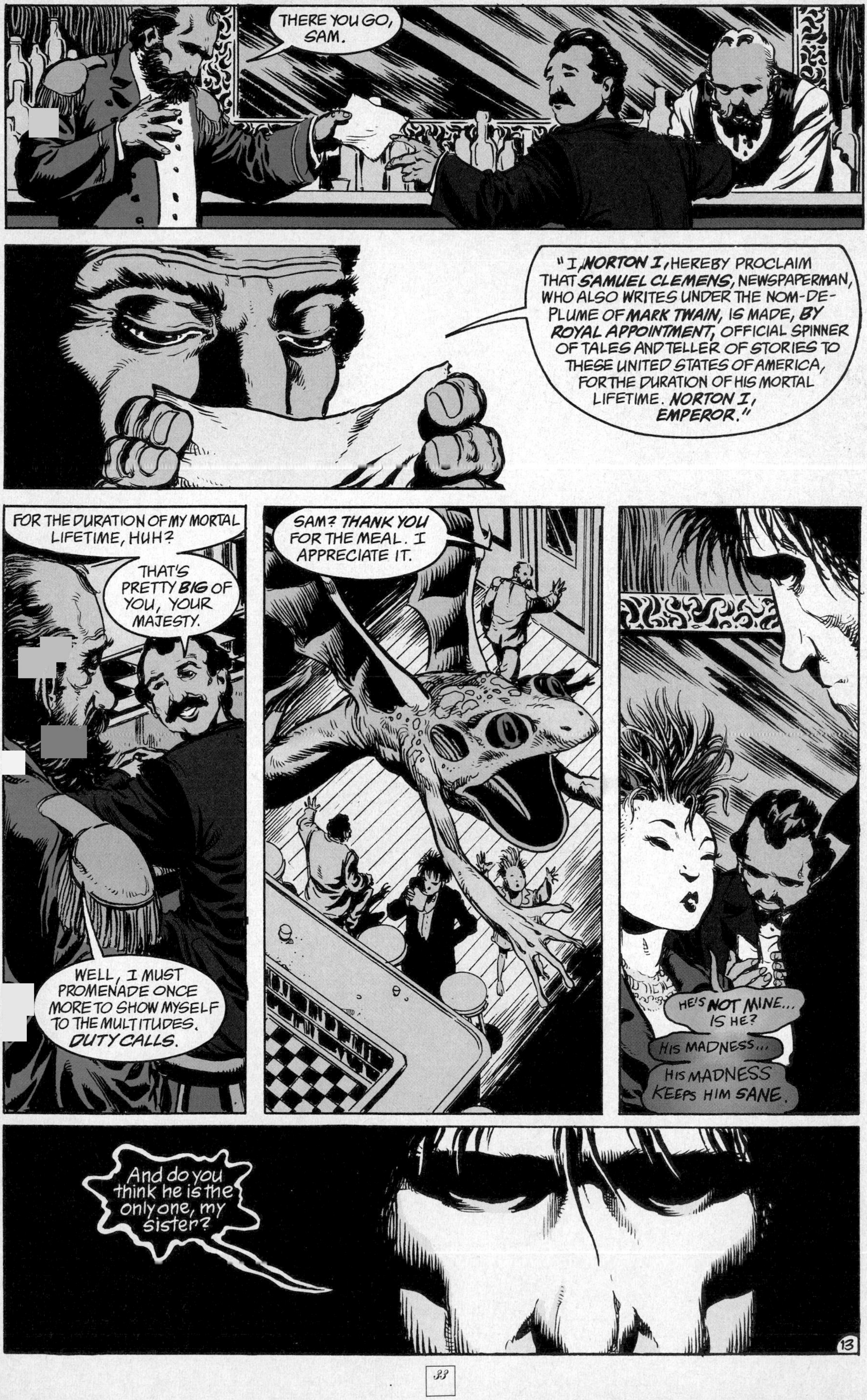
THERE YOU GO, SAM.
"I, NORTON I, HEREBY PROCLAIM THAT SAMUEL CLEMENS, NEWSPAPERMAN, WHO ALSO WRITES UNDER THE NOM-DE-PLUME OF MARK TWAIN, IS MADE, BY ROYAL APPOINTMENT, OFFICIAL SPINNER OF TALES AND TELLER OF STORIES TO THESE UNITED STATES OF AMERICA, FOR THE DURATION OF HIS MORTAL LIFETIME. NORTON I, EMPEROR."
FOR THE DURATION OF MY MORTAL LIFETIME, HUH?
THAT'S PRETTY BIG OF YOU, YOUR MAJESTY.
WELL, I MUST PROMENADE ONCE MORE TO SHOW MYSELF TO THE MULTITUDES. DUTY CALLS.
SAM? THANK YOU FOR THE MEAL. I APPRECIATE IT.
HE'S NOT MINE... IS HE?
HIS MADNESS...
HIS MADNESS KEEPS HIM SANE.
And do you think he is the only one, my sister?
13

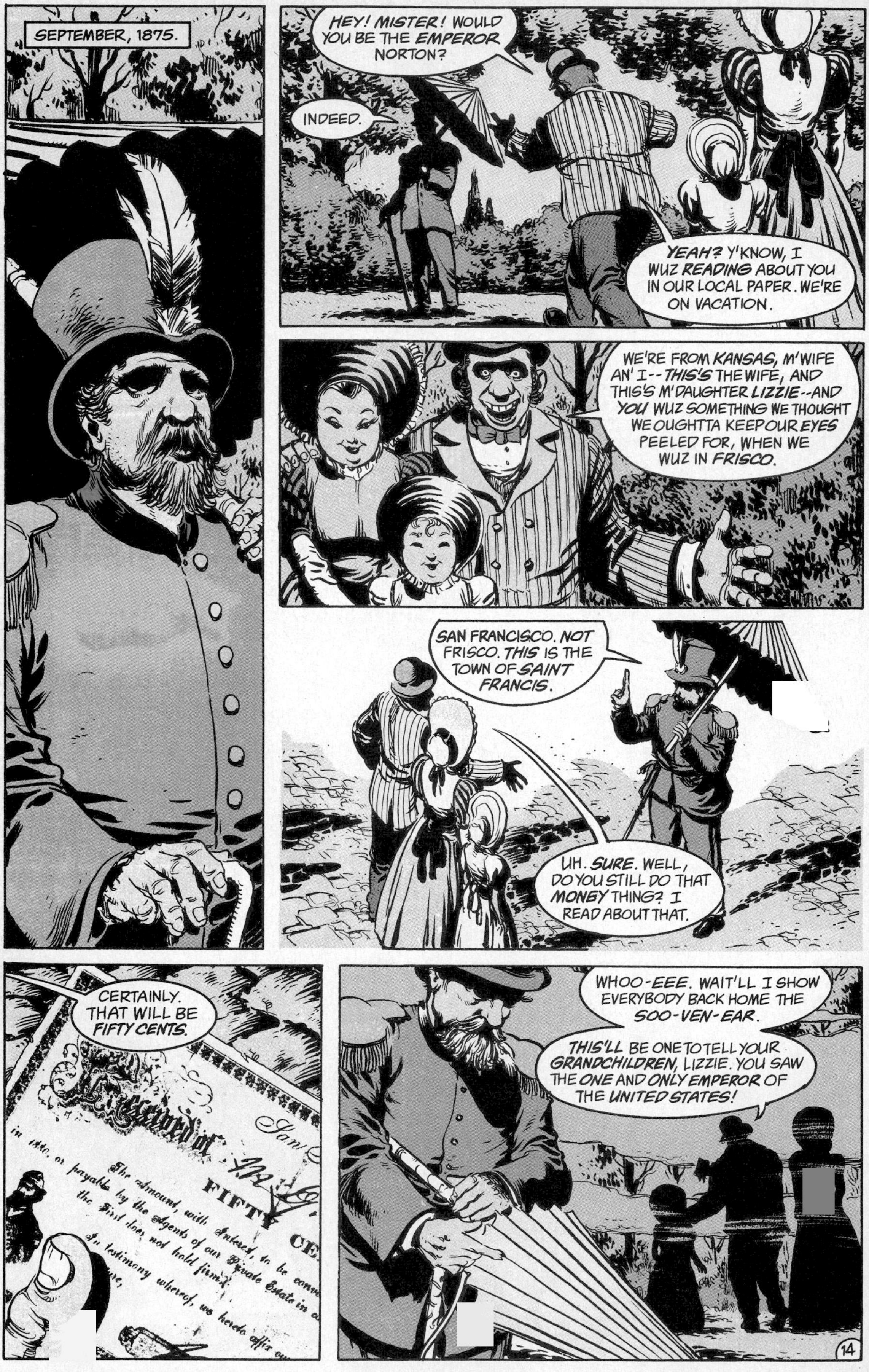
SEPTEMBER, 1875.
HEY! MISTER! WOULD YOU BE THE EMPEROR NORTON?
INDEED.
YEAH? Y'KNOW, I WUZ READING ABOUT YOU IN OUR LOCAL PAPER. WE'RE ON VACATION.
WE'RE FROM KANSAS, M'WIFE AN' I--THIS'S THE WIFE, AND THIS'S M'DAUGHTER LIZZIE--AND YOU WUZ SOMETHING WE THOUGHT WE OUGHTTA KEEP OUR EYES PEELED FOR, WHEN WE WUZ IN FRISCO.
SAN FRANCISCO. NOT FRISCO. THIS IS THE TOWN OF SAINT FRANCIS.
UH. SURE. WELL, DO YOU STILL DO THAT MONEY THING? I READ ABOUT THAT.
CERTAINLY. THAT WILL BE FIFTY CENTS.
WHOO-EEE. WAIT'LL I SHOW EVERYBODY BACK HOME THE SOO-VEN-EAR.
THIS'LL BE ONE TO TELL YOUR GRANDCHILDREN, LIZZIE. YOU SAW THE ONE AND ONLY EMPEROR OF THE UNITED STATES!

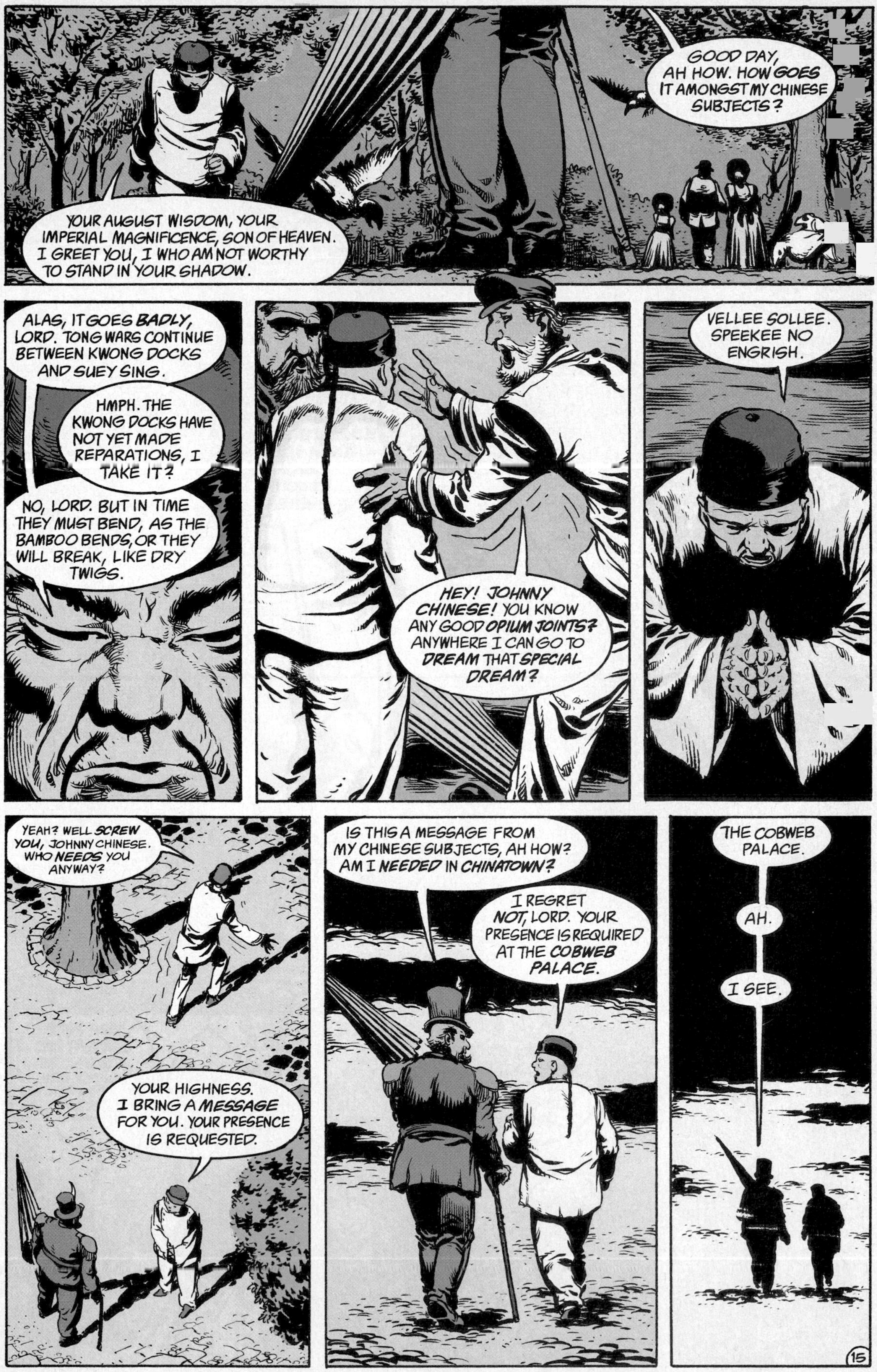
GOOD DAY, AH HOW. HOW GOES IT AMONGST MY CHINESE SUBJECTS?
YOUR AUGUST WISDOM, YOUR IMPERIAL MAGNIFICENCE, SON OF HEAVEN. I GREET YOU, I WHO AM NOT WORTHY TO STAND IN YOUR SHADOW.
ALAS, IT GOES BADLY, LORD. TONG WARS CONTINUE BETWEEN KWONG DOCKS AND SUEY SING.
HMPH. THE KWONG DOCKS HAVE NOT YET MADE REPARATIONS, I TAKE IT?
NO, LORD. BUT IN TIME THEY MUST BEND, AS THE BAMBOO BENDS, OR THEY WILL BREAK, LIKE DRY TWIGS.
HEY! JOHNNY CHINESE! YOU KNOW ANY GOOD OPIUM JOINTS? ANYWHERE I CAN GO TO DREAM THAT SPECIAL DREAM?
VELLEE SOLLEE. SPEEKEE NO ENGRISH.
YEAH? WELL SCREW YOU, JOHNNY CHINESE. WHO NEEDS YOU ANYWAY?
YOUR HIGHNESS. I BRING A MESSAGE FOR YOU. YOUR PRESENCE IS REQUESTED.
IS THIS A MESSAGE FROM MY CHINESE SUBJECTS, AH HOW? AM I NEEDED IN CHINATOWN?
I REGRET NOT, LORD. YOUR PRESENCE IS REQUIRED AT THE COBWEB PALACE.
THE COBWEB PALACE.
AH.
I SEE.
15

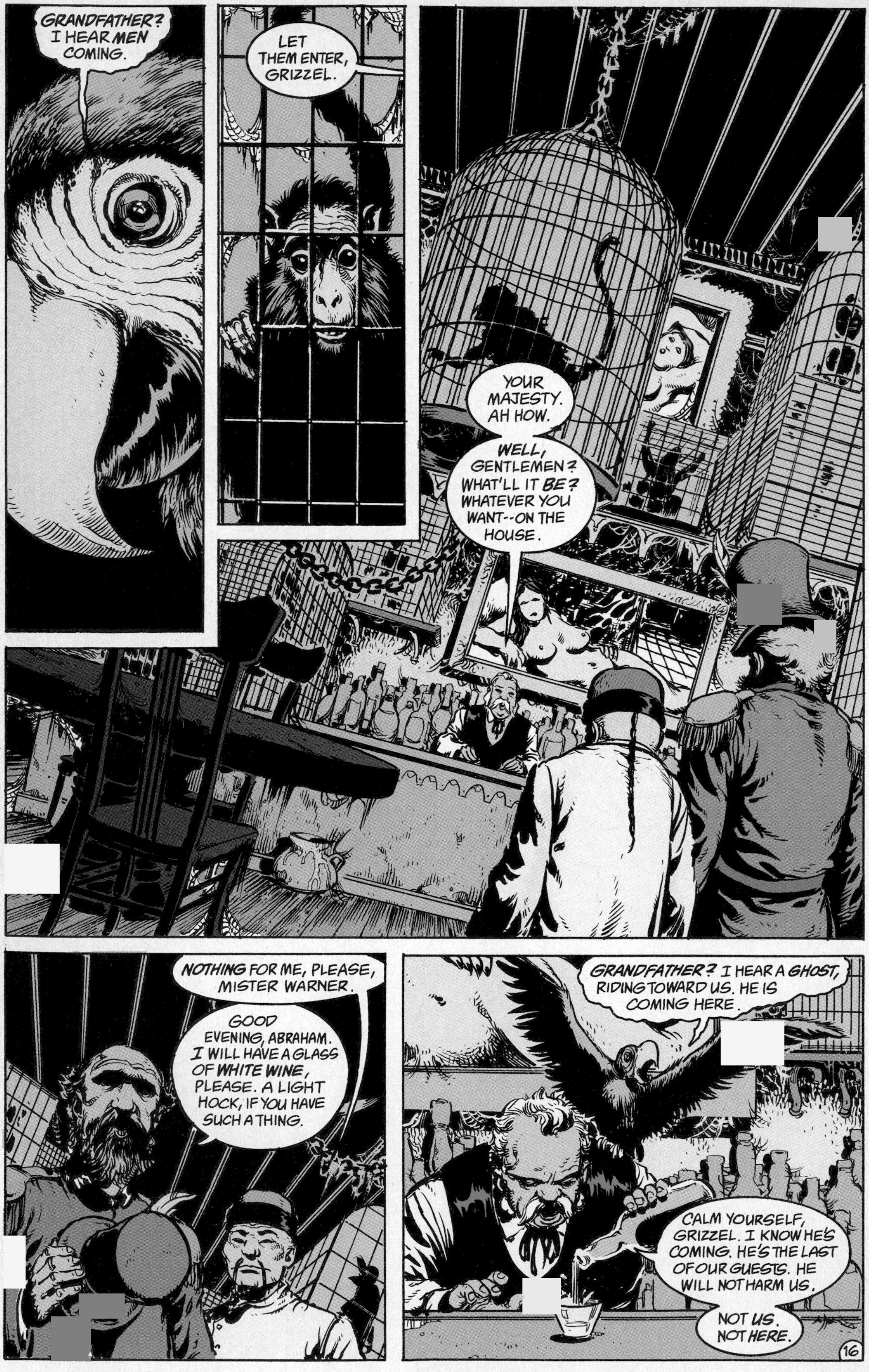
GRANDFATHER? I HEAR MEN COMING.
LET THEM ENTER, GRIZZEL.
YOUR MAJESTY. AH HOW.
WELL, GENTLEMEN? WHAT'LL IT BE? WHATEVER YOU WANT--ON THE HOUSE.
NOTHING FOR ME, PLEASE, MISTER WARNER.
GOOD EVENING, ABRAHAM. I WILL HAVE A GLASS OF WHITE WINE, PLEASE. A LIGHT HOCK, IF YOU HAVE SUCH A THING.
GRANDFATHER? I HEAR A GHOST, RIDING TOWARD US. HE IS COMING HERE.
CALM YOURSELF, GRIZZEL. I KNOW HE'S COMING. HE'S THE LAST OF OUR GUESTS. HE WILL NOT HARM US.
NOT US. NOT HERE.
16

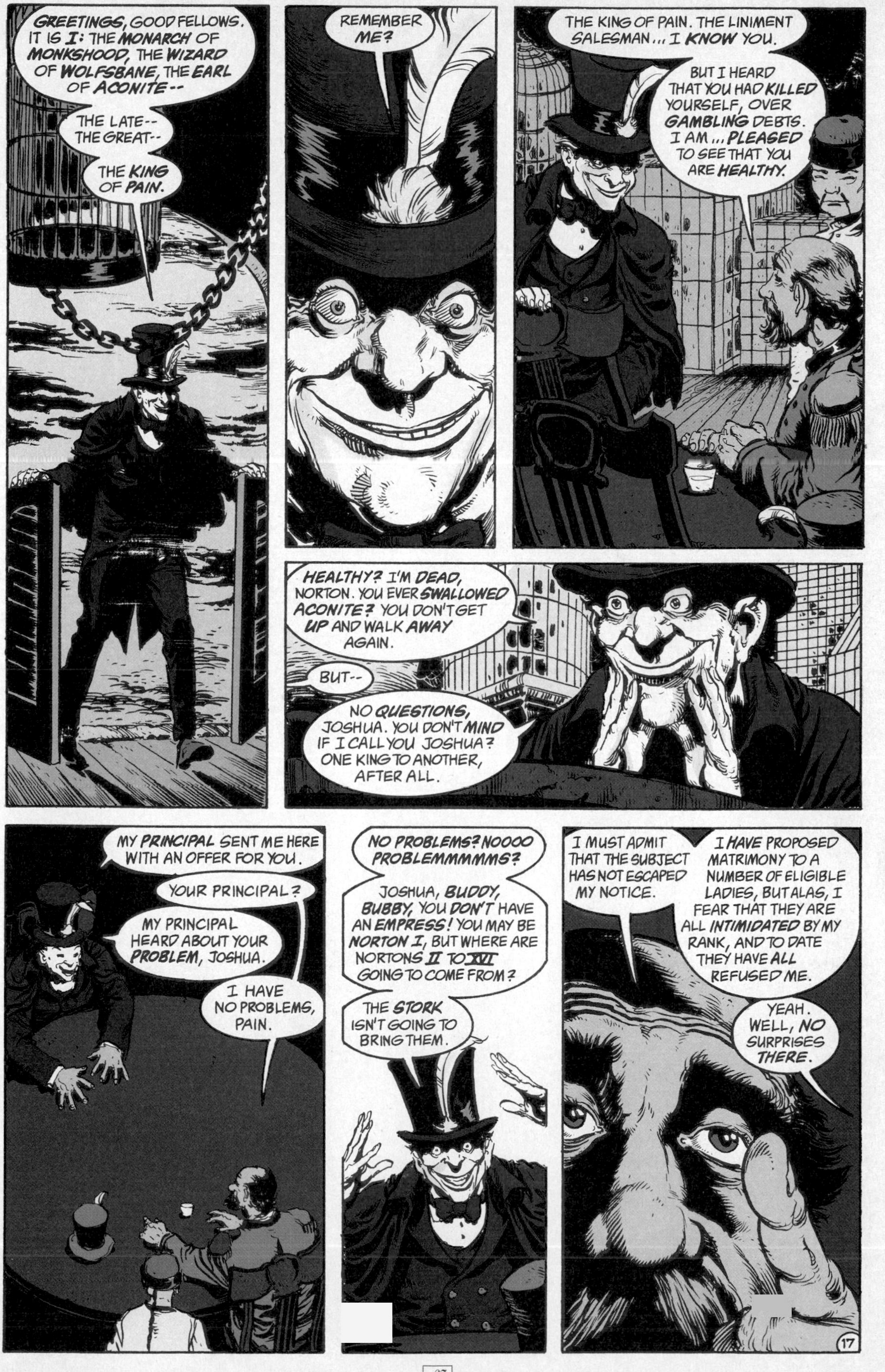
GREETINGS, GOOD FELLOWS. IT IS I: THE MONARCH OF MONKSHOOD, THE WIZARD OF WOLFSBANE, THE EARL OF ACONITE--
THE LATE-- THE GREAT--
THE KING OF PAIN.
REMEMBER ME?
THE KING OF PAIN. THE LINIMENT SALESMAN... I KNOW YOU.
BUT I HEARD THAT YOU HAD KILLED YOURSELF, OVER GAMBLING DEBTS. I AM... PLEASED TO SEE THAT YOU ARE HEALTHY.
HEALTHY? I'M DEAD, NORTON. YOU EVER SWALLOWED ACONITE? YOU DON'T GET UP AND WALK AWAY AGAIN.
BUT--
NO QUESTIONS, JOSHUA. YOU DON'T MIND IF I CALL YOU JOSHUA? ONE KING TO ANOTHER, AFTER ALL.
MY PRINCIPAL SENT ME HERE WITH AN OFFER FOR YOU.
YOUR PRINCIPAL?
MY PRINCIPAL HEARD ABOUT YOUR PROBLEM, JOSHUA.
I HAVE NO PROBLEMS, PAIN.
NO PROBLEMS? NOOOO PROBLEMMMMMS?
JOSHUA, BUDDY, BUBBY, YOU DON'T HAVE AN EMPRESS! YOU MAY BE NORTON I, BUT WHERE ARE NORTONS II TO XVI GOING TO COME FROM?
THE STORK ISN'T GOING TO BRING THEM.
I MUST ADMIT THAT THE SUBJECT HAS NOT ESCAPED MY NOTICE.
I HAVE PROPOSED MATRIMONY TO A NUMBER OF ELIGIBLE LADIES, BUT ALAS, I FEAR THAT THEY ARE ALL INTIMIDATED BY MY RANK, AND TO DATE THEY HAVE ALL REFUSED ME.
YEAH. WELL, NO SURPRISES THERE.
17

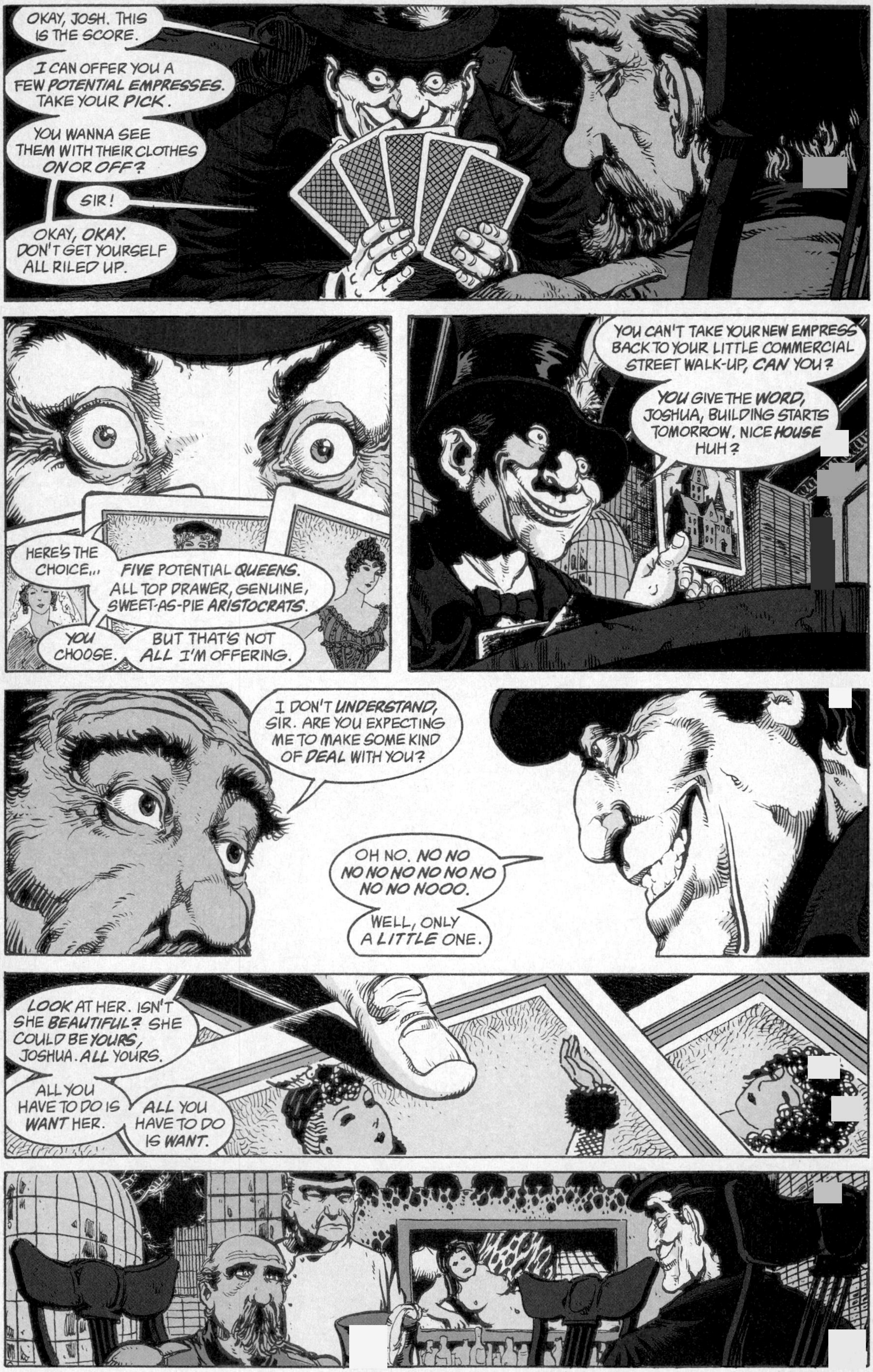
OKAY, JOSH. THIS IS THE SCORE.
I CAN OFFER YOU A FEW POTENTIAL EMPRESSES. TAKE YOUR PICK.
YOU WANNA SEE THEM WITH THEIR CLOTHES ON OR OFF?
SIR!
OKAY, OKAY. DON'T GET YOURSELF ALL RILED UP.
HERE'S THE CHOICE...
FIVE POTENTIAL QUEENS. ALL TOP DRAWER, GENUINE, SWEET-AS-PIE ARISTOCRATS.
YOU CHOOSE.
BUT THAT'S NOT ALL I'M OFFERING.
YOU CAN'T TAKE YOUR NEW EMPRESS BACK TO YOUR LITTLE COMMERCIAL STREET WALK-UP, CAN YOU?
YOU GIVE THE WORD, JOSHUA, BUILDING STARTS TOMORROW. NICE HOUSE HUH?
I DON'T UNDERSTAND, SIR. ARE YOU EXPECTING ME TO MAKE SOME KIND OF DEAL WITH YOU?
OH NO. NO NO NO NO NO NO NO NO NO NO NOOO.
WELL, ONLY A LITTLE ONE.
LOOK AT HER. ISN'T SHE BEAUTIFUL? SHE COULD BE YOURS, JOSHUA. ALL YOURS.
ALL YOU HAVE TO DO IS WANT HER.
ALL YOU HAVE TO DO IS WANT.

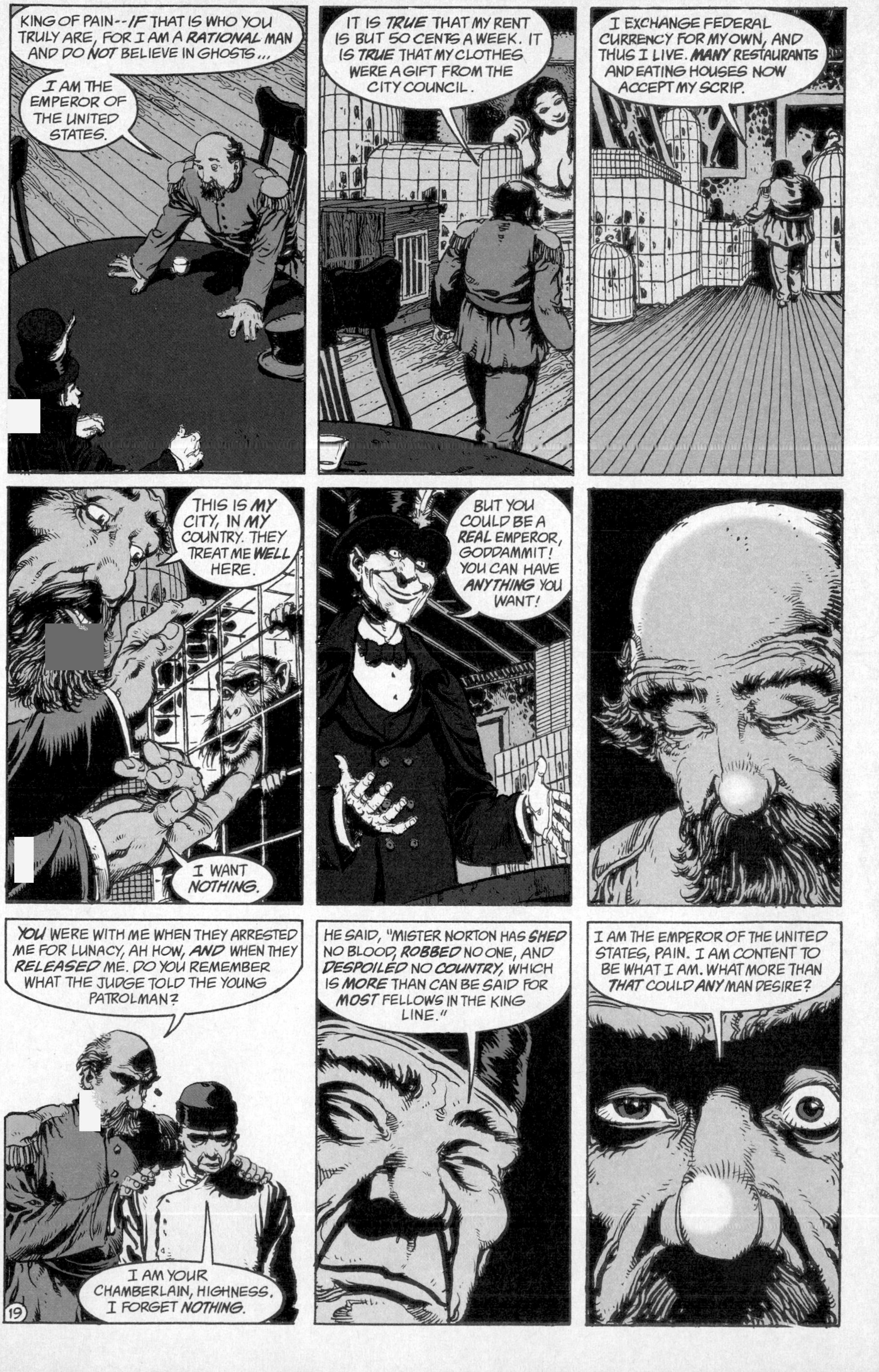
KING OF PAIN--*IF* THAT IS WHO YOU TRULY ARE, FOR I AM A *RATIONAL* MAN AND DO *NOT* BELIEVE IN GHOSTS...
I AM THE EMPEROR OF THE UNITED STATES.
IT IS *TRUE* THAT MY RENT IS BUT 50 CENTS A WEEK. IT IS *TRUE* THAT MY CLOTHES WERE A GIFT FROM THE CITY COUNCIL.
I EXCHANGE FEDERAL CURRENCY FOR MY OWN, AND THUS I LIVE. *MANY* RESTAURANTS AND EATING HOUSES NOW ACCEPT MY SCRIP.
THIS IS *MY* CITY, IN *MY* COUNTRY. THEY TREAT ME *WELL* HERE.
I WANT *NOTHING*.
BUT YOU COULD BE A *REAL* EMPEROR, GODDAMMIT! YOU CAN HAVE *ANYTHING* YOU WANT!
YOU WERE WITH ME WHEN THEY ARRESTED ME FOR LUNACY, AH HOW, *AND* WHEN THEY *RELEASED* ME. DO YOU REMEMBER WHAT THE JUDGE TOLD THE YOUNG PATROLMAN?
I AM YOUR CHAMBERLAIN, HIGHNESS. I FORGET *NOTHING*.
HE SAID, "MISTER NORTON HAS *SHED* NO BLOOD, *ROBBED* NO ONE, AND *DESPOILED* NO *COUNTRY*, WHICH IS *MORE* THAN CAN BE SAID FOR *MOST* FELLOWS IN THE KING LINE."
I AM THE EMPEROR OF THE UNITED STATES, PAIN. I AM CONTENT TO BE WHAT I AM. WHAT MORE THAN *THAT* COULD *ANY* MAN DESIRE?

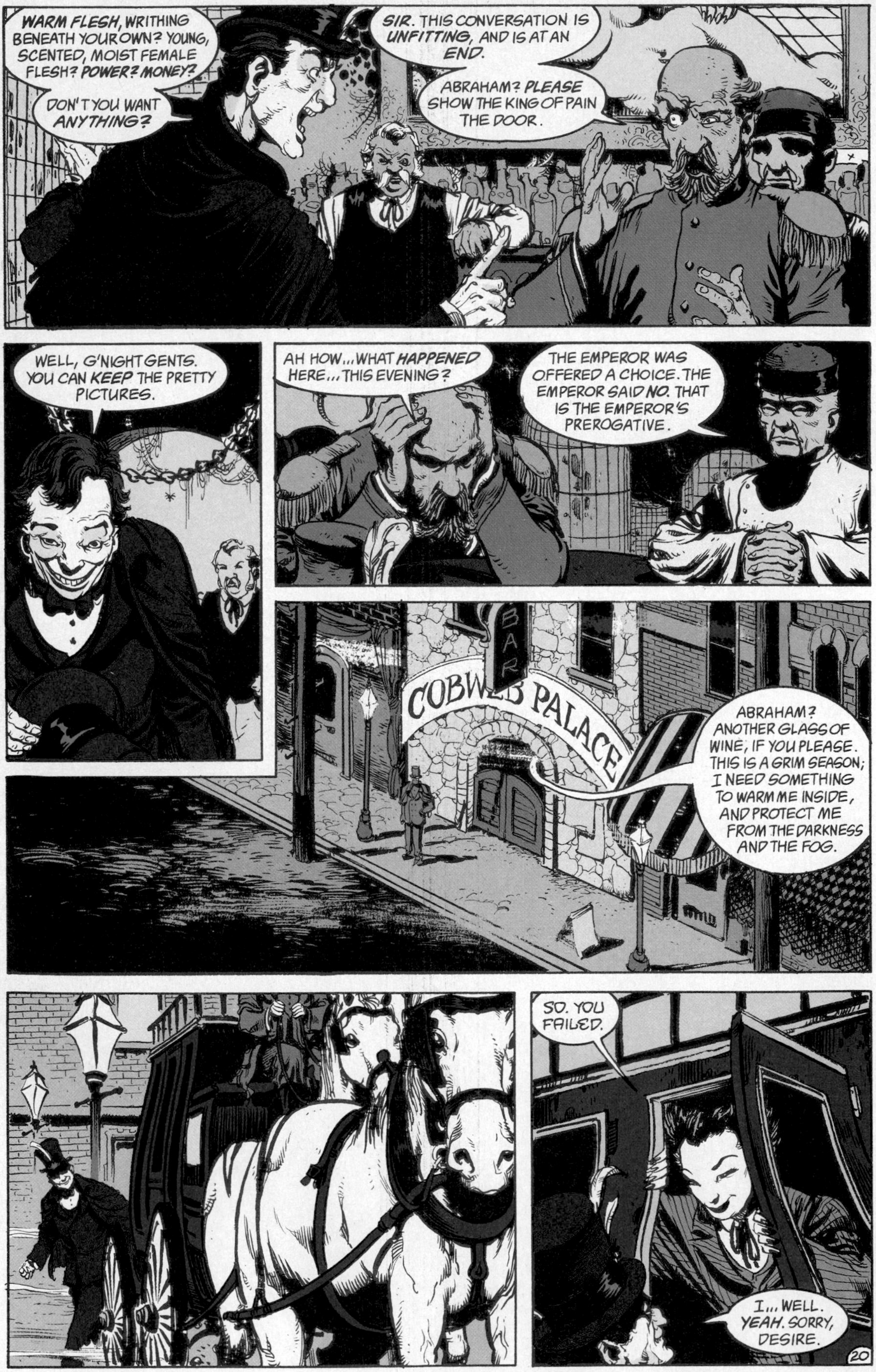

WARM FLESH, WRITHING BENEATH YOUR OWN? YOUNG, SCENTED, MOIST FEMALE FLESH? POWER? MONEY?
DON'T YOU WANT ANYTHING?
SIR. THIS CONVERSATION IS UNFITTING, AND IS AT AN END.
ABRAHAM? PLEASE SHOW THE KING OF PAIN THE DOOR.
WELL, G'NIGHT GENTS. YOU CAN KEEP THE PRETTY PICTURES.
AH HOW...WHAT HAPPENED HERE... THIS EVENING?
THE EMPEROR WAS OFFERED A CHOICE. THE EMPEROR SAID NO. THAT IS THE EMPEROR'S PREROGATIVE.
BAR
COBWEB PALACE
ABRAHAM? ANOTHER GLASS OF WINE, IF YOU PLEASE. THIS IS A GRIM SEASON; I NEED SOMETHING TO WARM ME INSIDE, AND PROTECT ME FROM THE DARKNESS AND THE FOG.
SO. YOU FAILED.
I... WELL. YEAH. SORRY, DESIRE.

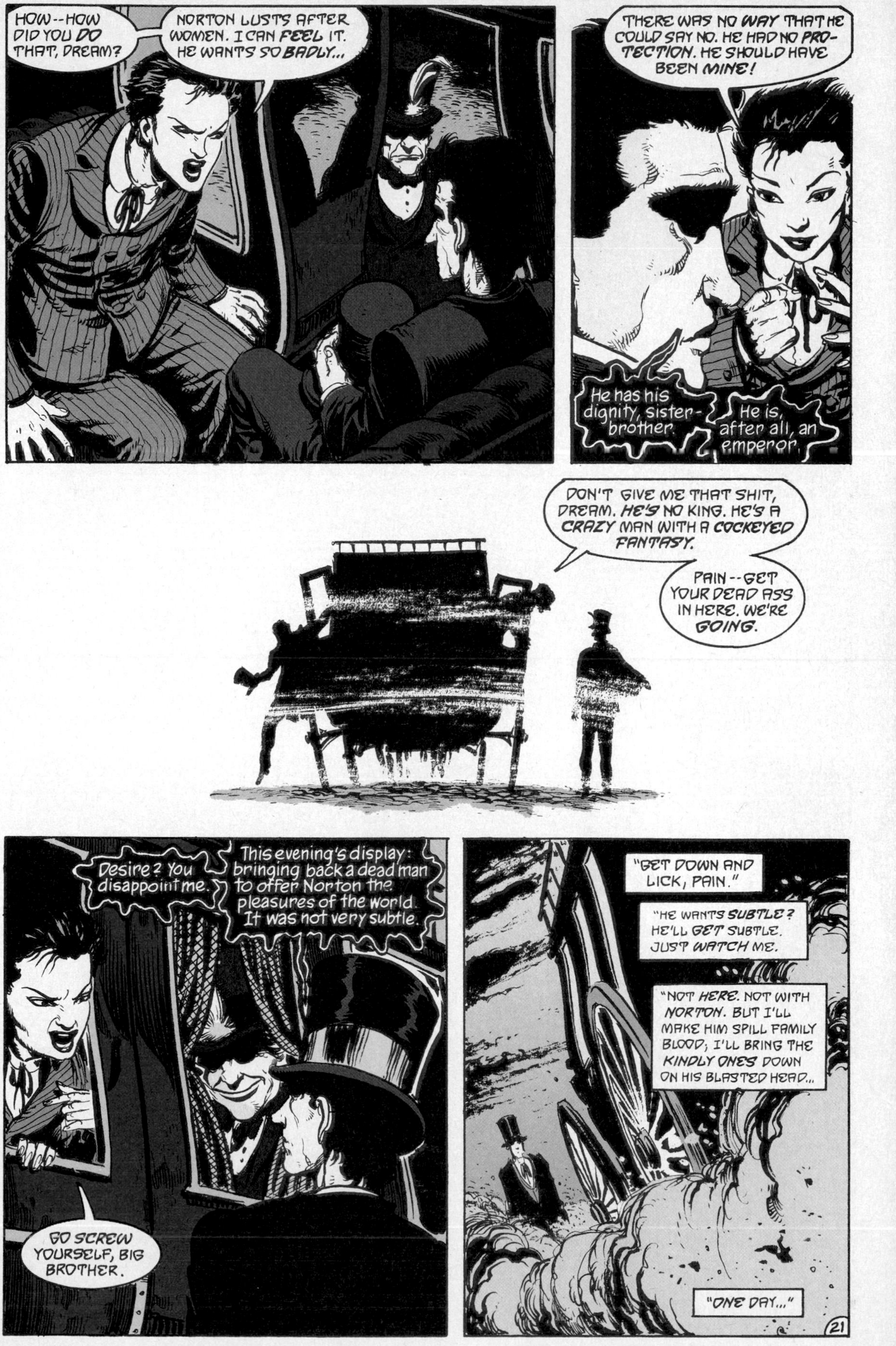
HOW--HOW DID YOU DO THAT, DREAM?
NORTON LUSTS AFTER WOMEN. I CAN FEEL IT. HE WANTS SO BADLY...
THERE WAS NO WAY THAT HE COULD SAY NO. HE HAD NO PROTECTION. HE SHOULD HAVE BEEN MINE!
He has his dignity, sister-brother.
He is, after all, an emperor.
DON'T GIVE ME THAT SHIT, DREAM. HE'S NO KING. HE'S A CRAZY MAN WITH A COCKEYED FANTASY.
PAIN--GET YOUR DEAD ASS IN HERE. WE'RE GOING.
Desire? You disappoint me.
This evening's display: bringing back a dead man to offer Norton the pleasures of the world. It was not very subtle.
GO SCREW YOURSELF, BIG BROTHER.
"GET DOWN AND LICK, PAIN."
"HE WANTS SUBTLE? HE'LL GET SUBTLE. JUST WATCH ME.
"NOT HERE. NOT WITH NORTON. BUT I'LL MAKE HIM SPILL FAMILY BLOOD; I'LL BRING THE KINDLY ONES DOWN ON HIS BLASTED HEAD...
"ONE DAY..."
21

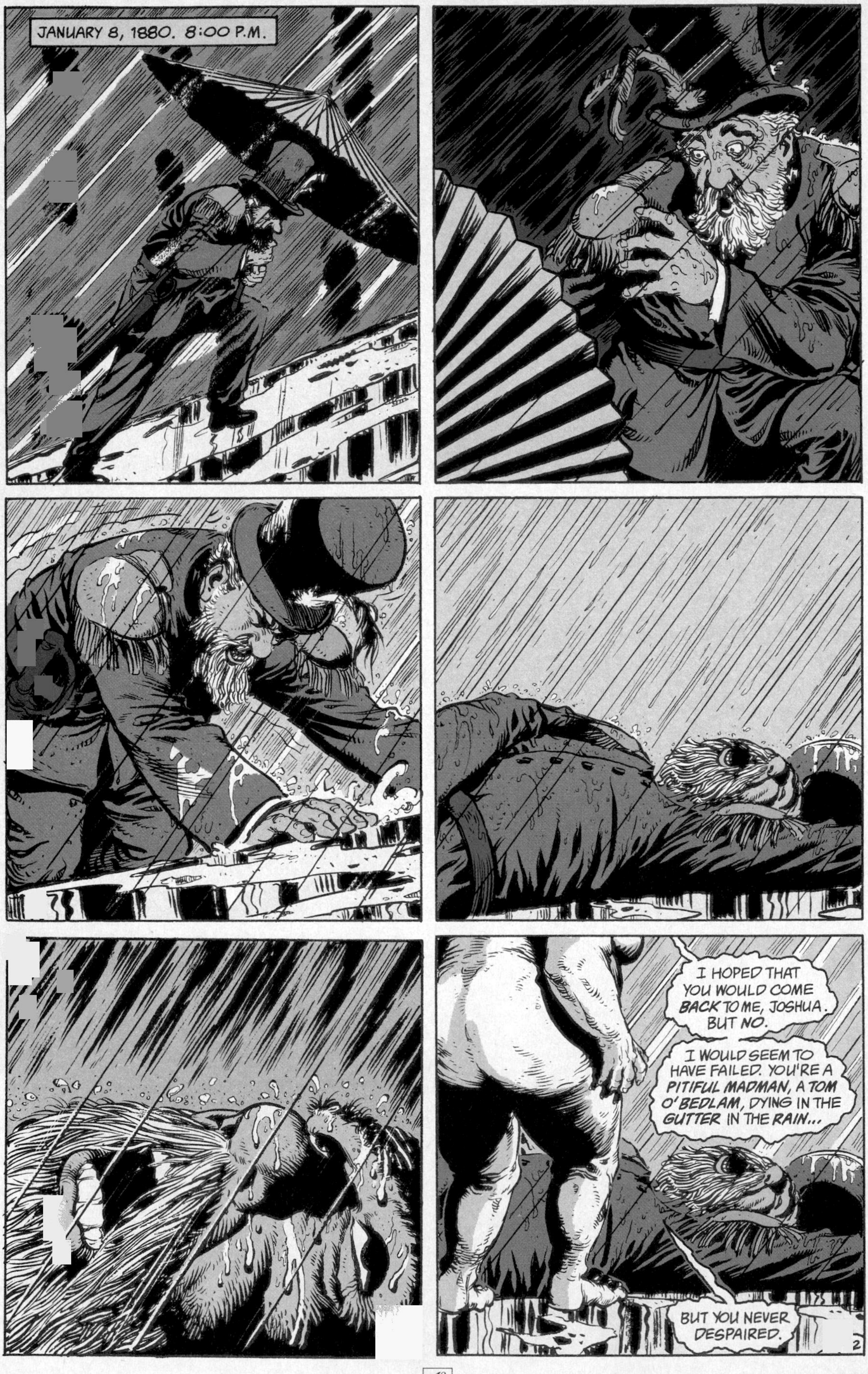
JANUARY 8, 1880. 8:00 P.M.
I HOPED THAT YOU WOULD COME BACK TO ME, JOSHUA. BUT NO.
I WOULD SEEM TO HAVE FAILED. YOU'RE A PITIFUL MADMAN, A TOM O'BEDLAM, DYING IN THE GUTTER IN THE RAIN...
BUT YOU NEVER DESPAIRED.
2

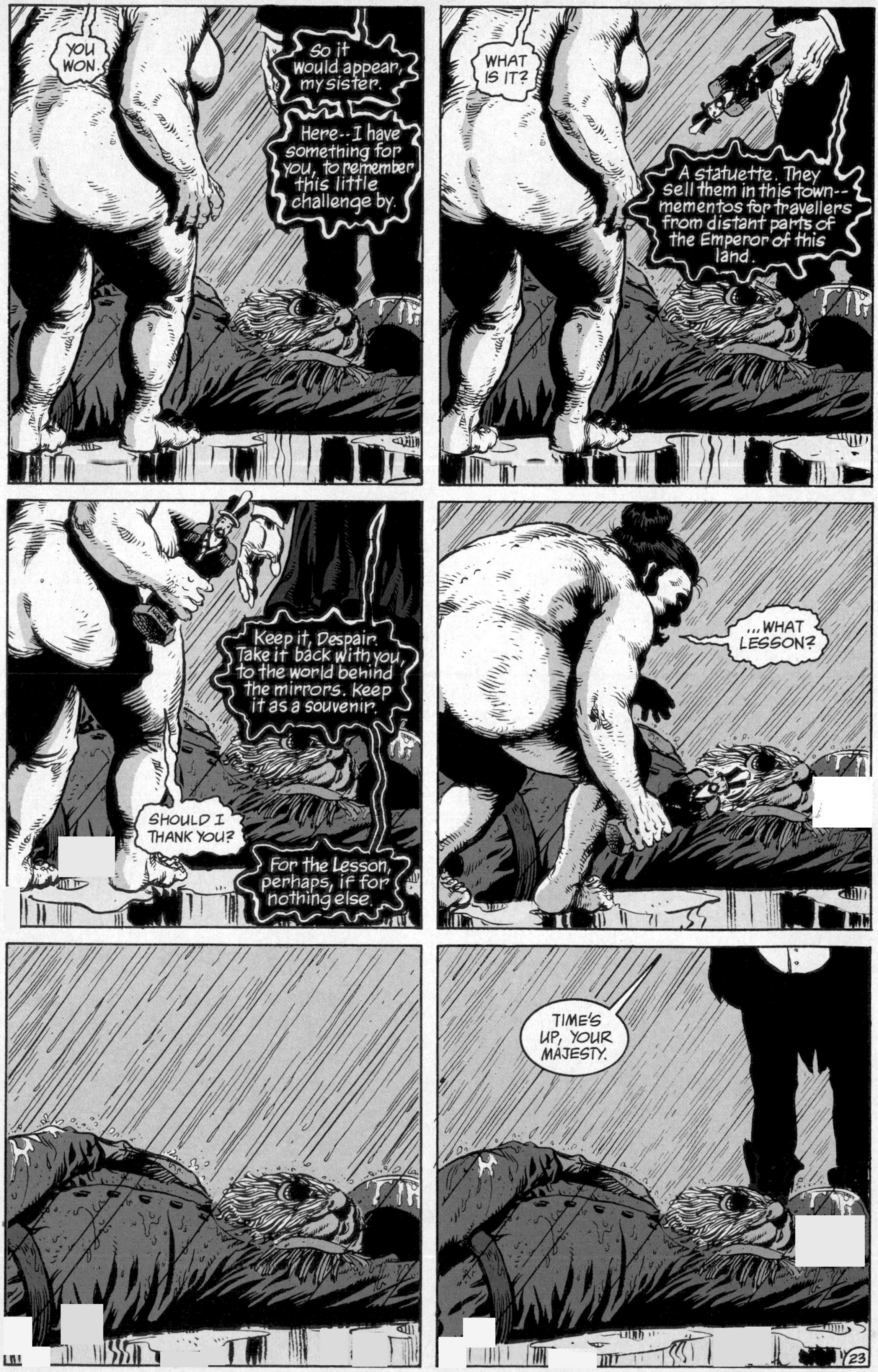
YOU WON.
So it would appear, my sister.
Here--I have something for you, to remember this little challenge by.
WHAT IS IT?
A statuette. They sell them in this town--mementos for travellers from distant parts of the Emperor of this land.
Keep it, Despair. Take it back with you, to the world behind the mirrors. Keep it as a souvenir.
SHOULD I THANK YOU?
For the Lesson, perhaps, if for nothing else.
...WHAT LESSON?
TIME'S UP, YOUR MAJESTY.
23

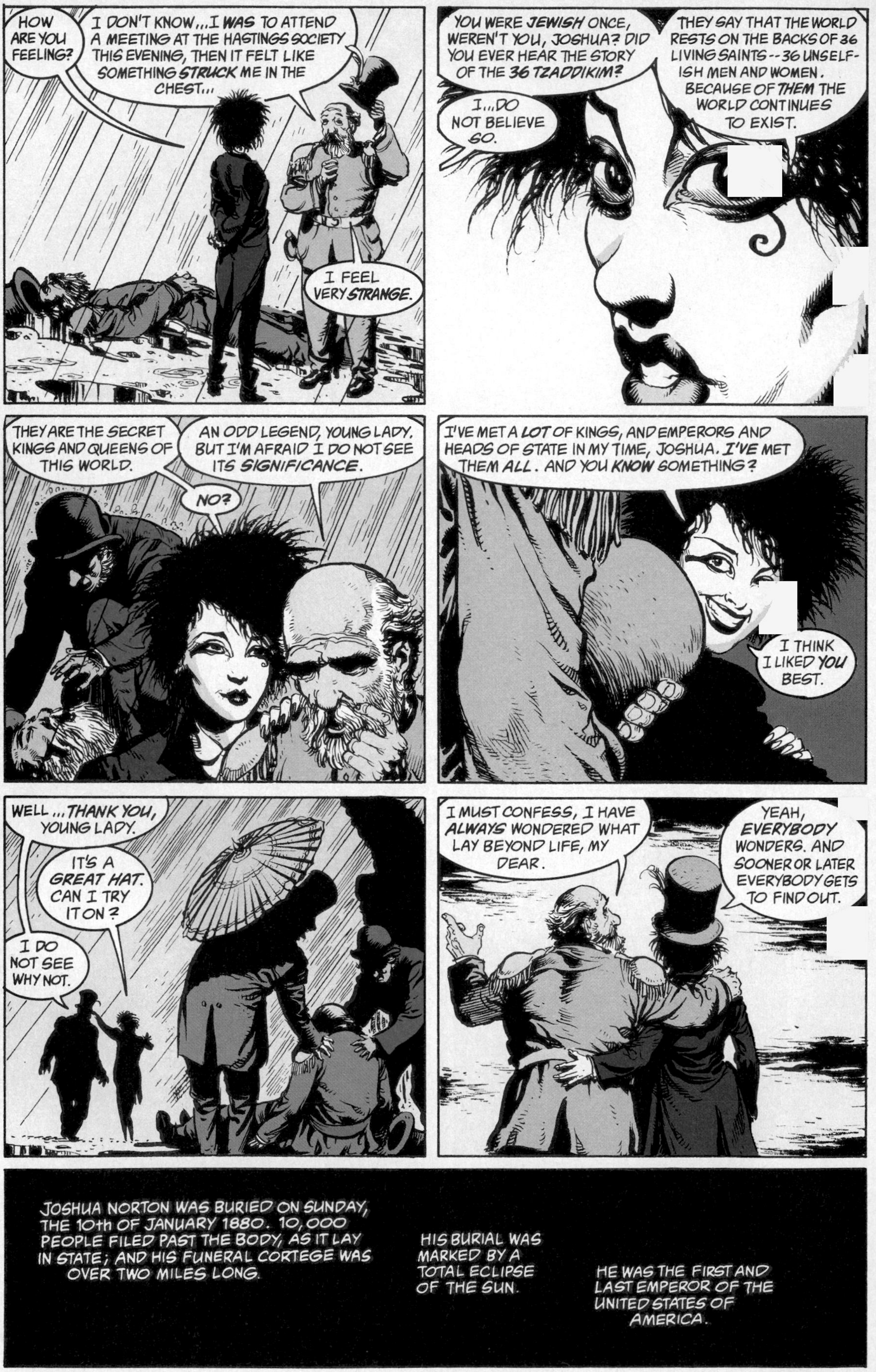
HOW ARE YOU FEELING?
I DON'T KNOW,...I WAS TO ATTEND A MEETING AT THE HASTINGS SOCIETY THIS EVENING, THEN IT FELT LIKE SOMETHING STRUCK ME IN THE CHEST...
I FEEL VERY STRANGE.
YOU WERE JEWISH ONCE, WEREN'T YOU, JOSHUA? DID YOU EVER HEAR THE STORY OF THE 36 TZADDIKIM?
I...DO NOT BELIEVE SO.
THEY SAY THAT THE WORLD RESTS ON THE BACKS OF 36 LIVING SAINTS--36 UNSELFISH MEN AND WOMEN. BECAUSE OF THEM THE WORLD CONTINUES TO EXIST.
THEY ARE THE SECRET KINGS AND QUEENS OF THIS WORLD.
AN ODD LEGEND, YOUNG LADY. BUT I'M AFRAID I DO NOT SEE ITS SIGNIFICANCE.
NO?
I'VE MET A LOT OF KINGS, AND EMPERORS AND HEADS OF STATE IN MY TIME, JOSHUA. I'VE MET THEM ALL. AND YOU KNOW SOMETHING?
I THINK I LIKED YOU BEST.
WELL ...THANK YOU, YOUNG LADY.
IT'S A GREAT HAT. CAN I TRY IT ON?
I DO NOT SEE WHY NOT.
I MUST CONFESS, I HAVE ALWAYS WONDERED WHAT LAY BEYOND LIFE, MY DEAR.
YEAH, EVERYBODY WONDERS. AND SOONER OR LATER EVERYBODY GETS TO FIND OUT.
JOSHUA NORTON WAS BURIED ON SUNDAY, THE 10th OF JANUARY 1880. 10,000 PEOPLE FILED PAST THE BODY, AS IT LAY IN STATE; AND HIS FUNERAL CORTEGE WAS OVER TWO MILES LONG.
HIS BURIAL WAS MARKED BY A TOTAL ECLIPSE OF THE SUN.
HE WAS THE FIRST AND LAST EMPEROR OF THE UNITED STATES OF AMERICA.

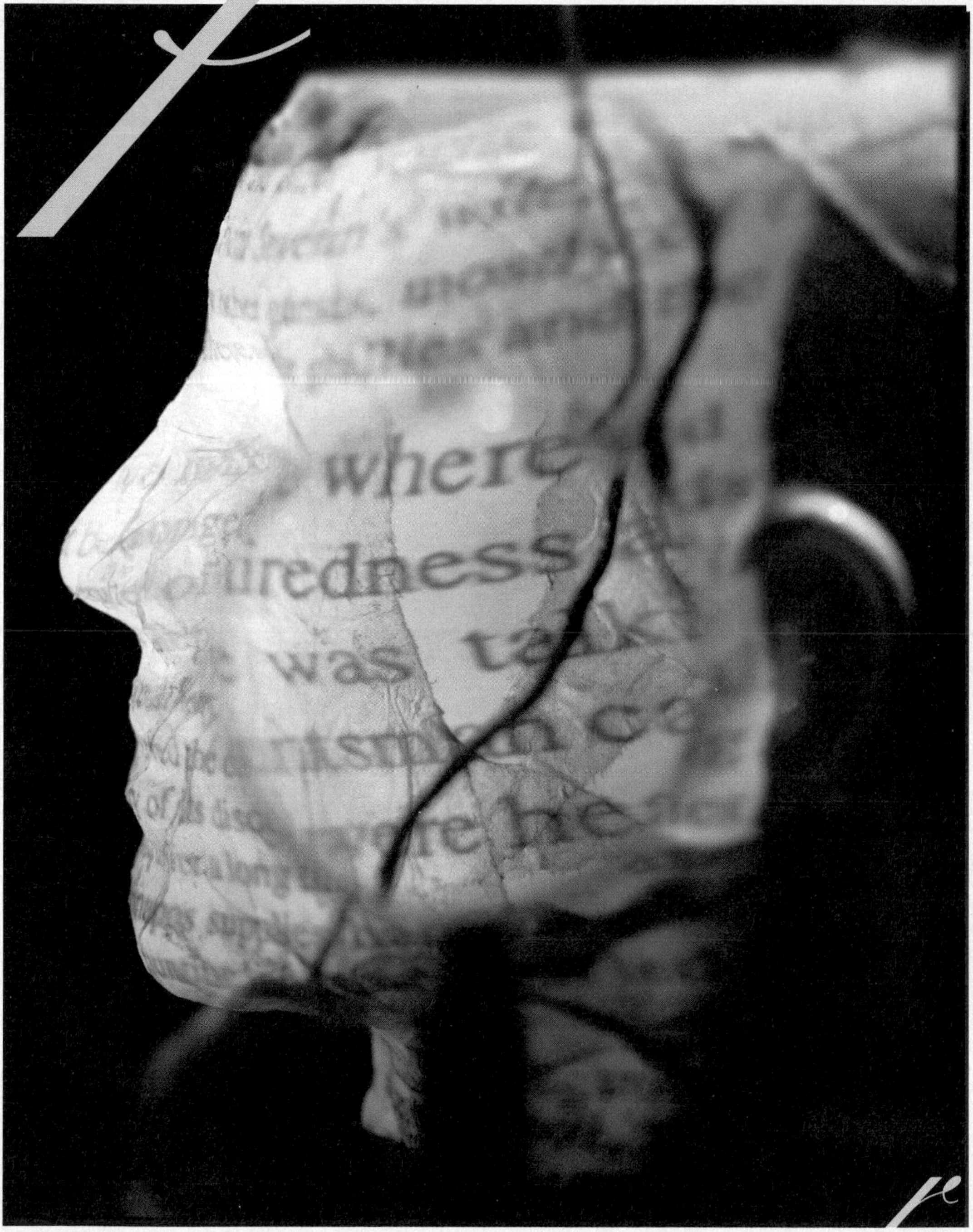
where
was

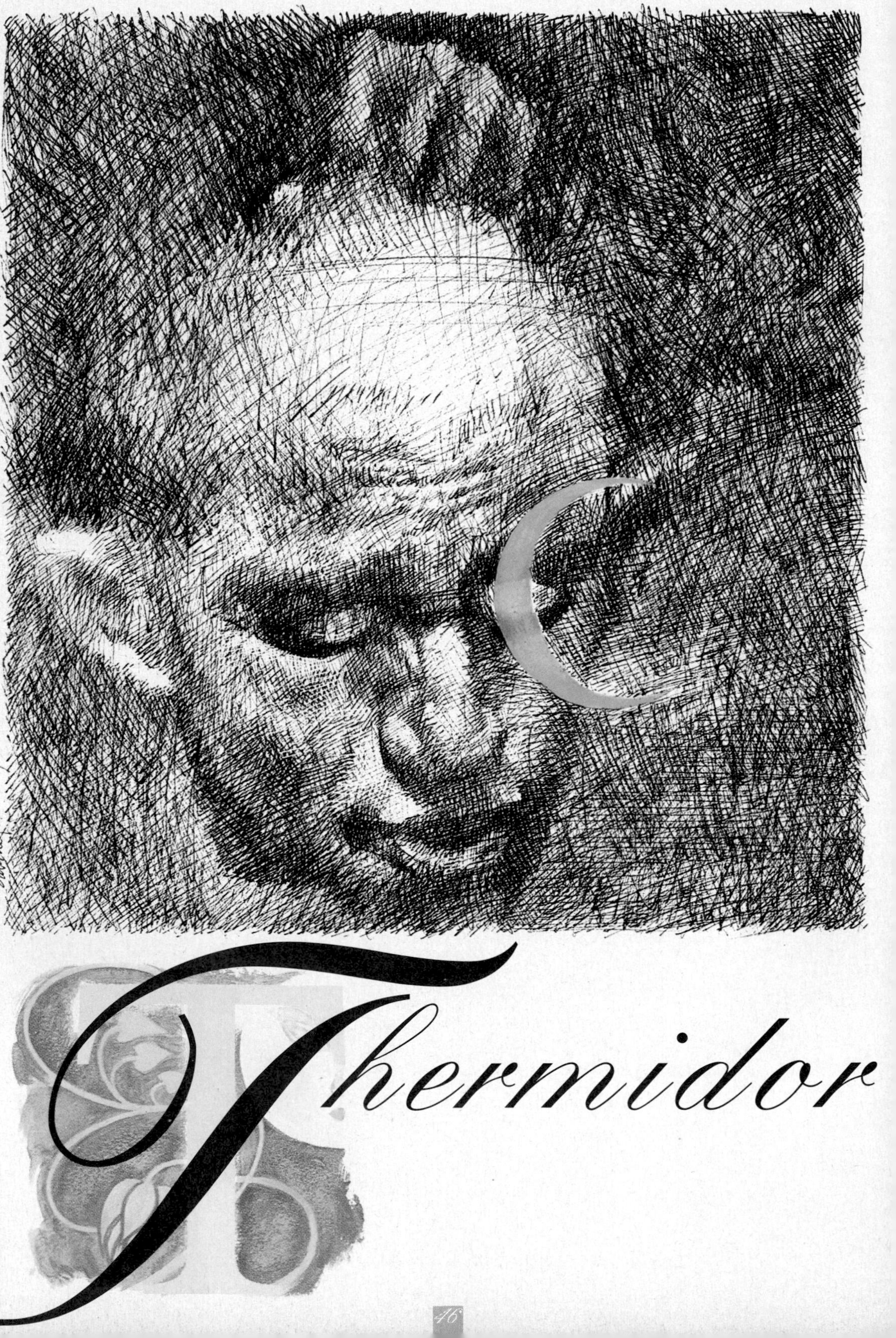

Thermidor

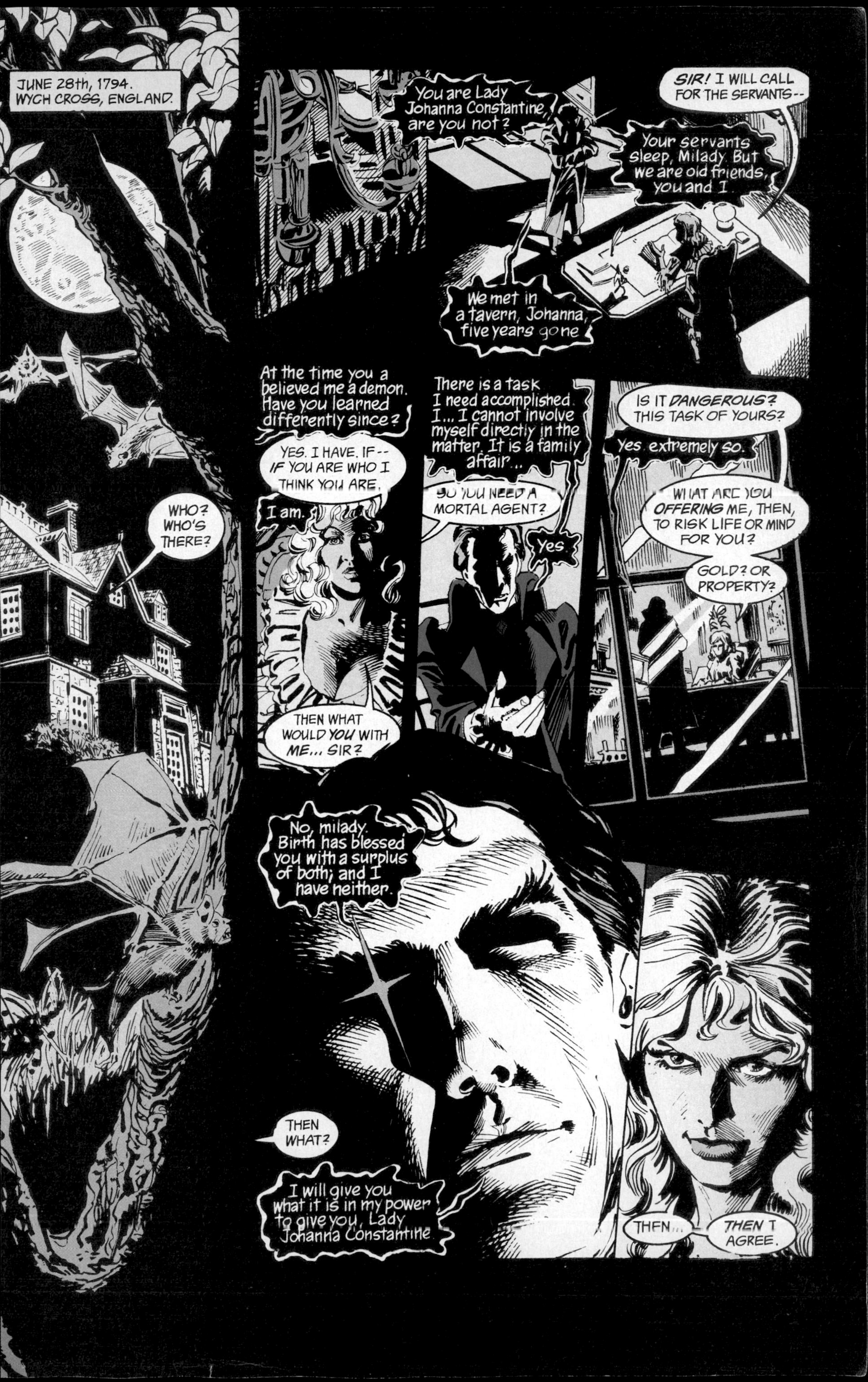

JUNE 28th, 1794. WYCH CROSS, ENGLAND.
WHO? WHO'S THERE?
You are Lady Johanna Constantine, are you not?
SIR! I WILL CALL FOR THE SERVANTS--
Your servants sleep, Milady. But we are old friends, you and I.
We met in a tavern, Johanna, five years gone.
At the time you a believed me a demon. Have you learned differently since?
YES. I HAVE. IF-- IF YOU ARE WHO I THINK YOU ARE.
I am.
THEN WHAT WOULD YOU WITH ME... SIR?
There is a task I need accomplished. I... I cannot involve myself directly in the matter. It is a family affair...
SO YOU NEED A MORTAL AGENT?
Yes.
IS IT DANGEROUS? THIS TASK OF YOURS?
Yes. extremely so.
WHAT ARE YOU OFFERING ME, THEN, TO RISK LIFE OR MIND FOR YOU?
GOLD? OR PROPERTY?
No, milady. Birth has blessed you with a surplus of both; and I have neither.
THEN WHAT?
I will give you what it is in my power to give you, Lady Johanna Constantine.
THEN...
THEN I AGREE.

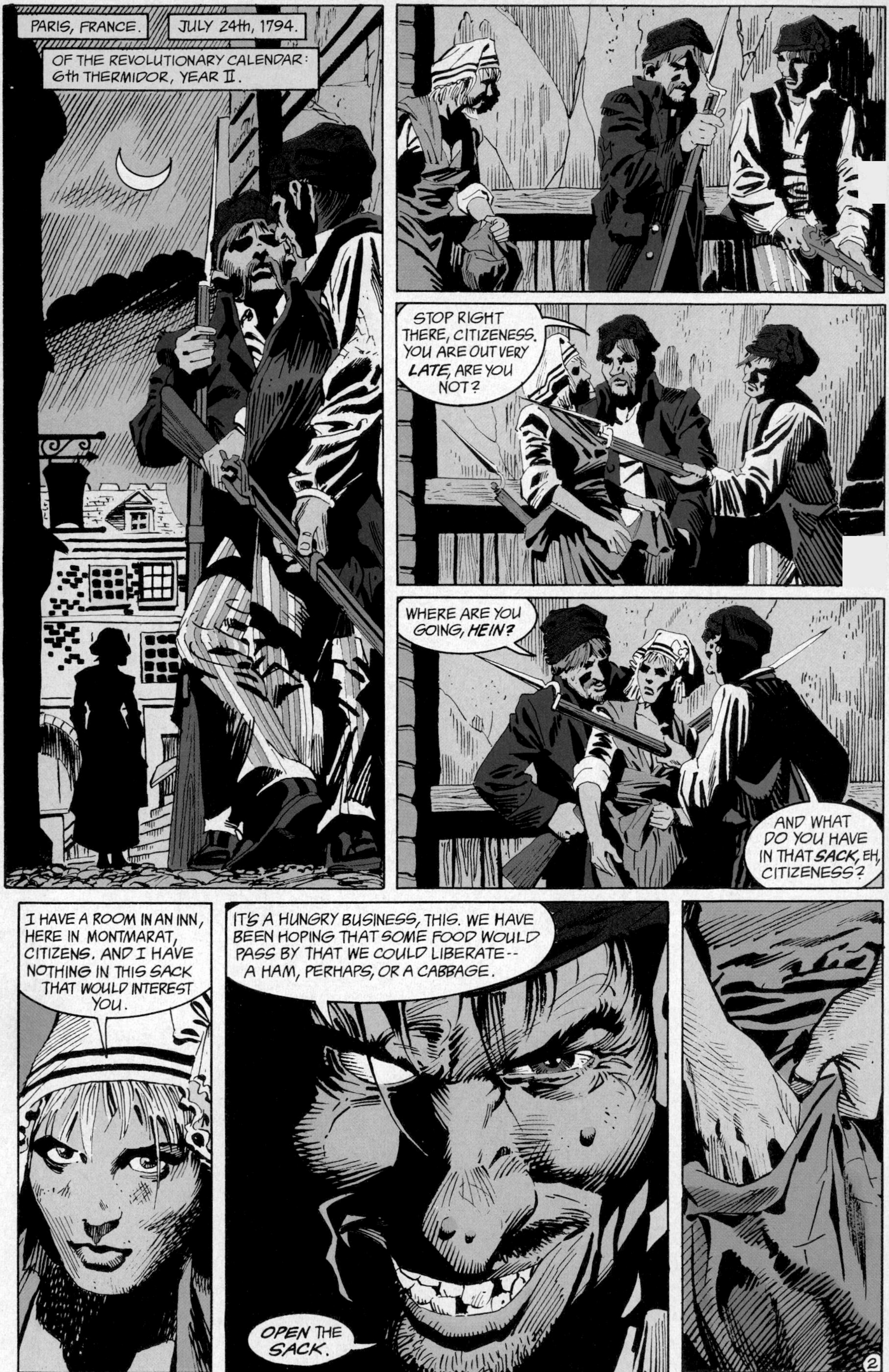

PARIS, FRANCE.
JULY 24th, 1794.
OF THE REVOLUTIONARY CALENDAR: 6th THERMIDOR, YEAR II.
STOP RIGHT THERE, CITIZENESS. YOU ARE OUT VERY LATE, ARE YOU NOT?
WHERE ARE YOU GOING, HEIN?
AND WHAT DO YOU HAVE IN THAT SACK, EH, CITIZENESS?
I HAVE A ROOM IN AN INN, HERE IN MONTMARAT, CITIZENS. AND I HAVE NOTHING IN THIS SACK THAT WOULD INTEREST YOU.
IT'S A HUNGRY BUSINESS, THIS. WE HAVE BEEN HOPING THAT SOME FOOD WOULD PASS BY THAT WE COULD LIBERATE-- A HAM, PERHAPS, OR A CABBAGE.
OPEN THE SACK.
2

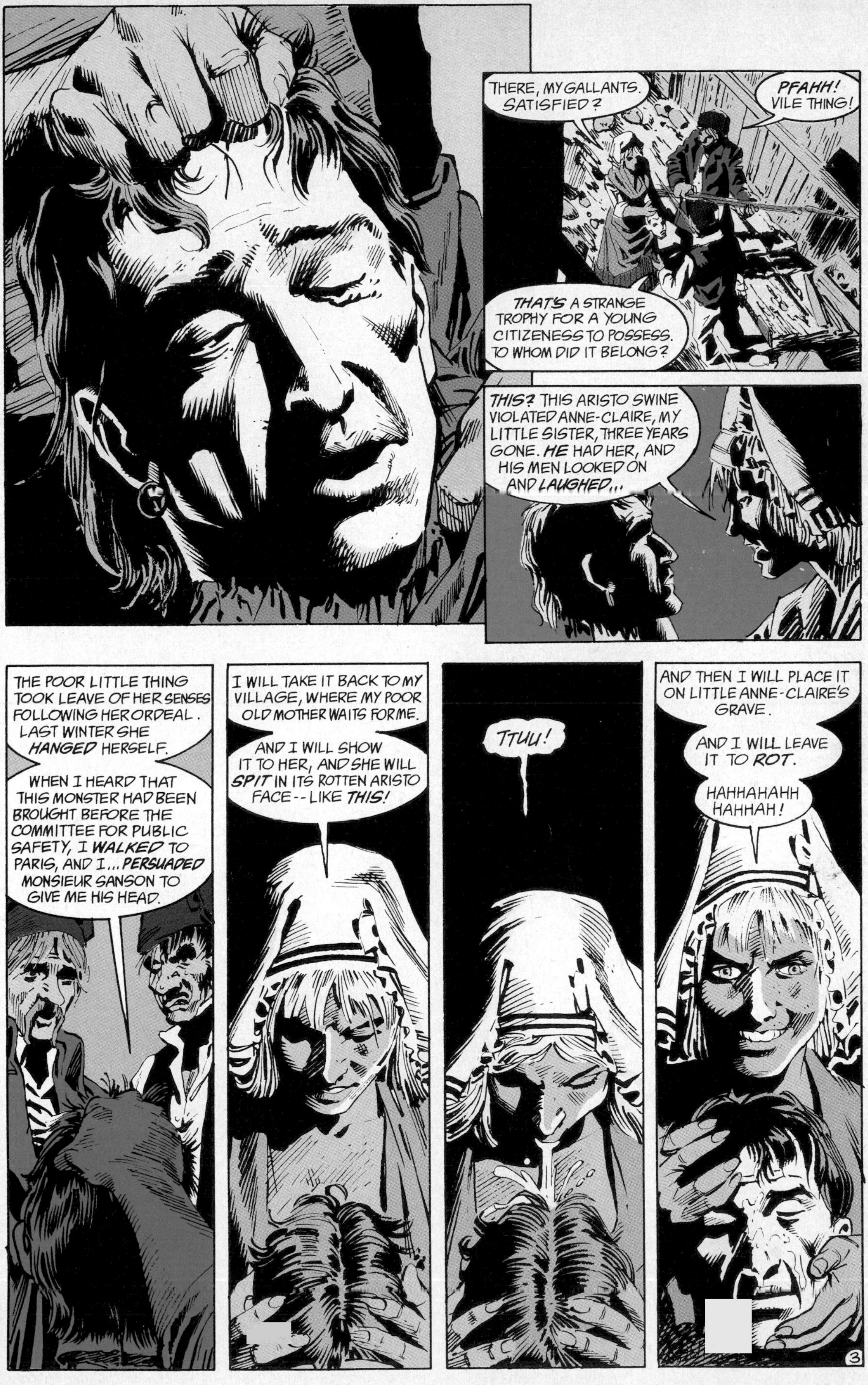
THERE, MY GALLANTS. SATISFIED?
PFAHH! VILE THING!
THAT'S A STRANGE TROPHY FOR A YOUNG CITIZENESS TO POSSESS. TO WHOM DID IT BELONG?
THIS? THIS ARISTO SWINE VIOLATED ANNE-CLAIRE, MY LITTLE SISTER, THREE YEARS GONE. HE HAD HER, AND HIS MEN LOOKED ON AND LAUGHED...
THE POOR LITTLE THING TOOK LEAVE OF HER SENSES FOLLOWING HER ORDEAL. LAST WINTER SHE HANGED HERSELF.
WHEN I HEARD THAT THIS MONSTER HAD BEEN BROUGHT BEFORE THE COMMITTEE FOR PUBLIC SAFETY, I WALKED TO PARIS, AND I... PERSUADED MONSIEUR SANSON TO GIVE ME HIS HEAD.
I WILL TAKE IT BACK TO MY VILLAGE, WHERE MY POOR OLD MOTHER WAITS FOR ME.
AND I WILL SHOW IT TO HER, AND SHE WILL SPIT IN ITS ROTTEN ARISTO FACE -- LIKE THIS!
TTUU!
AND THEN I WILL PLACE IT ON LITTLE ANNE-CLAIRE'S GRAVE.
AND I WILL LEAVE IT TO ROT.
HAHHAHAHH HAHHAH!

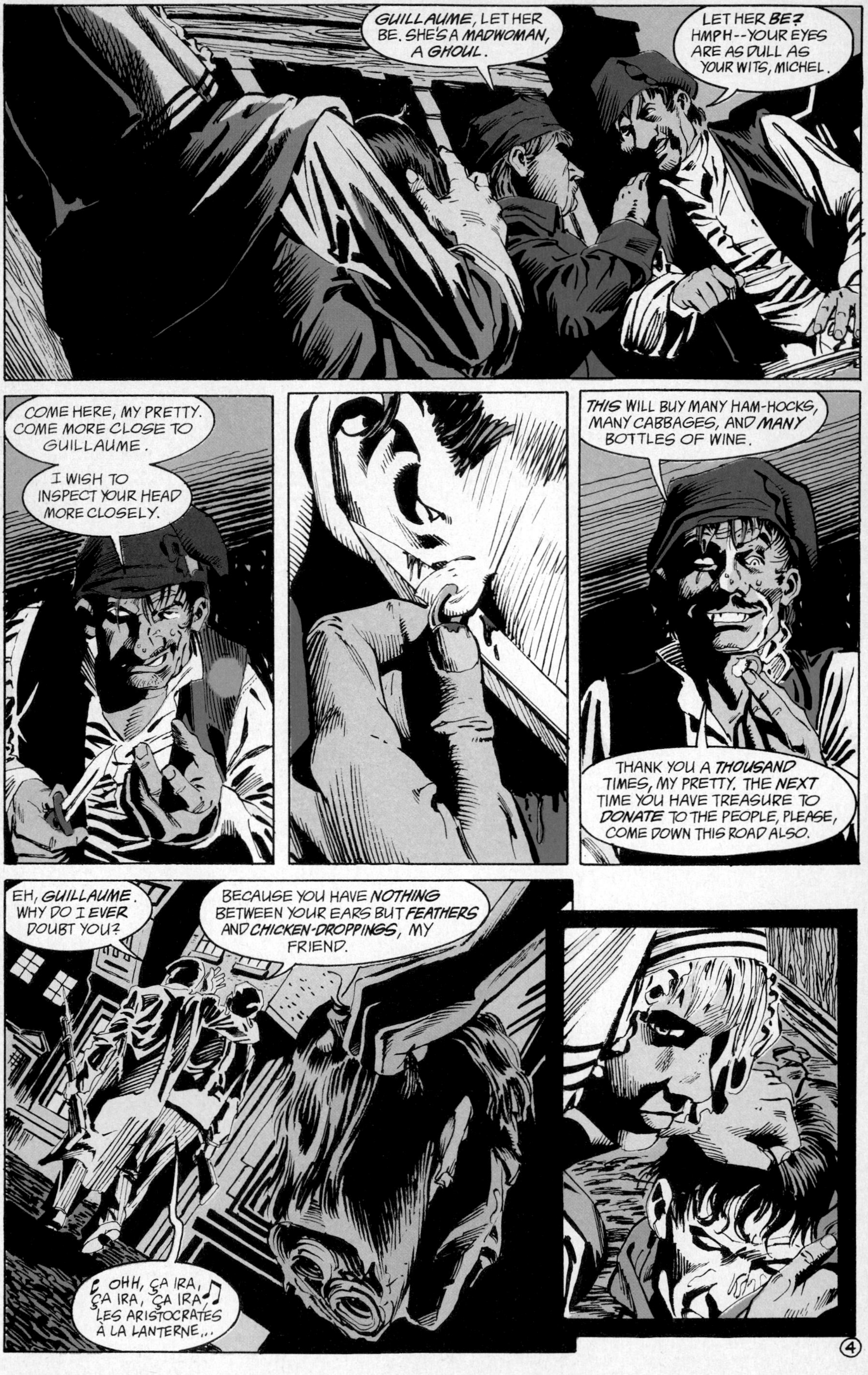
GUILLAUME, LET HER BE. SHE'S A MADWOMAN, A GHOUL.
LET HER BE? HMPH--YOUR EYES ARE AS DULL AS YOUR WITS, MICHEL.
COME HERE, MY PRETTY. COME MORE CLOSE TO GUILLAUME.
I WISH TO INSPECT YOUR HEAD MORE CLOSELY.
THIS WILL BUY MANY HAM-HOCKS, MANY CABBAGES, AND MANY BOTTLES OF WINE.
THANK YOU A THOUSAND TIMES, MY PRETTY. THE NEXT TIME YOU HAVE TREASURE TO DONATE TO THE PEOPLE, PLEASE, COME DOWN THIS ROAD ALSO.
EH, GUILLAUME. WHY DO I EVER DOUBT YOU?
BECAUSE YOU HAVE NOTHING BETWEEN YOUR EARS BUT FEATHERS AND CHICKEN-DROPPINGS, MY FRIEND.
OHH, ÇA IRA, ÇA IRA, ÇA IRA LES ARISTOCRATES À LA LANTERNE...

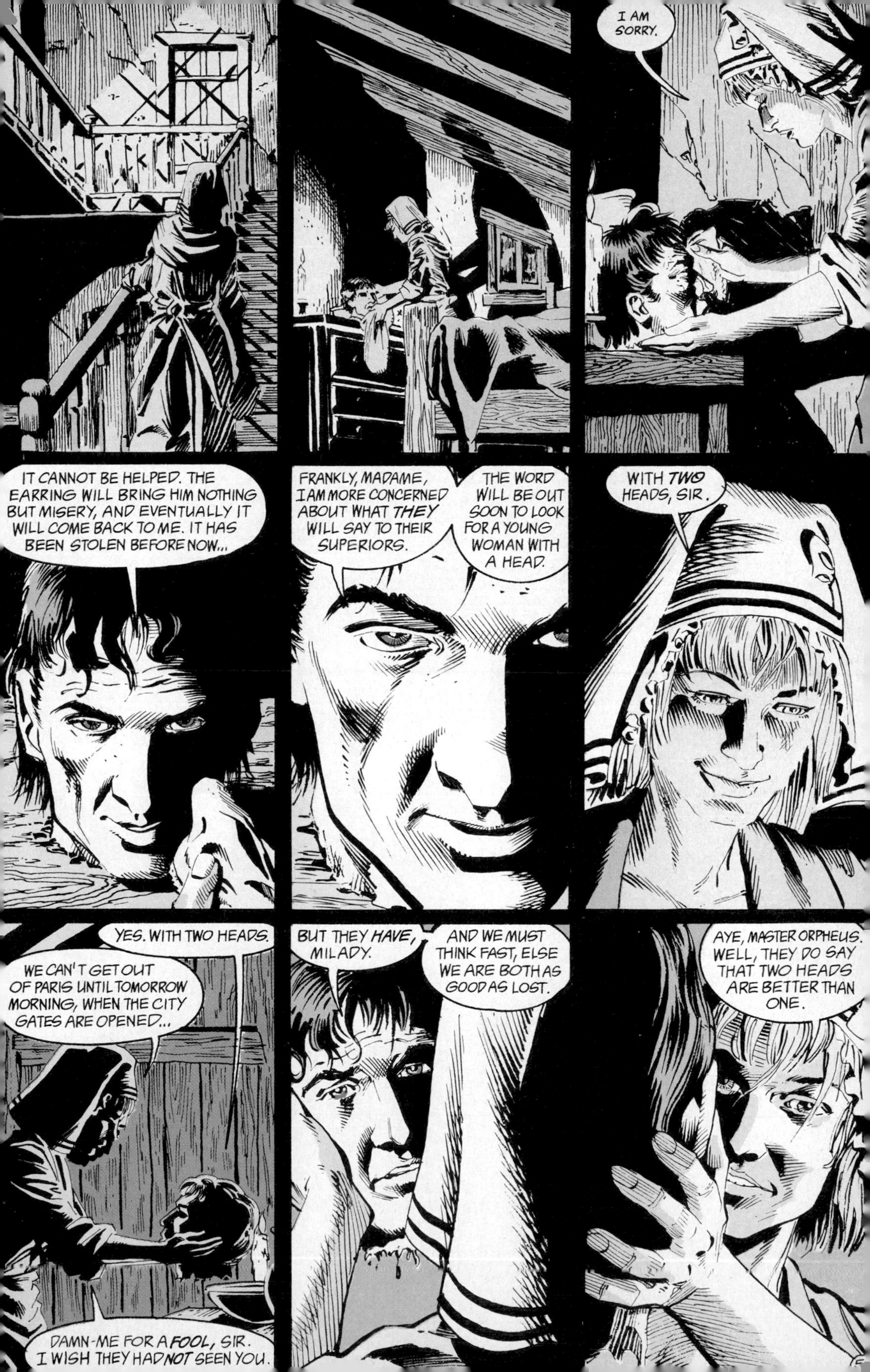
I AM SORRY.
IT CANNOT BE HELPED. THE EARRING WILL BRING HIM NOTHING BUT MISERY, AND EVENTUALLY IT WILL COME BACK TO ME. IT HAS BEEN STOLEN BEFORE NOW...
FRANKLY, MADAME, I AM MORE CONCERNED ABOUT WHAT THEY WILL SAY TO THEIR SUPERIORS.
THE WORD WILL BE OUT SOON TO LOOK FOR A YOUNG WOMAN WITH A HEAD.
WITH TWO HEADS, SIR.
YES. WITH TWO HEADS.
WE CAN'T GET OUT OF PARIS UNTIL TOMORROW MORNING, WHEN THE CITY GATES ARE OPENED...
DAMN-ME FOR A FOOL, SIR. I WISH THEY HAD NOT SEEN YOU.
BUT THEY HAVE, MILADY.
AND WE MUST THINK FAST, ELSE WE ARE BOTH AS GOOD AS LOST.
AYE, MASTER ORPHEUS. WELL, THEY DO SAY THAT TWO HEADS ARE BETTER THAN ONE.

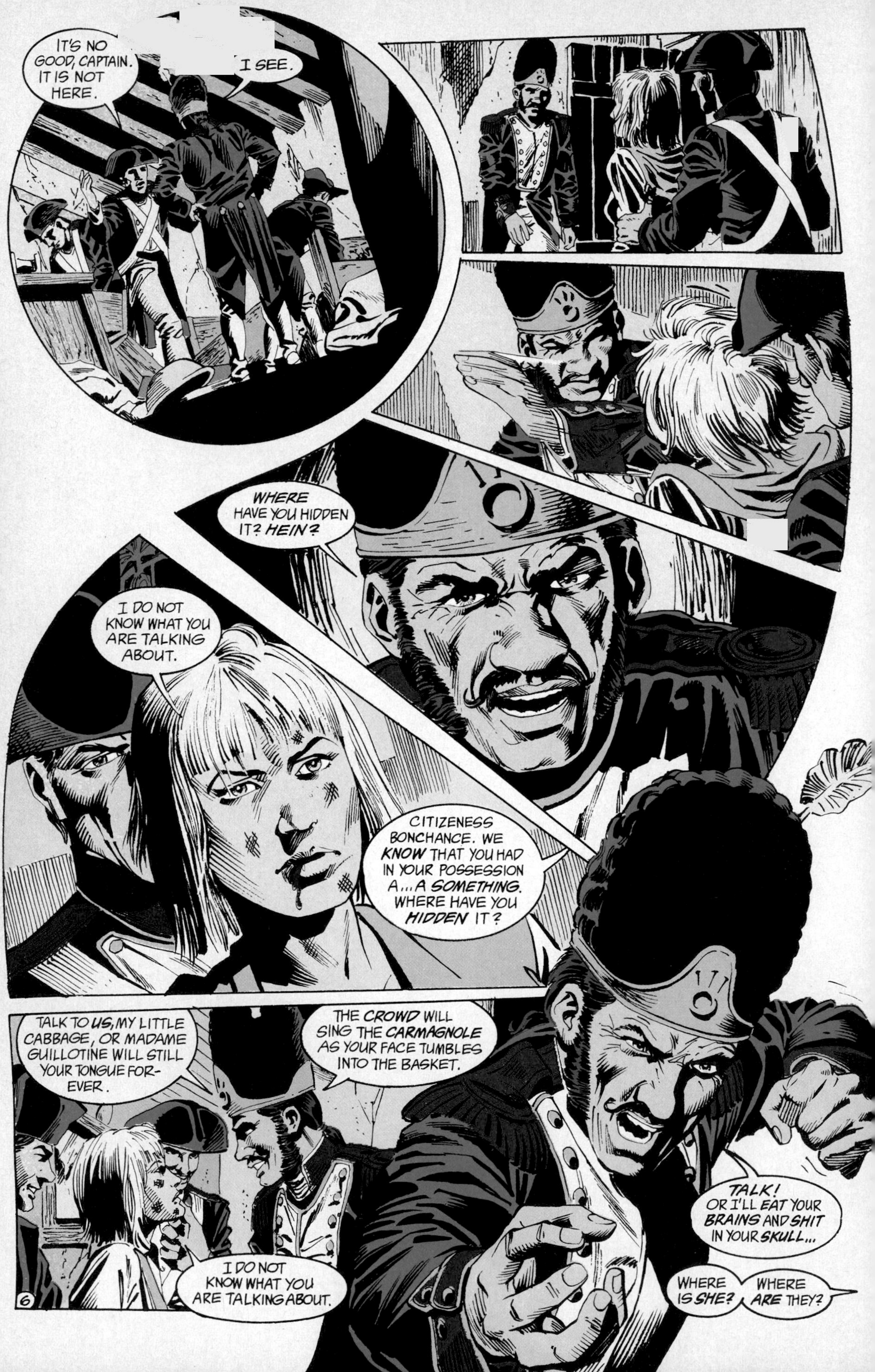
IT'S NO GOOD, CAPTAIN. IT IS NOT HERE.
I SEE.
WHERE HAVE YOU HIDDEN IT? HEIN?
I DO NOT KNOW WHAT YOU ARE TALKING ABOUT.
CITIZENESS BONCHANCE. WE KNOW THAT YOU HAD IN YOUR POSSESSION A...A SOMETHING. WHERE HAVE YOU HIDDEN IT?
TALK TO US, MY LITTLE CABBAGE, OR MADAME GUILLOTINE WILL STILL YOUR TONGUE FOR-EVER.
THE CROWD WILL SING THE CARMAGNOLE AS YOUR FACE TUMBLES INTO THE BASKET.
I DO NOT KNOW WHAT YOU ARE TALKING ABOUT.
TALK! OR I'LL EAT YOUR BRAINS AND SHIT IN YOUR SKULL...
WHERE IS SHE?
WHERE ARE THEY?
6

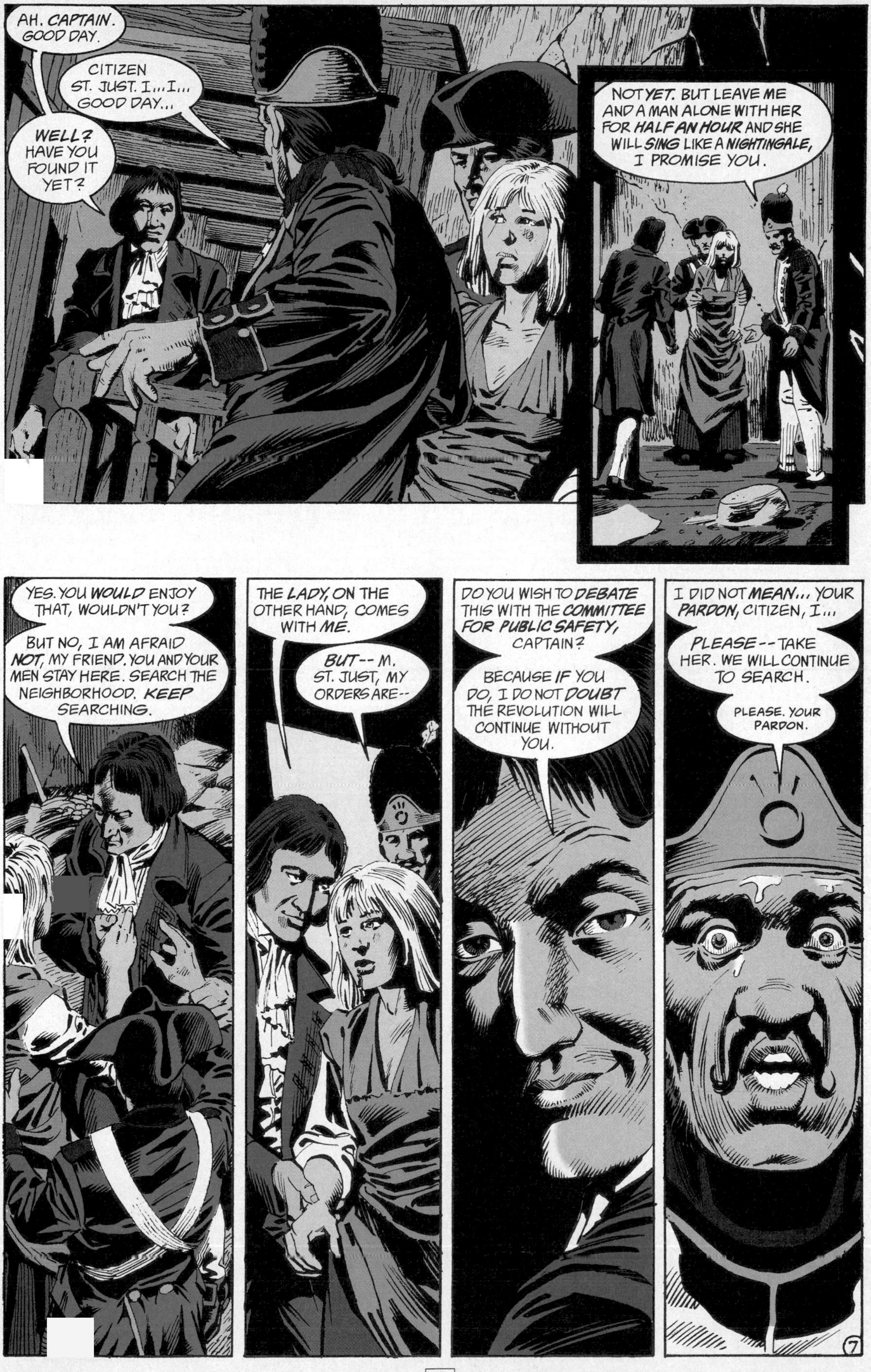
AH. CAPTAIN. GOOD DAY.
CITIZEN ST. JUST. I...I... GOOD DAY...
WELL? HAVE YOU FOUND IT YET?
NOT YET. BUT LEAVE ME AND A MAN ALONE WITH HER FOR HALF AN HOUR AND SHE WILL SING LIKE A NIGHTINGALE, I PROMISE YOU.
YES. YOU WOULD ENJOY THAT, WOULDN'T YOU?
BUT NO, I AM AFRAID NOT, MY FRIEND. YOU AND YOUR MEN STAY HERE. SEARCH THE NEIGHBORHOOD. KEEP SEARCHING.
THE LADY, ON THE OTHER HAND, COMES WITH ME.
BUT-- M. ST. JUST, MY ORDERS ARE--
DO YOU WISH TO DEBATE THIS WITH THE COMMITTEE FOR PUBLIC SAFETY, CAPTAIN?
BECAUSE IF YOU DO, I DO NOT DOUBT THE REVOLUTION WILL CONTINUE WITHOUT YOU.
I DID NOT MEAN... YOUR PARDON, CITIZEN, I...
PLEASE -- TAKE HER. WE WILL CONTINUE TO SEARCH.
PLEASE. YOUR PARDON.
7

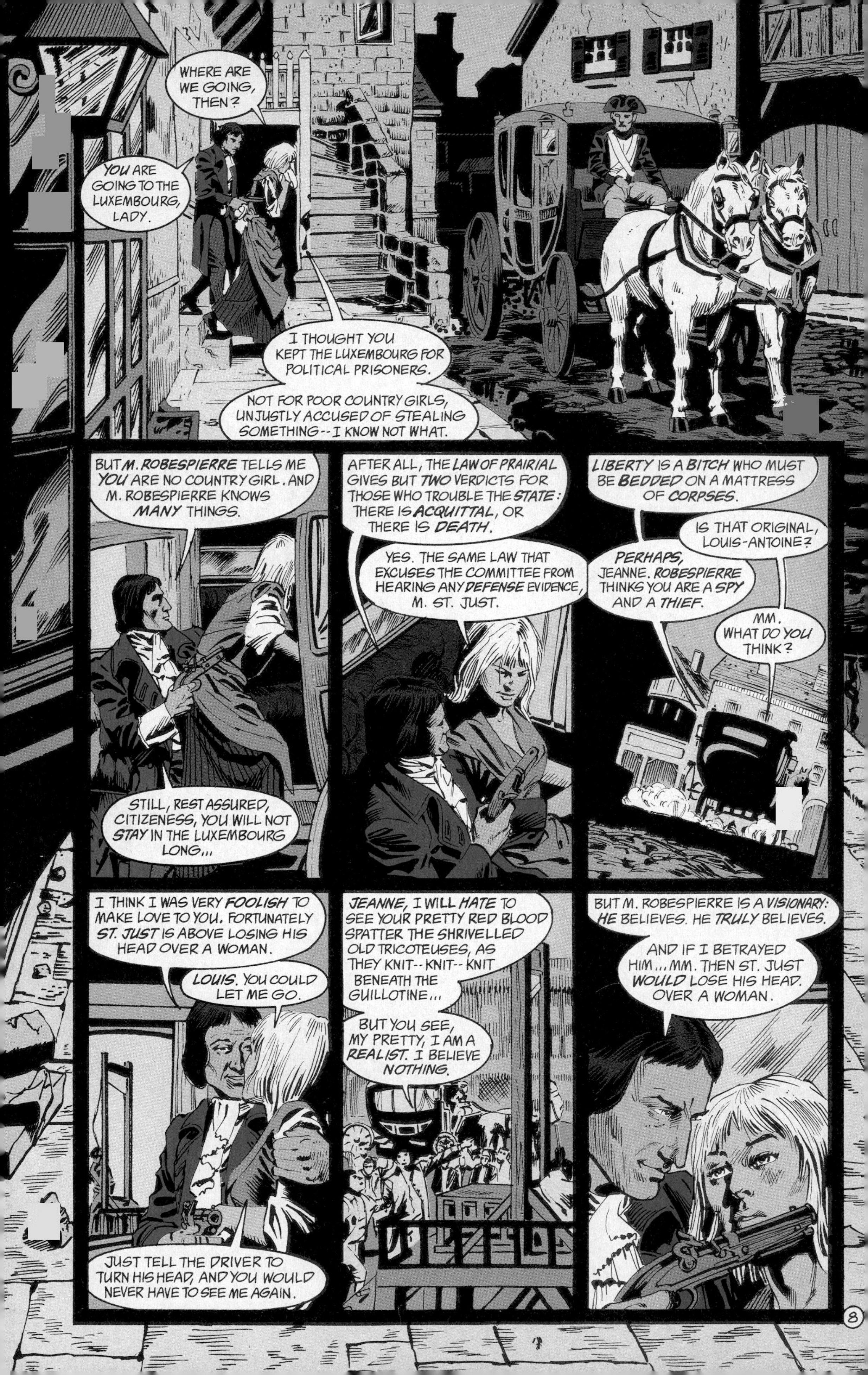
WHERE ARE WE GOING, THEN?
YOU ARE GOING TO THE LUXEMBOURG, LADY.
I THOUGHT YOU KEPT THE LUXEMBOURG FOR POLITICAL PRISONERS.
NOT FOR POOR COUNTRY GIRLS, UNJUSTLY ACCUSED OF STEALING SOMETHING-- I KNOW NOT WHAT.
BUT M. ROBESPIERRE TELLS ME YOU ARE NO COUNTRY GIRL. AND M. ROBESPIERRE KNOWS MANY THINGS.
STILL, REST ASSURED, CITIZENESS, YOU WILL NOT STAY IN THE LUXEMBOURG LONG...
AFTER ALL, THE LAW OF PRAIRIAL GIVES BUT TWO VERDICTS FOR THOSE WHO TROUBLE THE STATE: THERE IS ACQUITTAL, OR THERE IS DEATH.
YES. THE SAME LAW THAT EXCUSES THE COMMITTEE FROM HEARING ANY DEFENSE EVIDENCE, M. ST. JUST.
LIBERTY IS A BITCH WHO MUST BE BEDDED ON A MATTRESS OF CORPSES.
IS THAT ORIGINAL, LOUIS-ANTOINE?
PERHAPS, JEANNE. ROBESPIERRE THINKS YOU ARE A SPY AND A THIEF.
MM. WHAT DO YOU THINK?
I THINK I WAS VERY FOOLISH TO MAKE LOVE TO YOU. FORTUNATELY ST. JUST IS ABOVE LOSING HIS HEAD OVER A WOMAN.
LOUIS. YOU COULD LET ME GO.
JUST TELL THE DRIVER TO TURN HIS HEAD, AND YOU WOULD NEVER HAVE TO SEE ME AGAIN.
JEANNE, I WILL HATE TO SEE YOUR PRETTY RED BLOOD SPATTER THE SHRIVELLED OLD TRICOTEUSES, AS THEY KNIT-- KNIT-- KNIT BENEATH THE GUILLOTINE...
BUT YOU SEE, MY PRETTY, I AM A REALIST. I BELIEVE NOTHING.
BUT M. ROBESPIERRE IS A VISIONARY: HE BELIEVES. HE TRULY BELIEVES.
AND IF I BETRAYED HIM... MM. THEN ST. JUST WOULD LOSE HIS HEAD. OVER A WOMAN.

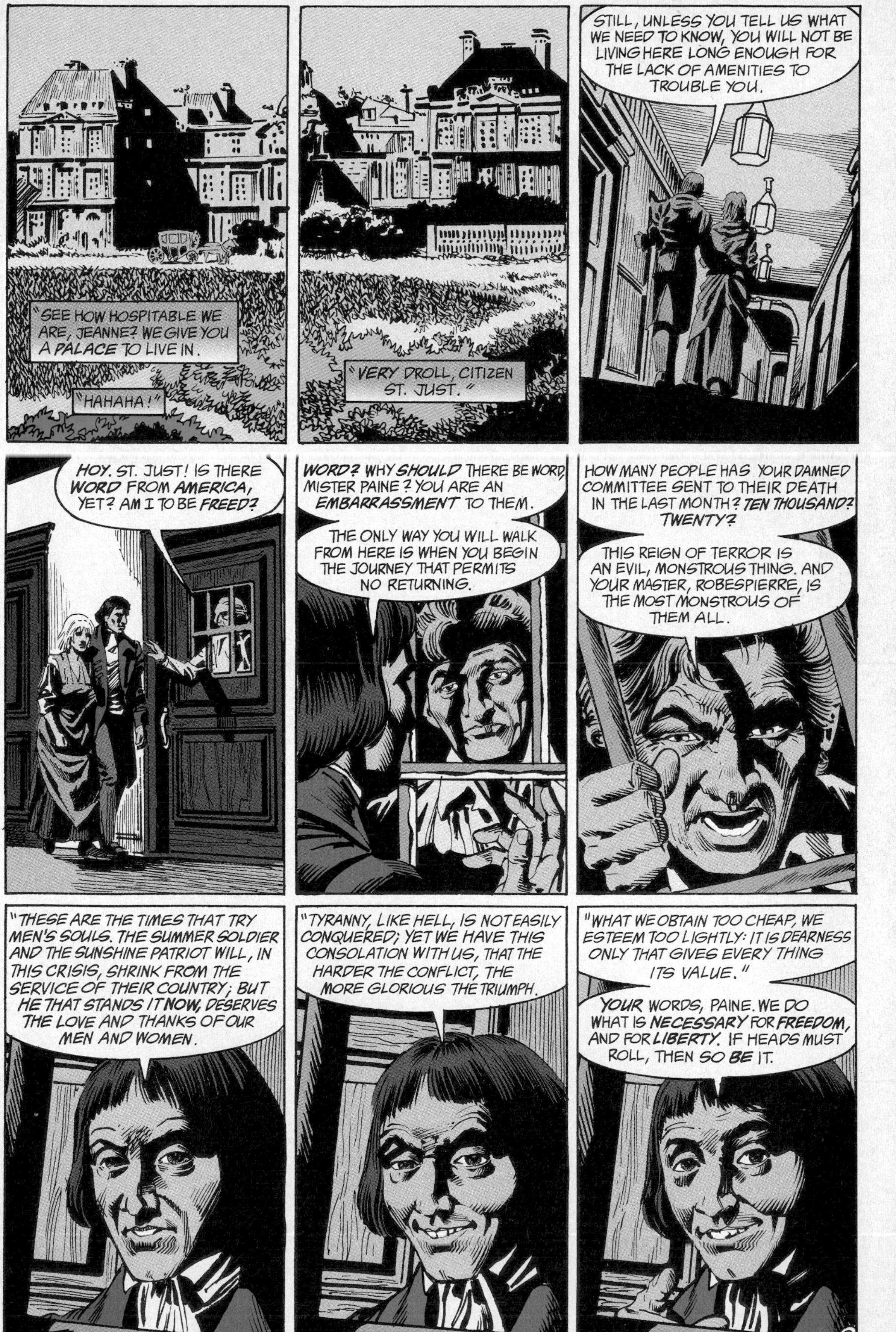

"SEE HOW HOSPITABLE WE ARE, JEANNE? WE GIVE YOU A PALACE TO LIVE IN.
"HAHAHA!"
"VERY DROLL, CITIZEN ST. JUST."
STILL, UNLESS YOU TELL US WHAT WE NEED TO KNOW, YOU WILL NOT BE LIVING HERE LONG ENOUGH FOR THE LACK OF AMENITIES TO TROUBLE YOU.
HOY. ST. JUST! IS THERE WORD FROM AMERICA, YET? AM I TO BE FREED?
WORD? WHY SHOULD THERE BE WORD, MISTER PAINE? YOU ARE AN EMBARRASSMENT TO THEM.
THE ONLY WAY YOU WILL WALK FROM HERE IS WHEN YOU BEGIN THE JOURNEY THAT PERMITS NO RETURNING.
HOW MANY PEOPLE HAS YOUR DAMNED COMMITTEE SENT TO THEIR DEATH IN THE LAST MONTH? TEN THOUSAND? TWENTY?
THIS REIGN OF TERROR IS AN EVIL, MONSTROUS THING. AND YOUR MASTER, ROBESPIERRE, IS THE MOST MONSTROUS OF THEM ALL.
"THESE ARE THE TIMES THAT TRY MEN'S SOULS. THE SUMMER SOLDIER AND THE SUNSHINE PATRIOT WILL, IN THIS CRISIS, SHRINK FROM THE SERVICE OF THEIR COUNTRY; BUT HE THAT STANDS IT NOW, DESERVES THE LOVE AND THANKS OF OUR MEN AND WOMEN.
"TYRANNY, LIKE HELL, IS NOT EASILY CONQUERED; YET WE HAVE THIS CONSOLATION WITH US, THAT THE HARDER THE CONFLICT, THE MORE GLORIOUS THE TRIUMPH.
"WHAT WE OBTAIN TOO CHEAP, WE ESTEEM TOO LIGHTLY: IT IS DEARNESS ONLY THAT GIVES EVERY THING ITS VALUE."
YOUR WORDS, PAINE. WE DO WHAT IS NECESSARY FOR FREEDOM, AND FOR LIBERTY. IF HEADS MUST ROLL, THEN SO BE IT.
9

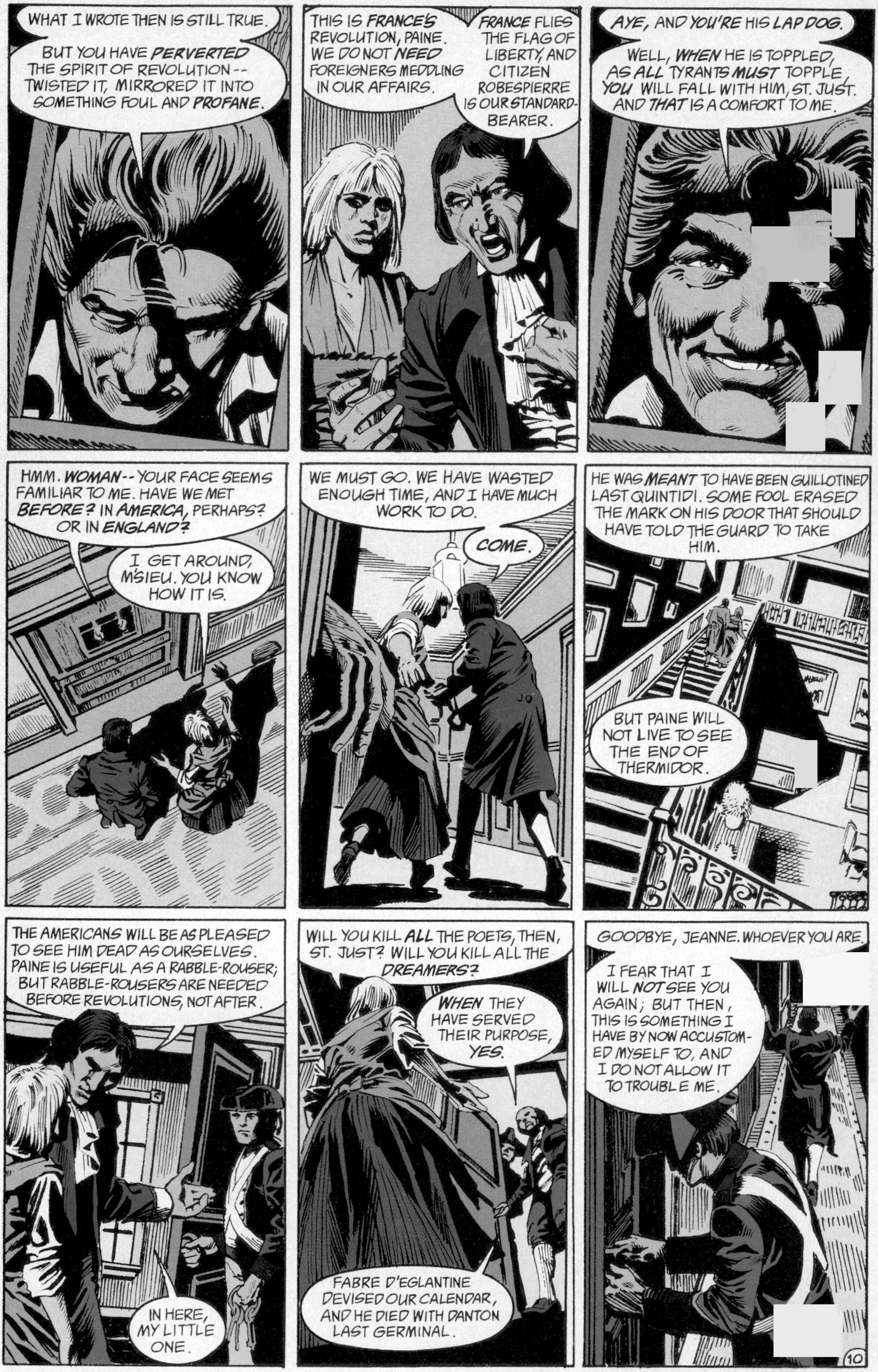
WHAT I WROTE THEN IS STILL TRUE.
BUT YOU HAVE **PERVERTED** THE SPIRIT OF REVOLUTION -- TWISTED IT, MIRRORED IT INTO SOMETHING FOUL AND **PROFANE**.
THIS IS **FRANCE'S** REVOLUTION, PAINE. WE DO NOT **NEED** FOREIGNERS MEDDLING IN OUR AFFAIRS.
FRANCE FLIES THE FLAG OF LIBERTY, AND CITIZEN ROBESPIERRE IS OUR STANDARD-BEARER.
AYE, AND **YOU'RE** HIS **LAP DOG**.
WELL, **WHEN** HE IS TOPPLED, AS **ALL** TYRANTS **MUST** TOPPLE, **YOU** WILL FALL WITH HIM, ST. JUST. AND **THAT** IS A COMFORT TO ME.
HMM. **WOMAN** -- YOUR FACE SEEMS FAMILIAR TO ME. HAVE WE MET **BEFORE**? IN **AMERICA**, PERHAPS? OR IN **ENGLAND**?
I GET AROUND, M'SIEU. YOU KNOW HOW IT IS.
WE MUST GO. WE HAVE WASTED ENOUGH TIME, AND I HAVE MUCH WORK TO DO.
COME.
HE WAS **MEANT** TO HAVE BEEN GUILLOTINED LAST QUINTIDI. SOME FOOL ERASED THE MARK ON HIS DOOR THAT SHOULD HAVE TOLD THE GUARD TO TAKE HIM.
BUT PAINE WILL NOT LIVE TO SEE THE END OF THERMIDOR.
THE AMERICANS WILL BE AS PLEASED TO SEE HIM DEAD AS OURSELVES. PAINE IS USEFUL AS A RABBLE-ROUSER; BUT RABBLE-ROUSERS ARE NEEDED BEFORE REVOLUTIONS, NOT AFTER.
IN HERE, MY LITTLE ONE.
WILL YOU KILL **ALL** THE POETS, THEN, ST. JUST? WILL YOU KILL ALL THE **DREAMERS**?
WHEN THEY HAVE SERVED THEIR PURPOSE, **YES**.
FABRE D'EGLANTINE DEVISED OUR CALENDAR, AND HE DIED WITH DANTON LAST GERMINAL.
GOODBYE, JEANNE. WHOEVER YOU ARE.
I FEAR THAT I WILL **NOT** SEE YOU AGAIN; BUT THEN, THIS IS SOMETHING I HAVE BY NOW ACCUSTOMED MYSELF TO, AND I DO NOT ALLOW IT TO TROUBLE ME.
10

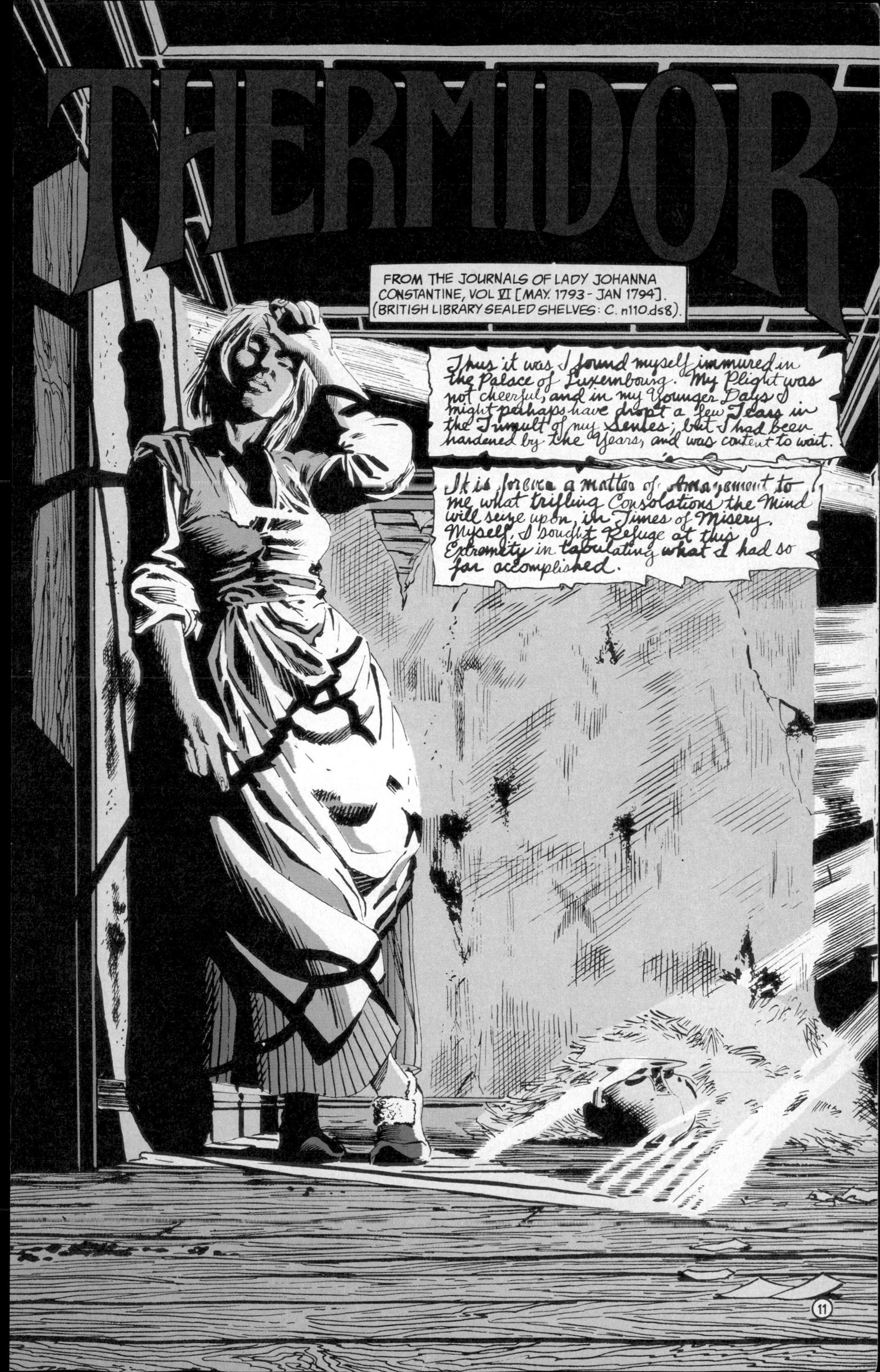
THERMIDOR
FROM THE JOURNALS OF LADY JOHANNA CONSTANTINE, VOL VI [MAY. 1793 - JAN 1794]. (BRITISH LIBRARY SEALED SHELVES: C. n110.ds8).
Thus it was I found myself immured in the Palace of Luxembourg. My Plight was not cheerful, and in my Younger Days I might perhaps have dropt a few Tears in the Tumult of my Sentes; but I had been hardened by the Years, and was content to wait.
It is forever a matter of Amazement to me what trifling Consolations the Mind will seize upon, in Times of Misery. Myself, I sought Refuge at this Extremity in tabulating what I had so far accomplished.

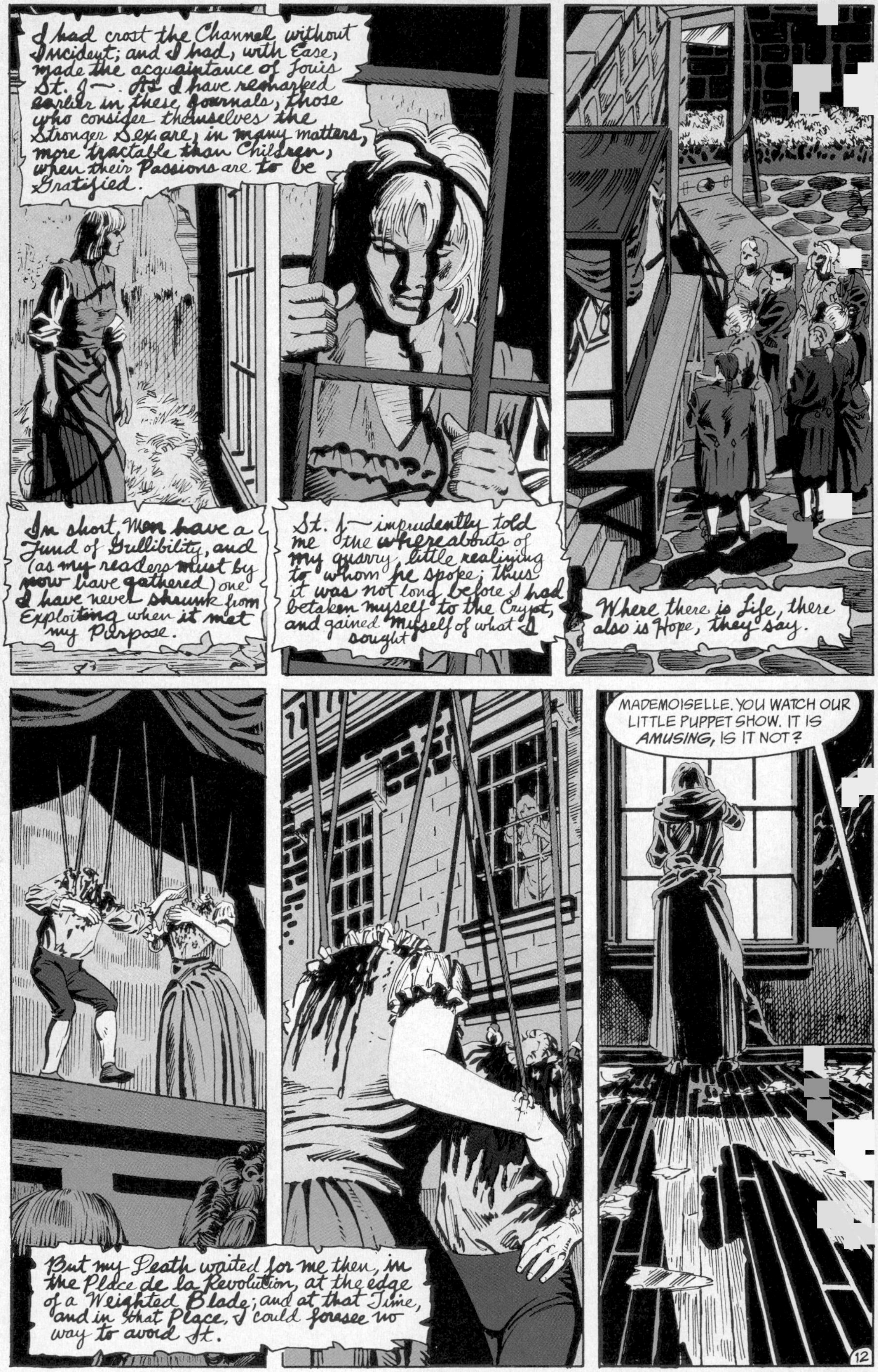
I had crost the Channel without Incident; and I had, with Ease, made the acquaintance of Louis St. J—. As I have remarked earlier in these Journals, those who consider themselves the Stronger Sex are, in many matters, more tractable than Children, when their Passions are to be Gratified.
In short, Men have a Fund of Gullibility, and (as my readers must by now have gathered) one I have never shrunk from Exploiting when it met my Purpose.
St. J— imprudently told me the whereabouts of my quarry, little realising to whom he spoke; thus it was not long before I had betaken myself to the Crypt, and gained myself of what I sought.
Where there is Life, there also is Hope, they say.
But my Death waited for me then, in the Place de la Revolution, at the edge of a Weighted Blade; and at that Time, and in that Place, I could forasee no way to avoid It.
MADEMOISELLE. YOU WATCH OUR LITTLE PUPPET SHOW. IT IS AMUSING, IS IT NOT?
12

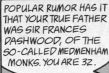

NOW, LET ME SEE. YOUR NAME IS *NOT* JEANNE BONCHANCE. IT IS JOHANNA CONSTANTINE. YOU ARE THE ONLY CHILD OF LORD GEORGE AND LADY HARRIET CONSTANTINE; YOUR TWIN SISTER DIED SOON AFTER YOUR BIRTH.

YOU HAVE *NEVER* MARRIED.

POPULAR RUMOR HAS IT THAT YOUR TRUE FATHER WAS SIR FRANCES DASHWOOD, OF THE SO-CALLED MEDMENHAM MONKS. YOU ARE 32.

YOU SPEAK PERFECT FRENCH. BUT THEN, YOU ARE THE PROTEGÉ OF THE SO-CALLED CHEVALIER D'EON, EXILE, SPY AND ENEMY OF FRANCE. AND HE--OR *SHE*--HAS TAUGHT YOU WELL.

D'EON TAUGHT YOU *FRENCH*. TAUGHT YOU SOMETHING OF ESPIONAGE. AND, *IF* THESE REPORTS ARE TO BE BELIEVED, TAUGHT YOU THE ART OF SUCCESSFULLY CROSS-DRESSING.

YOU HAVE BEEN *POSITIVELY* IDENTIFIED AS THE YOUNG ENGLISH CAPTAIN INVOLVED IN THE THEFT OF *CERTAIN* PAPERS FROM THE RUSSIAN IMPERIAL COURT IN 1786.

YOU WERE CERTAINLY INVOLVED IN THE SLAVE SCANDAL IN LOUISIANA THREE YEARS AGO. YOU WERE ALSO IN EGYPT, WHERE YOU NARROWLY ESCAPED BEING STRANGLED AS A WITCH.

YOU ARE NOW IN POSSESSION OF SOMETHING THAT BELONGS TO THE PEOPLE OF FRANCE. AN OBJECT OF *SUPERSTITION* AND *DECADENCE*. I WANT IT *BACK*, MADEMOISELLE CONSTANTINE.

GOOD DAY, CITIZEN ROBESPIERRE.

I DON'T KNOW *WHAT* YOU'RE TALKING ABOUT.

13

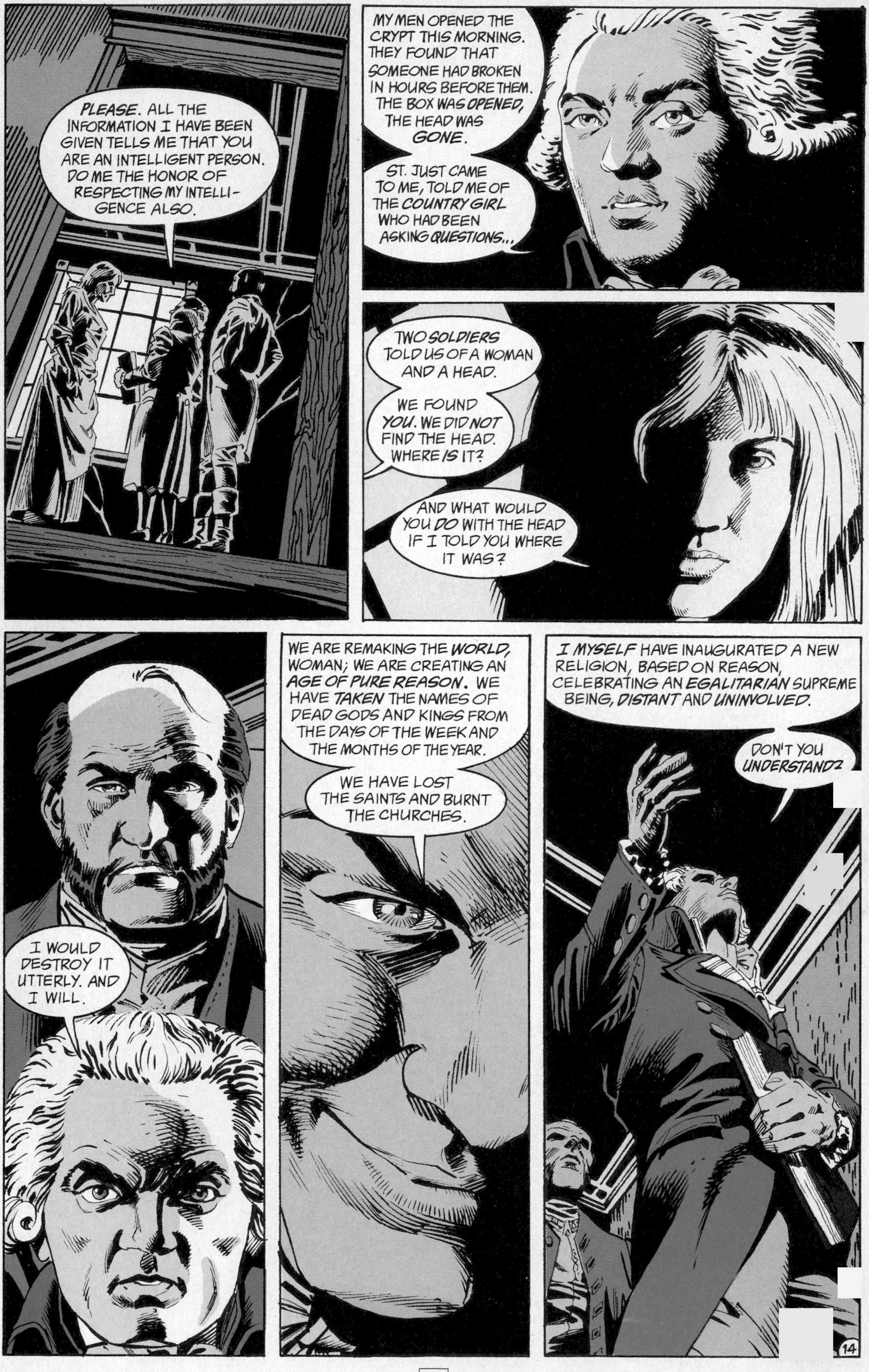
PLEASE. ALL THE INFORMATION I HAVE BEEN GIVEN TELLS ME THAT YOU ARE AN INTELLIGENT PERSON. DO ME THE HONOR OF RESPECTING MY INTELLIGENCE ALSO.
MY MEN OPENED THE CRYPT THIS MORNING. THEY FOUND THAT SOMEONE HAD BROKEN IN HOURS BEFORE THEM. THE BOX WAS OPENED, THE HEAD WAS GONE.
ST. JUST CAME TO ME, TOLD ME OF THE COUNTRY GIRL WHO HAD BEEN ASKING QUESTIONS...
TWO SOLDIERS TOLD US OF A WOMAN AND A HEAD.
WE FOUND YOU. WE DID NOT FIND THE HEAD. WHERE IS IT?
AND WHAT WOULD YOU DO WITH THE HEAD IF I TOLD YOU WHERE IT WAS?
I WOULD DESTROY IT UTTERLY. AND I WILL.
WE ARE REMAKING THE WORLD, WOMAN; WE ARE CREATING AN AGE OF PURE REASON. WE HAVE TAKEN THE NAMES OF DEAD GODS AND KINGS FROM THE DAYS OF THE WEEK AND THE MONTHS OF THE YEAR.
WE HAVE LOST THE SAINTS AND BURNT THE CHURCHES.
I MYSELF HAVE INAUGURATED A NEW RELIGION, BASED ON REASON, CELEBRATING AN EGALITARIAN SUPREME BEING, DISTANT AND UNINVOLVED.
DON'T YOU UNDERSTAND?
14

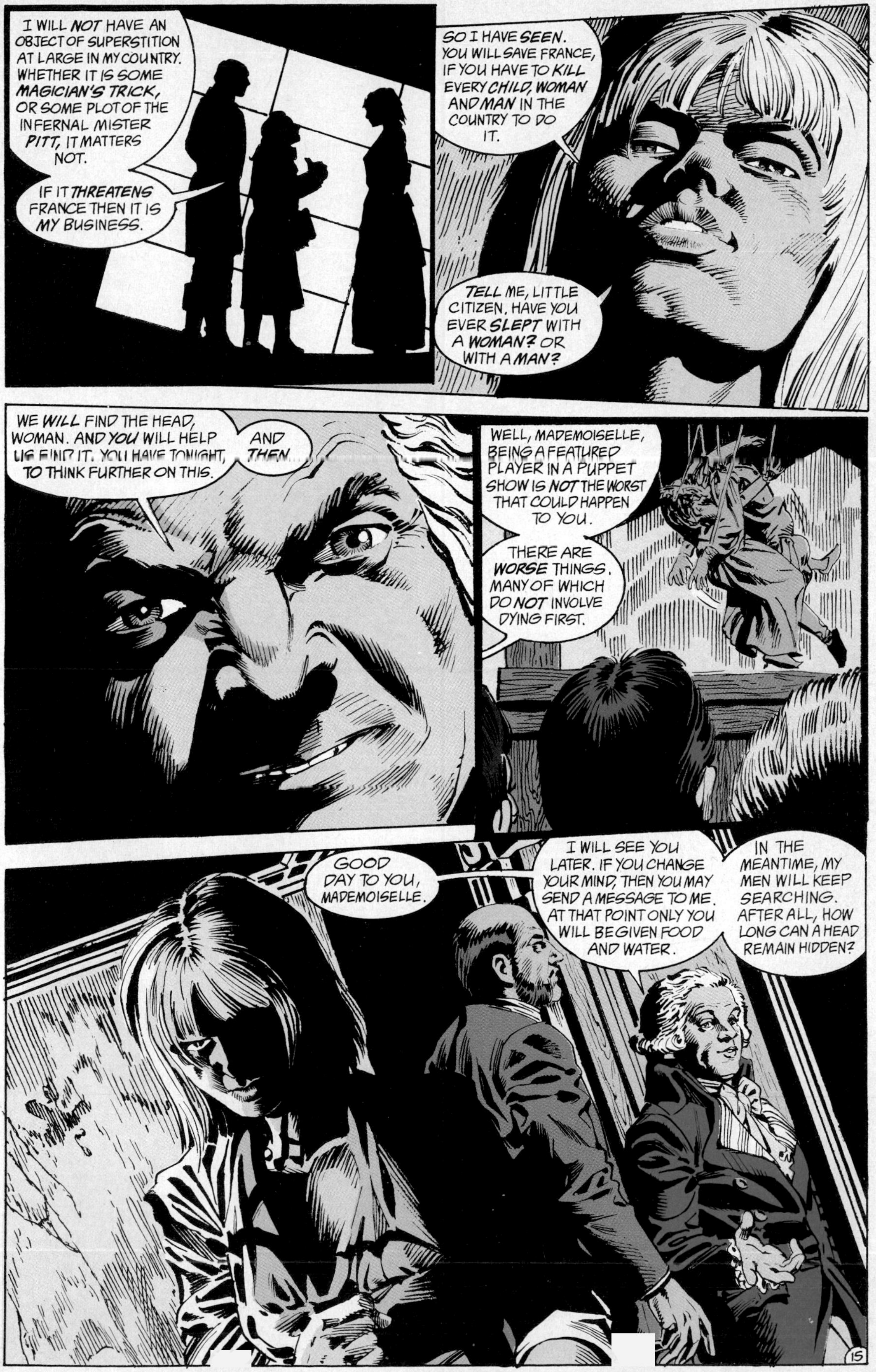
I WILL NOT HAVE AN OBJECT OF SUPERSTITION AT LARGE IN MY COUNTRY. WHETHER IT IS SOME MAGICIAN'S TRICK, OR SOME PLOT OF THE INFERNAL MISTER PITT, IT MATTERS NOT.
IF IT THREATENS FRANCE THEN IT IS MY BUSINESS.
SO I HAVE SEEN. YOU WILL SAVE FRANCE, IF YOU HAVE TO KILL EVERY CHILD, WOMAN AND MAN IN THE COUNTRY TO DO IT.
TELL ME, LITTLE CITIZEN, HAVE YOU EVER SLEPT WITH A WOMAN? OR WITH A MAN?
WE WILL FIND THE HEAD, WOMAN. AND YOU WILL HELP US FIND IT. YOU HAVE TONIGHT, TO THINK FURTHER ON THIS.
AND THEN...
WELL, MADEMOISELLE, BEING A FEATURED PLAYER IN A PUPPET SHOW IS NOT THE WORST THAT COULD HAPPEN TO YOU.
THERE ARE WORSE THINGS. MANY OF WHICH DO NOT INVOLVE DYING FIRST.
GOOD DAY TO YOU, MADEMOISELLE.
I WILL SEE YOU LATER. IF YOU CHANGE YOUR MIND, THEN YOU MAY SEND A MESSAGE TO ME. AT THAT POINT ONLY YOU WILL BE GIVEN FOOD AND WATER.
IN THE MEANTIME, MY MEN WILL KEEP SEARCHING. AFTER ALL, HOW LONG CAN A HEAD REMAIN HIDDEN?
15

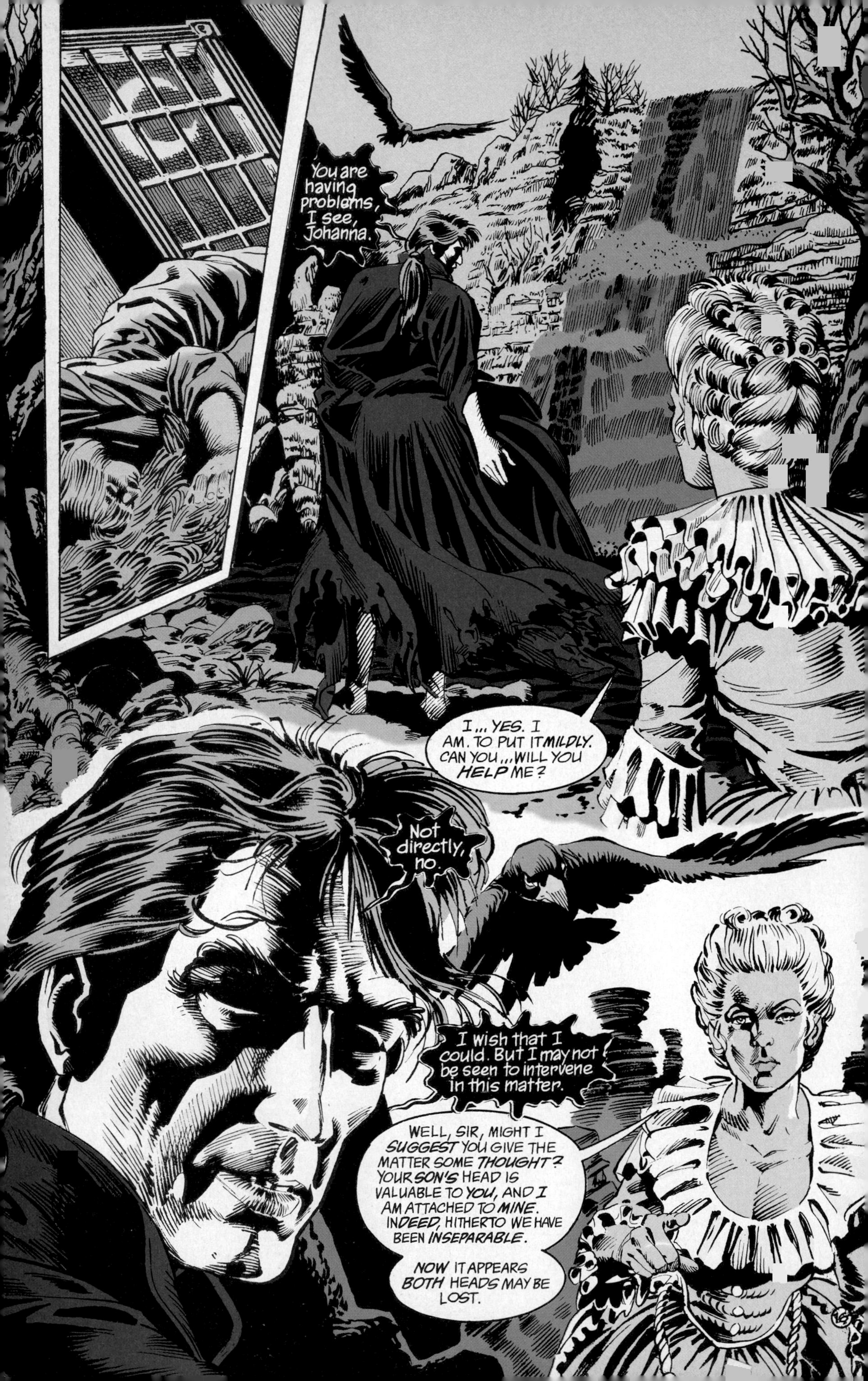
You are having problems, I see, Johanna.
I... YES. I AM. TO PUT IT MILDLY. CAN YOU... WILL YOU HELP ME?
Not directly, no.
I wish that I could. But I may not be seen to intervene in this matter.
WELL, SIR, MIGHT I SUGGEST YOU GIVE THE MATTER SOME THOUGHT? YOUR SON'S HEAD IS VALUABLE TO YOU, AND I AM ATTACHED TO MINE. INDEED, HITHERTO WE HAVE BEEN INSEPARABLE.
NOW IT APPEARS BOTH HEADS MAY BE LOST.
16

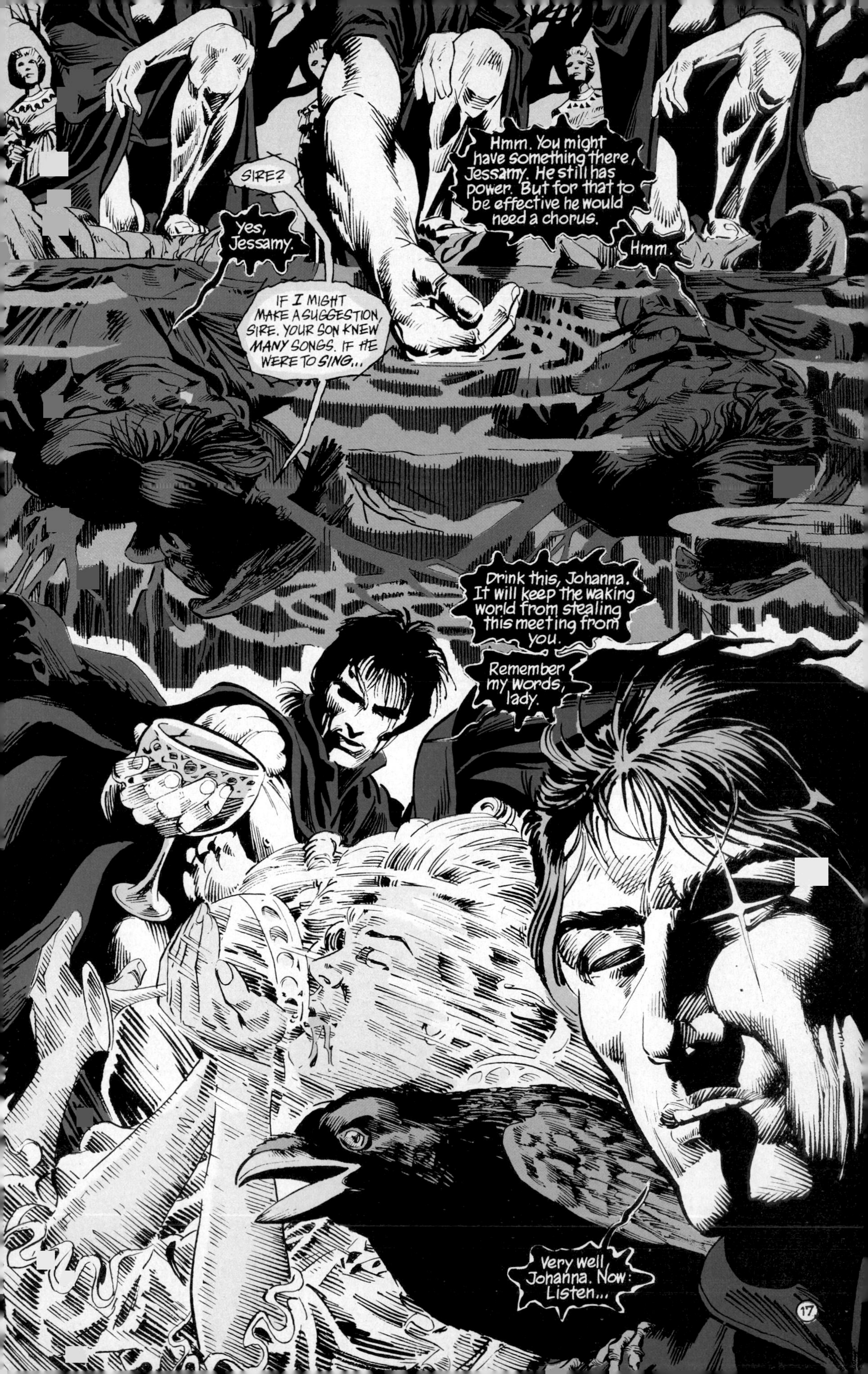
SIRE?
Yes, Jessamy.
IF I MIGHT MAKE A SUGGESTION, SIRE. YOUR SON KNEW MANY SONGS. IF HE WERE TO SING...
Hmm. You might have something there, Jessamy. He still has power. But for that to be effective he would need a chorus.
Hmm.
Drink this, Johanna. It will keep the waking world from stealing this meeting from you.
Remember my words, lady.
Very well Johanna. Now: Listen...

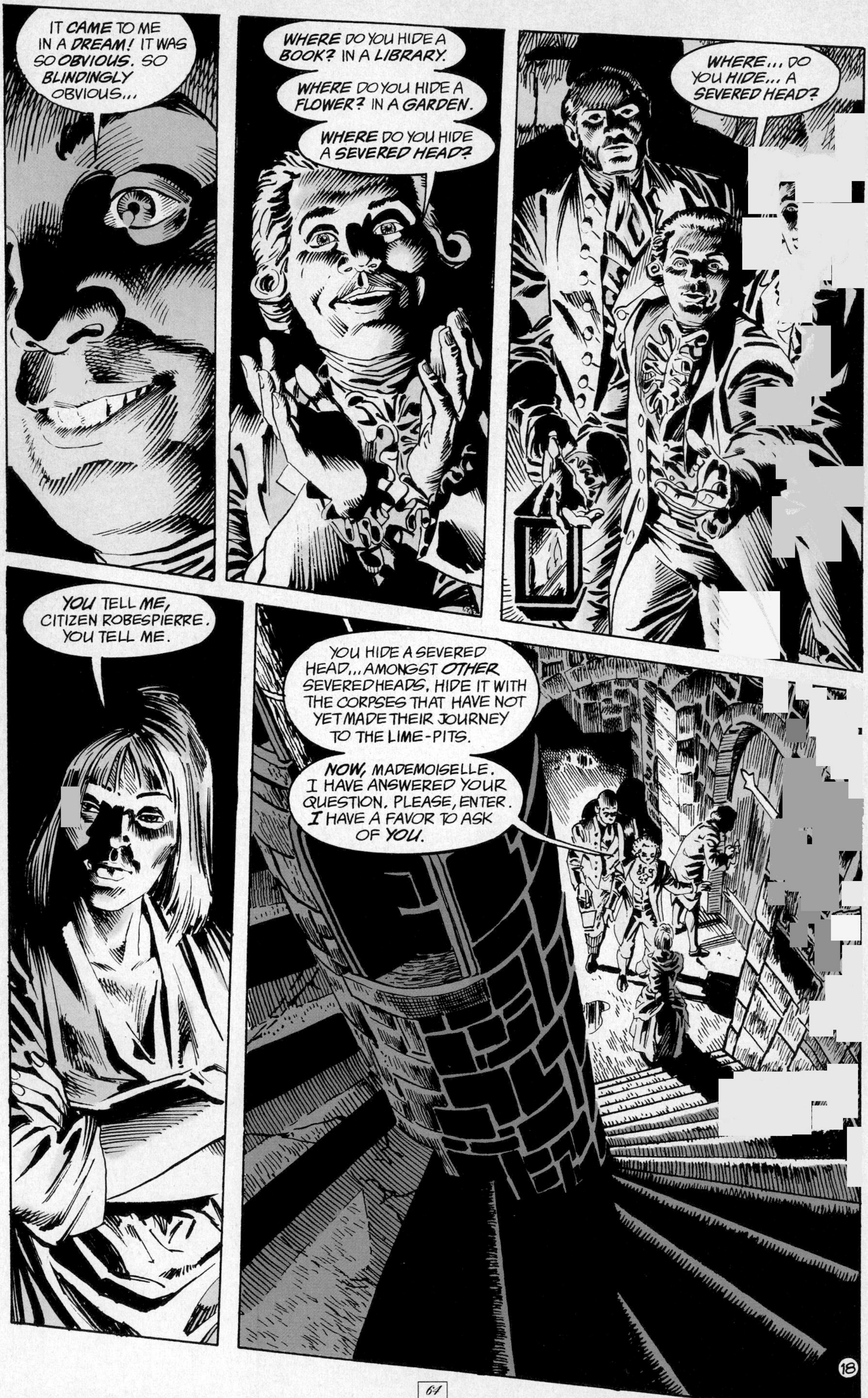
IT CAME TO ME IN A DREAM! IT WAS SO OBVIOUS. SO BLINDINGLY OBVIOUS...
WHERE DO YOU HIDE A BOOK? IN A LIBRARY.
WHERE DO YOU HIDE A FLOWER? IN A GARDEN.
WHERE DO YOU HIDE A SEVERED HEAD?
WHERE... DO YOU HIDE... A SEVERED HEAD?
YOU TELL ME, CITIZEN ROBESPIERRE. YOU TELL ME.
YOU HIDE A SEVERED HEAD... AMONGST OTHER SEVERED HEADS. HIDE IT WITH THE CORPSES THAT HAVE NOT YET MADE THEIR JOURNEY TO THE LIME-PITS.
NOW, MADEMOISELLE. I HAVE ANSWERED YOUR QUESTION. PLEASE, ENTER. I HAVE A FAVOR TO ASK OF YOU.
18

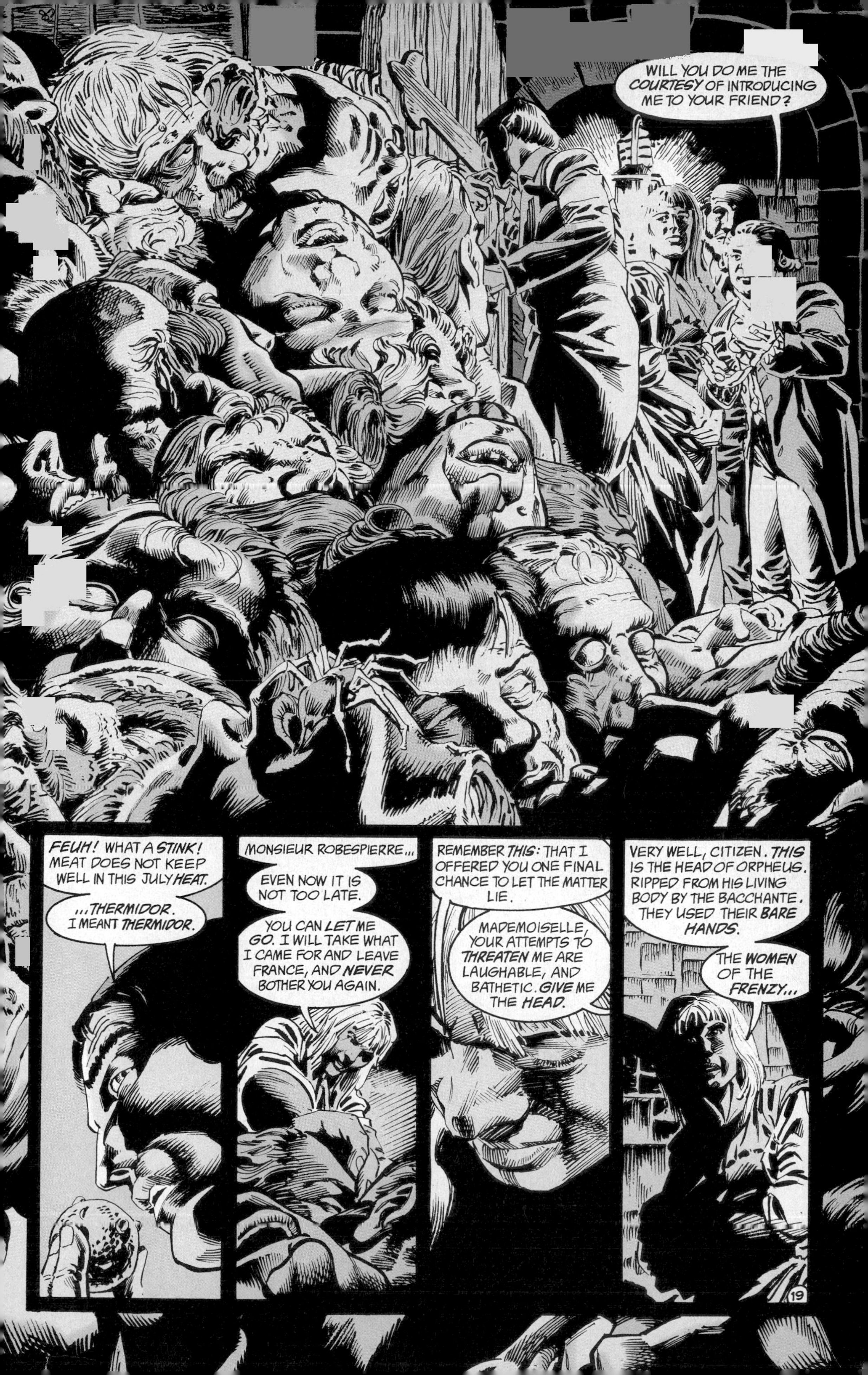
WILL YOU DO ME THE COURTESY OF INTRODUCING ME TO YOUR FRIEND?
FEUH! WHAT A STINK! MEAT DOES NOT KEEP WELL IN THIS JULY HEAT.
...THERMIDOR. I MEANT THERMIDOR.
MONSIEUR ROBESPIERRE...
EVEN NOW IT IS NOT TOO LATE.
YOU CAN LET ME GO. I WILL TAKE WHAT I CAME FOR AND LEAVE FRANCE, AND NEVER BOTHER YOU AGAIN.
REMEMBER THIS: THAT I OFFERED YOU ONE FINAL CHANCE TO LET THE MATTER LIE.
MADEMOISELLE, YOUR ATTEMPTS TO THREATEN ME ARE LAUGHABLE, AND BATHETIC. GIVE ME THE HEAD.
VERY WELL, CITIZEN. THIS IS THE HEAD OF ORPHEUS. RIPPED FROM HIS LIVING BODY BY THE BACCHANTE. THEY USED THEIR BARE HANDS.
THE WOMEN OF THE FRENZY...
19

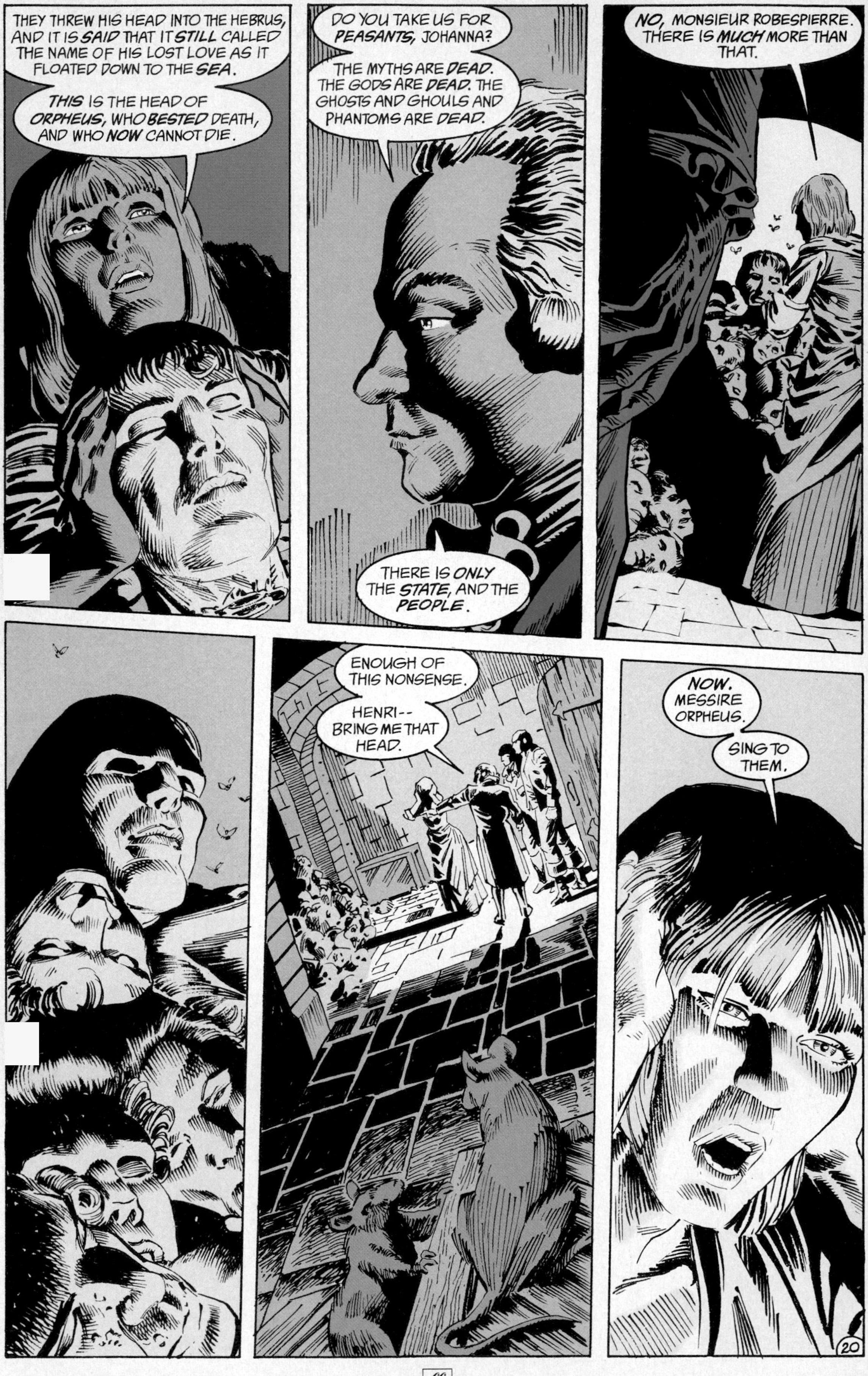
THEY THREW HIS HEAD INTO THE HEBRUS, AND IT IS SAID THAT IT STILL CALLED THE NAME OF HIS LOST LOVE AS IT FLOATED DOWN TO THE SEA.
THIS IS THE HEAD OF ORPHEUS, WHO BESTED DEATH, AND WHO NOW CANNOT DIE.
DO YOU TAKE US FOR PEASANTS, JOHANNA?
THE MYTHS ARE DEAD. THE GODS ARE DEAD. THE GHOSTS AND GHOULS AND PHANTOMS ARE DEAD.
THERE IS ONLY THE STATE, AND THE PEOPLE.
NO, MONSIEUR ROBESPIERRE. THERE IS MUCH MORE THAN THAT.
ENOUGH OF THIS NONSENSE.
HENRI-- BRING ME THAT HEAD.
NOW. MESSIRE ORPHEUS.
SING TO THEM.
20

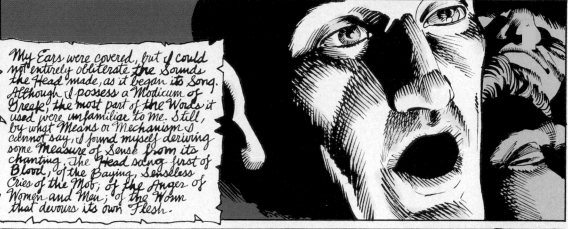

My Ears were covered, but I could not entirely obliterate the Sounds the Head made, as it began its Song. Although I possess a Modicum of Greek, the most part of the Words it used were unfamiliar to me. Still, by what Means or Mechanism I cannot say, I found myself deriving some Measure of Sense from its chanting. The Head sang first of Blood, of the Baying, Senseless Cries of the Mob; of the Anger of Women and Men; of the Worm that devours its own Flesh.

Then it sang of Freedom, of Liberty, of Love. And as it sang, I gazed in Dumbfoundment, for other Voices were also Raised in muffled Unison. Discordant Voices, Harsh Voices, the Voices of the Dead; and my friend (for so I now bethought him) no longer sang Alone.

The Ghastly Chorus sang of those who lead; of those who by Virtue or Circumstance, are Raised above the Crowd; who Manipulate the Commonality will-they or nil-they, as a Puppet-master tugs on the Strings of a Marionette, or a Romany Traveller pulls the Leash of his Dancing Bear. It sang of a dream—and of the Ending of the Dream.

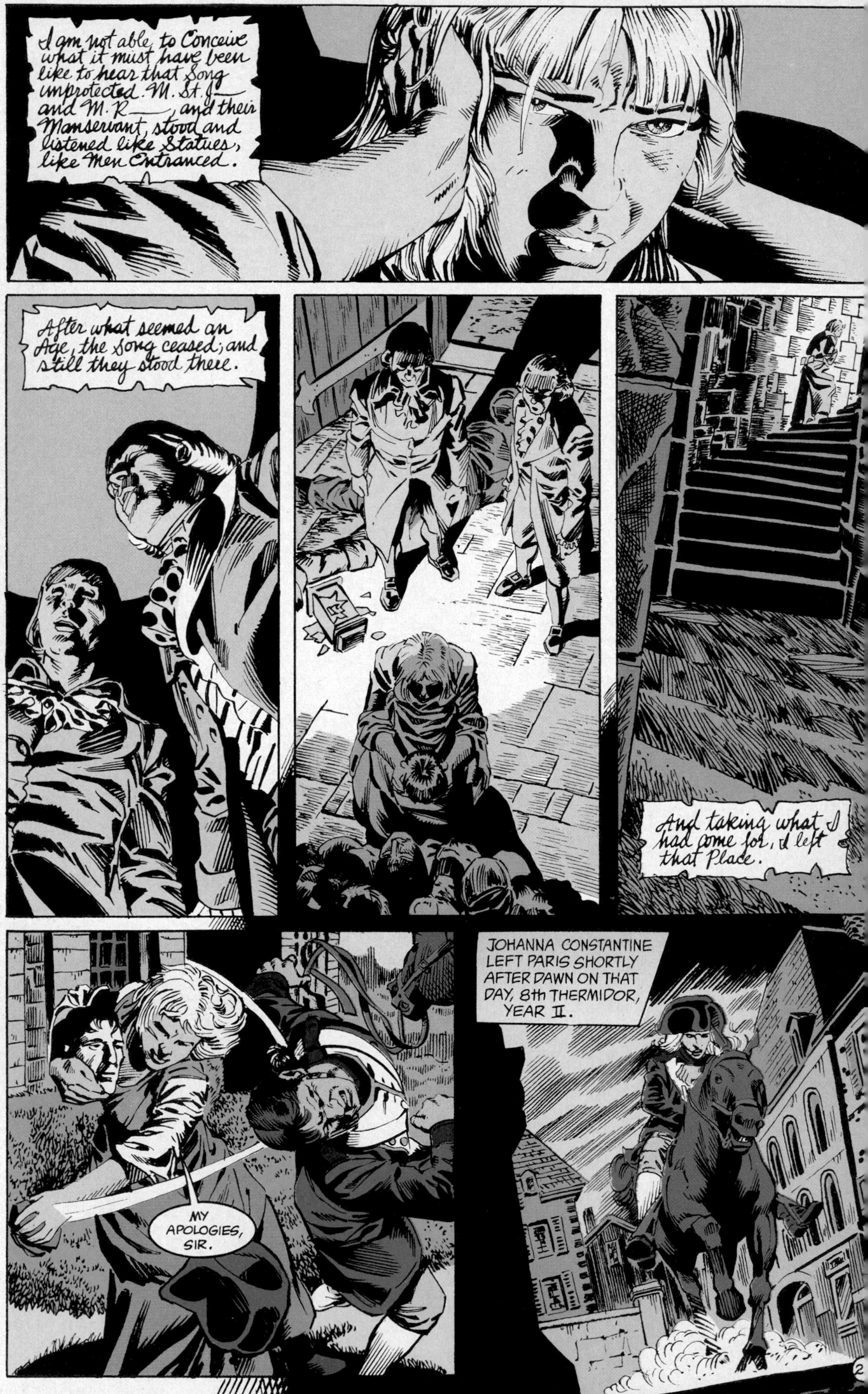
I am not able to Conceive what it must have been like to hear that Song unprotected. M. St. J— and M. R—, and their Manservant, stood and listened like Statues, like Men Entranced.
After what seemed an Age, the Song ceased; and still they stood there.
And taking what I had come for, I left that Place.
MY APOLOGIES, SIR.
JOHANNA CONSTANTINE LEFT PARIS SHORTLY AFTER DAWN ON THAT DAY, 8th THERMIDOR, YEAR II.

ON THE 9th THERMIDOR, LOUIS-ANTOINE ST. JUST, THE GREAT ORATOR, FALTERED DURING HIS SPEECH BEFORE THE NATIONAL CONVENTION, AND FELL SILENT.

MAXMILIEN ROBESPIERRE, THE MOST POWERFUL MAN IN FRANCE, THEN ATTEMPTED TO SPEAK. UNTIL THAT POINT HE HAD BEEN LISTENED TO WITH AWE, OR FEAR, OR SILENCE.

NOW, FOR THE FIRST TIME, HE FOUND HIMSELF LAUGHED AT, AND, ALSO FOR THE FIRST TIME, HE WAS LOST FOR WORDS.

THAT NIGHT HE AND HIS FACTION WERE DEPOSED AND ARRESTED, AND DURING THE ARREST ROBESPIERRE WAS SHOT IN THE JAW. OR PERHAPS HE FUMBLED A SUICIDE ATTEMPT. THE TRUTH HERE IS A MATTER OF CONJECTURE.

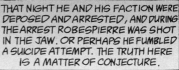

IT IS, HOWEVER, A MATTER OF RECORD THAT THE NEXT DAY, HIS SHATTERED JAW BOUND BY A PAPER BANDAGE, HE WATCHED ST. JUST STEP UP, SILENTLY, TO THE GUILLOTINE.

AND IT IS ALSO A MATTER OF RECORD THAT, IN THE END, MONSIEUR SANSON, THE EXECUTIONER, RIPPED OFF THE PAPER BANDAGE THAT HELD HIS JAW TOGETHER.

AND THAT ROBESPIERRE'S FINAL WORDLESS SCREAM OF PAIN WAS CUT OFF, WITH HIS HEAD, BY THE FALL OF THE WEIGHTED BLADE.

THE TERROR DIED WITH HIM.

23

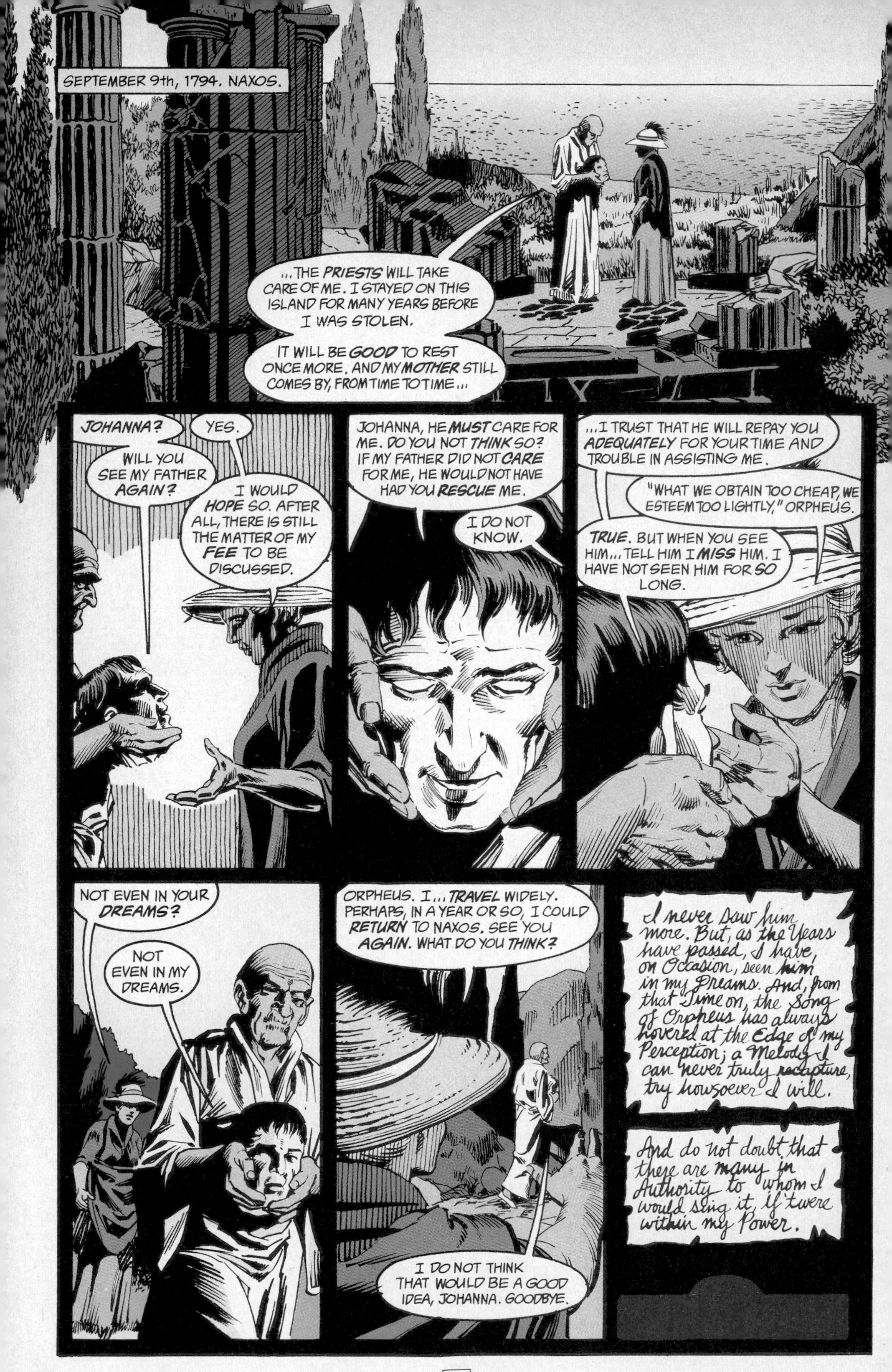
SEPTEMBER 9th, 1794. NAXOS.
...THE PRIESTS WILL TAKE CARE OF ME. I STAYED ON THIS ISLAND FOR MANY YEARS BEFORE I WAS STOLEN.
IT WILL BE GOOD TO REST ONCE MORE. AND MY MOTHER STILL COMES BY, FROM TIME TO TIME...
JOHANNA?
YES.
WILL YOU SEE MY FATHER AGAIN?
I WOULD HOPE SO. AFTER ALL, THERE IS STILL THE MATTER OF MY FEE TO BE DISCUSSED.
JOHANNA, HE MUST CARE FOR ME. DO YOU NOT THINK SO? IF MY FATHER DID NOT CARE FOR ME, HE WOULD NOT HAVE HAD YOU RESCUE ME.
I DO NOT KNOW.
...I TRUST THAT HE WILL REPAY YOU ADEQUATELY FOR YOUR TIME AND TROUBLE IN ASSISTING ME.
"WHAT WE OBTAIN TOO CHEAP, WE ESTEEM TOO LIGHTLY," ORPHEUS.
TRUE. BUT WHEN YOU SEE HIM... TELL HIM I MISS HIM. I HAVE NOT SEEN HIM FOR SO LONG.
NOT EVEN IN YOUR DREAMS?
NOT EVEN IN MY DREAMS.
ORPHEUS. I... TRAVEL WIDELY. PERHAPS, IN A YEAR OR SO, I COULD RETURN TO NAXOS. SEE YOU AGAIN. WHAT DO YOU THINK?
I DO NOT THINK THAT WOULD BE A GOOD IDEA, JOHANNA. GOODBYE.
I never saw him more. But, as the Years have passed, I have, on Occasion, seen him in my Dreams. And, from that Time on, the Song of Orpheus has always hovered at the Edge of my Perception; a Melody I can never truly recapture, try howsoever I will.
And do not doubt that there are many in Authority to whom I would sing it, if 'twere within my Power.

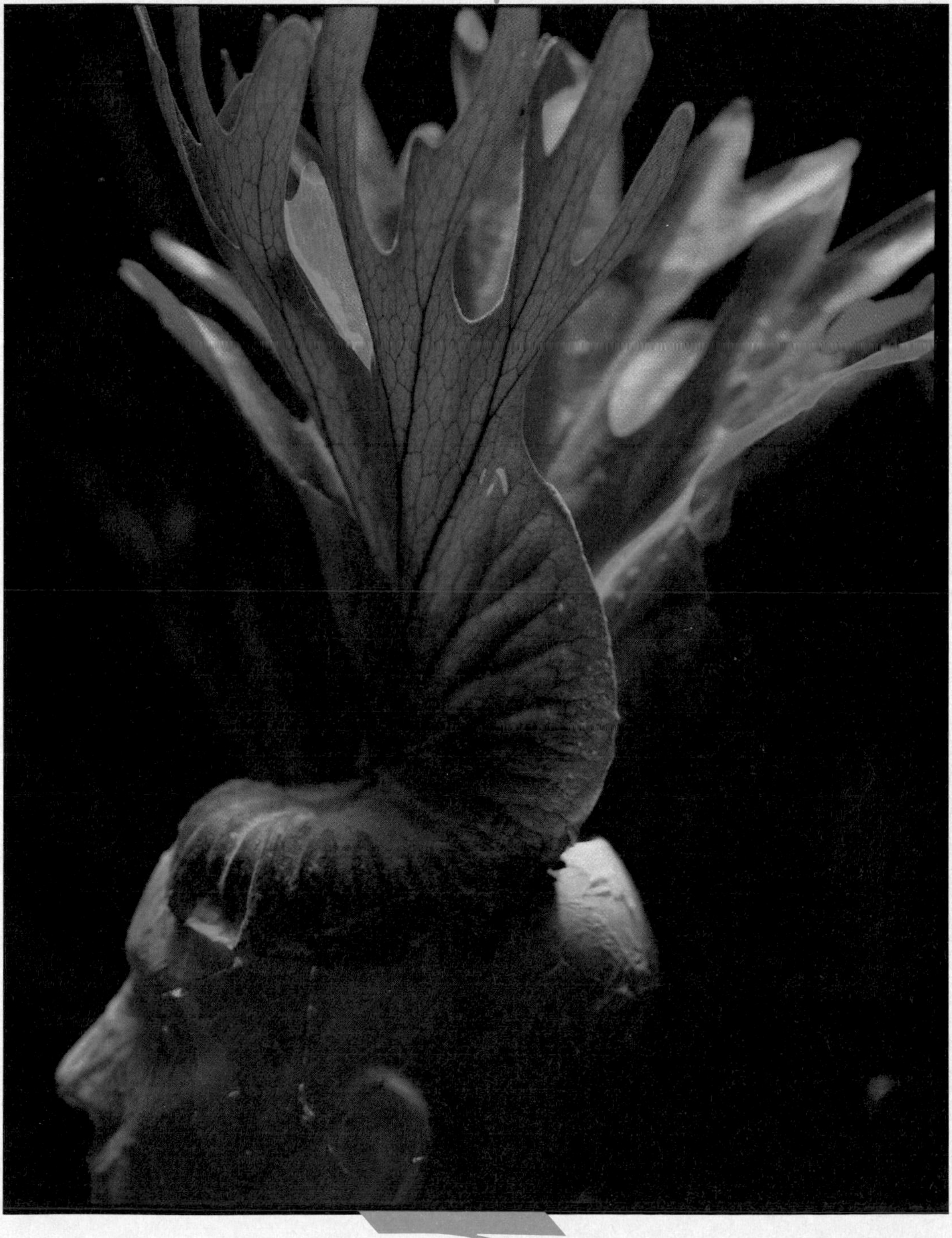

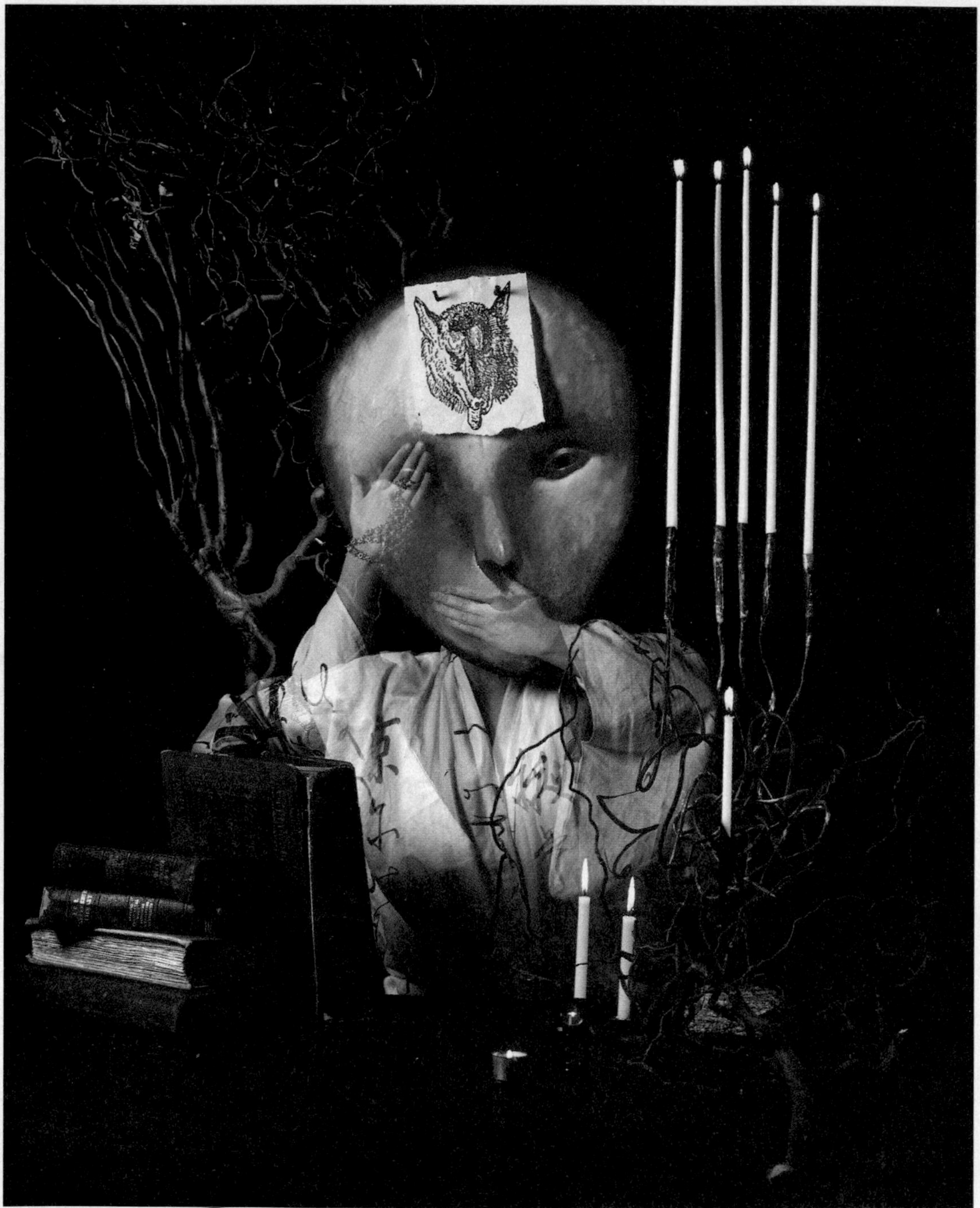

the Hunt

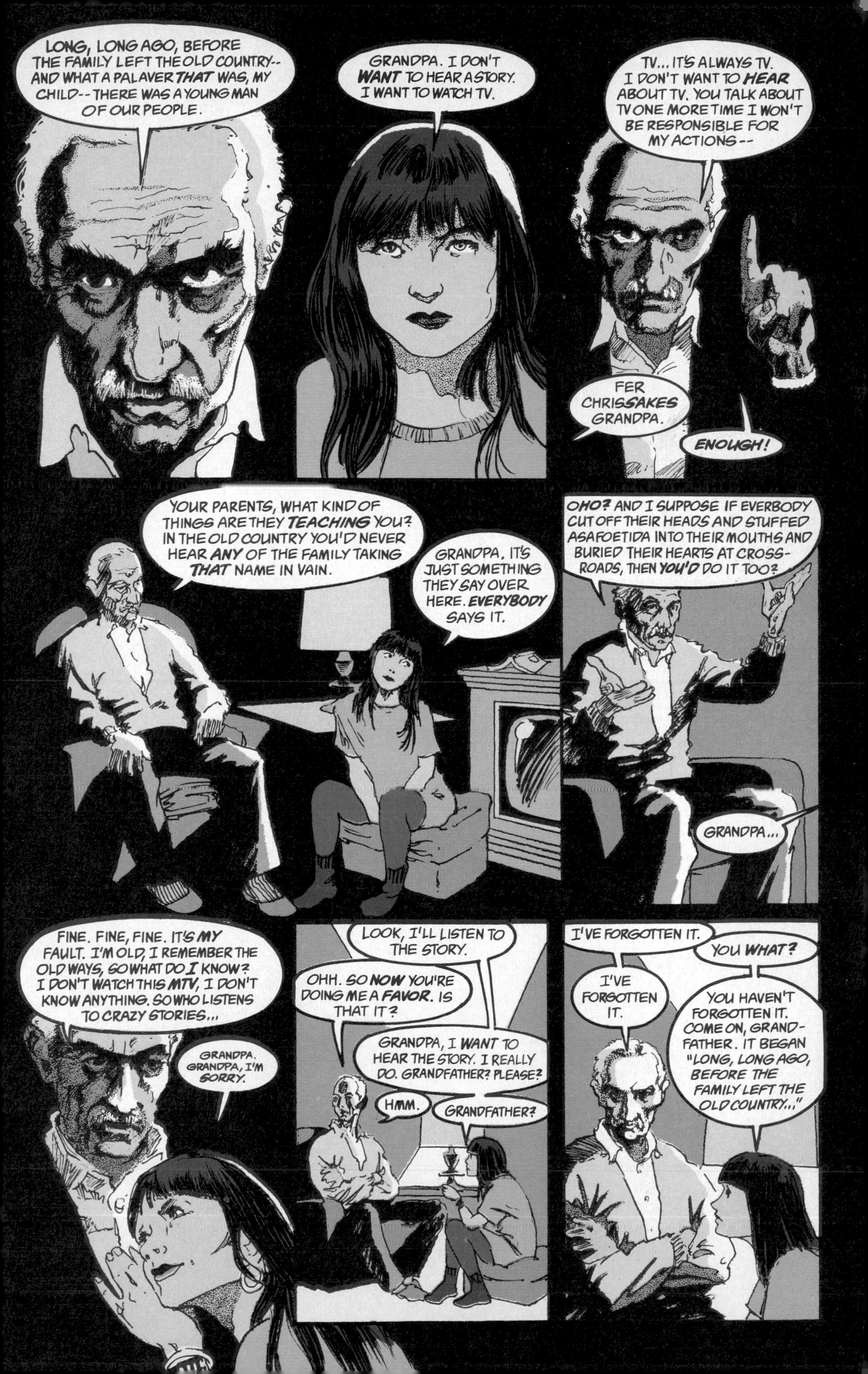
LONG, LONG AGO, BEFORE THE FAMILY LEFT THE OLD COUNTRY-- AND WHAT A PALAVER THAT WAS, MY CHILD-- THERE WAS A YOUNG MAN OF OUR PEOPLE.
GRANDPA. I DON'T WANT TO HEAR A STORY. I WANT TO WATCH TV.
TV... IT'S ALWAYS TV. I DON'T WANT TO HEAR ABOUT TV. YOU TALK ABOUT TV ONE MORE TIME I WON'T BE RESPONSIBLE FOR MY ACTIONS --
FER CHRISSAKES GRANDPA.
ENOUGH!
YOUR PARENTS, WHAT KIND OF THINGS ARE THEY TEACHING YOU? IN THE OLD COUNTRY YOU'D NEVER HEAR ANY OF THE FAMILY TAKING THAT NAME IN VAIN.
GRANDPA, IT'S JUST SOMETHING THEY SAY OVER HERE. EVERYBODY SAYS IT.
OHO? AND I SUPPOSE IF EVERBODY CUT OFF THEIR HEADS AND STUFFED ASAFOETIDA INTO THEIR MOUTHS AND BURIED THEIR HEARTS AT CROSS-ROADS, THEN YOU'D DO IT TOO?
GRANDPA...
FINE. FINE, FINE. IT'S MY FAULT. I'M OLD, I REMEMBER THE OLD WAYS, SO WHAT DO I KNOW? I DON'T WATCH THIS MTV, I DON'T KNOW ANYTHING. SO WHO LISTENS TO CRAZY STORIES...
GRANDPA. GRANDPA, I'M SORRY.
LOOK, I'LL LISTEN TO THE STORY.
OHH. SO NOW YOU'RE DOING ME A FAVOR. IS THAT IT?
GRANDPA, I WANT TO HEAR THE STORY. I REALLY DO. GRANDFATHER? PLEASE?
HMM.
GRANDFATHER?
I'VE FORGOTTEN IT.
YOU WHAT?
I'VE FORGOTTEN IT.
YOU HAVEN'T FORGOTTEN IT. COME ON, GRANDFATHER. IT BEGAN "LONG, LONG AGO, BEFORE THE FAMILY LEFT THE OLD COUNTRY..."

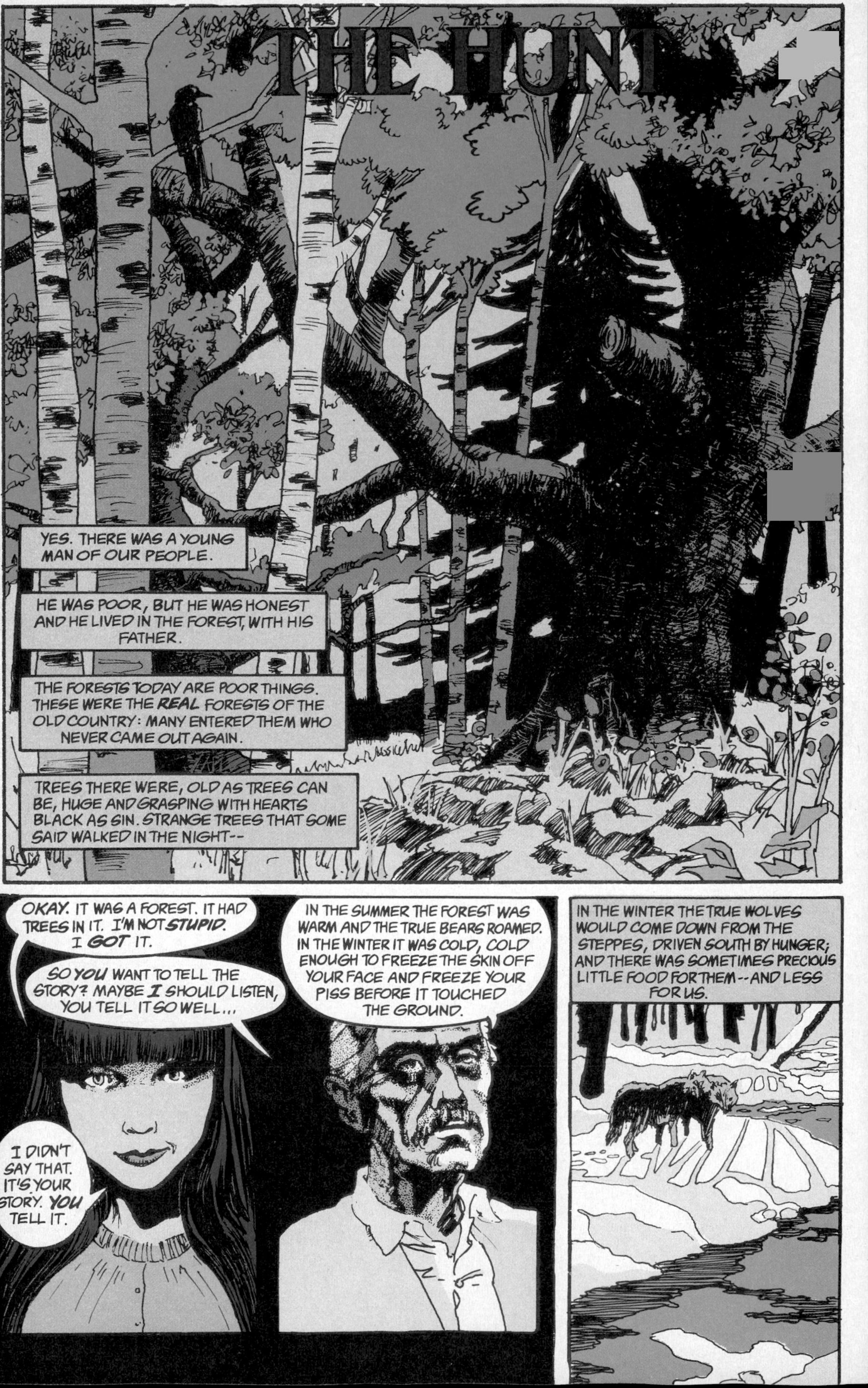
THE HUNT
YES. THERE WAS A YOUNG MAN OF OUR PEOPLE.
HE WAS POOR, BUT HE WAS HONEST AND HE LIVED IN THE FOREST, WITH HIS FATHER.
THE FORESTS TODAY ARE POOR THINGS. THESE WERE THE REAL FORESTS OF THE OLD COUNTRY: MANY ENTERED THEM WHO NEVER CAME OUT AGAIN.
TREES THERE WERE, OLD AS TREES CAN BE, HUGE AND GRASPING WITH HEARTS BLACK AS SIN. STRANGE TREES THAT SOME SAID WALKED IN THE NIGHT--
OKAY. IT WAS A FOREST. IT HAD TREES IN IT. I'M NOT STUPID. I GOT IT.
SO YOU WANT TO TELL THE STORY? MAYBE I SHOULD LISTEN, YOU TELL IT SO WELL...
I DIDN'T SAY THAT. IT'S YOUR STORY. YOU TELL IT.
IN THE SUMMER THE FOREST WAS WARM AND THE TRUE BEARS ROAMED. IN THE WINTER IT WAS COLD, COLD ENOUGH TO FREEZE THE SKIN OFF YOUR FACE AND FREEZE YOUR PISS BEFORE IT TOUCHED THE GROUND.
IN THE WINTER THE TRUE WOLVES WOULD COME DOWN FROM THE STEPPES, DRIVEN SOUTH BY HUNGER; AND THERE WAS SOMETIMES PRECIOUS LITTLE FOOD FOR THEM--AND LESS FOR US.

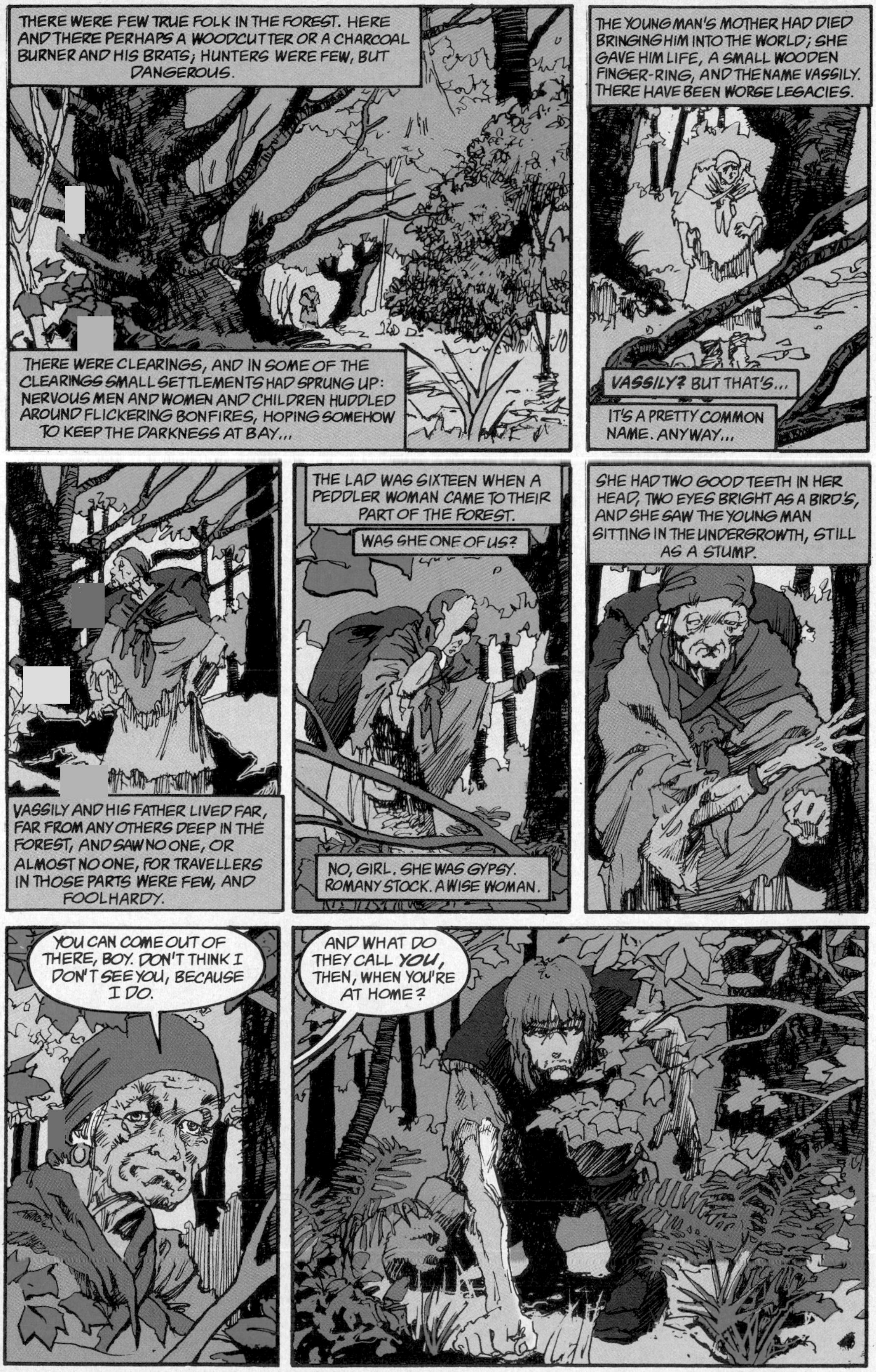
THERE WERE FEW TRUE FOLK IN THE FOREST. HERE AND THERE PERHAPS A WOODCUTTER OR A CHARCOAL BURNER AND HIS BRATS; HUNTERS WERE FEW, BUT DANGEROUS.
THERE WERE CLEARINGS, AND IN SOME OF THE CLEARINGS SMALL SETTLEMENTS HAD SPRUNG UP: NERVOUS MEN AND WOMEN AND CHILDREN HUDDLED AROUND FLICKERING BONFIRES, HOPING SOMEHOW TO KEEP THE DARKNESS AT BAY...
THE YOUNG MAN'S MOTHER HAD DIED BRINGING HIM INTO THE WORLD; SHE GAVE HIM LIFE, A SMALL WOODEN FINGER-RING, AND THE NAME VASSILY. THERE HAVE BEEN WORSE LEGACIES.
VASSILY? BUT THAT'S...
IT'S A PRETTY COMMON NAME. ANYWAY...
VASSILY AND HIS FATHER LIVED FAR, FAR FROM ANY OTHERS DEEP IN THE FOREST, AND SAW NO ONE, OR ALMOST NO ONE, FOR TRAVELLERS IN THOSE PARTS WERE FEW, AND FOOLHARDY.
THE LAD WAS SIXTEEN WHEN A PEDDLER WOMAN CAME TO THEIR PART OF THE FOREST.
WAS SHE ONE OF US?
NO, GIRL. SHE WAS GYPSY. ROMANY STOCK. A WISE WOMAN.
SHE HAD TWO GOOD TEETH IN HER HEAD, TWO EYES BRIGHT AS A BIRD'S, AND SHE SAW THE YOUNG MAN SITTING IN THE UNDERGROWTH, STILL AS A STUMP.
YOU CAN COME OUT OF THERE, BOY. DON'T THINK I DON'T SEE YOU, BECAUSE I DO.
AND WHAT DO THEY CALL YOU, THEN, WHEN YOU'RE AT HOME?

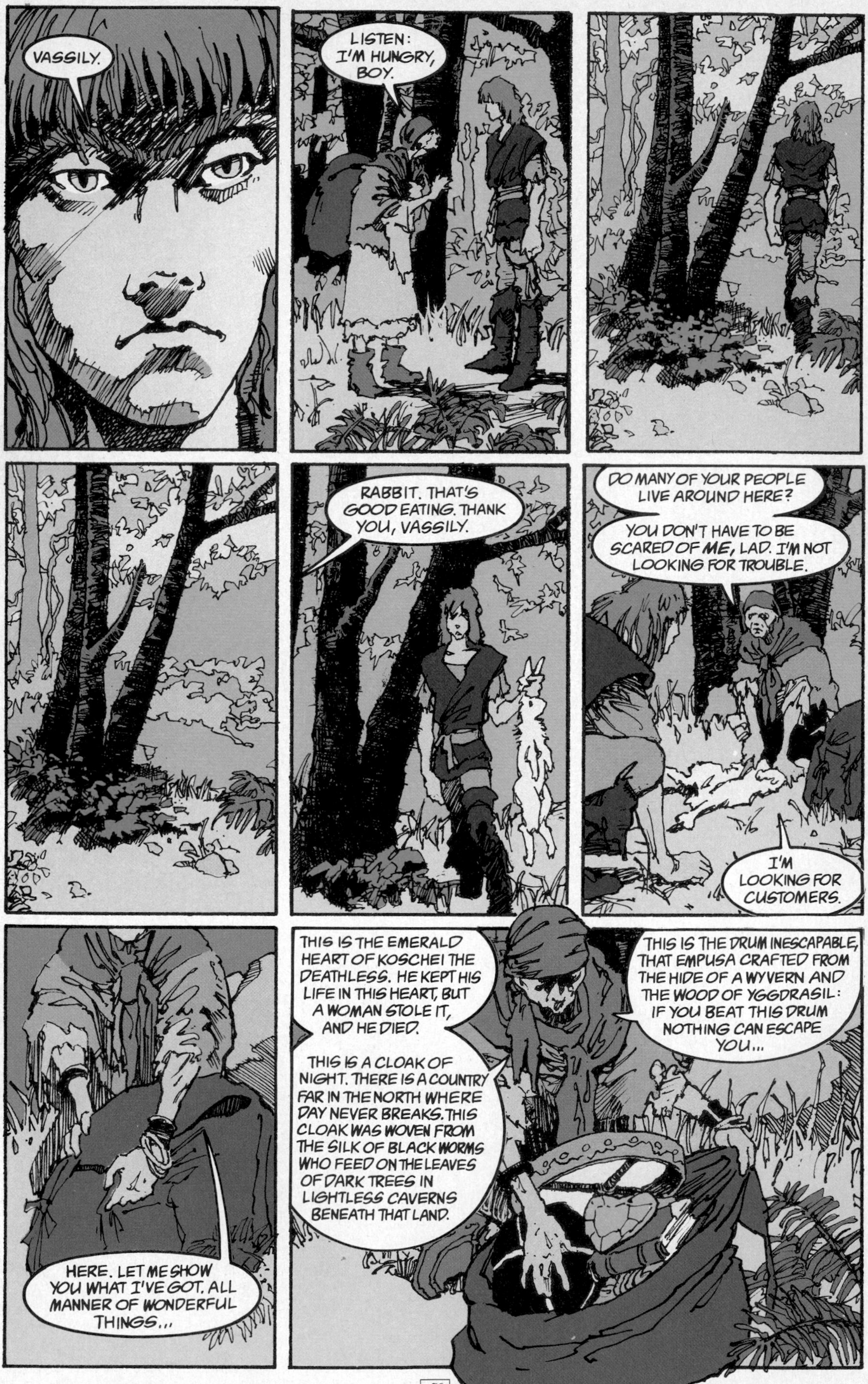

VASSILY.
LISTEN: I'M HUNGRY, BOY.
RABBIT. THAT'S GOOD EATING. THANK YOU, VASSILY.
DO MANY OF YOUR PEOPLE LIVE AROUND HERE?
YOU DON'T HAVE TO BE SCARED OF ME, LAD. I'M NOT LOOKING FOR TROUBLE.
I'M LOOKING FOR CUSTOMERS.
HERE. LET ME SHOW YOU WHAT I'VE GOT. ALL MANNER OF WONDERFUL THINGS...
THIS IS THE EMERALD HEART OF KOSCHEI THE DEATHLESS. HE KEPT HIS LIFE IN THIS HEART, BUT A WOMAN STOLE IT, AND HE DIED.
THIS IS A CLOAK OF NIGHT. THERE IS A COUNTRY FAR IN THE NORTH WHERE DAY NEVER BREAKS. THIS CLOAK WAS WOVEN FROM THE SILK OF BLACK WORMS WHO FEED ON THE LEAVES OF DARK TREES IN LIGHTLESS CAVERNS BENEATH THAT LAND.
THIS IS THE DRUM INESCAPABLE, THAT EMPUSA CRAFTED FROM THE HIDE OF A WYVERN AND THE WOOD OF YGGDRASIL: IF YOU BEAT THIS DRUM NOTHING CAN ESCAPE YOU...

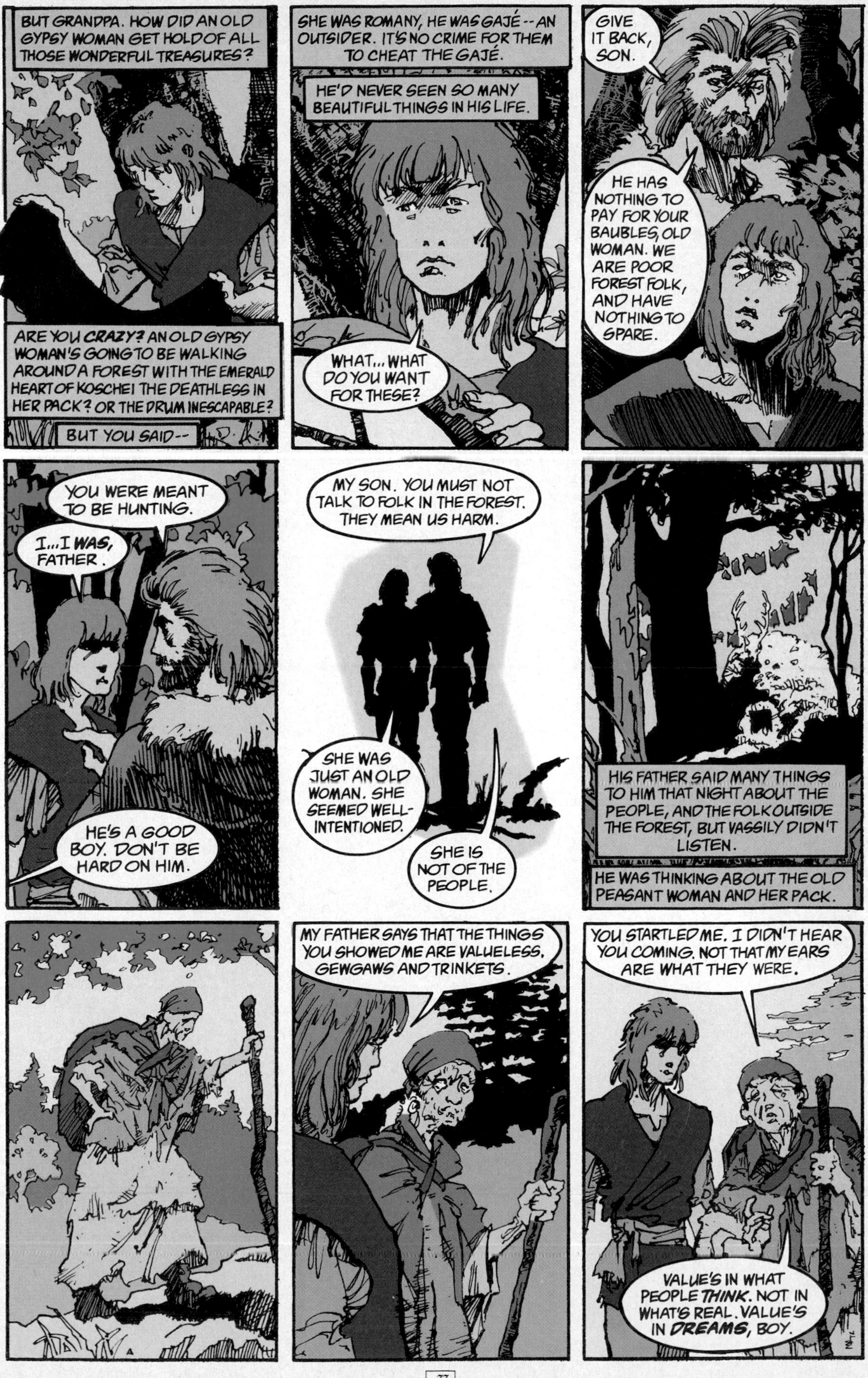

BUT GRANDPA. HOW DID AN OLD GYPSY WOMAN GET HOLD OF ALL THOSE WONDERFUL TREASURES?
ARE YOU CRAZY? AN OLD GYPSY WOMAN'S GOING TO BE WALKING AROUND A FOREST WITH THE EMERALD HEART OF KOSCHEI THE DEATHLESS IN HER PACK? OR THE DRUM INESCAPABLE?
BUT YOU SAID--
SHE WAS ROMANY, HE WAS GAJÉ--AN OUTSIDER. IT'S NO CRIME FOR THEM TO CHEAT THE GAJÉ.
HE'D NEVER SEEN SO MANY BEAUTIFUL THINGS IN HIS LIFE.
WHAT... WHAT DO YOU WANT FOR THESE?
GIVE IT BACK, SON.
HE HAS NOTHING TO PAY FOR YOUR BAUBLES, OLD WOMAN. WE ARE POOR FOREST FOLK, AND HAVE NOTHING TO SPARE.
YOU WERE MEANT TO BE HUNTING.
I... I WAS, FATHER.
HE'S A GOOD BOY. DON'T BE HARD ON HIM.
MY SON. YOU MUST NOT TALK TO FOLK IN THE FOREST. THEY MEAN US HARM.
SHE WAS JUST AN OLD WOMAN. SHE SEEMED WELL-INTENTIONED.
SHE IS NOT OF THE PEOPLE.
HIS FATHER SAID MANY THINGS TO HIM THAT NIGHT ABOUT THE PEOPLE, AND THE FOLK OUTSIDE THE FOREST, BUT VASSILY DIDN'T LISTEN.
HE WAS THINKING ABOUT THE OLD PEASANT WOMAN AND HER PACK.
MY FATHER SAYS THAT THE THINGS YOU SHOWED ME ARE VALUELESS. GEWGAWS AND TRINKETS.
YOU STARTLED ME. I DIDN'T HEAR YOU COMING. NOT THAT MY EARS ARE WHAT THEY WERE.
VALUE'S IN WHAT PEOPLE THINK. NOT IN WHAT'S REAL. VALUE'S IN DREAMS, BOY.

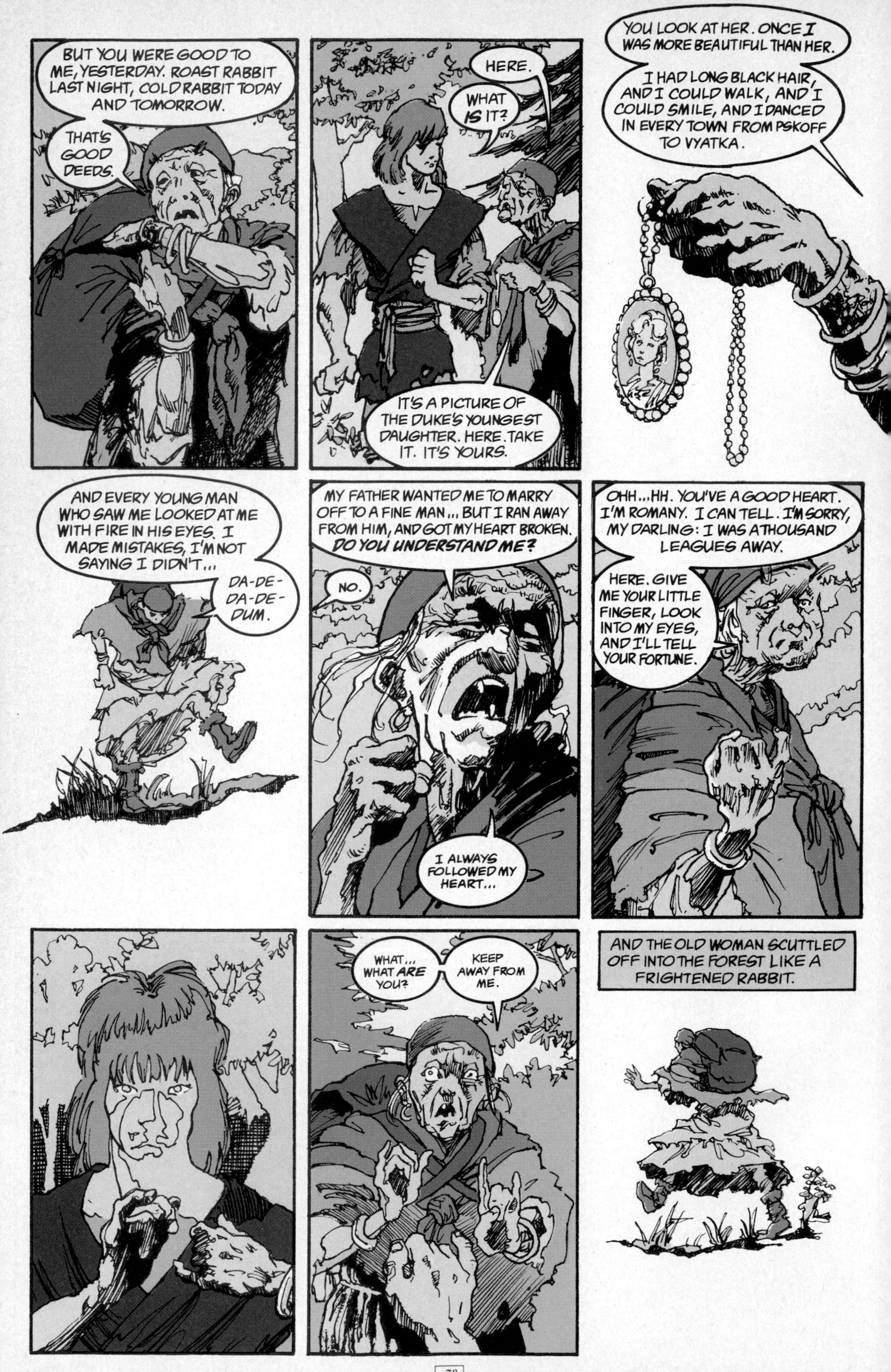
BUT YOU WERE GOOD TO ME, YESTERDAY. ROAST RABBIT LAST NIGHT, COLD RABBIT TODAY AND TOMORROW.
THAT'S GOOD DEEDS.
HERE.
WHAT IS IT?
IT'S A PICTURE OF THE DUKE'S YOUNGEST DAUGHTER. HERE. TAKE IT. IT'S YOURS.
YOU LOOK AT HER. ONCE I WAS MORE BEAUTIFUL THAN HER.
I HAD LONG BLACK HAIR, AND I COULD WALK, AND I COULD SMILE, AND I DANCED IN EVERY TOWN FROM PSKOFF TO VYATKA.
AND EVERY YOUNG MAN WHO SAW ME LOOKED AT ME WITH FIRE IN HIS EYES. I MADE MISTAKES, I'M NOT SAYING I DIDN'T...
DA-DE-DA-DE-DUM.
MY FATHER WANTED ME TO MARRY OFF TO A FINE MAN... BUT I RAN AWAY FROM HIM, AND GOT MY HEART BROKEN. DO YOU UNDERSTAND ME?
NO.
I ALWAYS FOLLOWED MY HEART...
OHH...HH. YOU'VE A GOOD HEART. I'M ROMANY. I CAN TELL. I'M SORRY, MY DARLING: I WAS A THOUSAND LEAGUES AWAY.
HERE. GIVE ME YOUR LITTLE FINGER, LOOK INTO MY EYES, AND I'LL TELL YOUR FORTUNE.
WHAT... WHAT ARE YOU?
KEEP AWAY FROM ME.
AND THE OLD WOMAN SCUTTLED OFF INTO THE FOREST LIKE A FRIGHTENED RABBIT.

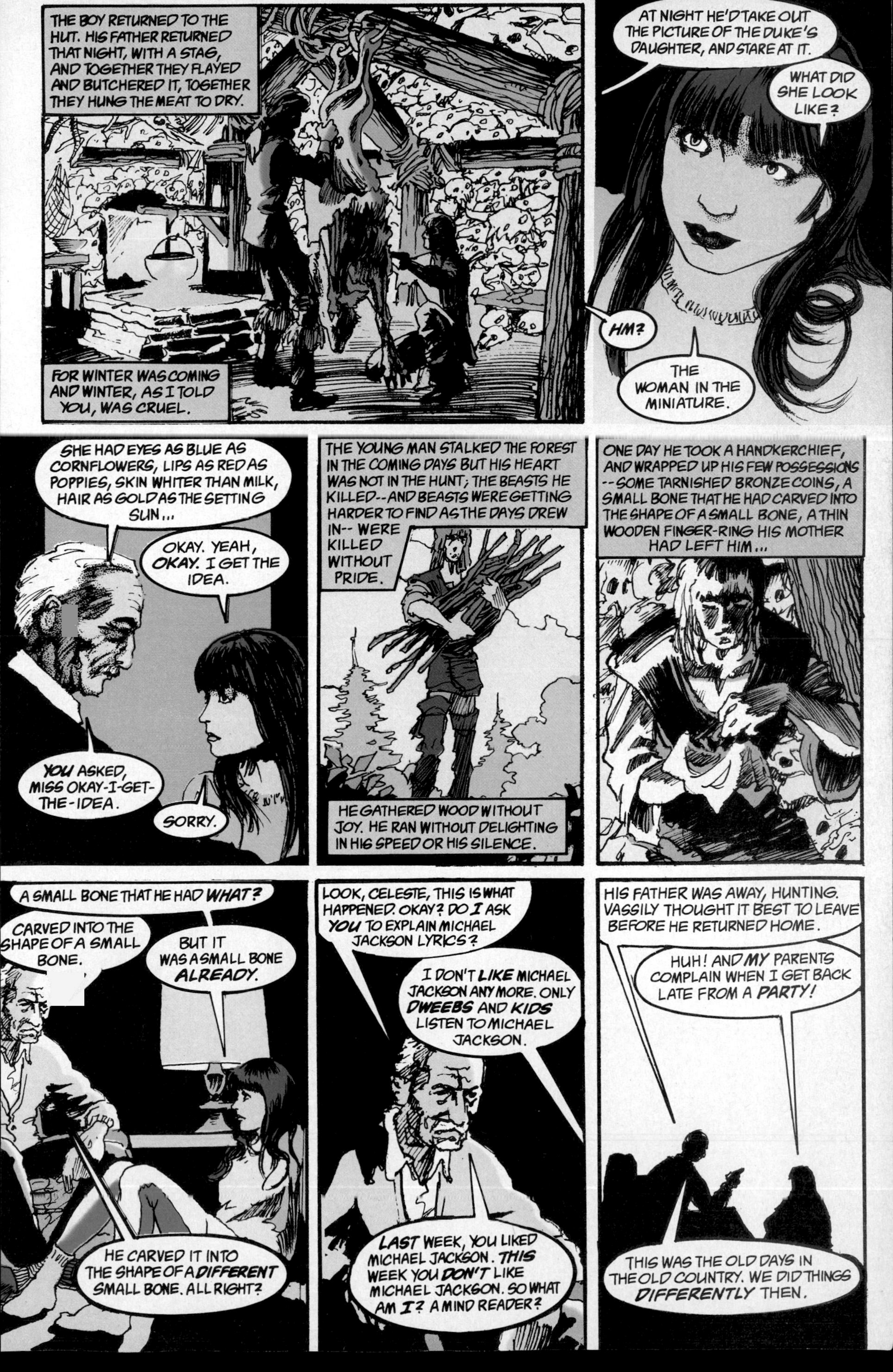
THE BOY RETURNED TO THE HUT. HIS FATHER RETURNED THAT NIGHT, WITH A STAG, AND TOGETHER THEY FLAYED AND BUTCHERED IT, TOGETHER THEY HUNG THE MEAT TO DRY.
FOR WINTER WAS COMING AND WINTER, AS I TOLD YOU, WAS CRUEL.
AT NIGHT HE'D TAKE OUT THE PICTURE OF THE DUKE'S DAUGHTER, AND STARE AT IT.
WHAT DID SHE LOOK LIKE?
HM?
THE WOMAN IN THE MINIATURE.
SHE HAD EYES AS BLUE AS CORNFLOWERS, LIPS AS RED AS POPPIES, SKIN WHITER THAN MILK, HAIR AS GOLD AS THE SETTING SUN...
OKAY. YEAH, OKAY. I GET THE IDEA.
YOU ASKED, MISS OKAY-I-GET-THE-IDEA.
SORRY.
THE YOUNG MAN STALKED THE FOREST IN THE COMING DAYS BUT HIS HEART WAS NOT IN THE HUNT; THE BEASTS HE KILLED--AND BEASTS WERE GETTING HARDER TO FIND AS THE DAYS DREW IN-- WERE KILLED WITHOUT PRIDE.
HE GATHERED WOOD WITHOUT JOY. HE RAN WITHOUT DELIGHTING IN HIS SPEED OR HIS SILENCE.
ONE DAY HE TOOK A HANDKERCHIEF, AND WRAPPED UP HIS FEW POSSESSIONS --SOME TARNISHED BRONZE COINS, A SMALL BONE THAT HE HAD CARVED INTO THE SHAPE OF A SMALL BONE, A THIN WOODEN FINGER-RING HIS MOTHER HAD LEFT HIM...
A SMALL BONE THAT HE HAD WHAT?
CARVED INTO THE SHAPE OF A SMALL BONE.
BUT IT WAS A SMALL BONE ALREADY.
HE CARVED IT INTO THE SHAPE OF A DIFFERENT SMALL BONE. ALL RIGHT?
LOOK, CELESTE, THIS IS WHAT HAPPENED. OKAY? DO I ASK YOU TO EXPLAIN MICHAEL JACKSON LYRICS?
I DON'T LIKE MICHAEL JACKSON ANY MORE. ONLY DWEEBS AND KIDS LISTEN TO MICHAEL JACKSON.
LAST WEEK, YOU LIKED MICHAEL JACKSON. THIS WEEK YOU DON'T LIKE MICHAEL JACKSON. SO WHAT AM I? A MIND READER?
HIS FATHER WAS AWAY, HUNTING. VASSILY THOUGHT IT BEST TO LEAVE BEFORE HE RETURNED HOME.
HUH! AND MY PARENTS COMPLAIN WHEN I GET BACK LATE FROM A PARTY!
THIS WAS THE OLD DAYS IN THE OLD COUNTRY. WE DID THINGS DIFFERENTLY THEN.

THE LAD SET OFF INTO THE FOREST.

AND SOME LEAGUES OFF, HE ENCOUNTERED THE PEDDLER WOMAN, FOR THE LAST TIME.

HER BODY WAS ALREADY COLD, AND THE BLOOD ON HER THROAT HAD HARDENED TO A BLACK CRUST.

DAYS LATER HE REACHED THE FOREST BORDERS.

WE DON'T SEE MANY PEDDLERS IN THESE PARTS. WHICH WAY DID YOU COME?

THROUGH THE OLD FOREST.

THE *DEVIL* YOU HAVE! DON'T YOU KNOW THAT FOREST IS HOME TO GHOULS AND OGRES? YOU WERE LUCKY TO ESCAPE WITH YOUR LIFE.

I SAW NOTHING THAT COULD HAVE HURT ME.

THE *DEVIL* YOU SAY.

WELL, WHAT ARE YOU SELLING, PEDDLER BOY?

AN EMERALD. A LITTLE DRUM. A SHIRT... A BOOK. OTHER THINGS.

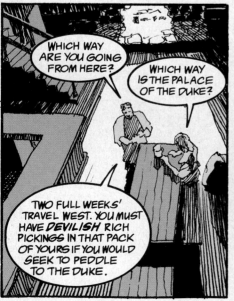

WHICH WAY ARE YOU GOING FROM HERE?

WHICH WAY IS THE PALACE OF THE DUKE?

TWO FULL WEEKS' TRAVEL WEST. YOU MUST HAVE *DEVILISH* RICH PICKINGS IN THAT PACK OF YOURS IF YOU WOULD SEEK TO PEDDLE TO THE DUKE.

VASSILY ATE LIGHTLY OF THE INN'S INDIFFERENT FOOD, THEN WENT UP TO HIS ROOM. HE BOLTED THE DOOR.

THE LEGS OF THE BED WERE BOLTED TO THE FLOOR, AND IT COULD NOT BE MOVED. HE WENT TO SLEEP ON THE HARD FLOOR, IN THE OPPOSITE CORNER OF THE ROOM.

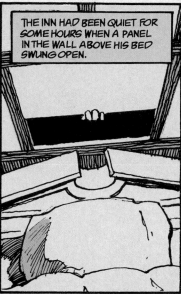

THE INN HAD BEEN QUIET FOR SOME HOURS WHEN A PANEL IN THE WALL ABOVE HIS BED SWUNG OPEN.

THERE WAS A MOMENT OF SILENCE, AND THEN, THROUGH THE HIDDEN DOORWAY IN THE WALL, VASSILY SAW THE INNKEEPER.

VASSILY HAD LEARNED A VALUABLE LESSON THAT NIGHT.

BEFORE HE LEFT THE INN HE TOOK BACK THE COIN HE HAD GIVEN THE INNKEEPER FOR HIS FOOD AND LODGING, FEELING QUITE JUSTIFIED IN SO DOING.

HE SET OFF DUE WEST, AWAY FROM THE SUNRISE, WELL-RESTED AND WELL-FED.

TWO DAYS OF TRAVEL, AND AN EARLY SNOW WAS BEGINNING TO FALL, WHEN UP TO HIM ON THE ROAD COMES THE TALLEST, THINNEST MAN THAT VASSILY HAD EVER SEEN.

"WHERE ARE YOU BOUND, YOUNG PEDDLER?" ASKS THE MAN.

"I'M BOUND WHERE MY FEET TAKE ME, AND WHERE MY HEART WILLS," SAID THE YOUNG MAN.

AND WHAT DO YOU HAVE IN YOUR PACK, YOUNG PEDDLER?

ODDMENTS AND TRINKETS, SIR. NOTHING OF ANY VALUE.

VALUE'S IN THE MIND OF THE BUYER, NOT THE PEDDLER.

AND IS THERE ANYTHING YOU'D BE SEEKING?

INDEED THERE IS. I'M LOOKING FOR A BOOK. I THOUGHT PERHAPS YOU COULD SELL IT TO ME.

AND WHAT WOULD I BE DOING WITH A BOOK?

YOU AREN'T THE FIRST TO CARRY THAT PACK, YOUNG MAN, ARE YOU?

SO, HAVE YOU MY BOOK?

I HAVE MANY THINGS, INCLUDING WHAT I HAVE BEEN ASSURED IS IN ALL PROBABILITY THE EMERALD HEART OF KOSCHEI THE DEATHLESS.

ACCORDING TO POPULAR REPORT, KOSCHEI THE DEATHLESS KEPT HIS HEART IN A DUCK EGG; AND IT WAS DESTROYED BY A YOUNG GALLANT, TWO HUNDRED YEARS AGO.

NO, IT'S THE BOOK I'M INTERESTED IN. WHAT'S YOUR PRICE?

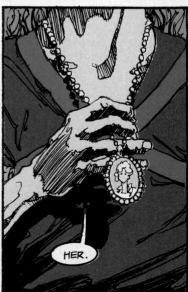

HER.

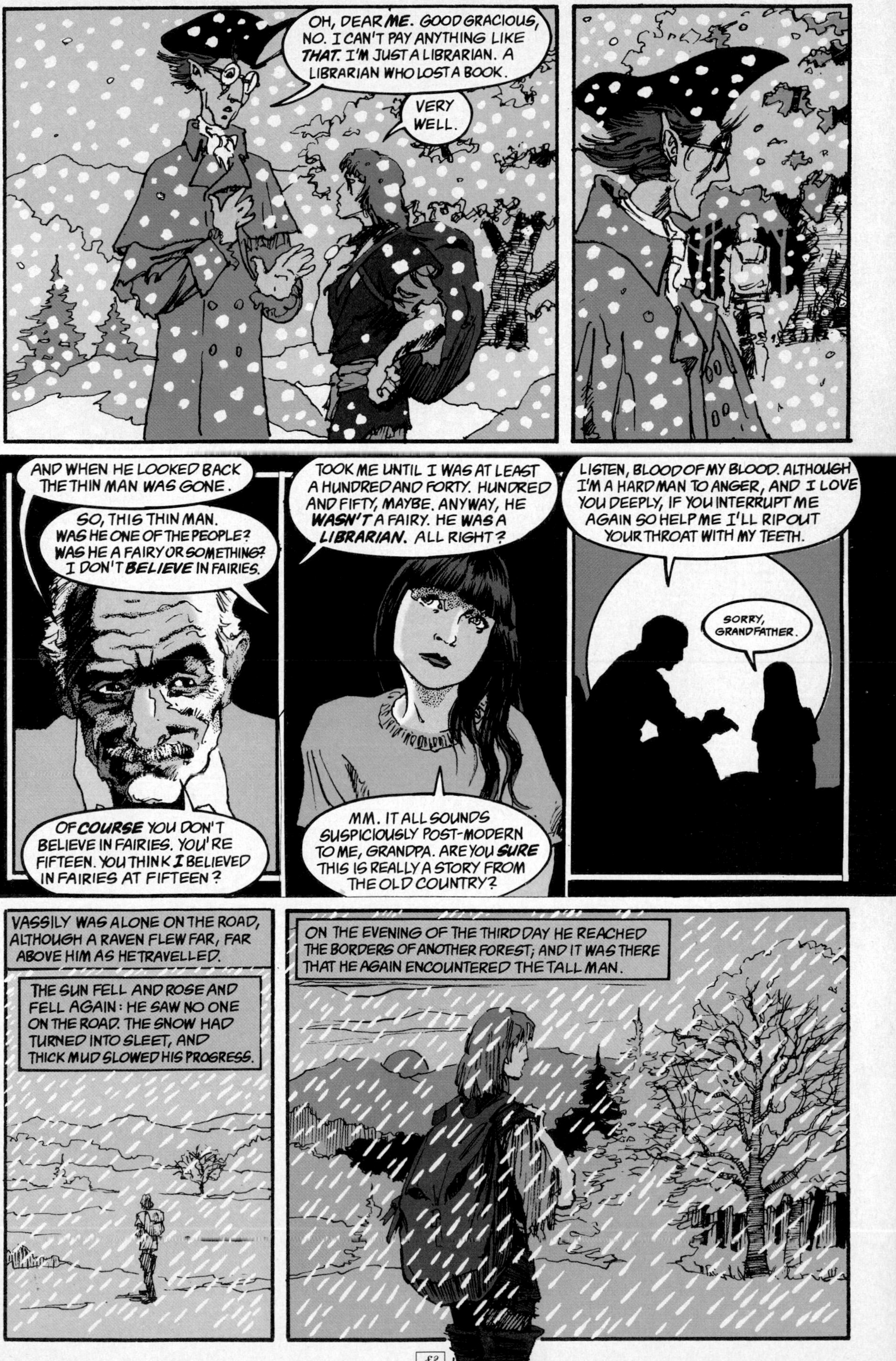
OH, DEAR ME. GOOD GRACIOUS, NO. I CAN'T PAY ANYTHING LIKE THAT. I'M JUST A LIBRARIAN. A LIBRARIAN WHO LOST A BOOK.
VERY WELL.
AND WHEN HE LOOKED BACK THE THIN MAN WAS GONE.
SO, THIS THIN MAN. WAS HE ONE OF THE PEOPLE? WAS HE A FAIRY OR SOMETHING? I DON'T BELIEVE IN FAIRIES.
OF COURSE YOU DON'T BELIEVE IN FAIRIES. YOU'RE FIFTEEN. YOU THINK I BELIEVED IN FAIRIES AT FIFTEEN?
TOOK ME UNTIL I WAS AT LEAST A HUNDRED AND FORTY. HUNDRED AND FIFTY, MAYBE. ANYWAY, HE WASN'T A FAIRY. HE WAS A LIBRARIAN. ALL RIGHT?
MM. IT ALL SOUNDS SUSPICIOUSLY POST-MODERN TO ME, GRANDPA. ARE YOU SURE THIS IS REALLY A STORY FROM THE OLD COUNTRY?
LISTEN, BLOOD OF MY BLOOD. ALTHOUGH I'M A HARD MAN TO ANGER, AND I LOVE YOU DEEPLY, IF YOU INTERRUPT ME AGAIN SO HELP ME I'LL RIP OUT YOUR THROAT WITH MY TEETH.
SORRY, GRANDFATHER.
VASSILY WAS ALONE ON THE ROAD, ALTHOUGH A RAVEN FLEW FAR, FAR ABOVE HIM AS HE TRAVELLED.
THE SUN FELL AND ROSE AND FELL AGAIN: HE SAW NO ONE ON THE ROAD. THE SNOW HAD TURNED INTO SLEET, AND THICK MUD SLOWED HIS PROGRESS.
ON THE EVENING OF THE THIRD DAY HE REACHED THE BORDERS OF ANOTHER FOREST; AND IT WAS THERE THAT HE AGAIN ENCOUNTERED THE TALL MAN.

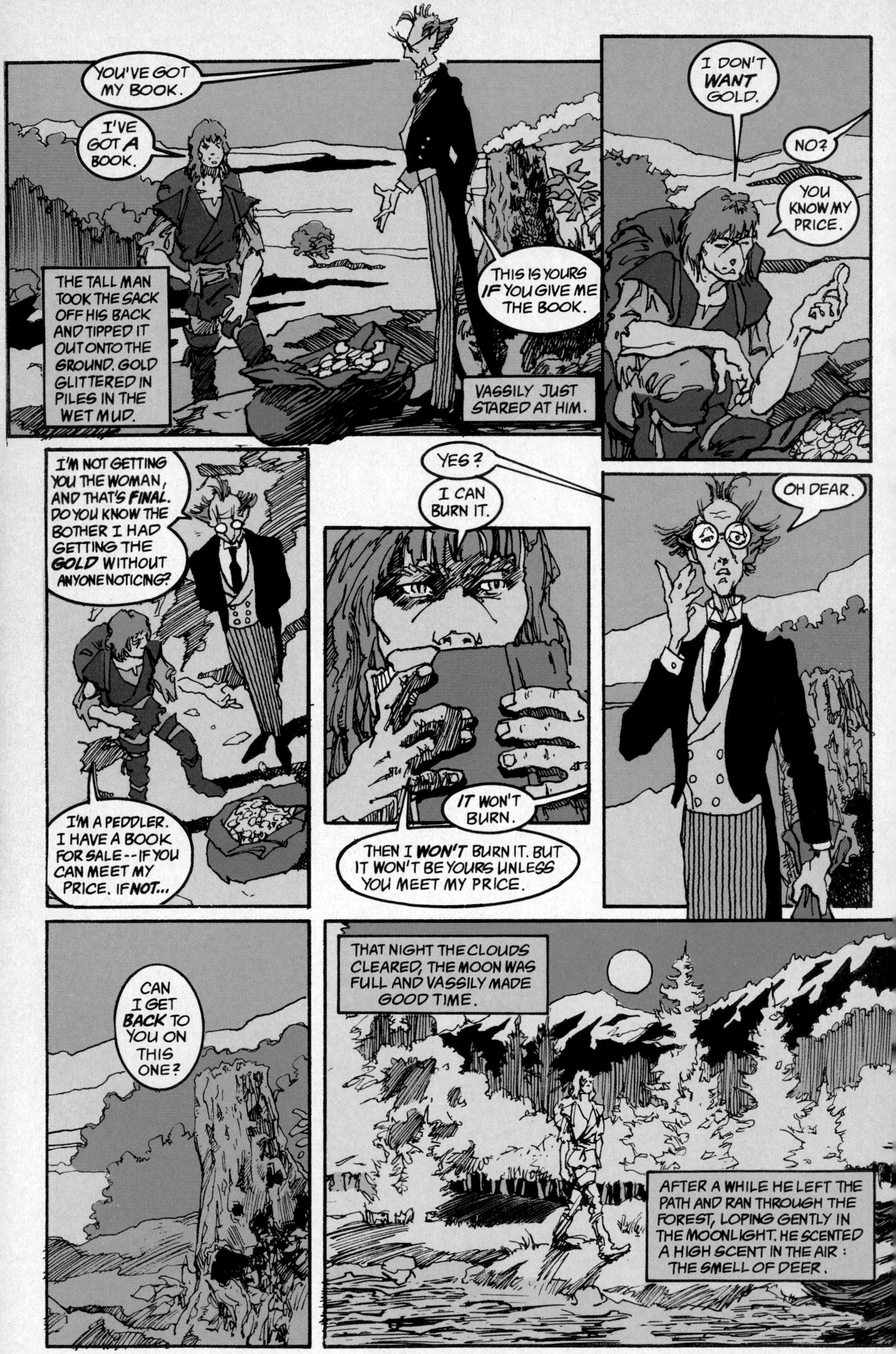

YOU'VE GOT MY BOOK.
I'VE GOT A BOOK.
THE TALL MAN TOOK THE SACK OFF HIS BACK AND TIPPED IT OUT ONTO THE GROUND. GOLD GLITTERED IN PILES IN THE WET MUD.
THIS IS YOURS IF YOU GIVE ME THE BOOK.
VASSILY JUST STARED AT HIM.
I DON'T WANT GOLD.
NO?
YOU KNOW MY PRICE.
I'M NOT GETTING YOU THE WOMAN, AND THAT'S FINAL. DO YOU KNOW THE BOTHER I HAD GETTING THE GOLD WITHOUT ANYONE NOTICING?
I'M A PEDDLER. I HAVE A BOOK FOR SALE--IF YOU CAN MEET MY PRICE. IF NOT...
YES?
I CAN BURN IT.
IT WON'T BURN.
THEN I WON'T BURN IT. BUT IT WON'T BE YOURS UNLESS YOU MEET MY PRICE.
OH DEAR.
CAN I GET BACK TO YOU ON THIS ONE?
THAT NIGHT THE CLOUDS CLEARED, THE MOON WAS FULL AND VASSILY MADE GOOD TIME.
AFTER A WHILE HE LEFT THE PATH AND RAN THROUGH THE FOREST, LOPING GENTLY IN THE MOONLIGHT. HE SCENTED A HIGH SCENT IN THE AIR: THE SMELL OF DEER.

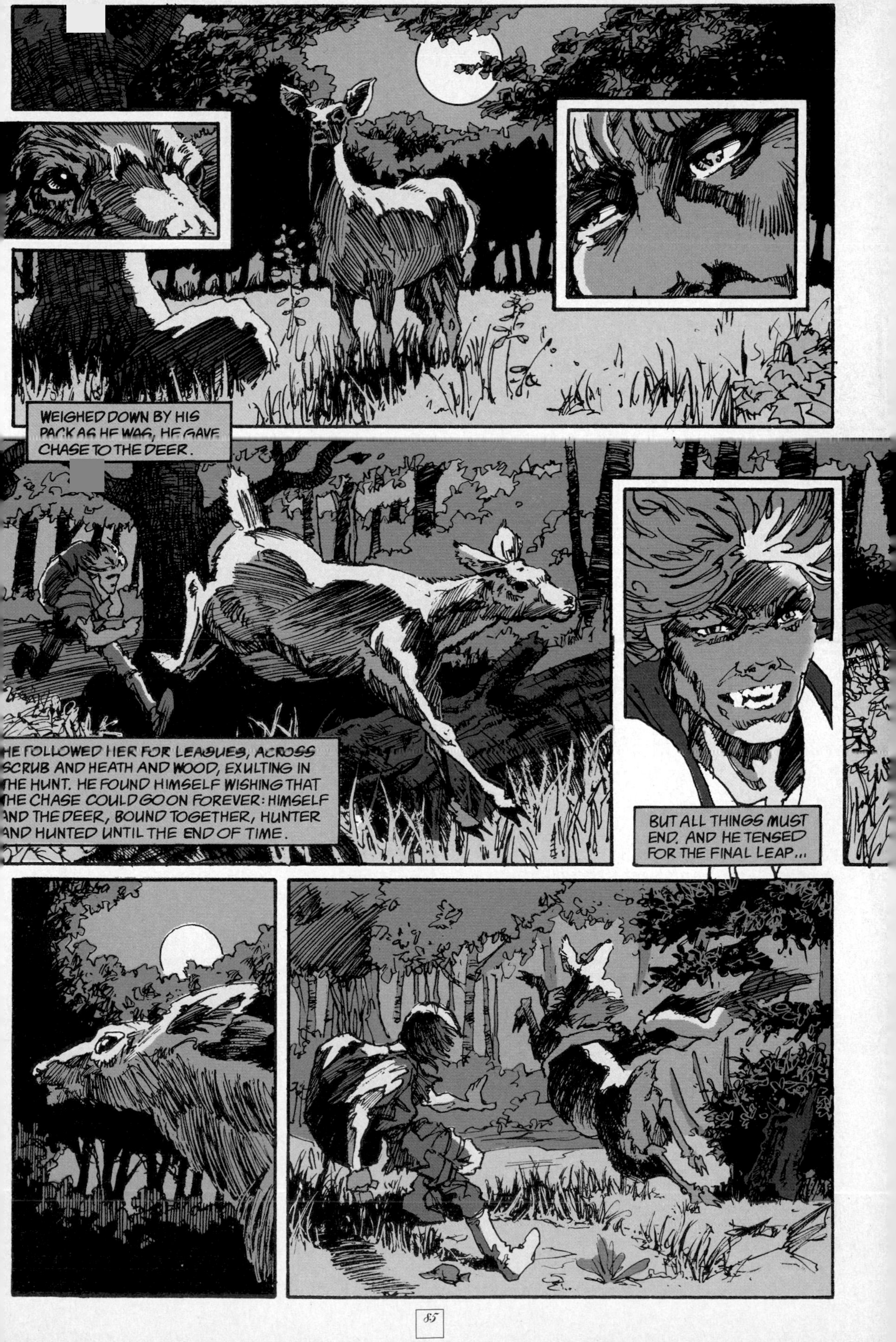
WEIGHED DOWN BY HIS PACK AS HE WAS, HE GAVE CHASE TO THE DEER.
HE FOLLOWED HER FOR LEAGUES, ACROSS SCRUB AND HEATH AND WOOD, EXULTING IN THE HUNT. HE FOUND HIMSELF WISHING THAT THE CHASE COULD GO ON FOREVER: HIMSELF AND THE DEER, BOUND TOGETHER, HUNTER AND HUNTED UNTIL THE END OF TIME.
BUT ALL THINGS MUST END. AND HE TENSED FOR THE FINAL LEAP...

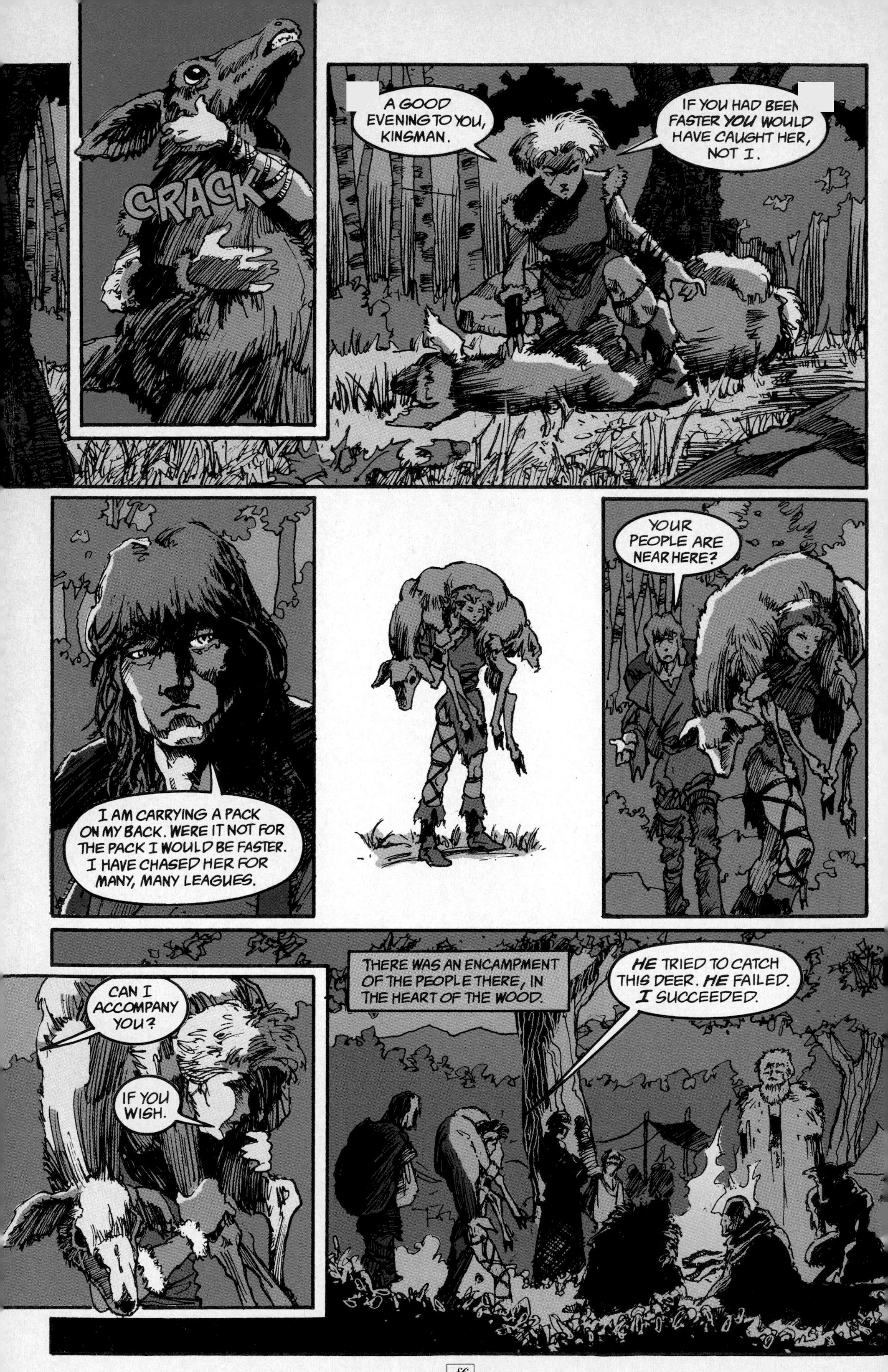
CRACK
A GOOD EVENING TO YOU, KINSMAN.
IF YOU HAD BEEN FASTER YOU WOULD HAVE CAUGHT HER, NOT I.
I AM CARRYING A PACK ON MY BACK. WERE IT NOT FOR THE PACK I WOULD BE FASTER. I HAVE CHASED HER FOR MANY, MANY LEAGUES.
YOUR PEOPLE ARE NEAR HERE?
CAN I ACCOMPANY YOU?
IF YOU WISH.
THERE WAS AN ENCAMPMENT OF THE PEOPLE THERE, IN THE HEART OF THE WOOD.
HE TRIED TO CATCH THIS DEER. HE FAILED. I SUCCEEDED.

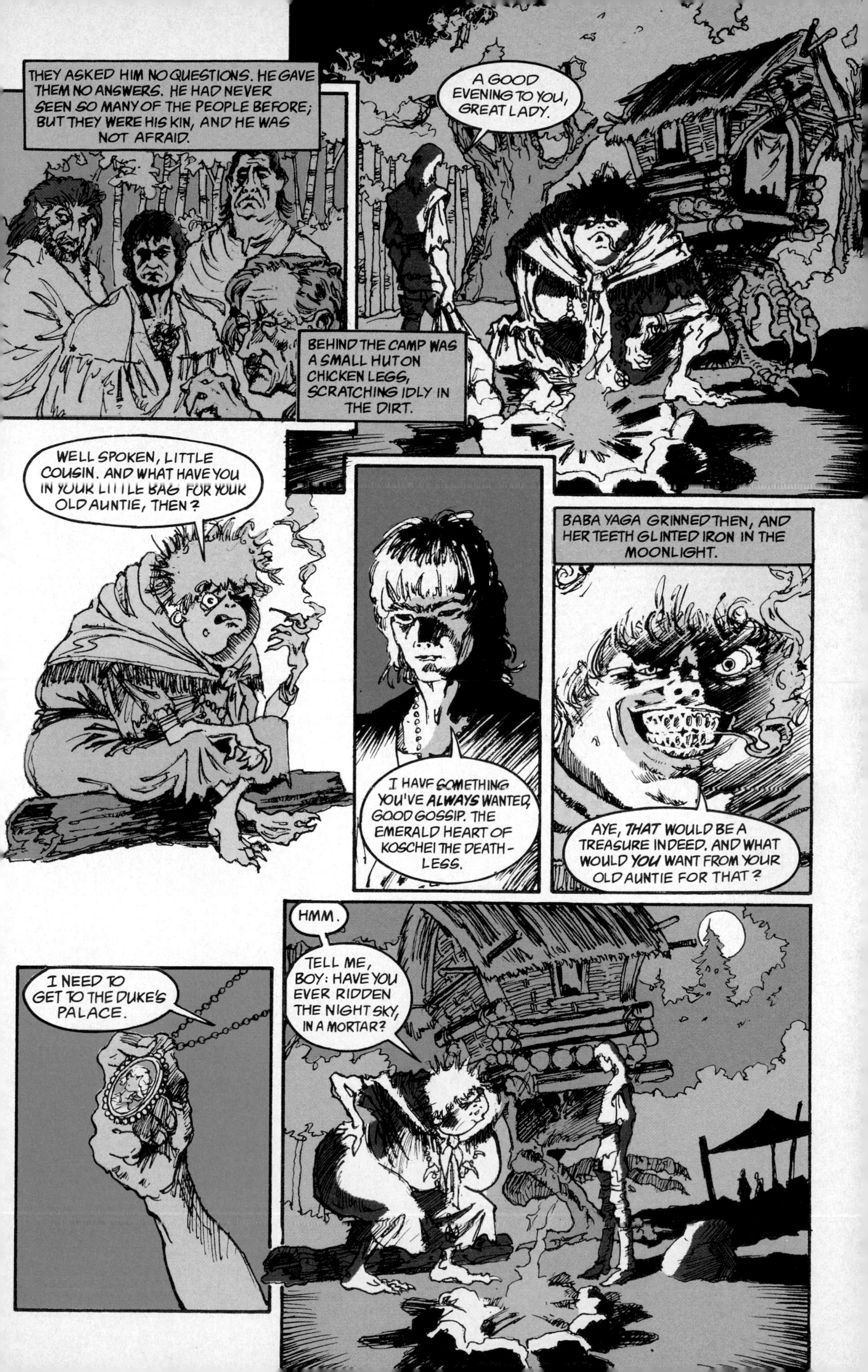
THEY ASKED HIM NO QUESTIONS. HE GAVE THEM NO ANSWERS. HE HAD NEVER SEEN SO MANY OF THE PEOPLE BEFORE; BUT THEY WERE HIS KIN, AND HE WAS NOT AFRAID.
A GOOD EVENING TO YOU, GREAT LADY.
BEHIND THE CAMP WAS A SMALL HUT ON CHICKEN LEGS, SCRATCHING IDLY IN THE DIRT.
WELL SPOKEN, LITTLE COUSIN. AND WHAT HAVE YOU IN YOUR LITTLE BAG FOR YOUR OLD AUNTIE, THEN?
I HAVE SOMETHING YOU'VE ALWAYS WANTED, GOOD GOSSIP. THE EMERALD HEART OF KOSCHEI THE DEATH-LESS.
BABA YAGA GRINNED THEN, AND HER TEETH GLINTED IRON IN THE MOONLIGHT.
AYE, THAT WOULD BE A TREASURE INDEED. AND WHAT WOULD YOU WANT FROM YOUR OLD AUNTIE FOR THAT?
I NEED TO GET TO THE DUKE'S PALACE.
HMM.
TELL ME, BOY: HAVE YOU EVER RIDDEN THE NIGHT SKY, IN A MORTAR?

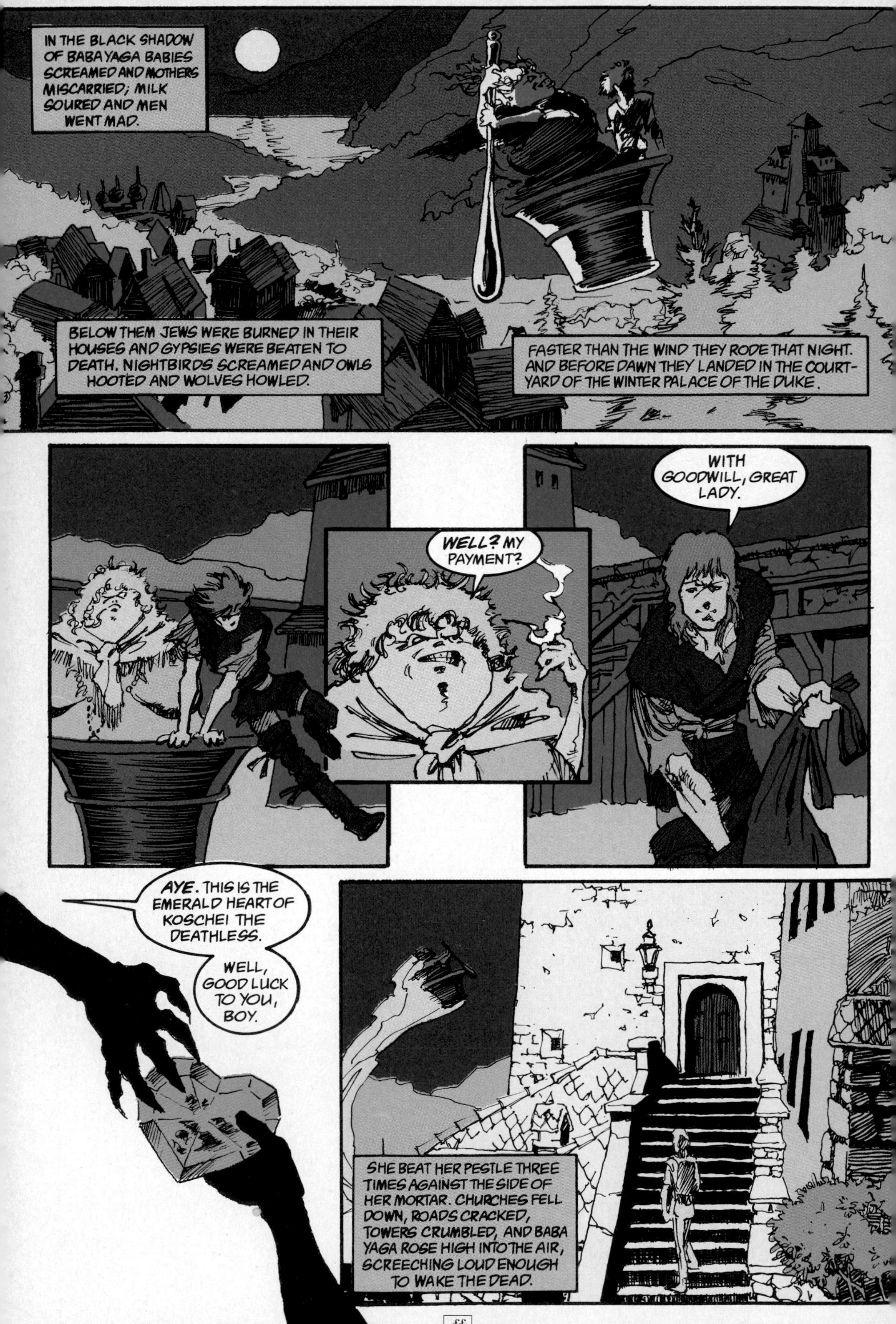
IN THE BLACK SHADOW OF BABA YAGA BABIES SCREAMED AND MOTHERS MISCARRIED; MILK SOURED AND MEN WENT MAD.
BELOW THEM JEWS WERE BURNED IN THEIR HOUSES AND GYPSIES WERE BEATEN TO DEATH. NIGHTBIRDS SCREAMED AND OWLS HOOTED AND WOLVES HOWLED.
FASTER THAN THE WIND THEY RODE THAT NIGHT. AND BEFORE DAWN THEY LANDED IN THE COURTYARD OF THE WINTER PALACE OF THE DUKE.
WELL? MY PAYMENT?
WITH GOODWILL, GREAT LADY.
AYE. THIS IS THE EMERALD HEART OF KOSCHEI THE DEATHLESS.
WELL, GOOD LUCK TO YOU, BOY.
SHE BEAT HER PESTLE THREE TIMES AGAINST THE SIDE OF HER MORTAR. CHURCHES FELL DOWN, ROADS CRACKED, TOWERS CRUMBLED, AND BABA YAGA ROSE HIGH INTO THE AIR, SCREECHING LOUD ENOUGH TO WAKE THE DEAD.

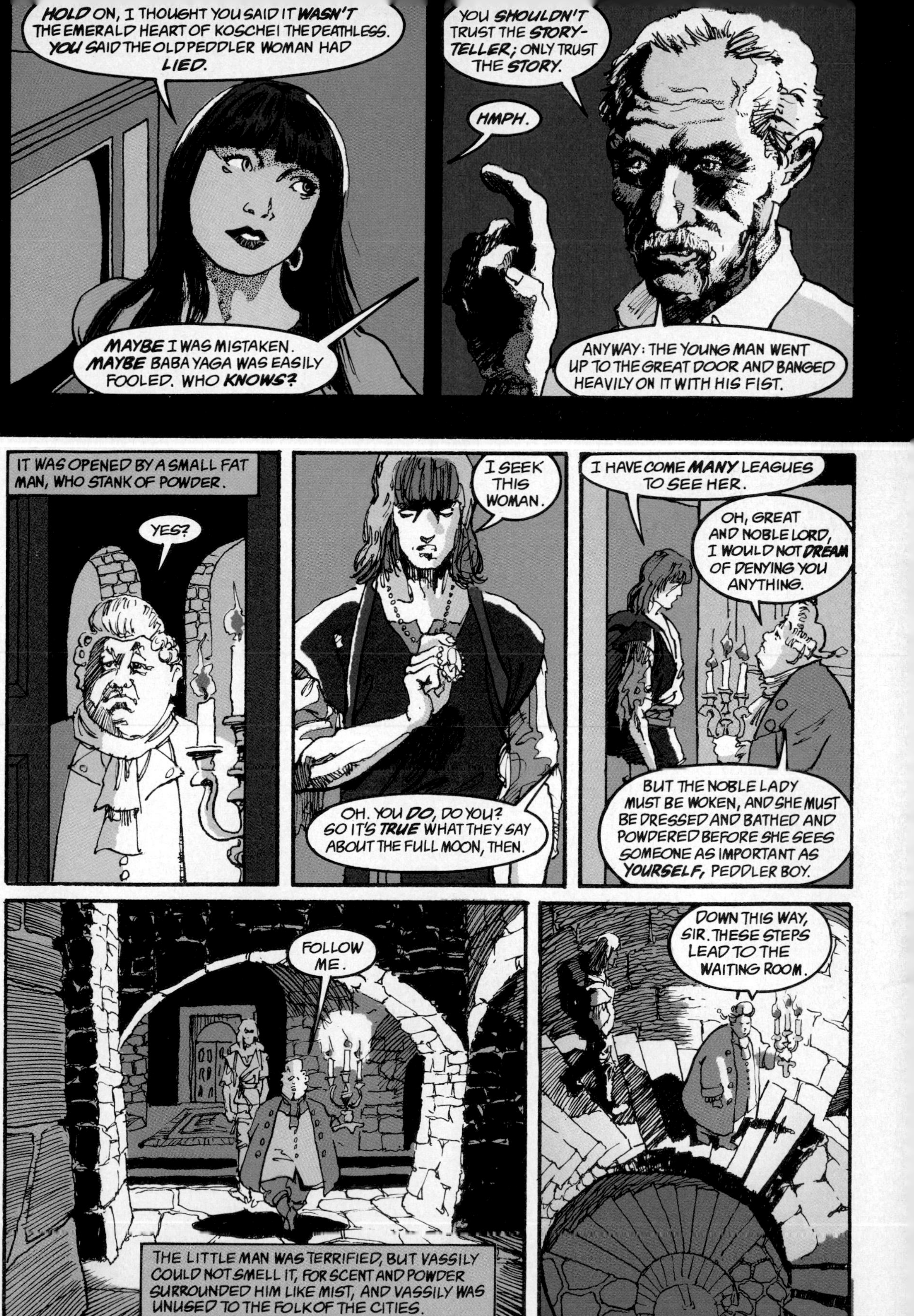
HOLD ON, I THOUGHT YOU SAID IT WASN'T THE EMERALD HEART OF KOSCHEI THE DEATHLESS. YOU SAID THE OLD PEDDLER WOMAN HAD LIED.
MAYBE I WAS MISTAKEN. MAYBE BABA YAGA WAS EASILY FOOLED. WHO KNOWS?
YOU SHOULDN'T TRUST THE STORY-TELLER; ONLY TRUST THE STORY.
HMPH.
ANYWAY: THE YOUNG MAN WENT UP TO THE GREAT DOOR AND BANGED HEAVILY ON IT WITH HIS FIST.
IT WAS OPENED BY A SMALL FAT MAN, WHO STANK OF POWDER.
YES?
I SEEK THIS WOMAN.
OH. YOU DO, DO YOU? SO IT'S TRUE WHAT THEY SAY ABOUT THE FULL MOON, THEN.
I HAVE COME MANY LEAGUES TO SEE HER.
OH, GREAT AND NOBLE LORD, I WOULD NOT DREAM OF DENYING YOU ANYTHING.
BUT THE NOBLE LADY MUST BE WOKEN, AND SHE MUST BE DRESSED AND BATHED AND POWDERED BEFORE SHE SEES SOMEONE AS IMPORTANT AS YOURSELF, PEDDLER BOY.
FOLLOW ME.
THE LITTLE MAN WAS TERRIFIED, BUT VASSILY COULD NOT SMELL IT, FOR SCENT AND POWDER SURROUNDED HIM LIKE MIST, AND VASSILY WAS UNUSED TO THE FOLK OF THE CITIES.
DOWN THIS WAY, SIR. THESE STEPS LEAD TO THE WAITING ROOM.

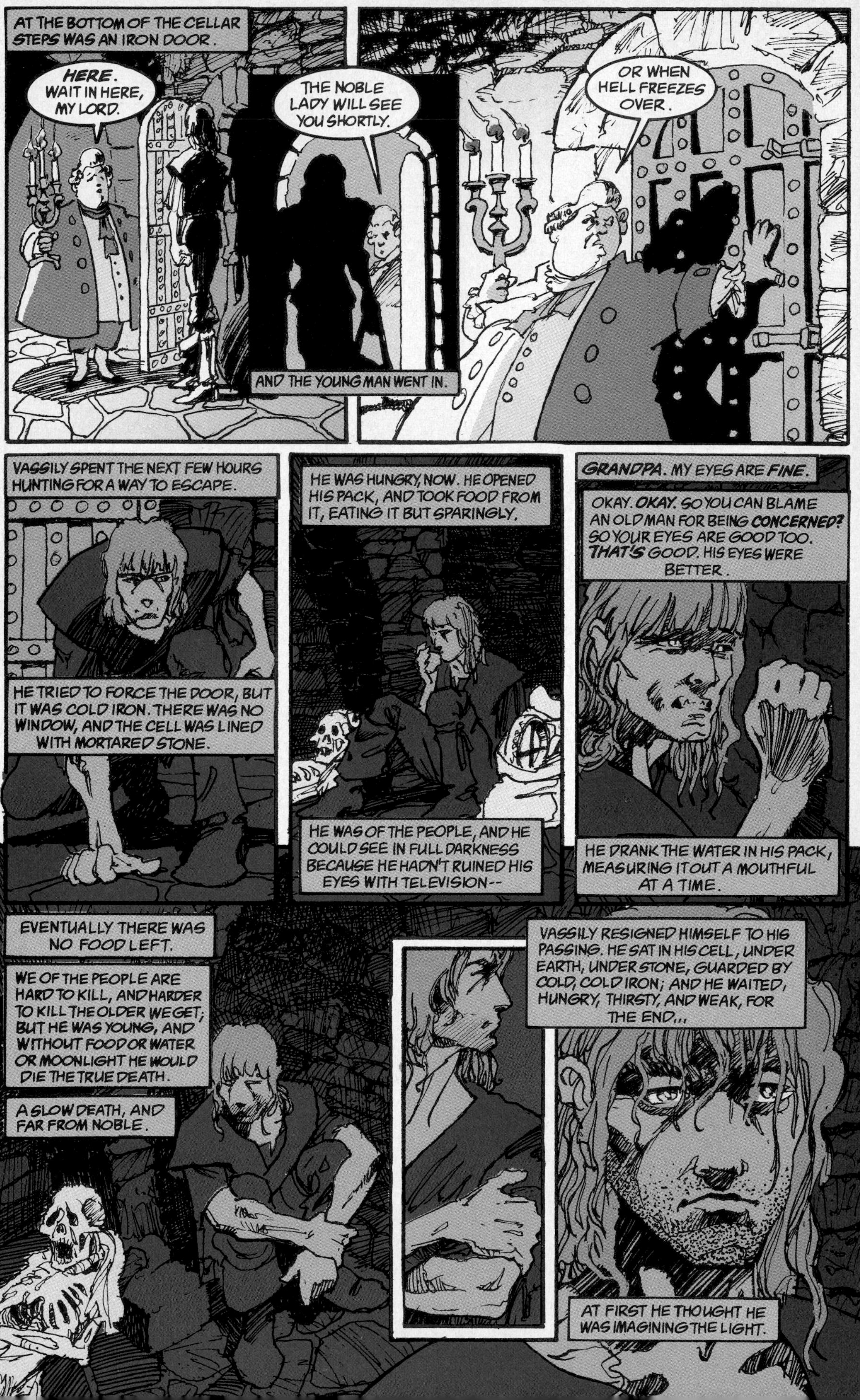
AT THE BOTTOM OF THE CELLAR STEPS WAS AN IRON DOOR.
HERE. WAIT IN HERE, MY LORD.
THE NOBLE LADY WILL SEE YOU SHORTLY.
AND THE YOUNG MAN WENT IN.
OR WHEN HELL FREEZES OVER.
VASSILY SPENT THE NEXT FEW HOURS HUNTING FOR A WAY TO ESCAPE.
HE TRIED TO FORCE THE DOOR, BUT IT WAS COLD IRON. THERE WAS NO WINDOW, AND THE CELL WAS LINED WITH MORTARED STONE.
HE WAS HUNGRY, NOW. HE OPENED HIS PACK, AND TOOK FOOD FROM IT, EATING IT BUT SPARINGLY.
HE WAS OF THE PEOPLE, AND HE COULD SEE IN FULL DARKNESS BECAUSE HE HADN'T RUINED HIS EYES WITH TELEVISION--
GRANDPA. MY EYES ARE FINE.
OKAY. OKAY. SO YOU CAN BLAME AN OLD MAN FOR BEING CONCERNED? SO YOUR EYES ARE GOOD TOO. THAT'S GOOD. HIS EYES WERE BETTER.
HE DRANK THE WATER IN HIS PACK, MEASURING IT OUT A MOUTHFUL AT A TIME.
EVENTUALLY THERE WAS NO FOOD LEFT.
WE OF THE PEOPLE ARE HARD TO KILL, AND HARDER TO KILL THE OLDER WE GET; BUT HE WAS YOUNG, AND WITHOUT FOOD OR WATER OR MOONLIGHT HE WOULD DIE THE TRUE DEATH.
A SLOW DEATH, AND FAR FROM NOBLE.
VASSILY RESIGNED HIMSELF TO HIS PASSING. HE SAT IN HIS CELL, UNDER EARTH, UNDER STONE, GUARDED BY COLD, COLD IRON; AND HE WAITED, HUNGRY, THIRSTY, AND WEAK, FOR THE END...
AT FIRST HE THOUGHT HE WAS IMAGINING THE LIGHT.

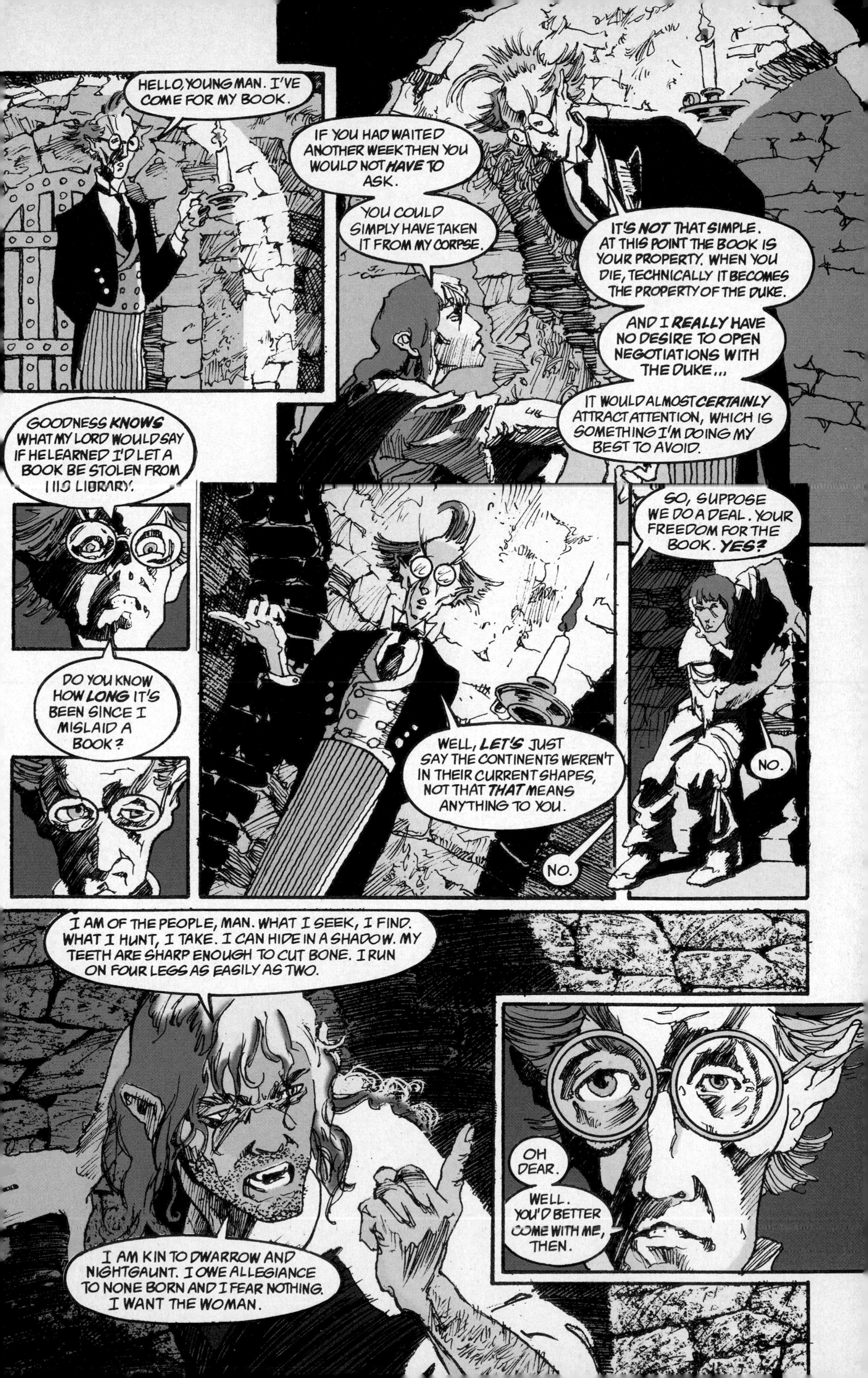
HELLO, YOUNG MAN. I'VE COME FOR MY BOOK.
IF YOU HAD WAITED ANOTHER WEEK THEN YOU WOULD NOT HAVE TO ASK.
YOU COULD SIMPLY HAVE TAKEN IT FROM MY CORPSE.
IT'S NOT THAT SIMPLE. AT THIS POINT THE BOOK IS YOUR PROPERTY. WHEN YOU DIE, TECHNICALLY IT BECOMES THE PROPERTY OF THE DUKE.
AND I REALLY HAVE NO DESIRE TO OPEN NEGOTIATIONS WITH THE DUKE...
IT WOULD ALMOST CERTAINLY ATTRACT ATTENTION, WHICH IS SOMETHING I'M DOING MY BEST TO AVOID.
GOODNESS KNOWS WHAT MY LORD WOULD SAY IF HE LEARNED I'D LET A BOOK BE STOLEN FROM HIS LIBRARY.
DO YOU KNOW HOW LONG IT'S BEEN SINCE I MISLAID A BOOK?
WELL, LET'S JUST SAY THE CONTINENTS WEREN'T IN THEIR CURRENT SHAPES, NOT THAT THAT MEANS ANYTHING TO YOU.
NO.
SO, SUPPOSE WE DO A DEAL. YOUR FREEDOM FOR THE BOOK. YES?
NO.
I AM OF THE PEOPLE, MAN. WHAT I SEEK, I FIND. WHAT I HUNT, I TAKE. I CAN HIDE IN A SHADOW. MY TEETH ARE SHARP ENOUGH TO CUT BONE. I RUN ON FOUR LEGS AS EASILY AS TWO.
I AM KIN TO DWARROW AND NIGHTGAUNT. I OWE ALLEGIANCE TO NONE BORN AND I FEAR NOTHING. I WANT THE WOMAN.
OH DEAR.
WELL. YOU'D BETTER COME WITH ME, THEN.

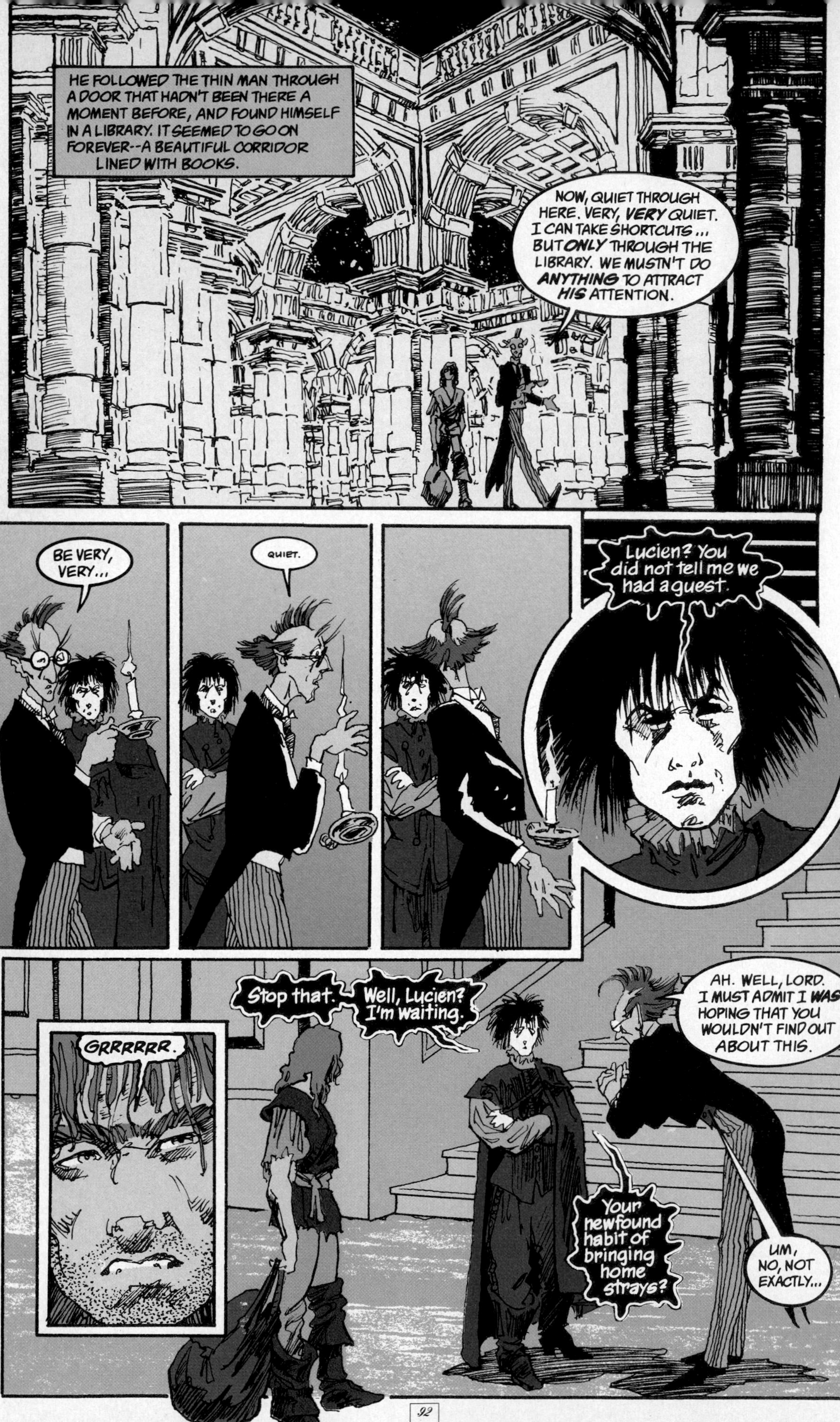
HE FOLLOWED THE THIN MAN THROUGH A DOOR THAT HADN'T BEEN THERE A MOMENT BEFORE, AND FOUND HIMSELF IN A LIBRARY. IT SEEMED TO GO ON FOREVER--A BEAUTIFUL CORRIDOR LINED WITH BOOKS.
NOW, QUIET THROUGH HERE. VERY, VERY QUIET. I CAN TAKE SHORTCUTS ... BUT ONLY THROUGH THE LIBRARY. WE MUSTN'T DO ANYTHING TO ATTRACT HIS ATTENTION.
BE VERY, VERY...
QUIET.
Lucien? You did not tell me we had a guest.
GRRRRRR.
Stop that.
Well, Lucien? I'm waiting.
AH. WELL, LORD. I MUST ADMIT I WAS HOPING THAT YOU WOULDN'T FIND OUT ABOUT THIS.
Your newfound habit of bringing home strays?
UM, NO, NOT EXACTLY...

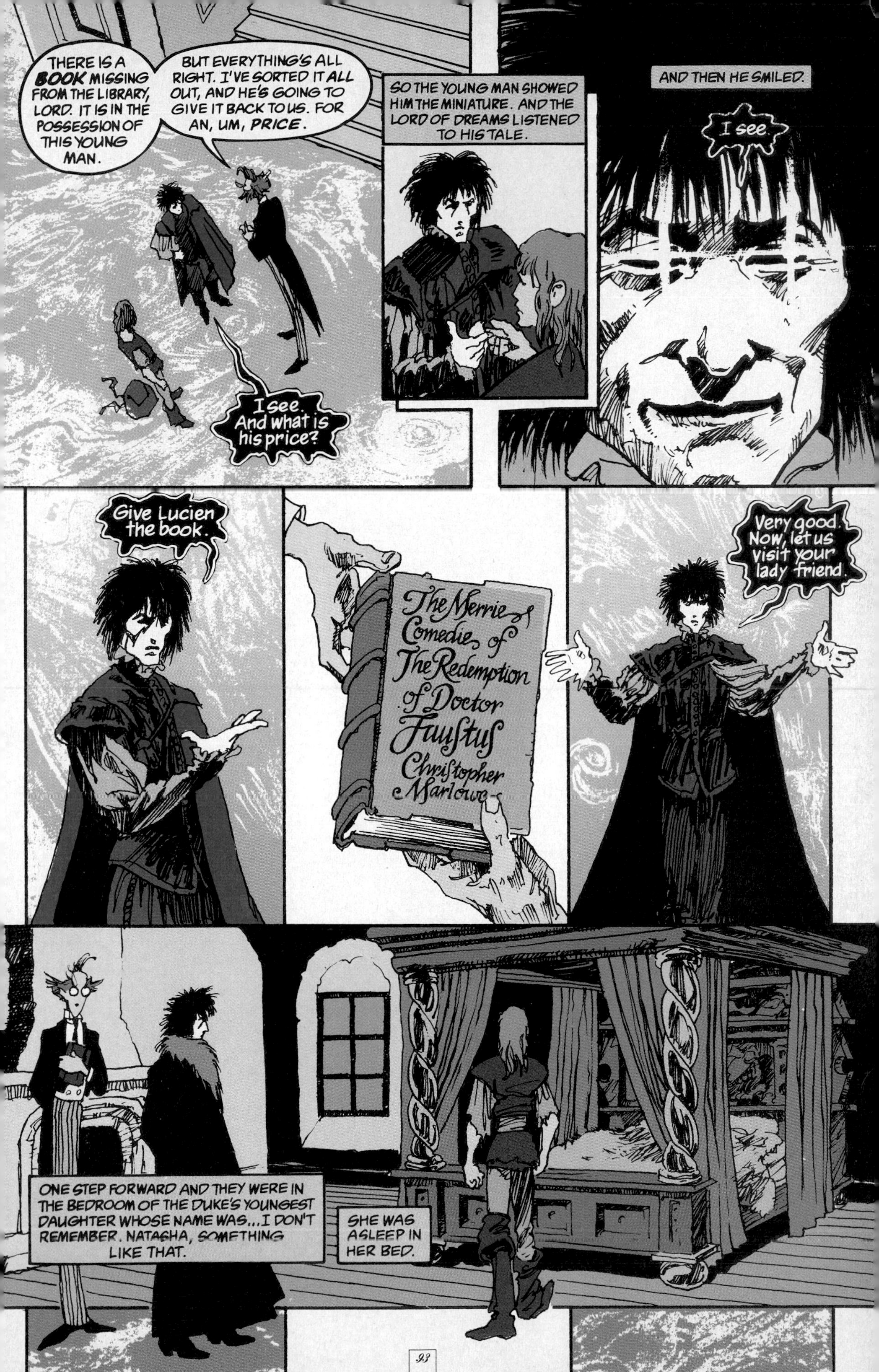
THERE IS A BOOK MISSING FROM THE LIBRARY, LORD. IT IS IN THE POSSESSION OF THIS YOUNG MAN.
BUT EVERYTHING'S ALL RIGHT. I'VE SORTED IT ALL OUT, AND HE'S GOING TO GIVE IT BACK TO US. FOR AN, UM, PRICE.
I see. And what is his price?
SO THE YOUNG MAN SHOWED HIM THE MINIATURE. AND THE LORD OF DREAMS LISTENED TO HIS TALE.
AND THEN HE SMILED.
I see.
Give Lucien the book.
The Merrie Comedie of The Redemption of Doctor Faustus Christopher Marlowe
Very good. Now, let us visit your lady friend.
ONE STEP FORWARD AND THEY WERE IN THE BEDROOM OF THE DUKE'S YOUNGEST DAUGHTER WHOSE NAME WAS... I DON'T REMEMBER. NATASHA, SOMETHING LIKE THAT.
SHE WAS ASLEEP IN HER BED.

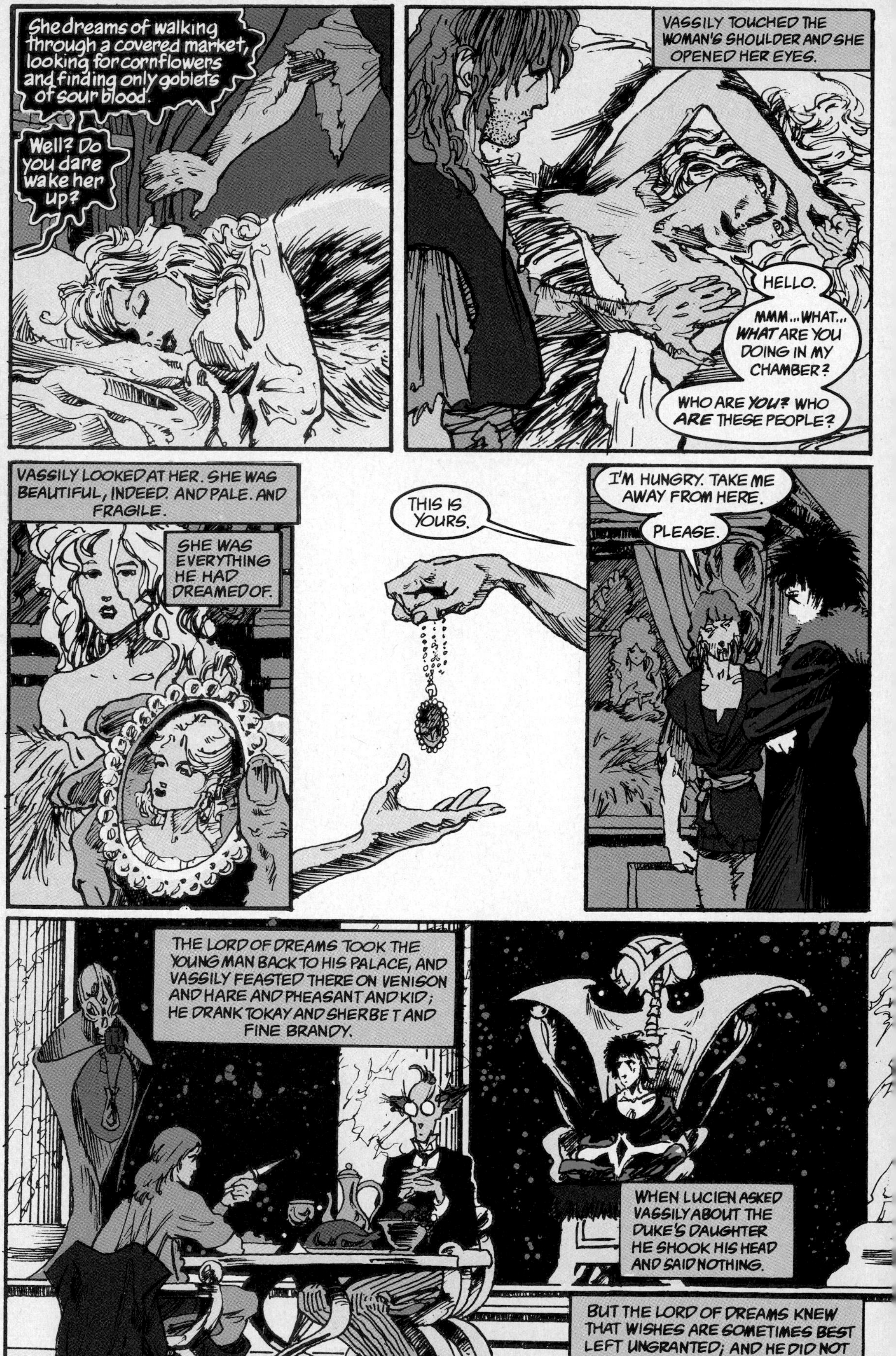
She dreams of walking through a covered market, looking for cornflowers and finding only gobiets of sour blood.
Well? Do you dare wake her up?
VASSILY TOUCHED THE WOMAN'S SHOULDER AND SHE OPENED HER EYES.
HELLO.
MMM... WHAT... WHAT ARE YOU DOING IN MY CHAMBER?
WHO ARE YOU? WHO ARE THESE PEOPLE?
VASSILY LOOKED AT HER. SHE WAS BEAUTIFUL, INDEED. AND PALE. AND FRAGILE.
SHE WAS EVERYTHING HE HAD DREAMED OF.
THIS IS YOURS.
I'M HUNGRY. TAKE ME AWAY FROM HERE.
PLEASE.
THE LORD OF DREAMS TOOK THE YOUNG MAN BACK TO HIS PALACE, AND VASSILY FEASTED THERE ON VENISON AND HARE AND PHEASANT AND KID; HE DRANK TOKAY AND SHERBET AND FINE BRANDY.
WHEN LUCIEN ASKED VASSILY ABOUT THE DUKE'S DAUGHTER HE SHOOK HIS HEAD AND SAID NOTHING.
BUT THE LORD OF DREAMS KNEW THAT WISHES ARE SOMETIMES BEST LEFT UNGRANTED; AND HE DID NOT NEED TO ASK.

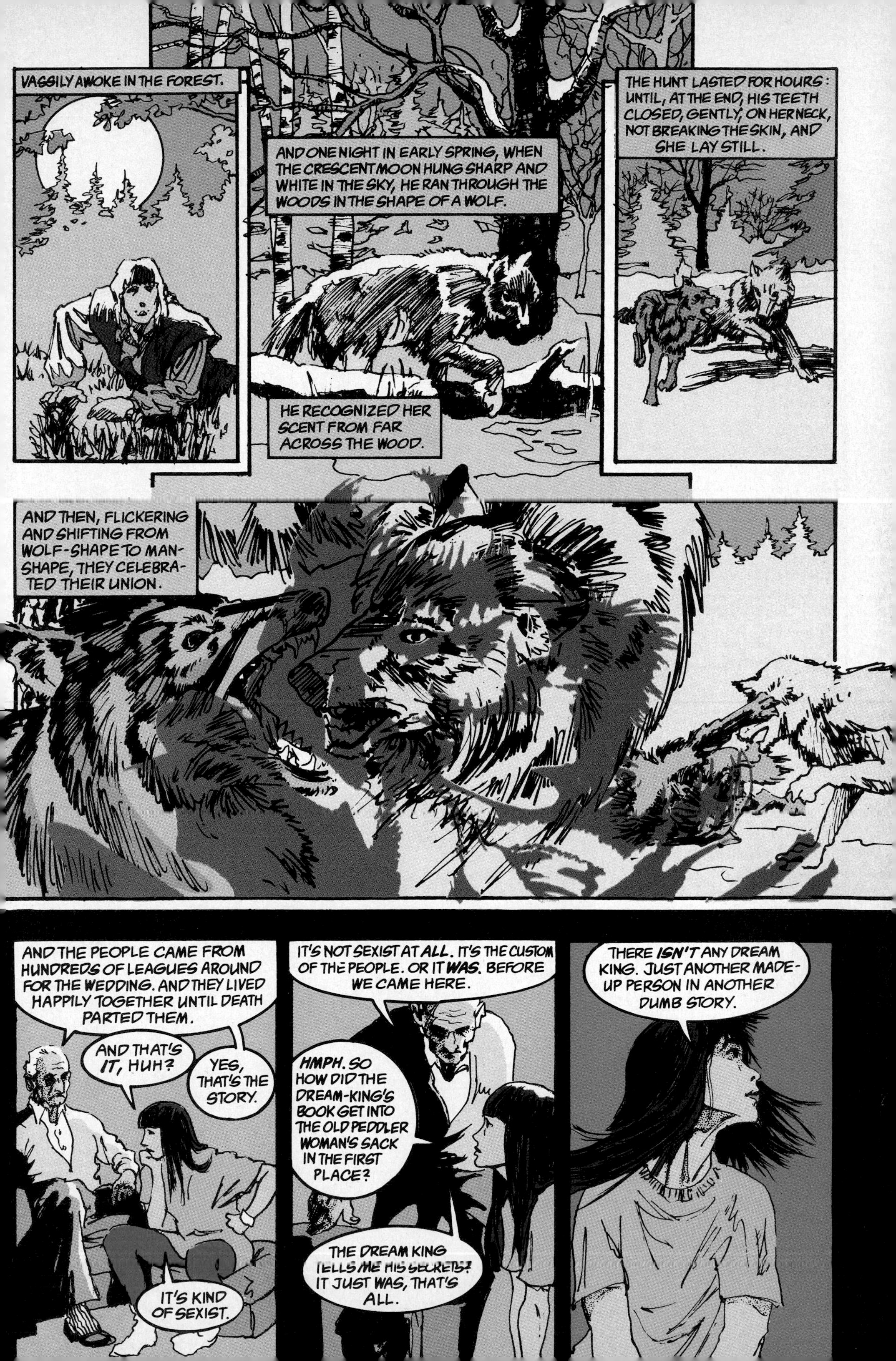
VASSILY AWOKE IN THE FOREST.
AND ONE NIGHT IN EARLY SPRING, WHEN THE CRESCENT MOON HUNG SHARP AND WHITE IN THE SKY, HE RAN THROUGH THE WOODS IN THE SHAPE OF A WOLF.
HE RECOGNIZED HER SCENT FROM FAR ACROSS THE WOOD.
THE HUNT LASTED FOR HOURS: UNTIL, AT THE END, HIS TEETH CLOSED, GENTLY, ON HER NECK, NOT BREAKING THE SKIN, AND SHE LAY STILL.
AND THEN, FLICKERING AND SHIFTING FROM WOLF-SHAPE TO MAN-SHAPE, THEY CELEBRATED THEIR UNION.
AND THE PEOPLE CAME FROM HUNDREDS OF LEAGUES AROUND FOR THE WEDDING. AND THEY LIVED HAPPILY TOGETHER UNTIL DEATH PARTED THEM.
AND THAT'S IT, HUH?
YES, THAT'S THE STORY.
IT'S KIND OF SEXIST.
IT'S NOT SEXIST AT ALL. IT'S THE CUSTOM OF THE PEOPLE. OR IT WAS. BEFORE WE CAME HERE.
HMPH. SO HOW DID THE DREAM-KING'S BOOK GET INTO THE OLD PEDDLER WOMAN'S SACK IN THE FIRST PLACE?
THE DREAM KING TELLS ME HIS SECRETS? IT JUST WAS, THAT'S ALL.
THERE ISN'T ANY DREAM KING. JUST ANOTHER MADE-UP PERSON IN ANOTHER DUMB STORY.

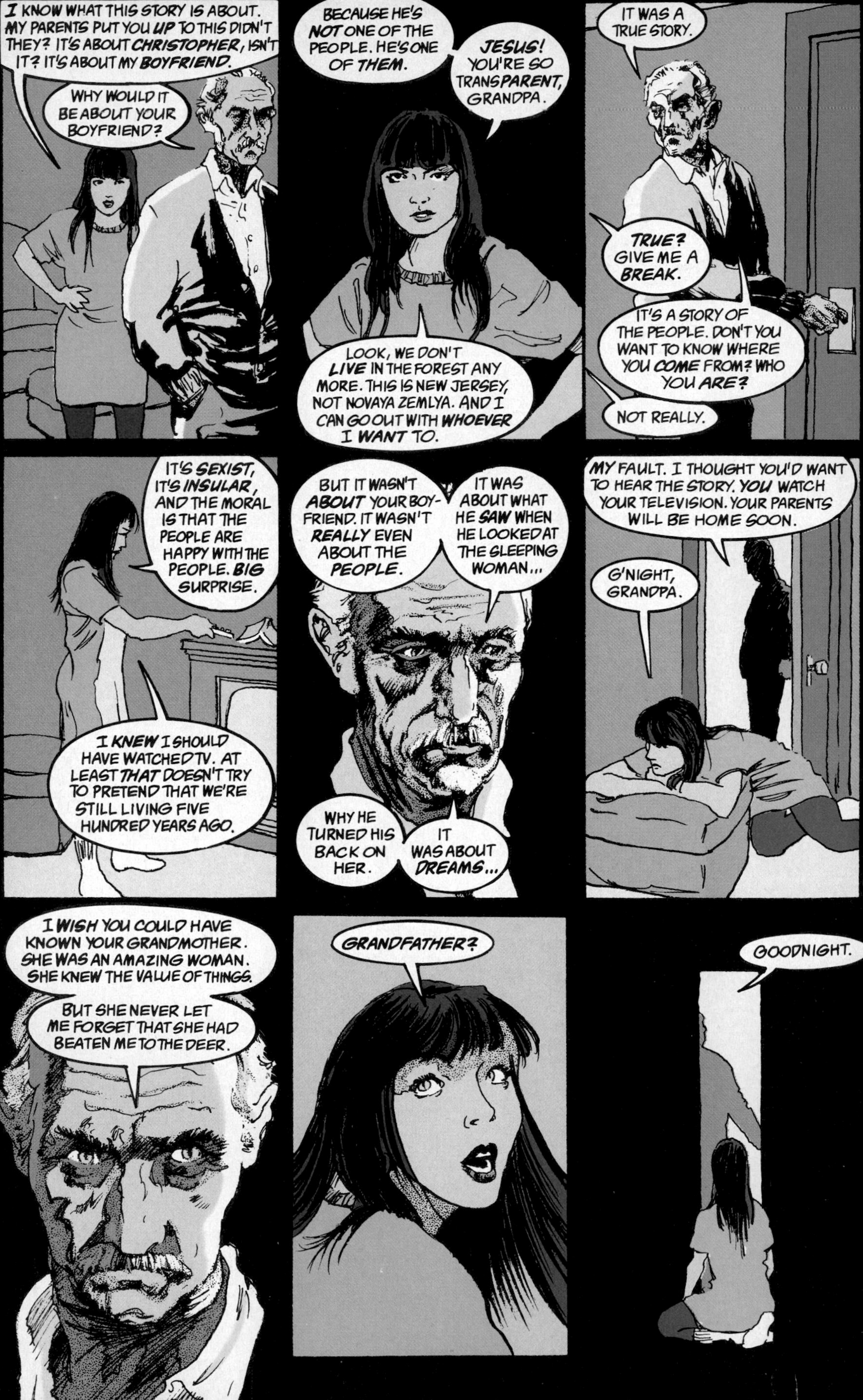
I KNOW WHAT THIS STORY IS ABOUT. MY PARENTS PUT YOU UP TO THIS DIDN'T THEY? IT'S ABOUT CHRISTOPHER, ISN'T IT? IT'S ABOUT MY BOYFRIEND.
WHY WOULD IT BE ABOUT YOUR BOYFRIEND?
BECAUSE HE'S NOT ONE OF THE PEOPLE. HE'S ONE OF THEM.
JESUS! YOU'RE SO TRANSPARENT, GRANDPA.
LOOK, WE DON'T LIVE IN THE FOREST ANY MORE. THIS IS NEW JERSEY, NOT NOVAYA ZEMLYA. AND I CAN GO OUT WITH WHOEVER I WANT TO.
IT WAS A TRUE STORY.
TRUE? GIVE ME A BREAK.
IT'S A STORY OF THE PEOPLE. DON'T YOU WANT TO KNOW WHERE YOU COME FROM? WHO YOU ARE?
NOT REALLY.
IT'S SEXIST, IT'S INSULAR, AND THE MORAL IS THAT THE PEOPLE ARE HAPPY WITH THE PEOPLE. BIG SURPRISE.
I KNEW I SHOULD HAVE WATCHED TV. AT LEAST THAT DOESN'T TRY TO PRETEND THAT WE'RE STILL LIVING FIVE HUNDRED YEARS AGO.
BUT IT WASN'T ABOUT YOUR BOY-FRIEND. IT WASN'T REALLY EVEN ABOUT THE PEOPLE.
IT WAS ABOUT WHAT HE SAW WHEN HE LOOKED AT THE SLEEPING WOMAN...
WHY HE TURNED HIS BACK ON HER.
IT WAS ABOUT DREAMS...
MY FAULT. I THOUGHT YOU'D WANT TO HEAR THE STORY. YOU WATCH YOUR TELEVISION. YOUR PARENTS WILL BE HOME SOON.
G'NIGHT, GRANDPA.
I WISH YOU COULD HAVE KNOWN YOUR GRANDMOTHER. SHE WAS AN AMAZING WOMAN. SHE KNEW THE VALUE OF THINGS.
BUT SHE NEVER LET ME FORGET THAT SHE HAD BEATEN ME TO THE DEER.
GRANDFATHER?
GOODNIGHT.

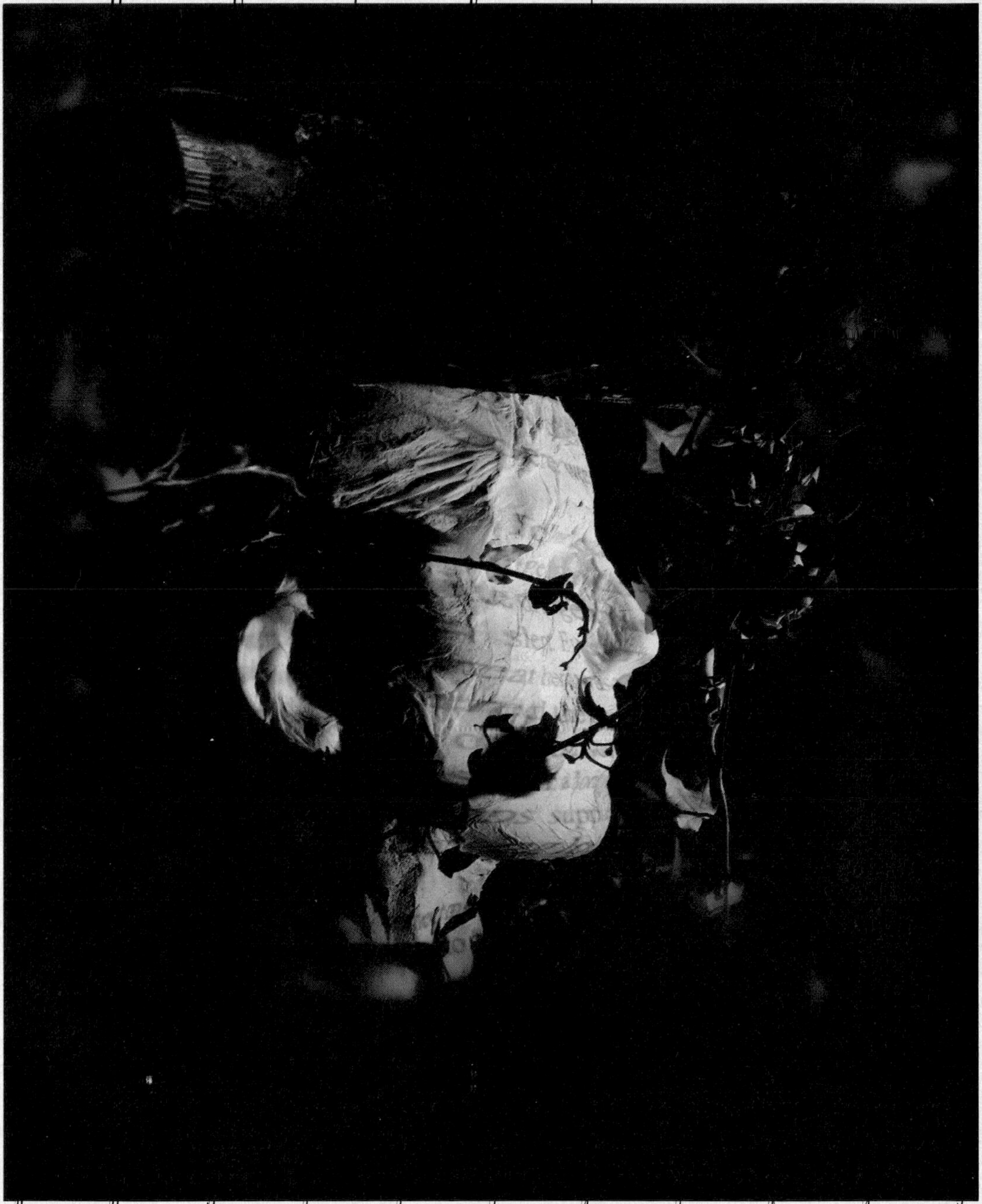

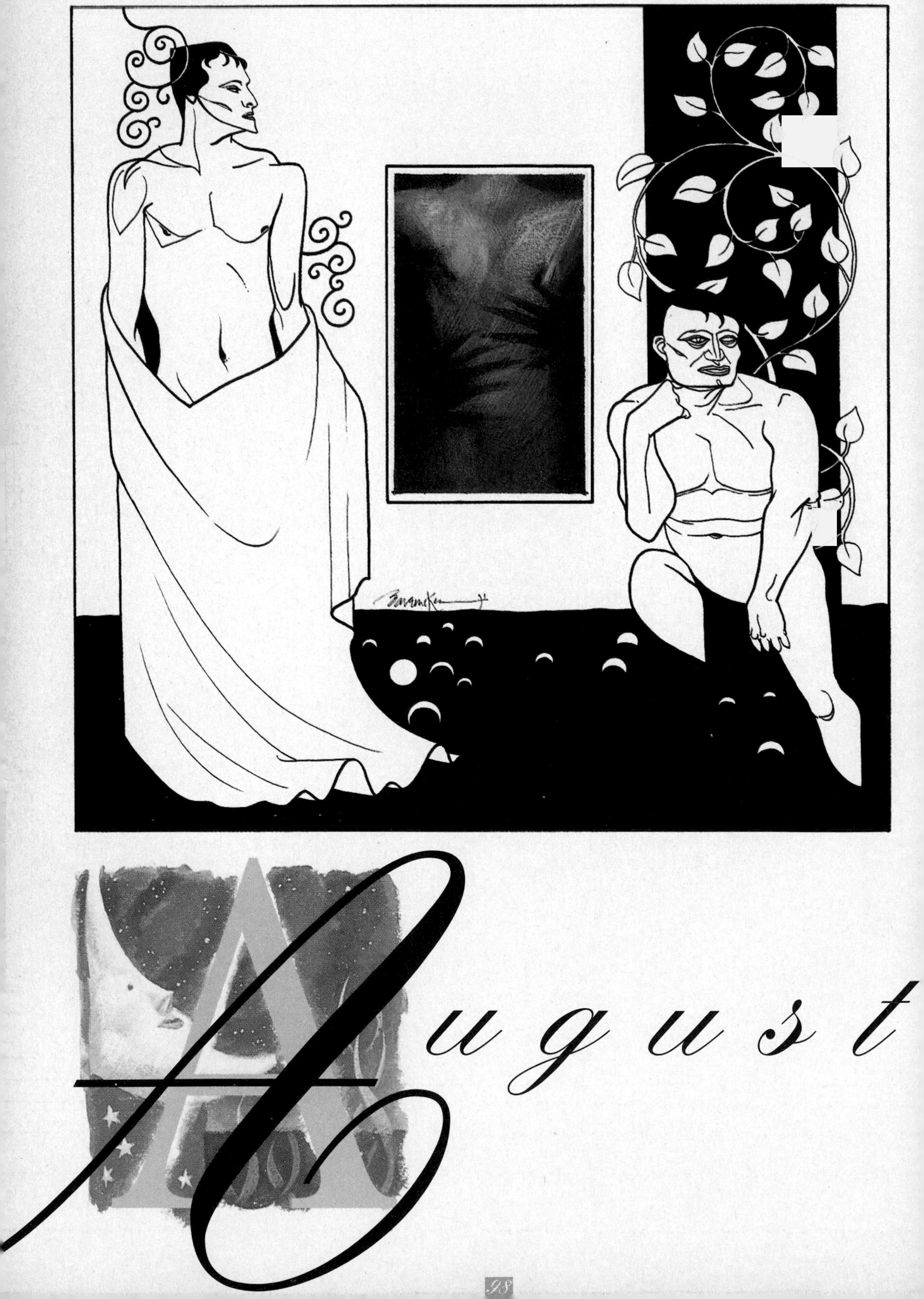

August

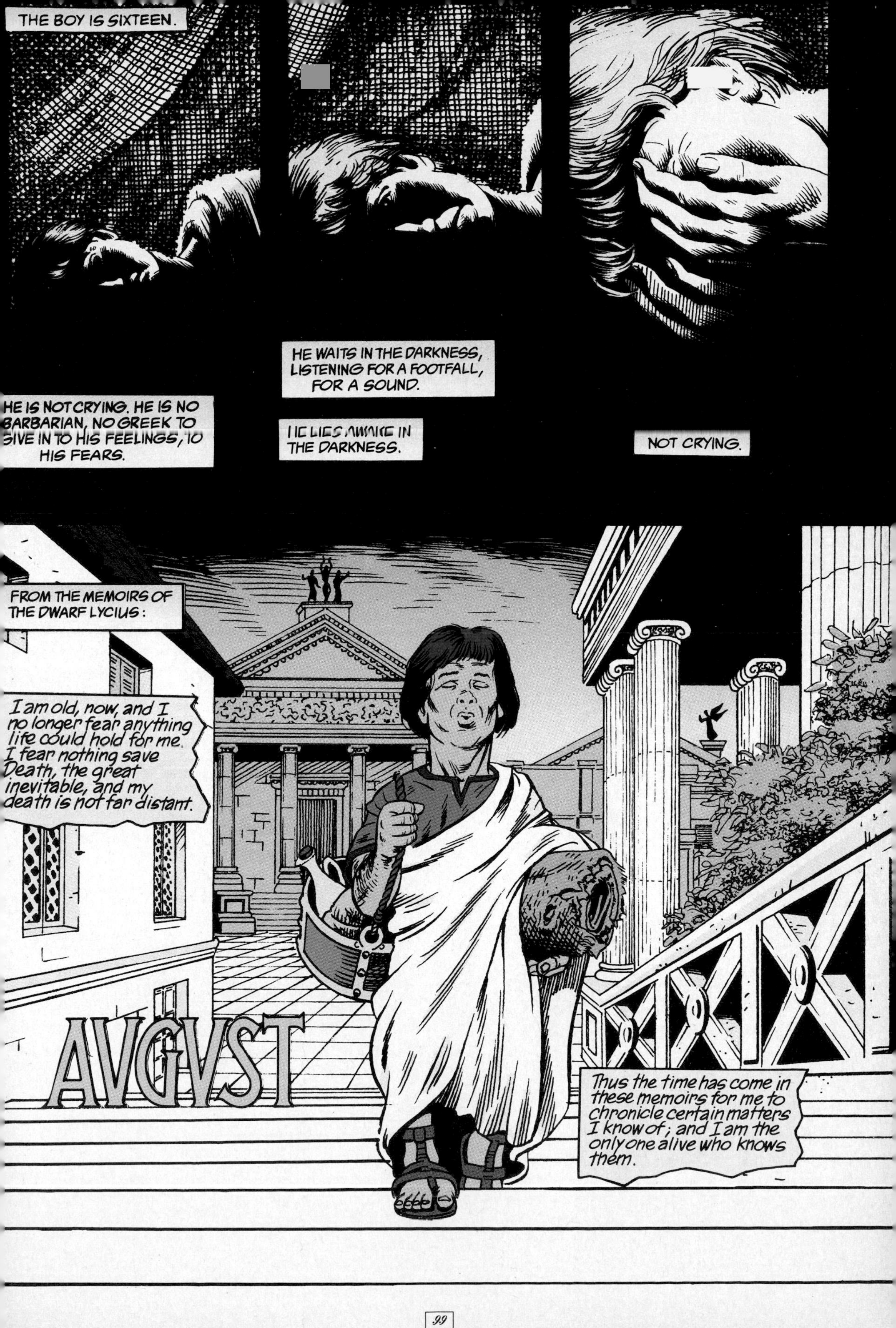
THE BOY IS SIXTEEN.
HE WAITS IN THE DARKNESS, LISTENING FOR A FOOTFALL, FOR A SOUND.
HE IS NOT CRYING. HE IS NO BARBARIAN, NO GREEK TO GIVE IN TO HIS FEELINGS, TO HIS FEARS.
HE LIES AWAKE IN THE DARKNESS.
NOT CRYING.
FROM THE MEMOIRS OF THE DWARF LYCIUS:
I am old, now, and I no longer fear anything life could hold for me. I fear nothing save Death, the great inevitable, and my death is not far distant.
AVGVST
Thus the time has come in these memoirs for me to chronicle certain matters I know of; and I am the only one alive who knows them.

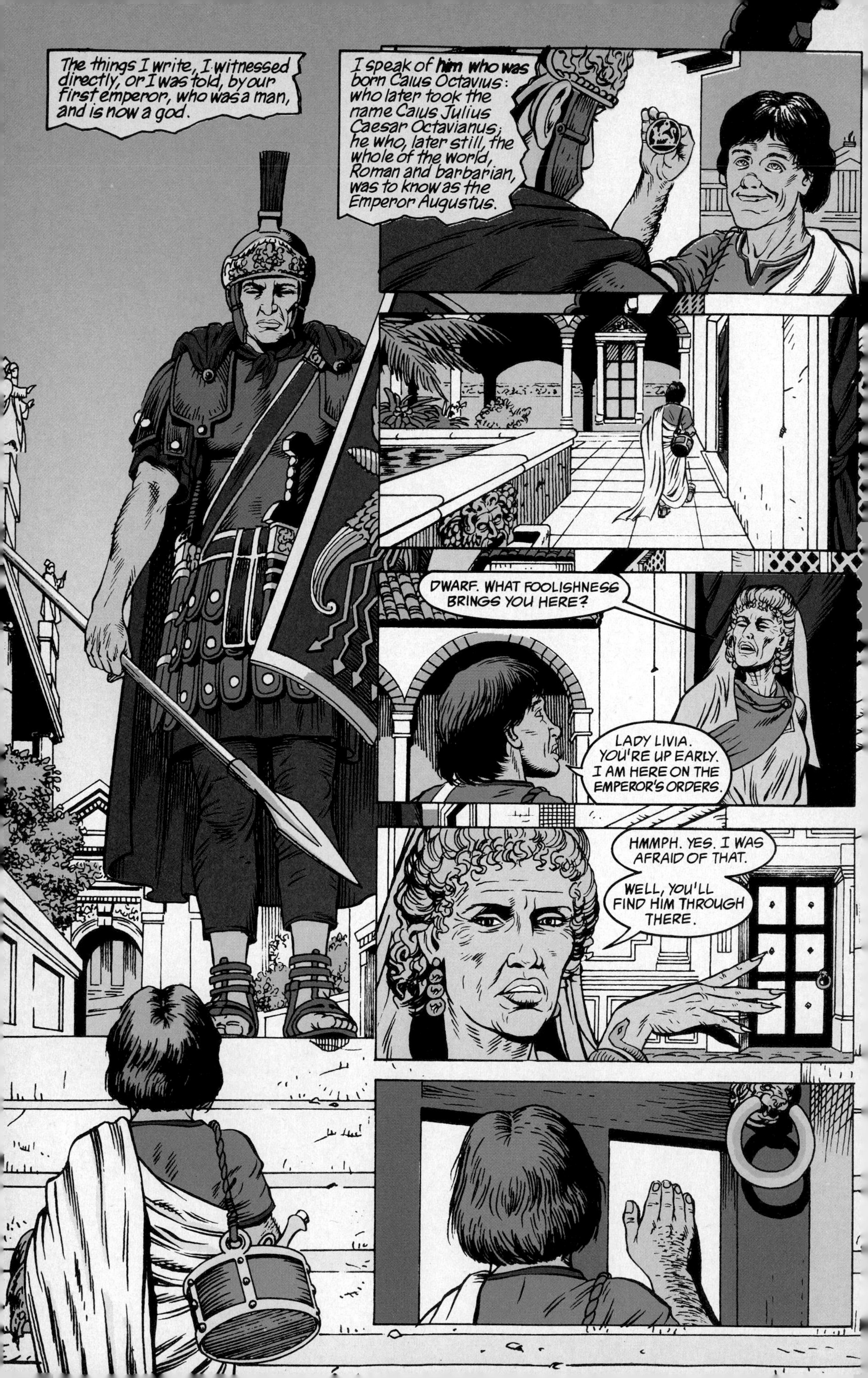
The things I write, I witnessed directly, or I was told, by our first emperor, who was a man, and is now a god.
I speak of **him who was** born Caius Octavius: who later took the name Caius Julius Caesar Octavianus; he who, later still, the whole of the world, Roman and barbarian, was to know as the Emperor Augustus.
DWARF. WHAT FOOLISHNESS BRINGS YOU HERE?
LADY LIVIA. YOU'RE UP EARLY. I AM HERE ON THE EMPEROR'S ORDERS.
HMMPH. YES. I WAS AFRAID OF THAT.
WELL, YOU'LL FIND HIM THROUGH THERE.

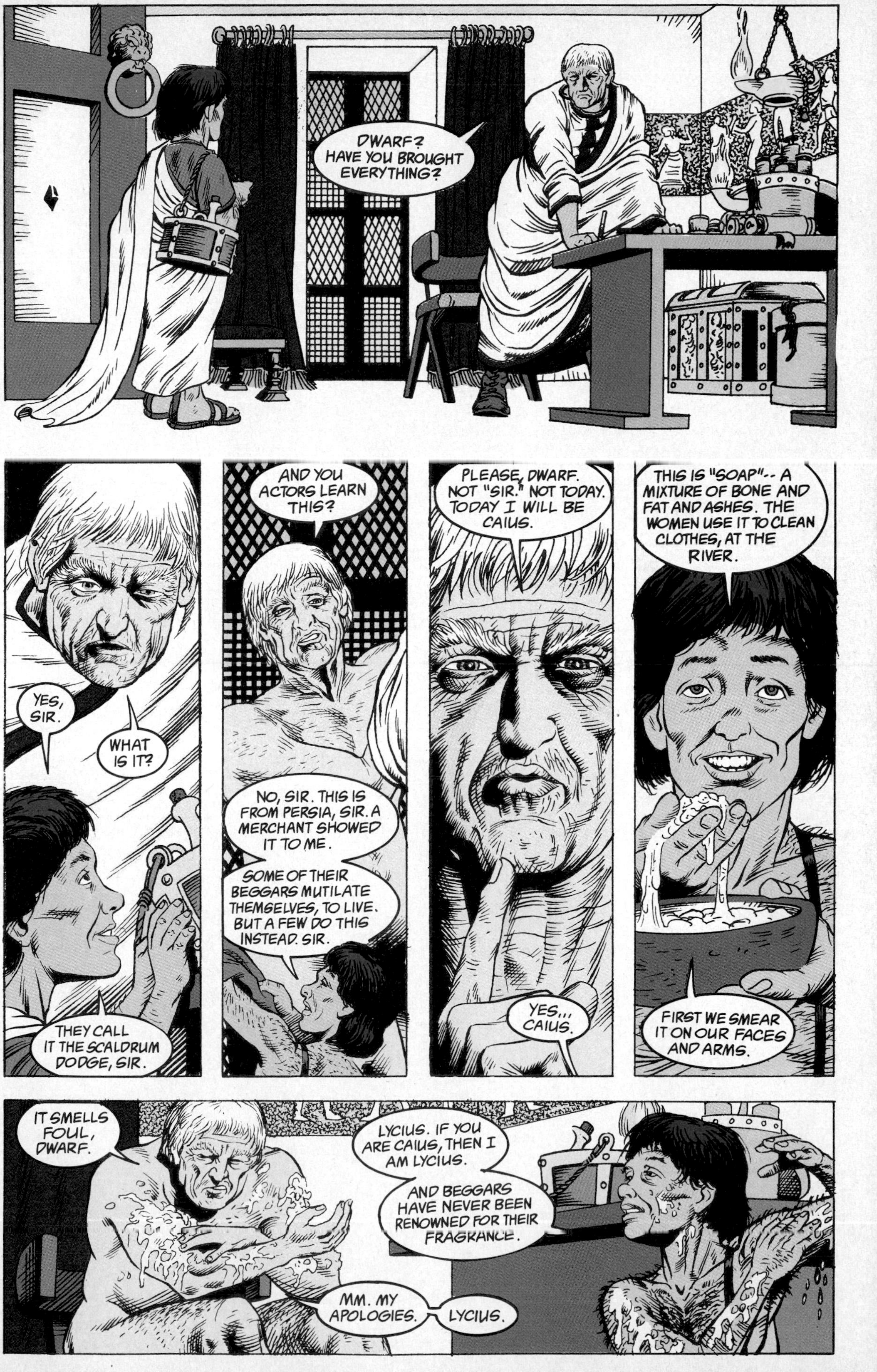
DWARF? HAVE YOU BROUGHT EVERYTHING?
YES, SIR.
WHAT IS IT?
THEY CALL IT THE SCALDRUM DODGE, SIR.
AND YOU ACTORS LEARN THIS?
NO, SIR. THIS IS FROM PERSIA, SIR. A MERCHANT SHOWED IT TO ME.
SOME OF THEIR BEGGARS MUTILATE THEMSELVES, TO LIVE. BUT A FEW DO THIS INSTEAD. SIR.
PLEASE, DWARF. NOT "SIR." NOT TODAY. TODAY I WILL BE CAIUS.
YES... CAIUS.
THIS IS "SOAP"-- A MIXTURE OF BONE AND FAT AND ASHES. THE WOMEN USE IT TO CLEAN CLOTHES, AT THE RIVER.
FIRST WE SMEAR IT ON OUR FACES AND ARMS.
IT SMELLS FOUL, DWARF.
LYCIUS. IF YOU ARE CAIUS, THEN I AM LYCIUS.
AND BEGGARS HAVE NEVER BEEN RENOWNED FOR THEIR FRAGRANCE.
MM. MY APOLOGIES.
LYCIUS.

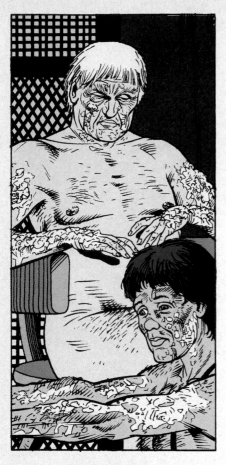

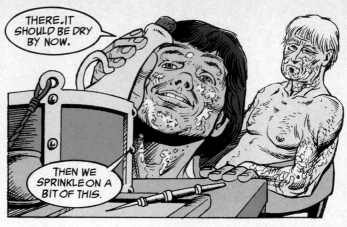

THERE. IT SHOULD BE DRY BY NOW.

THEN WE SPRINKLE ON A BIT OF THIS.

FAUGH. IT SMELLS LIKE VINEGAR.

IT IS VINEGAR. SEE? THE SOAP BLISTERS -- AND TO ANY PASSER-BY, YOUR SKIN APPEARS BURNED AND ULCERATED.

REMARKABLE. QUICKER THAN BOILED ASPARAGUS.

NOW: LET US SEE WHAT THE MARKET HAS IN STORE FOR US.

WELL? ARE YOU READY, SIR?

CAIUS. PLEASE. REMEMBER THAT TODAY WE ARE BEGGARS TOGETHER, FRIEND LYCIUS.

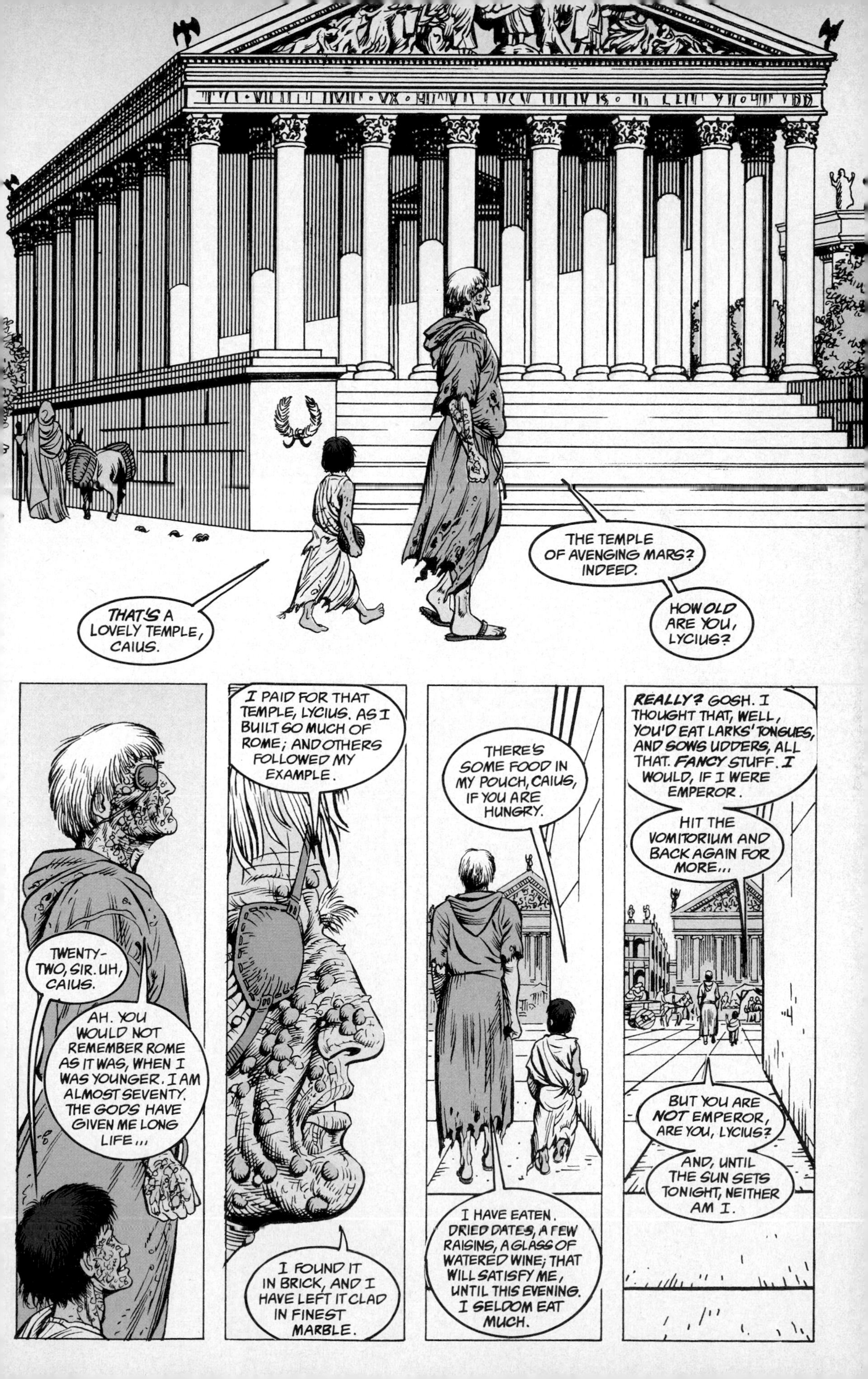
THAT'S A LOVELY TEMPLE, CAIUS.
THE TEMPLE OF AVENGING MARS? INDEED.
HOW OLD ARE YOU, LYCIUS?
TWENTY-TWO, SIR. UH, CAIUS.
AH. YOU WOULD NOT REMEMBER ROME AS IT WAS, WHEN I WAS YOUNGER. I AM ALMOST SEVENTY. THE GODS HAVE GIVEN ME LONG LIFE...
I PAID FOR THAT TEMPLE, LYCIUS. AS I BUILT SO MUCH OF ROME; AND OTHERS FOLLOWED MY EXAMPLE.
I FOUND IT IN BRICK, AND I HAVE LEFT IT CLAD IN FINEST MARBLE.
THERE'S SOME FOOD IN MY POUCH, CAIUS, IF YOU ARE HUNGRY.
I HAVE EATEN. DRIED DATES, A FEW RAISINS, A GLASS OF WATERED WINE; THAT WILL SATISFY ME, UNTIL THIS EVENING. I SELDOM EAT MUCH.
REALLY? GOSH. I THOUGHT THAT, WELL, YOU'D EAT LARKS' TONGUES, AND SOWS UDDERS, ALL THAT. FANCY STUFF. I WOULD, IF I WERE EMPEROR.
HIT THE VOMITORIUM AND BACK AGAIN FOR MORE...
BUT YOU ARE NOT EMPEROR, ARE YOU, LYCIUS?
AND, UNTIL THE SUN SETS TONIGHT, NEITHER AM I.

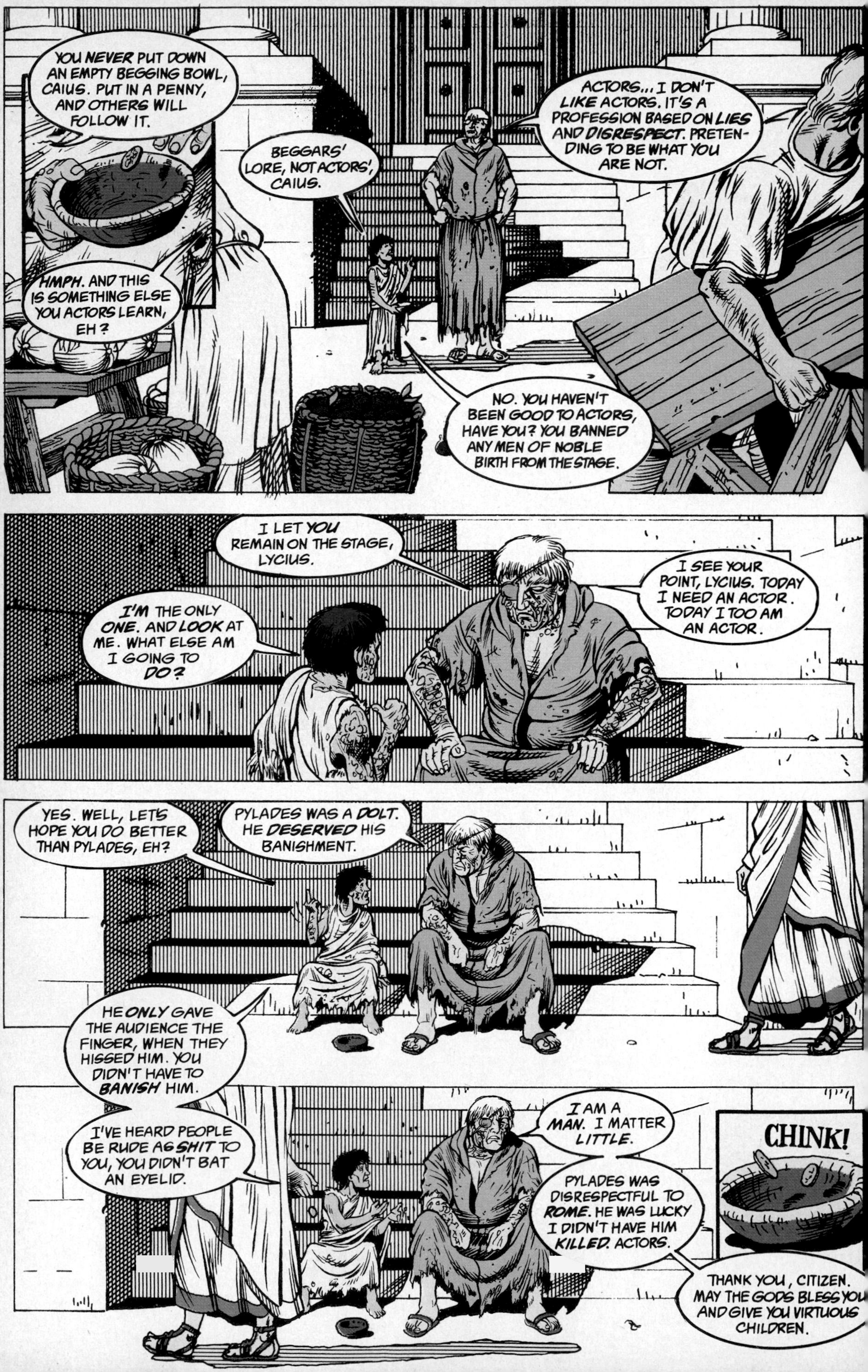
YOU NEVER PUT DOWN AN EMPTY BEGGING BOWL, CAIUS. PUT IN A PENNY, AND OTHERS WILL FOLLOW IT.
BEGGARS' LORE, NOT ACTORS', CAIUS.
ACTORS... I DON'T LIKE ACTORS. IT'S A PROFESSION BASED ON LIES AND DISRESPECT. PRETENDING TO BE WHAT YOU ARE NOT.
HMPH. AND THIS IS SOMETHING ELSE YOU ACTORS LEARN, EH?
NO. YOU HAVEN'T BEEN GOOD TO ACTORS, HAVE YOU? YOU BANNED ANY MEN OF NOBLE BIRTH FROM THE STAGE.
I LET YOU REMAIN ON THE STAGE, LYCIUS.
I'M THE ONLY ONE. AND LOOK AT ME. WHAT ELSE AM I GOING TO DO?
I SEE YOUR POINT, LYCIUS. TODAY I NEED AN ACTOR. TODAY I TOO AM AN ACTOR.
YES. WELL, LET'S HOPE YOU DO BETTER THAN PYLADES, EH?
PYLADES WAS A DOLT. HE DESERVED HIS BANISHMENT.
HE ONLY GAVE THE AUDIENCE THE FINGER, WHEN THEY HISSED HIM. YOU DIDN'T HAVE TO BANISH HIM.
I'VE HEARD PEOPLE BE RUDE AS SHIT TO YOU, YOU DIDN'T BAT AN EYELID.
I AM A MAN. I MATTER LITTLE.
PYLADES WAS DISRESPECTFUL TO ROME. HE WAS LUCKY I DIDN'T HAVE HIM KILLED. ACTORS.
CHINK!
THANK YOU, CITIZEN. MAY THE GODS BLESS YOU AND GIVE YOU VIRTUOUS CHILDREN.

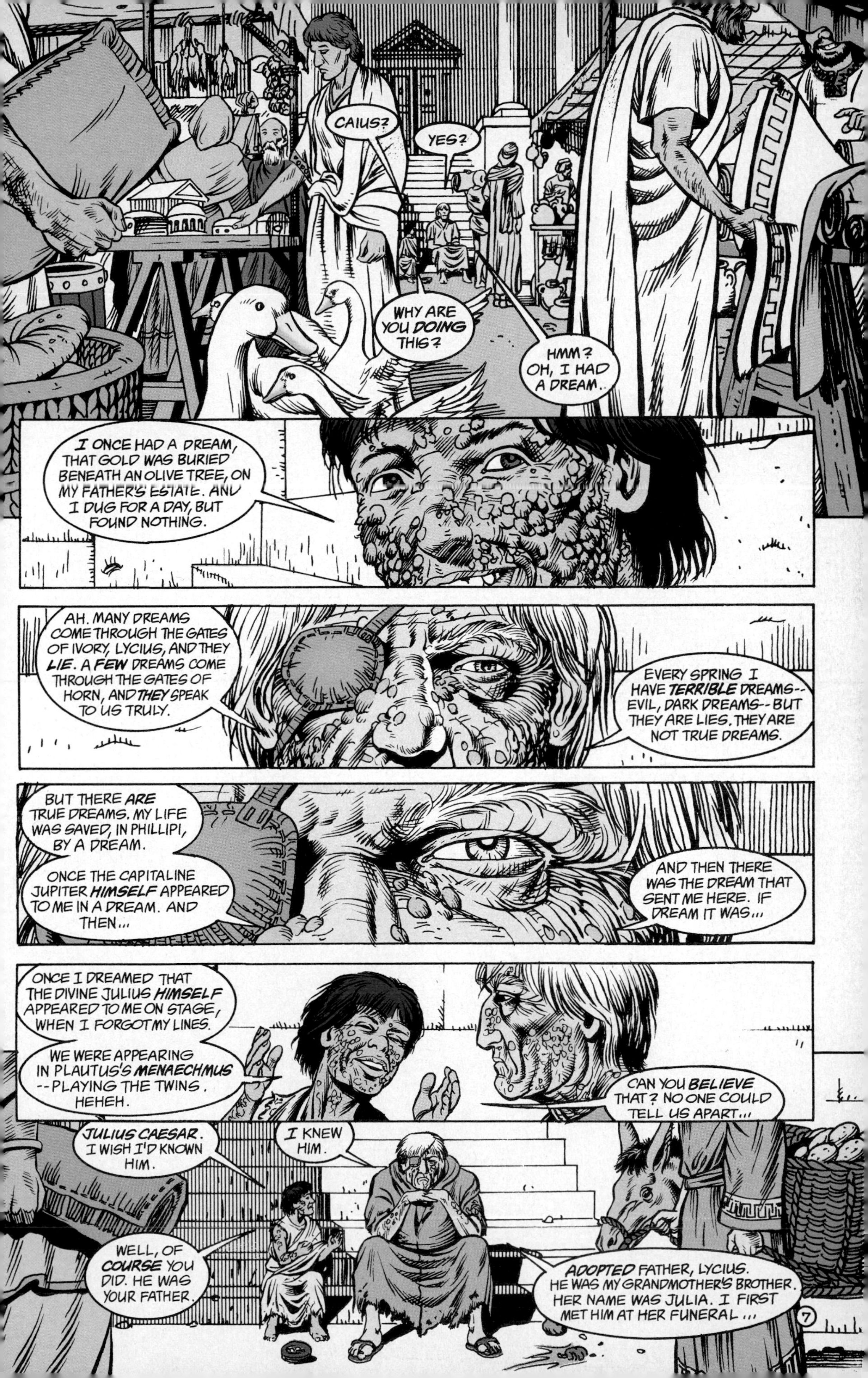
CAIUS?
YES?
WHY ARE YOU *DOING* THIS?
HMM? OH, I HAD A DREAM..
I ONCE HAD A DREAM, THAT GOLD WAS BURIED BENEATH AN OLIVE TREE, ON MY FATHER'S ESTATE. AND I DUG FOR A DAY, BUT FOUND NOTHING.
AH. MANY DREAMS COME THROUGH THE GATES OF IVORY, LYCIUS, AND THEY *LIE*. A *FEW* DREAMS COME THROUGH THE GATES OF HORN, AND *THEY* SPEAK TO US TRULY.
EVERY SPRING I HAVE *TERRIBLE* DREAMS-- EVIL, DARK DREAMS-- BUT THEY ARE LIES. THEY ARE NOT TRUE DREAMS.
BUT THERE *ARE* TRUE DREAMS. MY LIFE WAS SAVED, IN PHILLIPI, BY A DREAM.
ONCE THE CAPITALINE JUPITER *HIMSELF* APPEARED TO ME IN A DREAM. AND THEN...
AND THEN THERE WAS THE DREAM THAT SENT ME HERE. IF DREAM IT WAS...
ONCE I DREAMED THAT THE DIVINE JULIUS *HIMSELF* APPEARED TO ME ON STAGE, WHEN I FORGOT MY LINES.
WE WERE APPEARING IN PLAUTUS'S *MENAECHMUS* --PLAYING THE TWINS. HEHEH.
CAN YOU *BELIEVE* THAT? NO ONE COULD TELL US APART...
JULIUS CAESAR. I WISH I'D KNOWN HIM.
I KNEW HIM.
WELL, OF *COURSE* YOU DID. HE WAS YOUR FATHER.
ADOPTED FATHER, LYCIUS. HE WAS MY GRANDMOTHER'S BROTHER. HER NAME WAS JULIA. I FIRST MET HIM AT HER FUNERAL...

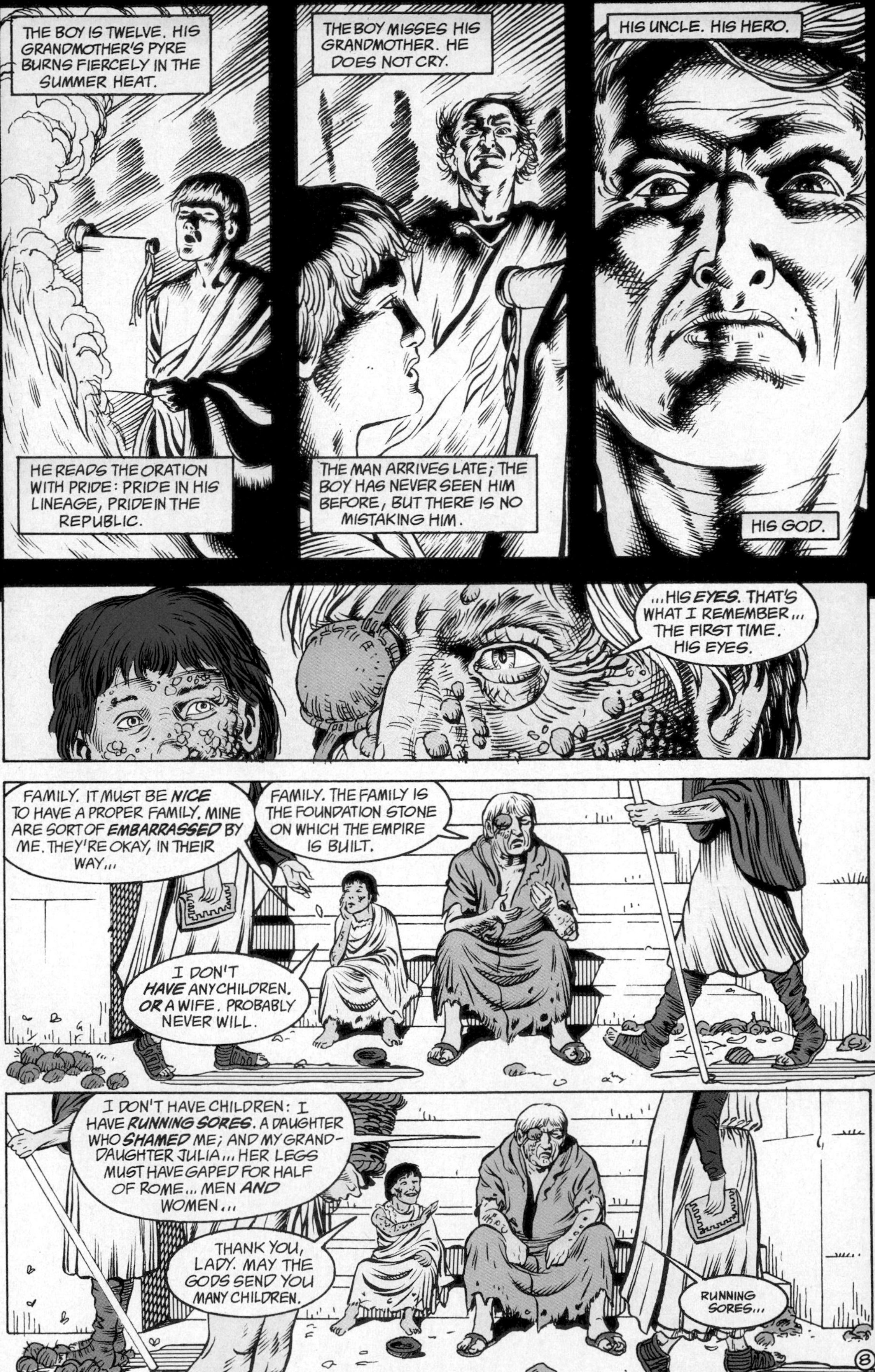

THE BOY IS TWELVE. HIS GRANDMOTHER'S PYRE BURNS FIERCELY IN THE SUMMER HEAT.
HE READS THE ORATION WITH PRIDE: PRIDE IN HIS LINEAGE, PRIDE IN THE REPUBLIC.
THE BOY MISSES HIS GRANDMOTHER. HE DOES NOT CRY.
THE MAN ARRIVES LATE; THE BOY HAS NEVER SEEN HIM BEFORE, BUT THERE IS NO MISTAKING HIM.
HIS UNCLE. HIS HERO.
HIS GOD.
...HIS EYES. THAT'S WHAT I REMEMBER... THE FIRST TIME. HIS EYES.
FAMILY. IT MUST BE NICE TO HAVE A PROPER FAMILY. MINE ARE SORT OF EMBARRASSED BY ME. THEY'RE OKAY, IN THEIR WAY...
FAMILY. THE FAMILY IS THE FOUNDATION STONE ON WHICH THE EMPIRE IS BUILT.
I DON'T HAVE ANY CHILDREN. OR A WIFE. PROBABLY NEVER WILL.
I DON'T HAVE CHILDREN: I HAVE RUNNING SORES. A DAUGHTER WHO SHAMED ME; AND MY GRAND-DAUGHTER JULIA... HER LEGS MUST HAVE GAPED FOR HALF OF ROME... MEN AND WOMEN...
THANK YOU, LADY. MAY THE GODS SEND YOU MANY CHILDREN.
RUNNING SORES...

ARUM'T YOU GOING TO GIVE HIM A COIN, MARCUS?

WHY? IF IT IS THE GODS' WILL THAT HE CANNOT WORK, THEN LET THE GODS FEED HIM AND GIVE HIM COINS.

HE'D PISS HIMSELF IF HE KNEW WHO YOU REALLY WERE.

UNDOUBTEDLY. BUT HE HAD A POINT. WE CANNOT DEFY THE GODS.

MM. I HAVE THREE DUTIES, LYCIUS. I AM HEAD OF THE STATE. I AM HEAD OF THE ARMY. AND I AM THE CHIEF PRIEST.

I... SOMETIMES DOUBT THE GODS EXIST. I HAVE NEVER SEEN ONE...

EXCEPT... DURING MY ELEUSINEAN INITIATION, I THOUGHT I HEARD VOICES...

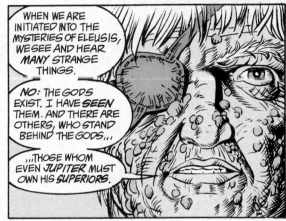

WHEN WE ARE INITIATED INTO THE MYSTERIES OF ELEUSIS, WE SEE AND HEAR MANY STRANGE THINGS.

NO: THE GODS EXIST. I HAVE SEEN THEM. AND THERE ARE OTHERS, WHO STAND BEHIND THE GODS...

...THOSE WHOM EVEN JUPITER MUST OWN HIS SUPERIORS.

EH? WHO COULD BE GREATER THAN JUPITER THE GREATEST AND MOST POWERFUL?

HM. FIRSTLY, TERMINUS, THE GOD OF BOUNDARIES. JUPITER MUST BOW TO HIM; BOUNDARIES ARE THE MOST IMPORTANT OF THINGS, LYCIUS.

AND SECONDLY... BUT I DO NOT KNOW WHO THEY ARE.

THEY ARE WHISPERED OF IN THE INNER MYSTERIES: THE SEVEN, WHO ARE NOT PRAYED TO, WHO ARE NOT GODS, WHO WERE NEVER MEN.

THE DIVINE JULIUS IS NOW A GOD. I WONDER WHAT IT'S LIKE, BEING A GOD.

I WILL BE A GOD, WHEN I DIE, LYCIUS. ALREADY THEY BEGIN TO WEAVE STORIES ABOUT ME, PRESAGING MY DIVINITY.

THEY SAY THAT MY MOTHER, ATIA, FELL ASLEEP AT THE TEMPLE OF APOLLO, AND A SNAKE MADE ITS WAY INTO HER WOMB, AND FERTILIZED HER.

AND IS IT TRUE?

OF COURSE NOT. MY MOTHER WAS ENTERED BY NOTHING MORE REMARKABLE THAN MY FATHER'S PENIS.

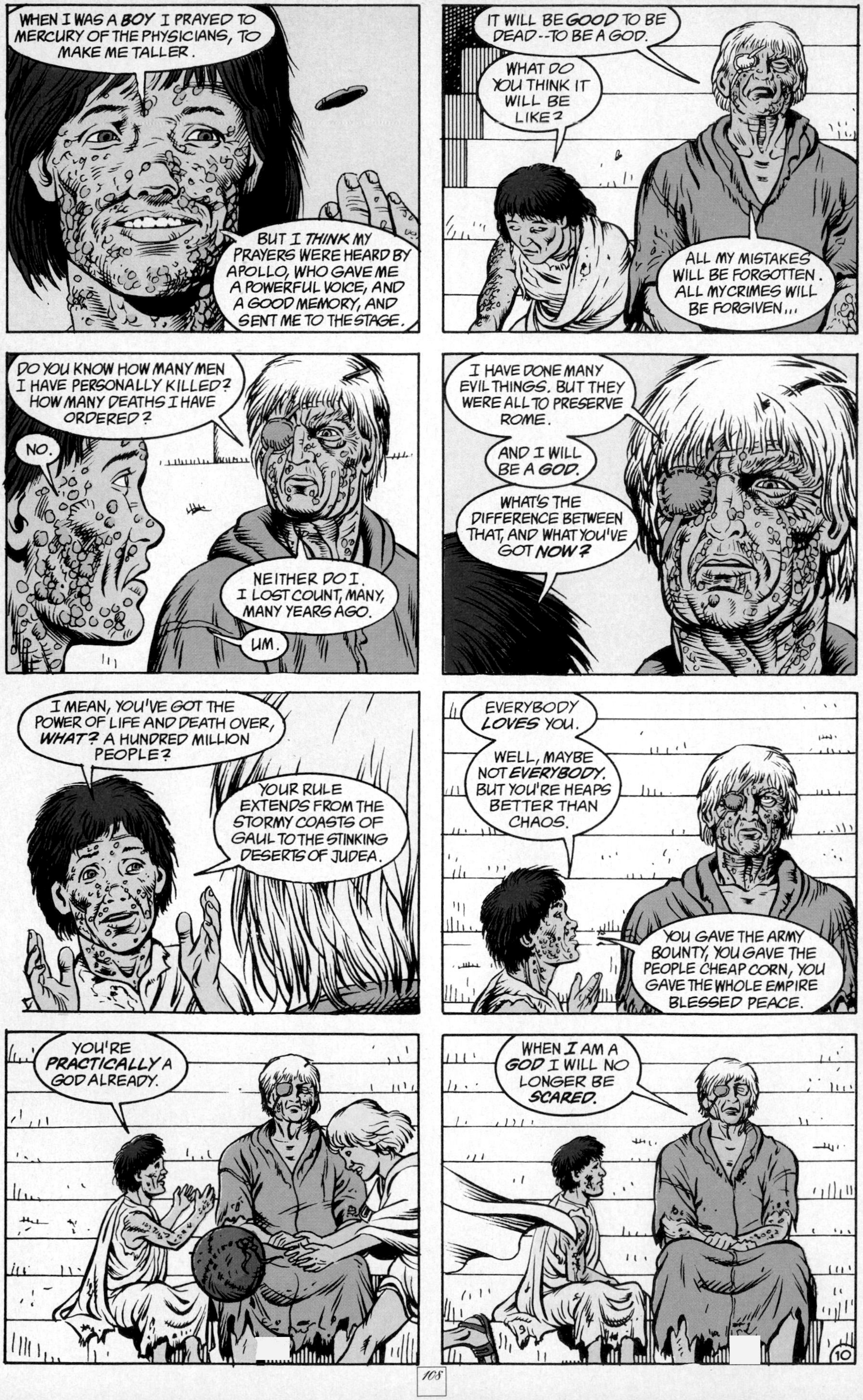
WHEN I WAS A BOY I PRAYED TO MERCURY OF THE PHYSICIANS, TO MAKE ME TALLER.
BUT I THINK MY PRAYERS WERE HEARD BY APOLLO, WHO GAVE ME A POWERFUL VOICE, AND A GOOD MEMORY, AND SENT ME TO THE STAGE.
IT WILL BE GOOD TO BE DEAD--TO BE A GOD.
WHAT DO YOU THINK IT WILL BE LIKE?
ALL MY MISTAKES WILL BE FORGOTTEN. ALL MY CRIMES WILL BE FORGIVEN...
DO YOU KNOW HOW MANY MEN I HAVE PERSONALLY KILLED? HOW MANY DEATHS I HAVE ORDERED?
NO.
NEITHER DO I. I LOST COUNT, MANY, MANY YEARS AGO.
UM.
I HAVE DONE MANY EVIL THINGS. BUT THEY WERE ALL TO PRESERVE ROME.
AND I WILL BE A GOD.
WHAT'S THE DIFFERENCE BETWEEN THAT, AND WHAT YOU'VE GOT NOW?
I MEAN, YOU'VE GOT THE POWER OF LIFE AND DEATH OVER, WHAT? A HUNDRED MILLION PEOPLE?
YOUR RULE EXTENDS FROM THE STORMY COASTS OF GAUL TO THE STINKING DESERTS OF JUDEA.
EVERYBODY LOVES YOU.
WELL, MAYBE NOT EVERYBODY. BUT YOU'RE HEAPS BETTER THAN CHAOS.
YOU GAVE THE ARMY BOUNTY, YOU GAVE THE PEOPLE CHEAP CORN, YOU GAVE THE WHOLE EMPIRE BLESSED PEACE.
YOU'RE PRACTICALLY A GOD ALREADY.
WHEN I AM A GOD I WILL NO LONGER BE SCARED.
10

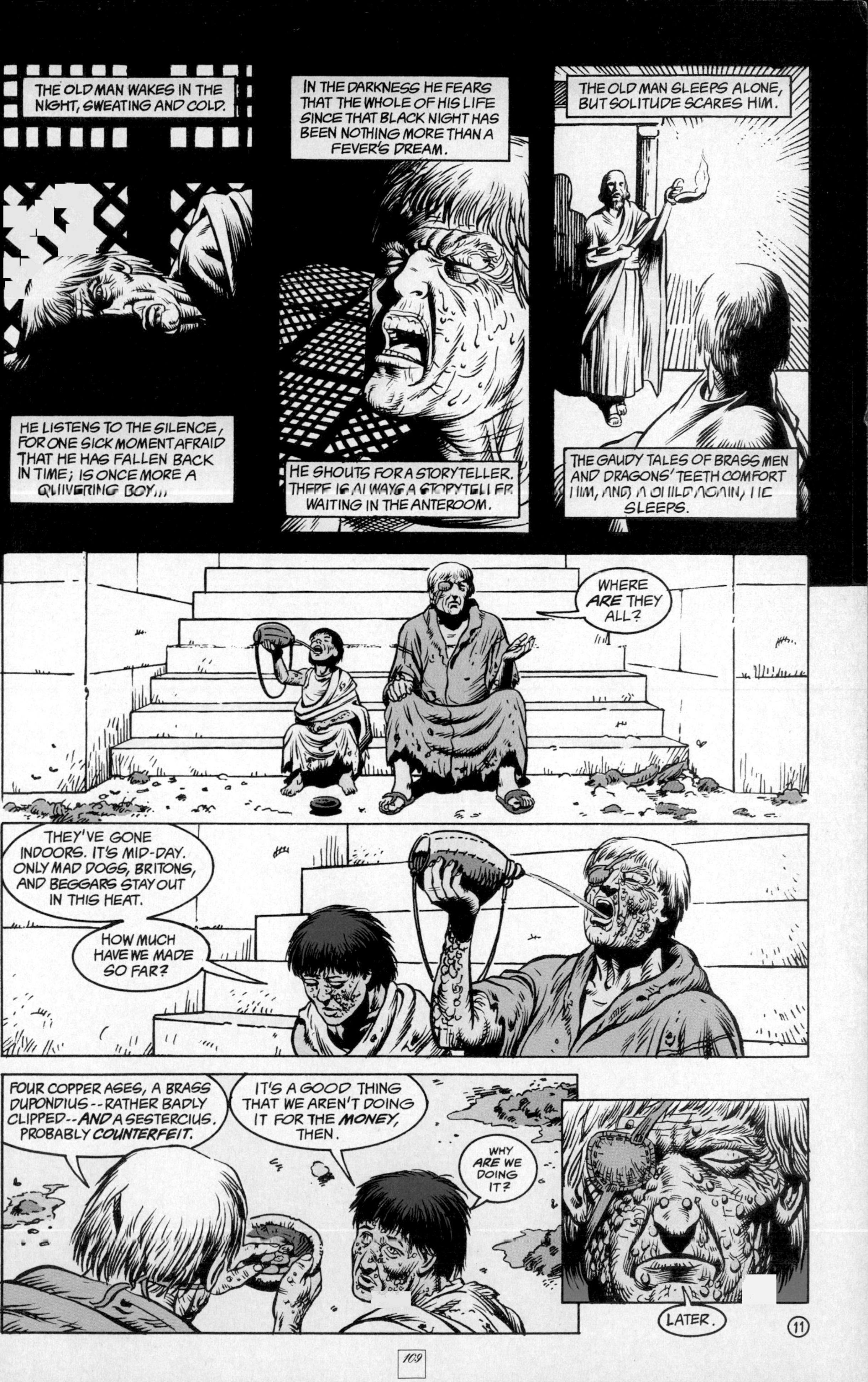
THE OLD MAN WAKES IN THE NIGHT, SWEATING AND COLD.
HE LISTENS TO THE SILENCE, FOR ONE SICK MOMENT AFRAID THAT HE HAS FALLEN BACK IN TIME; IS ONCE MORE A QUIVERING BOY...
IN THE DARKNESS HE FEARS THAT THE WHOLE OF HIS LIFE SINCE THAT BLACK NIGHT HAS BEEN NOTHING MORE THAN A FEVER'S DREAM.
HE SHOUTS FOR A STORYTELLER. THERE IS ALWAYS A STORYTELLER WAITING IN THE ANTEROOM.
THE OLD MAN SLEEPS ALONE, BUT SOLITUDE SCARES HIM.
THE GAUDY TALES OF BRASS MEN AND DRAGONS' TEETH COMFORT HIM, AND A CHILD AGAIN, HE SLEEPS.
WHERE ARE THEY ALL?
THEY'VE GONE INDOORS. IT'S MID-DAY. ONLY MAD DOGS, BRITONS, AND BEGGARS STAY OUT IN THIS HEAT.
HOW MUCH HAVE WE MADE SO FAR?
FOUR COPPER ASES, A BRASS DUPONDIUS--RATHER BADLY CLIPPED--AND A SESTERCIUS. PROBABLY COUNTERFEIT.
IT'S A GOOD THING THAT WE AREN'T DOING IT FOR THE MONEY, THEN.
WHY ARE WE DOING IT?
LATER.
11

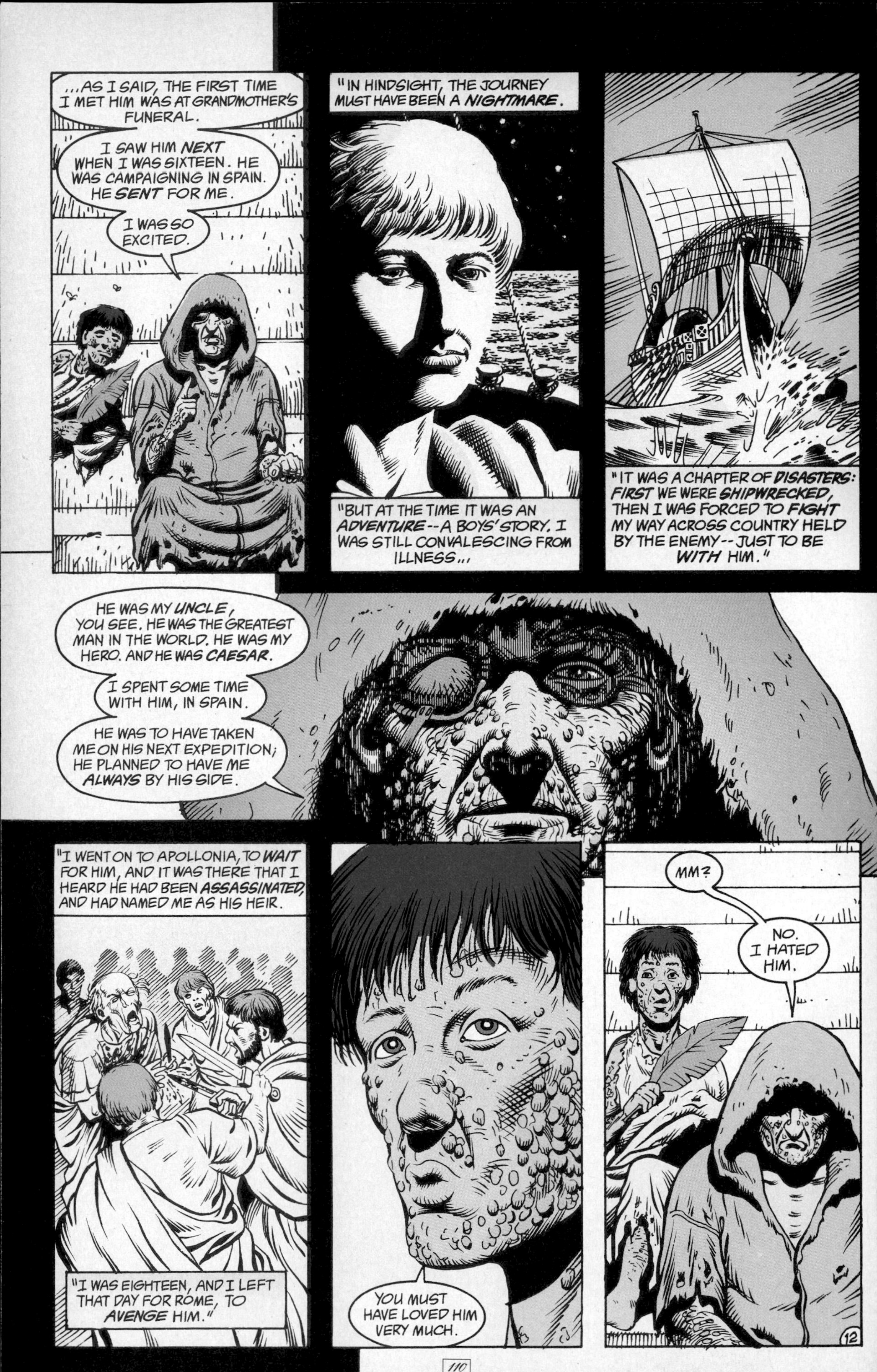

...AS I SAID, THE FIRST TIME I MET HIM WAS AT GRANDMOTHER'S FUNERAL.
I SAW HIM NEXT WHEN I WAS SIXTEEN. HE WAS CAMPAIGNING IN SPAIN. HE SENT FOR ME.
I WAS SO EXCITED.
"IN HINDSIGHT, THE JOURNEY MUST HAVE BEEN A NIGHTMARE.
"BUT AT THE TIME IT WAS AN ADVENTURE--A BOYS' STORY. I WAS STILL CONVALESCING FROM ILLNESS...
"IT WAS A CHAPTER OF DISASTERS: FIRST WE WERE SHIPWRECKED, THEN I WAS FORCED TO FIGHT MY WAY ACROSS COUNTRY HELD BY THE ENEMY--JUST TO BE WITH HIM."
HE WAS MY UNCLE, YOU SEE. HE WAS THE GREATEST MAN IN THE WORLD. HE WAS MY HERO. AND HE WAS CAESAR.
I SPENT SOME TIME WITH HIM, IN SPAIN.
HE WAS TO HAVE TAKEN ME ON HIS NEXT EXPEDITION; HE PLANNED TO HAVE ME ALWAYS BY HIS SIDE.
"I WENT ON TO APOLLONIA, TO WAIT FOR HIM, AND IT WAS THERE THAT I HEARD HE HAD BEEN ASSASSINATED, AND HAD NAMED ME AS HIS HEIR.
"I WAS EIGHTEEN, AND I LEFT THAT DAY FOR ROME, TO AVENGE HIM."
YOU MUST HAVE LOVED HIM VERY MUCH.
MM?
NO. I HATED HIM.
12

...WHAT WAS IT *LIKE,* LYCIUS? IN THE DAYS OF THE REPUBLIC?

IT WAS *CHAOS,* HELD AT BAY BY A HANDFUL OF MEN: *CICERO,* FOR EXAMPLE.

THE *LAWYER?* MY FATHER'S TOLD ME ABOUT HIM. HE WAS A GREAT MAN, WASN'T HE?

YES. A *FINE MIND,* AND AN *HONORABLE MAN.* THE LAST OF THE GIANTS.

CICERO... WHATEVER *HAPPENED* TO HIM?

I HAD HIM KILLED.

OH.

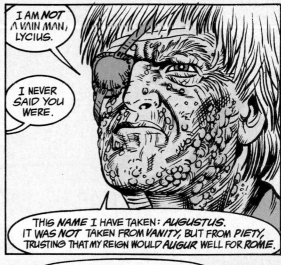

I AM *NOT* A VAIN MAN, LYCIUS.

I NEVER SAID YOU WERE.

THIS *NAME* I HAVE TAKEN: *AUGUSTUS.* IT WAS *NOT* TAKEN FROM *VANITY,* BUT FROM *PIETY,* TRUSTING THAT MY REIGN WOULD *AUGUR* WELL FOR *ROME.*

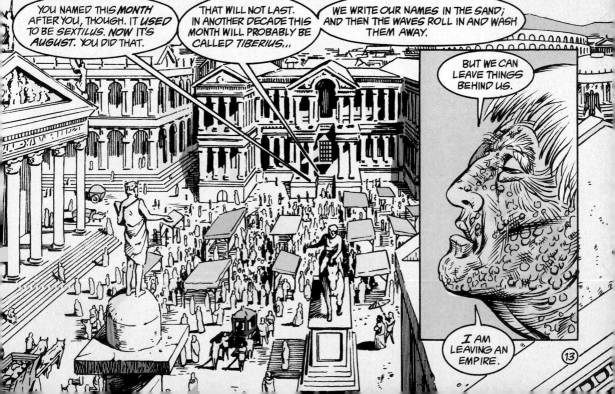

YOU NAMED THIS *MONTH* AFTER YOU, THOUGH. IT *USED* TO BE *SEXTILUS. NOW* IT'S *AUGUST.* YOU DID THAT.

THAT WILL NOT LAST. IN ANOTHER DECADE THIS MONTH WILL PROBABLY BE CALLED *TIBERIUS...*

WE WRITE OUR NAMES IN THE SAND; AND THEN THE WAVES ROLL IN AND WASH THEM AWAY.

BUT WE CAN LEAVE THINGS BEHIND US.

I AM LEAVING AN EMPIRE.

13

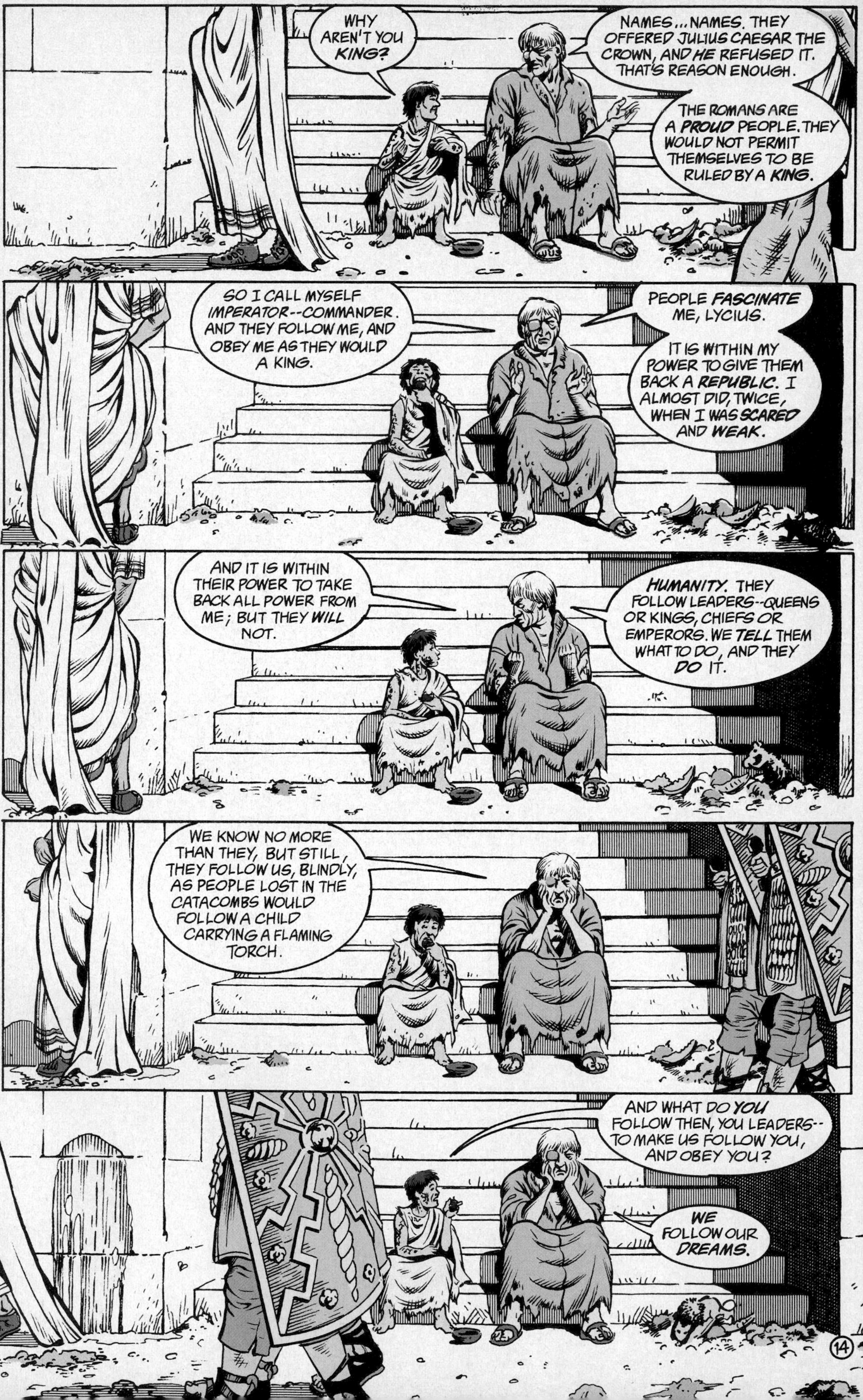
WHY AREN'T YOU KING?
NAMES... NAMES. THEY OFFERED JULIUS CAESAR THE CROWN, AND HE REFUSED IT. THAT'S REASON ENOUGH.
THE ROMANS ARE A PROUD PEOPLE. THEY WOULD NOT PERMIT THEMSELVES TO BE RULED BY A KING.
SO I CALL MYSELF IMPERATOR--COMMANDER. AND THEY FOLLOW ME, AND OBEY ME AS THEY WOULD A KING.
PEOPLE FASCINATE ME, LYCIUS.
IT IS WITHIN MY POWER TO GIVE THEM BACK A REPUBLIC. I ALMOST DID, TWICE, WHEN I WAS SCARED AND WEAK.
AND IT IS WITHIN THEIR POWER TO TAKE BACK ALL POWER FROM ME; BUT THEY WILL NOT.
HUMANITY. THEY FOLLOW LEADERS--QUEENS OR KINGS, CHIEFS OR EMPERORS. WE TELL THEM WHAT TO DO, AND THEY DO IT.
WE KNOW NO MORE THAN THEY, BUT STILL, THEY FOLLOW US, BLINDLY, AS PEOPLE LOST IN THE CATACOMBS WOULD FOLLOW A CHILD CARRYING A FLAMING TORCH.
AND WHAT DO YOU FOLLOW THEN, YOU LEADERS-- TO MAKE US FOLLOW YOU, AND OBEY YOU?
WE FOLLOW OUR DREAMS.

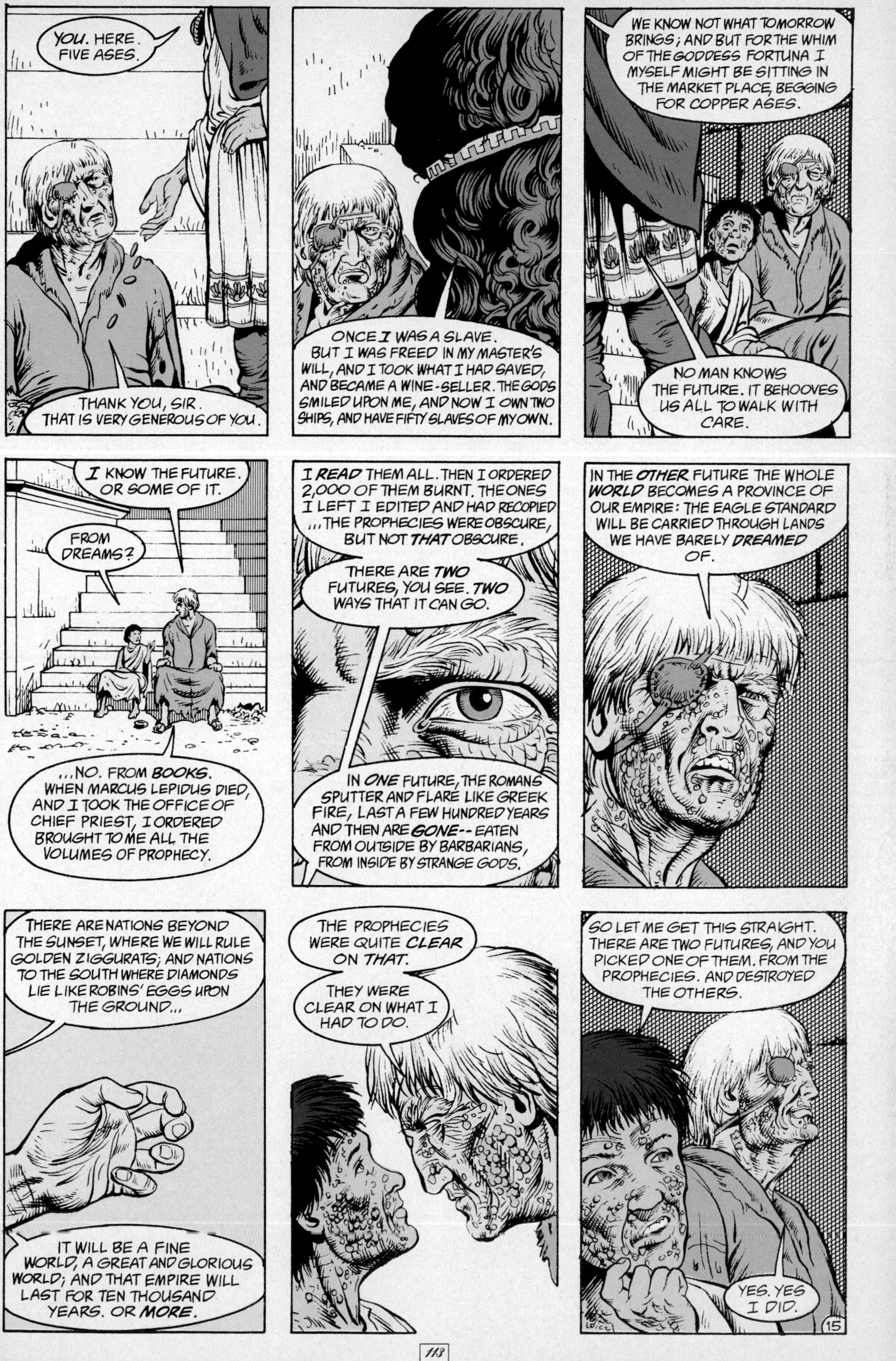
YOU. HERE. FIVE ASES.
THANK YOU, SIR. THAT IS VERY GENEROUS OF YOU.
ONCE I WAS A SLAVE. BUT I WAS FREED IN MY MASTER'S WILL, AND I TOOK WHAT I HAD SAVED, AND BECAME A WINE-SELLER. THE GODS SMILED UPON ME, AND NOW I OWN TWO SHIPS, AND HAVE FIFTY SLAVES OF MY OWN.
WE KNOW NOT WHAT TOMORROW BRINGS; AND BUT FOR THE WHIM OF THE GODDESS FORTUNA I MYSELF MIGHT BE SITTING IN THE MARKET PLACE, BEGGING FOR COPPER ASES.
NO MAN KNOWS THE FUTURE. IT BEHOOVES US ALL TO WALK WITH CARE.
I KNOW THE FUTURE. OR SOME OF IT.
FROM DREAMS?
...NO. FROM BOOKS. WHEN MARCUS LEPIDUS DIED, AND I TOOK THE OFFICE OF CHIEF PRIEST, I ORDERED BROUGHT TO ME ALL THE VOLUMES OF PROPHECY.
I READ THEM ALL. THEN I ORDERED 2,000 OF THEM BURNT. THE ONES I LEFT I EDITED AND HAD RECOPIED ...THE PROPHECIES WERE OBSCURE, BUT NOT THAT OBSCURE.
THERE ARE TWO FUTURES, YOU SEE. TWO WAYS THAT IT CAN GO.
IN ONE FUTURE, THE ROMANS SPUTTER AND FLARE LIKE GREEK FIRE, LAST A FEW HUNDRED YEARS AND THEN ARE GONE-- EATEN FROM OUTSIDE BY BARBARIANS, FROM INSIDE BY STRANGE GODS.
IN THE OTHER FUTURE THE WHOLE WORLD BECOMES A PROVINCE OF OUR EMPIRE: THE EAGLE STANDARD WILL BE CARRIED THROUGH LANDS WE HAVE BARELY DREAMED OF.
THERE ARE NATIONS BEYOND THE SUNSET, WHERE WE WILL RULE GOLDEN ZIGGURATS; AND NATIONS TO THE SOUTH WHERE DIAMONDS LIE LIKE ROBINS' EGGS UPON THE GROUND...
IT WILL BE A FINE WORLD, A GREAT AND GLORIOUS WORLD; AND THAT EMPIRE WILL LAST FOR TEN THOUSAND YEARS. OR MORE.
THE PROPHECIES WERE QUITE CLEAR ON THAT.
THEY WERE CLEAR ON WHAT I HAD TO DO.
SO LET ME GET THIS STRAIGHT. THERE ARE TWO FUTURES, AND YOU PICKED ONE OF THEM. FROM THE PROPHECIES. AND DESTROYED THE OTHERS.
YES. YES I DID.
15

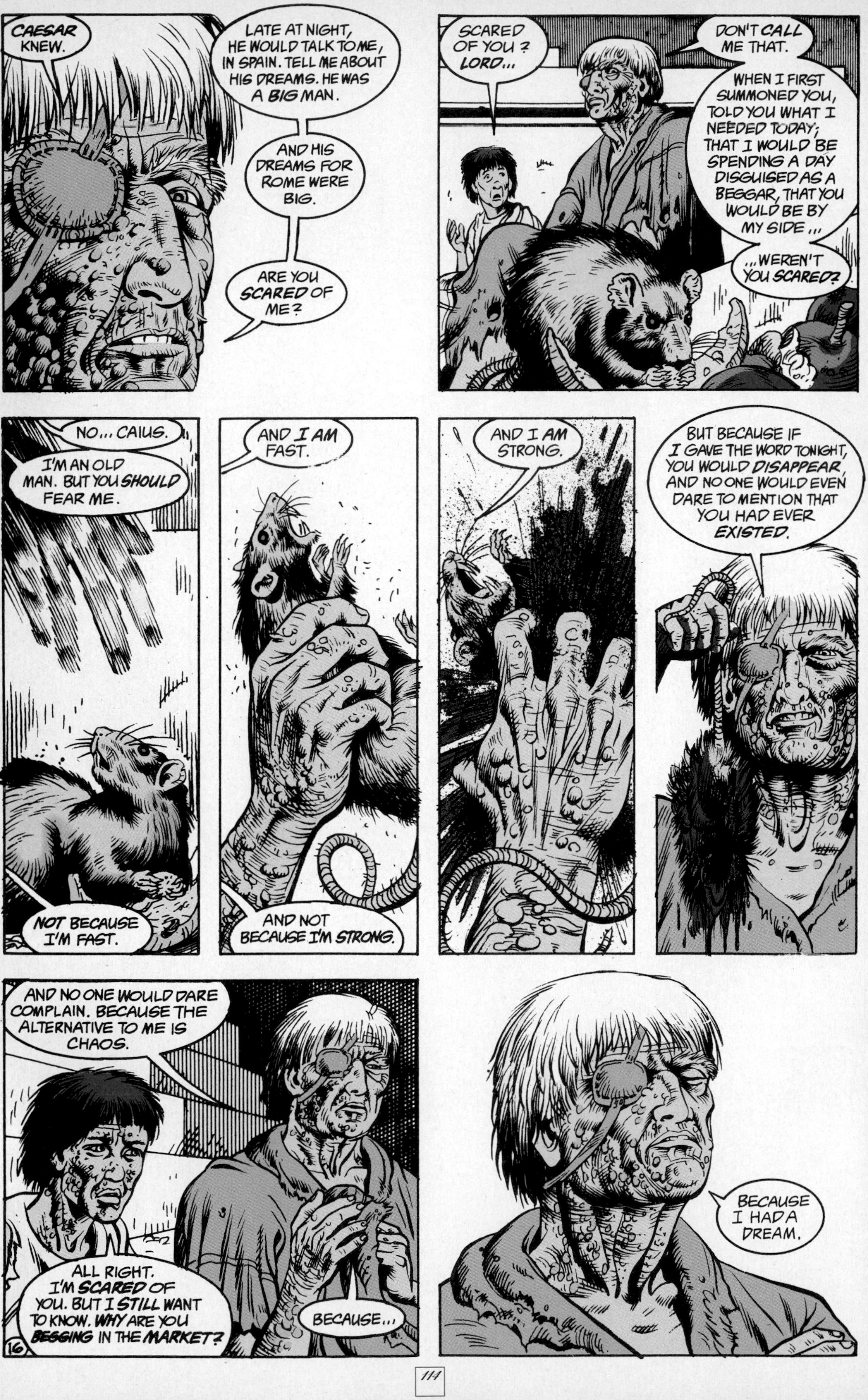
CAESAR KNEW.
LATE AT NIGHT, HE WOULD TALK TO ME, IN SPAIN. TELL ME ABOUT HIS DREAMS. HE WAS A BIG MAN.
AND HIS DREAMS FOR ROME WERE BIG.
ARE YOU SCARED OF ME?
SCARED OF YOU? LORD...
DON'T CALL ME THAT.
WHEN I FIRST SUMMONED YOU, TOLD YOU WHAT I NEEDED TODAY; THAT I WOULD BE SPENDING A DAY DISGUISED AS A BEGGAR, THAT YOU WOULD BE BY MY SIDE...
...WEREN'T YOU SCARED?
NO... CAIUS.
I'M AN OLD MAN. BUT YOU SHOULD FEAR ME.
NOT BECAUSE I'M FAST.
AND I AM FAST.
AND NOT BECAUSE I'M STRONG.
AND I AM STRONG.
BUT BECAUSE IF I GAVE THE WORD TONIGHT, YOU WOULD DISAPPEAR, AND NO ONE WOULD EVEN DARE TO MENTION THAT YOU HAD EVER EXISTED.
AND NO ONE WOULD DARE COMPLAIN. BECAUSE THE ALTERNATIVE TO ME IS CHAOS.
ALL RIGHT. I'M SCARED OF YOU. BUT I STILL WANT TO KNOW. WHY ARE YOU BEGGING IN THE MARKET?
BECAUSE...
16
BECAUSE I HAD A DREAM.

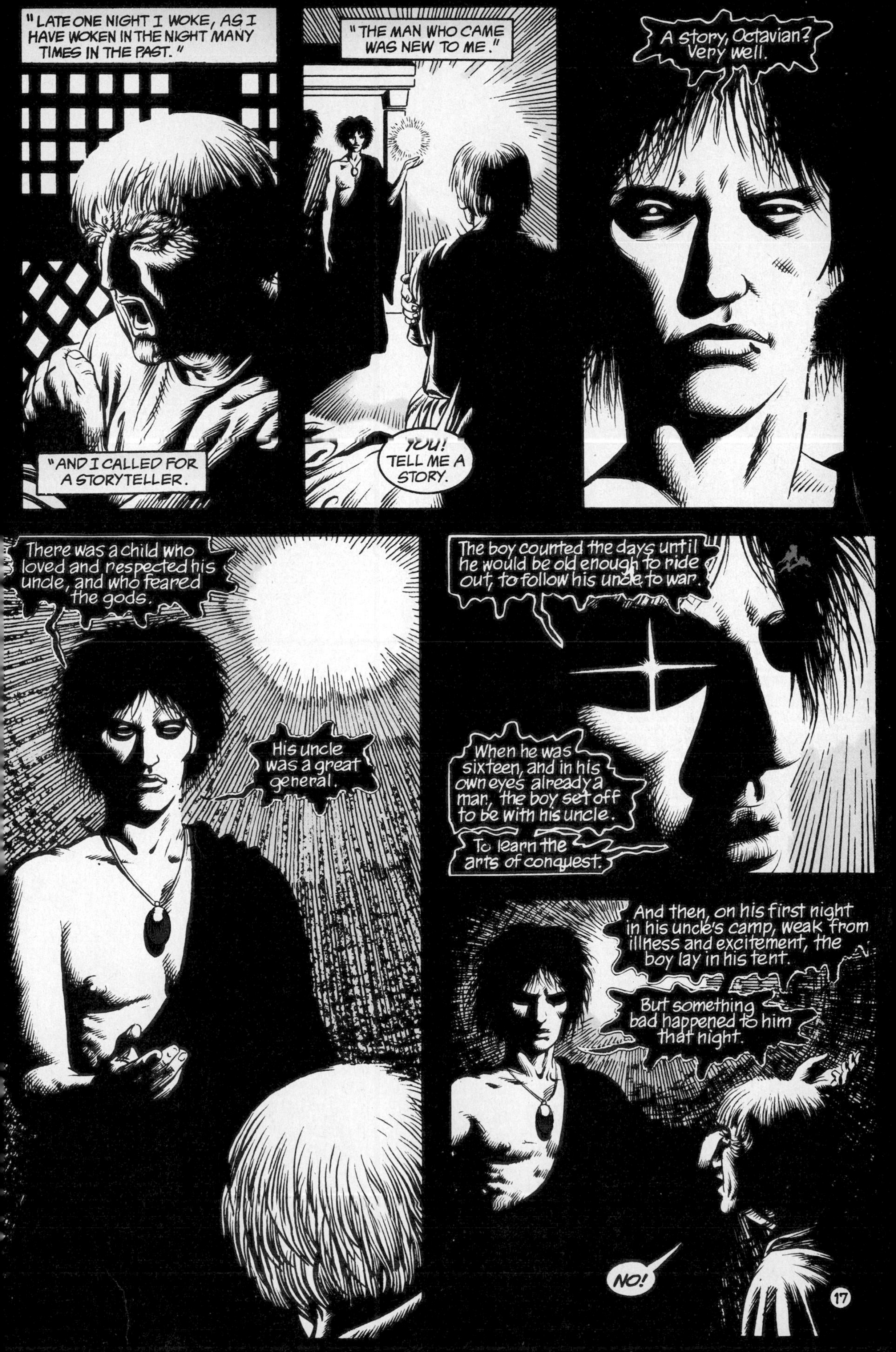
"LATE ONE NIGHT I WOKE, AS I HAVE WOKEN IN THE NIGHT MANY TIMES IN THE PAST."
"AND I CALLED FOR A STORYTELLER.
"THE MAN WHO CAME WAS NEW TO ME."
YOU! TELL ME A STORY.
A story, Octavian? Very well.
There was a child who loved and respected his uncle, and who feared the gods.
His uncle was a great general.
The boy counted the days until he would be old enough to ride out, to follow his uncle to war.
When he was sixteen, and in his own eyes already a man, the boy set off to be with his uncle.
To learn the arts of conquest.
And then, on his first night in his uncle's camp, weak from illness and excitement, the boy lay in his tent.
But something bad happened to him that night.
NO!

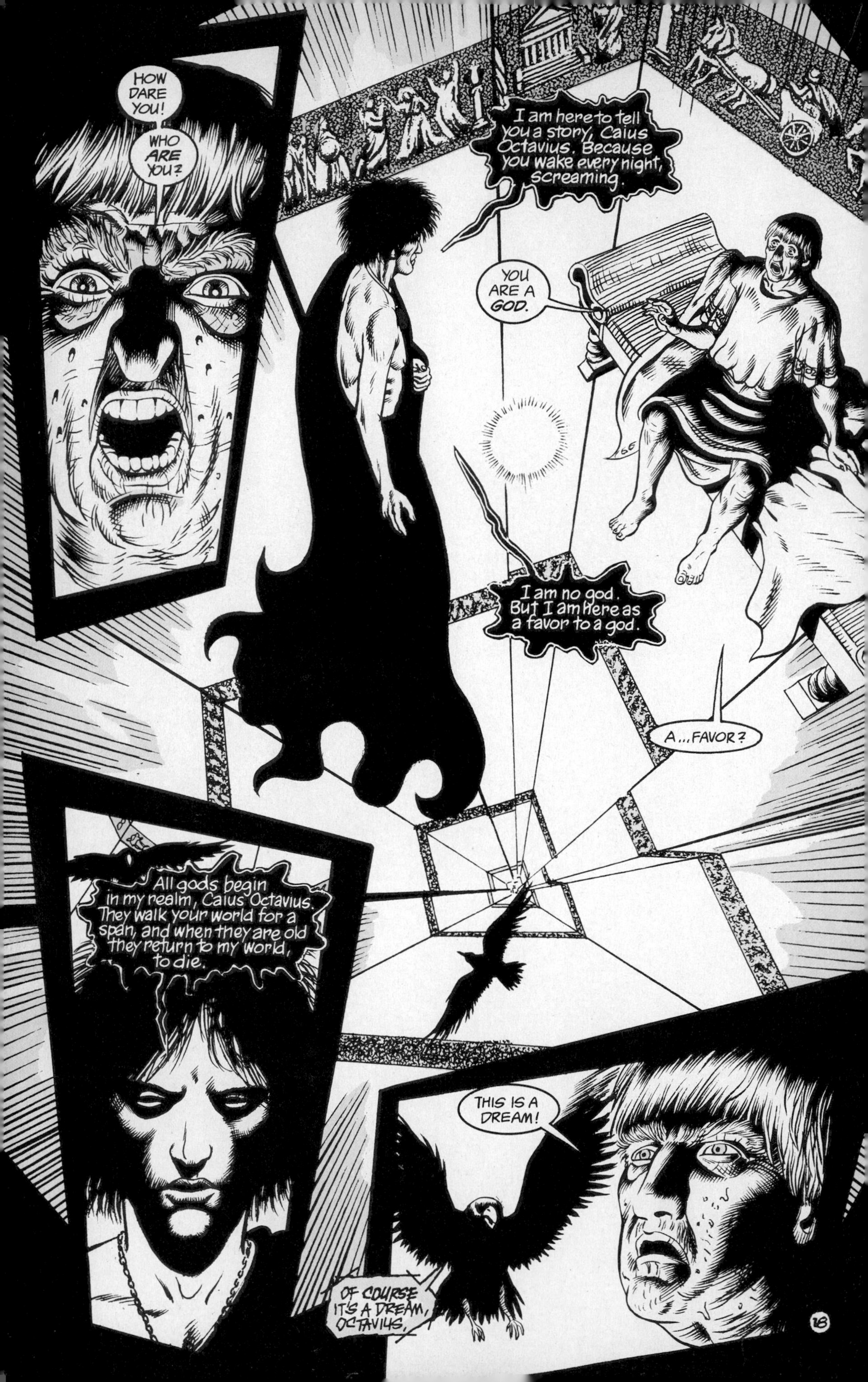
HOW DARE YOU!
WHO ARE YOU?
I am here to tell you a story, Caius Octavius. Because you wake every night, screaming.
YOU ARE A GOD.
I am no god. But I am here as a favor to a god.
A...FAVOR?
All gods begin in my realm, Caius Octavius. They walk your world for a span, and when they are old they return to my world, to die.
THIS IS A DREAM!
OF COURSE IT'S A DREAM, OCTAVIUS.
18

WHO ARE YOU?

WHEN I WAS A MAN, I WAS ARISTEAS OF MARMORA. BUT THAT WAS SEVEN HUNDRED YEARS AGO.

...THE POET, WHO BECAME APOLLO'S RAVEN?

THEN YOU *ARE* APOLLO? I PRAY YOU, BE NOT APOLLO OF THE TORMENTS, BUT APOLLO OF SOME GENTLER ASPECT.

I am not Apollo. I am no sun god. But poets and dreamers are my people, and it is not unheard-of for us to be confused.

I am no little Roman dream god, no god of rhyme and madness. I am myself.

WHAT WILL YOU... WHAT DO YOU *WANT* WITH ME, LORD?

There is a way out of your dilemma, Octavius.

MY DILEMMA?

Indeed.

I do not do this for you, little emperor. I do it for another, who has asked me to intercede on your behalf.

THE DIVINE JULIUS?

Terminus. He who walks the boundaries.

He requested that I counsel a way out of your difficulties.

19

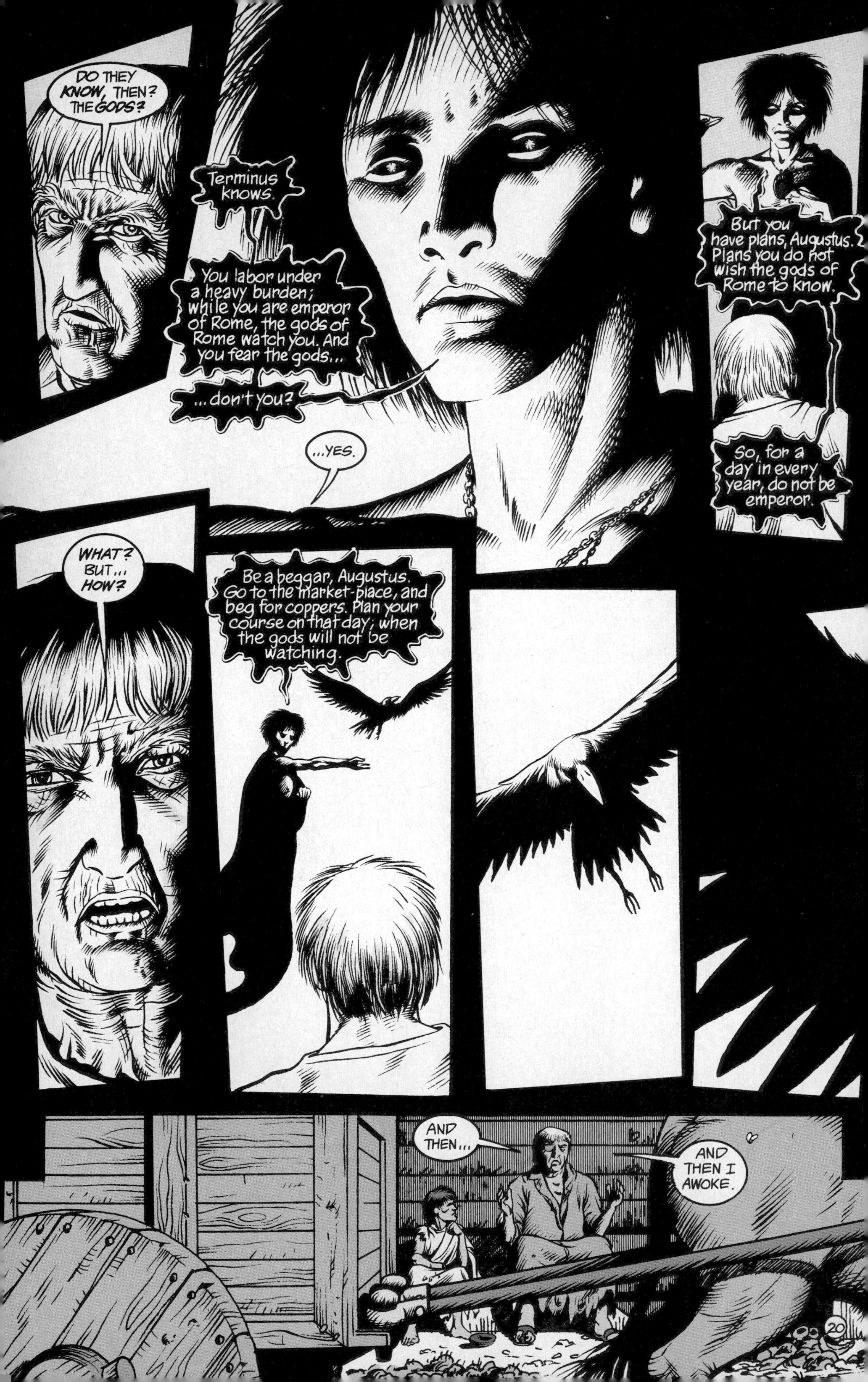

DO THEY KNOW, THEN? THE GODS?
Terminus knows.
You labor under a heavy burden; while you are emperor of Rome, the gods of Rome watch you. And you fear the gods...
...don't you?
...YES.
But you have plans, Augustus. Plans you do not wish the gods of Rome to know.
So, for a day in every year, do not be emperor.
WHAT? BUT... HOW?
Be a beggar, Augustus. Go to the market-place, and beg for coppers. Plan your course on that day; when the gods will not be watching.
AND THEN...
AND THEN I AWOKE.

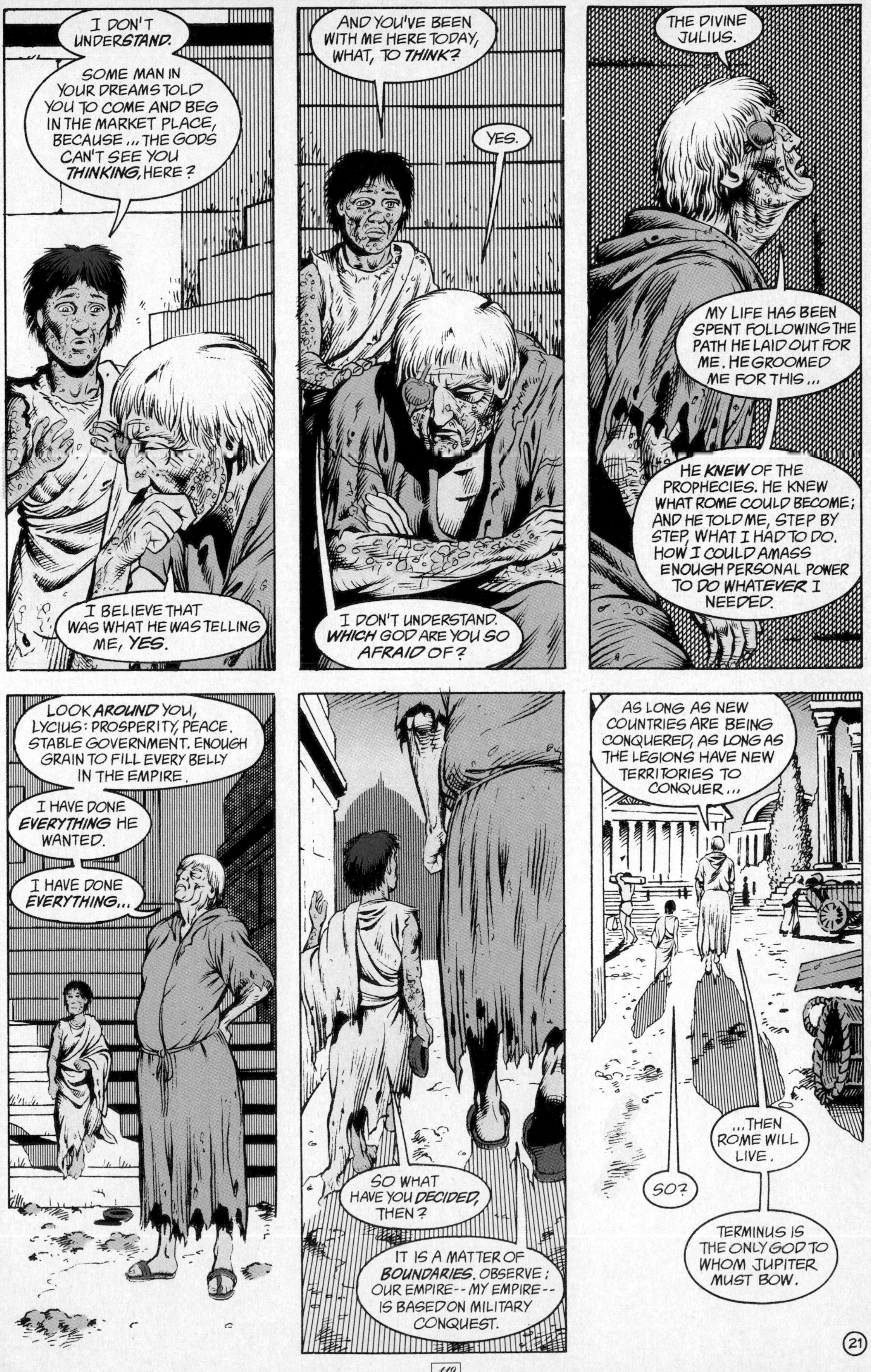
I DON'T UNDERSTAND.
SOME MAN IN YOUR DREAMS TOLD YOU TO COME AND BEG IN THE MARKET PLACE, BECAUSE ... THE GODS CAN'T SEE YOU THINKING, HERE?
I BELIEVE THAT WAS WHAT HE WAS TELLING ME, YES.
AND YOU'VE BEEN WITH ME HERE TODAY, WHAT, TO THINK?
YES.
I DON'T UNDERSTAND. WHICH GOD ARE YOU SO AFRAID OF?
THE DIVINE JULIUS.
MY LIFE HAS BEEN SPENT FOLLOWING THE PATH HE LAID OUT FOR ME. HE GROOMED ME FOR THIS ...
HE KNEW OF THE PROPHECIES. HE KNEW WHAT ROME COULD BECOME; AND HE TOLD ME, STEP BY STEP, WHAT I HAD TO DO. HOW I COULD AMASS ENOUGH PERSONAL POWER TO DO WHATEVER I NEEDED.
LOOK AROUND YOU, LYCIUS: PROSPERITY, PEACE. STABLE GOVERNMENT. ENOUGH GRAIN TO FILL EVERY BELLY IN THE EMPIRE.
I HAVE DONE EVERYTHING HE WANTED.
I HAVE DONE EVERYTHING...
SO WHAT HAVE YOU DECIDED, THEN?
IT IS A MATTER OF BOUNDARIES. OBSERVE: OUR EMPIRE-- MY EMPIRE-- IS BASED ON MILITARY CONQUEST.
AS LONG AS NEW COUNTRIES ARE BEING CONQUERED, AS LONG AS THE LEGIONS HAVE NEW TERRITORIES TO CONQUER...
...THEN ROME WILL LIVE.
SO?
TERMINUS IS THE ONLY GOD TO WHOM JUPITER MUST BOW.
21

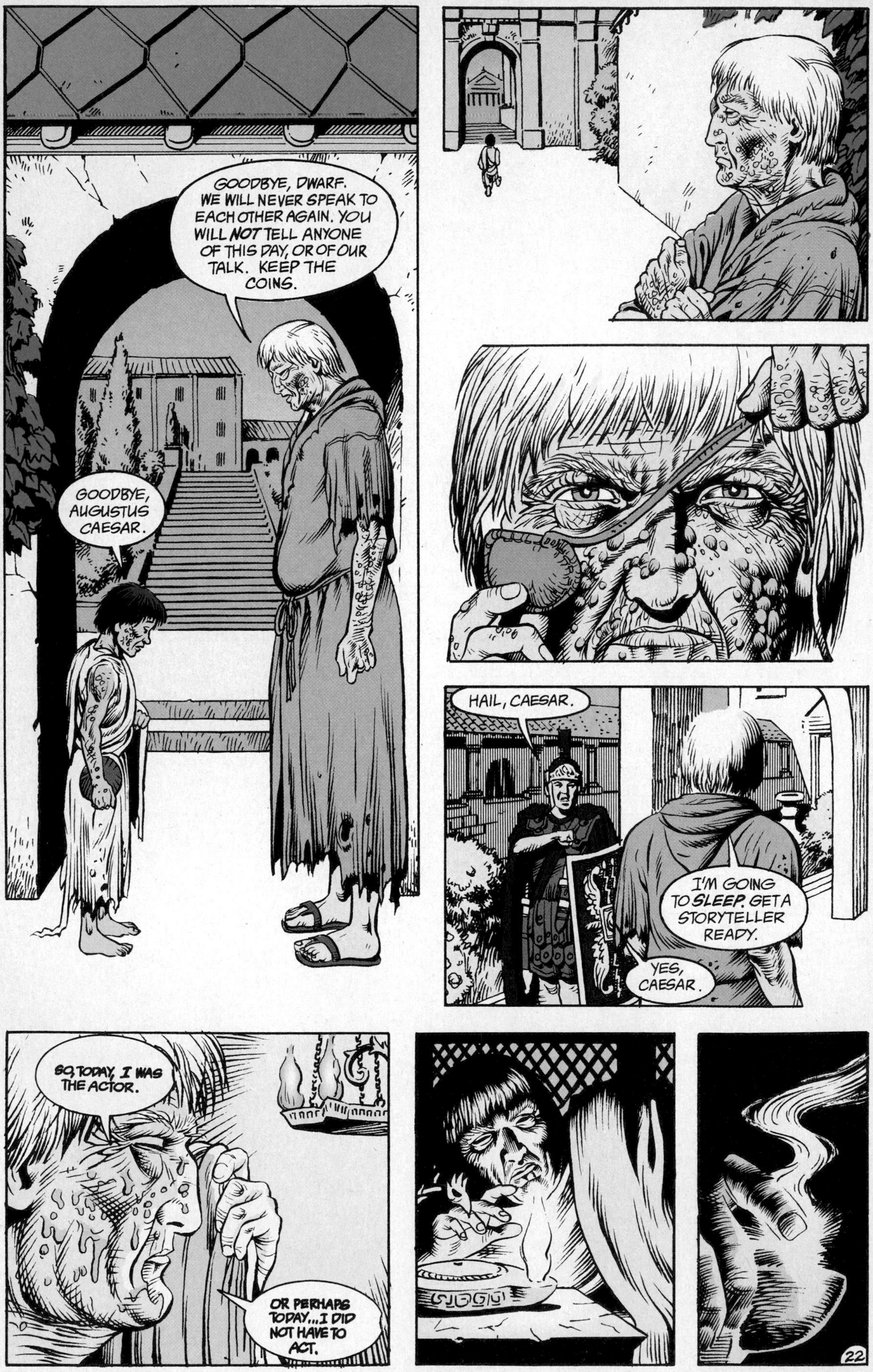
GOODBYE, DWARF. WE WILL NEVER SPEAK TO EACH OTHER AGAIN. YOU WILL NOT TELL ANYONE OF THIS DAY, OR OF OUR TALK. KEEP THE COINS.
GOODBYE, AUGUSTUS CAESAR.
HAIL, CAESAR.
I'M GOING TO SLEEP. GET A STORYTELLER READY.
YES, CAESAR.
SO, TODAY, I WAS THE ACTOR.
OR PERHAPS TODAY... I DID NOT HAVE TO ACT.
22

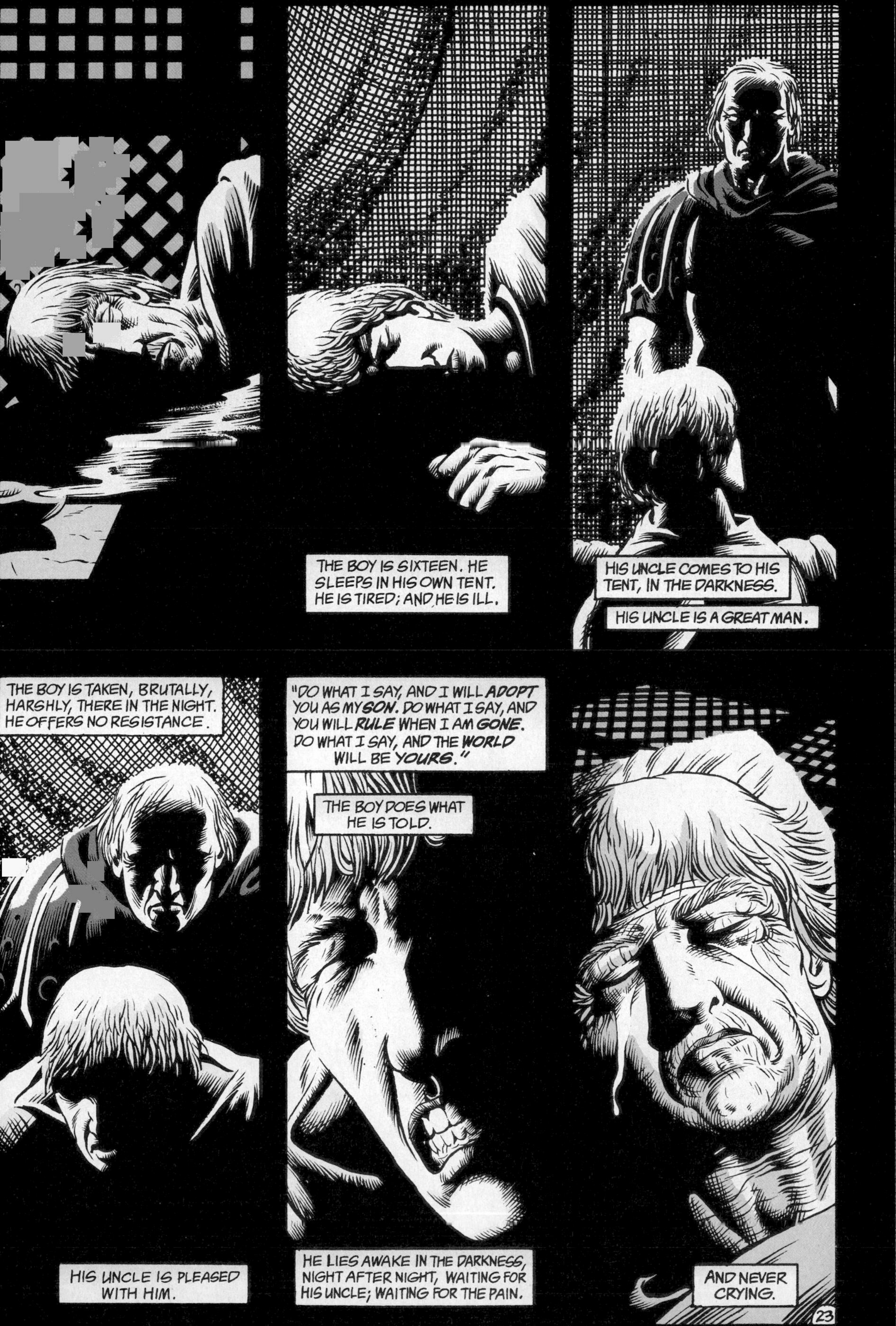
THE BOY IS SIXTEEN. HE SLEEPS IN HIS OWN TENT. HE IS TIRED; AND HE IS ILL.
HIS UNCLE COMES TO HIS TENT, IN THE DARKNESS.
HIS UNCLE IS A GREAT MAN.
THE BOY IS TAKEN, BRUTALLY, HARSHLY, THERE IN THE NIGHT. HE OFFERS NO RESISTANCE.
HIS UNCLE IS PLEASED WITH HIM.
"DO WHAT I SAY, AND I WILL ADOPT YOU AS MY SON. DO WHAT I SAY, AND YOU WILL RULE WHEN I AM GONE. DO WHAT I SAY, AND THE WORLD WILL BE YOURS."
THE BOY DOES WHAT HE IS TOLD.
HE LIES AWAKE IN THE DARKNESS, NIGHT AFTER NIGHT, WAITING FOR HIS UNCLE; WAITING FOR THE PAIN.
AND NEVER CRYING.
23

That, then, is a true account of the day I spent with the Emperor of Rome, in the month that still bears his name.

I passed him in the market, two years later, to the day. And I tossed him a copper. And he smiled at me.

I am an old man, now, and Augustus Caesar has been dead for almost fifty years.

But since that day I have wondered, turning the question over and over in my mind: what could he have been afraid of? And what was he trying to do?

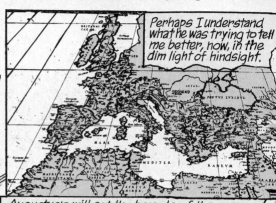

Perhaps I understand what he was trying to tell me better, now, in the dim light of hindsight.

Augustus's will set the bounds of the empire; forbade any further expansion.

And in his will Augustus also appointed Tiberius as his successor. Our divine rulers have, since then, been successively evil, mad, foolish, and--now--all three.

Perhaps he achieved his goal, perhaps not.

But still I persist in wondering: what was Augustus afraid of? Why did he wake in the night, screaming...?

AVGVSTVS

Why was he angry? Why was he scared?

I do not know his secret; and Augustus has taken it with him.

To Olympus.

Or to the grave.

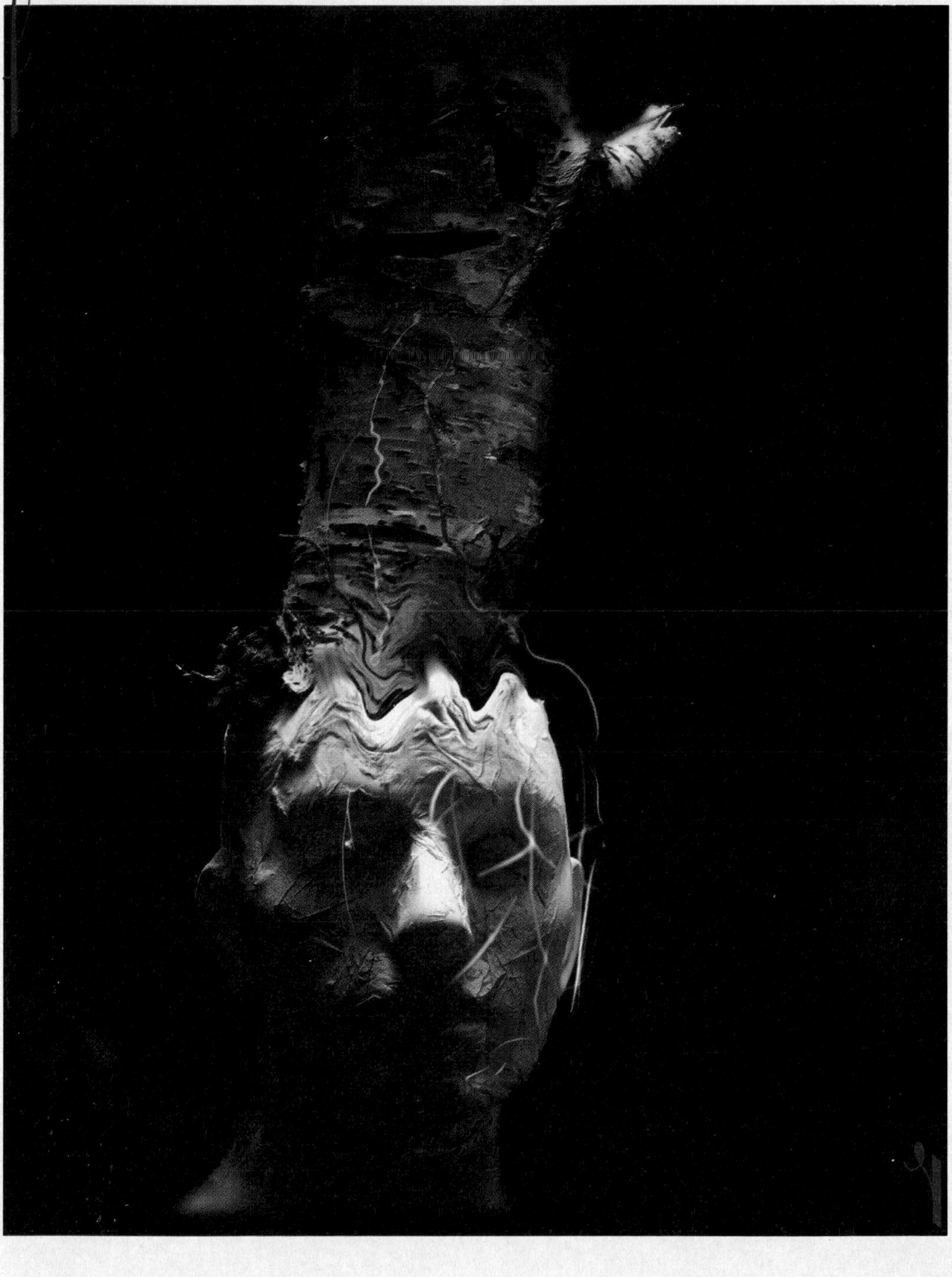

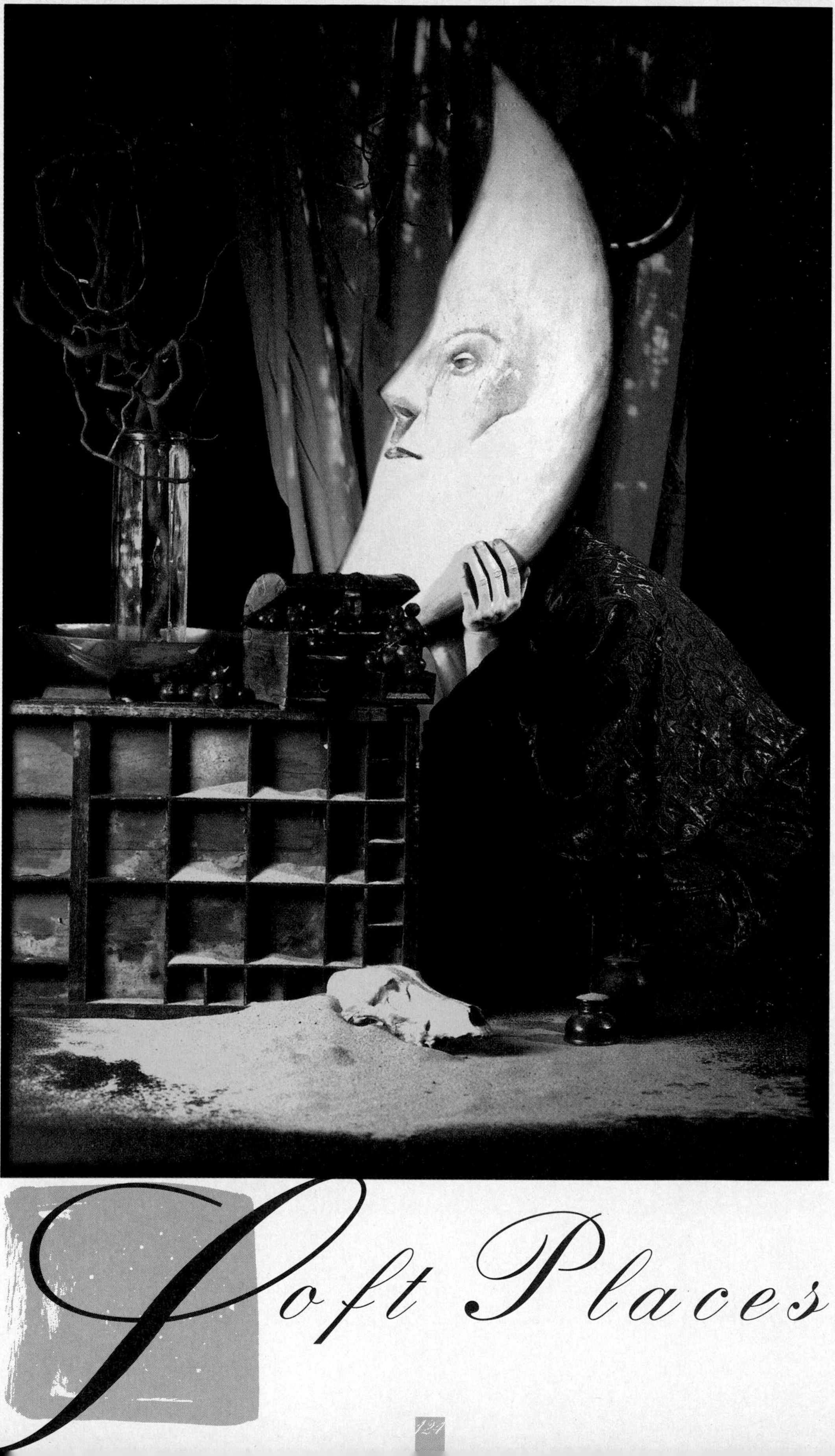

Soft Places

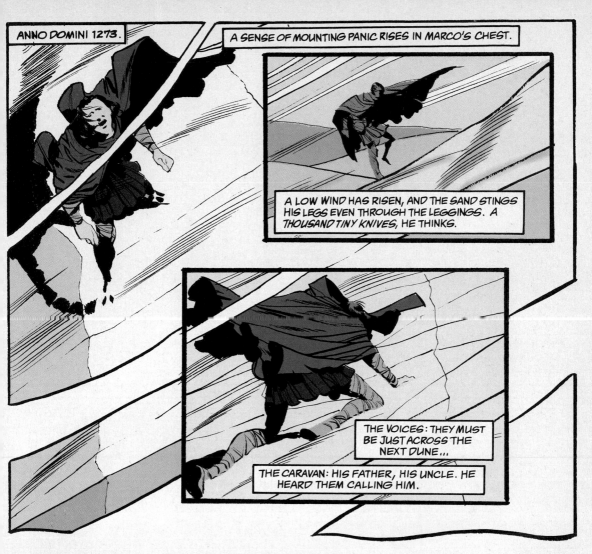

ANNO DOMINI 1273.

A SENSE OF MOUNTING PANIC RISES IN MARCO'S CHEST.

A LOW WIND HAS RISEN, AND THE SAND STINGS HIS LEGS EVEN THROUGH THE LEGGINGS. A *THOUSAND TINY KNIVES*, HE THINKS.

THE VOICES: THEY MUST BE JUST ACROSS THE NEXT DUNE...

THE CARAVAN: HIS FATHER, HIS UNCLE. HE HEARD THEM CALLING HIM.

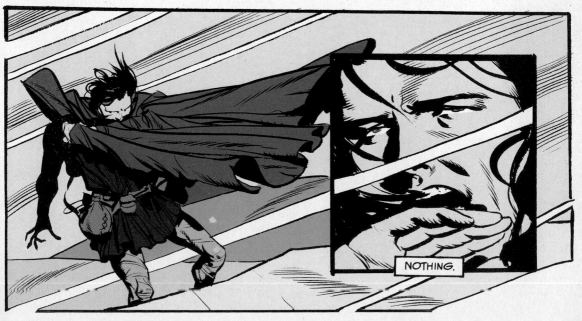

NOTHING.

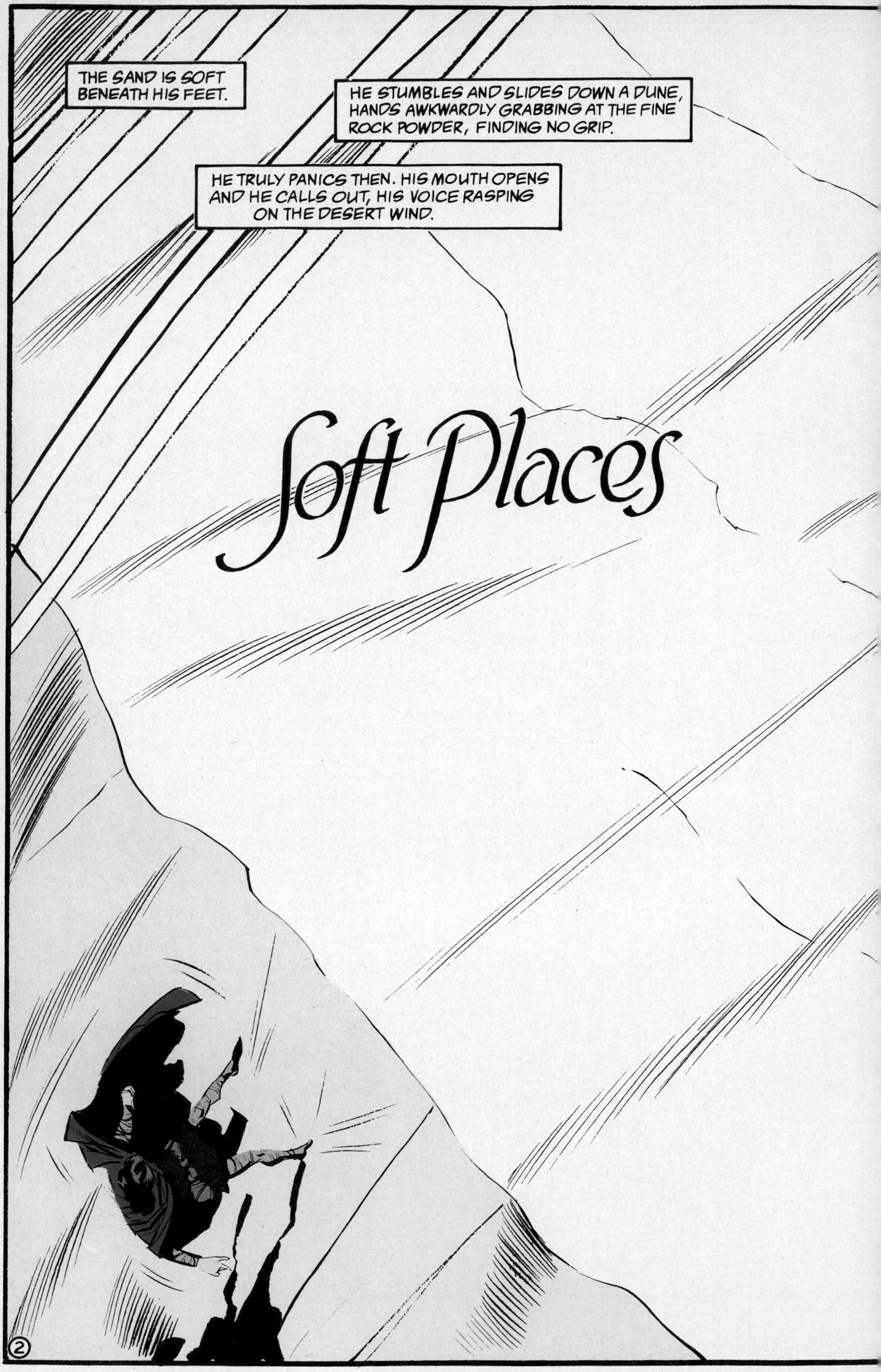
THE SAND IS SOFT BENEATH HIS FEET.
HE STUMBLES AND SLIDES DOWN A DUNE, HANDS AWKWARDLY GRABBING AT THE FINE ROCK POWDER, FINDING NO GRIP.
HE TRULY PANICS THEN. HIS MOUTH OPENS AND HE CALLS OUT, HIS VOICE RASPING ON THE DESERT WIND.
Soft Places
2

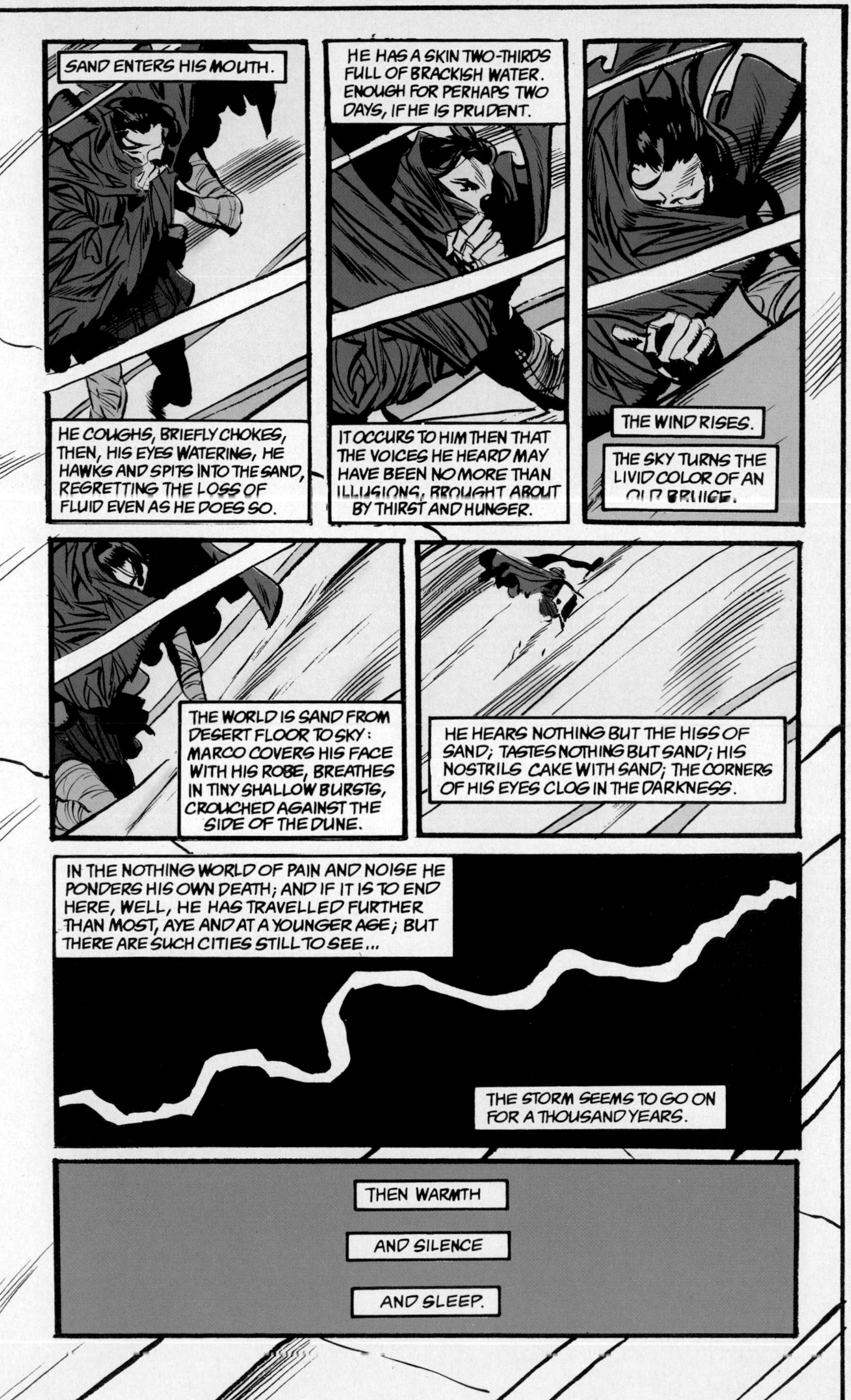
SAND ENTERS HIS MOUTH.
HE COUGHS, BRIEFLY CHOKES, THEN, HIS EYES WATERING, HE HAWKS AND SPITS INTO THE SAND, REGRETTING THE LOSS OF FLUID EVEN AS HE DOES SO.
HE HAS A SKIN TWO-THIRDS FULL OF BRACKISH WATER. ENOUGH FOR PERHAPS TWO DAYS, IF HE IS PRUDENT.
IT OCCURS TO HIM THEN THAT THE VOICES HE HEARD MAY HAVE BEEN NO MORE THAN ILLUSIONS, BROUGHT ABOUT BY THIRST AND HUNGER.
THE WIND RISES.
THE SKY TURNS THE LIVID COLOR OF AN OLD BRUISE.
THE WORLD IS SAND FROM DESERT FLOOR TO SKY: MARCO COVERS HIS FACE WITH HIS ROBE, BREATHES IN TINY SHALLOW BURSTS, CROUCHED AGAINST THE SIDE OF THE DUNE.
HE HEARS NOTHING BUT THE HISS OF SAND; TASTES NOTHING BUT SAND; HIS NOSTRILS CAKE WITH SAND; THE CORNERS OF HIS EYES CLOG IN THE DARKNESS.
IN THE NOTHING WORLD OF PAIN AND NOISE HE PONDERS HIS OWN DEATH; AND IF IT IS TO END HERE, WELL, HE HAS TRAVELLED FURTHER THAN MOST, AYE AND AT A YOUNGER AGE; BUT THERE ARE SUCH CITIES STILL TO SEE...
THE STORM SEEMS TO GO ON FOR A THOUSAND YEARS.
THEN WARMTH
AND SILENCE
AND SLEEP.
3

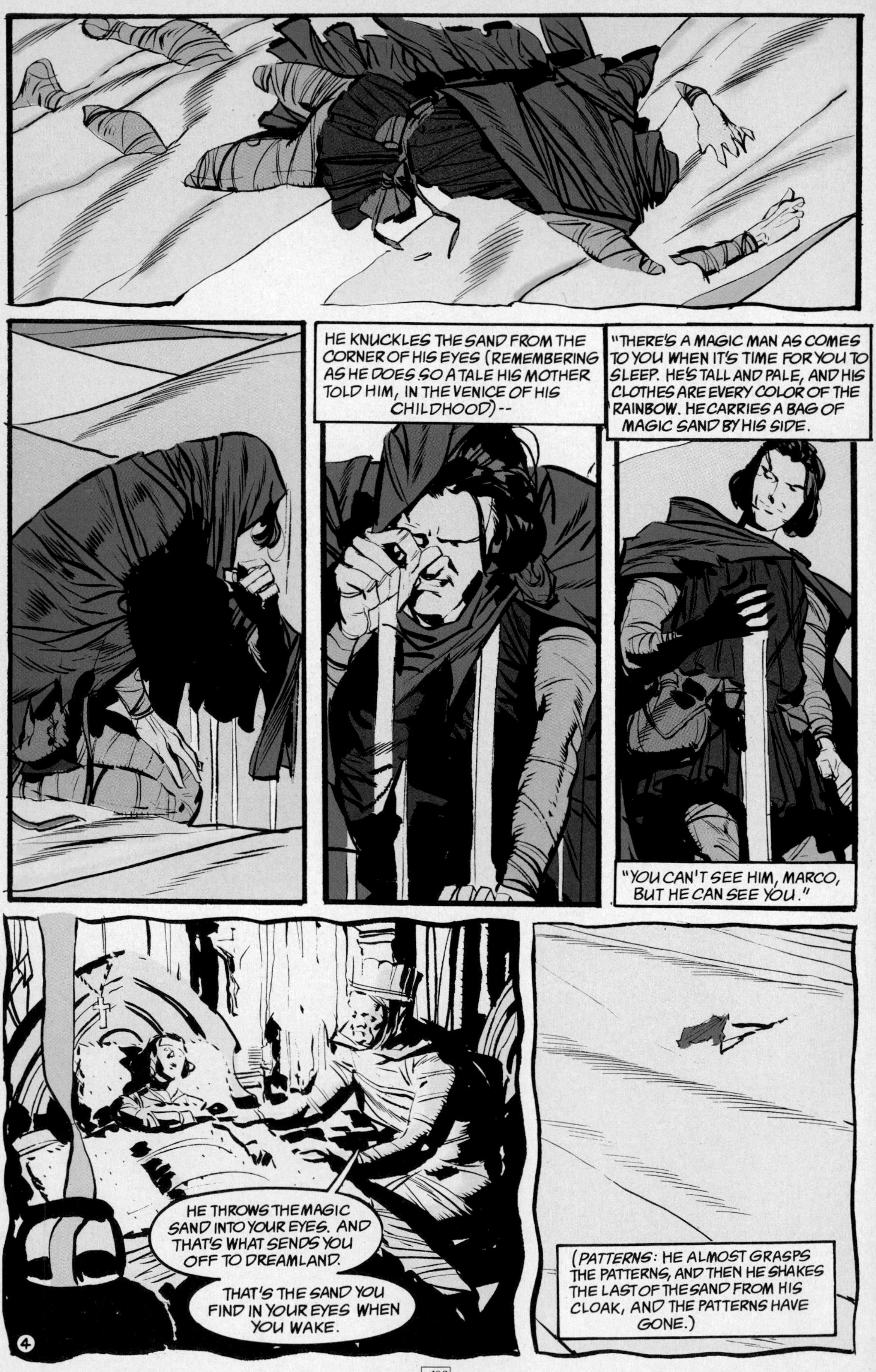
HE KNUCKLES THE SAND FROM THE CORNER OF HIS EYES (REMEMBERING AS HE DOES SO A TALE HIS MOTHER TOLD HIM, IN THE VENICE OF HIS CHILDHOOD)--
"THERE'S A MAGIC MAN AS COMES TO YOU WHEN IT'S TIME FOR YOU TO SLEEP. HE'S TALL AND PALE, AND HIS CLOTHES ARE EVERY COLOR OF THE RAINBOW. HE CARRIES A BAG OF MAGIC SAND BY HIS SIDE.
"YOU CAN'T SEE HIM, MARCO, BUT HE CAN SEE YOU."
HE THROWS THE MAGIC SAND INTO YOUR EYES. AND THAT'S WHAT SENDS YOU OFF TO DREAMLAND.
THAT'S THE SAND YOU FIND IN YOUR EYES WHEN YOU WAKE.
4
(PATTERNS: HE ALMOST GRASPS THE PATTERNS, AND THEN HE SHAKES THE LAST OF THE SAND FROM HIS CLOAK, AND THE PATTERNS HAVE GONE.)

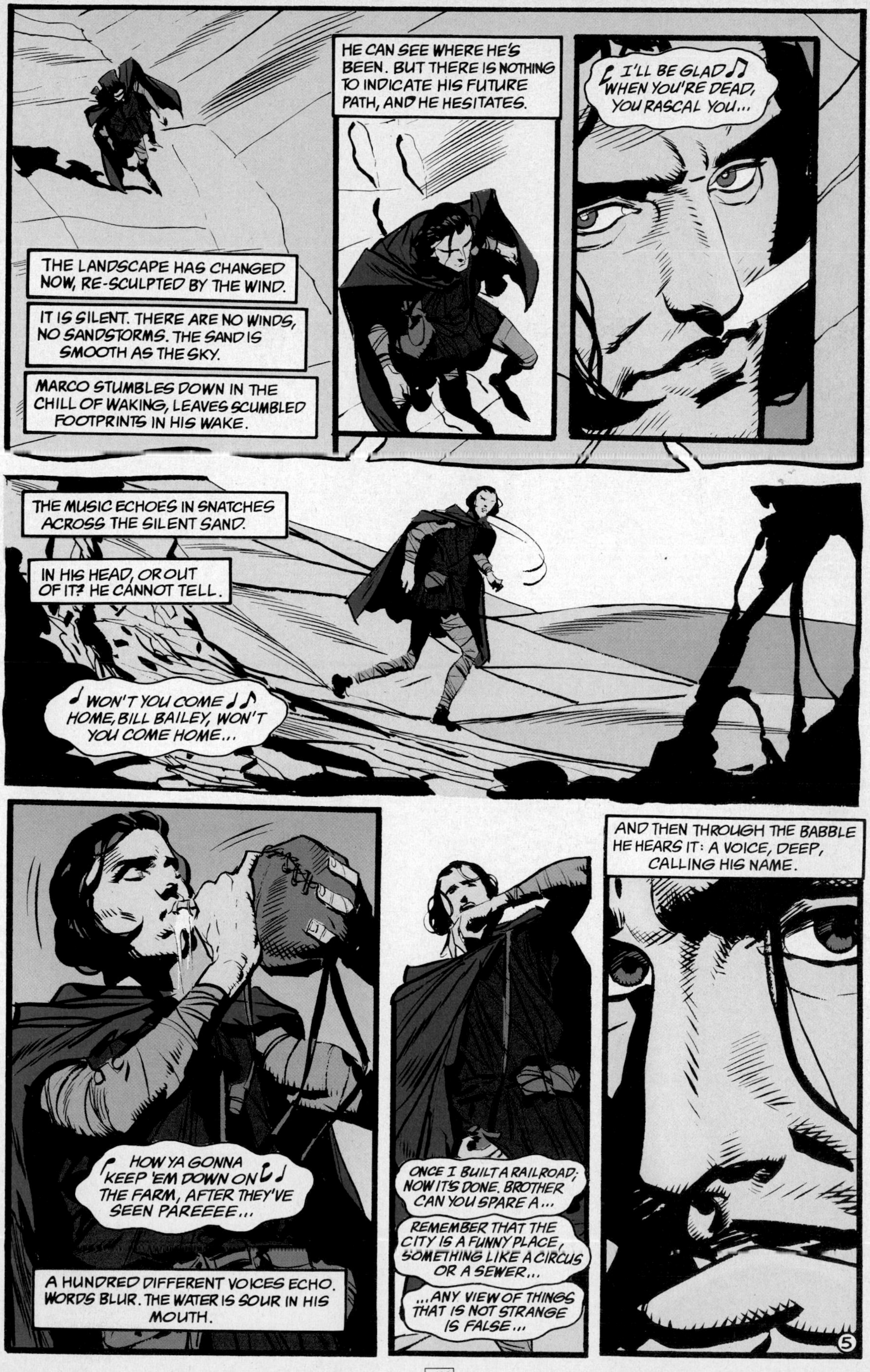
THE LANDSCAPE HAS CHANGED NOW, RE-SCULPTED BY THE WIND.
IT IS SILENT. THERE ARE NO WINDS, NO SANDSTORMS. THE SAND IS SMOOTH AS THE SKY.
MARCO STUMBLES DOWN IN THE CHILL OF WAKING, LEAVES SCUMBLED FOOTPRINTS IN HIS WAKE.
HE CAN SEE WHERE HE'S BEEN. BUT THERE IS NOTHING TO INDICATE HIS FUTURE PATH, AND HE HESITATES.
♪ I'LL BE GLAD ♫ WHEN YOU'RE DEAD, YOU RASCAL YOU...
THE MUSIC ECHOES IN SNATCHES ACROSS THE SILENT SAND.
IN HIS HEAD, OR OUT OF IT? HE CANNOT TELL.
♩ WON'T YOU COME ♩♪ HOME, BILL BAILEY, WON'T YOU COME HOME...
♪ HOW YA GONNA KEEP 'EM DOWN ON ♫♩ THE FARM, AFTER THEY'VE SEEN PAREEEE...
A HUNDRED DIFFERENT VOICES ECHO. WORDS BLUR. THE WATER IS SOUR IN HIS MOUTH.
ONCE I BUILT A RAILROAD; NOW IT'S DONE. BROTHER CAN YOU SPARE A...
REMEMBER THAT THE CITY IS A FUNNY PLACE, SOMETHING LIKE A CIRCUS OR A SEWER...
...ANY VIEW OF THINGS THAT IS NOT STRANGE IS FALSE...
AND THEN THROUGH THE BABBLE HE HEARS IT: A VOICE, DEEP, CALLING HIS NAME.
5

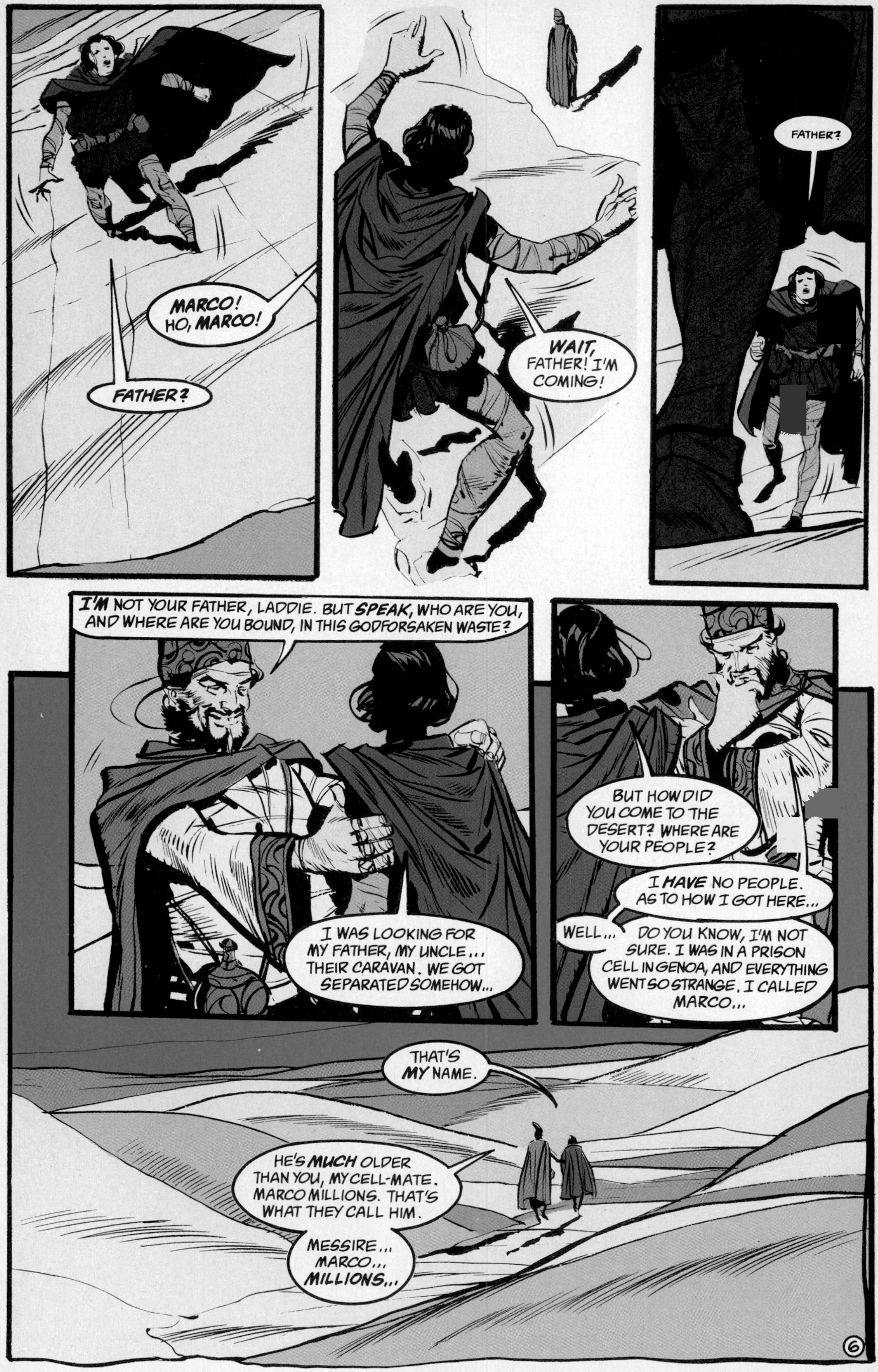
MARCO! HO, MARCO!
FATHER?
WAIT, FATHER! I'M COMING!
FATHER?
I'M NOT YOUR FATHER, LADDIE. BUT SPEAK, WHO ARE YOU, AND WHERE ARE YOU BOUND, IN THIS GODFORSAKEN WASTE?
I WAS LOOKING FOR MY FATHER, MY UNCLE... ...THEIR CARAVAN. WE GOT SEPARATED SOMEHOW...
BUT HOW DID YOU COME TO THE DESERT? WHERE ARE YOUR PEOPLE?
I HAVE NO PEOPLE. AS TO HOW I GOT HERE...
WELL...
DO YOU KNOW, I'M NOT SURE. I WAS IN A PRISON CELL IN GENOA, AND EVERYTHING WENT SO STRANGE. I CALLED MARCO...
THAT'S MY NAME.
HE'S MUCH OLDER THAN YOU, MY CELL-MATE. MARCO MILLIONS. THAT'S WHAT THEY CALL HIM.
MESSIRE... MARCO... MILLIONS...
6

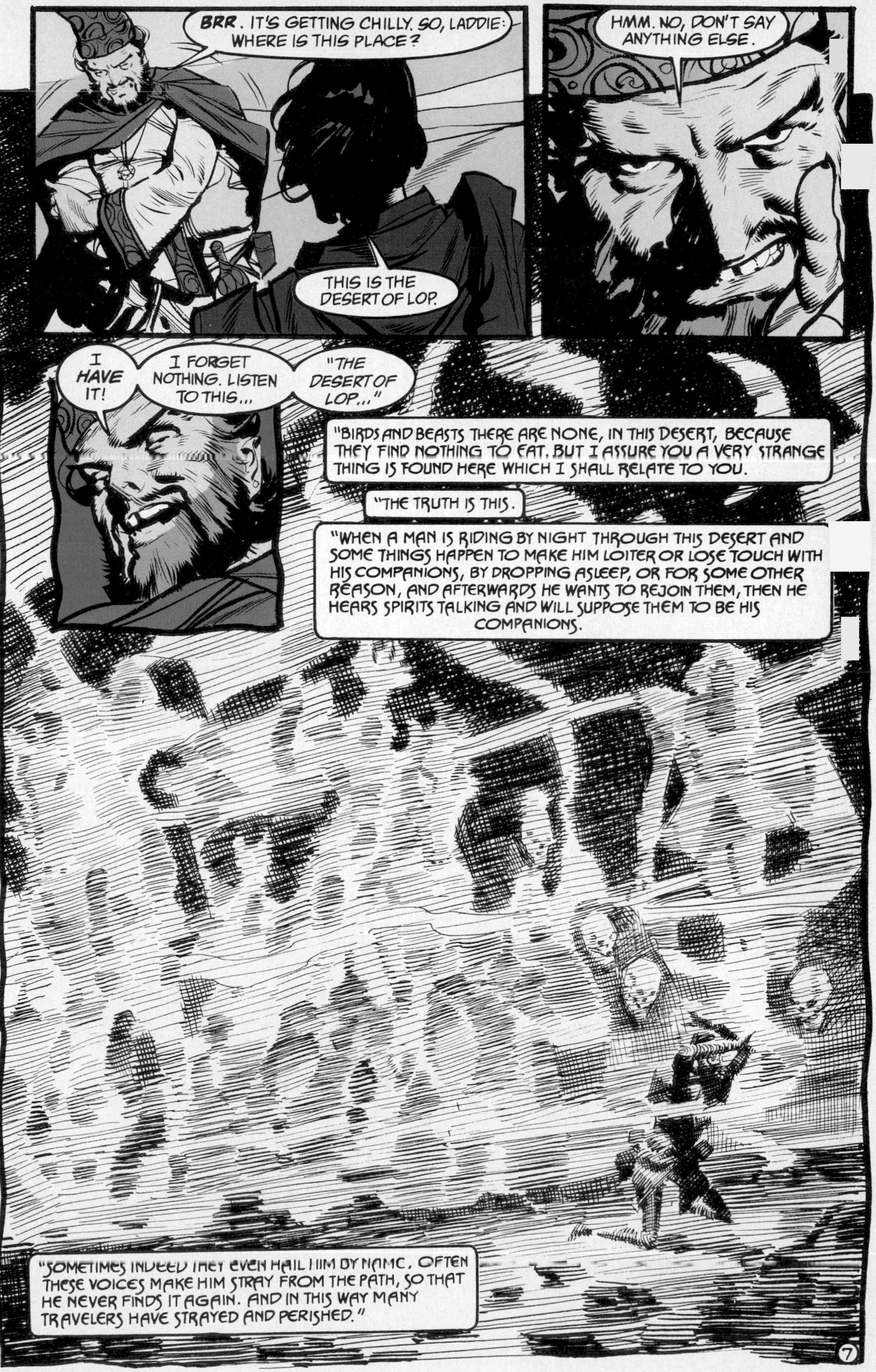
BRR. IT'S GETTING CHILLY. SO, LADDIE: WHERE IS THIS PLACE?
THIS IS THE DESERT OF LOP.
HMM. NO, DON'T SAY ANYTHING ELSE.
I HAVE IT!
I FORGET NOTHING. LISTEN TO THIS...
"THE DESERT OF LOP..."
"BIRDS AND BEASTS THERE ARE NONE, IN THIS DESERT, BECAUSE THEY FIND NOTHING TO EAT. BUT I ASSURE YOU A VERY STRANGE THING IS FOUND HERE WHICH I SHALL RELATE TO YOU.
"THE TRUTH IS THIS.
"WHEN A MAN IS RIDING BY NIGHT THROUGH THIS DESERT AND SOME THINGS HAPPEN TO MAKE HIM LOITER OR LOSE TOUCH WITH HIS COMPANIONS, BY DROPPING ASLEEP, OR FOR SOME OTHER REASON, AND AFTERWARDS HE WANTS TO REJOIN THEM, THEN HE HEARS SPIRITS TALKING AND WILL SUPPOSE THEM TO BE HIS COMPANIONS.
"SOMETIMES INDEED THEY EVEN HAIL HIM BY NAME. OFTEN THESE VOICES MAKE HIM STRAY FROM THE PATH, SO THAT HE NEVER FINDS IT AGAIN. AND IN THIS WAY MANY TRAVELERS HAVE STRAYED AND PERISHED."
7

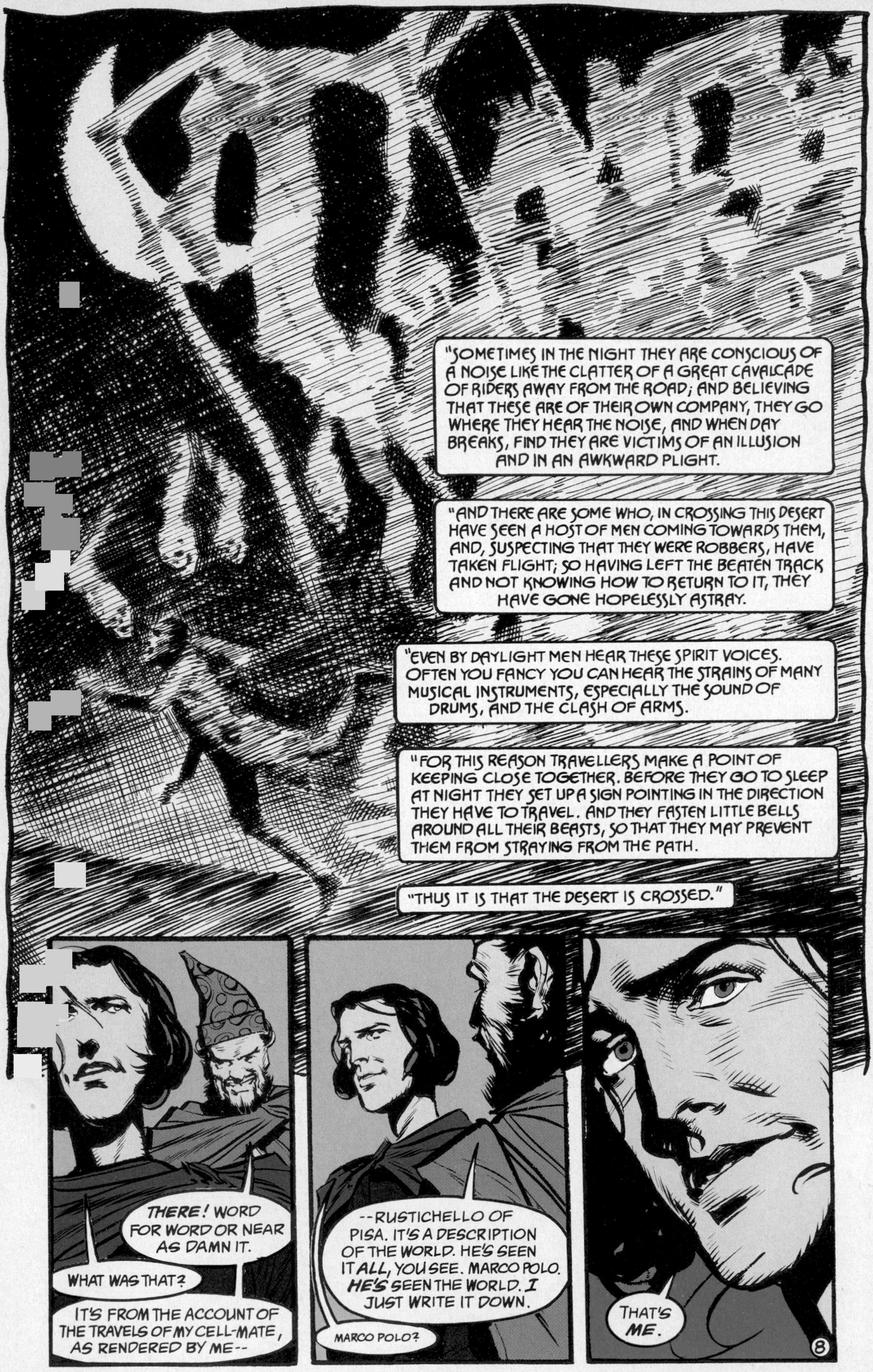
"SOMETIMES IN THE NIGHT THEY ARE CONSCIOUS OF A NOISE LIKE THE CLATTER OF A GREAT CAVALCADE OF RIDERS AWAY FROM THE ROAD; AND BELIEVING THAT THESE ARE OF THEIR OWN COMPANY, THEY GO WHERE THEY HEAR THE NOISE, AND WHEN DAY BREAKS, FIND THEY ARE VICTIMS OF AN ILLUSION AND IN AN AWKWARD PLIGHT.
"AND THERE ARE SOME WHO, IN CROSSING THIS DESERT HAVE SEEN A HOST OF MEN COMING TOWARDS THEM, AND, SUSPECTING THAT THEY WERE ROBBERS, HAVE TAKEN FLIGHT; SO HAVING LEFT THE BEATEN TRACK AND NOT KNOWING HOW TO RETURN TO IT, THEY HAVE GONE HOPELESSLY ASTRAY.
"EVEN BY DAYLIGHT MEN HEAR THESE SPIRIT VOICES. OFTEN YOU FANCY YOU CAN HEAR THE STRAINS OF MANY MUSICAL INSTRUMENTS, ESPECIALLY THE SOUND OF DRUMS, AND THE CLASH OF ARMS.
"FOR THIS REASON TRAVELLERS MAKE A POINT OF KEEPING CLOSE TOGETHER. BEFORE THEY GO TO SLEEP AT NIGHT THEY SET UP A SIGN POINTING IN THE DIRECTION THEY HAVE TO TRAVEL. AND THEY FASTEN LITTLE BELLS AROUND ALL THEIR BEASTS, SO THAT THEY MAY PREVENT THEM FROM STRAYING FROM THE PATH.
"THUS IT IS THAT THE DESERT IS CROSSED."
THERE! WORD FOR WORD OR NEAR AS DAMN IT.
WHAT WAS THAT?
IT'S FROM THE ACCOUNT OF THE TRAVELS OF MY CELL-MATE, AS RENDERED BY ME--
--RUSTICHELLO OF PISA. IT'S A DESCRIPTION OF THE WORLD. HE'S SEEN IT *ALL*, YOU SEE. MARCO POLO. *HE'S* SEEN THE WORLD. *I* JUST WRITE IT DOWN.
MARCO POLO?
THAT'S *ME*.
8

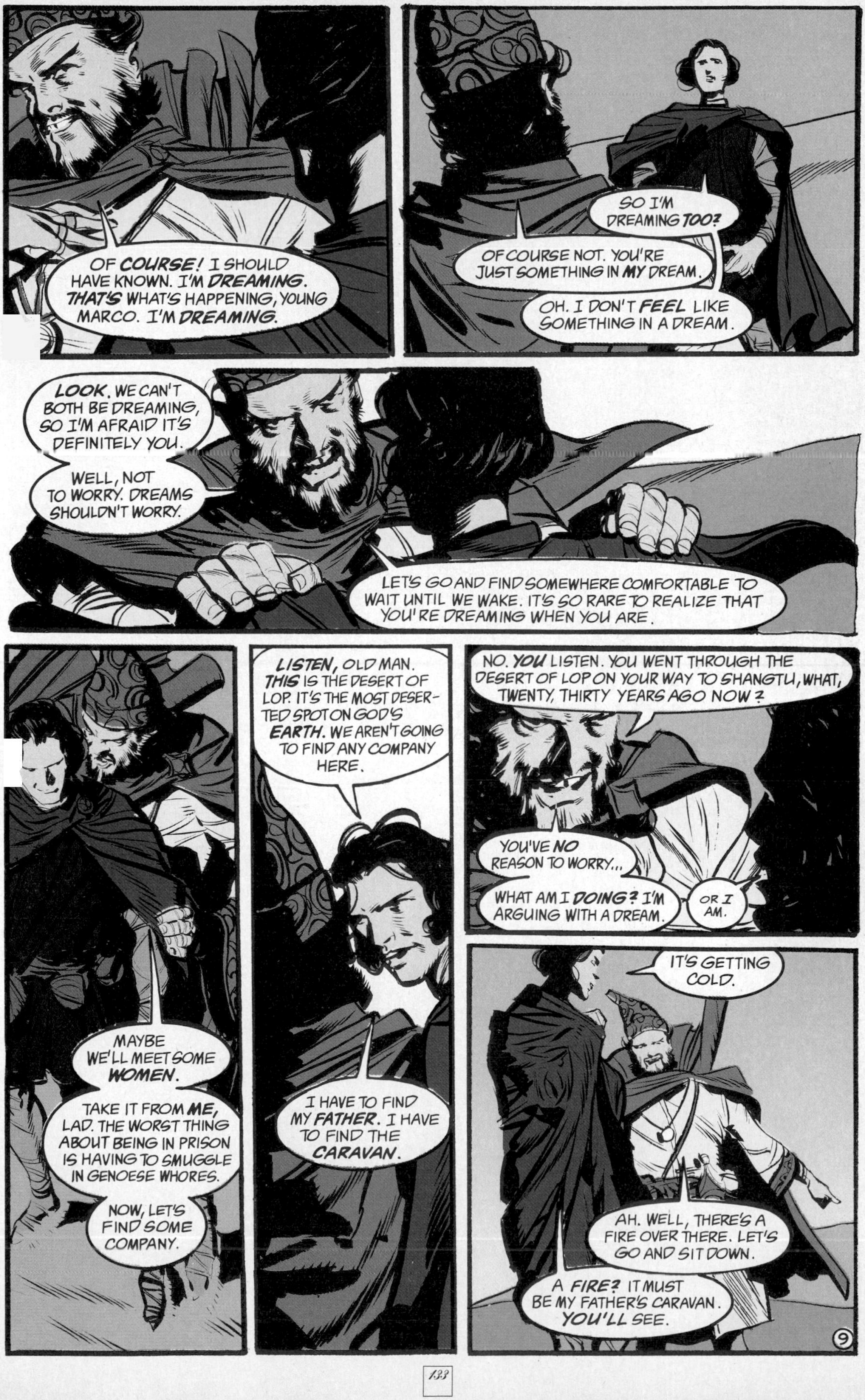

OF COURSE! I SHOULD HAVE KNOWN. I'M DREAMING. THAT'S WHAT'S HAPPENING, YOUNG MARCO. I'M DREAMING.
SO I'M DREAMING TOO?
OF COURSE NOT. YOU'RE JUST SOMETHING IN MY DREAM.
OH. I DON'T FEEL LIKE SOMETHING IN A DREAM.
LOOK. WE CAN'T BOTH BE DREAMING, SO I'M AFRAID IT'S DEFINITELY YOU.
WELL, NOT TO WORRY. DREAMS SHOULDN'T WORRY.
LET'S GO AND FIND SOMEWHERE COMFORTABLE TO WAIT UNTIL WE WAKE. IT'S SO RARE TO REALIZE THAT YOU'RE DREAMING WHEN YOU ARE.
MAYBE WE'LL MEET SOME WOMEN.
TAKE IT FROM ME, LAD. THE WORST THING ABOUT BEING IN PRISON IS HAVING TO SMUGGLE IN GENOESE WHORES.
NOW, LET'S FIND SOME COMPANY.
LISTEN, OLD MAN. THIS IS THE DESERT OF LOP. IT'S THE MOST DESERTED SPOT ON GOD'S EARTH. WE AREN'T GOING TO FIND ANY COMPANY HERE.
I HAVE TO FIND MY FATHER. I HAVE TO FIND THE CARAVAN.
NO. YOU LISTEN. YOU WENT THROUGH THE DESERT OF LOP ON YOUR WAY TO SHANGTU, WHAT, TWENTY, THIRTY YEARS AGO NOW?
YOU'VE NO REASON TO WORRY...
WHAT AM I DOING? I'M ARGUING WITH A DREAM.
OR I AM.
IT'S GETTING COLD.
AH. WELL, THERE'S A FIRE OVER THERE. LET'S GO AND SIT DOWN.
A FIRE? IT MUST BE MY FATHER'S CARAVAN. YOU'LL SEE.
9

HOLA! COME AND SIT DOWN, FRIENDS. COME AND WARM YOURSELVES.

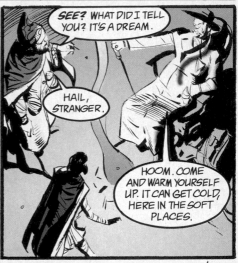

SEE? WHAT DID I TELL YOU? IT'S A DREAM.

HAIL, STRANGER.

HOOM. COME AND WARM YOURSELF UP. IT CAN GET COLD, HERE IN THE SOFT PLACES.

EXCUSE ME, SIR. MY FATHER, AND MY UNCLE. NICOLO AND MAFFEO POLO. THEY ARE WITH A CARAVAN. THEY ARE TRADERS, MERCHANTS.

HAVE YOU SEEN THEM?

I HAVEN'T SEEN ANYONE. I CAME OUT TO THE SOFT PLACES TO THINK. TO GET *AWAY* FROM MYSELF.

MESSIRE, HAVE YOU WINE?

WINE! A RUBY RED BEAUJOLAIS! A SWEET, TOPAZ-COLORED TOKAY! WHAT A *WONDERFUL* IDEA!

INDEED, WE WILL DRINK WINE, AND YOU WILL TELL ME YOUR STORIES. AND PERHAPS OTHER TRAVELLERS, EQUALLY AS CONGENIAL, WILL ARRIVE, AND WE WILL ENTERTAIN THEM, TOO.

10

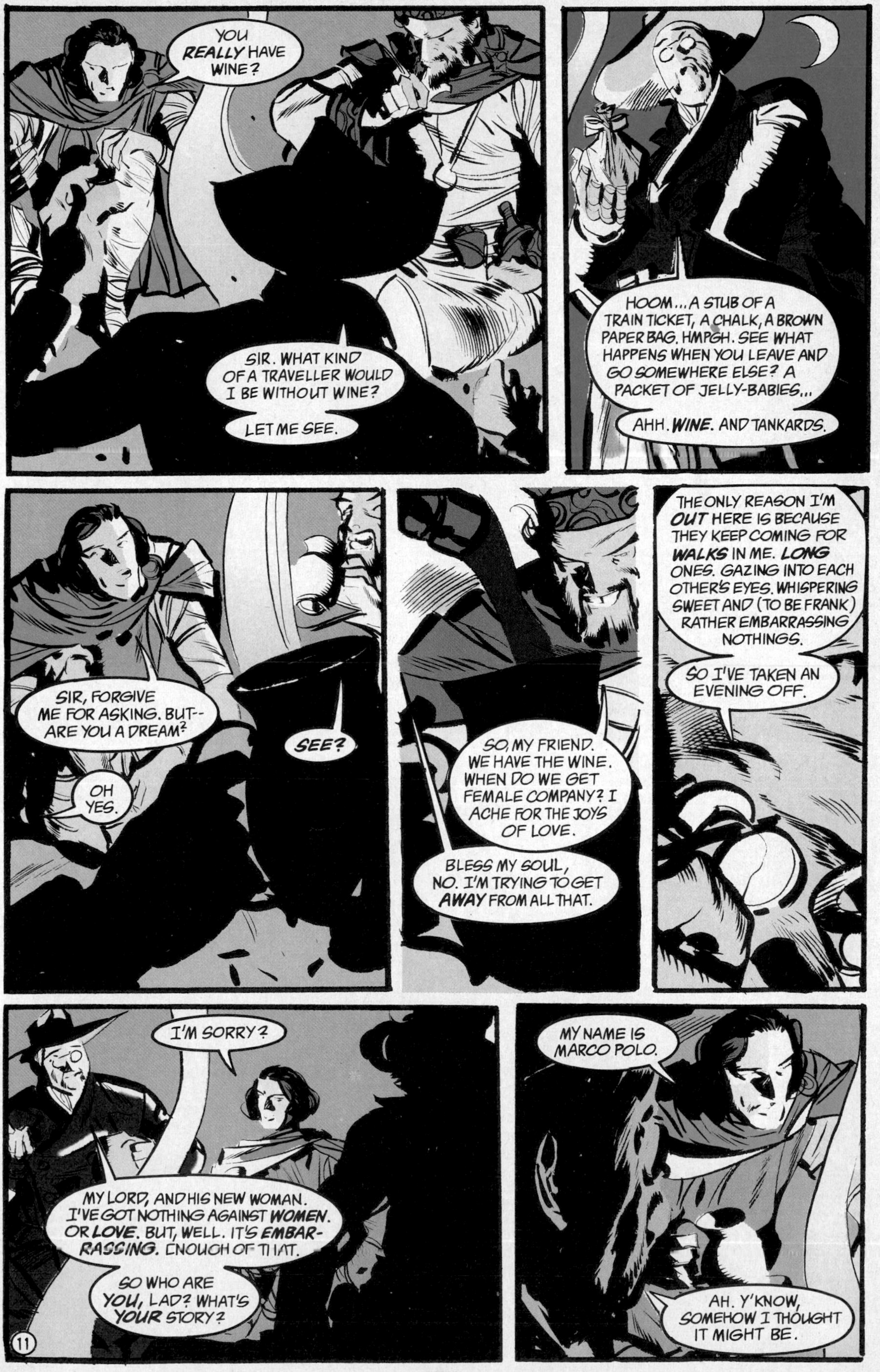
YOU REALLY HAVE WINE?
SIR. WHAT KIND OF A TRAVELLER WOULD I BE WITHOUT WINE?
LET ME SEE.
HOOM... A STUB OF A TRAIN TICKET, A CHALK, A BROWN PAPER BAG. HMPGH. SEE WHAT HAPPENS WHEN YOU LEAVE AND GO SOMEWHERE ELSE? A PACKET OF JELLY-BABIES...
AHH. WINE. AND TANKARDS.
SIR, FORGIVE ME FOR ASKING. BUT-- ARE YOU A DREAM?
OH YES.
SEE?
SO, MY FRIEND. WE HAVE THE WINE. WHEN DO WE GET FEMALE COMPANY? I ACHE FOR THE JOYS OF LOVE.
BLESS MY SOUL, NO. I'M TRYING TO GET AWAY FROM ALL THAT.
THE ONLY REASON I'M OUT HERE IS BECAUSE THEY KEEP COMING FOR WALKS IN ME. LONG ONES. GAZING INTO EACH OTHER'S EYES. WHISPERING SWEET AND (TO BE FRANK) RATHER EMBARRASSING NOTHINGS.
SO I'VE TAKEN AN EVENING OFF.
I'M SORRY?
MY LORD, AND HIS NEW WOMAN. I'VE GOT NOTHING AGAINST WOMEN. OR LOVE. BUT, WELL. IT'S EMBARRASSING. ENOUGH OF THAT.
SO WHO ARE YOU, LAD? WHAT'S YOUR STORY?
11
MY NAME IS MARCO POLO.
AH. Y'KNOW, SOMEHOW I THOUGHT IT MIGHT BE.

WHEN I WAS... VERY YOUNG... MY FATHER AND MY UNCLE WERE TRAVELLING IN CONSTANTINOPLE.

AS WARS BROKE OUT BEHIND THEM, THEY WERE FORCED TO CONTINUE ON TO THE EAST INTO UNCHARTED TERRITORY.

EVENTUALLY THEY REACHED THE COURT OF THE GREAT KING. KUBILAI KHAN HIMSELF, IN FAR CATHAY.

NOW, WHILE THE KHAN HIMSELF WAS A HEATHEN AND AN IDOLATER, HE LOOKED KINDLY UPON THE CHRISTIAN FAITH.

MY FATHER WISHED TO CONVERT THE KHAN TO THE TRUE FAITH-- AND THUS CONVERT ALL HIS EMPIRE, WHICH EXTENDS FROM THE LANDS OF NIGHT IN THE NORTH TO THE UTTERMOST ISLANDS OF THE EAST.

IMAGINE HOW MANY WOULD BE DRAWN INTO THE FAITH AT A STROKE, WHAT THAT WOULD DO TO THE WORLD...

"BUT THE KHAN HAS IDOLATER PRIESTS, WHO WORK MIRACLES FOR HIM. THEY ENSURE THAT IT IS ALWAYS SUMMER ABOVE HIS PALACE, THOUGH IT RAINS AND STORMS NEARBY.

"THEY CAUSE HIS FOOD AND WINE TO FLY INTO HIS HAND, SO NEVER A DROP IS SPILLED, AND NEVER A MAN TOUCHES THEM.

"'LOOK AT THEM,' SAID THE KHAN TO MY FATHER. 'THEY HAVE POWER EVEN *I* FEAR.'

"'SO THIS I SAY: GO BACK TO YOUR POPE AND TELL HIM TO SEND ME ONE HUNDRED CHRISTIAN MIRACLE WORKERS, WHO WILL SHOW MY PRIESTS THAT YOUR CHRIST CAN WORK MIRACLES AS GREAT AS THOSE OF THEIR GAUTAMA BUDDHA.'"

GOOD GRACIOUS. SO WHAT HAPPENED?

WELL, THEY CAME BACK. I WAS FIFTEEN. I CAN'T HAVE BEEN MORE THAN FOUR WHEN THEY LEFT.

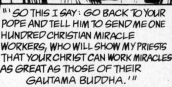

≥MUUUURP.≤ FRIEND? HAVE YOU MORE WINE?

⑫

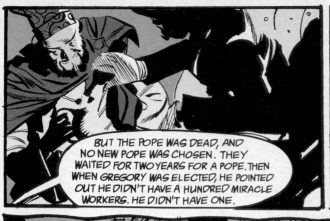

BUT THE POPE WAS DEAD, AND NO NEW POPE WAS CHOSEN. THEY WAITED FOR TWO YEARS FOR A POPE. THEN WHEN GREGORY WAS ELECTED, HE POINTED OUT HE DIDN'T HAVE A HUNDRED MIRACLE WORKERS. HE DIDN'T HAVE ONE.

THERE'S A TERRIBLY NICE FRANCISCAN IN SEVENTEENTH CENTURY ASSISI WHO CAN FLY. IQ OF SIXTY, AND PERHAPS A LITTLE TOO HEAVILY INTO SELF-MUTILATION, BUT HE CAN HONESTLY FLY.

SAINT JOSEPH OF COPERTINO. BIT AFTER YOUR TIME, HOOM. SORRY. PRAY CONTINUE.

"EVENTUALLY, WHEN I WAS SIXTEEN, WE SET OFF WITH TWO ELDERLY DOMINICAN PRIESTS."

"COULD *THEY* DO MIRACLES?"

"WELL, NOT SO YOU'D NOTICE. ONE OF THEM HAD A LITTLE THING HE DID WITH A CUP AND SOME BALLS, BUT IT WASN'T VERY IMPRESSIVE. THEY BOTH GAVE UP BEFORE WE REACHED SYRIA.

"THEY GOT SCARED. WE WENT ON."

WE'VE BEEN TRAVELLING FOR ALMOST TWO YEARS, NOW. AND KUBILAI KHAN HIMSELF WAITS ON THE OTHER SIDE OF THIS DESERT.

I HAVE SEEN *SUCH* CITIES...

YES! THAT WAS YOUR GENIUS!

BEING ABLE TO *DESCRIBE* CITIES. NOT JUST THE LAND, OR THE TRADE, BUT THE *SOUL* OF THE CITY. WHAT MADE IT *UNIQUELY* ITSELF...

KUBILAI KHAN STAYED IN HIS SUMMER PALACE IN SUMMER, AND HIS WINTER PALACE IN WINTER, LIKE A SPIDER, EDGING FROM ONE SIDE OF THE WEB TO ANOTHER.

AND *YOU* WENT OUT TO ALL THE CITIES IN HIS EMPIRE AND CAME HOME AND DESCRIBED THEM TO HIM.

⊰ UUURP. ⊱ I KNOW THE STORY, YOU SEE. I'M WRITING IT ALL DOWN FOR YOU. SO IT'LL BE REMEMBERED.

13

HOOM. *FOOD.* LET'S SEE WHAT WE CAN MANAGE.

WELL, THERE ARE JELLY BABIES. A BIT STICKY, BUT QUITE PALATABLE.

AND -- *GOOD LORD* -- SANDWICHES! I DO BELIEVE -- YES! -- CHEESE AND PICKLE.

SIR? I'M HUNGRY. HAVE YOU ANY FOOD?

HERE YOU GO.

GREAT LORD. MAY WE SPEAK TO YOU?

HOOM. I DON'T SEE WHY NOT.

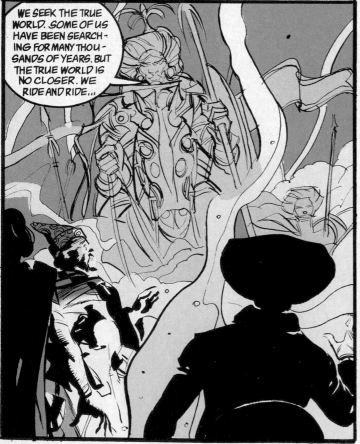

WE SEEK THE TRUE WORLD. SOME OF US HAVE BEEN SEARCH- ING FOR MANY THOU- SANDS OF YEARS. BUT THE TRUE WORLD IS NO CLOSER. WE RIDE AND RIDE...

I FEAR YOUR BUSINESS IS NOT WITH ME, FRIEND, BUT WITH MY MASTER.

14

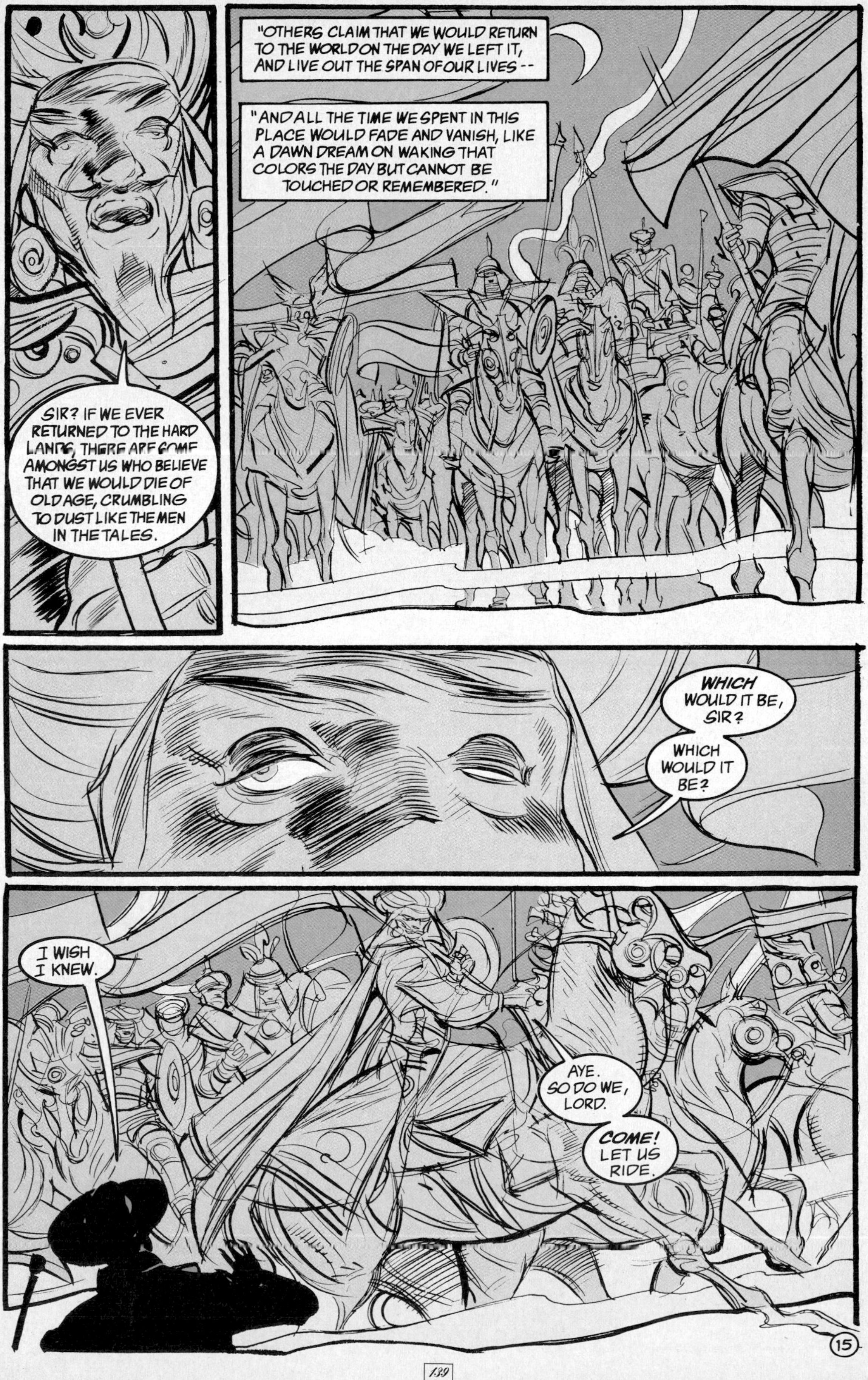

"OTHERS CLAIM THAT WE WOULD RETURN TO THE WORLD ON THE DAY WE LEFT IT, AND LIVE OUT THE SPAN OF OUR LIVES --
"AND ALL THE TIME WE SPENT IN THIS PLACE WOULD FADE AND VANISH, LIKE A DAWN DREAM ON WAKING THAT COLORS THE DAY BUT CANNOT BE TOUCHED OR REMEMBERED."
SIR? IF WE EVER RETURNED TO THE HARD LANDS, THERE ARE SOME AMONGST US WHO BELIEVE THAT WE WOULD DIE OF OLD AGE, CRUMBLING TO DUST LIKE THE MEN IN THE TALES.
WHICH WOULD IT BE, SIR?
WHICH WOULD IT BE?
I WISH I KNEW.
AYE. SO DO WE, LORD.
COME! LET US RIDE.
15

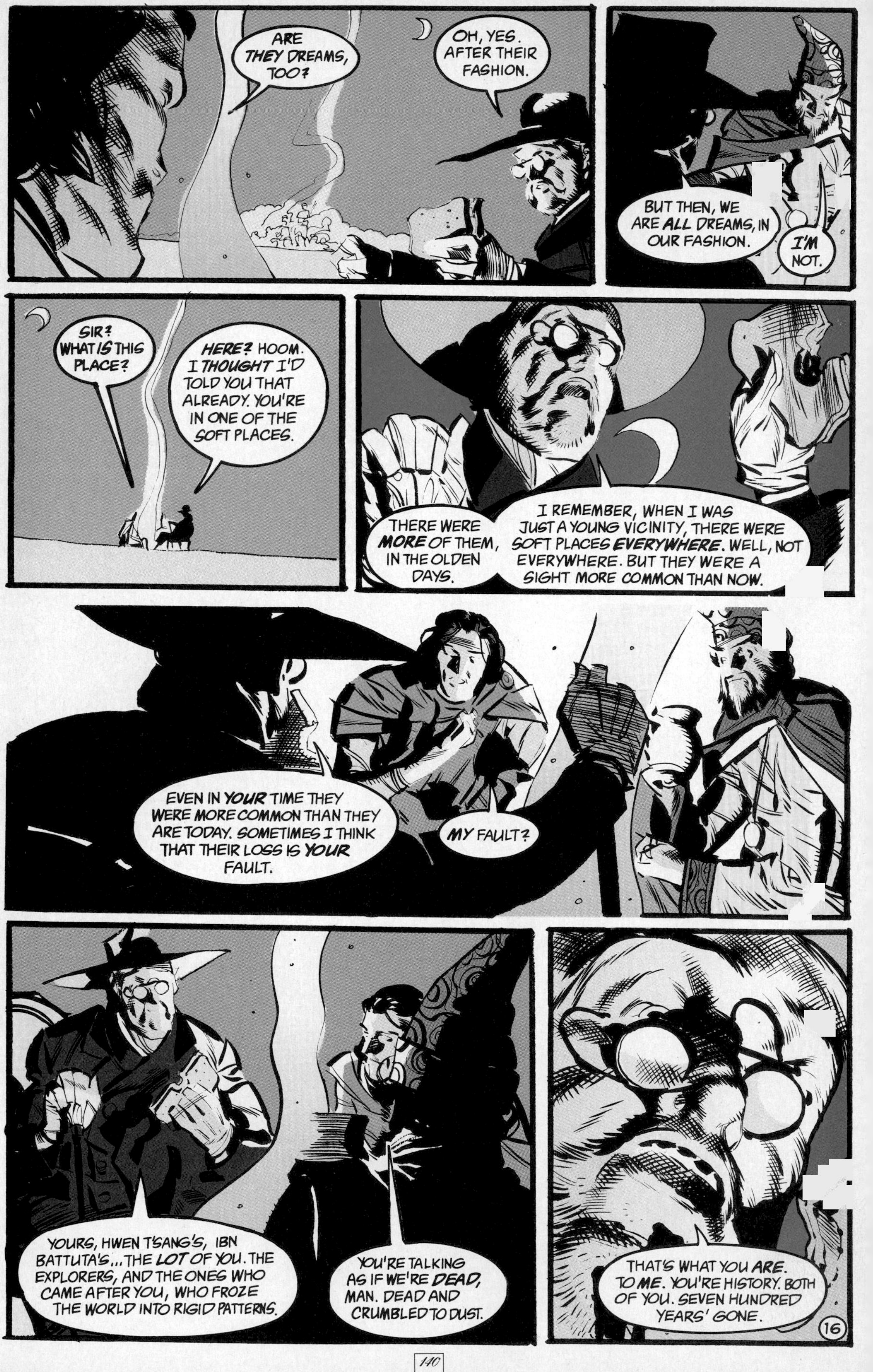
ARE THEY DREAMS, TOO?
OH, YES. AFTER THEIR FASHION.
BUT THEN, WE ARE ALL DREAMS, IN OUR FASHION.
I'M NOT.
SIR? WHAT IS THIS PLACE?
HERE? HOOM. I THOUGHT I'D TOLD YOU THAT ALREADY. YOU'RE IN ONE OF THE SOFT PLACES.
THERE WERE MORE OF THEM, IN THE OLDEN DAYS.
I REMEMBER, WHEN I WAS JUST A YOUNG VICINITY, THERE WERE SOFT PLACES EVERYWHERE. WELL, NOT EVERYWHERE. BUT THEY WERE A SIGHT MORE COMMON THAN NOW.
EVEN IN YOUR TIME THEY WERE MORE COMMON THAN THEY ARE TODAY. SOMETIMES I THINK THAT THEIR LOSS IS YOUR FAULT.
MY FAULT?
YOURS, HWEN T'SANG'S, IBN BATTUTA'S... THE LOT OF YOU. THE EXPLORERS, AND THE ONES WHO CAME AFTER YOU, WHO FROZE THE WORLD INTO RIGID PATTERNS.
YOU'RE TALKING AS IF WE'RE DEAD, MAN. DEAD AND CRUMBLED TO DUST.
THAT'S WHAT YOU ARE. TO ME. YOU'RE HISTORY. BOTH OF YOU. SEVEN HUNDRED YEARS' GONE.
16

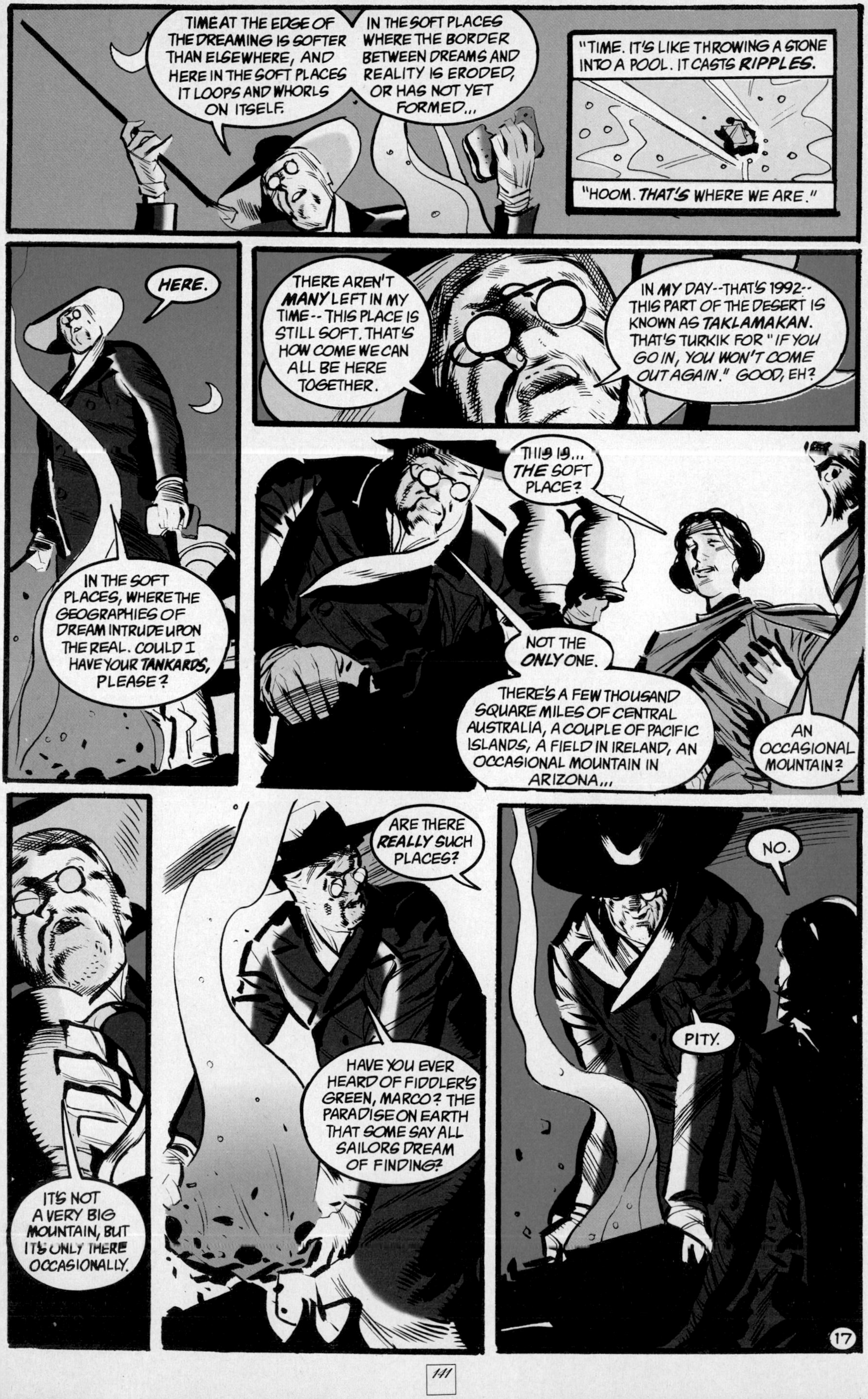

TIME AT THE EDGE OF THE DREAMING IS SOFTER THAN ELSEWHERE, AND HERE IN THE SOFT PLACES IT LOOPS AND WHORLS ON ITSELF.
IN THE SOFT PLACES WHERE THE BORDER BETWEEN DREAMS AND REALITY IS ERODED, OR HAS NOT YET FORMED...
"TIME. IT'S LIKE THROWING A STONE INTO A POOL. IT CASTS RIPPLES.
"HOOM. THAT'S WHERE WE ARE."
HERE.
IN THE SOFT PLACES, WHERE THE GEOGRAPHIES OF DREAM INTRUDE UPON THE REAL. COULD I HAVE YOUR TANKARDS, PLEASE?
THERE AREN'T MANY LEFT IN MY TIME -- THIS PLACE IS STILL SOFT. THAT'S HOW COME WE CAN ALL BE HERE TOGETHER.
IN MY DAY--THAT'S 1992-- THIS PART OF THE DESERT IS KNOWN AS TAKLAMAKAN. THAT'S TURKIK FOR "IF YOU GO IN, YOU WON'T COME OUT AGAIN." GOOD, EH?
THIS IS... THE SOFT PLACE?
NOT THE ONLY ONE.
THERE'S A FEW THOUSAND SQUARE MILES OF CENTRAL AUSTRALIA, A COUPLE OF PACIFIC ISLANDS, A FIELD IN IRELAND, AN OCCASIONAL MOUNTAIN IN ARIZONA...
AN OCCASIONAL MOUNTAIN?
IT'S NOT A VERY BIG MOUNTAIN, BUT IT'S ONLY THERE OCCASIONALLY.
ARE THERE REALLY SUCH PLACES?
HAVE YOU EVER HEARD OF FIDDLER'S GREEN, MARCO? THE PARADISE ON EARTH THAT SOME SAY ALL SAILORS DREAM OF FINDING?
NO.
PITY.
17

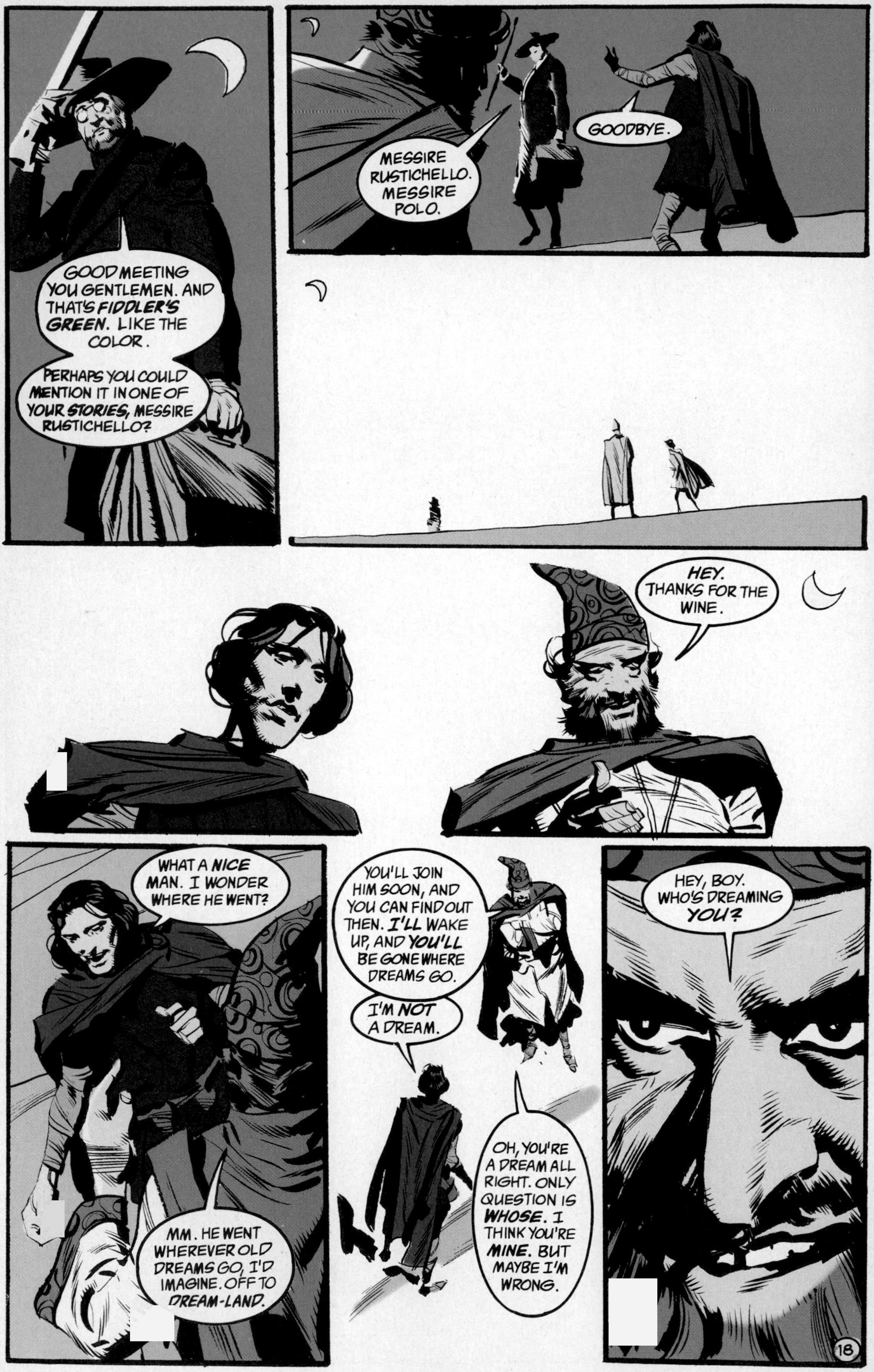

GOOD MEETING YOU GENTLEMEN. AND THAT'S FIDDLER'S GREEN. LIKE THE COLOR.
PERHAPS YOU COULD MENTION IT IN ONE OF YOUR STORIES, MESSIRE RUSTICHELLO?
MESSIRE RUSTICHELLO. MESSIRE POLO.
GOODBYE.
HEY. THANKS FOR THE WINE.
WHAT A NICE MAN. I WONDER WHERE HE WENT?
MM. HE WENT WHEREVER OLD DREAMS GO, I'D IMAGINE. OFF TO DREAM-LAND.
YOU'LL JOIN HIM SOON, AND YOU CAN FIND OUT THEN. I'LL WAKE UP, AND YOU'LL BE GONE WHERE DREAMS GO.
I'M NOT A DREAM.
OH, YOU'RE A DREAM ALL RIGHT. ONLY QUESTION IS WHOSE. I THINK YOU'RE MINE. BUT MAYBE I'M WRONG.
HEY, BOY. WHO'S DREAMING YOU?
18

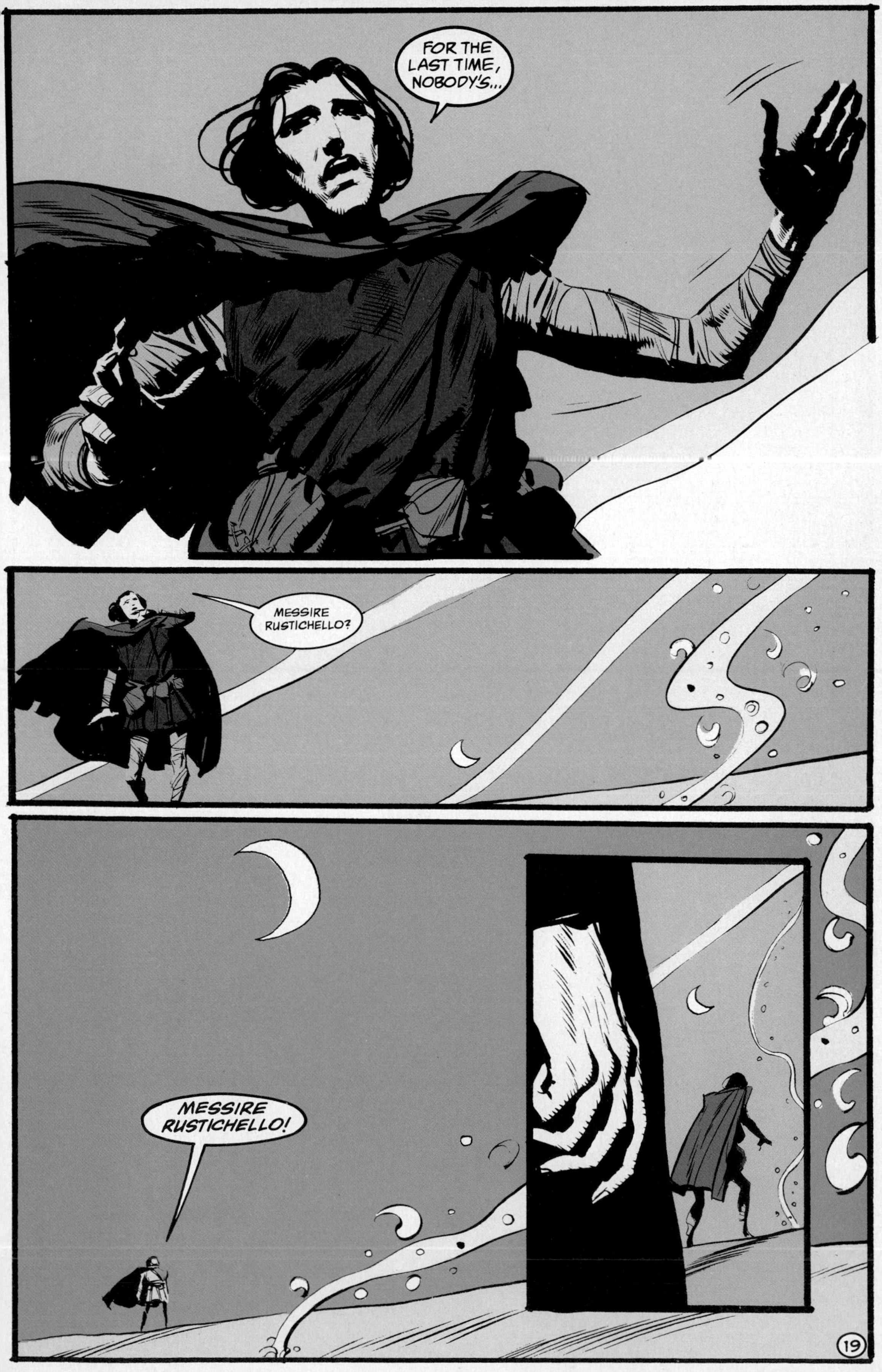
FOR THE LAST TIME, NOBODY'S...
MESSIRE RUSTICHELLO?
MESSIRE RUSTICHELLO!
19

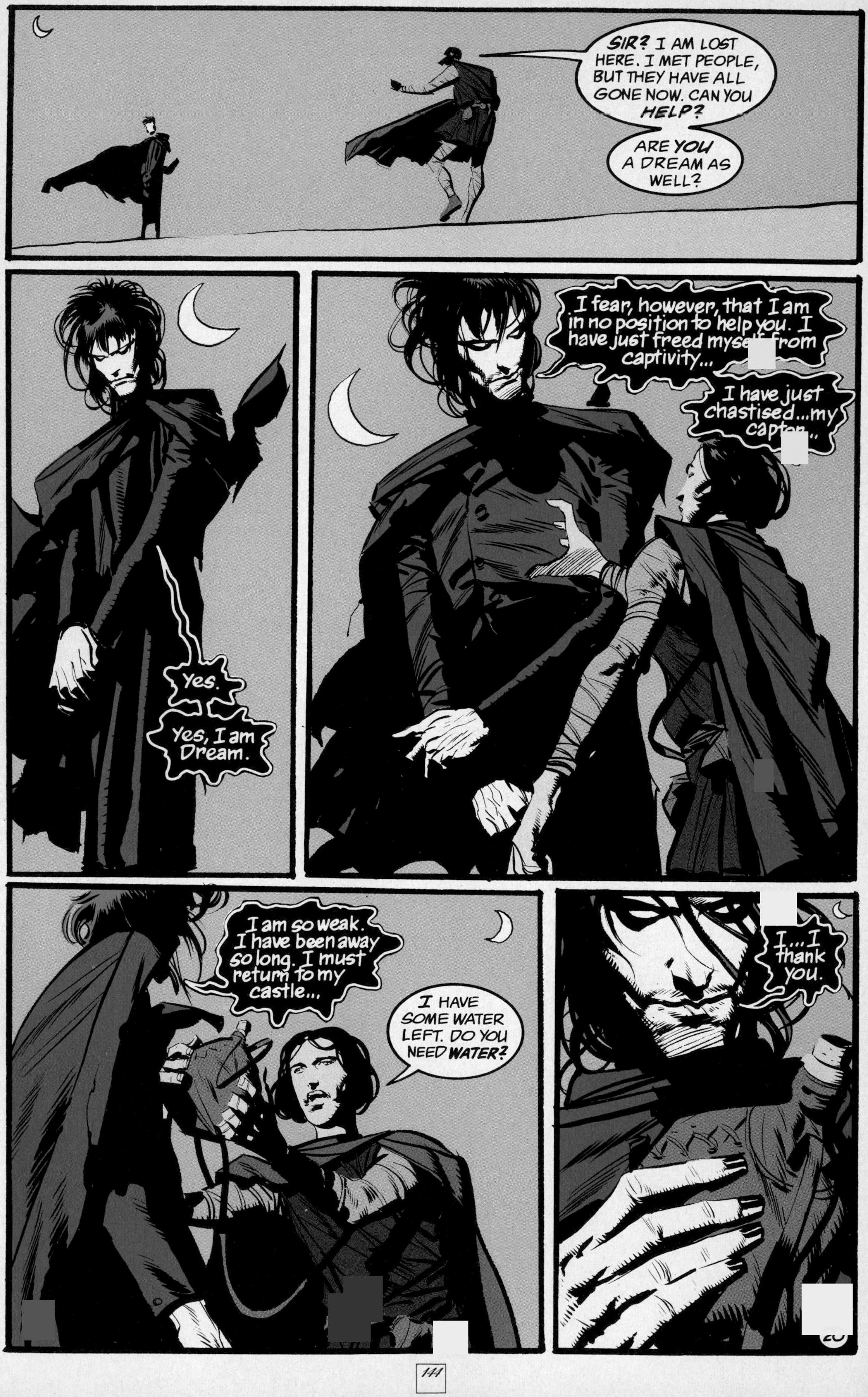
SIR? I AM LOST HERE. I MET PEOPLE, BUT THEY HAVE ALL GONE NOW. CAN YOU HELP?
ARE YOU A DREAM AS WELL?
Yes.
Yes, I am Dream.
I fear, however, that I am in no position to help you. I have just freed mys from captivity...
I have just chastised...my capt ..
I am so weak. I have been away so long. I must return to my castle...
I HAVE SOME WATER LEFT. DO YOU NEED WATER?
I...I thank you.

SIR? ARE *YOU* THE LORD OF THIS PLACE?

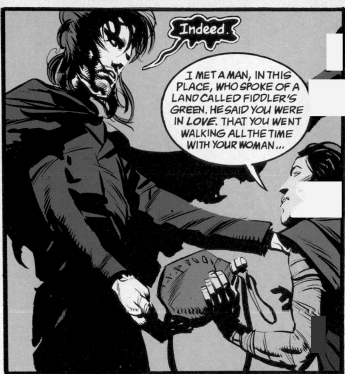

Indeed.

I MET A MAN, IN THIS PLACE, WHO SPOKE OF A LAND CALLED FIDDLER'S GREEN. HE SAID YOU WERE IN *LOVE*. THAT YOU WENT WALKING ALL THE TIME WITH YOUR WOMAN...

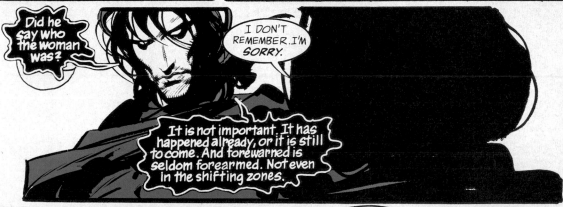

Did he say who the woman was?

I DON'T REMEMBER. I'M *SORRY*.

It is not important. It has happened already, or it is still to come. And forewarned is seldom forearmed. Not even in the shifting zones.

THE MAN I MENTIONED, HE SAID THIS WAS CALLED A SOFT PLACE.

Yes. That is a valid name. The soft places of the world. The shifting places...

The...

YOU LOOK *TERRIBLE*. WHITE AS THE MAN IN THE *MOON*. ARE YOU *ALWAYS* SO PALE?

That depends on who's watching.

SORRY?

No matter.

21

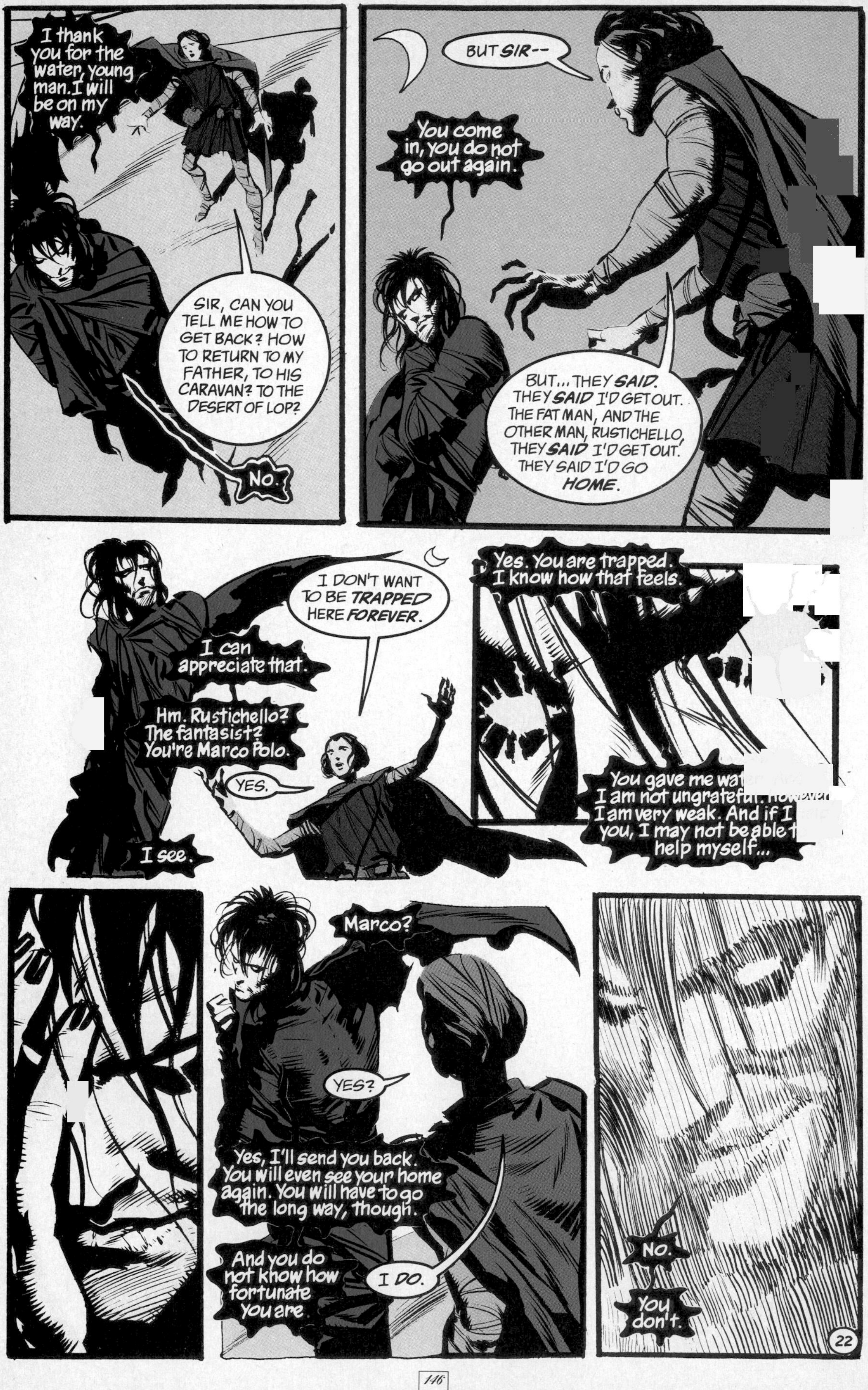

I thank you for the water, young man. I will be on my way.
SIR, CAN YOU TELL ME HOW TO GET BACK? HOW TO RETURN TO MY FATHER, TO HIS CARAVAN? TO THE DESERT OF LOP?
No.
BUT SIR--
You come in, you do not go out again.
BUT... THEY SAID. THEY SAID I'D GET OUT. THE FAT MAN, AND THE OTHER MAN, RUSTICHELLO, THEY SAID I'D GET OUT. THEY SAID I'D GO HOME.
I DON'T WANT TO BE TRAPPED HERE FOREVER.
I can appreciate that.
Hm. Rustichello? The fantasist? You're Marco Polo.
YES.
I see.
Yes. You are trapped. I know how that feels.
You gave me wat I am not ungrateful. I am very weak. And if I you, I may not be able help myself...
Marco?
YES?
Yes, I'll send you back. You will even see your home again. You will have to go the long way, though.
And you do not know how fortunate you are.
I DO.
No.
You don't.
22

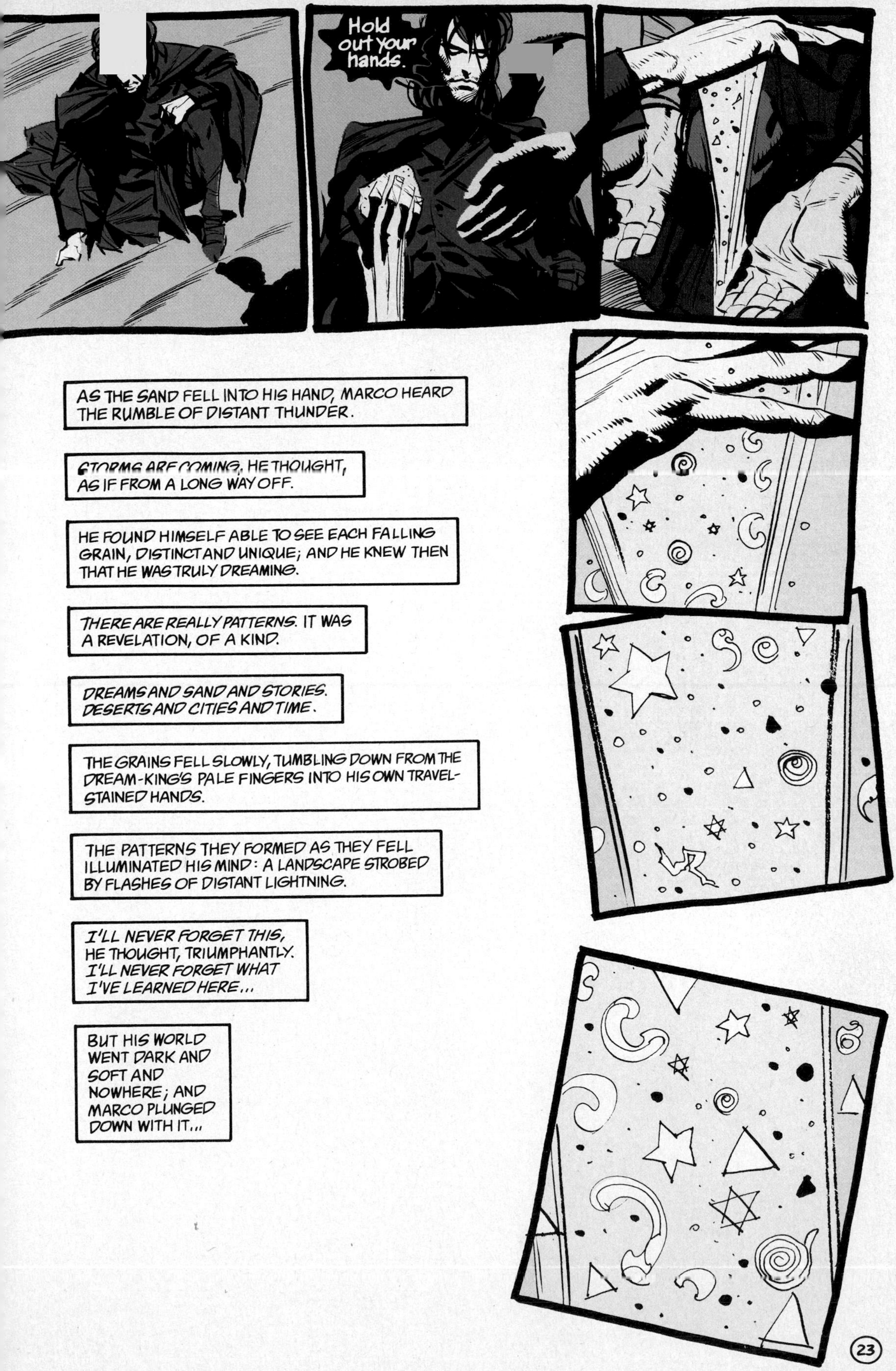
Hold out your hands.
AS THE SAND FELL INTO HIS HAND, MARCO HEARD THE RUMBLE OF DISTANT THUNDER.
STORMS ARE COMING, HE THOUGHT, AS IF FROM A LONG WAY OFF.
HE FOUND HIMSELF ABLE TO SEE EACH FALLING GRAIN, DISTINCT AND UNIQUE; AND HE KNEW THEN THAT HE WAS TRULY DREAMING.
THERE ARE REALLY PATTERNS. IT WAS A REVELATION, OF A KIND.
DREAMS AND SAND AND STORIES. DESERTS AND CITIES AND TIME.
THE GRAINS FELL SLOWLY, TUMBLING DOWN FROM THE DREAM-KING'S PALE FINGERS INTO HIS OWN TRAVEL-STAINED HANDS.
THE PATTERNS THEY FORMED AS THEY FELL ILLUMINATED HIS MIND: A LANDSCAPE STROBED BY FLASHES OF DISTANT LIGHTNING.
I'LL NEVER FORGET THIS, HE THOUGHT, TRIUMPHANTLY. I'LL NEVER FORGET WHAT I'VE LEARNED HERE...
BUT HIS WORLD WENT DARK AND SOFT AND NOWHERE; AND MARCO PLUNGED DOWN WITH IT...
23

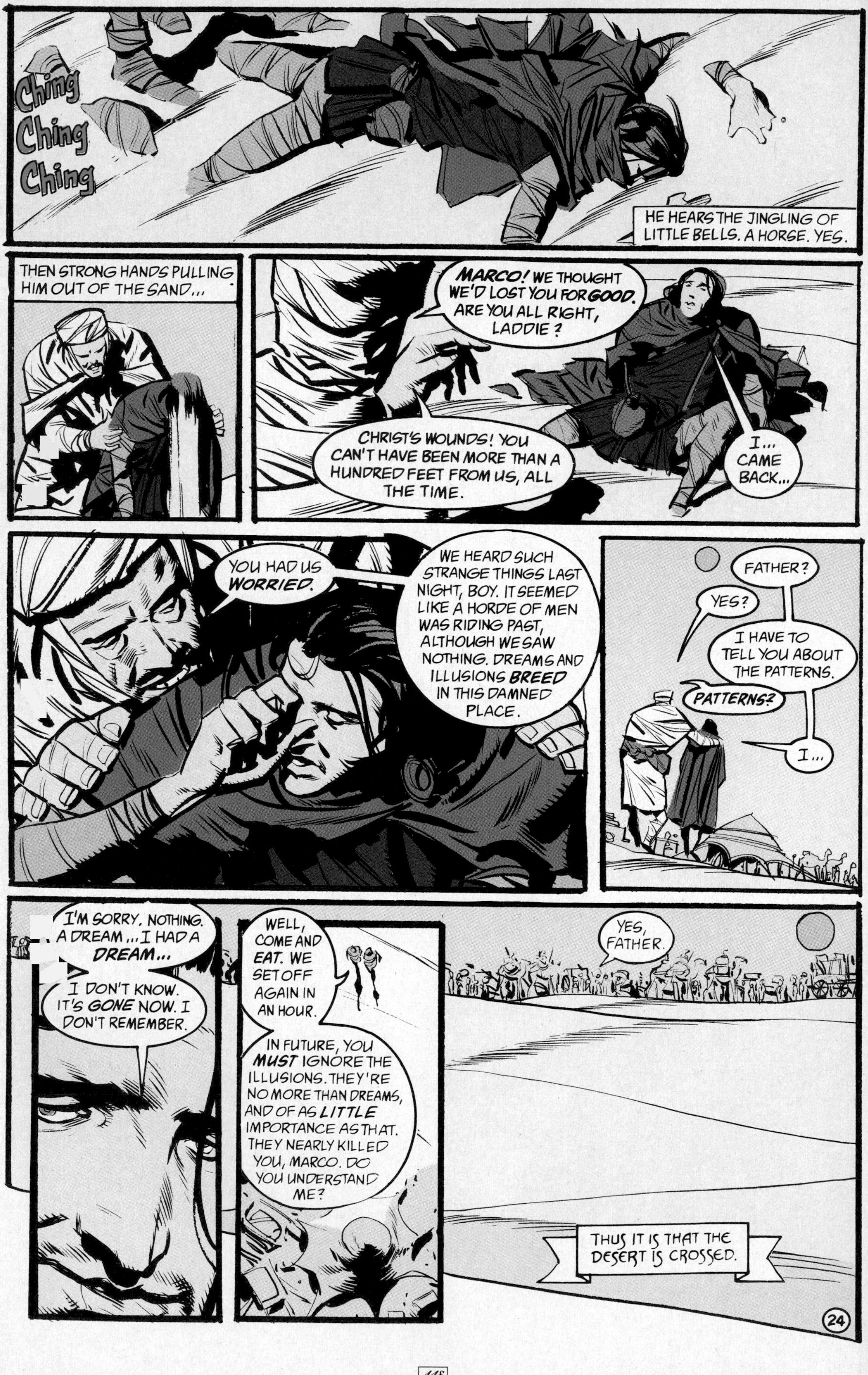

Ching Ching Ching
HE HEARS THE JINGLING OF LITTLE BELLS. A HORSE. YES.
THEN STRONG HANDS PULLING HIM OUT OF THE SAND...
MARCO! WE THOUGHT WE'D LOST YOU FOR GOOD. ARE YOU ALL RIGHT, LADDIE?
CHRIST'S WOUNDS! YOU CAN'T HAVE BEEN MORE THAN A HUNDRED FEET FROM US, ALL THE TIME.
I... CAME BACK...
YOU HAD US WORRIED.
WE HEARD SUCH STRANGE THINGS LAST NIGHT, BOY. IT SEEMED LIKE A HORDE OF MEN WAS RIDING PAST, ALTHOUGH WE SAW NOTHING. DREAMS AND ILLUSIONS BREED IN THIS DAMNED PLACE.
FATHER?
YES?
I HAVE TO TELL YOU ABOUT THE PATTERNS.
PATTERNS?
I...
I'M SORRY. NOTHING. A DREAM... I HAD A DREAM...
I DON'T KNOW. IT'S GONE NOW. I DON'T REMEMBER.
WELL, COME AND EAT. WE SET OFF AGAIN IN AN HOUR.
IN FUTURE, YOU MUST IGNORE THE ILLUSIONS. THEY'RE NO MORE THAN DREAMS, AND OF AS LITTLE IMPORTANCE AS THAT. THEY NEARLY KILLED YOU, MARCO. DO YOU UNDERSTAND ME?
YES, FATHER.
THUS IT IS THAT THE DESERT IS CROSSED.
24

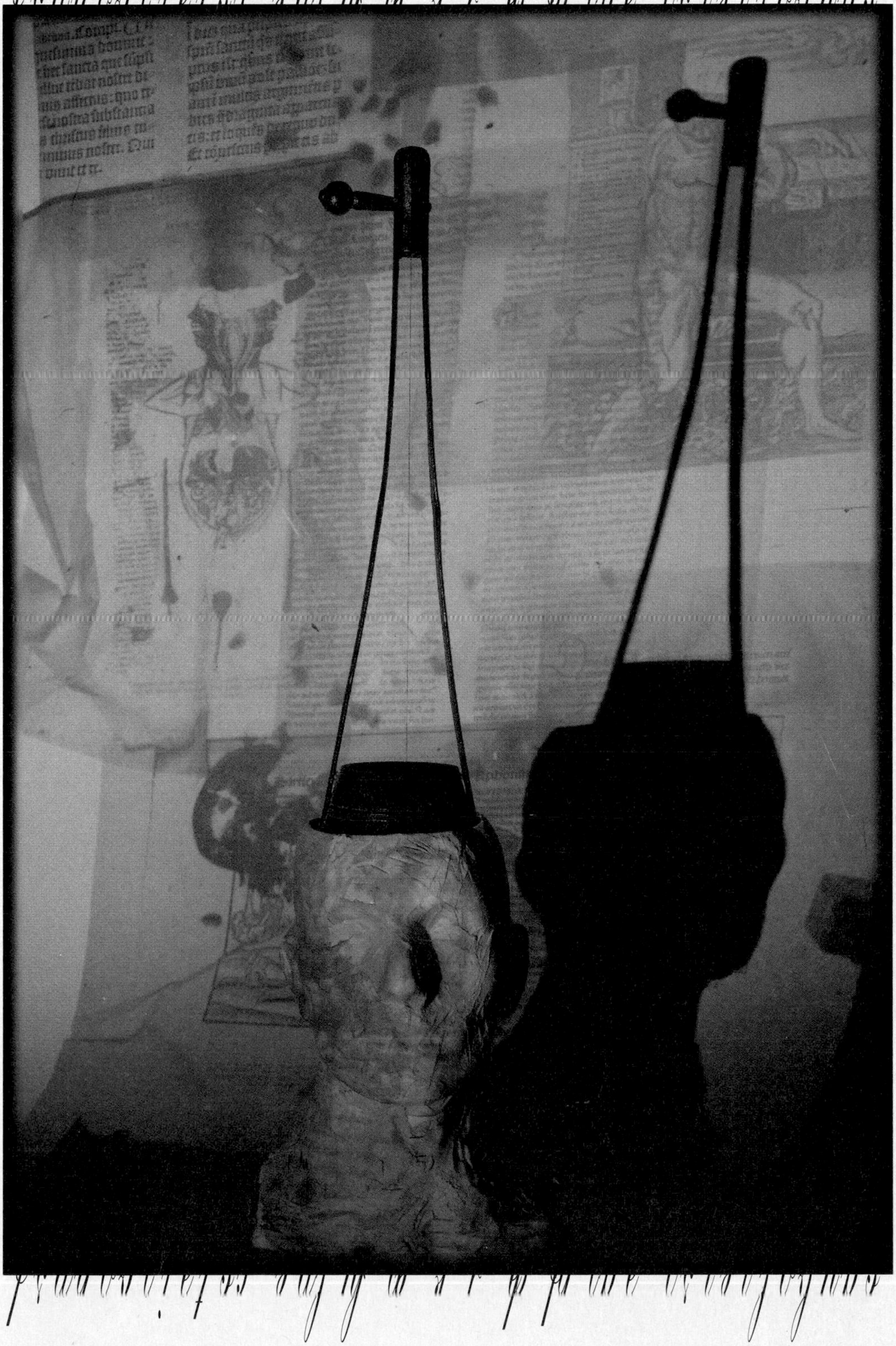

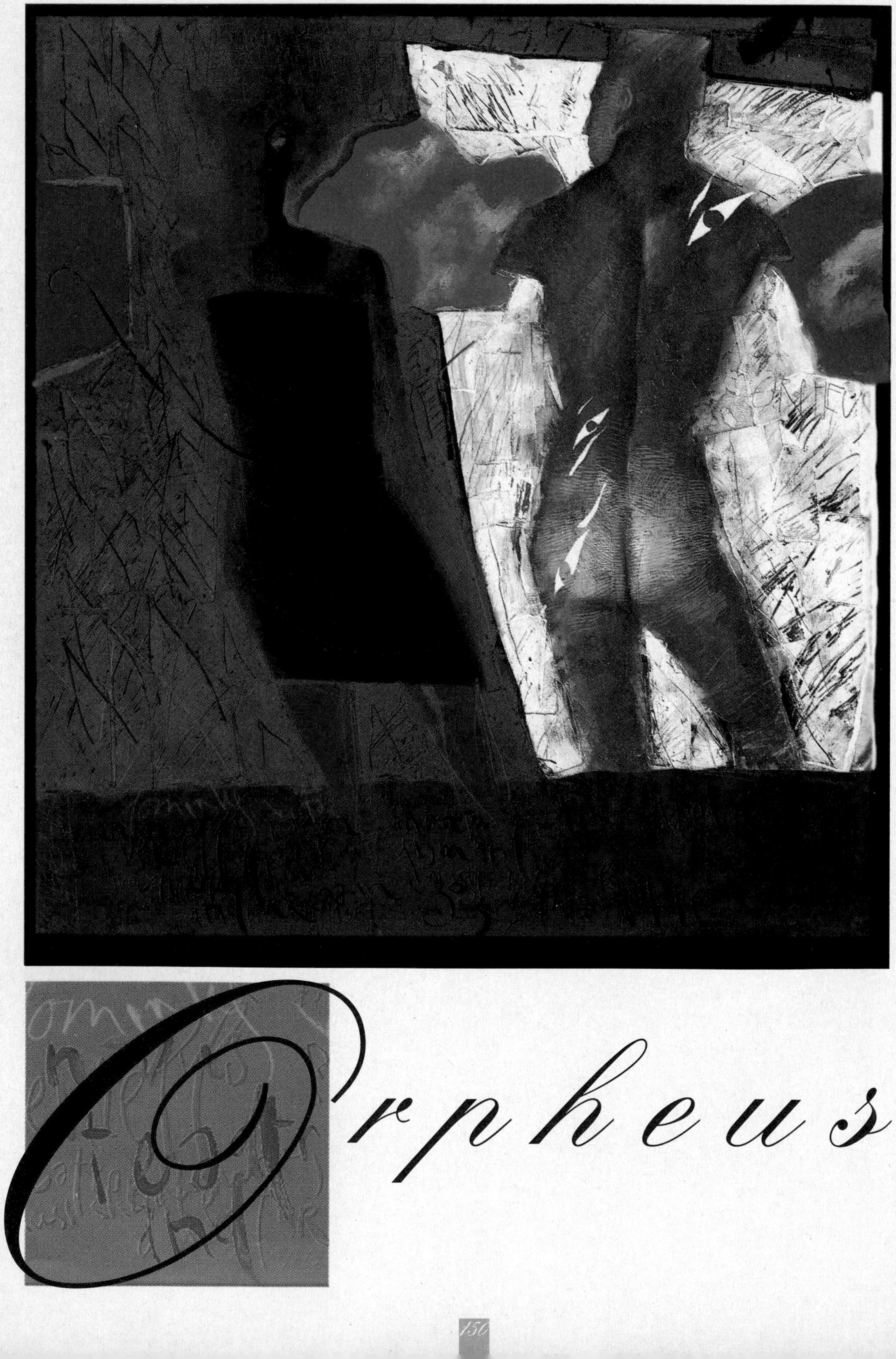

Orpheus

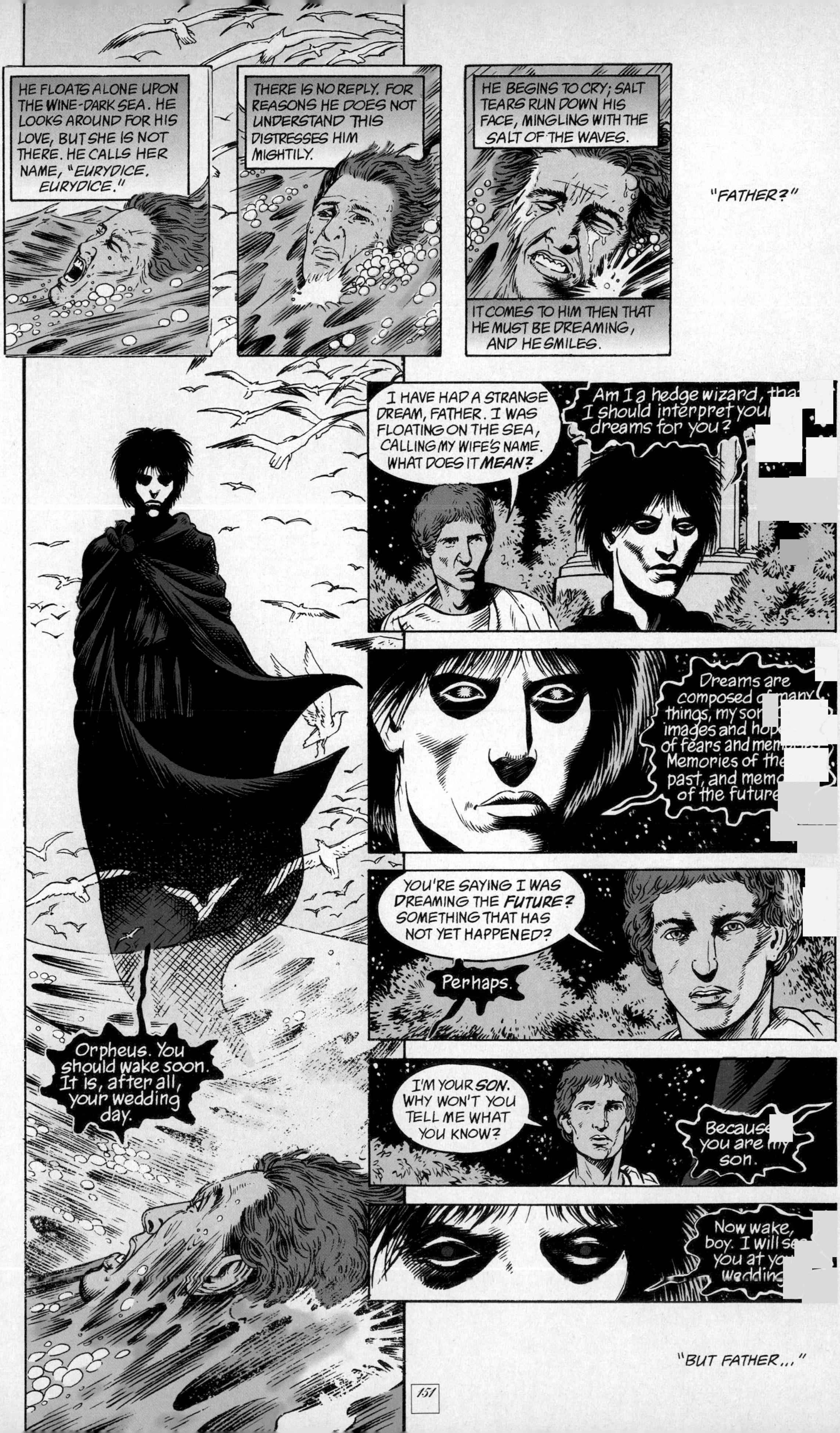
HE FLOATS ALONE UPON THE WINE-DARK SEA. HE LOOKS AROUND FOR HIS LOVE, BUT SHE IS NOT THERE. HE CALLS HER NAME, "EURYDICE. EURYDICE."
THERE IS NO REPLY. FOR REASONS HE DOES NOT UNDERSTAND THIS DISTRESSES HIM MIGHTILY.
HE BEGINS TO CRY; SALT TEARS RUN DOWN HIS FACE, MINGLING WITH THE SALT OF THE WAVES.
IT COMES TO HIM THEN THAT HE MUST BE DREAMING, AND HE SMILES.
"FATHER?"
I HAVE HAD A STRANGE DREAM, FATHER. I WAS FLOATING ON THE SEA, CALLING MY WIFE'S NAME. WHAT DOES IT MEAN?
Am I a hedge wizard, tha I should interpret you dreams for you?
Dreams are composed o many things, my so images and hop of fears and mem Memories of the past, and memo of the future
YOU'RE SAYING I WAS DREAMING THE FUTURE? SOMETHING THAT HAS NOT YET HAPPENED?
Perhaps.
I'M YOUR SON. WHY WON'T YOU TELL ME WHAT YOU KNOW?
Because you are m son.
Now wake, boy. I will se you at yo wedding
Orpheus. You should wake soon. It is, after all, your wedding day.
"BUT FATHER..."

THE SONG OF ORPHEUS

C·H·A·P·T·E·R O·N·E

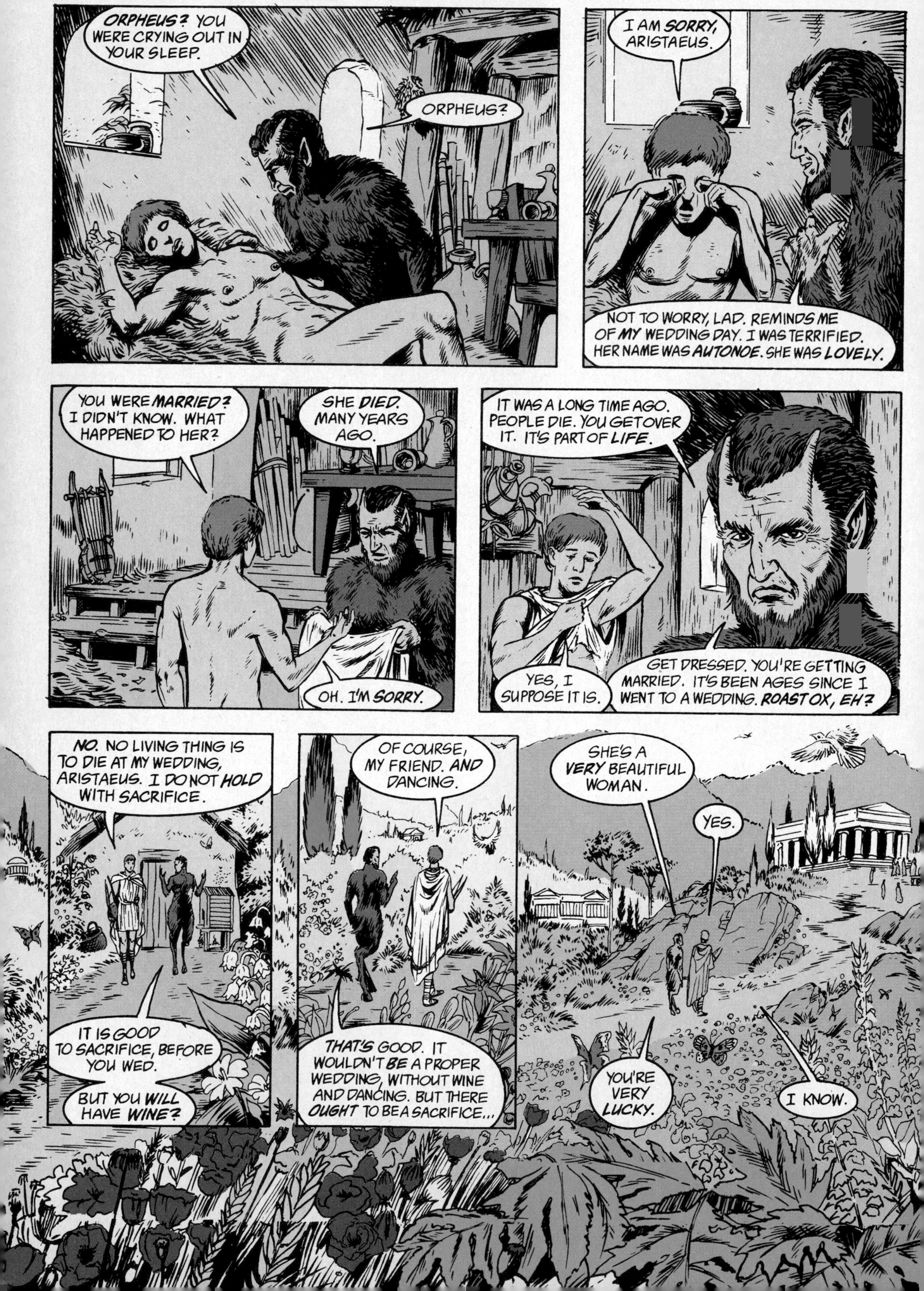
ORPHEUS? YOU WERE CRYING OUT IN YOUR SLEEP.
ORPHEUS?
I AM SORRY, ARISTAEUS.
NOT TO WORRY, LAD. REMINDS ME OF MY WEDDING DAY. I WAS TERRIFIED. HER NAME WAS AUTONOE. SHE WAS LOVELY.
YOU WERE MARRIED? I DIDN'T KNOW. WHAT HAPPENED TO HER?
SHE DIED. MANY YEARS AGO.
OH. I'M SORRY.
IT WAS A LONG TIME AGO. PEOPLE DIE. YOU GET OVER IT. IT'S PART OF LIFE.
YES, I SUPPOSE IT IS.
GET DRESSED. YOU'RE GETTING MARRIED. IT'S BEEN AGES SINCE I WENT TO A WEDDING. ROAST OX, EH?
NO. NO LIVING THING IS TO DIE AT MY WEDDING, ARISTAEUS. I DO NOT HOLD WITH SACRIFICE.
IT IS GOOD TO SACRIFICE, BEFORE YOU WED.
BUT YOU WILL HAVE WINE?
OF COURSE, MY FRIEND. AND DANCING.
THAT'S GOOD. IT WOULDN'T BE A PROPER WEDDING, WITHOUT WINE AND DANCING. BUT THERE OUGHT TO BE A SACRIFICE...
SHE'S A VERY BEAUTIFUL WOMAN.
YES.
YOU'RE VERY LUCKY.
I KNOW.

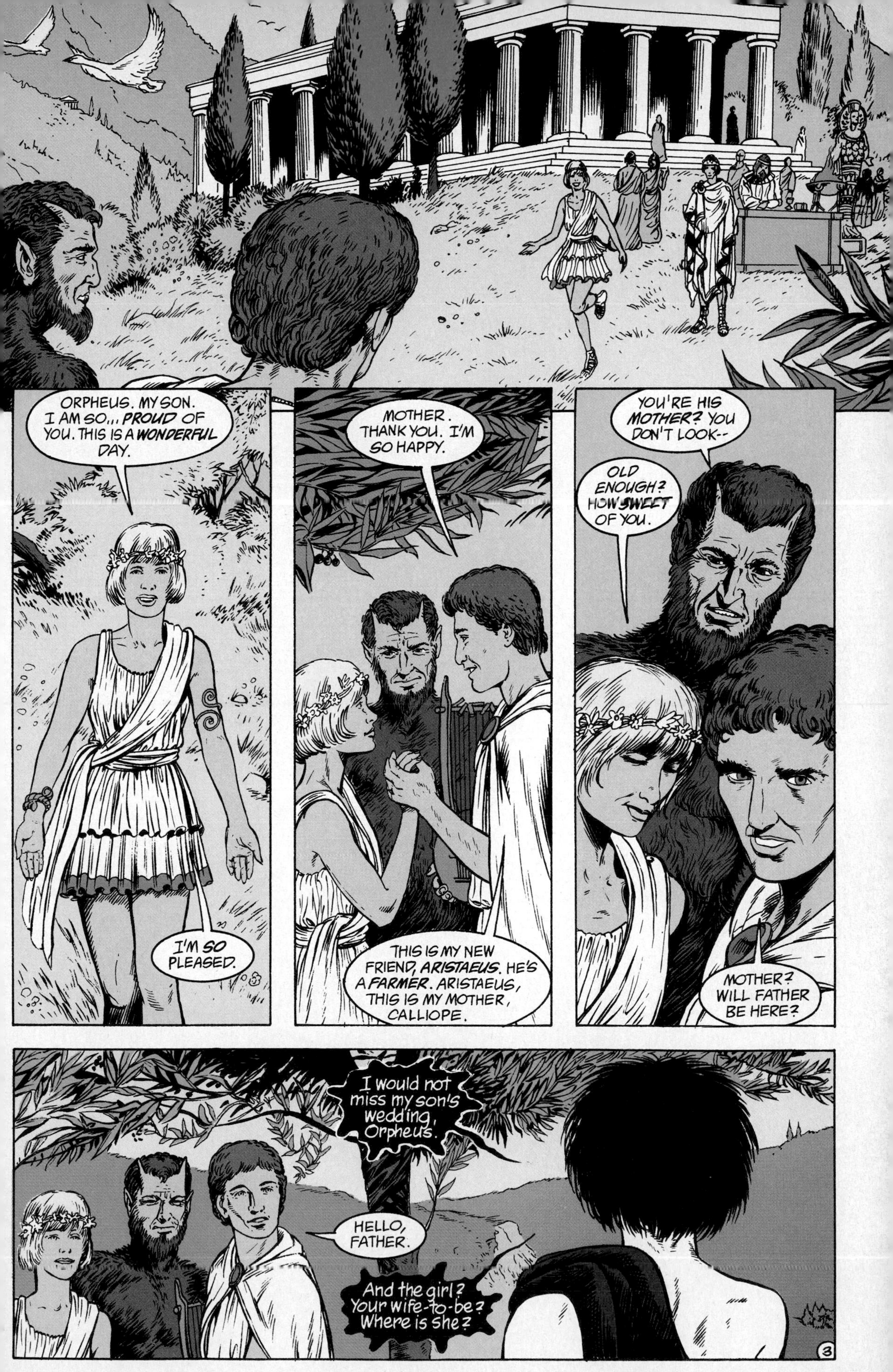
ORPHEUS. MY SON. I AM SO... PROUD OF YOU. THIS IS A WONDERFUL DAY.
I'M SO PLEASED.
MOTHER. THANK YOU. I'M SO HAPPY.
THIS IS MY NEW FRIEND, ARISTAEUS. HE'S A FARMER. ARISTAEUS, THIS IS MY MOTHER, CALLIOPE.
YOU'RE HIS MOTHER? YOU DON'T LOOK--
OLD ENOUGH? HOW SWEET OF YOU.
MOTHER? WILL FATHER BE HERE?
I would not miss my son's wedding, Orpheus.
HELLO, FATHER.
And the girl? Your wife-to-be? Where is she?
3

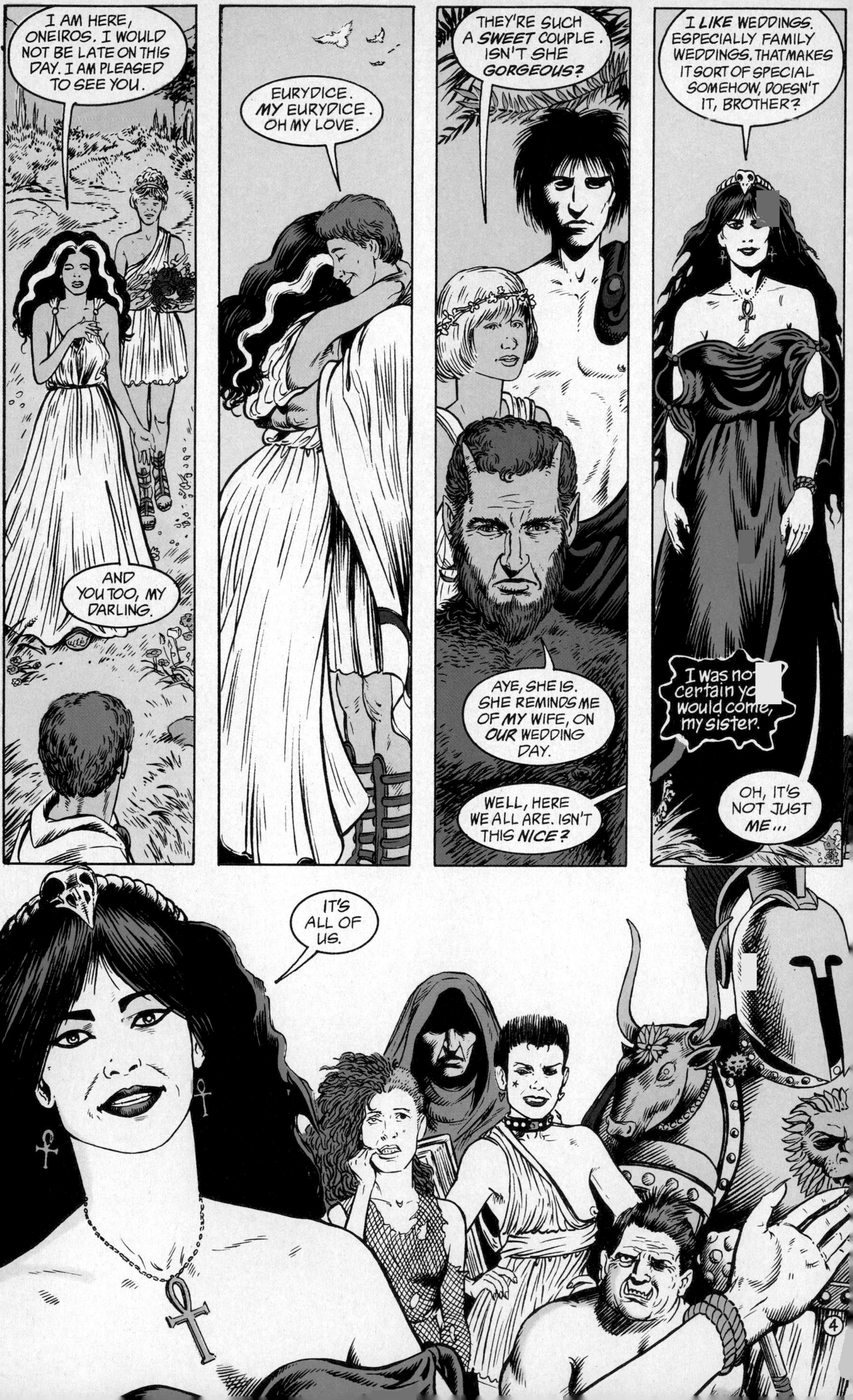
I AM HERE, ONEIROS. I WOULD NOT BE LATE ON THIS DAY. I AM PLEASED TO SEE YOU.
AND YOU TOO, MY DARLING.
EURYDICE. MY EURYDICE. OH MY LOVE.
THEY'RE SUCH A SWEET COUPLE. ISN'T SHE GORGEOUS?
AYE, SHE IS. SHE REMINDS ME OF MY WIFE, ON OUR WEDDING DAY.
WELL, HERE WE ALL ARE. ISN'T THIS NICE?
I LIKE WEDDINGS. ESPECIALLY FAMILY WEDDINGS. THAT MAKES IT SORT OF SPECIAL SOMEHOW, DOESN'T IT, BROTHER?
I was no certain yo would come, my sister.
OH, IT'S NOT JUST ME...
IT'S ALL OF US.
4

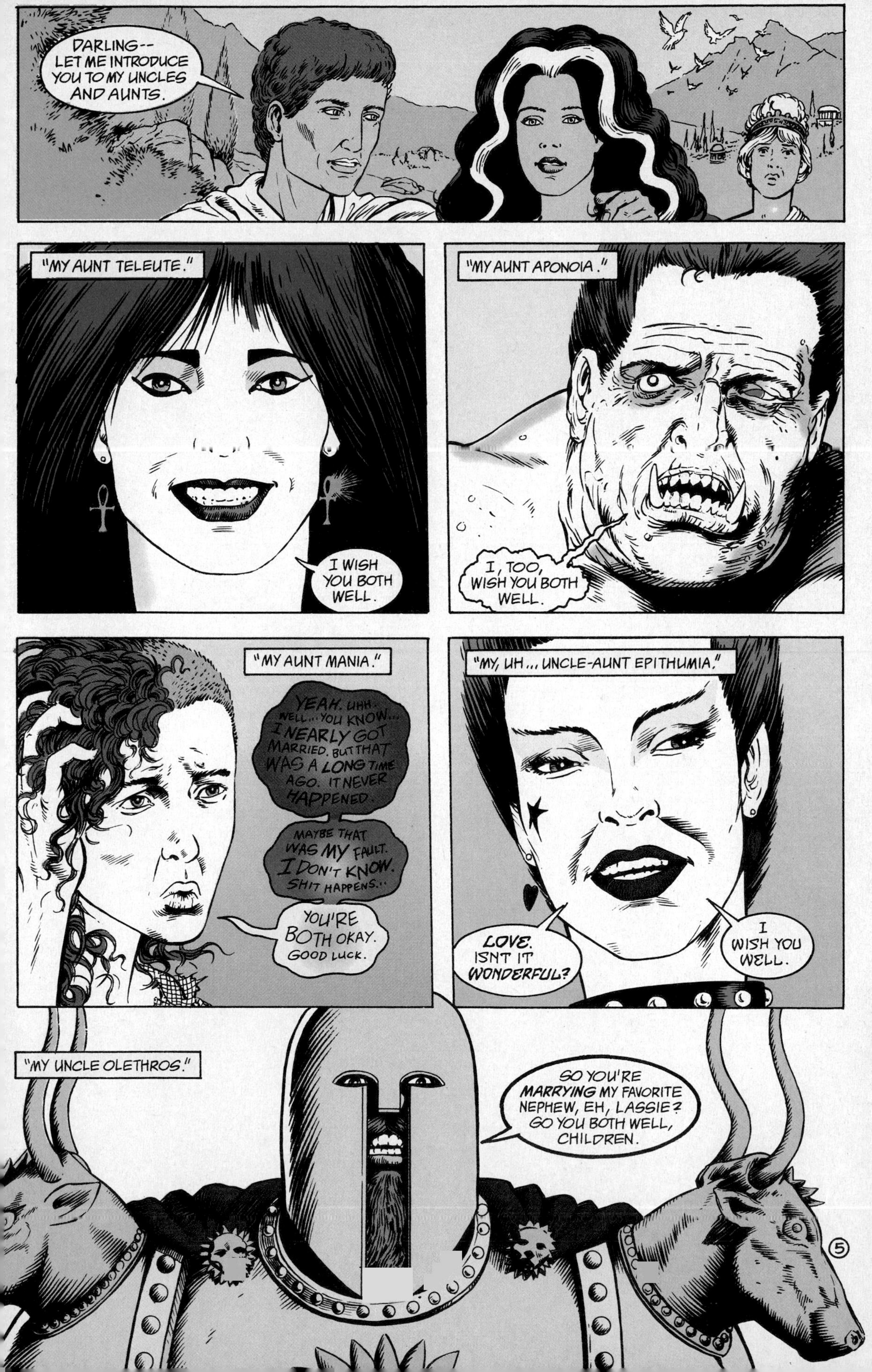
DARLING-- LET ME INTRODUCE YOU TO MY UNCLES AND AUNTS.
"MY AUNT TELEUTE."
I WISH YOU BOTH WELL.
"MY AUNT APONOIA."
I, TOO, WISH YOU BOTH WELL.
"MY AUNT MANIA."
YEAH. UHH. WELL... YOU KNOW... I NEARLY GOT MARRIED. BUT THAT WAS A LONG TIME AGO. IT NEVER HAPPENED.
MAYBE THAT WAS MY FAULT. I DON'T KNOW. SHIT HAPPENS...
YOU'RE BOTH OKAY. GOOD LUCK.
"MY, UH... UNCLE-AUNT EPITHUMIA."
LOVE. ISN'T IT WONDERFUL?
I WISH YOU WELL.
"MY UNCLE OLETHROS."
SO YOU'RE MARRYING MY FAVORITE NEPHEW, EH, LASSIE? GO YOU BOTH WELL, CHILDREN.

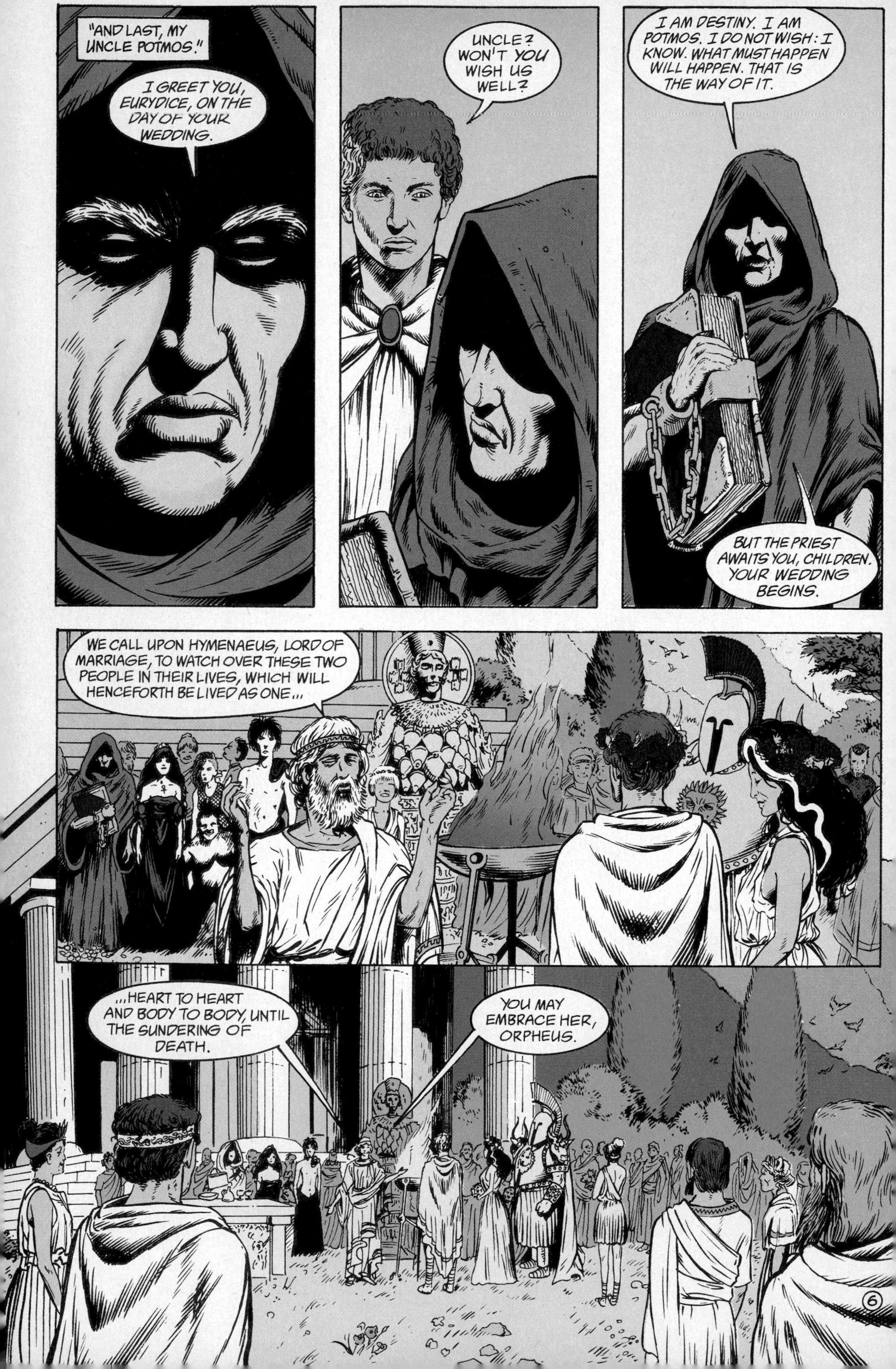
"AND LAST, MY UNCLE POTMOS."
I GREET YOU, EURYDICE, ON THE DAY OF YOUR WEDDING.
UNCLE? WON'T YOU WISH US WELL?
I AM DESTINY. I AM POTMOS. I DO NOT WISH: I KNOW. WHAT MUST HAPPEN WILL HAPPEN. THAT IS THE WAY OF IT.
BUT THE PRIEST AWAITS YOU, CHILDREN. YOUR WEDDING BEGINS.
WE CALL UPON HYMENAEUS, LORD OF MARRIAGE, TO WATCH OVER THESE TWO PEOPLE IN THEIR LIVES, WHICH WILL HENCEFORTH BE LIVED AS ONE...
...HEART TO HEART AND BODY TO BODY, UNTIL THE SUNDERING OF DEATH.
YOU MAY EMBRACE HER, ORPHEUS.

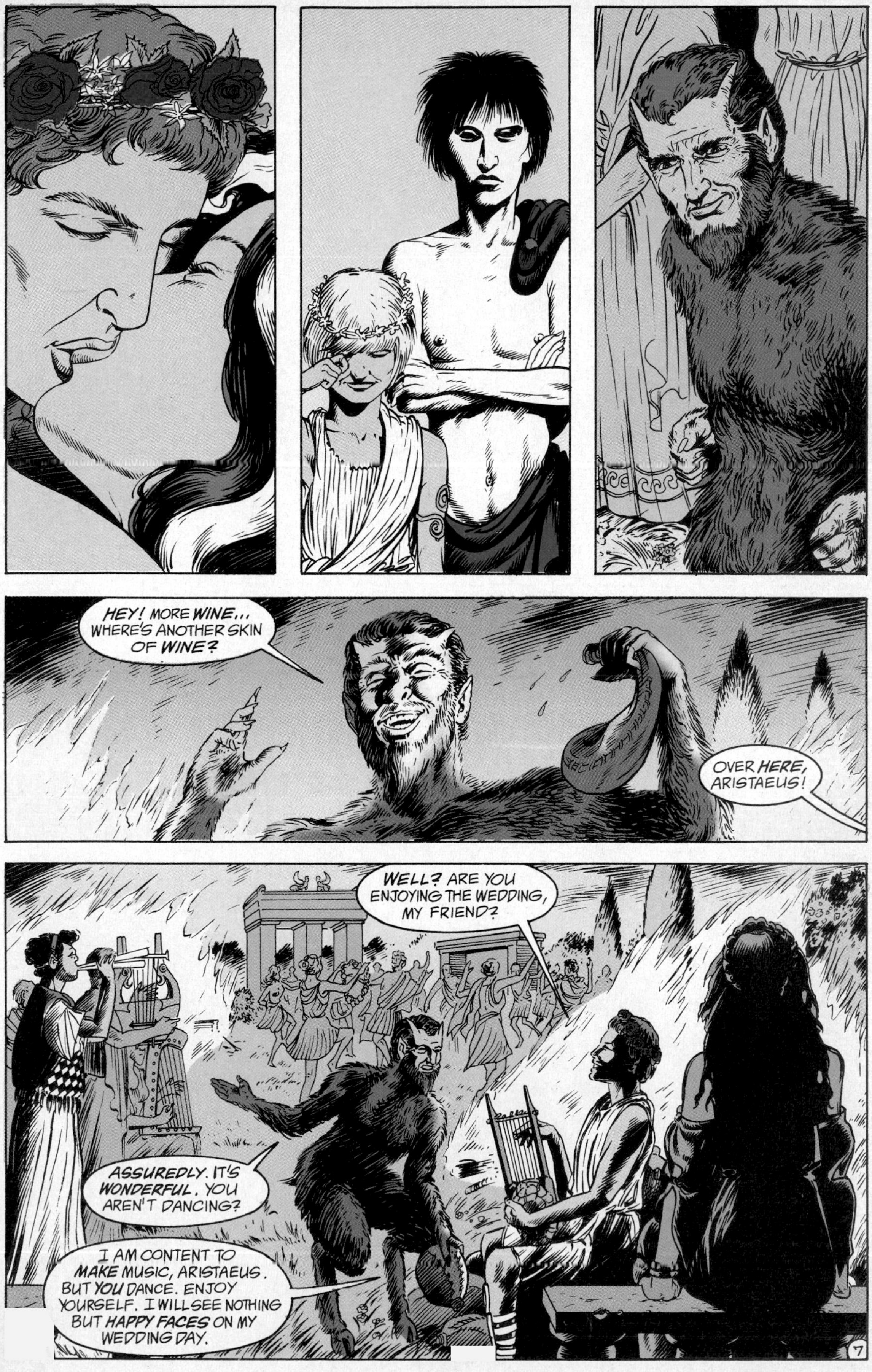
HEY! MORE WINE... WHERE'S ANOTHER SKIN OF WINE?
OVER HERE, ARISTAEUS!
WELL? ARE YOU ENJOYING THE WEDDING, MY FRIEND?
ASSUREDLY. IT'S WONDERFUL. YOU AREN'T DANCING?
I AM CONTENT TO MAKE MUSIC, ARISTAEUS. BUT YOU DANCE. ENJOY YOURSELF. I WILL SEE NOTHING BUT HAPPY FACES ON MY WEDDING DAY.
7

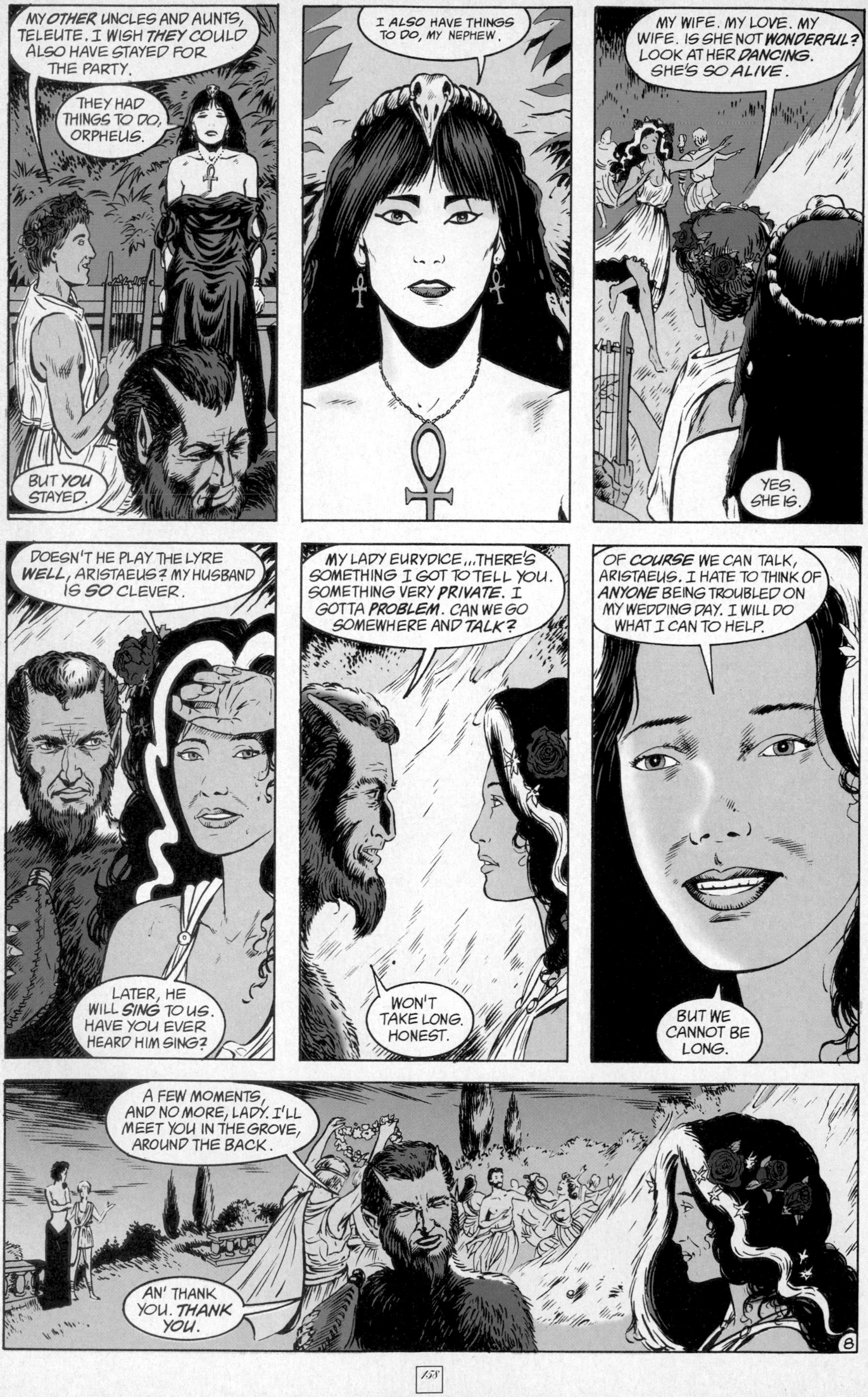
MY OTHER UNCLES AND AUNTS, TELEUTE. I WISH THEY COULD ALSO HAVE STAYED FOR THE PARTY.
THEY HAD THINGS TO DO, ORPHEUS.
BUT YOU STAYED.
I ALSO HAVE THINGS TO DO, MY NEPHEW.
MY WIFE. MY LOVE. MY WIFE. IS SHE NOT WONDERFUL? LOOK AT HER DANCING. SHE'S SO ALIVE.
YES. SHE IS.
DOESN'T HE PLAY THE LYRE WELL, ARISTAEUS? MY HUSBAND IS SO CLEVER.
LATER, HE WILL SING TO US. HAVE YOU EVER HEARD HIM SING?
MY LADY EURYDICE... THERE'S SOMETHING I GOT TO TELL YOU. SOMETHING VERY PRIVATE. I GOTTA PROBLEM. CAN WE GO SOMEWHERE AND TALK?
WON'T TAKE LONG. HONEST.
OF COURSE WE CAN TALK, ARISTAEUS. I HATE TO THINK OF ANYONE BEING TROUBLED ON MY WEDDING DAY. I WILL DO WHAT I CAN TO HELP.
BUT WE CANNOT BE LONG.
A FEW MOMENTS, AND NO MORE, LADY. I'LL MEET YOU IN THE GROVE, AROUND THE BACK.
AN' THANK YOU. THANK YOU.
8

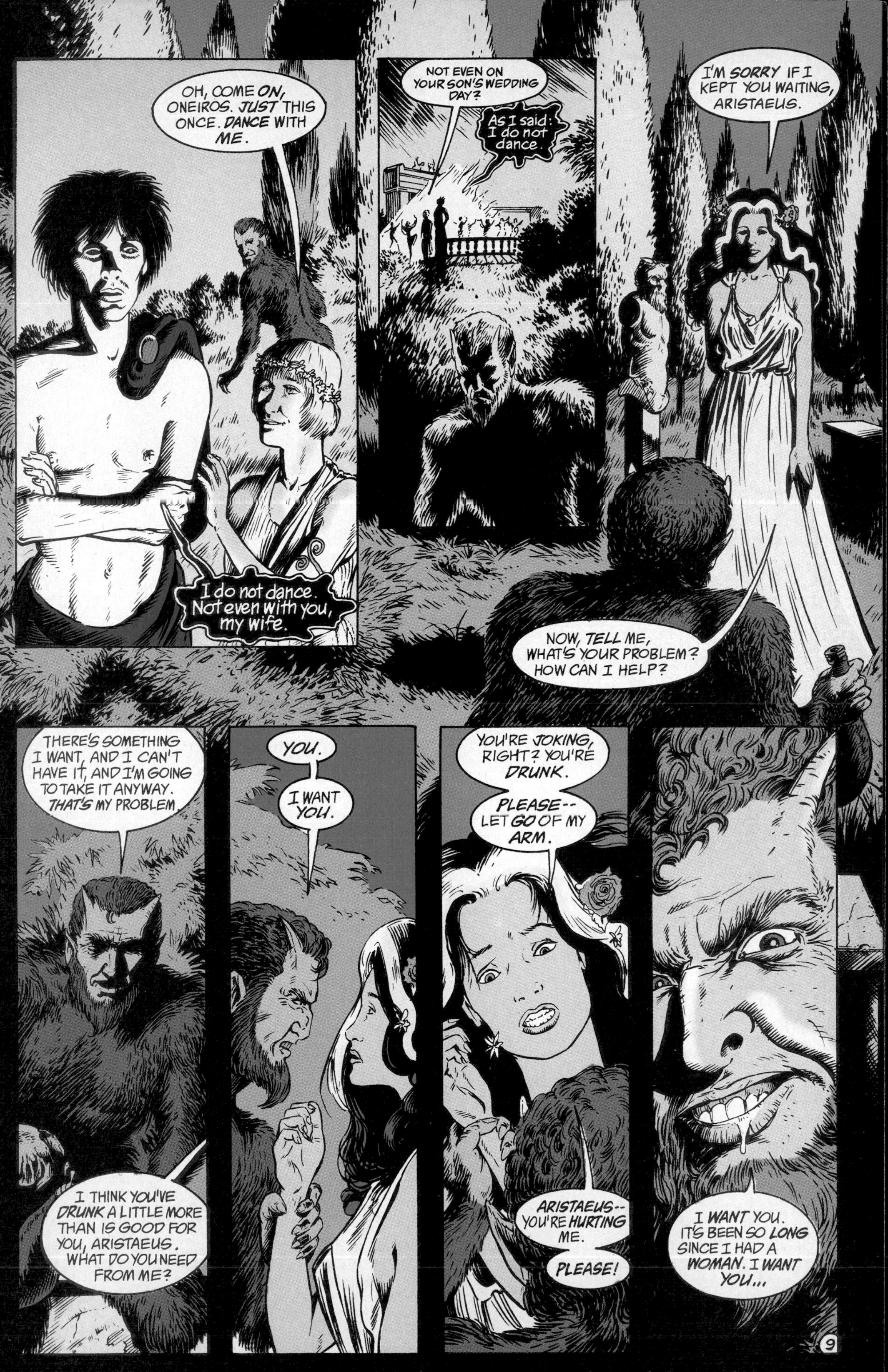
OH, COME ON, ONEIROS. JUST THIS ONCE. DANCE WITH ME.
I do not dance. Not even with you, my wife.
NOT EVEN ON YOUR SON'S WEDDING DAY?
As I said: I do not dance.
I'M SORRY IF I KEPT YOU WAITING, ARISTAEUS.
NOW, TELL ME, WHAT'S YOUR PROBLEM? HOW CAN I HELP?
THERE'S SOMETHING I WANT, AND I CAN'T HAVE IT, AND I'M GOING TO TAKE IT ANYWAY. THAT'S MY PROBLEM.
I THINK YOU'VE DRUNK A LITTLE MORE THAN IS GOOD FOR YOU, ARISTAEUS. WHAT DO YOU NEED FROM ME?
YOU.
I WANT YOU.
YOU'RE JOKING, RIGHT? YOU'RE DRUNK.
PLEASE-- LET GO OF MY ARM.
ARISTAEUS-- YOU'RE HURTING ME.
PLEASE!
I WANT YOU. IT'S BEEN SO LONG SINCE I HAD A WOMAN. I WANT YOU...

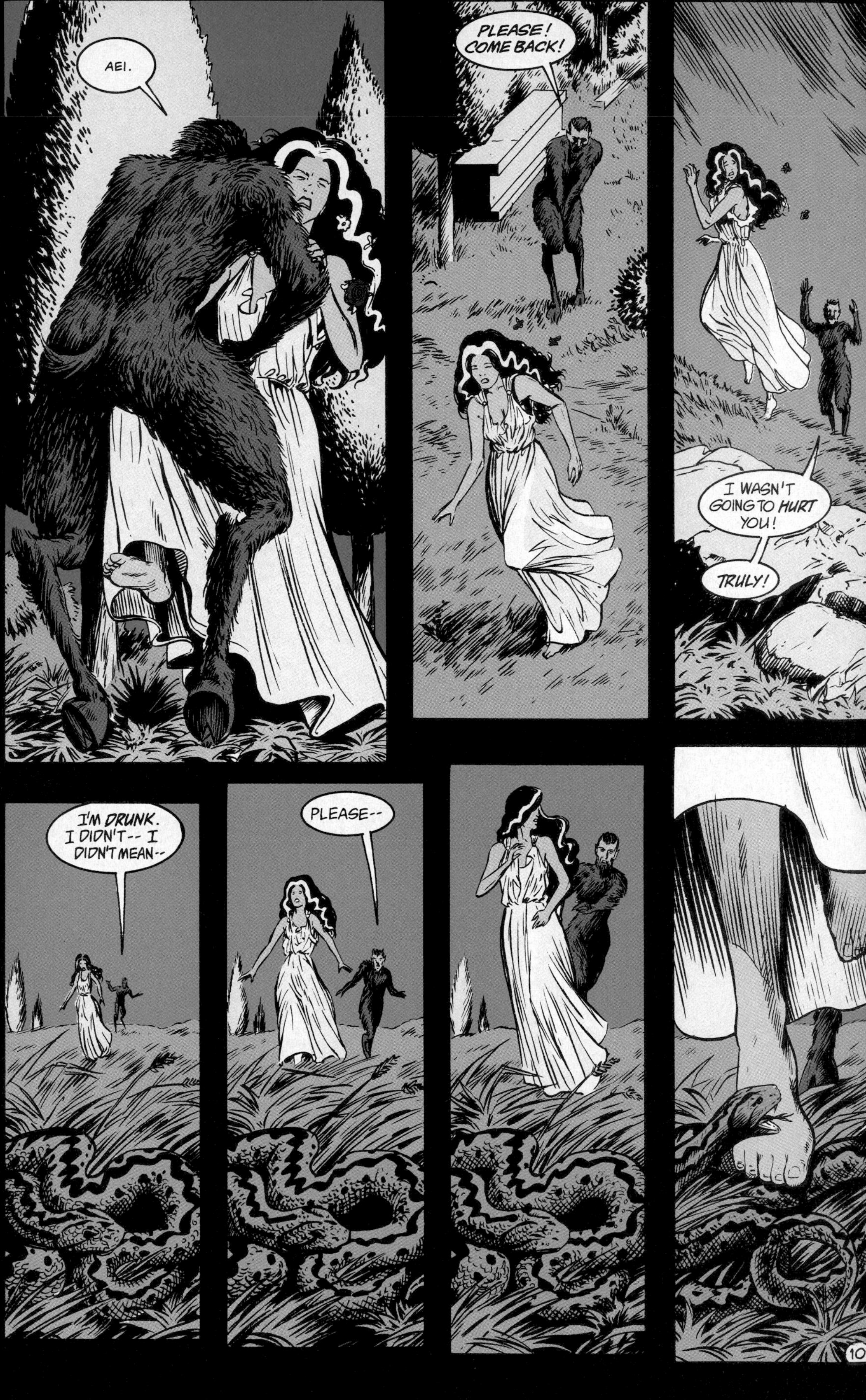
AEI.
PLEASE! COME BACK!
I WASN'T GOING TO HURT YOU!
TRULY!
I'M DRUNK. I DIDN'T-- I DIDN'T MEAN--
PLEASE--
10

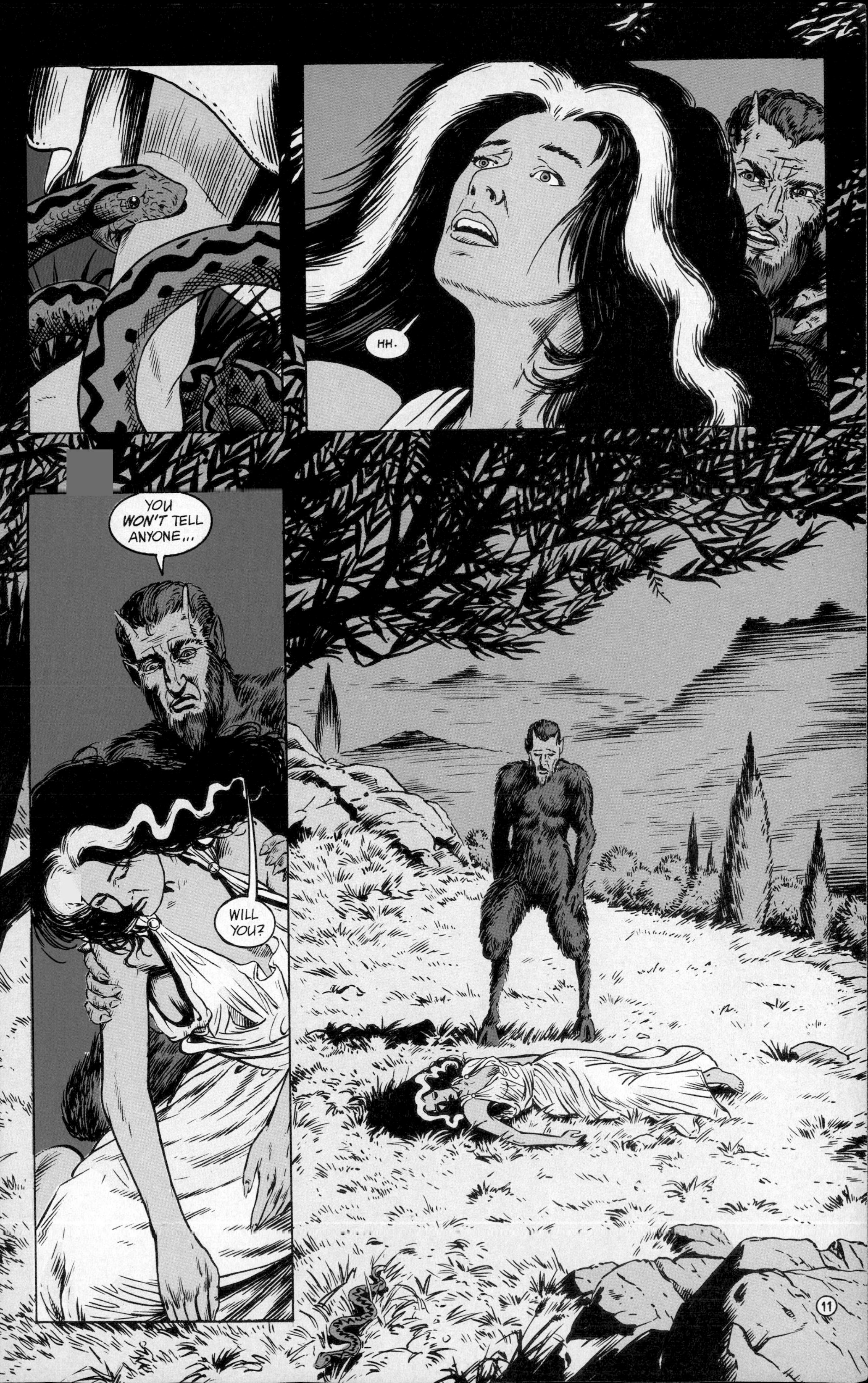
HH.
YOU WON'T TELL ANYONE...
WILL YOU?

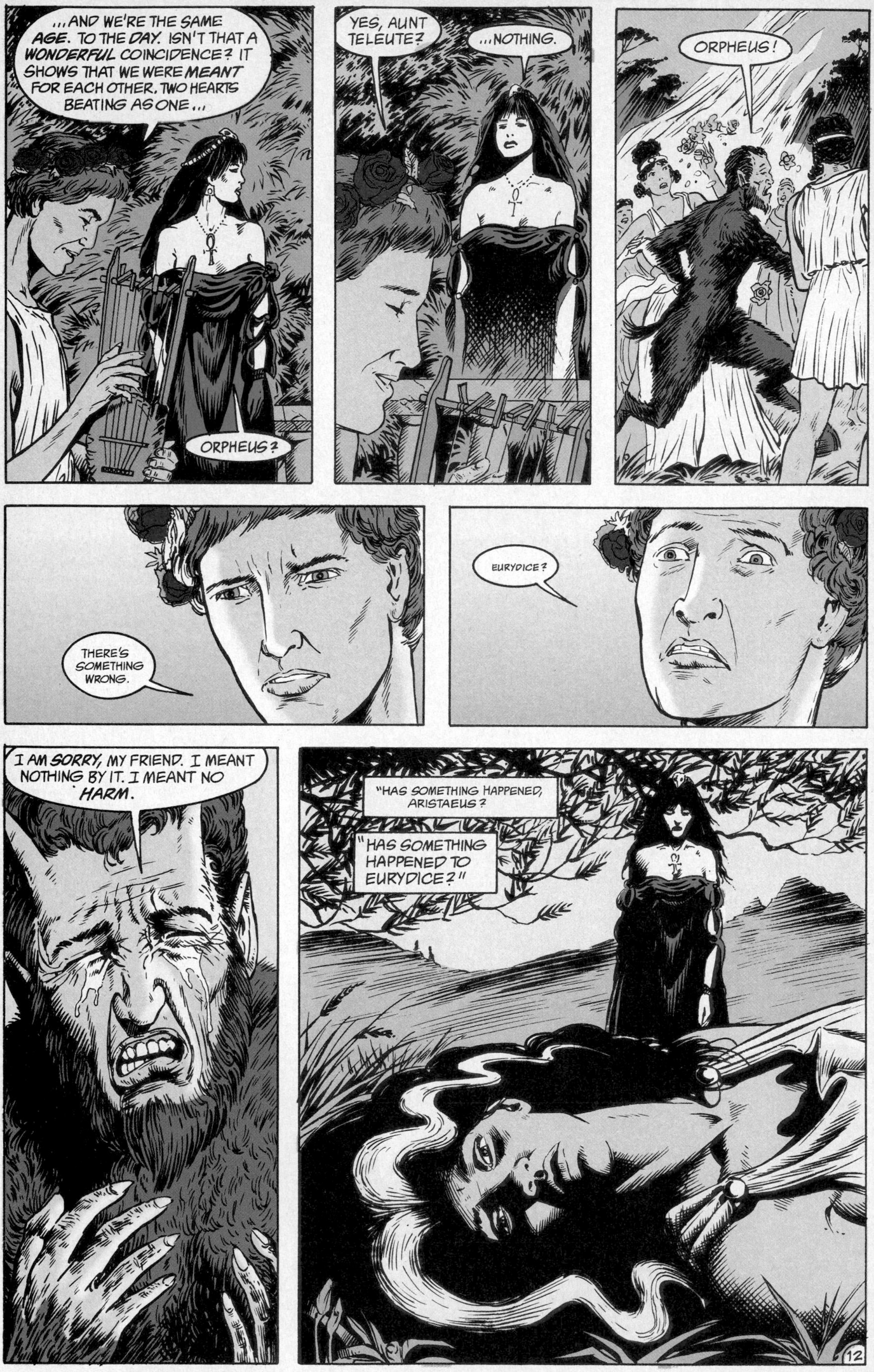
...AND WE'RE THE SAME AGE. TO THE DAY. ISN'T THAT A WONDERFUL COINCIDENCE? IT SHOWS THAT WE WERE MEANT FOR EACH OTHER. TWO HEARTS BEATING AS ONE...
ORPHEUS?
YES, AUNT TELEUTE?
...NOTHING.
ORPHEUS!
THERE'S SOMETHING WRONG.
EURYDICE?
I AM SORRY, MY FRIEND. I MEANT NOTHING BY IT. I MEANT NO HARM.
"HAS SOMETHING HAPPENED, ARISTAEUS?
"HAS SOMETHING HAPPENED TO EURYDICE?"
12

THE SONG OF ORPHEUS

CHAPTER TWO

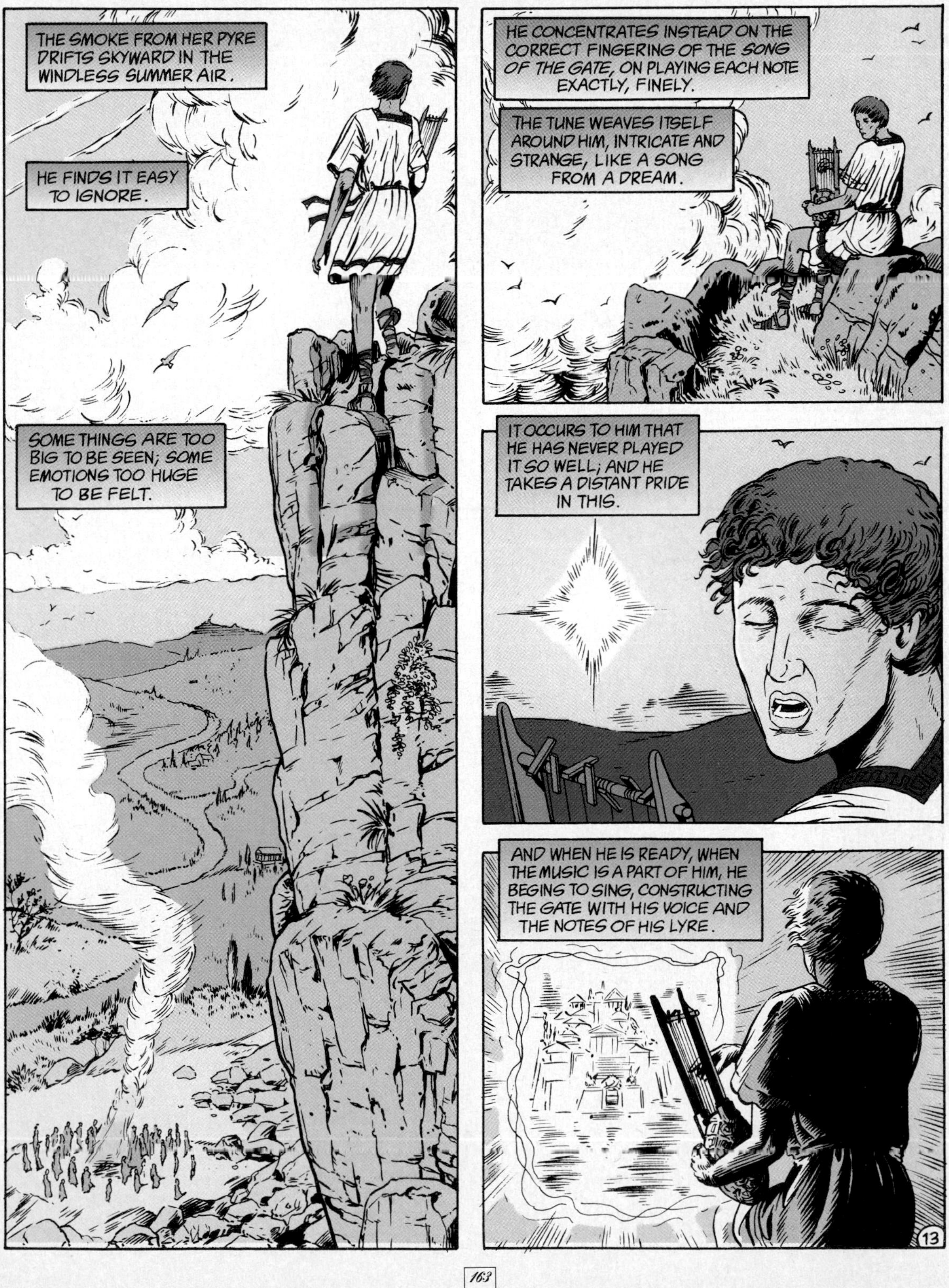

THE SMOKE FROM HER PYRE DRIFTS SKYWARD IN THE WINDLESS SUMMER AIR.
HE FINDS IT EASY TO IGNORE.
SOME THINGS ARE TOO BIG TO BE SEEN; SOME EMOTIONS TOO HUGE TO BE FELT.
HE CONCENTRATES INSTEAD ON THE CORRECT FINGERING OF THE SONG OF THE GATE, ON PLAYING EACH NOTE EXACTLY, FINELY.
THE TUNE WEAVES ITSELF AROUND HIM, INTRICATE AND STRANGE, LIKE A SONG FROM A DREAM.
IT OCCURS TO HIM THAT HE HAS NEVER PLAYED IT SO WELL; AND HE TAKES A DISTANT PRIDE IN THIS.
AND WHEN HE IS READY, WHEN THE MUSIC IS A PART OF HIM, HE BEGINS TO SING, CONSTRUCTING THE GATE WITH HIS VOICE AND THE NOTES OF HIS LYRE.
13

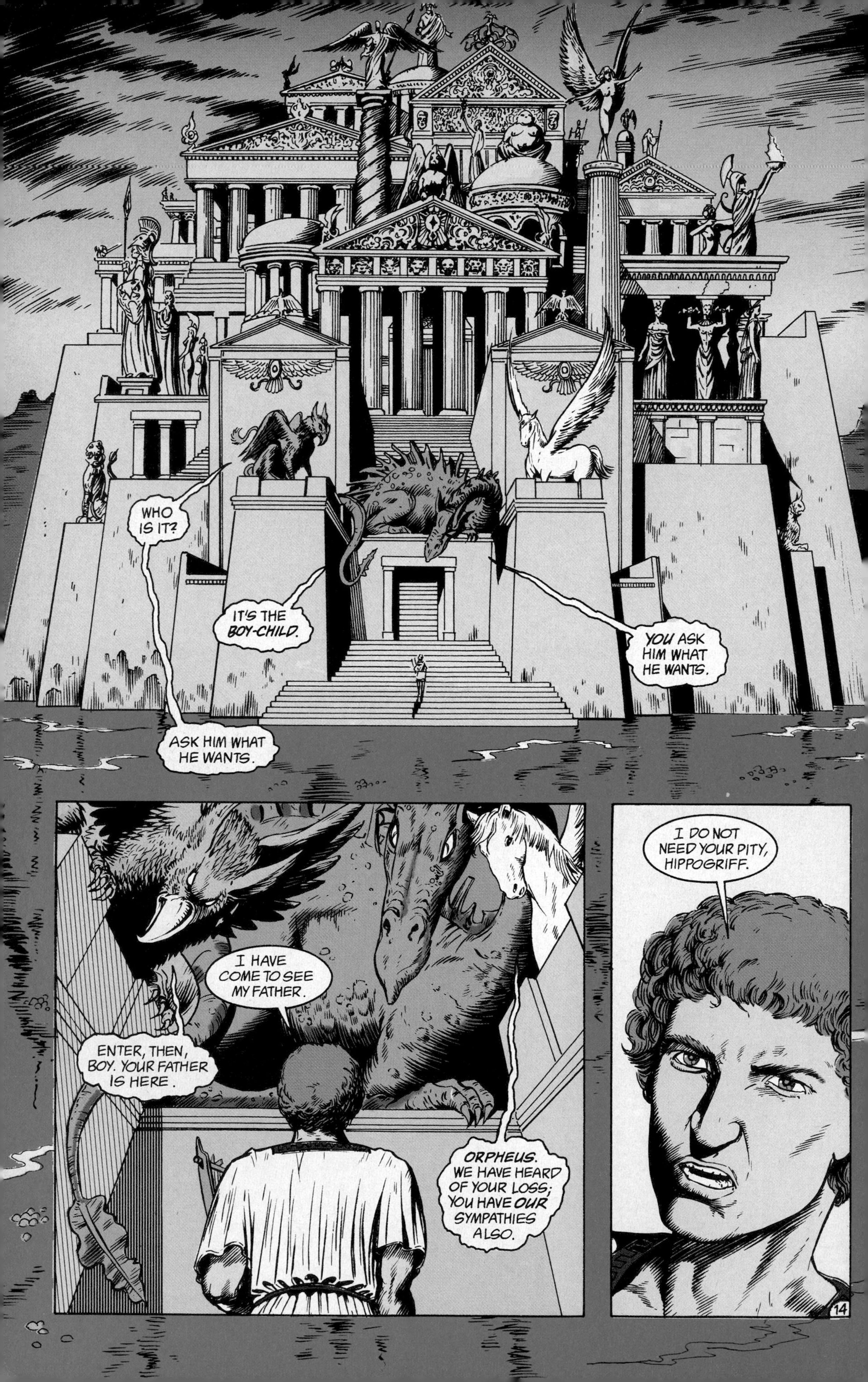
WHO IS IT?
IT'S THE BOY-CHILD.
YOU ASK HIM WHAT HE WANTS.
ASK HIM WHAT HE WANTS.
I HAVE COME TO SEE MY FATHER.
ENTER, THEN, BOY. YOUR FATHER IS HERE.
ORPHEUS. WE HAVE HEARD OF YOUR LOSS; YOU HAVE OUR SYMPATHIES ALSO.
I DO NOT NEED YOUR PITY, HIPPOGRIFF.
14

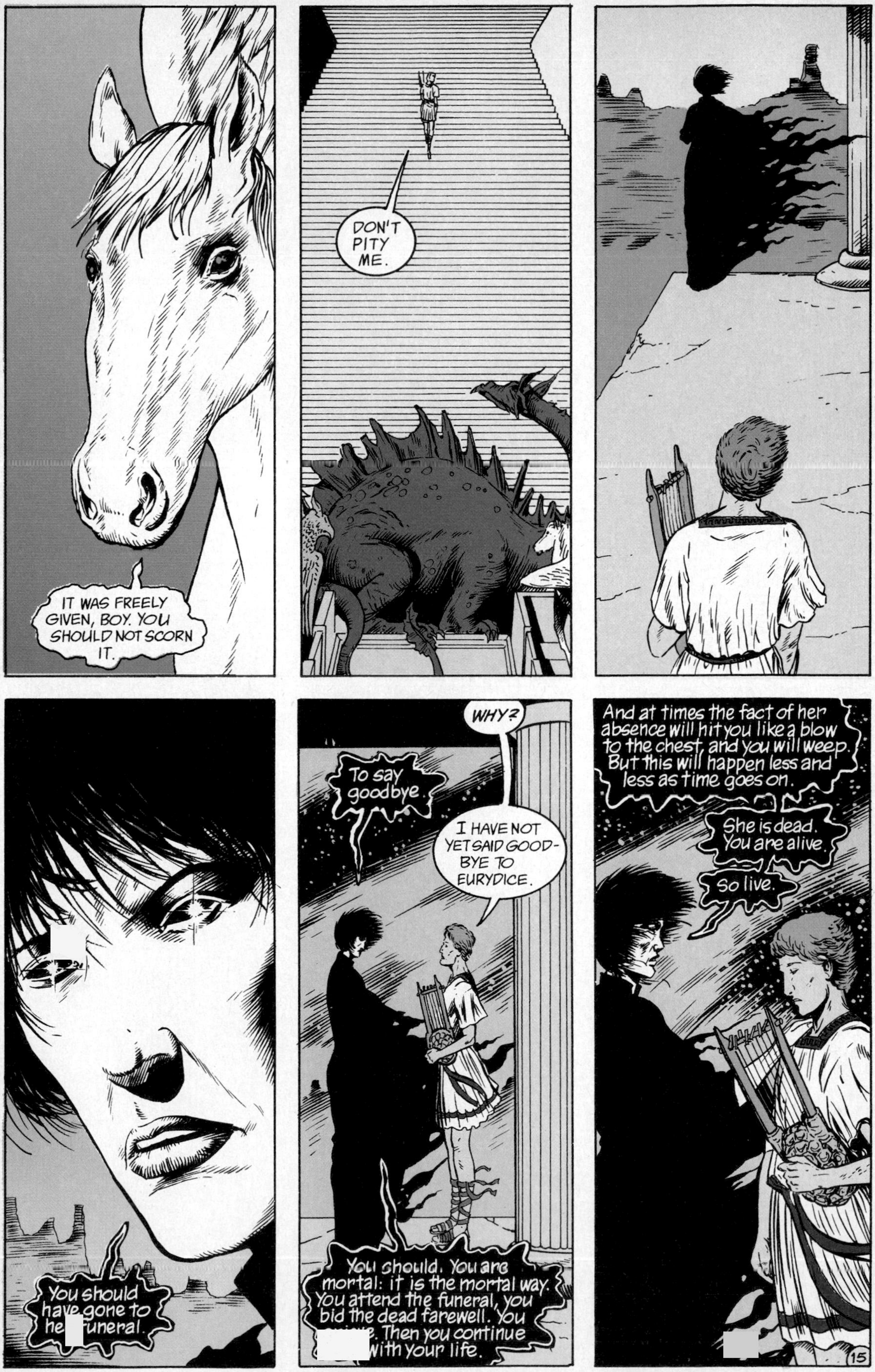
IT WAS FREELY GIVEN, BOY. YOU SHOULD NOT SCORN IT.
DON'T PITY ME.
You should have gone to he uneral.
WHY?
To say goodbye.
I HAVE NOT YET SAID GOOD-BYE TO EURYDICE.
You should. You are mortal: it is the mortal way. You attend the funeral, you bid the dead farewell. You . Then you continue with your life.
And at times the fact of her absence will hit you like a blow to the chest, and you will weep. But this will happen less and less as time goes on.
She is dead. You are alive.
So live.
15

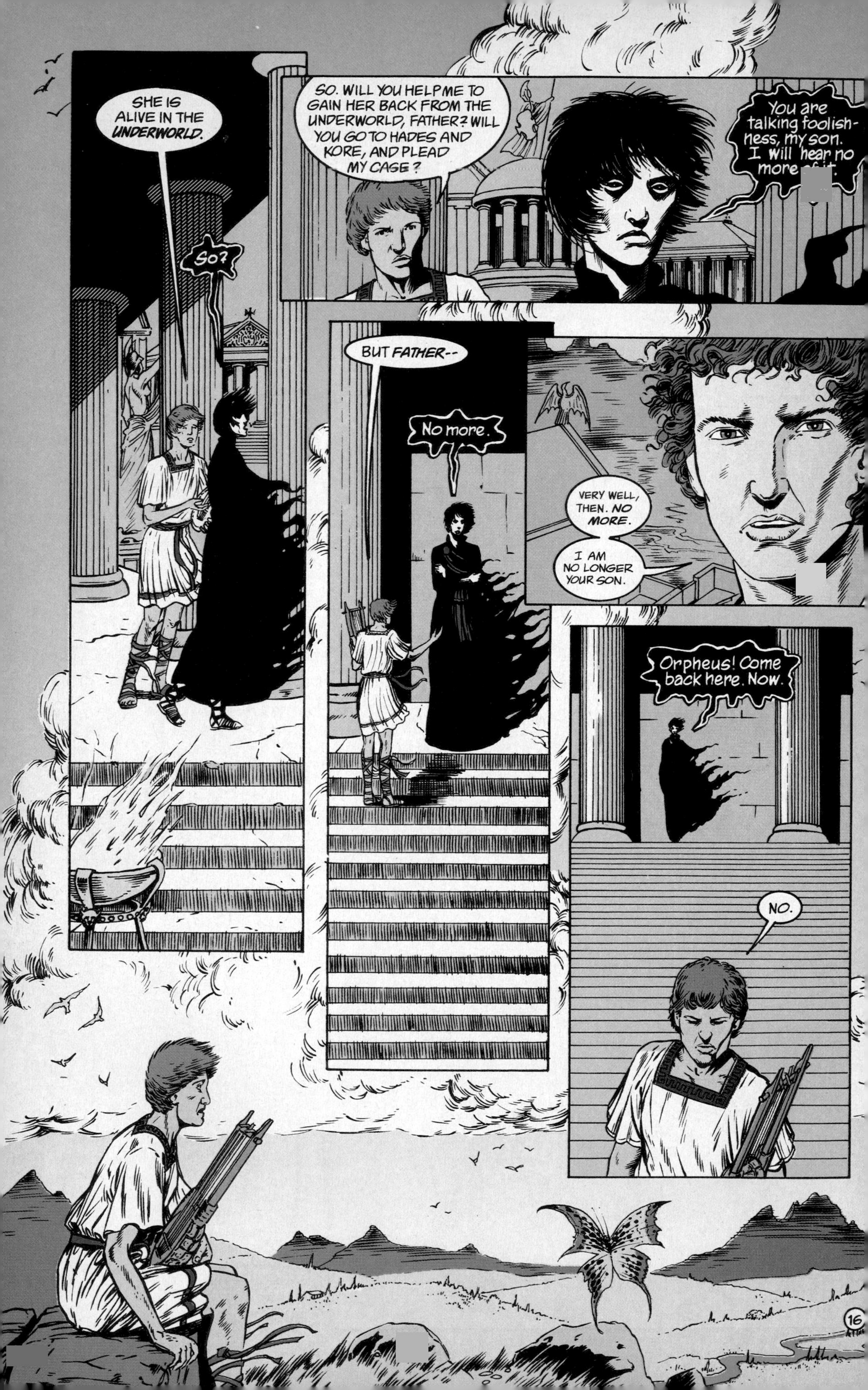
SHE IS ALIVE IN THE *UNDERWORLD*.
So?
SO. WILL YOU HELP ME TO GAIN HER BACK FROM THE UNDERWORLD, FATHER? WILL YOU GO TO HADES AND KORE, AND PLEAD MY CASE?
You are talking foolishness, my son. I will hear no more
BUT *FATHER*--
No more.
VERY WELL, THEN. *NO MORE*.
I AM NO LONGER YOUR SON.
Orpheus! Come back here. Now.
NO.

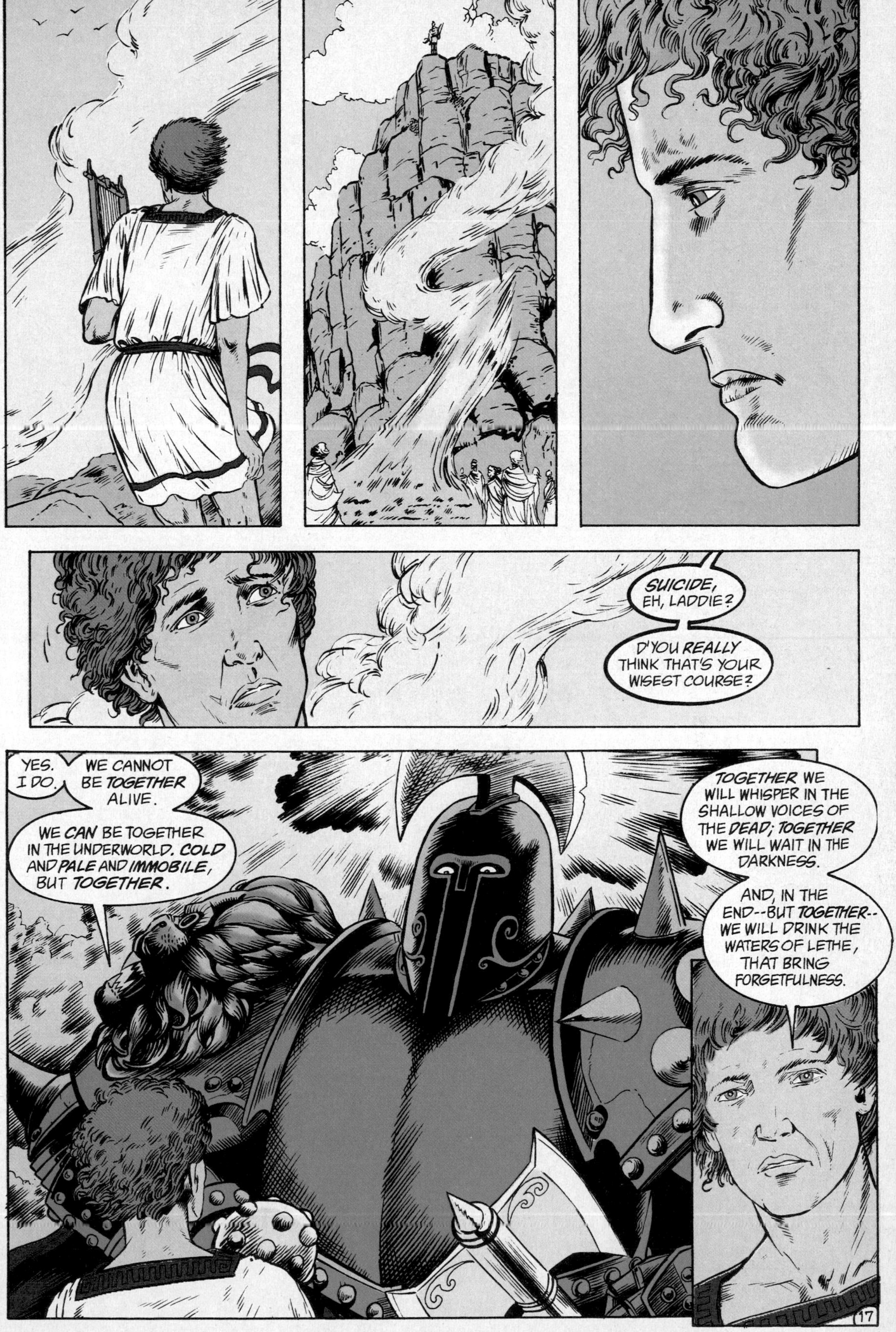
SUICIDE, EH, LADDIE?
D'YOU REALLY THINK THAT'S YOUR WISEST COURSE?
YES. I DO.
WE CANNOT BE TOGETHER ALIVE.
WE CAN BE TOGETHER IN THE UNDERWORLD. COLD AND PALE AND IMMOBILE, BUT TOGETHER.
TOGETHER WE WILL WHISPER IN THE SHALLOW VOICES OF THE DEAD; TOGETHER WE WILL WAIT IN THE DARKNESS.
AND, IN THE END--BUT TOGETHER--WE WILL DRINK THE WATERS OF LETHE, THAT BRING FORGETFULNESS.
17

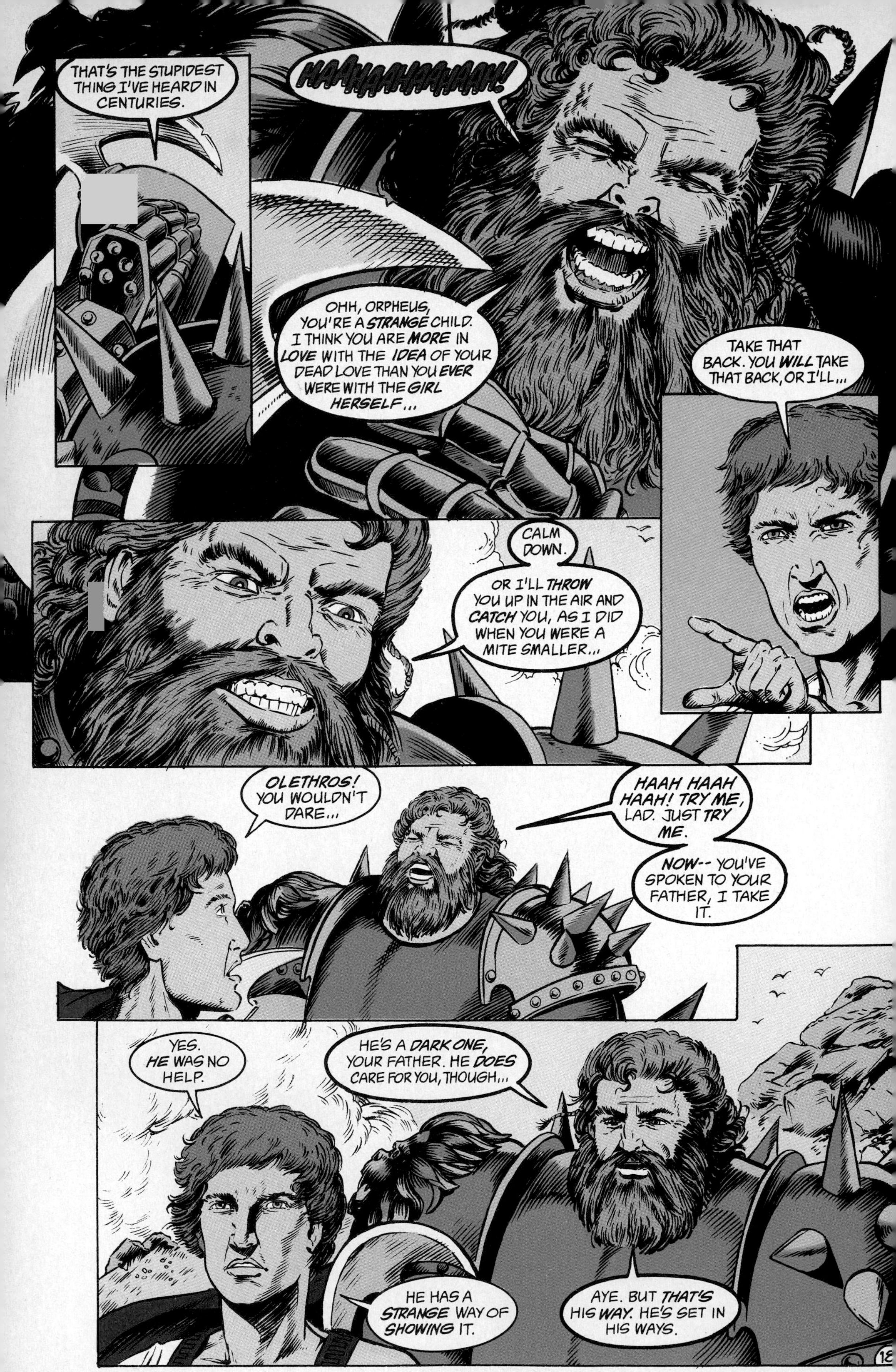
THAT'S THE STUPIDEST THING I'VE HEARD IN CENTURIES.
HAAHAAHAAHAAH!
OHH, ORPHEUS, YOU'RE A STRANGE CHILD. I THINK YOU ARE MORE IN LOVE WITH THE IDEA OF YOUR DEAD LOVE THAN YOU EVER WERE WITH THE GIRL HERSELF...
TAKE THAT BACK. YOU WILL TAKE THAT BACK, OR I'LL...
CALM DOWN.
OR I'LL THROW YOU UP IN THE AIR AND CATCH YOU, AS I DID WHEN YOU WERE A MITE SMALLER...
OLETHROS! YOU WOULDN'T DARE...
HAAH HAAH HAAH! TRY ME, LAD. JUST TRY ME.
NOW-- YOU'VE SPOKEN TO YOUR FATHER, I TAKE IT.
YES. HE WAS NO HELP.
HE'S A DARK ONE, YOUR FATHER. HE DOES CARE FOR YOU, THOUGH...
HE HAS A STRANGE WAY OF SHOWING IT.
AYE. BUT THAT'S HIS WAY. HE'S SET IN HIS WAYS.
18

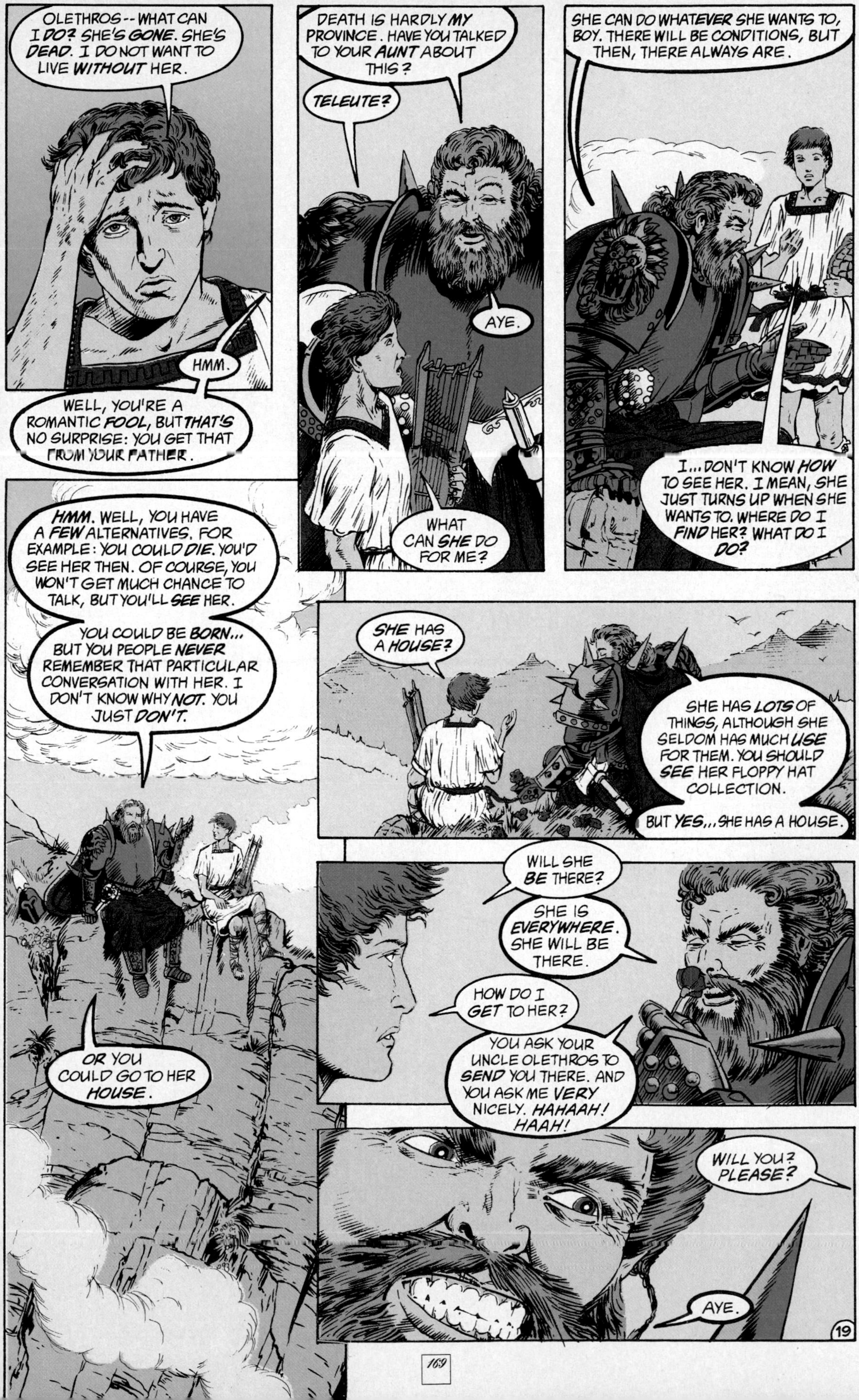
OLETHROS--WHAT CAN I DO? SHE'S GONE. SHE'S DEAD. I DO NOT WANT TO LIVE WITHOUT HER.
HMM.
WELL, YOU'RE A ROMANTIC FOOL, BUT THAT'S NO SURPRISE: YOU GET THAT FROM YOUR FATHER.
DEATH IS HARDLY MY PROVINCE. HAVE YOU TALKED TO YOUR AUNT ABOUT THIS?
TELEUTE?
AYE.
WHAT CAN SHE DO FOR ME?
SHE CAN DO WHATEVER SHE WANTS TO, BOY. THERE WILL BE CONDITIONS, BUT THEN, THERE ALWAYS ARE.
I... DON'T KNOW HOW TO SEE HER. I MEAN, SHE JUST TURNS UP WHEN SHE WANTS TO. WHERE DO I FIND HER? WHAT DO I DO?
HMM. WELL, YOU HAVE A FEW ALTERNATIVES. FOR EXAMPLE: YOU COULD DIE. YOU'D SEE HER THEN. OF COURSE, YOU WON'T GET MUCH CHANCE TO TALK, BUT YOU'LL SEE HER.
YOU COULD BE BORN... BUT YOU PEOPLE NEVER REMEMBER THAT PARTICULAR CONVERSATION WITH HER. I DON'T KNOW WHY NOT. YOU JUST DON'T.
OR YOU COULD GO TO HER HOUSE.
SHE HAS A HOUSE?
SHE HAS LOTS OF THINGS, ALTHOUGH SHE SELDOM HAS MUCH USE FOR THEM. YOU SHOULD SEE HER FLOPPY HAT COLLECTION.
BUT YES... SHE HAS A HOUSE.
WILL SHE BE THERE?
SHE IS EVERYWHERE. SHE WILL BE THERE.
HOW DO I GET TO HER?
YOU ASK YOUR UNCLE OLETHROS TO SEND YOU THERE. AND YOU ASK ME VERY NICELY. HAHAAAH! HAAH!
WILL YOU? PLEASE?
AYE.
19

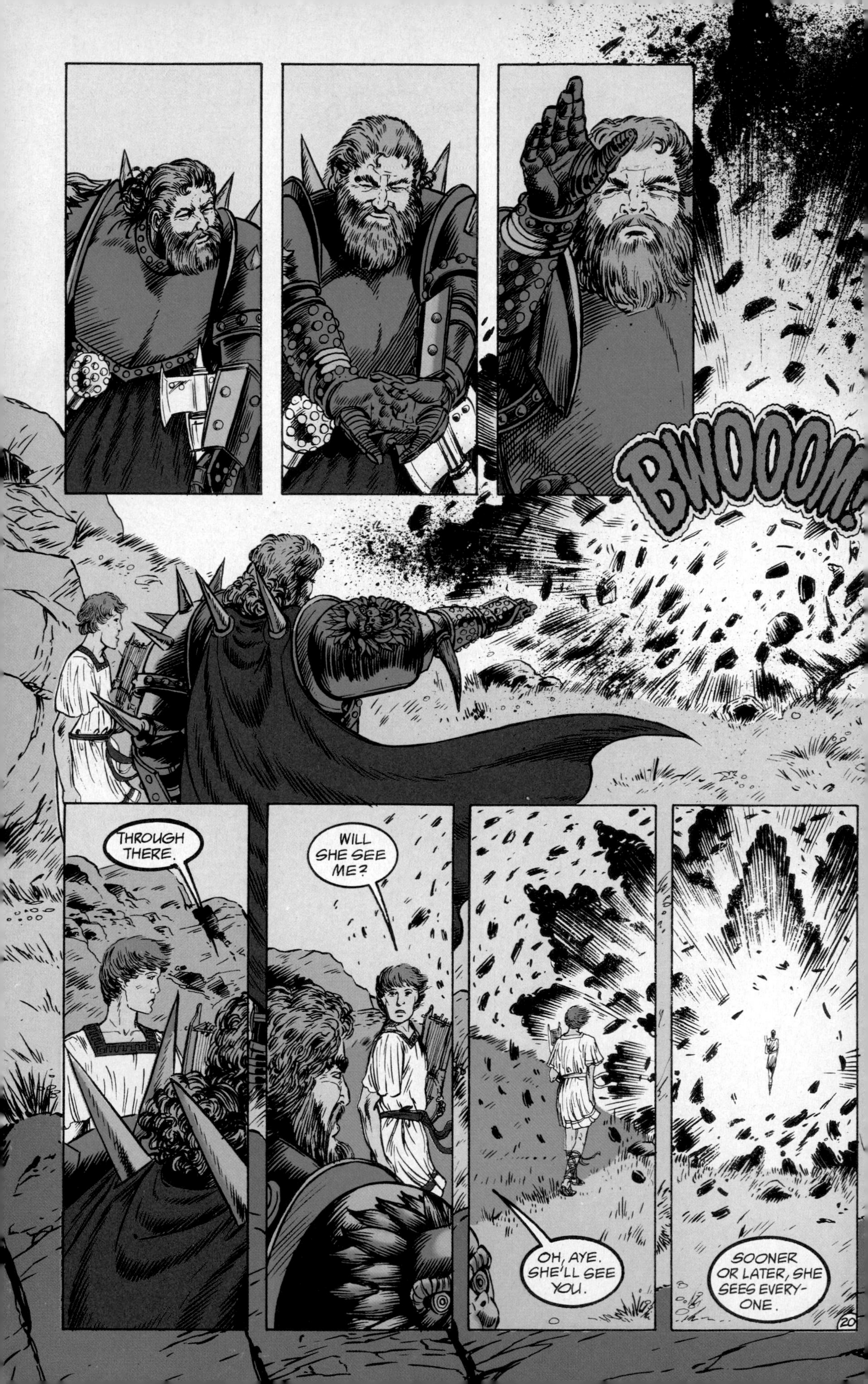
BWOOOM!
THROUGH THERE.
WILL SHE SEE ME?
OH, AYE. SHE'LL SEE YOU.
SOONER OR LATER, SHE SEES EVERY-ONE.
20

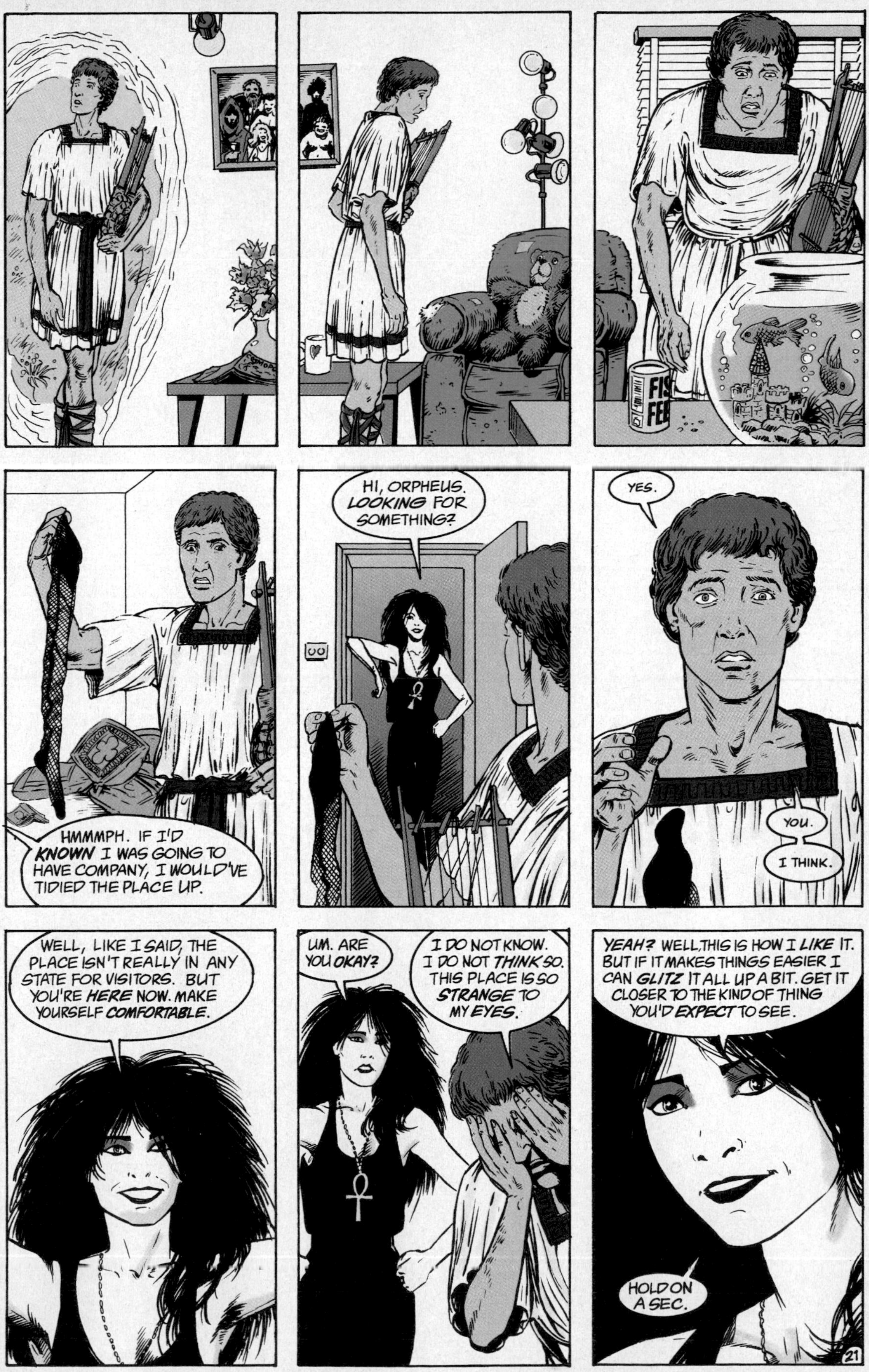
HMMMPH. IF I'D KNOWN I WAS GOING TO HAVE COMPANY, I WOULD'VE TIDIED THE PLACE UP.
HI, ORPHEUS. LOOKING FOR SOMETHING?
YES.
YOU.
I THINK.
WELL, LIKE I SAID, THE PLACE ISN'T REALLY IN ANY STATE FOR VISITORS. BUT YOU'RE HERE NOW. MAKE YOURSELF COMFORTABLE.
UM. ARE YOU OKAY?
I DO NOT KNOW. I DO NOT THINK SO. THIS PLACE IS SO STRANGE TO MY EYES.
YEAH? WELL, THIS IS HOW I LIKE IT. BUT IF IT MAKES THINGS EASIER I CAN GLITZ IT ALL UP A BIT. GET IT CLOSER TO THE KIND OF THING YOU'D EXPECT TO SEE.
HOLD ON A SEC.
21

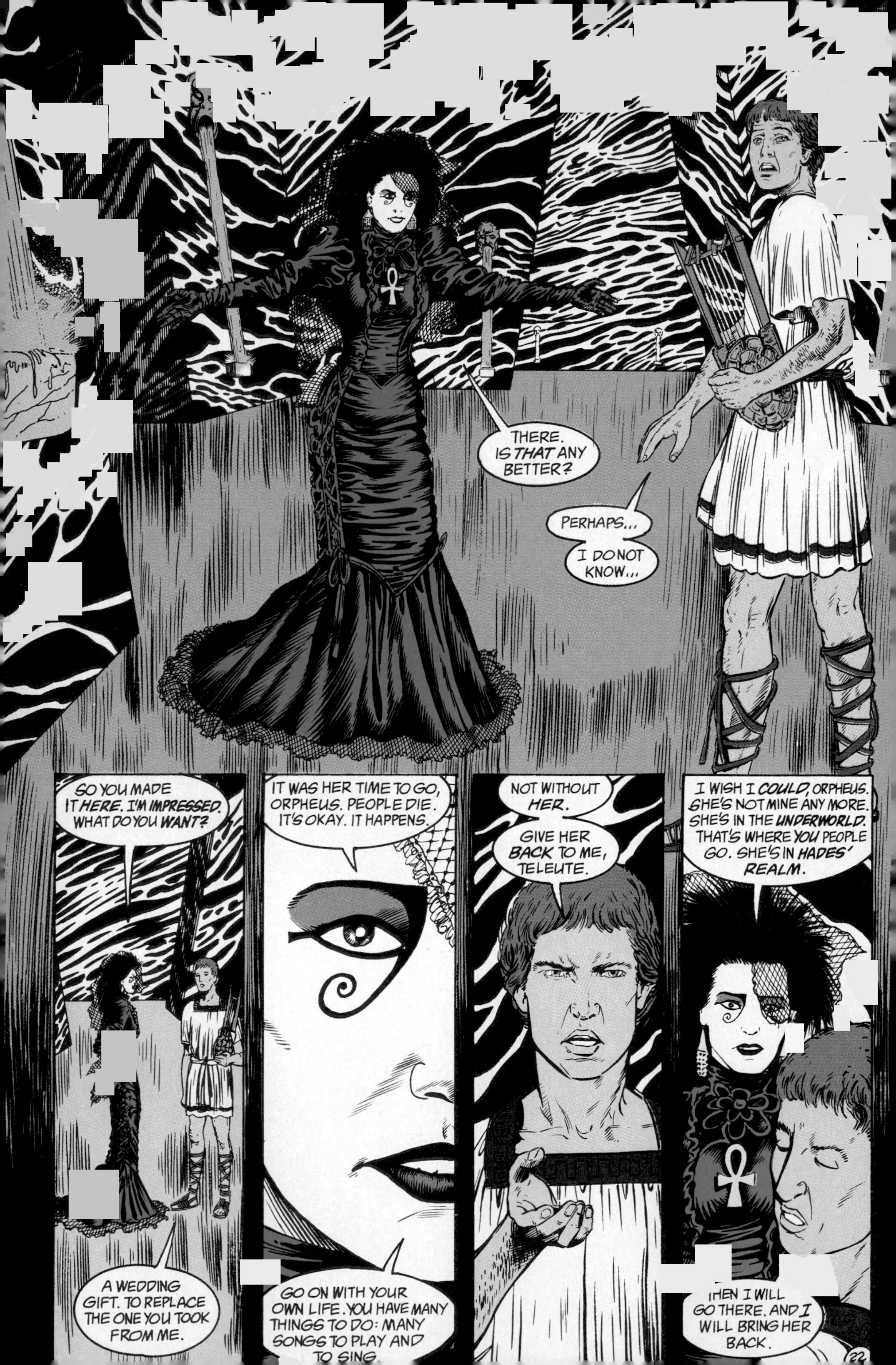
THERE. IS *THAT* ANY BETTER?
PERHAPS...
I DO NOT KNOW...
SO YOU MADE IT *HERE*. I'M *IMPRESSED*. WHAT DO YOU *WANT*?
A WEDDING GIFT. TO REPLACE THE ONE YOU TOOK FROM ME.
IT WAS HER TIME TO GO, ORPHEUS. PEOPLE DIE. IT'S OKAY. IT HAPPENS.
GO ON WITH YOUR OWN LIFE. YOU HAVE MANY THINGS TO DO: MANY SONGS TO PLAY AND TO SING.
NOT WITHOUT *HER*.
GIVE HER *BACK* TO ME, TELEUTE.
I WISH I *COULD*, ORPHEUS. SHE'S NOT MINE ANY MORE. SHE'S IN THE *UNDERWORLD*. THAT'S WHERE *YOU* PEOPLE GO. SHE'S IN *HADES' REALM*.
THEN I WILL GO THERE. AND *I* WILL BRING HER BACK.

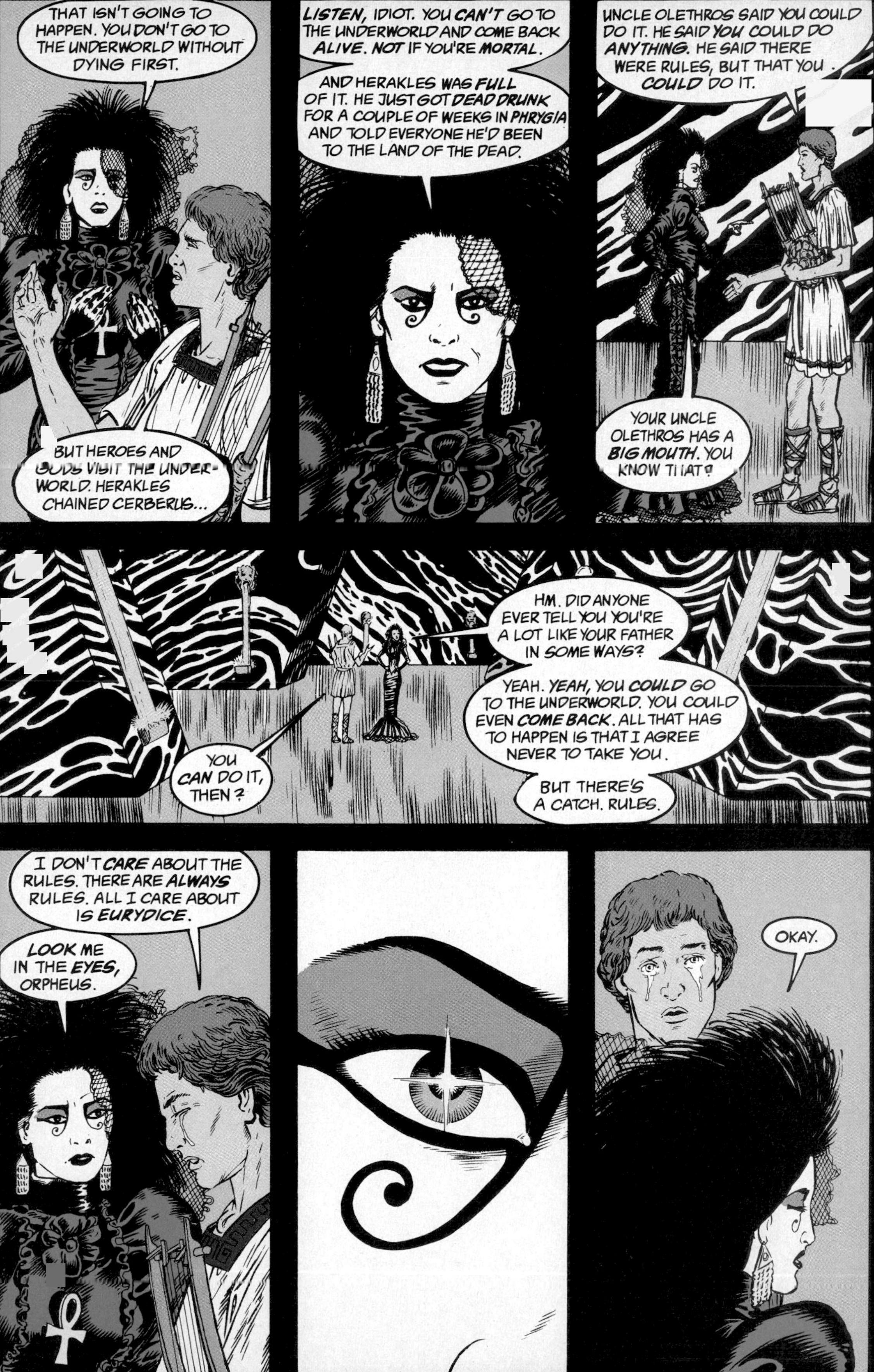
THAT ISN'T GOING TO HAPPEN. YOU DON'T GO TO THE UNDERWORLD WITHOUT DYING FIRST.
BUT HEROES AND GODS VISIT THE UNDERWORLD. HERAKLES CHAINED CERBERUS...
LISTEN, IDIOT. YOU CAN'T GO TO THE UNDERWORLD AND COME BACK ALIVE. NOT IF YOU'RE MORTAL.
AND HERAKLES WAS FULL OF IT. HE JUST GOT DEAD DRUNK FOR A COUPLE OF WEEKS IN PHRYGIA AND TOLD EVERYONE HE'D BEEN TO THE LAND OF THE DEAD.
UNCLE OLETHROS SAID YOU COULD DO IT. HE SAID YOU COULD DO ANYTHING. HE SAID THERE WERE RULES, BUT THAT YOU COULD DO IT.
YOUR UNCLE OLETHROS HAS A BIG MOUTH. YOU KNOW THAT?
YOU CAN DO IT, THEN?
HM. DID ANYONE EVER TELL YOU YOU'RE A LOT LIKE YOUR FATHER IN SOME WAYS?
YEAH. YEAH, YOU COULD GO TO THE UNDERWORLD. YOU COULD EVEN COME BACK. ALL THAT HAS TO HAPPEN IS THAT I AGREE NEVER TO TAKE YOU.
BUT THERE'S A CATCH. RULES.
I DON'T CARE ABOUT THE RULES. THERE ARE ALWAYS RULES. ALL I CARE ABOUT IS EURYDICE.
LOOK ME IN THE EYES, ORPHEUS.
OKAY.

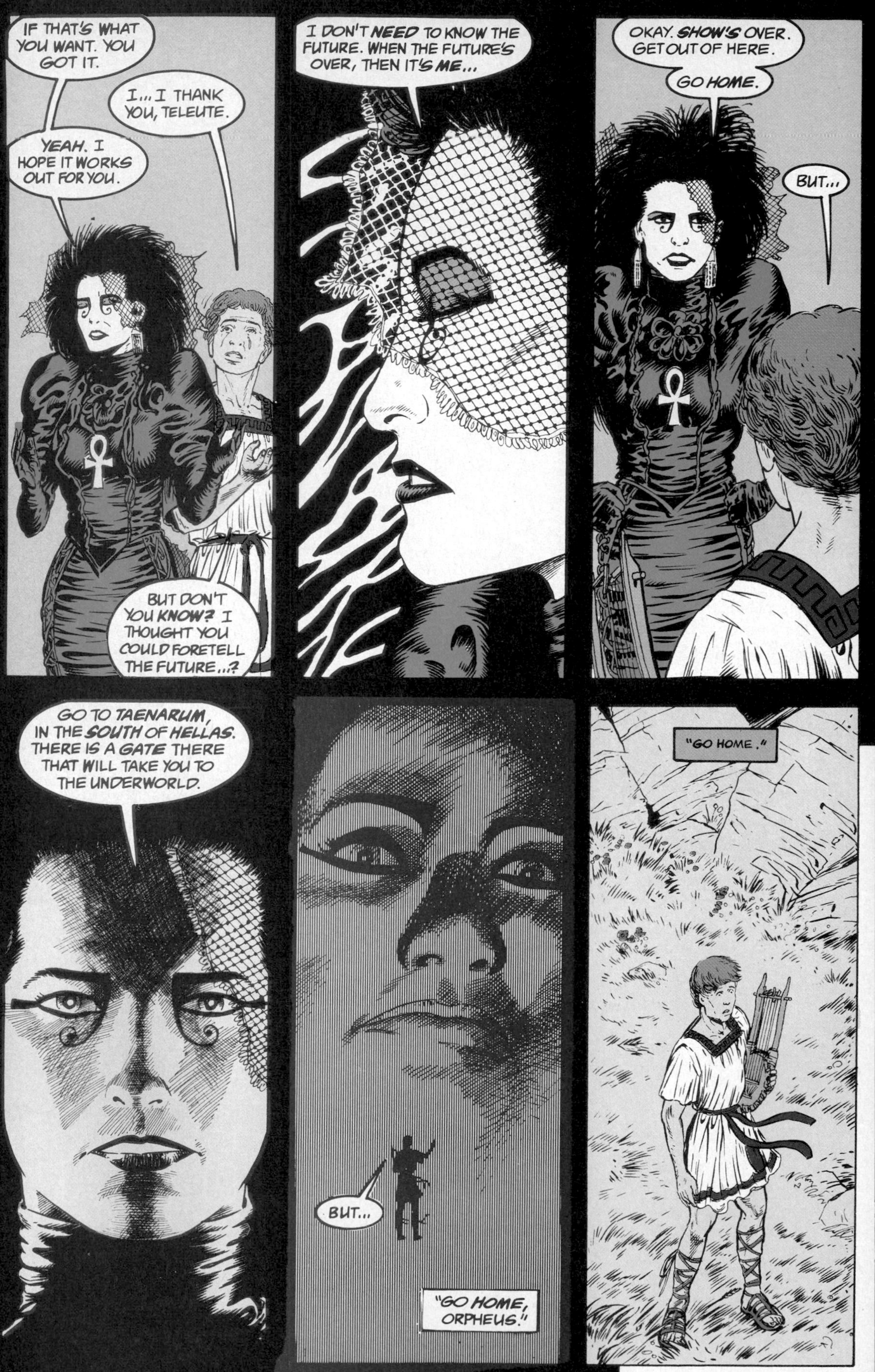
IF THAT'S WHAT YOU WANT. YOU GOT IT.
I... I THANK YOU, TELEUTE.
YEAH. I HOPE IT WORKS OUT FOR YOU.
BUT DON'T YOU KNOW? I THOUGHT YOU COULD FORETELL THE FUTURE...?
I DON'T NEED TO KNOW THE FUTURE. WHEN THE FUTURE'S OVER, THEN IT'S ME...
OKAY. SHOW'S OVER. GET OUT OF HERE.
GO HOME.
BUT...
GO TO TAENARUM, IN THE SOUTH OF HELLAS. THERE IS A GATE THERE THAT WILL TAKE YOU TO THE UNDERWORLD.
BUT...
"GO HOME, ORPHEUS."
"GO HOME."

THE SONG OF ORPHEUS

C·H·A·P·T·E·R T·H·R·E·E

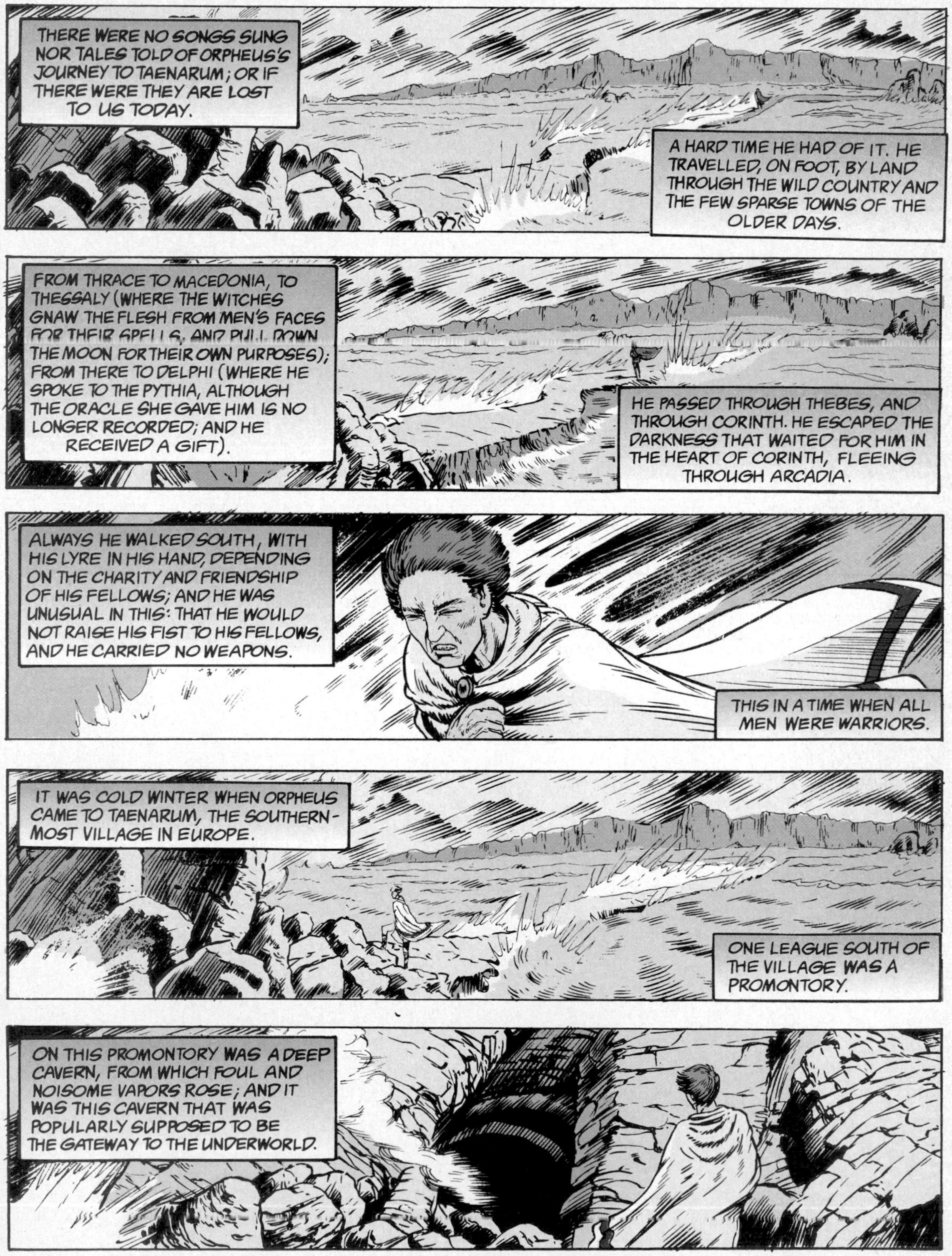
THERE WERE NO SONGS SUNG NOR TALES TOLD OF ORPHEUS'S JOURNEY TO TAENARUM; OR IF THERE WERE THEY ARE LOST TO US TODAY.
A HARD TIME HE HAD OF IT. HE TRAVELLED, ON FOOT, BY LAND THROUGH THE WILD COUNTRY AND THE FEW SPARSE TOWNS OF THE OLDER DAYS.
FROM THRACE TO MACEDONIA, TO THESSALY (WHERE THE WITCHES GNAW THE FLESH FROM MEN'S FACES FOR THEIR SPELLS, AND PULL DOWN THE MOON FOR THEIR OWN PURPOSES); FROM THERE TO DELPHI (WHERE HE SPOKE TO THE PYTHIA, ALTHOUGH THE ORACLE SHE GAVE HIM IS NO LONGER RECORDED; AND HE RECEIVED A GIFT).
HE PASSED THROUGH THEBES, AND THROUGH CORINTH. HE ESCAPED THE DARKNESS THAT WAITED FOR HIM IN THE HEART OF CORINTH, FLEEING THROUGH ARCADIA.
ALWAYS HE WALKED SOUTH, WITH HIS LYRE IN HIS HAND, DEPENDING ON THE CHARITY AND FRIENDSHIP OF HIS FELLOWS; AND HE WAS UNUSUAL IN THIS: THAT HE WOULD NOT RAISE HIS FIST TO HIS FELLOWS, AND HE CARRIED NO WEAPONS.
THIS IN A TIME WHEN ALL MEN WERE WARRIORS.
IT WAS COLD WINTER WHEN ORPHEUS CAME TO TAENARUM, THE SOUTHERN-MOST VILLAGE IN EUROPE.
ONE LEAGUE SOUTH OF THE VILLAGE WAS A PROMONTORY.
ON THIS PROMONTORY WAS A DEEP CAVERN, FROM WHICH FOUL AND NOISOME VAPORS ROSE; AND IT WAS THIS CAVERN THAT WAS POPULARLY SUPPOSED TO BE THE GATEWAY TO THE UNDERWORLD.

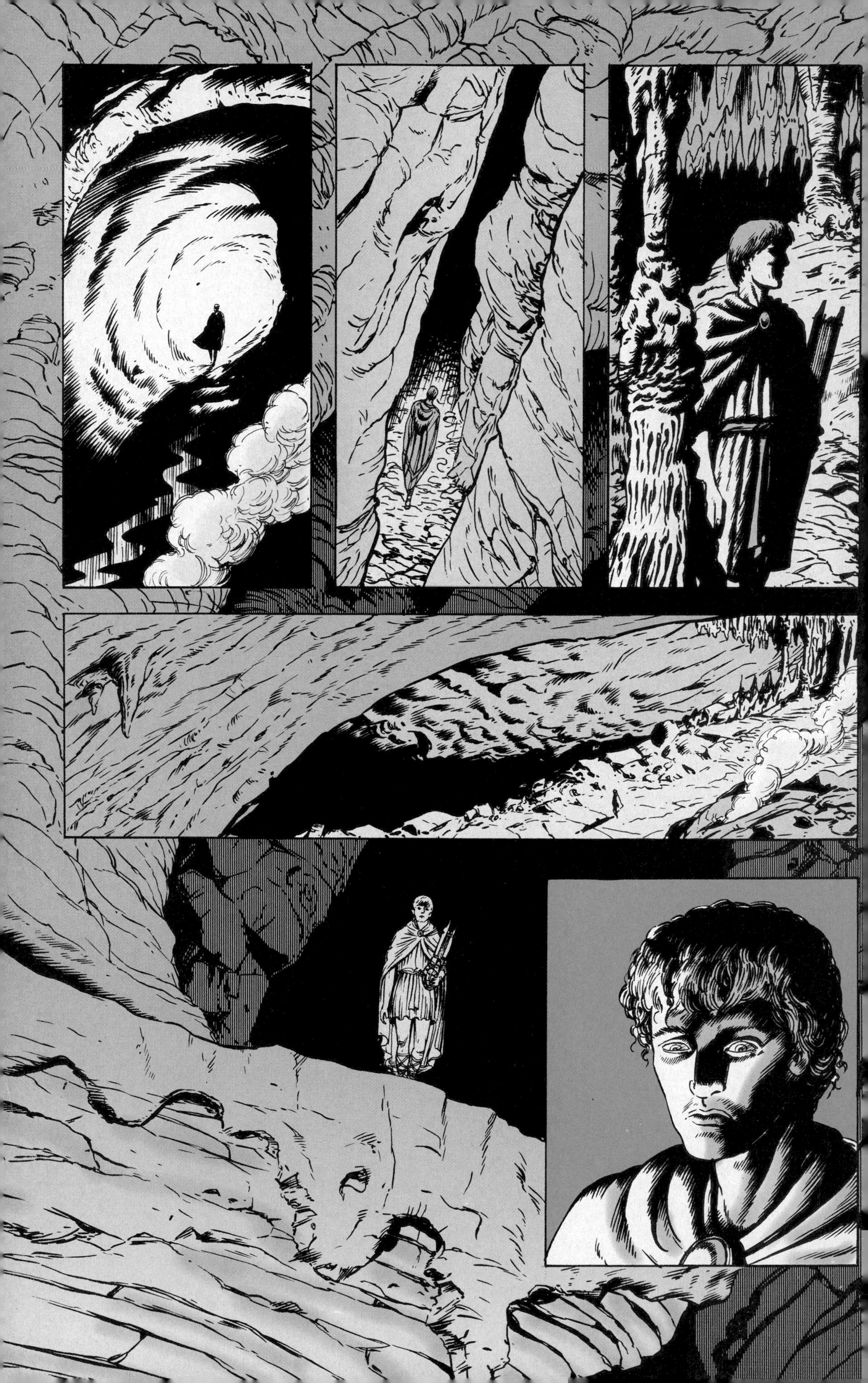

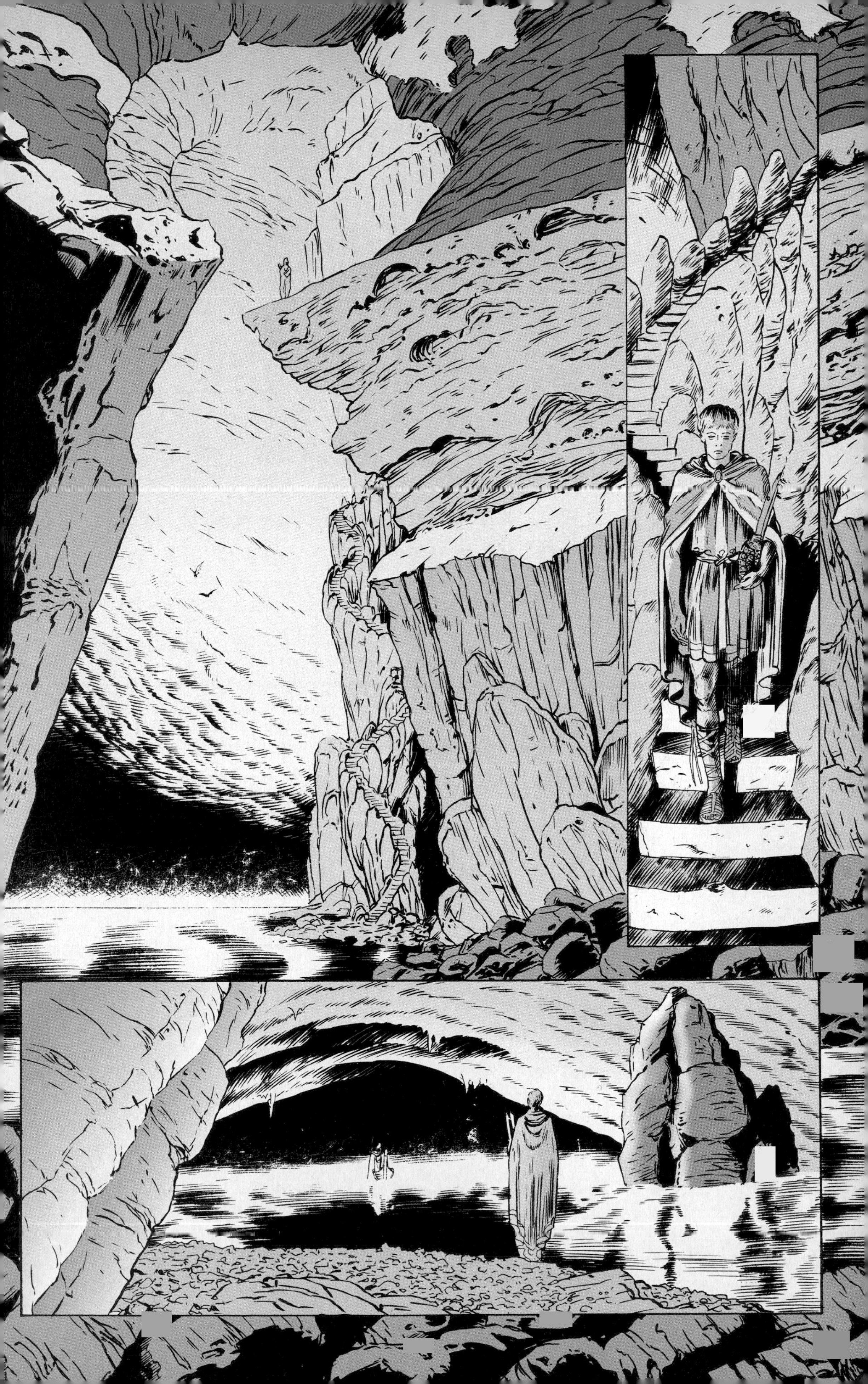

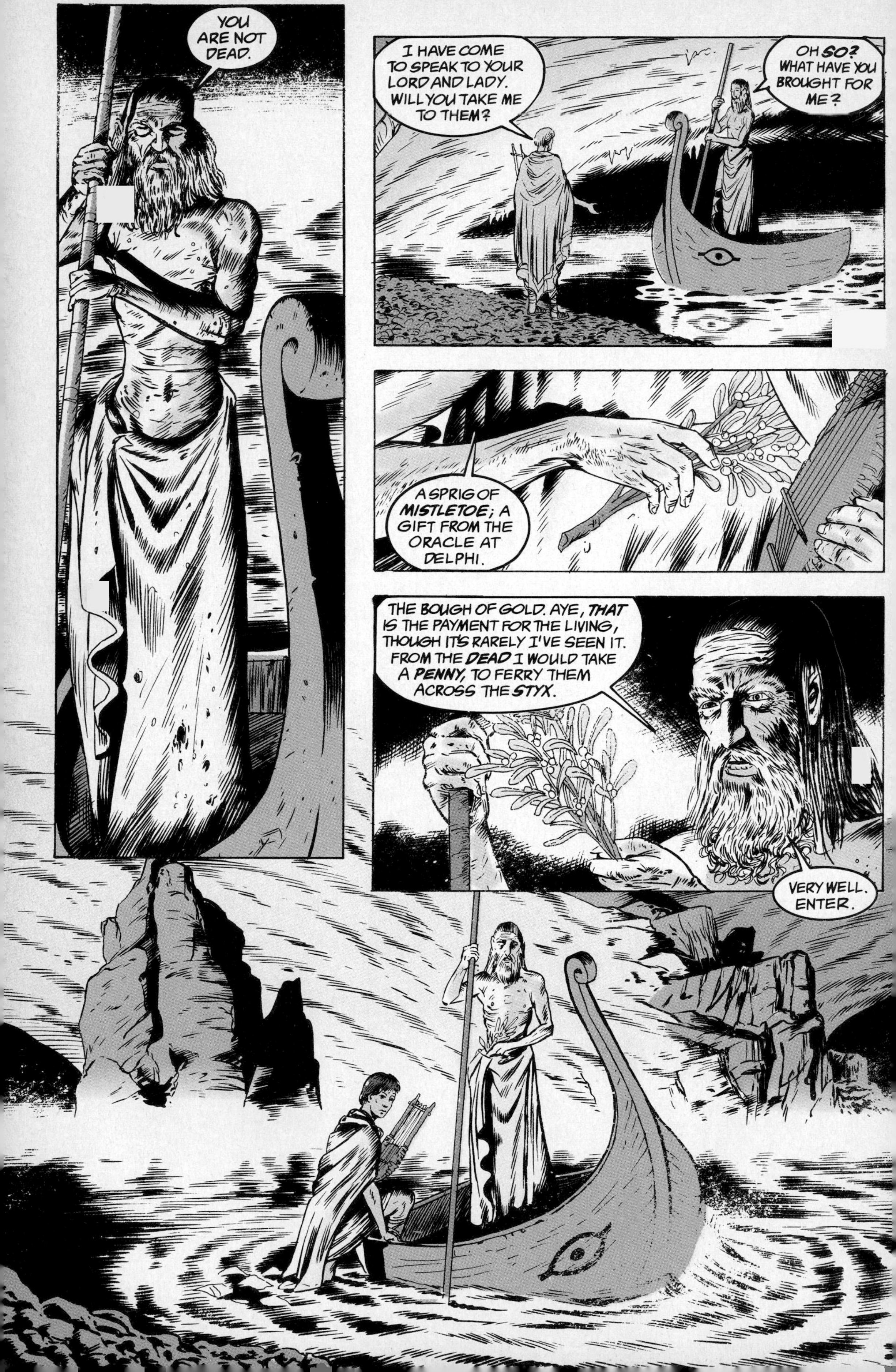
YOU ARE NOT DEAD.
I HAVE COME TO SPEAK TO YOUR LORD AND LADY. WILL YOU TAKE ME TO THEM?
OH SO? WHAT HAVE YOU BROUGHT FOR ME?
A SPRIG OF MISTLETOE; A GIFT FROM THE ORACLE AT DELPHI.
THE BOUGH OF GOLD. AYE, THAT IS THE PAYMENT FOR THE LIVING, THOUGH IT'S RARELY I'VE SEEN IT. FROM THE DEAD I WOULD TAKE A PENNY, TO FERRY THEM ACROSS THE STYX.
VERY WELL. ENTER.

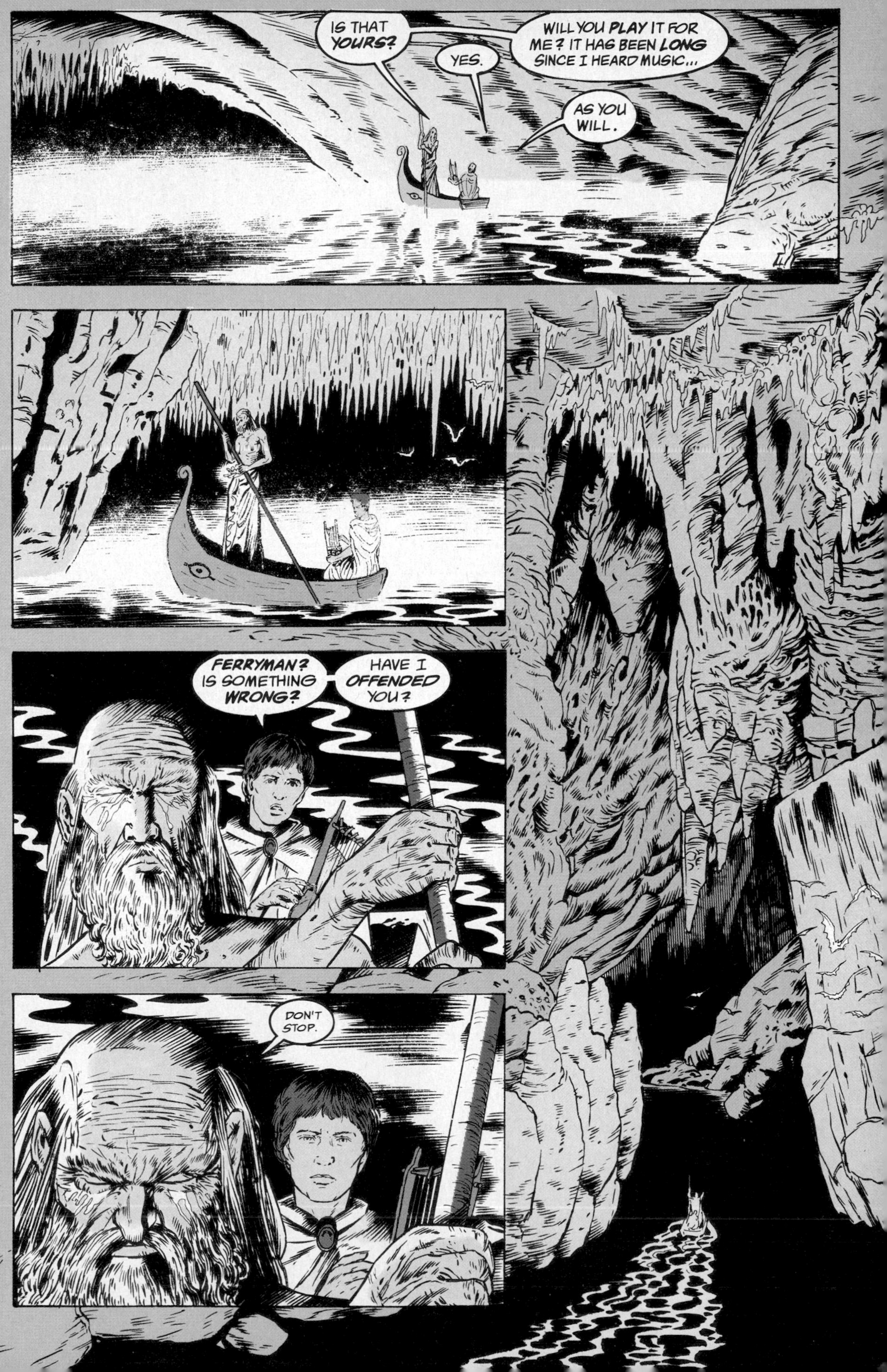
IS THAT YOURS?
YES.
WILL YOU PLAY IT FOR ME? IT HAS BEEN LONG SINCE I HEARD MUSIC...
AS YOU WILL.
FERRYMAN? IS SOMETHING WRONG?
HAVE I OFFENDED YOU?
DON'T STOP.

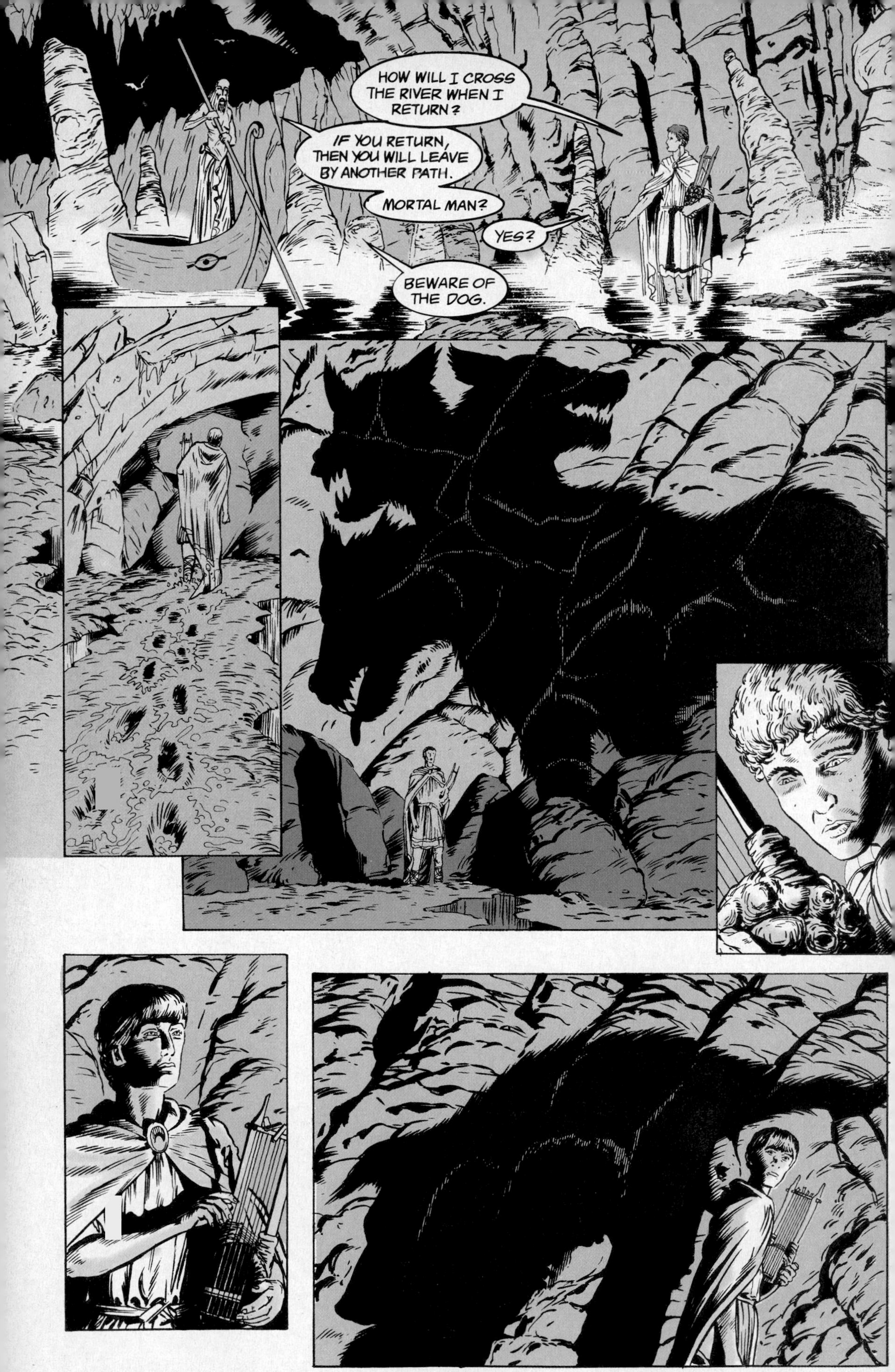
HOW WILL I CROSS THE RIVER WHEN I RETURN?
IF YOU RETURN, THEN YOU WILL LEAVE BY ANOTHER PATH.
MORTAL MAN?
YES?
BEWARE OF THE DOG.

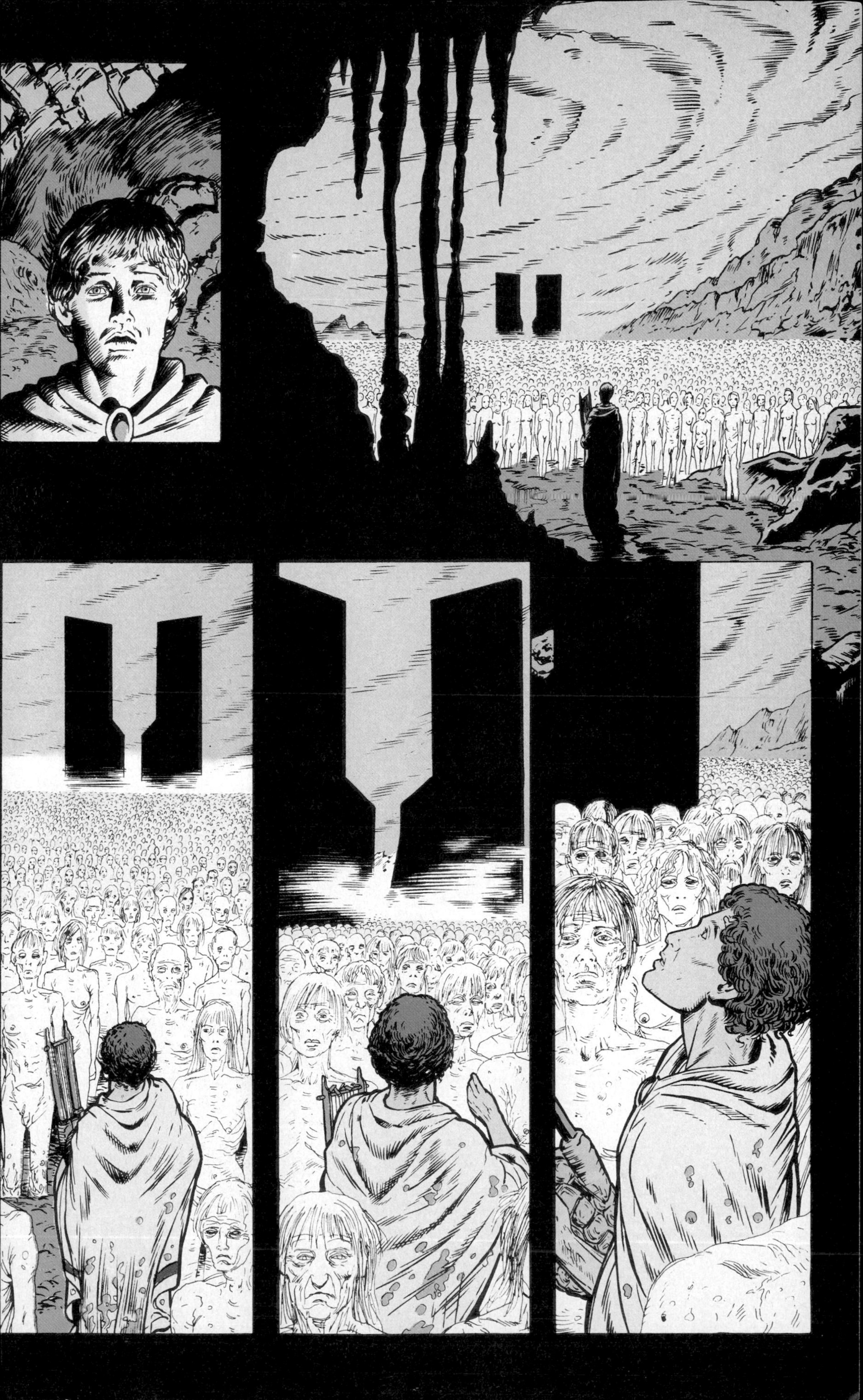

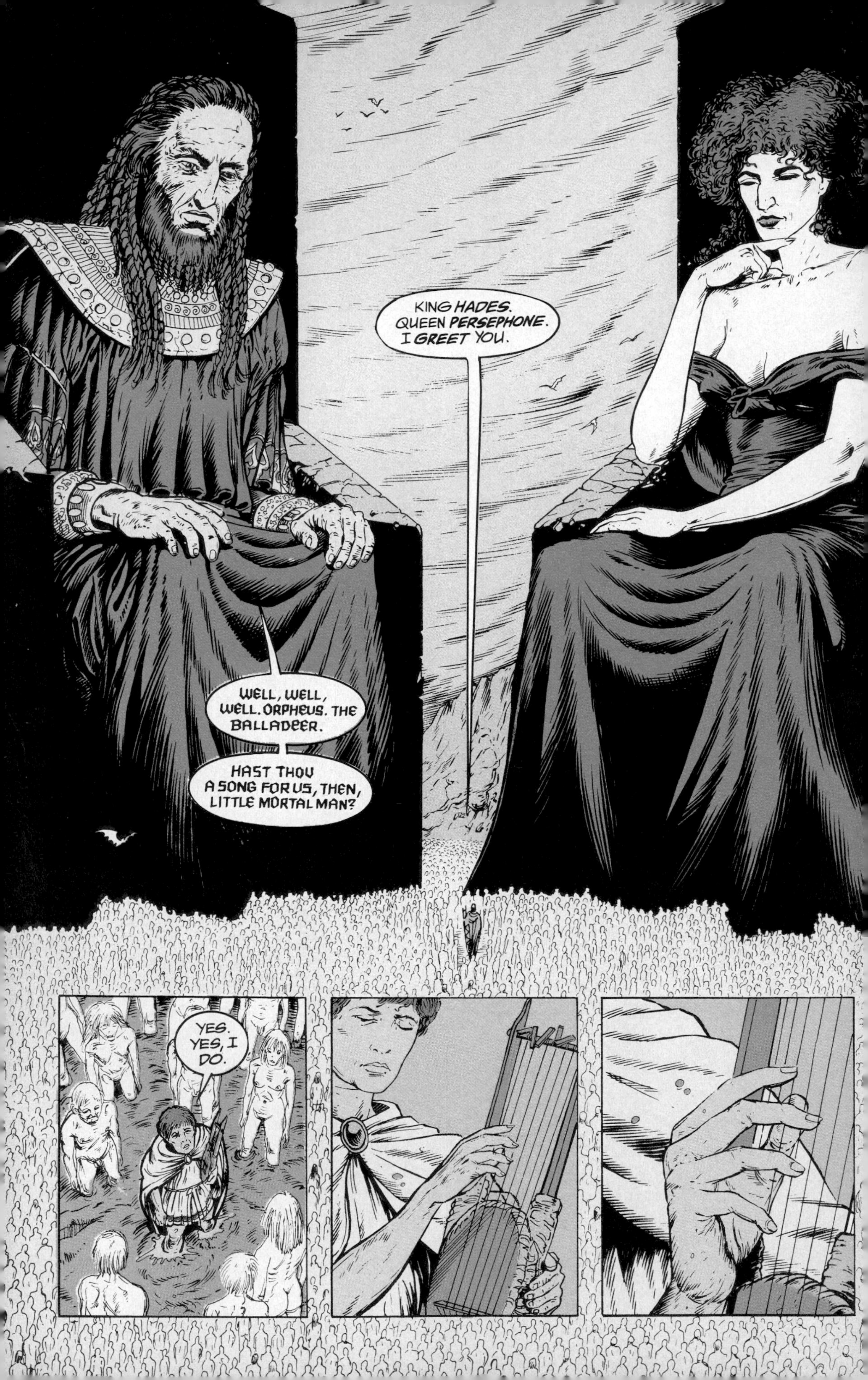
KING HADES. QUEEN PERSEPHONE. I GREET YOU.
WELL, WELL, WELL. ORPHEUS. THE BALLADEER.
HAST THOU A SONG FOR US, THEN, LITTLE MORTAL MAN?
YES. YES, I DO.

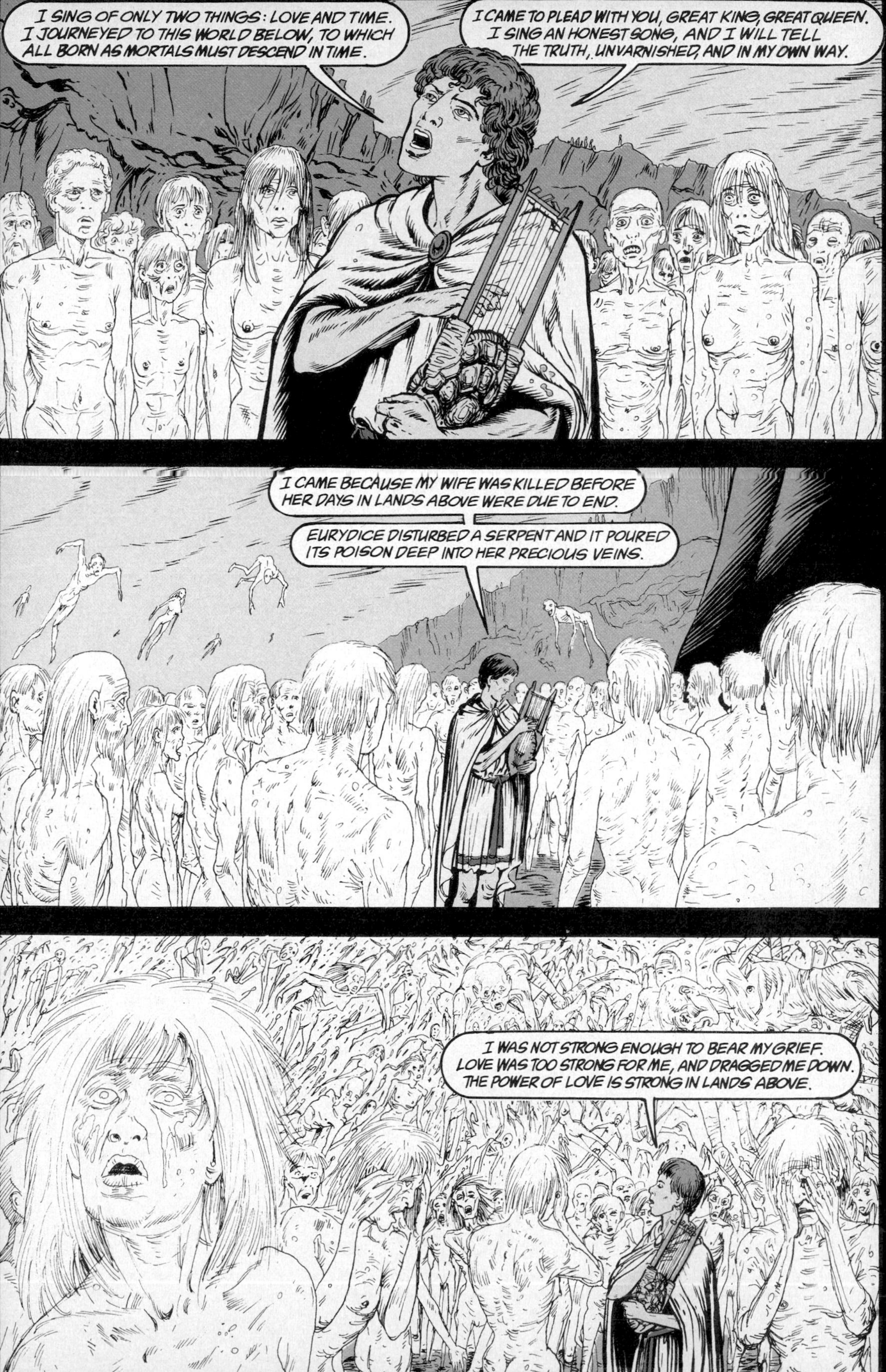
I SING OF ONLY TWO THINGS: LOVE AND TIME. I JOURNEYED TO THIS WORLD BELOW, TO WHICH ALL BORN AS MORTALS MUST DESCEND IN TIME.
I CAME TO PLEAD WITH YOU, GREAT KING, GREAT QUEEN. I SING AN HONEST SONG, AND I WILL TELL THE TRUTH, UNVARNISHED, AND IN MY OWN WAY.
I CAME BECAUSE MY WIFE WAS KILLED BEFORE HER DAYS IN LANDS ABOVE WERE DUE TO END.
EURYDICE DISTURBED A SERPENT AND IT POURED ITS POISON DEEP INTO HER PRECIOUS VEINS.
I WAS NOT STRONG ENOUGH TO BEAR MY GRIEF. LOVE WAS TOO STRONG FOR ME, AND DRAGGED ME DOWN. THE POWER OF LOVE IS STRONG IN LANDS ABOVE.

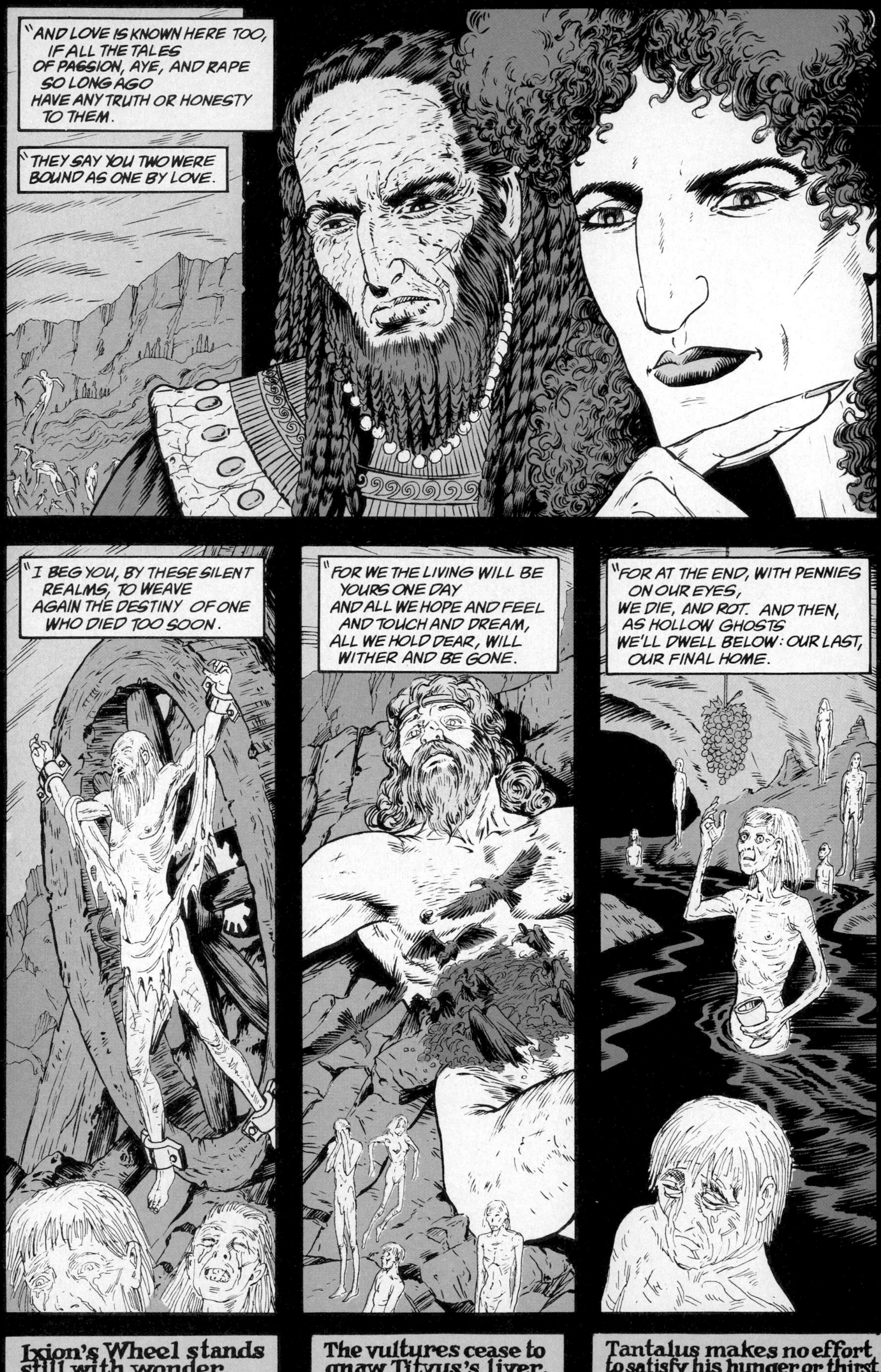
"AND LOVE IS KNOWN HERE TOO, IF ALL THE TALES OF PASSION, AYE, AND RAPE SO LONG AGO HAVE ANY TRUTH OR HONESTY TO THEM.
"THEY SAY YOU TWO WERE BOUND AS ONE BY LOVE.
"I BEG YOU, BY THESE SILENT REALMS, TO WEAVE AGAIN THE DESTINY OF ONE WHO DIED TOO SOON.
Ixion's Wheel stands still with wonder.
"FOR WE THE LIVING WILL BE YOURS ONE DAY AND ALL WE HOPE AND FEEL AND TOUCH AND DREAM, ALL WE HOLD DEAR, WILL WITHER AND BE GONE.
The vultures cease to gnaw Tityus's liver.
"FOR AT THE END, WITH PENNIES ON OUR EYES, WE DIE, AND ROT. AND THEN, AS HOLLOW GHOSTS WE'LL DWELL BELOW: OUR LAST, OUR FINAL HOME.
Tantalus makes no effort to satisfy his hunger or thirst.

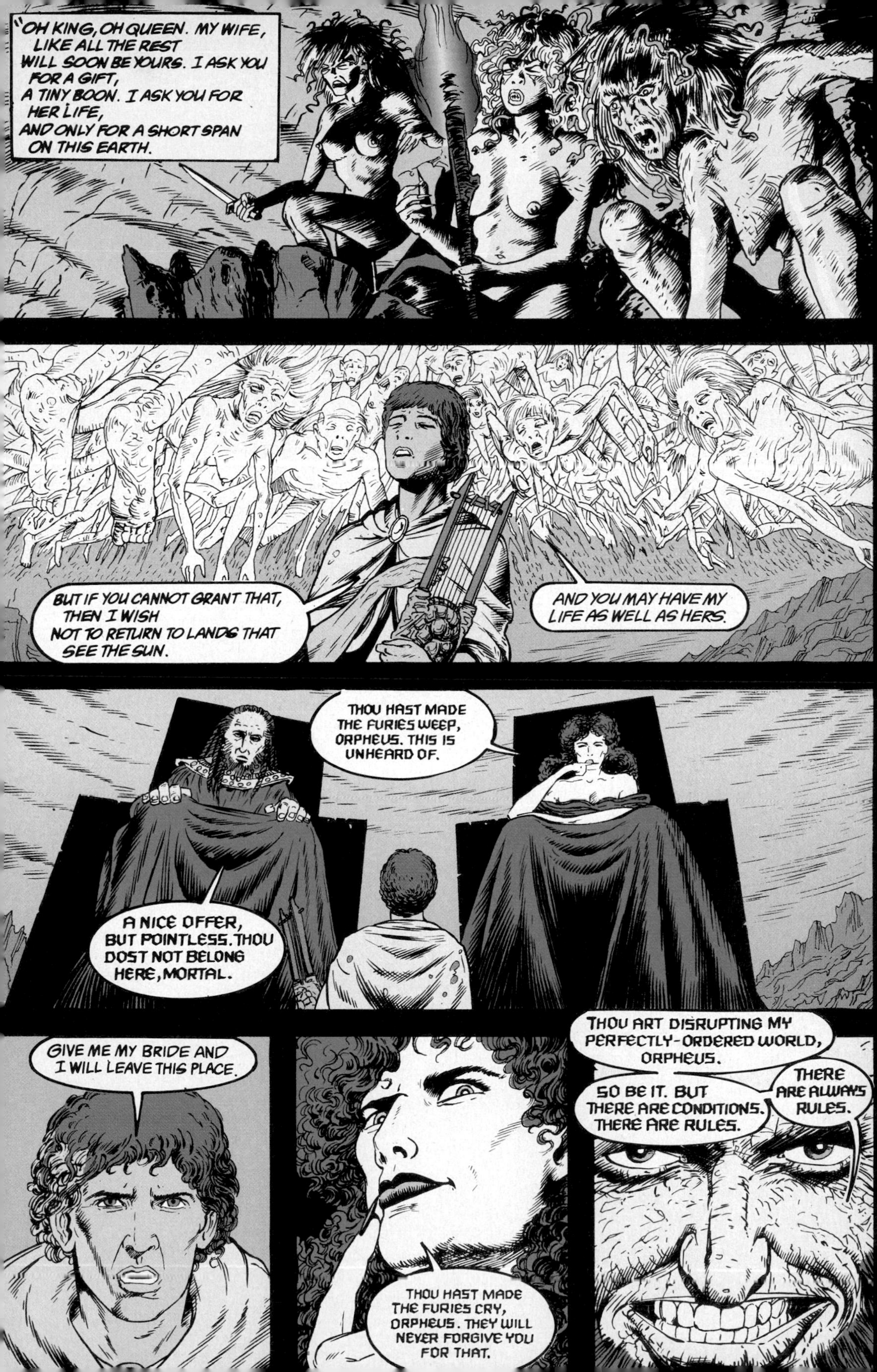
"OH KING, OH QUEEN. MY WIFE, LIKE ALL THE REST WILL SOON BE YOURS. I ASK YOU FOR A GIFT, A TINY BOON. I ASK YOU FOR HER LIFE, AND ONLY FOR A SHORT SPAN ON THIS EARTH.
BUT IF YOU CANNOT GRANT THAT, THEN I WISH NOT TO RETURN TO LANDS THAT SEE THE SUN.
AND YOU MAY HAVE MY LIFE AS WELL AS HERS.
THOU HAST MADE THE FURIES WEEP, ORPHEUS. THIS IS UNHEARD OF.
A NICE OFFER, BUT POINTLESS. THOU DOST NOT BELONG HERE, MORTAL.
GIVE ME MY BRIDE AND I WILL LEAVE THIS PLACE.
THOU HAST MADE THE FURIES CRY, ORPHEUS. THEY WILL NEVER FORGIVE YOU FOR THAT.
THOU ART DISRUPTING MY PERFECTLY-ORDERED WORLD, ORPHEUS.
SO BE IT. BUT THERE ARE CONDITIONS. THERE ARE RULES.
THERE ARE ALWAYS RULES.

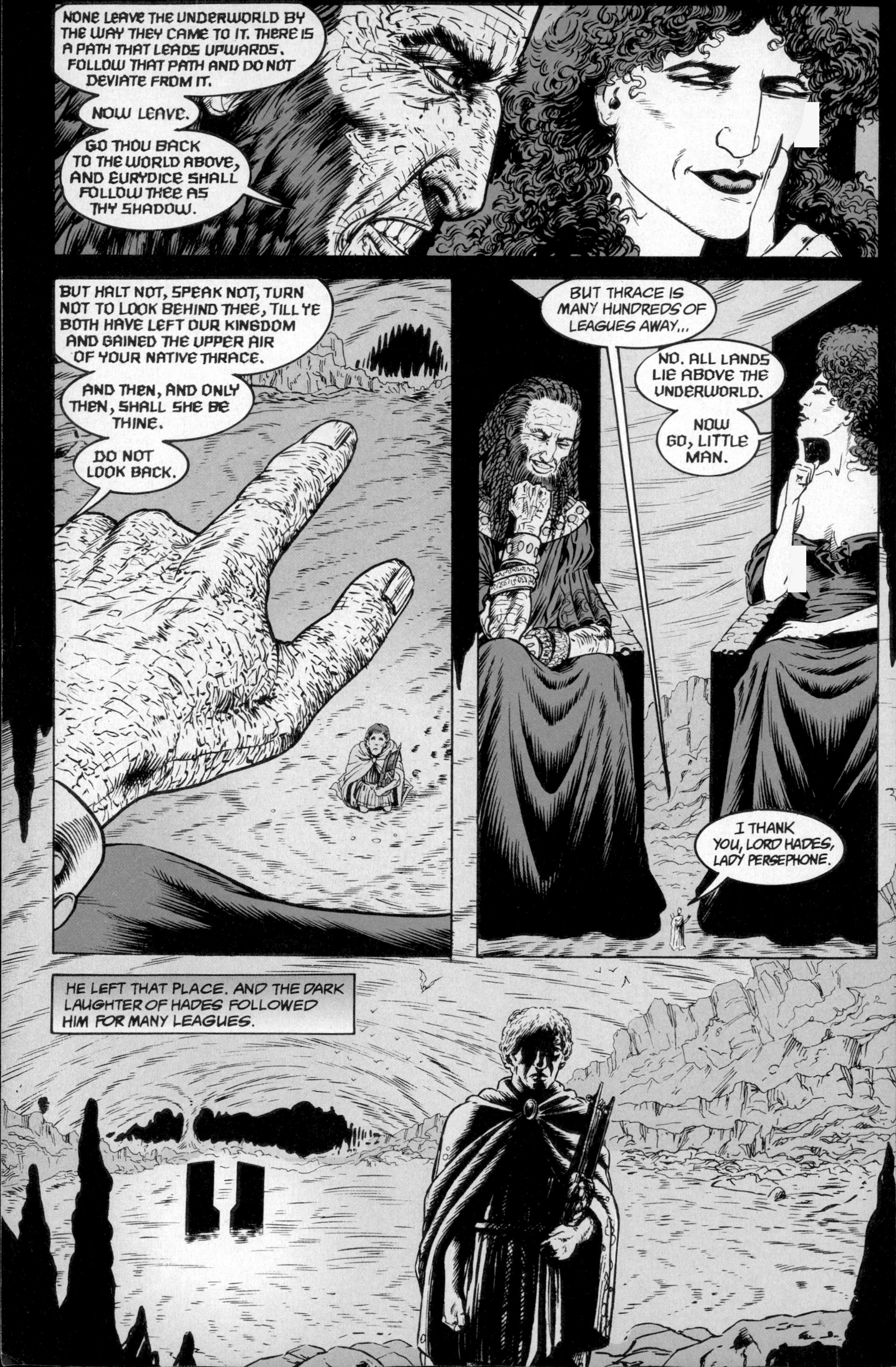
NONE LEAVE THE UNDERWORLD BY THE WAY THEY CAME TO IT. THERE IS A PATH THAT LEADS UPWARDS. FOLLOW THAT PATH AND DO NOT DEVIATE FROM IT.
NOW LEAVE.
GO THOU BACK TO THE WORLD ABOVE, AND EURYDICE SHALL FOLLOW THEE AS THY SHADOW.
BUT HALT NOT, SPEAK NOT, TURN NOT TO LOOK BEHIND THEE, TILL YE BOTH HAVE LEFT OUR KINGDOM AND GAINED THE UPPER AIR OF YOUR NATIVE THRACE.
AND THEN, AND ONLY THEN, SHALL SHE BE THINE.
DO NOT LOOK BACK.
BUT THRACE IS MANY HUNDREDS OF LEAGUES AWAY...
NO. ALL LANDS LIE ABOVE THE UNDERWORLD.
NOW GO, LITTLE MAN.
I THANK YOU, LORD HADES, LADY PERSEPHONE.
HE LEFT THAT PLACE. AND THE DARK LAUGHTER OF HADES FOLLOWED HIM FOR MANY LEAGUES.

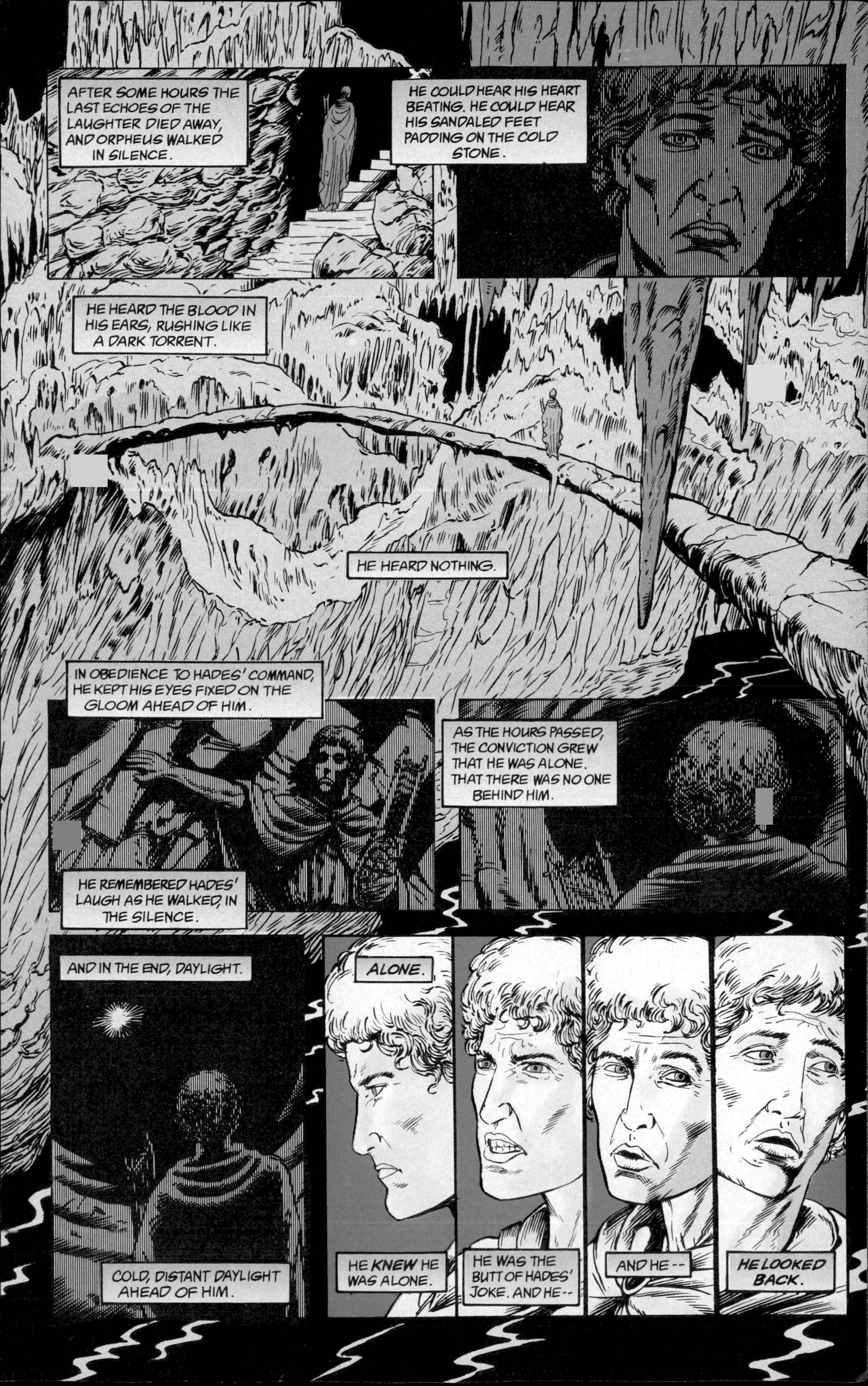
AFTER SOME HOURS THE LAST ECHOES OF THE LAUGHTER DIED AWAY, AND ORPHEUS WALKED IN SILENCE.
HE COULD HEAR HIS HEART BEATING. HE COULD HEAR HIS SANDALED FEET PADDING ON THE COLD STONE.
HE HEARD THE BLOOD IN HIS EARS, RUSHING LIKE A DARK TORRENT.
HE HEARD NOTHING.
IN OBEDIENCE TO HADES' COMMAND, HE KEPT HIS EYES FIXED ON THE GLOOM AHEAD OF HIM.
HE REMEMBERED HADES' LAUGH AS HE WALKED, IN THE SILENCE.
AS THE HOURS PASSED, THE CONVICTION GREW THAT HE WAS ALONE, THAT THERE WAS NO ONE BEHIND HIM.
AND IN THE END, DAYLIGHT.
COLD, DISTANT DAYLIGHT AHEAD OF HIM.
ALONE.
HE KNEW HE WAS ALONE.
HE WAS THE BUTT OF HADES' JOKE. AND HE--
AND HE--
HE LOOKED BACK.

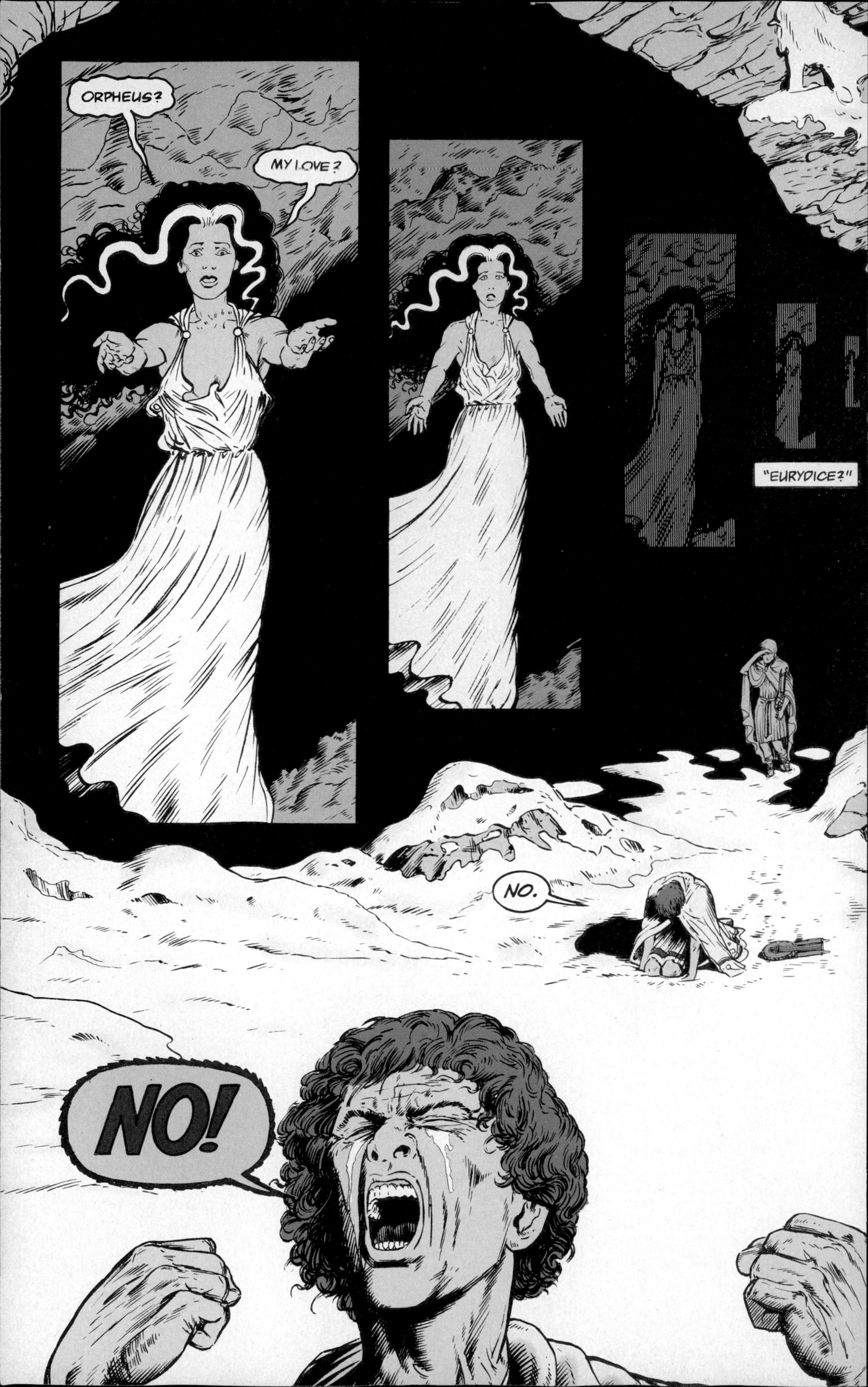
ORPHEUS?
MY LOVE?
"EURYDICE?"
NO.
NO!

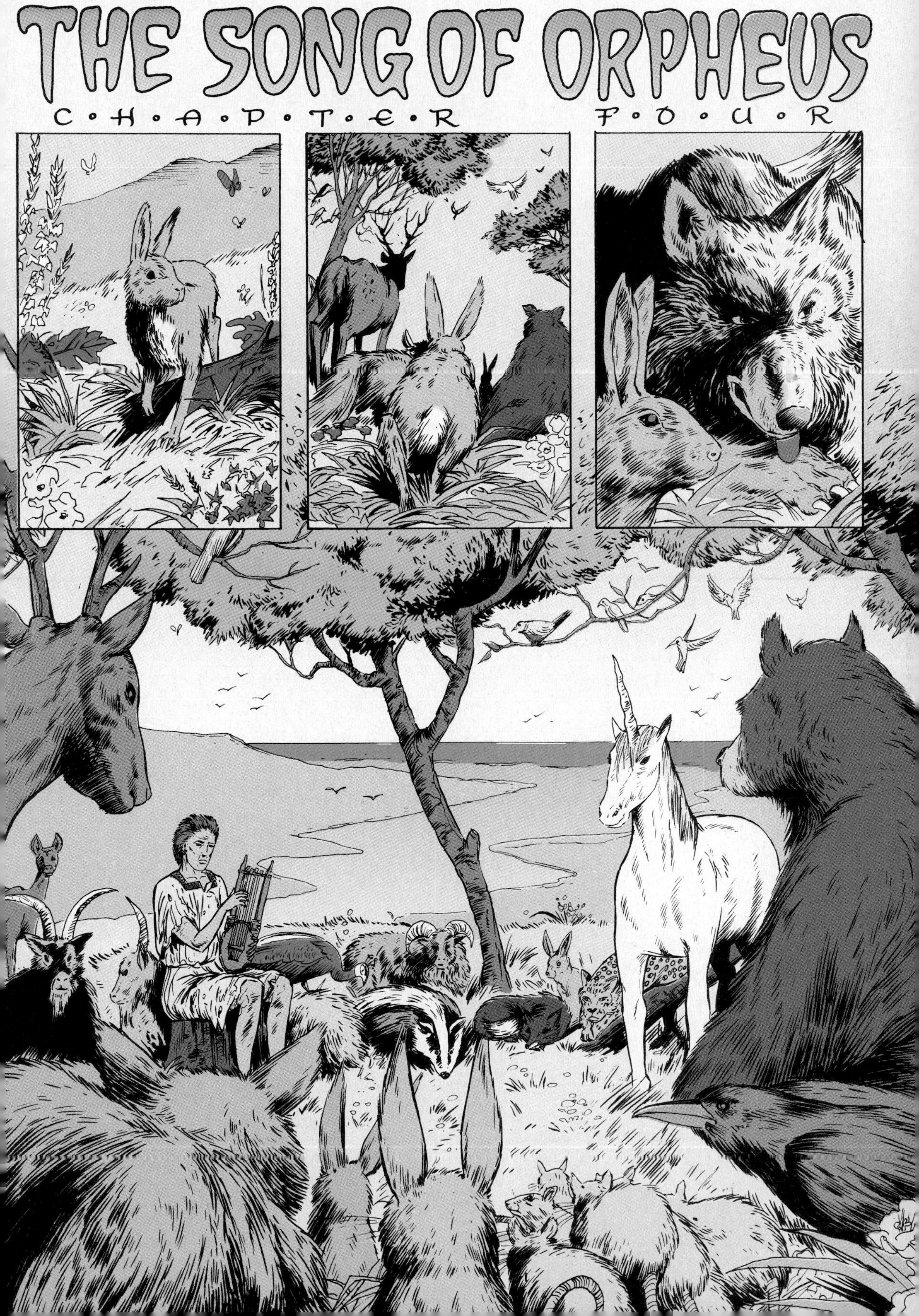
THE SONG OF ORPHEUS
C•H•A•P•T•E•R F•O•U•R

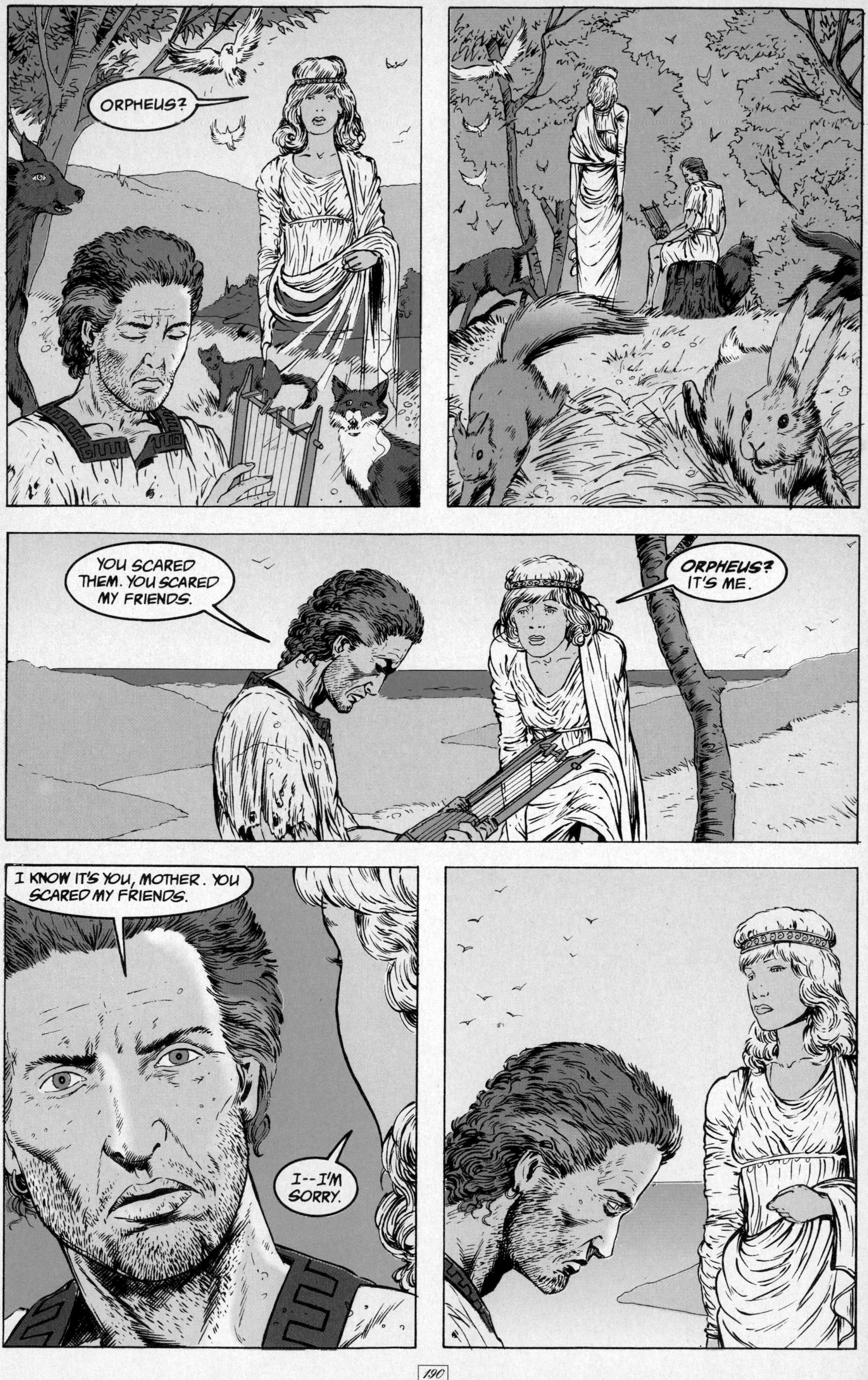
ORPHEUS?
YOU SCARED THEM. YOU SCARED MY FRIENDS.
ORPHEUS? IT'S ME.
I KNOW IT'S YOU, MOTHER. YOU SCARED MY FRIENDS.
I--I'M SORRY.

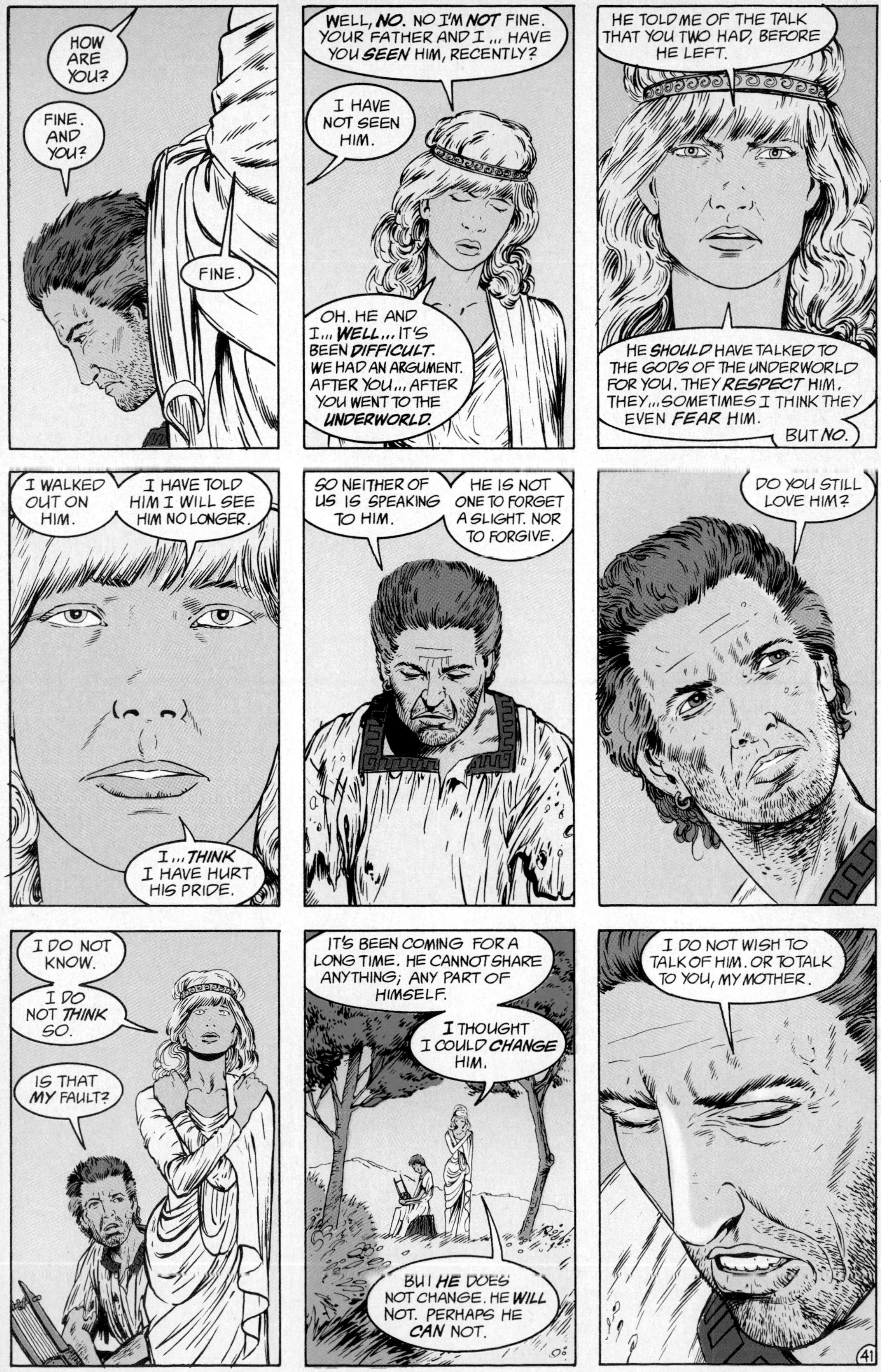
HOW ARE YOU?
FINE. AND YOU?
FINE.
WELL, NO. NO I'M NOT FINE. YOUR FATHER AND I ... HAVE YOU SEEN HIM, RECENTLY?
I HAVE NOT SEEN HIM.
OH. HE AND I... WELL... IT'S BEEN DIFFICULT. WE HAD AN ARGUMENT. AFTER YOU... AFTER YOU WENT TO THE UNDERWORLD.
HE TOLD ME OF THE TALK THAT YOU TWO HAD, BEFORE HE LEFT.
HE SHOULD HAVE TALKED TO THE GODS OF THE UNDERWORLD FOR YOU. THEY RESPECT HIM. THEY...SOMETIMES I THINK THEY EVEN FEAR HIM.
BUT NO.
I WALKED OUT ON HIM.
I HAVE TOLD HIM I WILL SEE HIM NO LONGER.
I...THINK I HAVE HURT HIS PRIDE.
SO NEITHER OF US IS SPEAKING TO HIM.
HE IS NOT ONE TO FORGET A SLIGHT. NOR TO FORGIVE.
DO YOU STILL LOVE HIM?
I DO NOT KNOW.
I DO NOT THINK SO.
IS THAT MY FAULT?
IT'S BEEN COMING FOR A LONG TIME. HE CANNOT SHARE ANYTHING; ANY PART OF HIMSELF.
I THOUGHT I COULD CHANGE HIM.
BUT HE DOES NOT CHANGE. HE WILL NOT. PERHAPS HE CAN NOT.
I DO NOT WISH TO TALK OF HIM. OR TO TALK TO YOU, MY MOTHER.
41

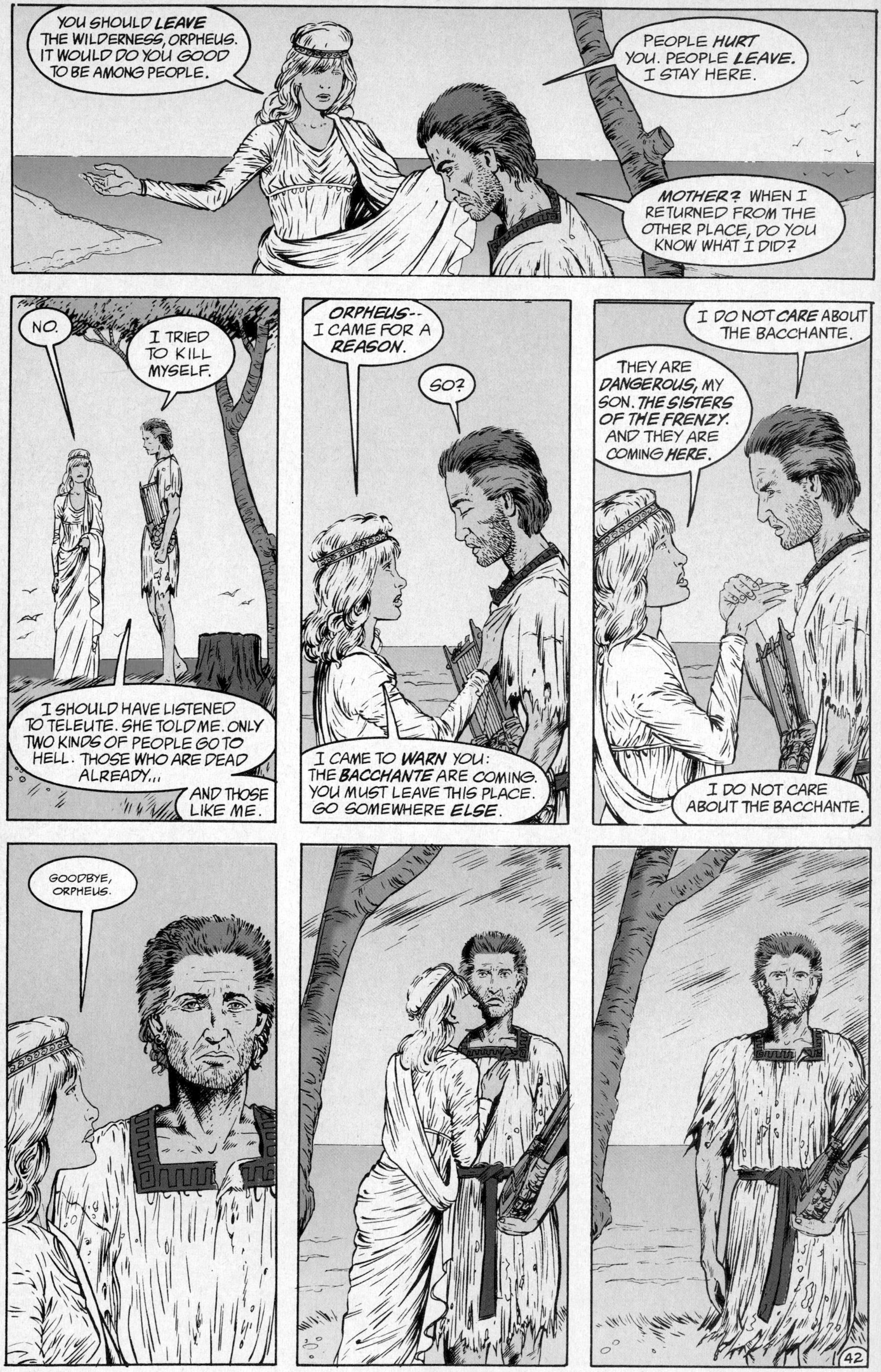

YOU SHOULD LEAVE THE WILDERNESS, ORPHEUS. IT WOULD DO YOU GOOD TO BE AMONG PEOPLE.
PEOPLE HURT YOU. PEOPLE LEAVE. I STAY HERE.
MOTHER? WHEN I RETURNED FROM THE OTHER PLACE, DO YOU KNOW WHAT I DID?
NO.
I TRIED TO KILL MYSELF.
I SHOULD HAVE LISTENED TO TELEUTE. SHE TOLD ME. ONLY TWO KINDS OF PEOPLE GO TO HELL. THOSE WHO ARE DEAD ALREADY...
AND THOSE LIKE ME.
ORPHEUS-- I CAME FOR A REASON.
SO?
I CAME TO WARN YOU: THE BACCHANTE ARE COMING. YOU MUST LEAVE THIS PLACE. GO SOMEWHERE ELSE.
I DO NOT CARE ABOUT THE BACCHANTE.
THEY ARE DANGEROUS, MY SON. THE SISTERS OF THE FRENZY. AND THEY ARE COMING HERE.
I DO NOT CARE ABOUT THE BACCHANTE.
GOODBYE, ORPHEUS.
42

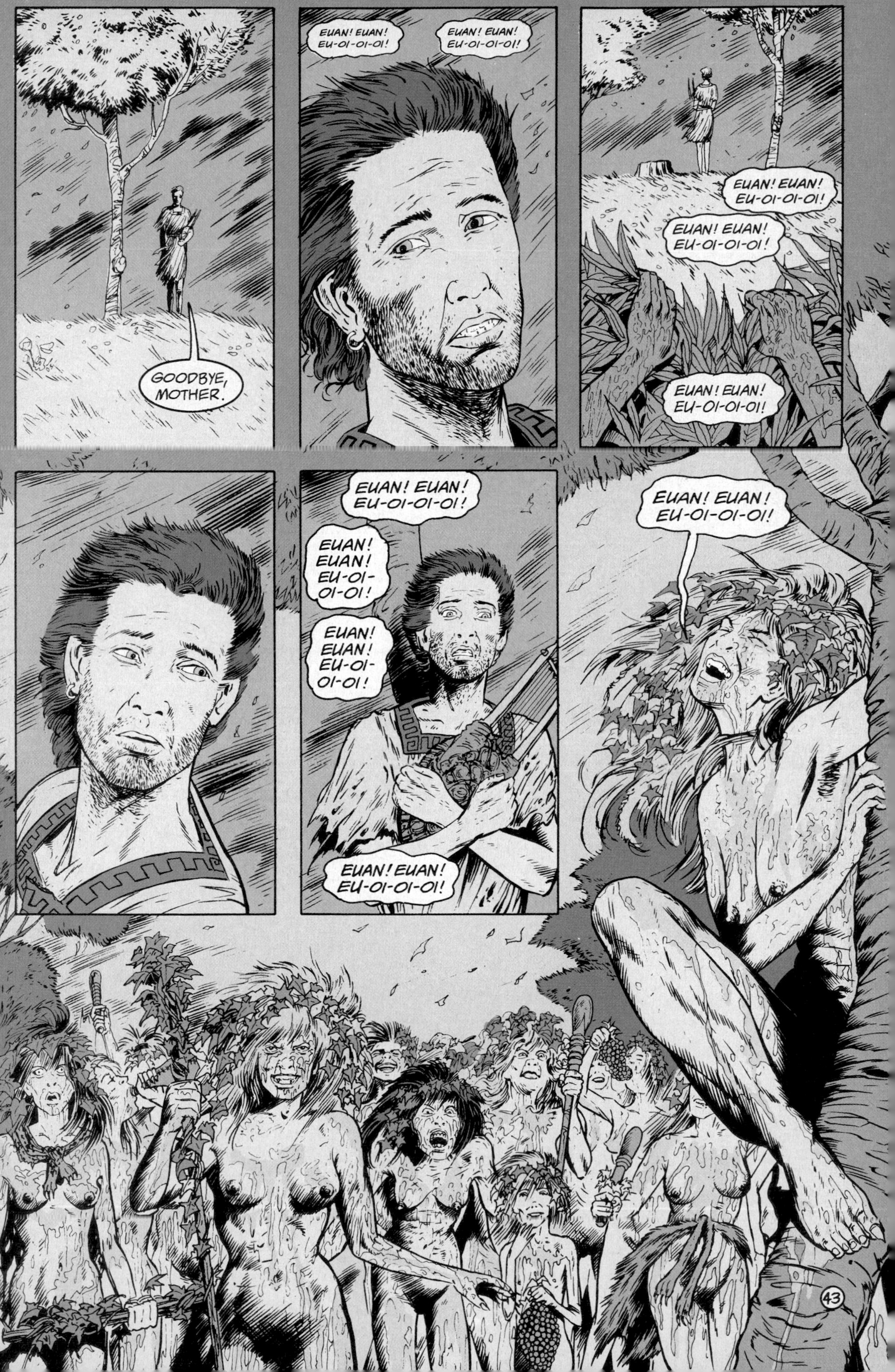
GOODBYE, MOTHER.
EUAN! EUAN! EU-OI-OI-OI!
EUAN! EUAN! EU-OI-OI-OI!
EUAN! EUAN! EU-OI-OI-OI!
EUAN! EUAN! EU-OI-OI-OI!
EUAN! EUAN! EU-OI-OI-OI!
EUAN! EUAN! EU-OI-OI-OI!
EUAN! EUAN! EU-OI-OI-OI!
EUAN! EUAN! EU-OI-OI-OI!
EUAN! EUAN! EU-OI-OI-OI!
EUAN! EUAN! EU-OI-OI-OI!

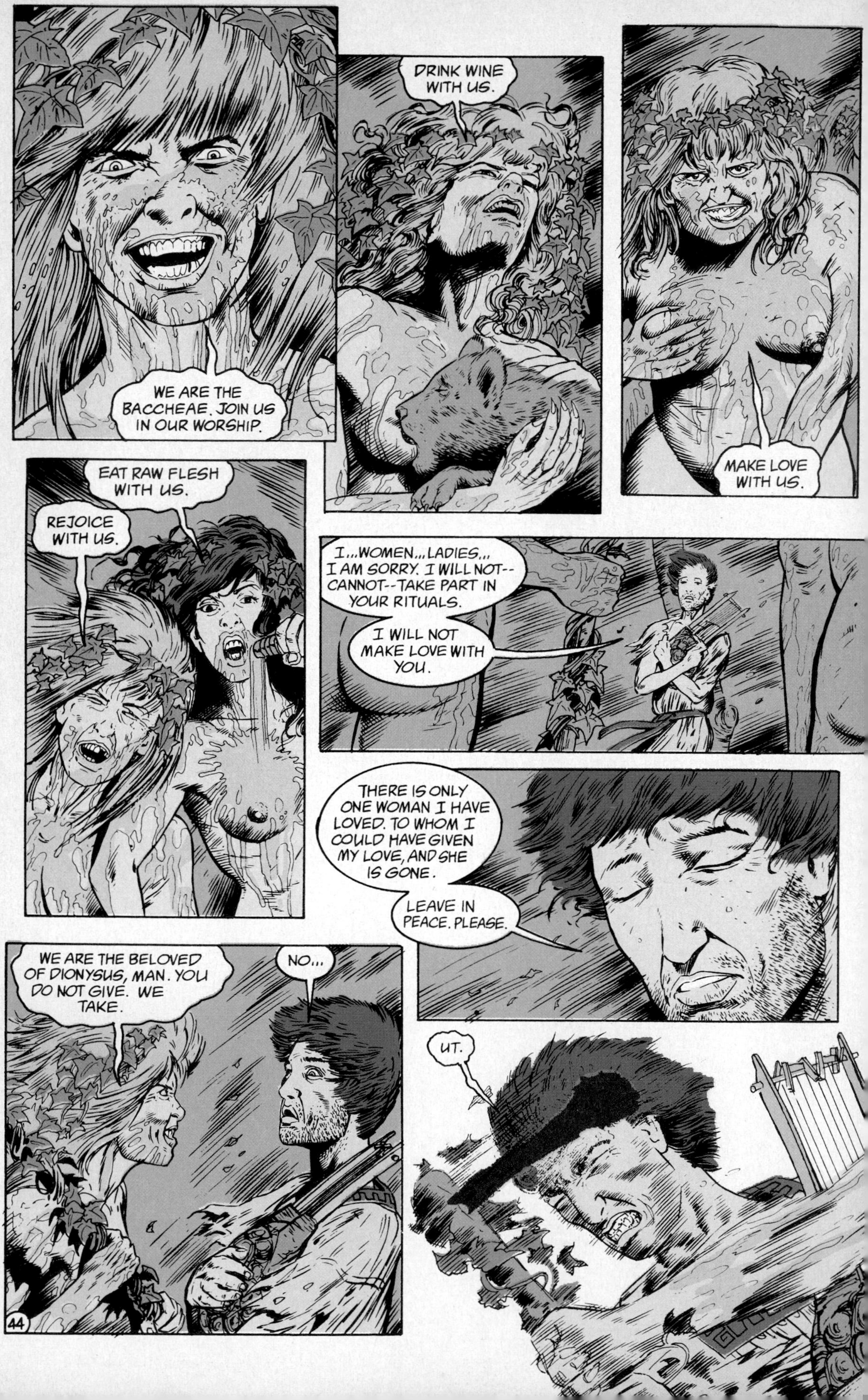
WE ARE THE BACCHEAE. JOIN US IN OUR WORSHIP.
DRINK WINE WITH US.
MAKE LOVE WITH US.
EAT RAW FLESH WITH US.
REJOICE WITH US.
I...WOMEN...LADIES... I AM SORRY. I WILL NOT-- CANNOT--TAKE PART IN YOUR RITUALS.
I WILL NOT MAKE LOVE WITH YOU.
THERE IS ONLY ONE WOMAN I HAVE LOVED. TO WHOM I COULD HAVE GIVEN MY LOVE, AND SHE IS GONE.
LEAVE IN PEACE. PLEASE.
WE ARE THE BELOVED OF DIONYSUS, MAN. YOU DO NOT GIVE. WE TAKE.
NO...
UT.

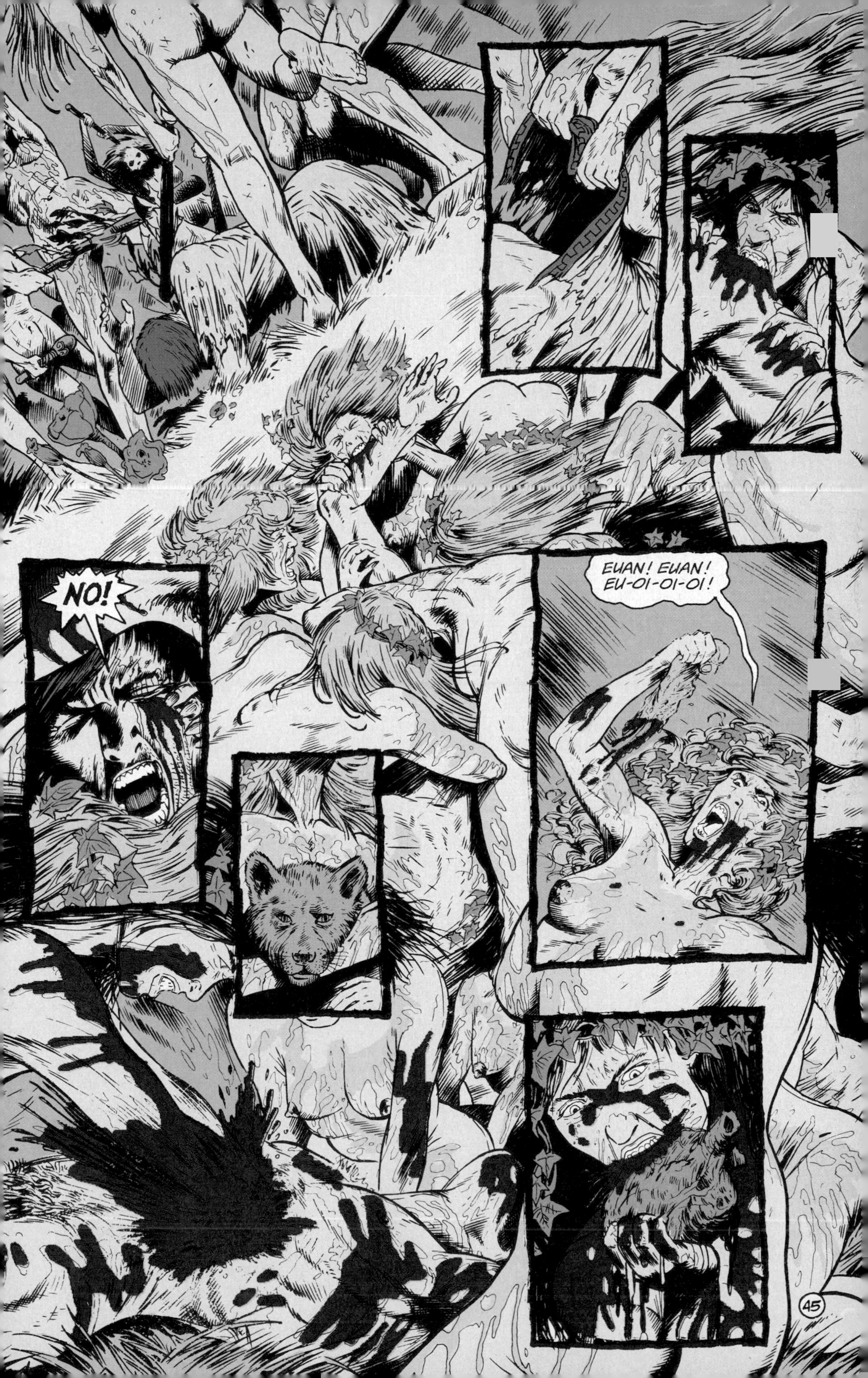
NO!
EUAN! EUAN!
EU-OI-OI-OI!

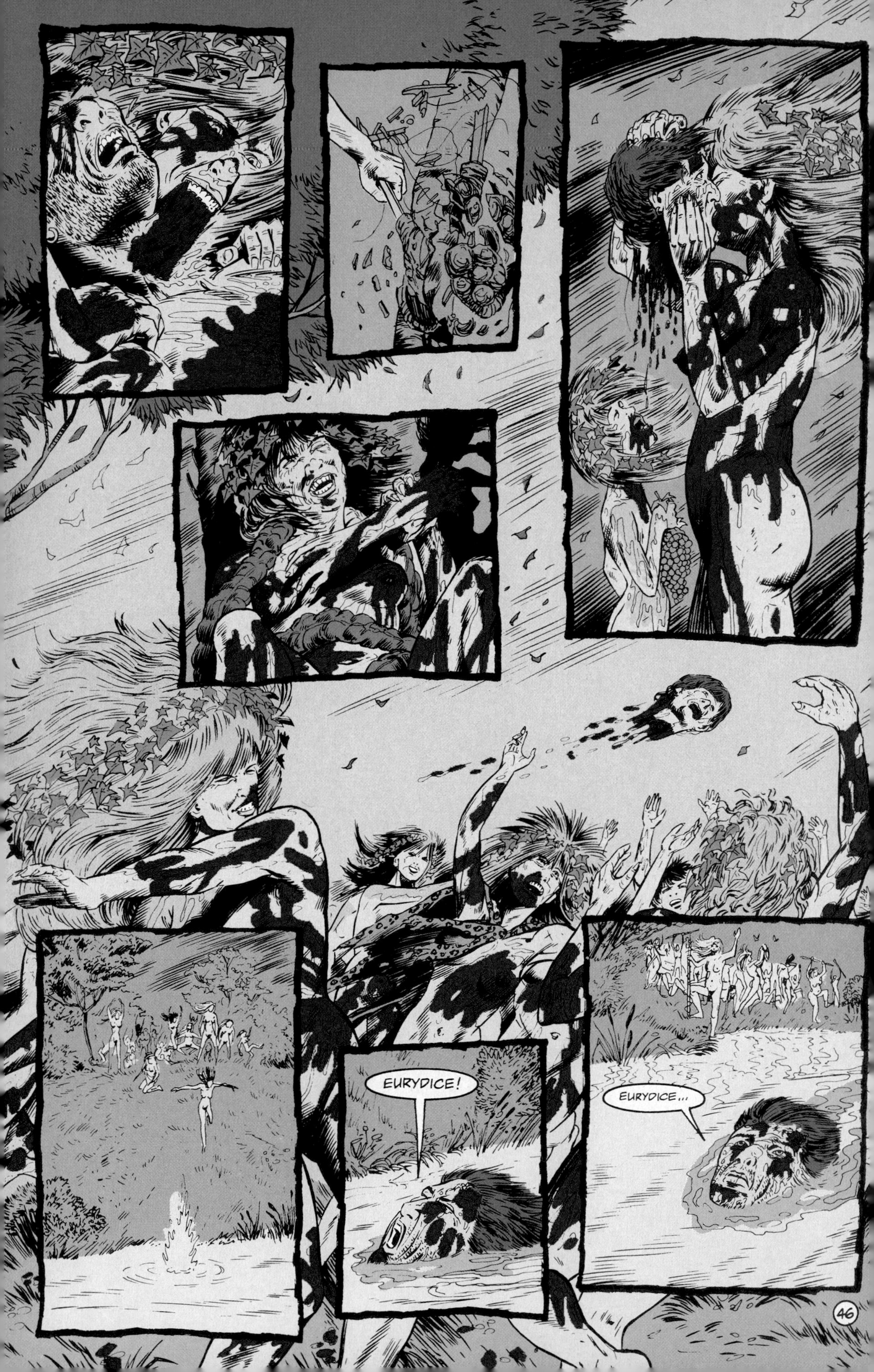
EURYDICE!
EURYDICE...

THE SONG OF ORPHEUS

E · P · I · L · O · G · U · E

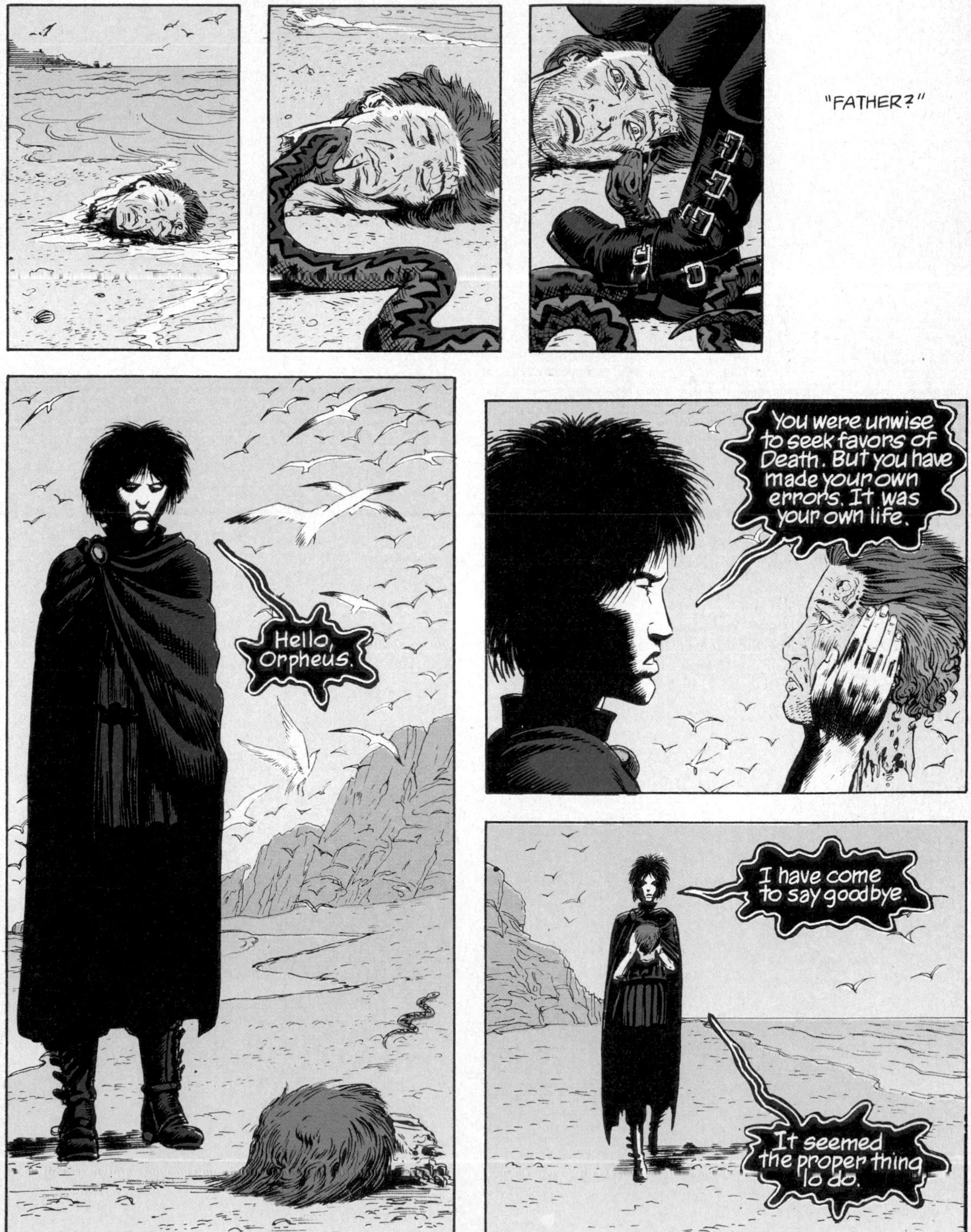
"FATHER?"
Hello, Orpheus.
You were unwise to seek favors of Death. But you have made your own errors. It was your own life.
I have come to say goodbye.
It seemed the proper thing to do.
47

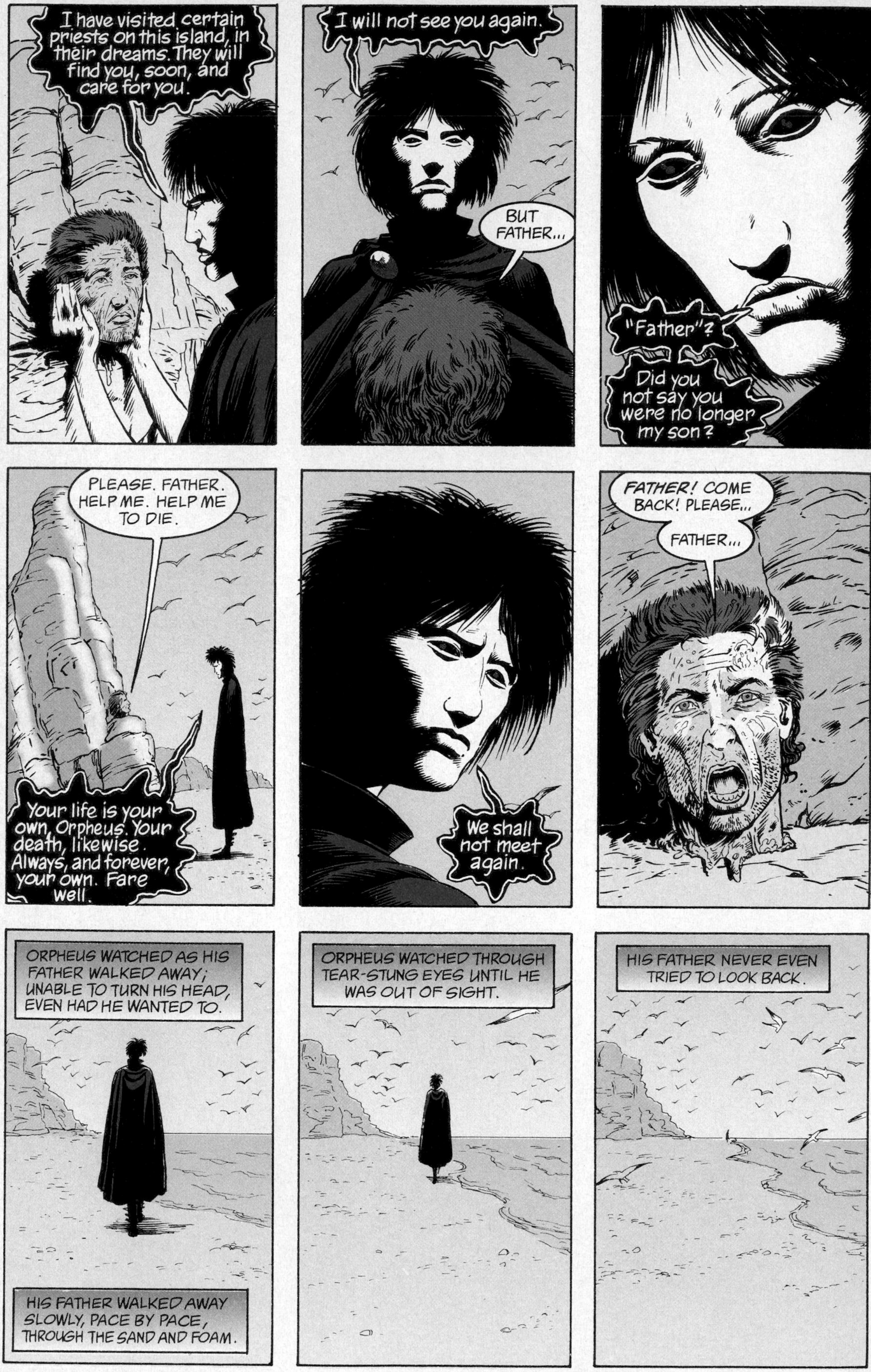
I have visited certain priests on this island, in their dreams. They will find you, soon, and care for you.
I will not see you again.
BUT FATHER...
"Father"?
Did you not say you were no longer my son?
PLEASE. FATHER. HELP ME. HELP ME TO DIE.
Your life is your own, Orpheus. Your death, likewise. Always, and forever, your own. Fare well.
We shall not meet again.
FATHER! COME BACK! PLEASE...
FATHER...
ORPHEUS WATCHED AS HIS FATHER WALKED AWAY; UNABLE TO TURN HIS HEAD, EVEN HAD HE WANTED TO.
HIS FATHER WALKED AWAY SLOWLY, PACE BY PACE, THROUGH THE SAND AND FOAM.
ORPHEUS WATCHED THROUGH TEAR-STUNG EYES UNTIL HE WAS OUT OF SIGHT.
HIS FATHER NEVER EVEN TRIED TO LOOK BACK.

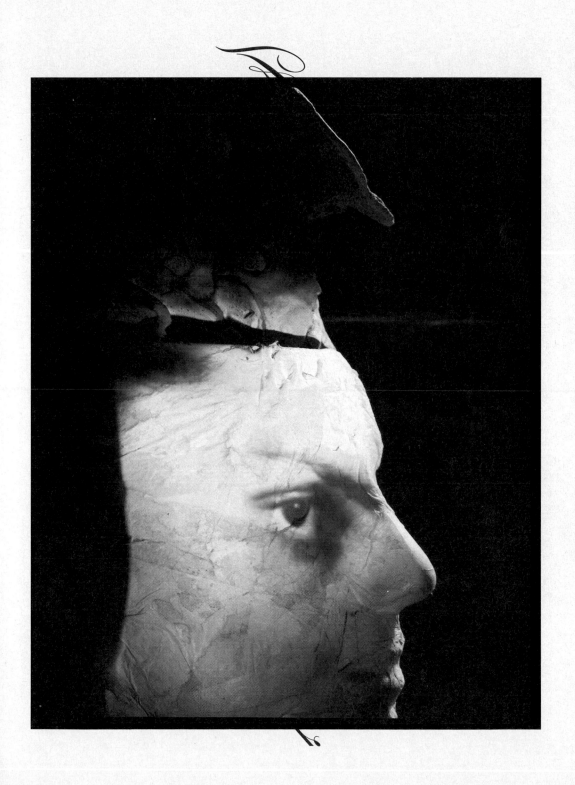

the *Parliament* of *Rooks*

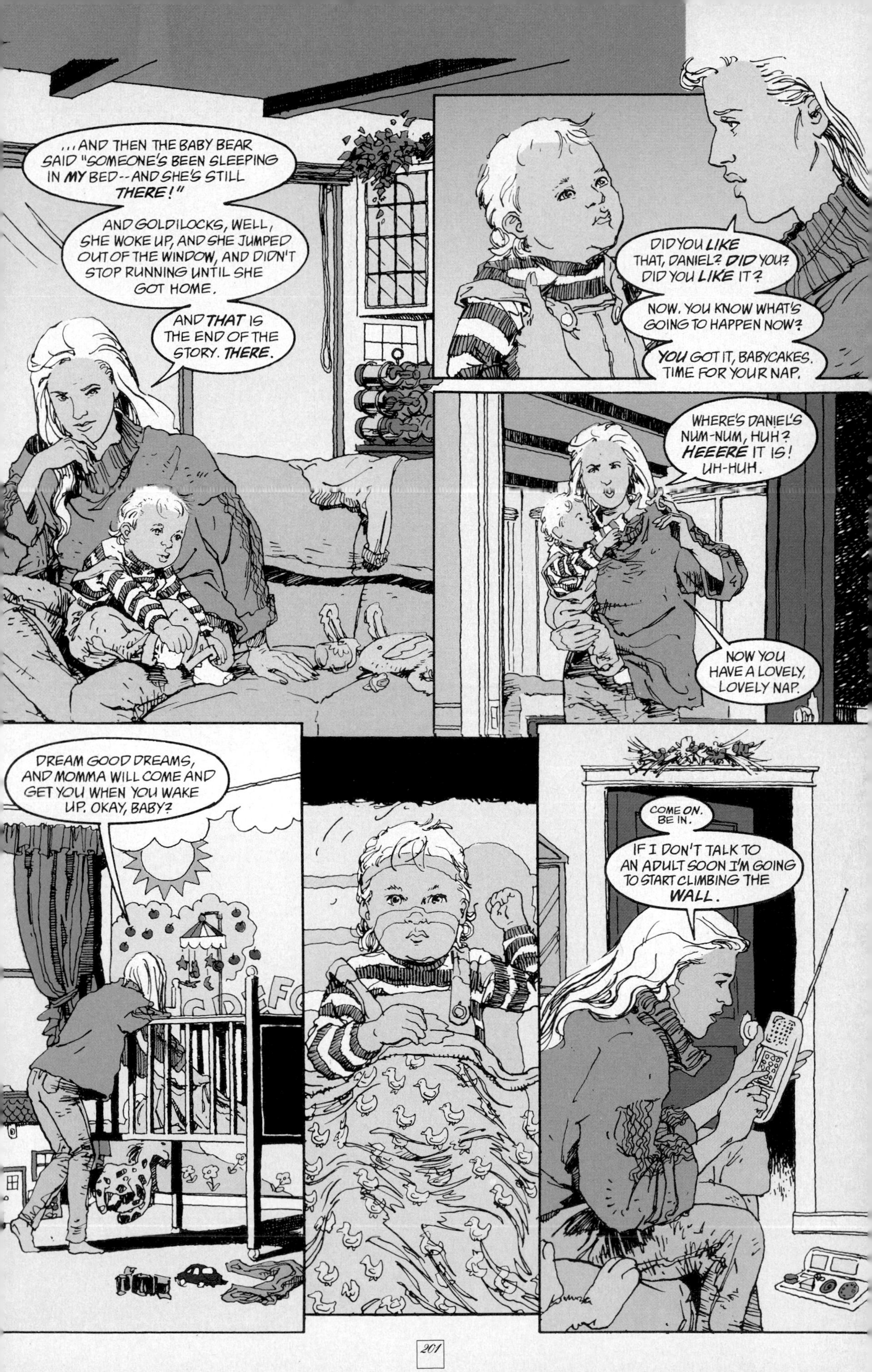
...AND THEN THE BABY BEAR SAID "SOMEONE'S BEEN SLEEPING IN MY BED--AND SHE'S STILL THERE!"
AND GOLDILOCKS, WELL, SHE WOKE UP, AND SHE JUMPED OUT OF THE WINDOW, AND DIDN'T STOP RUNNING UNTIL SHE GOT HOME.
AND THAT IS THE END OF THE STORY. THERE.
DID YOU LIKE THAT, DANIEL? DID YOU? DID YOU LIKE IT?
NOW. YOU KNOW WHAT'S GOING TO HAPPEN NOW?
YOU GOT IT, BABYCAKES. TIME FOR YOUR NAP.
WHERE'S DANIEL'S NUM-NUM, HUH? HEEERE IT IS! UH-HUH.
NOW YOU HAVE A LOVELY, LOVELY NAP.
DREAM GOOD DREAMS, AND MOMMA WILL COME AND GET YOU WHEN YOU WAKE UP. OKAY, BABY?
COME ON. BE IN.
IF I DON'T TALK TO AN ADULT SOON I'M GOING TO START CLIMBING THE WALL.

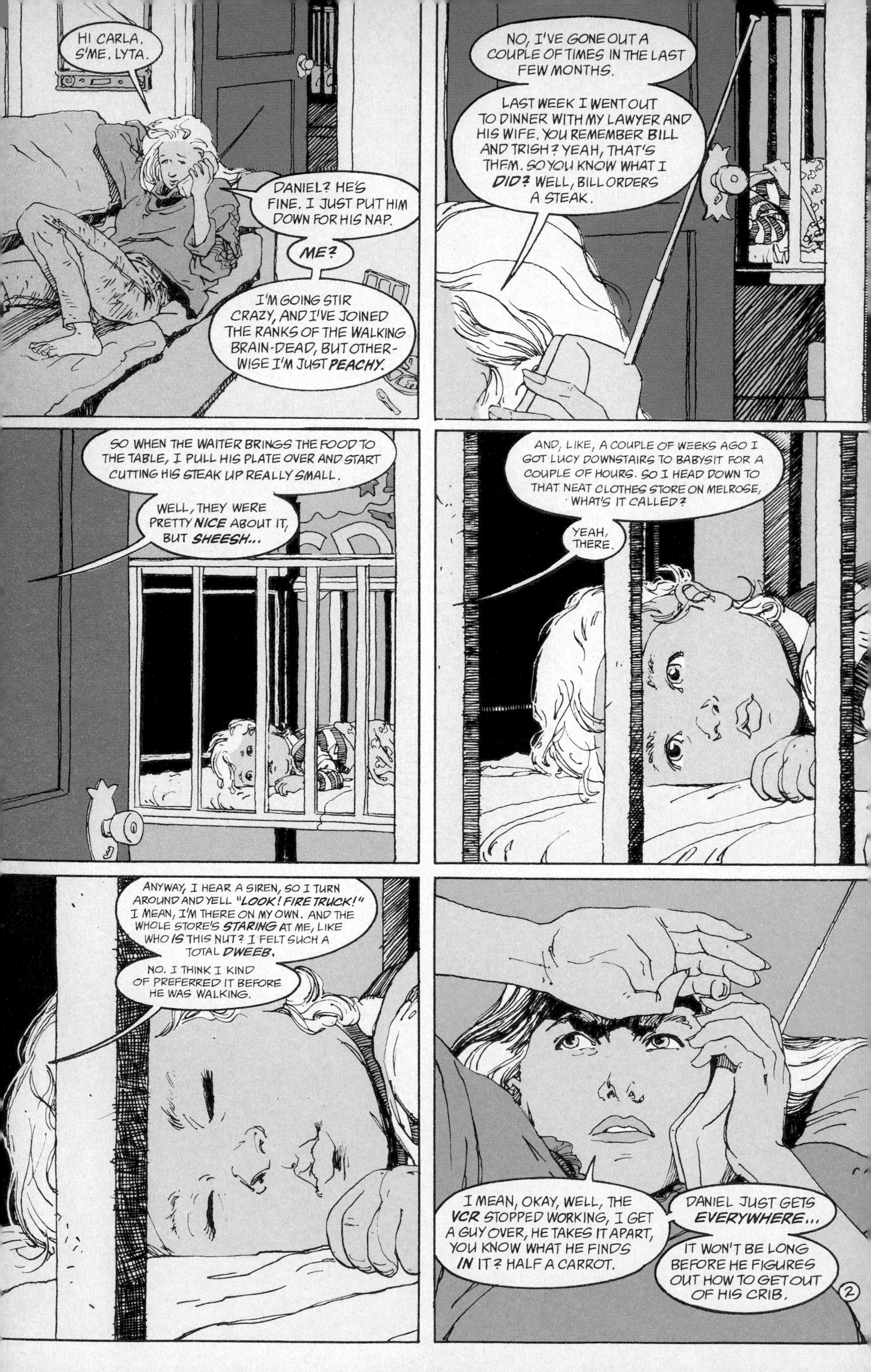
HI CARLA. S'ME. LYTA.
DANIEL? HE'S FINE. I JUST PUT HIM DOWN FOR HIS NAP.
ME?
I'M GOING STIR CRAZY, AND I'VE JOINED THE RANKS OF THE WALKING BRAIN-DEAD, BUT OTHERWISE I'M JUST PEACHY.
NO, I'VE GONE OUT A COUPLE OF TIMES IN THE LAST FEW MONTHS.
LAST WEEK I WENT OUT TO DINNER WITH MY LAWYER AND HIS WIFE. YOU REMEMBER BILL AND TRISH? YEAH, THAT'S THEM. SO YOU KNOW WHAT I DID? WELL, BILL ORDERS A STEAK.
SO WHEN THE WAITER BRINGS THE FOOD TO THE TABLE, I PULL HIS PLATE OVER AND START CUTTING HIS STEAK UP REALLY SMALL.
WELL, THEY WERE PRETTY NICE ABOUT IT, BUT SHEESH...
AND, LIKE, A COUPLE OF WEEKS AGO I GOT LUCY DOWNSTAIRS TO BABYSIT FOR A COUPLE OF HOURS. SO I HEAD DOWN TO THAT NEAT CLOTHES STORE ON MELROSE, WHAT'S IT CALLED?
YEAH, THERE.
ANYWAY, I HEAR A SIREN, SO I TURN AROUND AND YELL "LOOK! FIRE TRUCK!" I MEAN, I'M THERE ON MY OWN. AND THE WHOLE STORE'S STARING AT ME, LIKE WHO IS THIS NUT? I FELT SUCH A TOTAL DWEEB.
NO. I THINK I KIND OF PREFERRED IT BEFORE HE WAS WALKING.
I MEAN, OKAY, WELL, THE VCR STOPPED WORKING, I GET A GUY OVER, HE TAKES IT APART, YOU KNOW WHAT HE FINDS IN IT? HALF A CARROT.
DANIEL JUST GETS EVERYWHERE...
IT WON'T BE LONG BEFORE HE FIGURES OUT HOW TO GET OUT OF HIS CRIB.

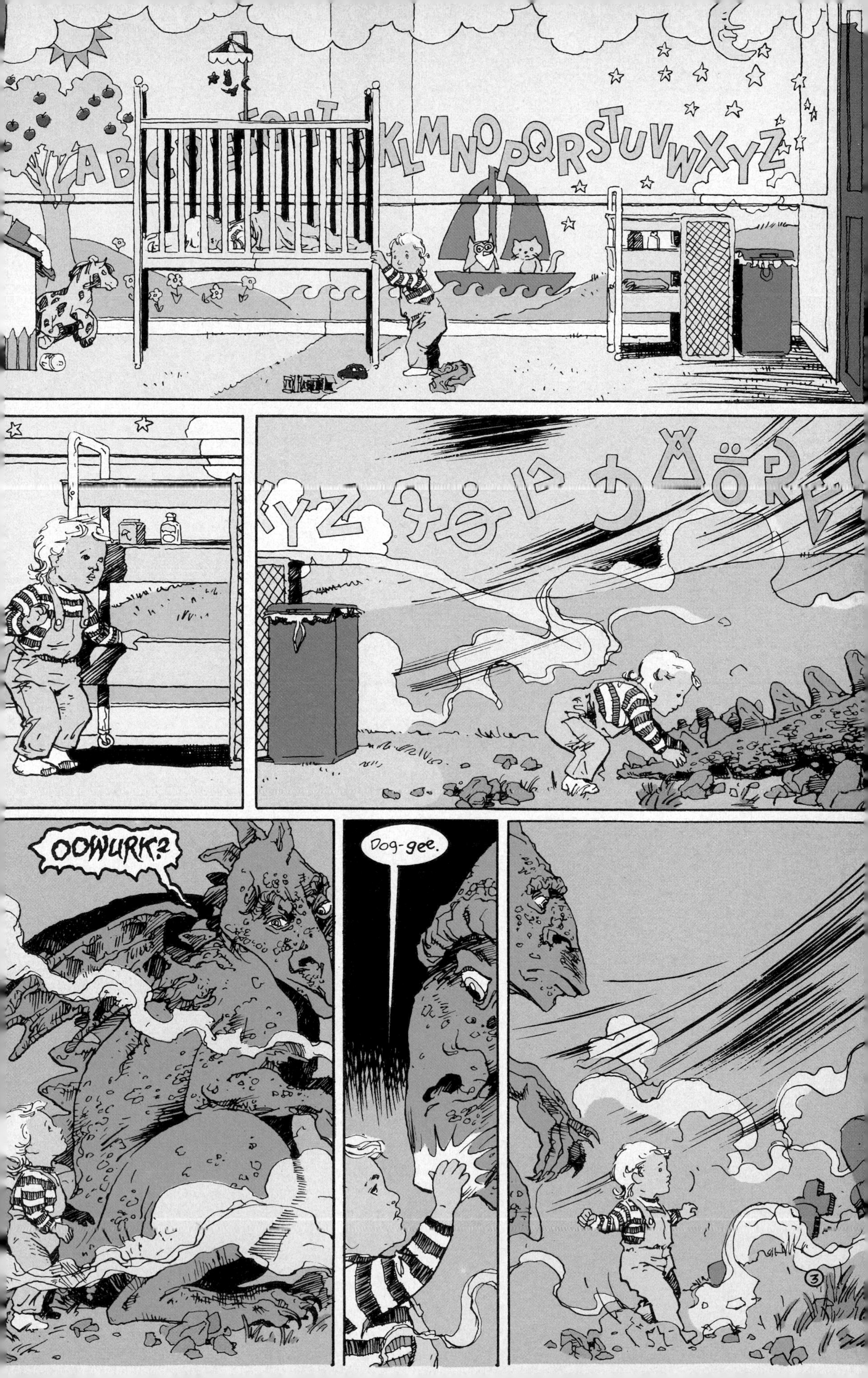
OOWURK?
Dog-gee.

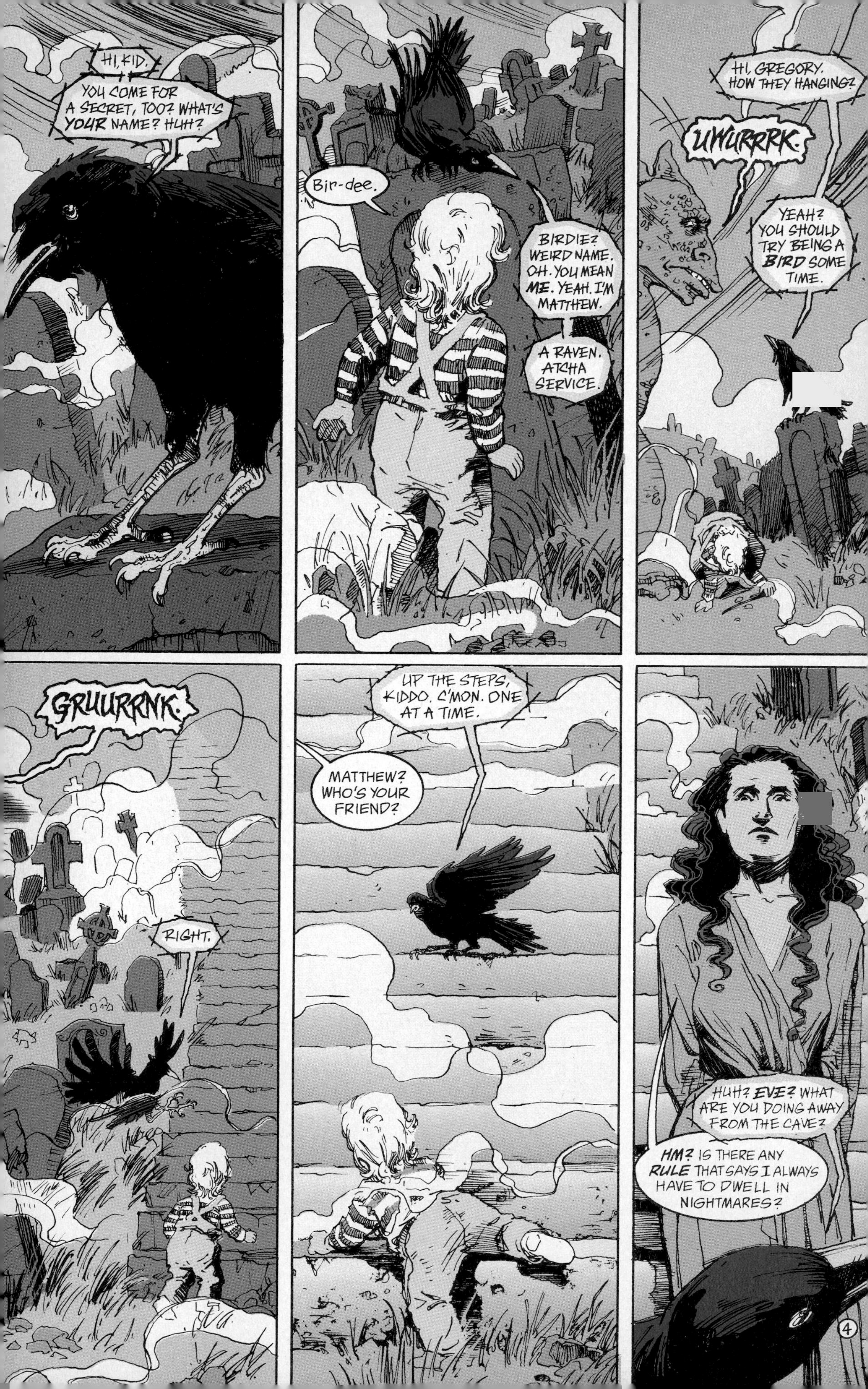
HI, KID.
YOU COME FOR A SECRET, TOO? WHAT'S YOUR NAME? HUH?
Bir-dee.
BIRDIE? WEIRD NAME. OH. YOU MEAN ME. YEAH. I'M MATTHEW.
A RAVEN. ATCHA SERVICE.
HI, GREGORY. HOW THEY HANGING?
UWURRRK.
YEAH? YOU SHOULD TRY BEING A BIRD SOME TIME.
GRUURRNK.
RIGHT.
UP THE STEPS, KIDDO. C'MON. ONE AT A TIME.
MATTHEW? WHO'S YOUR FRIEND?
HUH? EVE? WHAT ARE YOU DOING AWAY FROM THE CAVE?
HM? IS THERE ANY RULE THAT SAYS I ALWAYS HAVE TO DWELL IN NIGHTMARES?
4

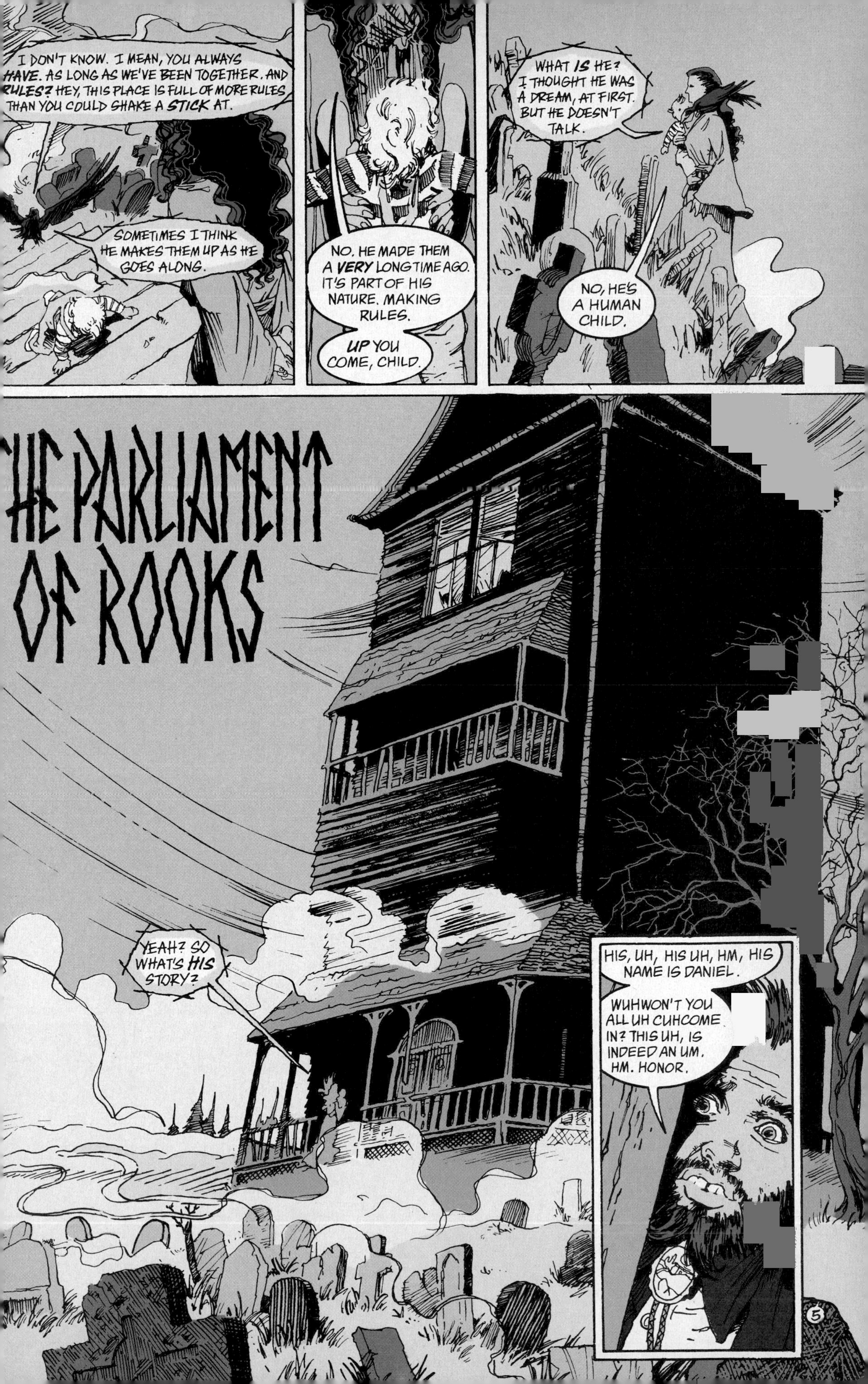
I DON'T KNOW. I MEAN, YOU ALWAYS HAVE. AS LONG AS WE'VE BEEN TOGETHER. AND RULES? HEY, THIS PLACE IS FULL OF MORE RULES THAN YOU COULD SHAKE A STICK AT.
SOMETIMES I THINK HE MAKES THEM UP AS HE GOES ALONG.
NO. HE MADE THEM A VERY LONG TIME AGO. IT'S PART OF HIS NATURE. MAKING RULES.
UP YOU COME, CHILD.
WHAT IS HE? I THOUGHT HE WAS A DREAM, AT FIRST. BUT HE DOESN'T TALK.
NO, HE'S A HUMAN CHILD.
THE PARLIAMENT OF ROOKS
YEAH? SO WHAT'S HIS STORY?
HIS, UH, HIS UH, HM, HIS NAME IS DANIEL.
WUHWON'T YOU ALL UH CUHCOME IN? THIS UH, IS INDEED AN UM. HM. HONOR.
5

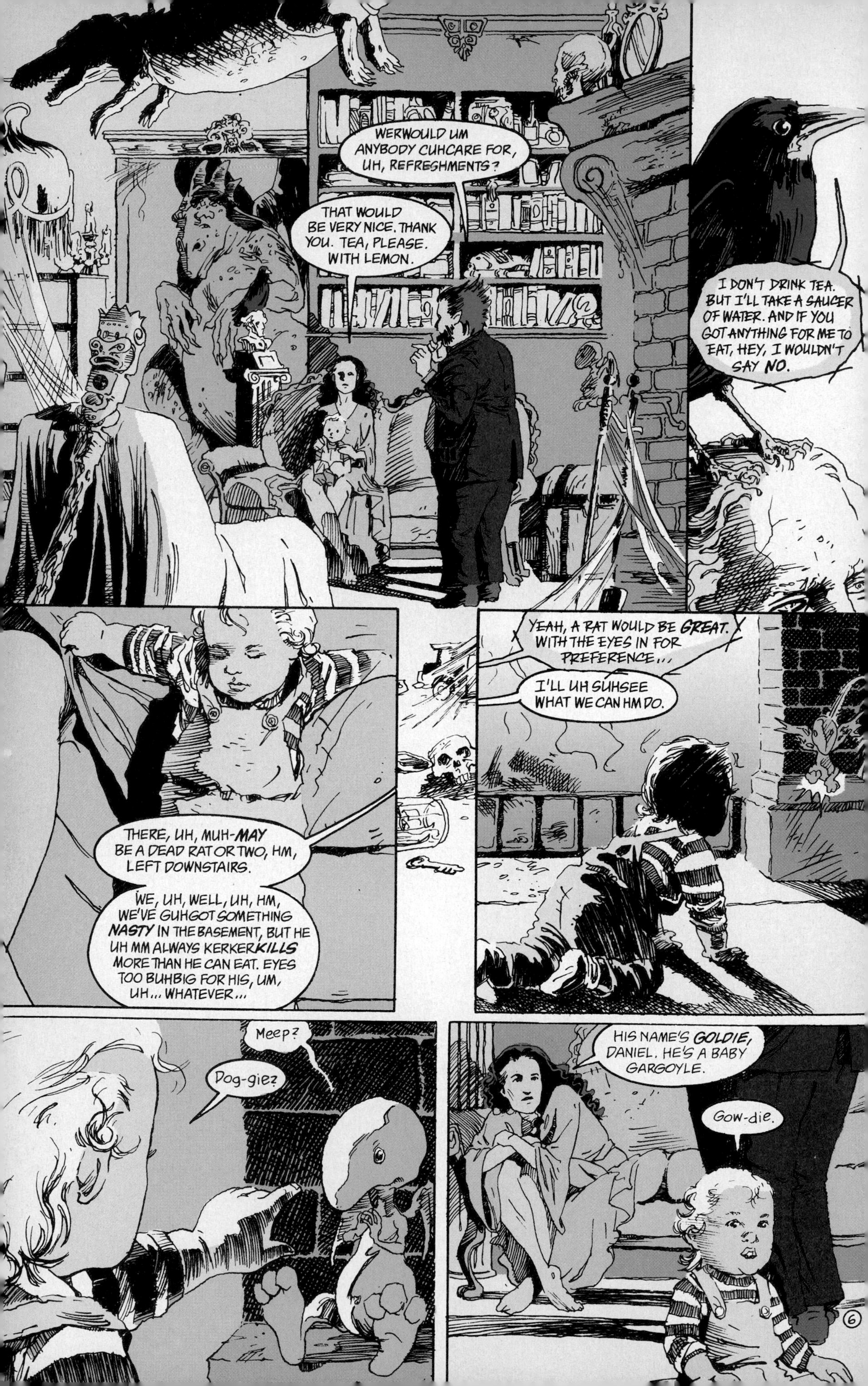
WERWOULD UM ANYBODY CUHCARE FOR, UH, REFRESHMENTS?
THAT WOULD BE VERY NICE. THANK YOU. TEA, PLEASE. WITH LEMON.
I DON'T DRINK TEA. BUT I'LL TAKE A SAUCER OF WATER. AND IF YOU GOT ANYTHING FOR ME TO EAT, HEY, I WOULDN'T SAY NO.
THERE, UH, MUH-MAY BE A DEAD RAT OR TWO, HM, LEFT DOWNSTAIRS.
WE, UH, WELL, UH, HM, WE'VE GUHGOT SOMETHING NASTY IN THE BASEMENT, BUT HE UH MM ALWAYS KERKERKILLS MORE THAN HE CAN EAT. EYES TOO BUHBIG FOR HIS, UM, UH... WHATEVER...
YEAH, A RAT WOULD BE GREAT. WITH THE EYES IN FOR PREFERENCE...
I'LL UH SUHSEE WHAT WE CAN HM DO.
Dog-gie?
Meep?
HIS NAME'S GOLDIE, DANIEL. HE'S A BABY GARGOYLE.
Gow-die.
6

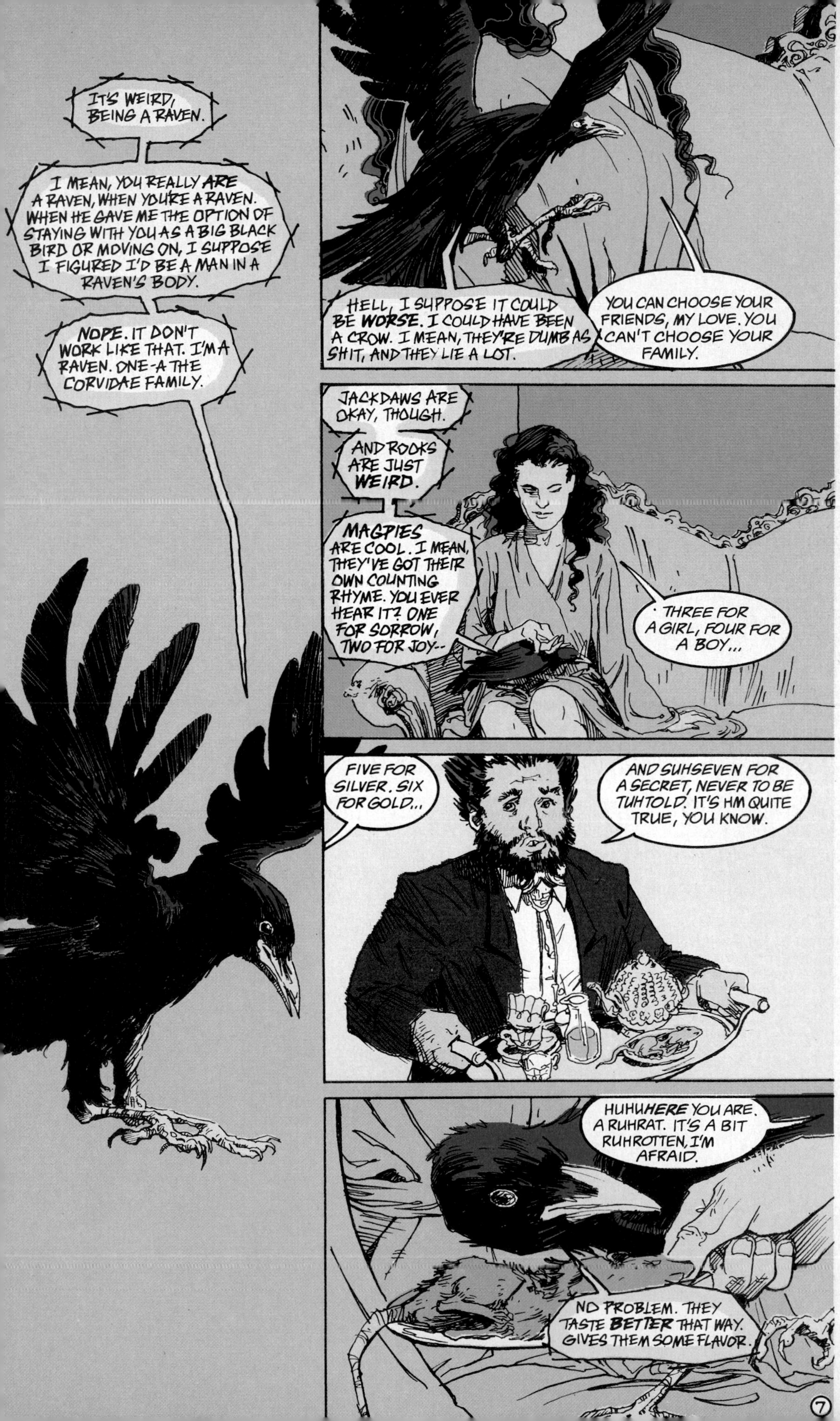
IT'S WEIRD, BEING A RAVEN.
I MEAN, YOU REALLY ARE A RAVEN, WHEN YOU'RE A RAVEN. WHEN HE GAVE ME THE OPTION OF STAYING WITH YOU AS A BIG BLACK BIRD OR MOVING ON, I SUPPOSE I FIGURED I'D BE A MAN IN A RAVEN'S BODY.
NOPE. IT DON'T WORK LIKE THAT. I'M A RAVEN. ONE-A THE CORVIDAE FAMILY.
HELL, I SUPPOSE IT COULD BE WORSE. I COULD HAVE BEEN A CROW. I MEAN, THEY'RE DUMB AS SHIT, AND THEY LIE A LOT.
YOU CAN CHOOSE YOUR FRIENDS, MY LOVE. YOU CAN'T CHOOSE YOUR FAMILY.
JACKDAWS ARE OKAY, THOUGH.
AND ROOKS ARE JUST WEIRD.
MAGPIES ARE COOL. I MEAN, THEY'VE GOT THEIR OWN COUNTING RHYME. YOU EVER HEAR IT? ONE FOR SORROW, TWO FOR JOY--
THREE FOR A GIRL, FOUR FOR A BOY...
FIVE FOR SILVER. SIX FOR GOLD...
AND SUHSEVEN FOR A SECRET, NEVER TO BE TUHTOLD. IT'S HM QUITE TRUE, YOU KNOW.
HUHUHERE YOU ARE. A RUHRAT. IT'S A BIT RUHROTTEN, I'M AFRAID.
NO PROBLEM. THEY TASTE BETTER THAT WAY. GIVES THEM SOME FLAVOR.

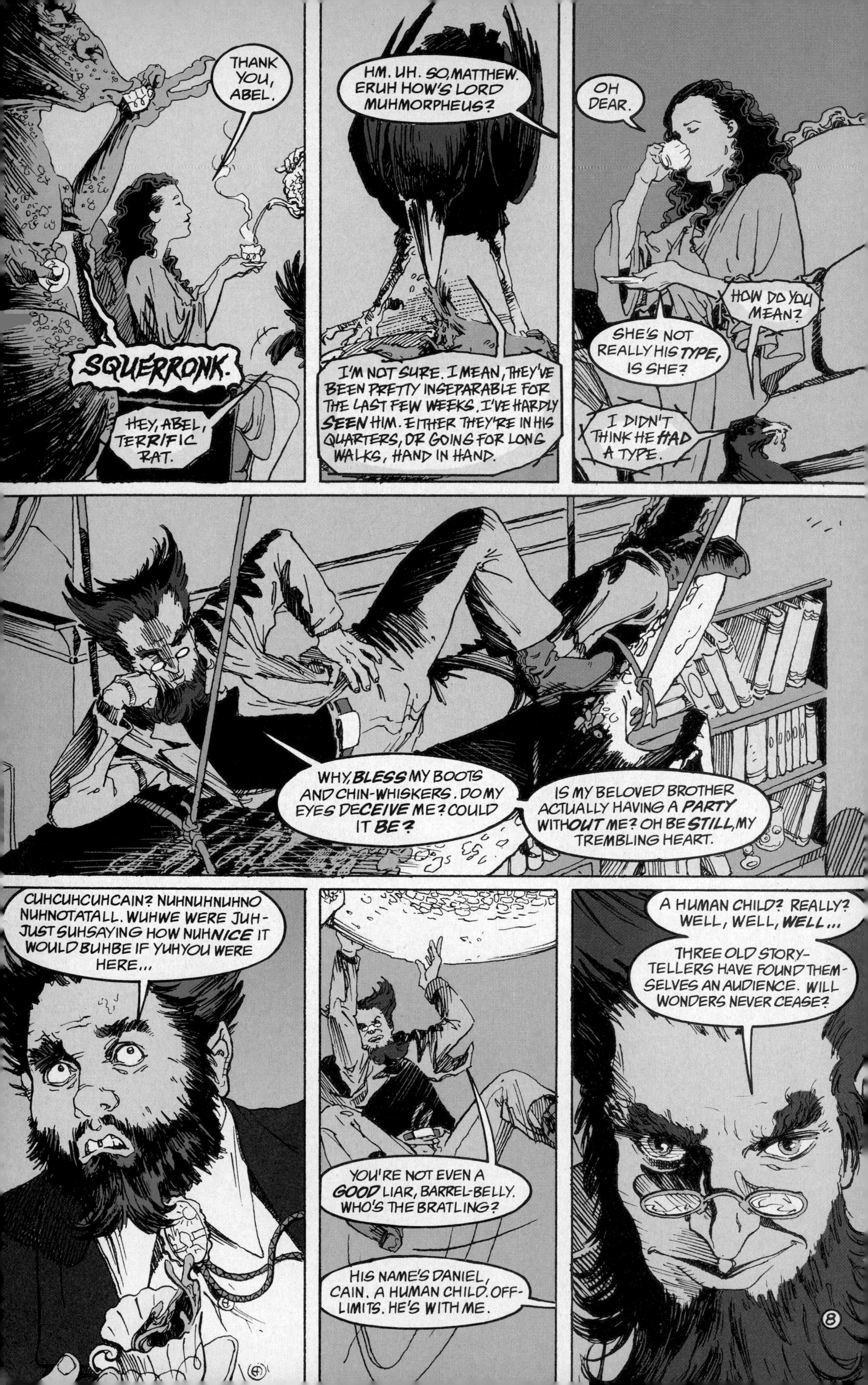
THANK YOU, ABEL.
SQUERRONK.
HEY, ABEL, TERRIFIC RAT.
HM. UH. SO, MATTHEW. ERUH HOW'S LORD MUHMORPHEUS?
I'M NOT SURE. I MEAN, THEY'VE BEEN PRETTY INSEPARABLE FOR THE LAST FEW WEEKS. I'VE HARDLY SEEN HIM. EITHER THEY'RE IN HIS QUARTERS, OR GOING FOR LONG WALKS, HAND IN HAND.
OH DEAR.
SHE'S NOT REALLY HIS TYPE, IS SHE?
HOW DO YOU MEAN?
I DIDN'T THINK HE HAD A TYPE.
WHY, BLESS MY BOOTS AND CHIN-WHISKERS. DO MY EYES DECEIVE ME? COULD IT BE?
IS MY BELOVED BROTHER ACTUALLY HAVING A PARTY WITHOUT ME? OH BE STILL, MY TREMBLING HEART.
CUHCUHCUHCAIN? NUHNUHNUHNO NUHNOTATALL. WUHWE WERE JUH-JUST SUHSAYING HOW NUHNICE IT WOULD BUHBE IF YUHYOU WERE HERE...
YOU'RE NOT EVEN A GOOD LIAR, BARREL-BELLY. WHO'S THE BRATLING?
HIS NAME'S DANIEL, CAIN. A HUMAN CHILD. OFF-LIMITS. HE'S WITH ME.
A HUMAN CHILD? REALLY? WELL, WELL, WELL...
THREE OLD STORY-TELLERS HAVE FOUND THEMSELVES AN AUDIENCE. WILL WONDERS NEVER CEASE?
8

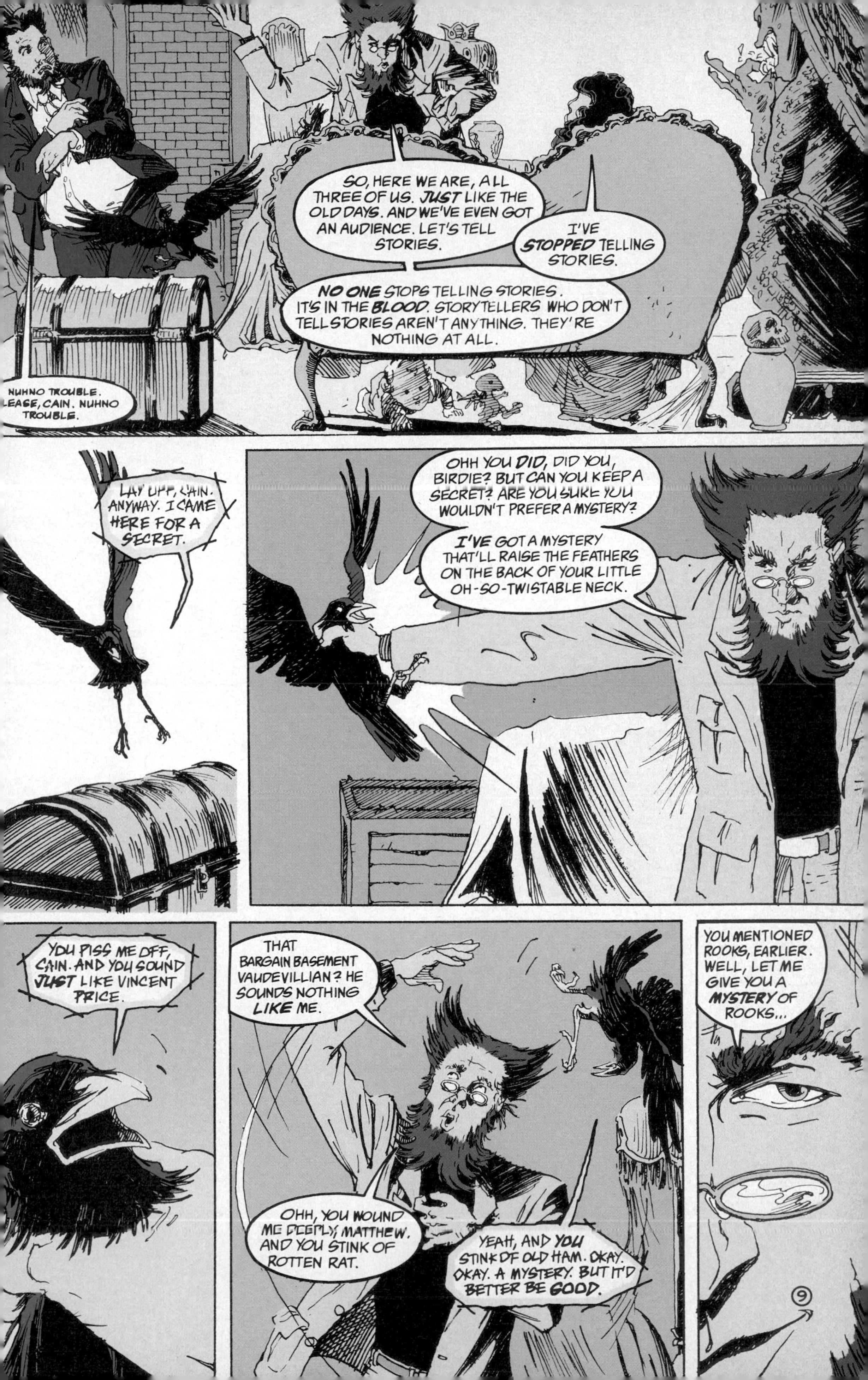
SO, HERE WE ARE, ALL THREE OF US. JUST LIKE THE OLD DAYS. AND WE'VE EVEN GOT AN AUDIENCE. LET'S TELL STORIES.
I'VE STOPPED TELLING STORIES.
NO ONE STOPS TELLING STORIES. IT'S IN THE BLOOD. STORYTELLERS WHO DON'T TELL STORIES AREN'T ANYTHING. THEY'RE NOTHING AT ALL.
NUHNO TROUBLE. LEASE, CAIN. NUHNO TROUBLE.
LAY OFF, CAIN. ANYWAY. I CAME HERE FOR A SECRET.
OHH YOU DID, DID YOU, BIRDIE? BUT CAN YOU KEEP A SECRET? ARE YOU SURE YOU WOULDN'T PREFER A MYSTERY?
I'VE GOT A MYSTERY THAT'LL RAISE THE FEATHERS ON THE BACK OF YOUR LITTLE OH-SO-TWISTABLE NECK.
YOU PISS ME OFF, CAIN. AND YOU SOUND JUST LIKE VINCENT PRICE.
THAT BARGAIN BASEMENT VAUDEVILLIAN? HE SOUNDS NOTHING LIKE ME.
OHH, YOU WOUND ME DEEPLY, MATTHEW. AND YOU STINK OF ROTTEN RAT.
YEAH, AND YOU STINK OF OLD HAM. OKAY. OKAY. A MYSTERY. BUT IT'D BETTER BE GOOD.
YOU MENTIONED ROOKS, EARLIER. WELL, LET ME GIVE YOU A MYSTERY OF ROOKS...
9

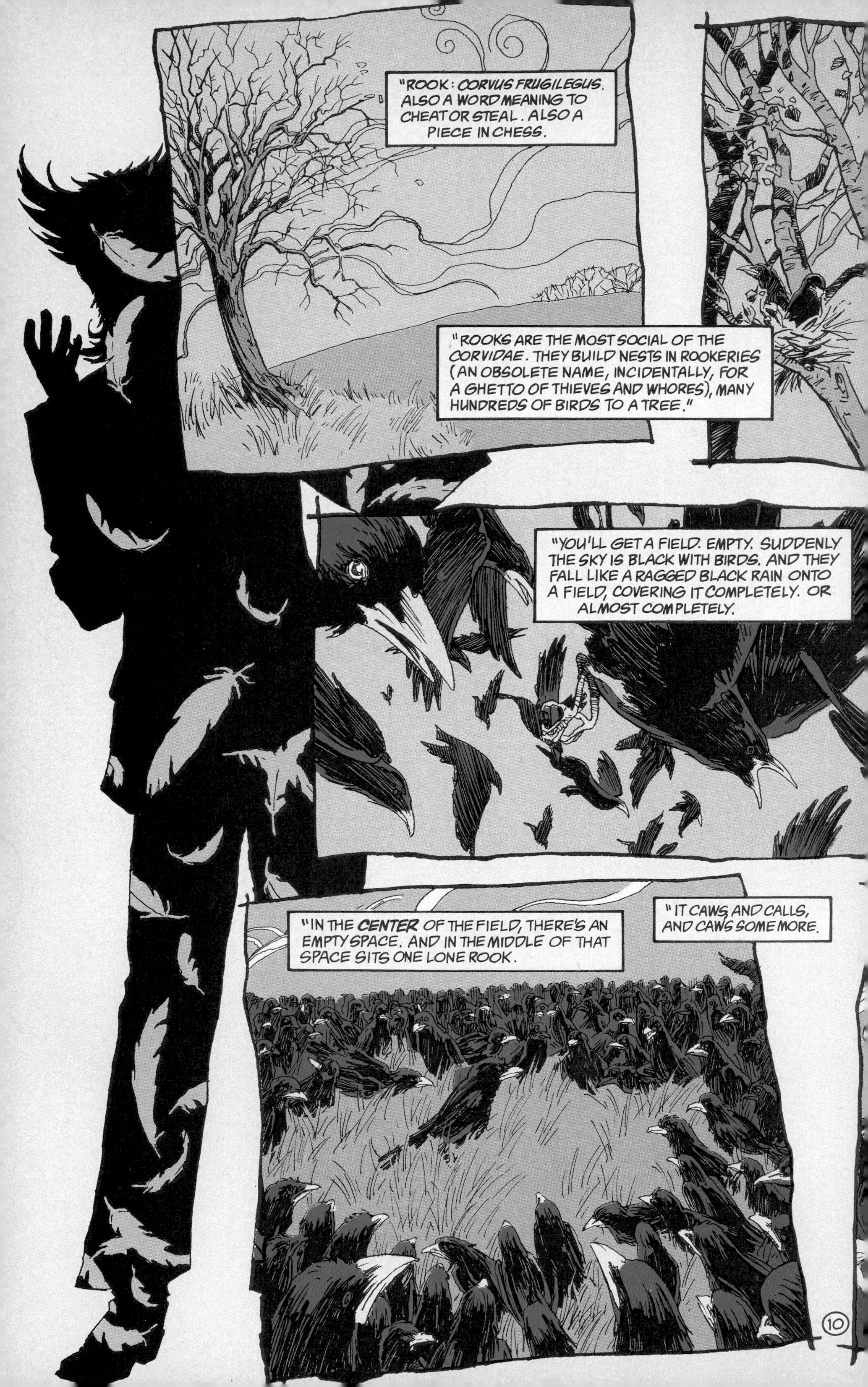
"ROOK: CORVUS FRUGILEGUS. ALSO A WORD MEANING TO CHEAT OR STEAL. ALSO A PIECE IN CHESS.
"ROOKS ARE THE MOST SOCIAL OF THE CORVIDAE. THEY BUILD NESTS IN ROOKERIES (AN OBSOLETE NAME, INCIDENTALLY, FOR A GHETTO OF THIEVES AND WHORES), MANY HUNDREDS OF BIRDS TO A TREE."
"YOU'LL GET A FIELD. EMPTY. SUDDENLY THE SKY IS BLACK WITH BIRDS. AND THEY FALL LIKE A RAGGED BLACK RAIN ONTO A FIELD, COVERING IT COMPLETELY. OR ALMOST COMPLETELY.
"IN THE CENTER OF THE FIELD, THERE'S AN EMPTY SPACE. AND IN THE MIDDLE OF THAT SPACE SITS ONE LONE ROOK.
"IT CAWS AND CALLS, AND CAWS SOME MORE.
10

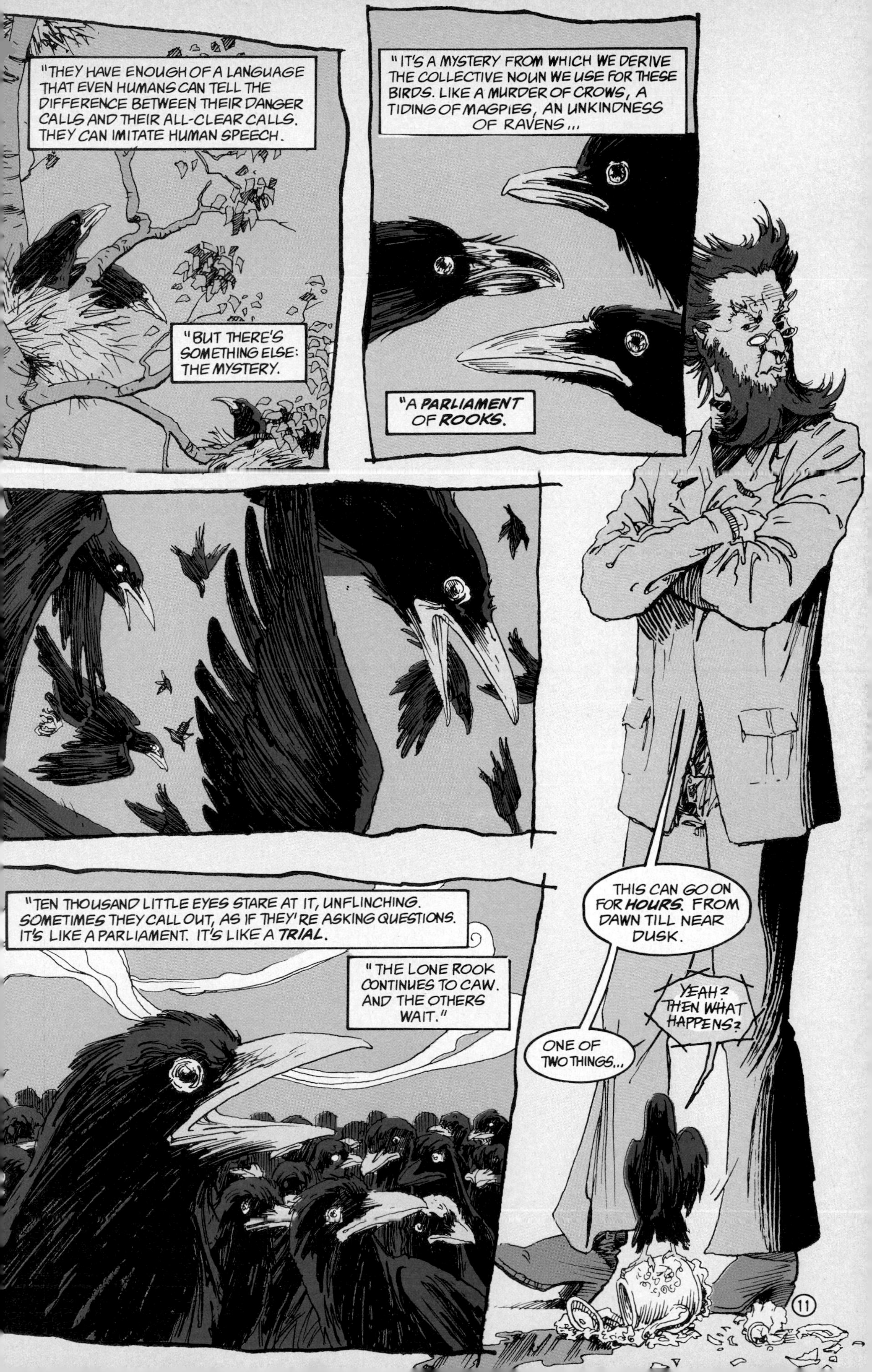
"THEY HAVE ENOUGH OF A LANGUAGE THAT EVEN HUMANS CAN TELL THE DIFFERENCE BETWEEN THEIR DANGER CALLS AND THEIR ALL-CLEAR CALLS. THEY CAN IMITATE HUMAN SPEECH.
"BUT THERE'S SOMETHING ELSE: THE MYSTERY.
"IT'S A MYSTERY FROM WHICH WE DERIVE THE COLLECTIVE NOUN WE USE FOR THESE BIRDS. LIKE A MURDER OF CROWS, A TIDING OF MAGPIES, AN UNKINDNESS OF RAVENS...
"A PARLIAMENT OF ROOKS.
"TEN THOUSAND LITTLE EYES STARE AT IT, UNFLINCHING. SOMETIMES THEY CALL OUT, AS IF THEY'RE ASKING QUESTIONS. IT'S LIKE A PARLIAMENT. IT'S LIKE A TRIAL.
"THE LONE ROOK CONTINUES TO CAW. AND THE OTHERS WAIT."
THIS CAN GO ON FOR HOURS. FROM DAWN TILL NEAR DUSK.
YEAH? THEN WHAT HAPPENS?
ONE OF TWO THINGS...
11

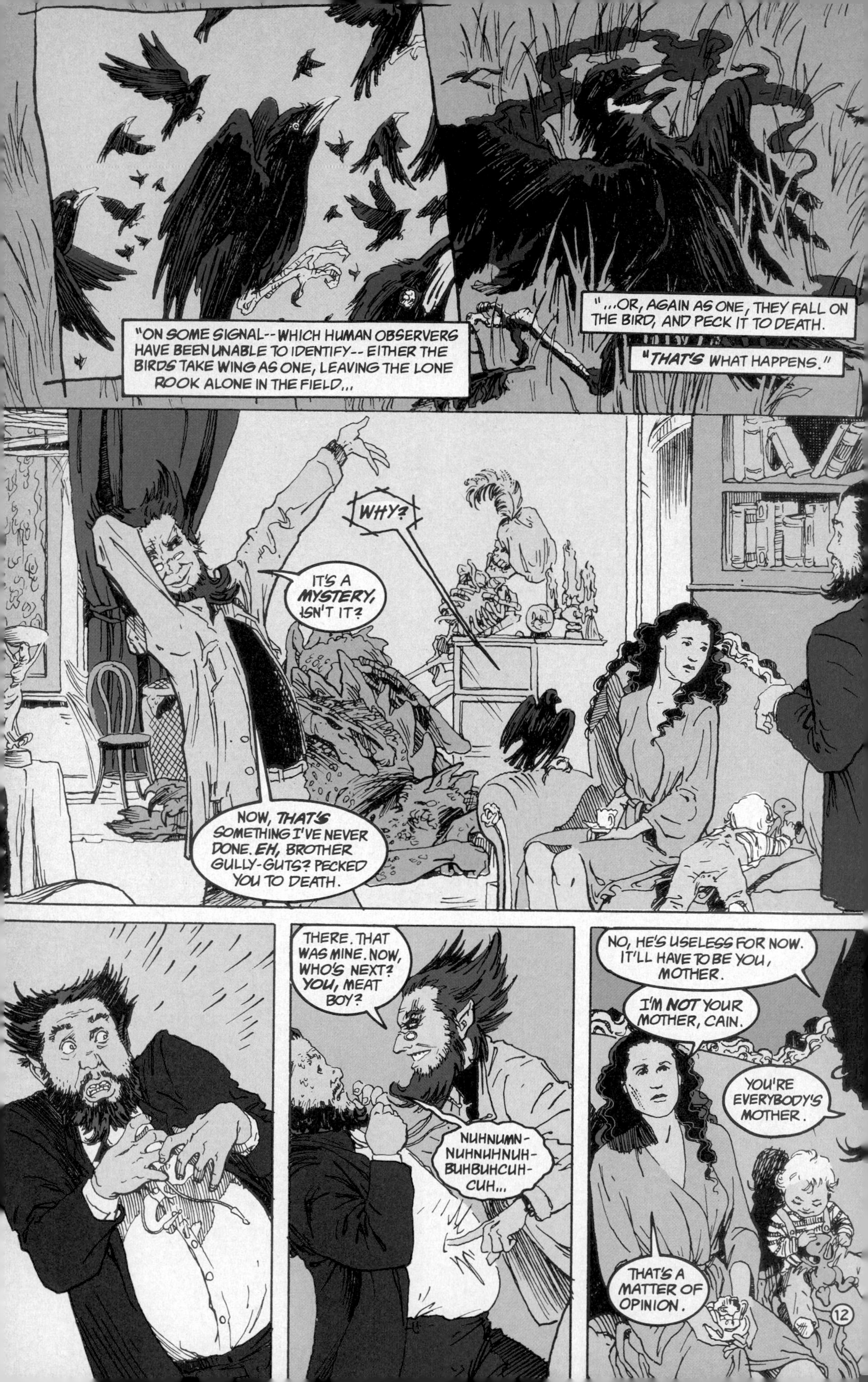
"ON SOME SIGNAL--WHICH HUMAN OBSERVERS HAVE BEEN UNABLE TO IDENTIFY--EITHER THE BIRDS TAKE WING AS ONE, LEAVING THE LONE ROOK ALONE IN THE FIELD...
"...OR, AGAIN AS ONE, THEY FALL ON THE BIRD, AND PECK IT TO DEATH.
"THAT'S WHAT HAPPENS."
WHY?
IT'S A MYSTERY, ISN'T IT?
NOW, THAT'S SOMETHING I'VE NEVER DONE. EH, BROTHER GULLY-GUTS? PECKED YOU TO DEATH.
THERE. THAT WAS MINE. NOW, WHO'S NEXT? YOU, MEAT BOY?
NUHNUMN-NUHNUHNUH-BUHBUHCUH-CUH...
NO, HE'S USELESS FOR NOW. IT'LL HAVE TO BE YOU, MOTHER.
I'M NOT YOUR MOTHER, CAIN.
YOU'RE EVERYBODY'S MOTHER.
THAT'S A MATTER OF OPINION.

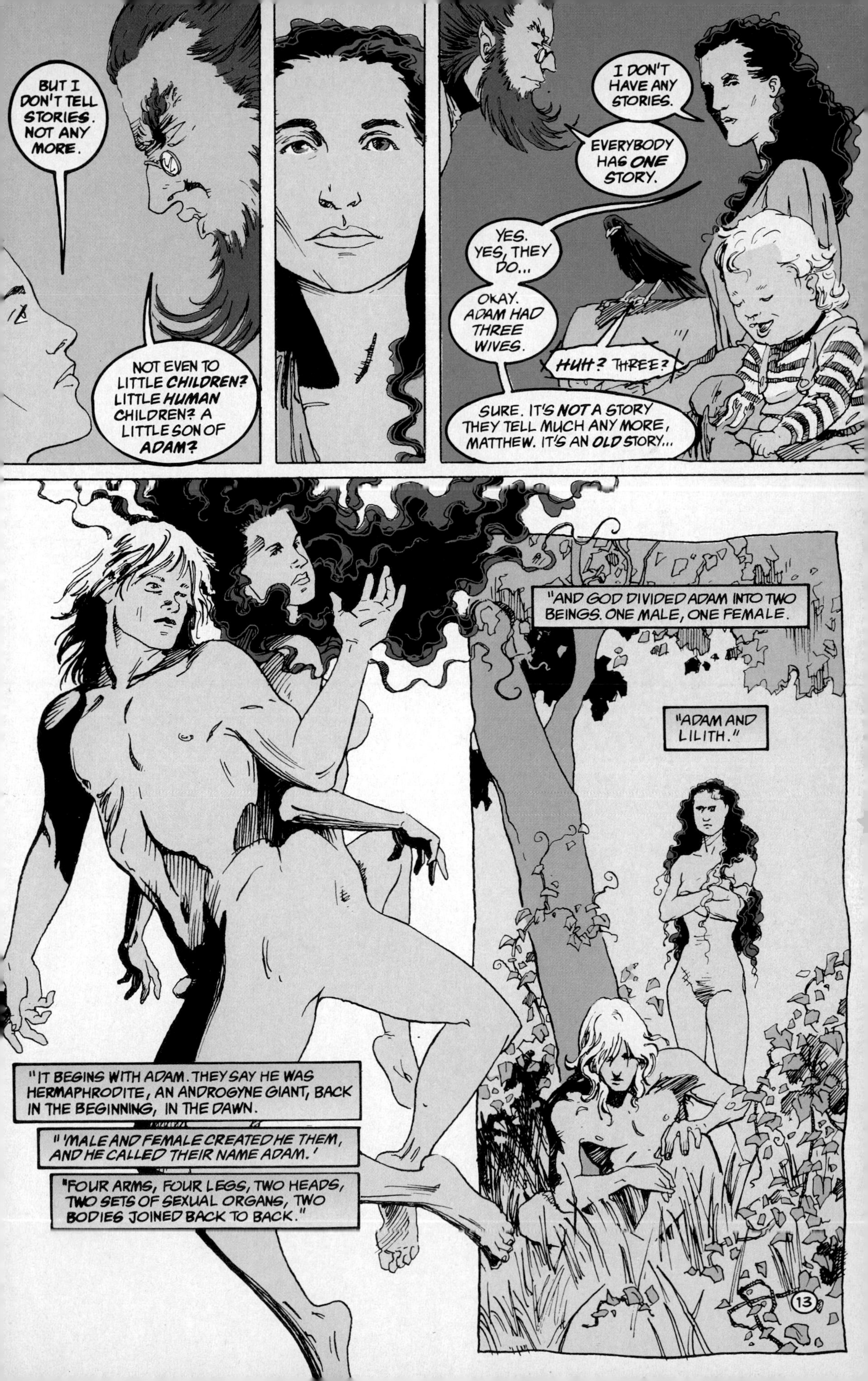
BUT I DON'T TELL STORIES. NOT ANY MORE.
NOT EVEN TO LITTLE CHILDREN? LITTLE HUMAN CHILDREN? A LITTLE SON OF ADAM?
I DON'T HAVE ANY STORIES.
EVERYBODY HAS ONE STORY.
YES. YES, THEY DO...
OKAY. ADAM HAD THREE WIVES.
HUH? THREE?
SURE. IT'S NOT A STORY THEY TELL MUCH ANY MORE, MATTHEW. IT'S AN OLD STORY...
"IT BEGINS WITH ADAM. THEY SAY HE WAS HERMAPHRODITE, AN ANDROGYNE GIANT, BACK IN THE BEGINNING, IN THE DAWN.
"'MALE AND FEMALE CREATED HE THEM, AND HE CALLED THEIR NAME ADAM.'
"FOUR ARMS, FOUR LEGS, TWO HEADS, TWO SETS OF SEXUAL ORGANS, TWO BODIES JOINED BACK TO BACK."
"AND GOD DIVIDED ADAM INTO TWO BEINGS. ONE MALE, ONE FEMALE.
"ADAM AND LILITH."
13

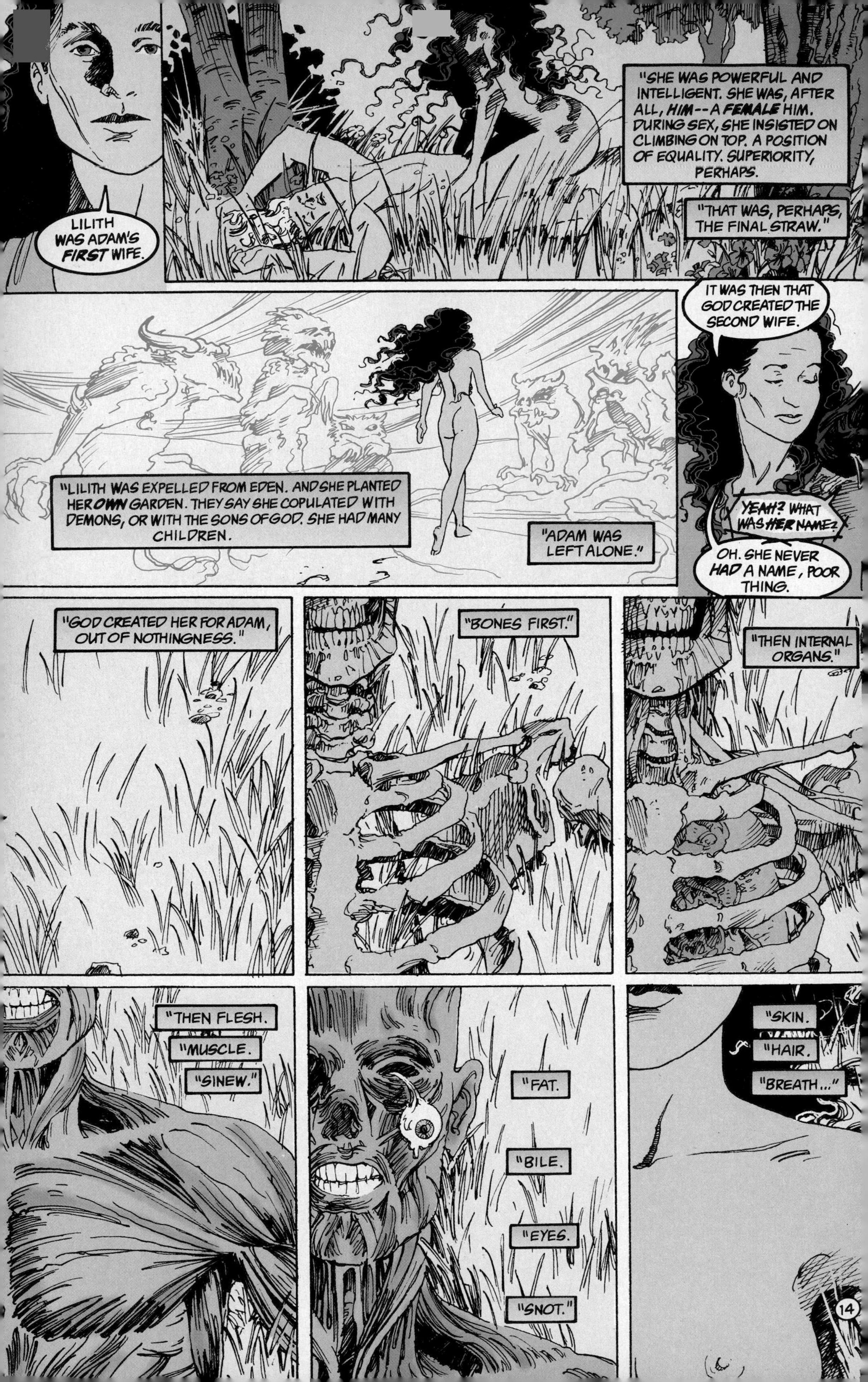

LILITH WAS ADAM'S FIRST WIFE.
"SHE WAS POWERFUL AND INTELLIGENT. SHE WAS, AFTER ALL, HIM--A FEMALE HIM. DURING SEX, SHE INSISTED ON CLIMBING ON TOP. A POSITION OF EQUALITY. SUPERIORITY, PERHAPS.
"THAT WAS, PERHAPS, THE FINAL STRAW."
"LILITH WAS EXPELLED FROM EDEN. AND SHE PLANTED HER OWN GARDEN. THEY SAY SHE COPULATED WITH DEMONS, OR WITH THE SONS OF GOD. SHE HAD MANY CHILDREN.
"ADAM WAS LEFT ALONE."
IT WAS THEN THAT GOD CREATED THE SECOND WIFE.
YEAH? WHAT WAS HER NAME?
OH. SHE NEVER HAD A NAME, POOR THING.
"GOD CREATED HER FOR ADAM, OUT OF NOTHINGNESS."
"BONES FIRST."
"THEN INTERNAL ORGANS."
"THEN FLESH.
"MUSCLE.
"SINEW."
"FAT.
"BILE.
"EYES.
"SNOT."
"SKIN.
"HAIR.
"BREATH..."

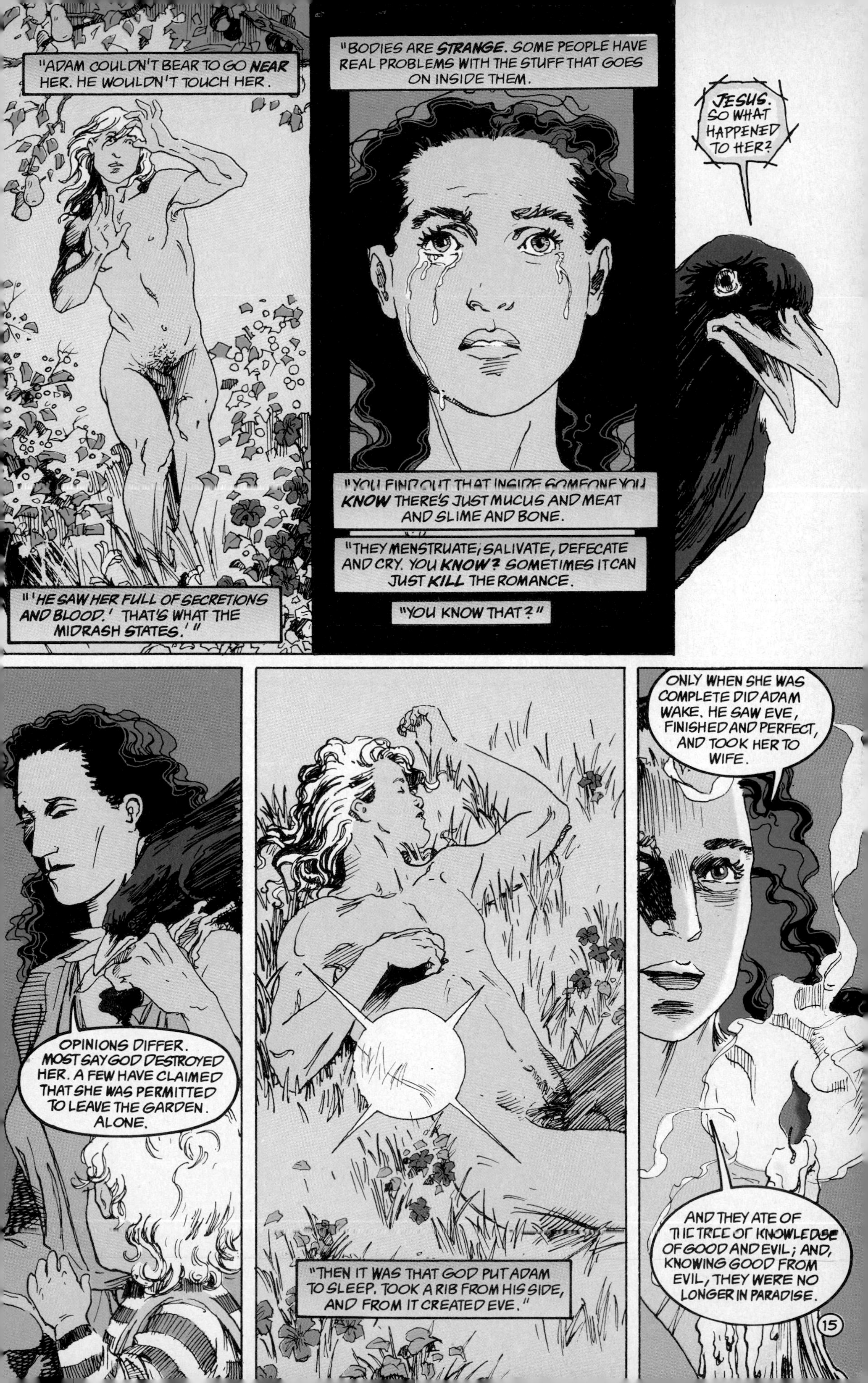

"ADAM COULDN'T BEAR TO GO NEAR HER. HE WOULDN'T TOUCH HER.
"'HE SAW HER FULL OF SECRETIONS AND BLOOD.' THAT'S WHAT THE MIDRASH STATES.'"
"BODIES ARE STRANGE. SOME PEOPLE HAVE REAL PROBLEMS WITH THE STUFF THAT GOES ON INSIDE THEM.
"YOU FIND OUT THAT INSIDE SOMEONE YOU KNOW THERE'S JUST MUCUS AND MEAT AND SLIME AND BONE.
"THEY MENSTRUATE; SALIVATE, DEFECATE AND CRY. YOU KNOW? SOMETIMES IT CAN JUST KILL THE ROMANCE.
"YOU KNOW THAT?"
JESUS. SO WHAT HAPPENED TO HER?
OPINIONS DIFFER. MOST SAY GOD DESTROYED HER. A FEW HAVE CLAIMED THAT SHE WAS PERMITTED TO LEAVE THE GARDEN. ALONE.
"THEN IT WAS THAT GOD PUT ADAM TO SLEEP. TOOK A RIB FROM HIS SIDE, AND FROM IT CREATED EVE."
ONLY WHEN SHE WAS COMPLETE DID ADAM WAKE. HE SAW EVE, FINISHED AND PERFECT, AND TOOK HER TO WIFE.
AND THEY ATE OF THE TREE OF KNOWLEDGE OF GOOD AND EVIL; AND, KNOWING GOOD FROM EVIL, THEY WERE NO LONGER IN PARADISE.

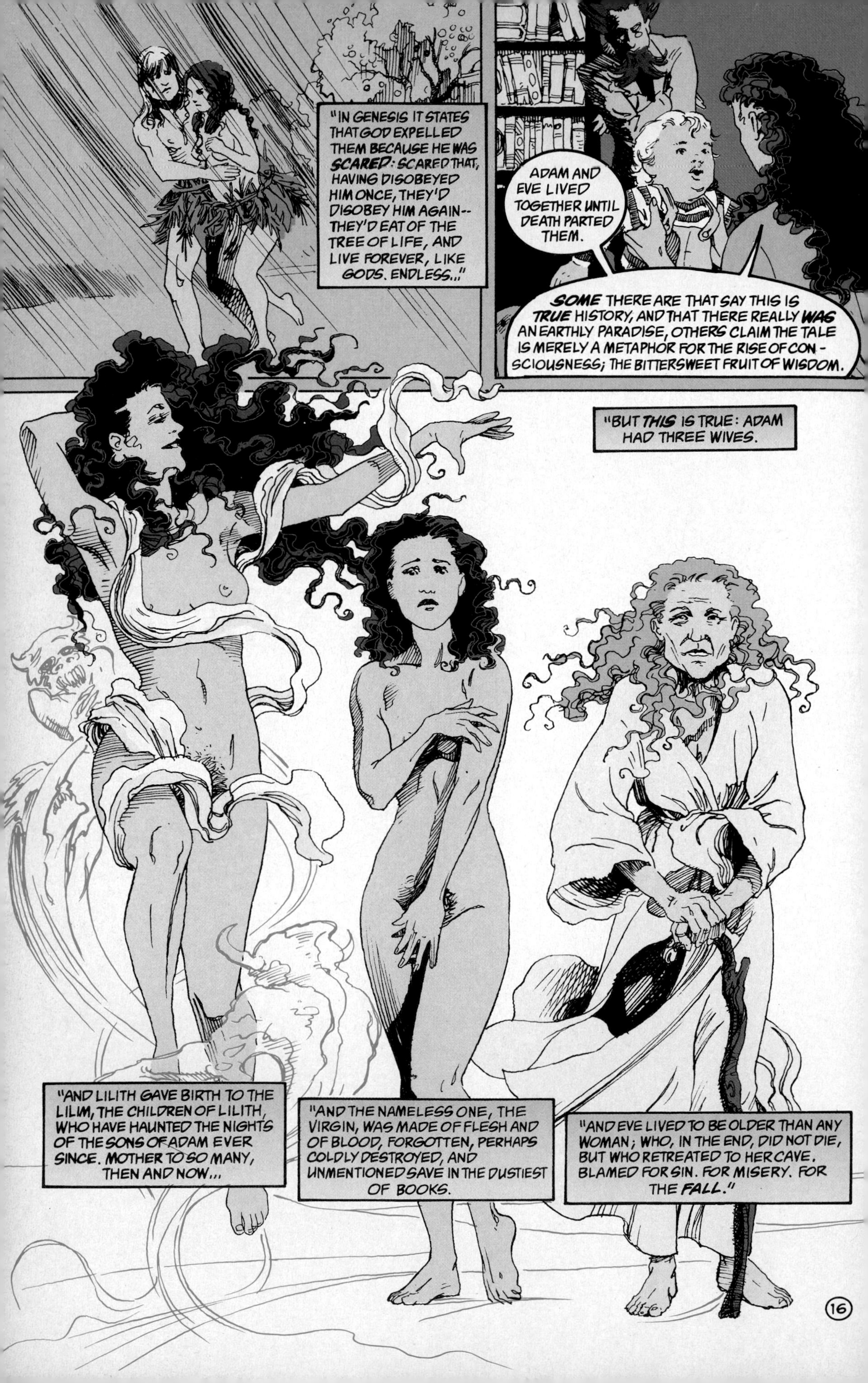
"IN GENESIS IT STATES THAT GOD EXPELLED THEM BECAUSE HE WAS SCARED: SCARED THAT, HAVING DISOBEYED HIM ONCE, THEY'D DISOBEY HIM AGAIN-- THEY'D EAT OF THE TREE OF LIFE, AND LIVE FOREVER, LIKE GODS. ENDLESS..."
ADAM AND EVE LIVED TOGETHER UNTIL DEATH PARTED THEM.
SOME THERE ARE THAT SAY THIS IS TRUE HISTORY, AND THAT THERE REALLY WAS AN EARTHLY PARADISE, OTHERS CLAIM THE TALE IS MERELY A METAPHOR FOR THE RISE OF CON-SCIOUSNESS; THE BITTERSWEET FRUIT OF WISDOM.
"BUT THIS IS TRUE: ADAM HAD THREE WIVES.
"AND LILITH GAVE BIRTH TO THE LILIM, THE CHILDREN OF LILITH, WHO HAVE HAUNTED THE NIGHTS OF THE SONS OF ADAM EVER SINCE. MOTHER TO SO MANY, THEN AND NOW...
"AND THE NAMELESS ONE, THE VIRGIN, WAS MADE OF FLESH AND OF BLOOD, FORGOTTEN, PERHAPS COLDLY DESTROYED, AND UNMENTIONED SAVE IN THE DUSTIEST OF BOOKS.
"AND EVE LIVED TO BE OLDER THAN ANY WOMAN; WHO, IN THE END, DID NOT DIE, BUT WHO RETREATED TO HER CAVE. BLAMED FOR SIN. FOR MISERY. FOR THE FALL."

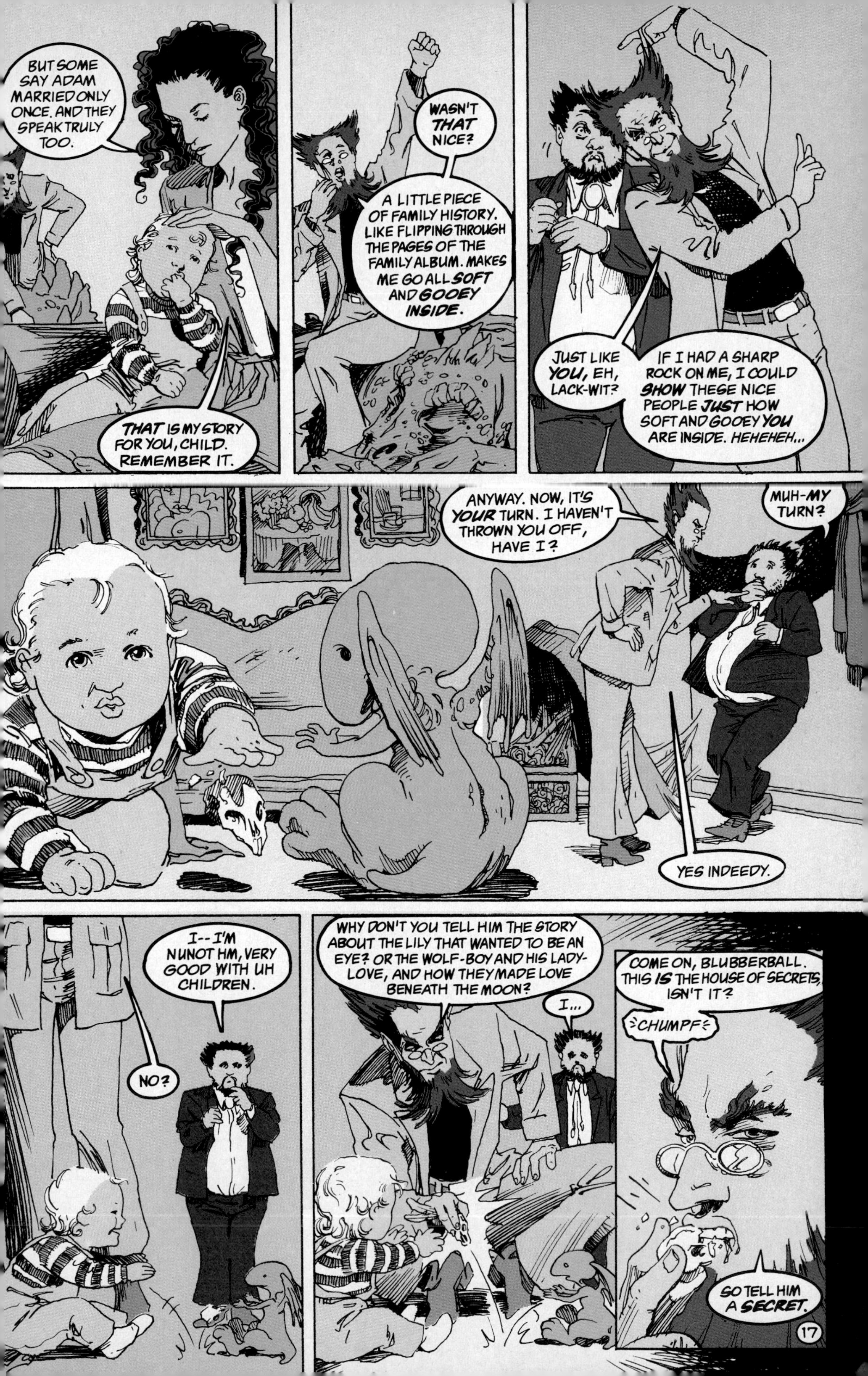
BUT SOME SAY ADAM MARRIED ONLY ONCE. AND THEY SPEAK TRULY TOO.
THAT IS MY STORY FOR YOU, CHILD. REMEMBER IT.
WASN'T THAT NICE?
A LITTLE PIECE OF FAMILY HISTORY. LIKE FLIPPING THROUGH THE PAGES OF THE FAMILY ALBUM. MAKES ME GO ALL SOFT AND GOOEY INSIDE.
JUST LIKE YOU, EH, LACK-WIT?
IF I HAD A SHARP ROCK ON ME, I COULD SHOW THESE NICE PEOPLE JUST HOW SOFT AND GOOEY YOU ARE INSIDE. HEHEHEH...
ANYWAY. NOW, IT'S YOUR TURN. I HAVEN'T THROWN YOU OFF, HAVE I?
MUH-MY TURN?
YES INDEEDY.
I-- I'M NUNOT HM, VERY GOOD WITH UH CHILDREN.
NO?
WHY DON'T YOU TELL HIM THE STORY ABOUT THE LILY THAT WANTED TO BE AN EYE? OR THE WOLF-BOY AND HIS LADY-LOVE, AND HOW THEY MADE LOVE BENEATH THE MOON?
I...
COME ON, BLUBBERBALL. THIS IS THE HOUSE OF SECRETS, ISN'T IT?
CHUMPF
SO TELL HIM A SECRET.

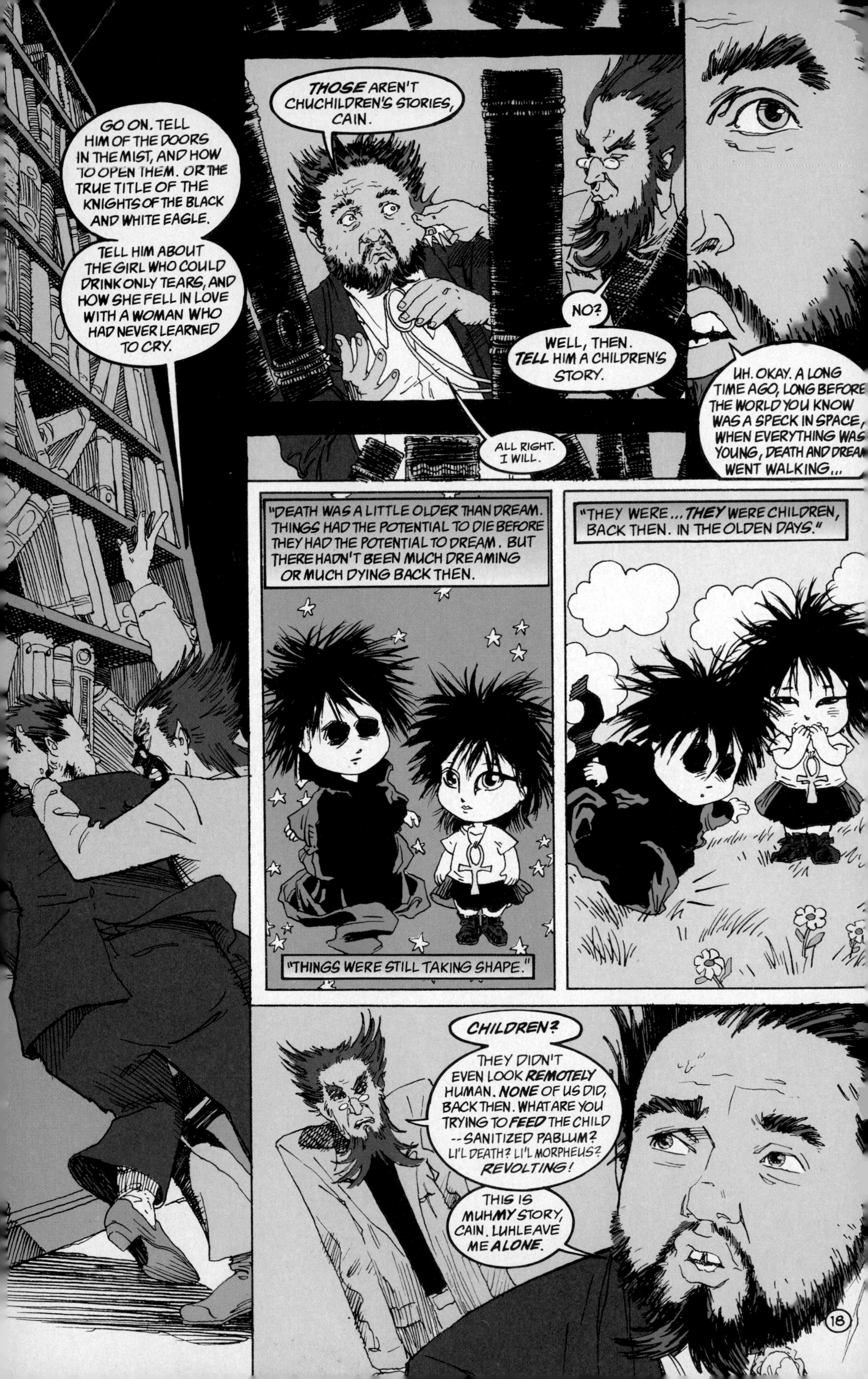

GO ON. TELL HIM OF THE DOORS IN THE MIST, AND HOW TO OPEN THEM. OR THE TRUE TITLE OF THE KNIGHTS OF THE BLACK AND WHITE EAGLE.
TELL HIM ABOUT THE GIRL WHO COULD DRINK ONLY TEARS, AND HOW SHE FELL IN LOVE WITH A WOMAN WHO HAD NEVER LEARNED TO CRY.
THOSE AREN'T CHUCHILDREN'S STORIES, CAIN.
NO?
WELL, THEN. TELL HIM A CHILDREN'S STORY.
ALL RIGHT. I WILL.
UH. OKAY. A LONG TIME AGO, LONG BEFORE THE WORLD YOU KNOW WAS A SPECK IN SPACE, WHEN EVERYTHING WAS YOUNG, DEATH AND DREAM WENT WALKING...
"DEATH WAS A LITTLE OLDER THAN DREAM. THINGS HAD THE POTENTIAL TO DIE BEFORE THEY HAD THE POTENTIAL TO DREAM. BUT THERE HADN'T BEEN MUCH DREAMING OR MUCH DYING BACK THEN.
"THINGS WERE STILL TAKING SHAPE."
"THEY WERE... THEY WERE CHILDREN, BACK THEN. IN THE OLDEN DAYS."
CHILDREN?
THEY DIDN'T EVEN LOOK REMOTELY HUMAN. NONE OF US DID, BACK THEN. WHAT ARE YOU TRYING TO FEED THE CHILD --SANITIZED PABLUM? LI'L DEATH? LI'L MORPHEUS? REVOLTING!
THIS IS MUHMY STORY, CAIN. LUHLEAVE ME ALONE.
18

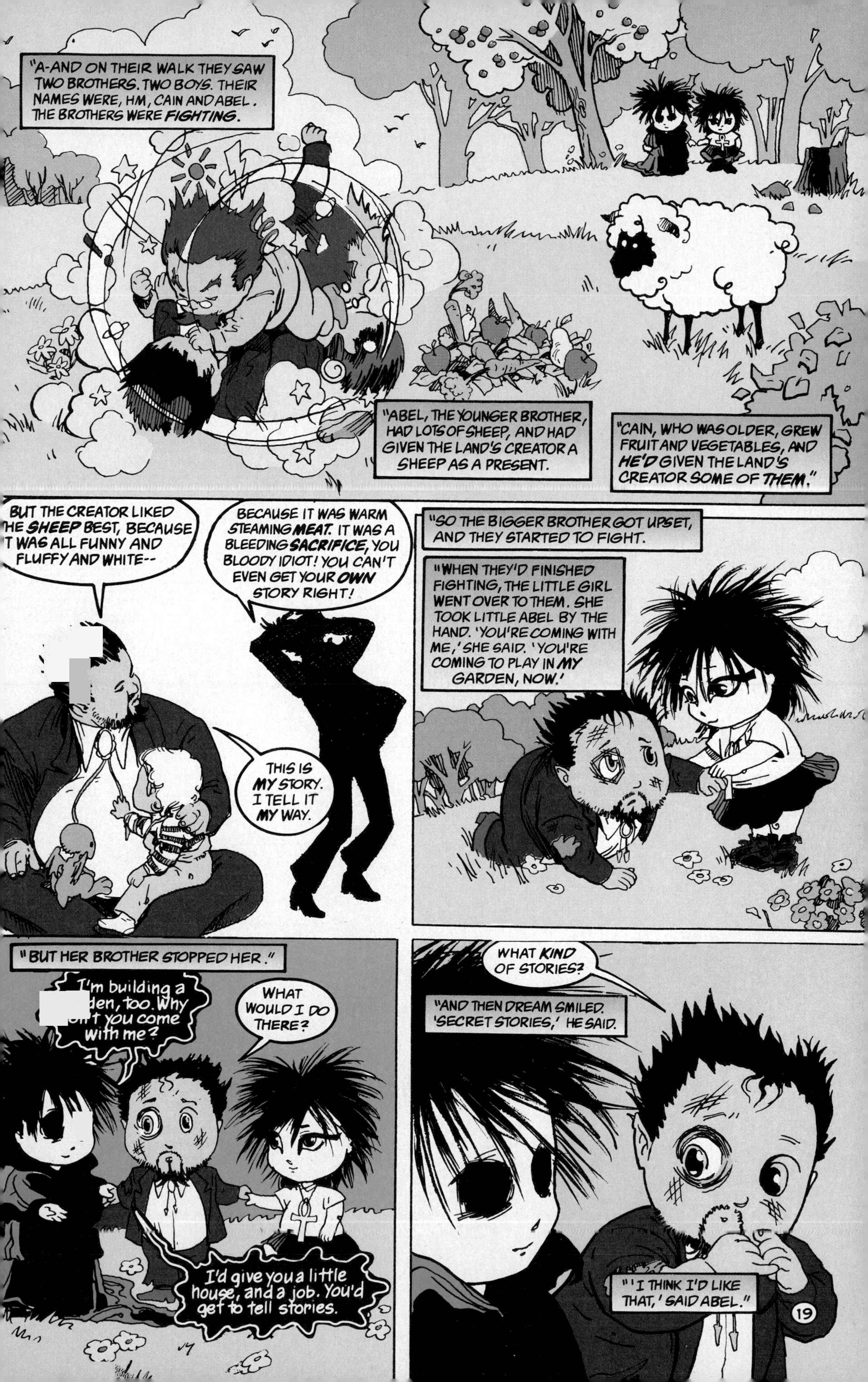
"A-AND ON THEIR WALK THEY SAW TWO BROTHERS. TWO BOYS. THEIR NAMES WERE, HM, CAIN AND ABEL. THE BROTHERS WERE FIGHTING.
"ABEL, THE YOUNGER BROTHER, HAD LOTS OF SHEEP, AND HAD GIVEN THE LAND'S CREATOR A SHEEP AS A PRESENT.
"CAIN, WHO WAS OLDER, GREW FRUIT AND VEGETABLES, AND HE'D GIVEN THE LAND'S CREATOR SOME OF THEM."
BUT THE CREATOR LIKED HE SHEEP BEST, BECAUSE T WAS ALL FUNNY AND FLUFFY AND WHITE--
BECAUSE IT WAS WARM STEAMING MEAT. IT WAS A BLEEDING SACRIFICE, YOU BLOODY IDIOT! YOU CAN'T EVEN GET YOUR OWN STORY RIGHT!
THIS IS MY STORY. I TELL IT MY WAY.
"SO THE BIGGER BROTHER GOT UPSET, AND THEY STARTED TO FIGHT.
"WHEN THEY'D FINISHED FIGHTING, THE LITTLE GIRL WENT OVER TO THEM. SHE TOOK LITTLE ABEL BY THE HAND. 'YOU'RE COMING WITH ME,' SHE SAID. 'YOU'RE COMING TO PLAY IN MY GARDEN, NOW.'
"BUT HER BROTHER STOPPED HER."
I'm building a den, too. Why n't you come with me?
WHAT WOULD I DO THERE?
I'd give you a little house, and a job. You'd get to tell stories.
WHAT KIND OF STORIES?
"AND THEN DREAM SMILED. 'SECRET STORIES,' HE SAID.
"'I THINK I'D LIKE THAT,' SAID ABEL."
19

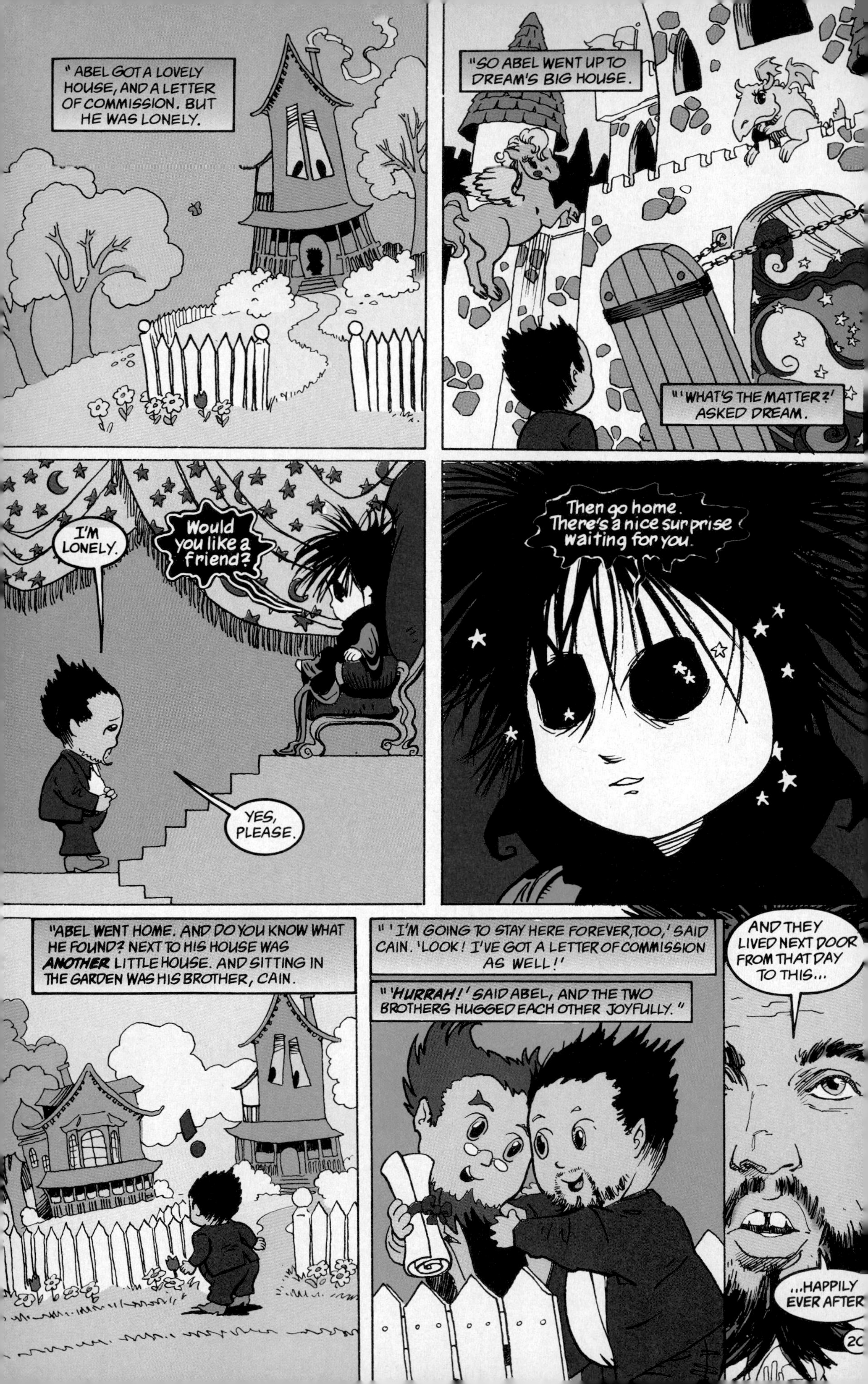
"ABEL GOT A LOVELY HOUSE, AND A LETTER OF COMMISSION. BUT HE WAS LONELY.
"SO ABEL WENT UP TO DREAM'S BIG HOUSE.
"'WHAT'S THE MATTER?' ASKED DREAM.
I'M LONELY.
Would you like a friend?
YES, PLEASE.
Then go home. There's a nice surprise waiting for you.
"ABEL WENT HOME. AND DO YOU KNOW WHAT HE FOUND? NEXT TO HIS HOUSE WAS ANOTHER LITTLE HOUSE. AND SITTING IN THE GARDEN WAS HIS BROTHER, CAIN.
"'I'M GOING TO STAY HERE FOREVER, TOO,' SAID CAIN. 'LOOK! I'VE GOT A LETTER OF COMMISSION AS WELL!'
"'HURRAH!' SAID ABEL, AND THE TWO BROTHERS HUGGED EACH OTHER JOYFULLY."
AND THEY LIVED NEXT DOOR FROM THAT DAY TO THIS...
...HAPPILY EVER AFTER
20

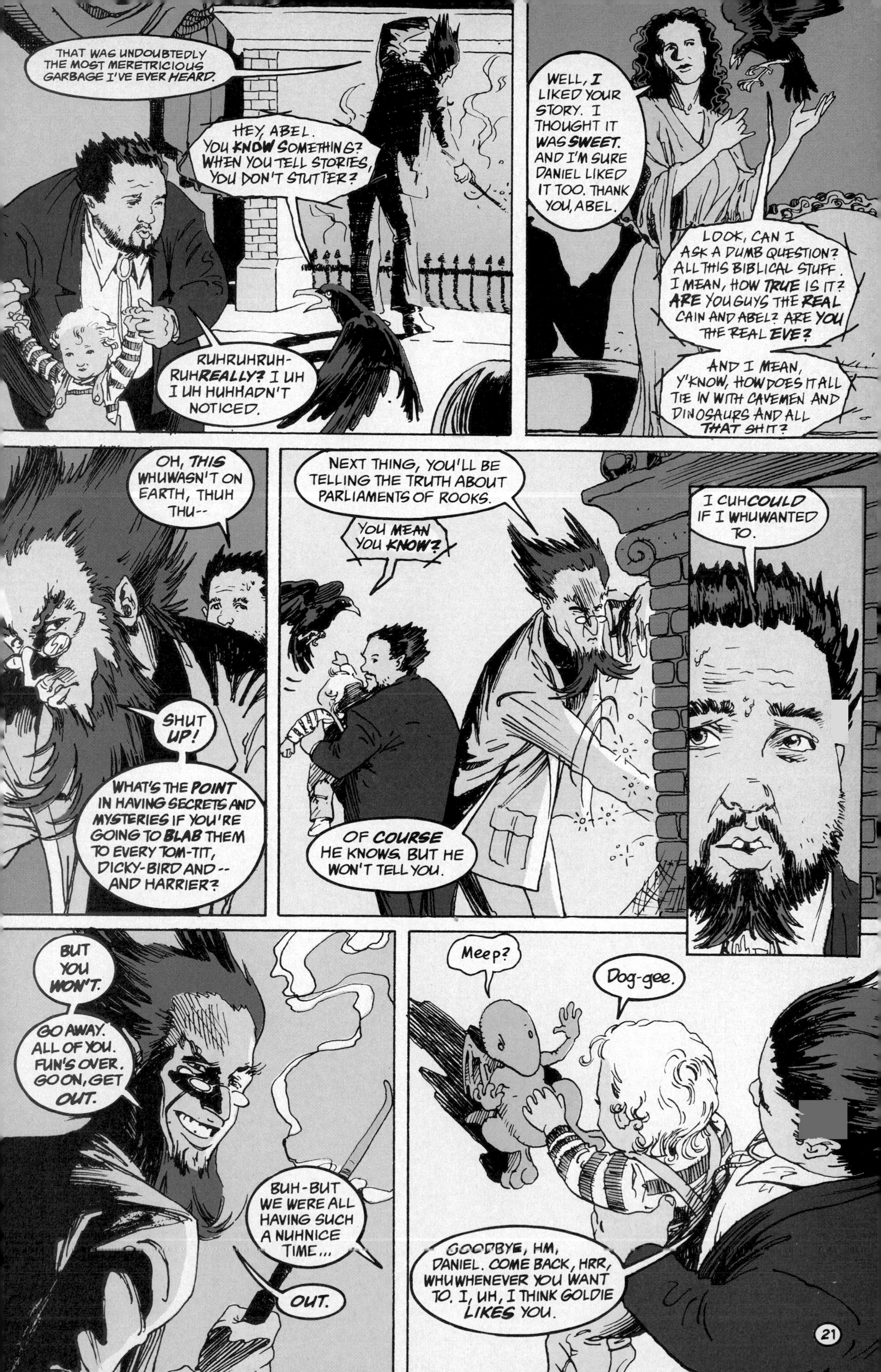
THAT WAS UNDOUBTEDLY THE MOST MERETRICIOUS GARBAGE I'VE EVER HEARD.
HEY, ABEL. YOU KNOW SOMETHING? WHEN YOU TELL STORIES, YOU DON'T STUTTER?
RUHRUHRUH-RUHREALLY? I UH I UH HUHHADN'T NOTICED.
WELL, I LIKED YOUR STORY. I THOUGHT IT WAS SWEET. AND I'M SURE DANIEL LIKED IT TOO. THANK YOU, ABEL.
LOOK, CAN I ASK A DUMB QUESTION? ALL THIS BIBLICAL STUFF. I MEAN, HOW TRUE IS IT? ARE YOU GUYS THE REAL CAIN AND ABEL? ARE YOU THE REAL EVE?
AND I MEAN, Y'KNOW, HOW DOES IT ALL TIE IN WITH CAVEMEN AND DINOSAURS AND ALL THAT SHIT?
OH, THIS WHUWASN'T ON EARTH, THUH THU--
SHUT UP!
WHAT'S THE POINT IN HAVING SECRETS AND MYSTERIES IF YOU'RE GOING TO BLAB THEM TO EVERY TOM-TIT, DICKY-BIRD AND -- AND HARRIER?
NEXT THING, YOU'LL BE TELLING THE TRUTH ABOUT PARLIAMENTS OF ROOKS.
YOU MEAN YOU KNOW?
OF COURSE HE KNOWS. BUT HE WON'T TELL YOU.
I CUHCOULD IF I WHUWANTED TO.
BUT YOU WON'T.
GO AWAY. ALL OF YOU. FUN'S OVER. GO ON, GET OUT.
BUH-BUT WE WERE ALL HAVING SUCH A NUHNICE TIME...
OUT.
Meep?
Dog-gee.
GOODBYE, HM, DANIEL. COME BACK, HRR, WHUWHENEVER YOU WANT TO. I, UH, I THINK GOLDIE LIKES YOU.

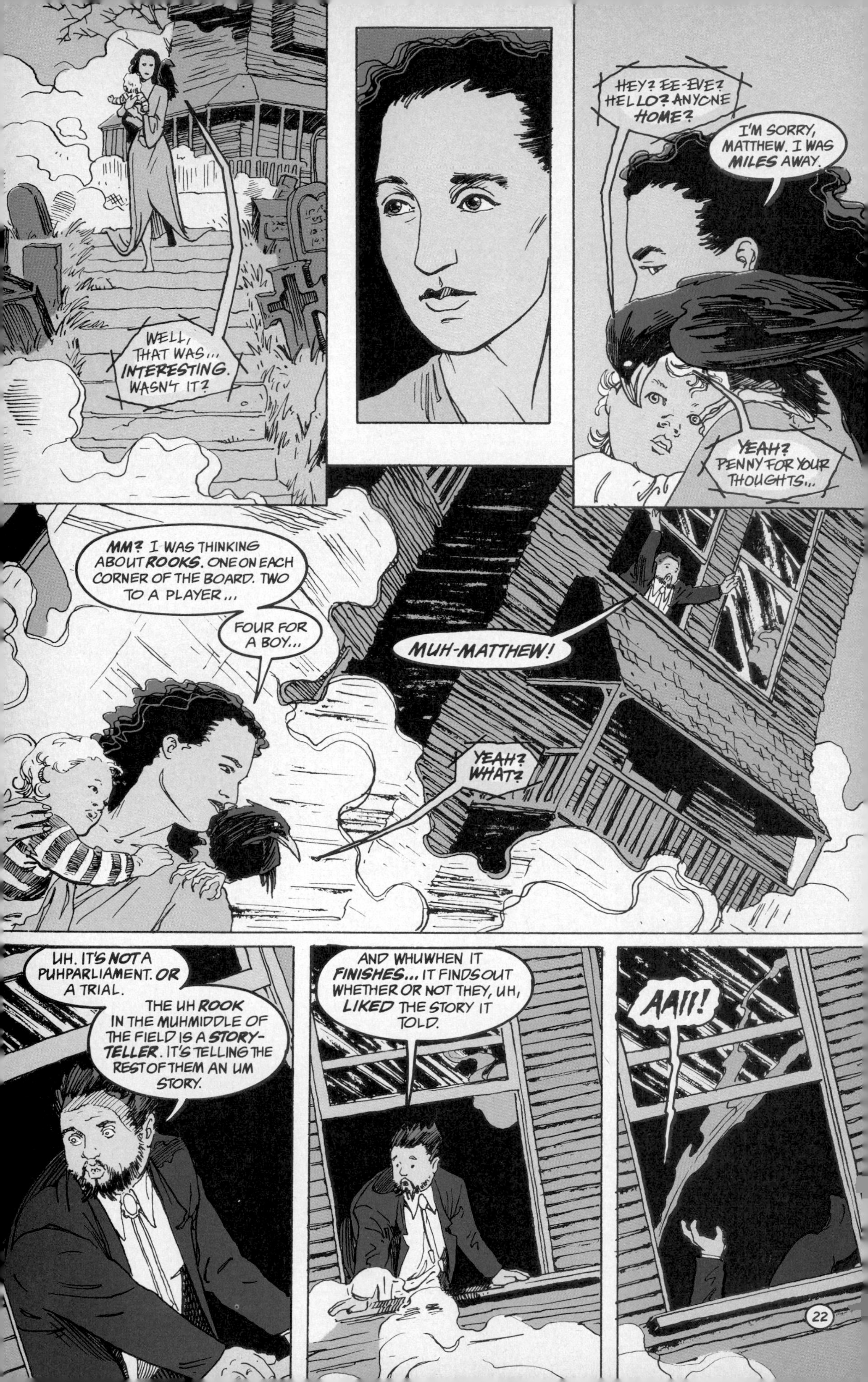
WELL, THAT WAS... INTERESTING. WASN'T IT?
HEY? EE-EVE? HELLO? ANYONE HOME?
I'M SORRY, MATTHEW. I WAS MILES AWAY.
YEAH? PENNY FOR YOUR THOUGHTS...
MM? I WAS THINKING ABOUT ROOKS. ONE ON EACH CORNER OF THE BOARD. TWO TO A PLAYER...
FOUR FOR A BOY...
MUH-MATTHEW!
YEAH? WHAT?
UH. IT'S NOT A PUHPARLIAMENT. OR A TRIAL.
THE UH ROOK IN THE MUHMIDDLE OF THE FIELD IS A STORY-TELLER. IT'S TELLING THE REST OF THEM AN UM STORY.
AND WHUWHEN IT FINISHES... IT FINDS OUT WHETHER OR NOT THEY, UH, LIKED THE STORY IT TOLD.
AAII!

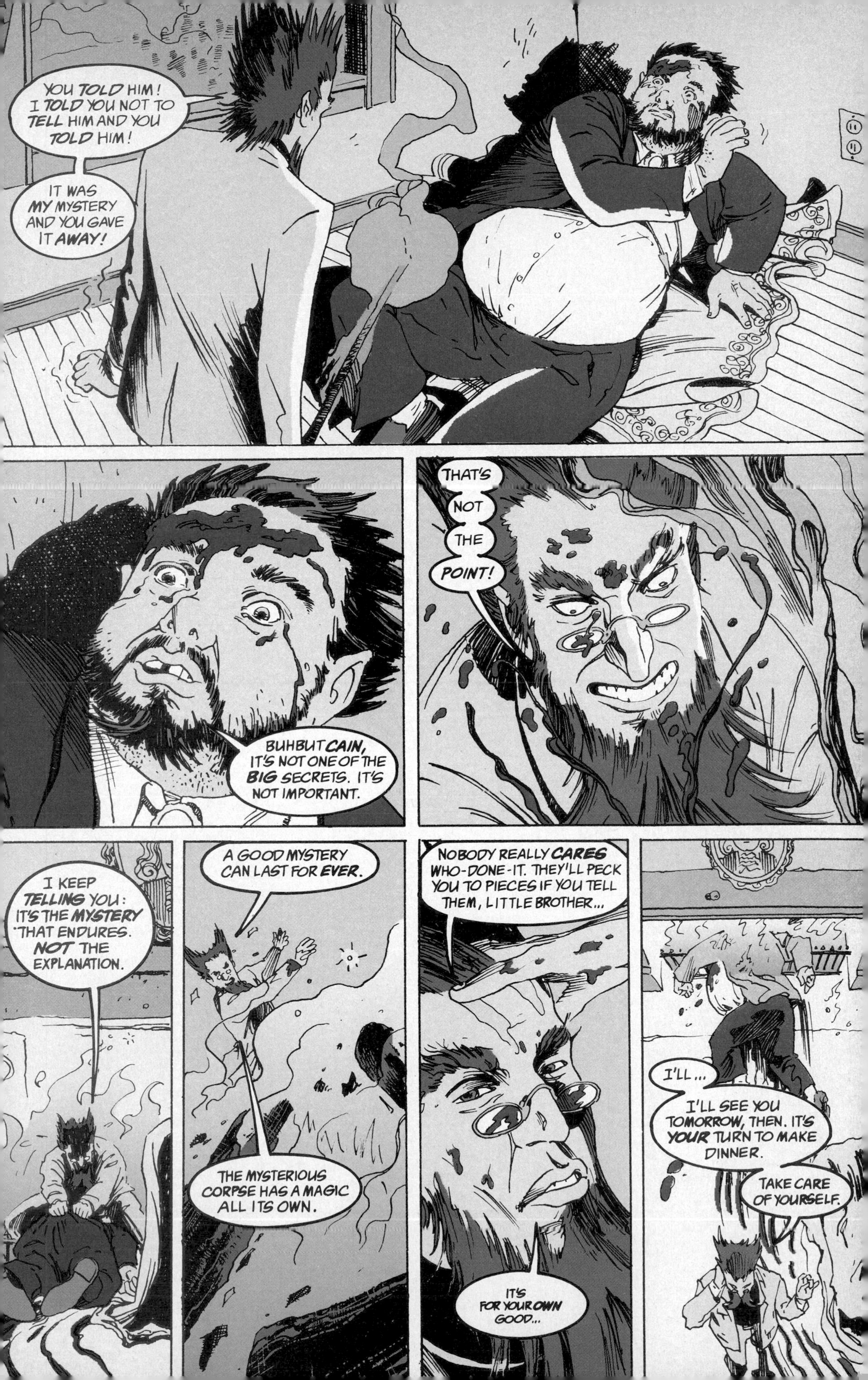
YOU TOLD HIM! I TOLD YOU NOT TO TELL HIM AND YOU TOLD HIM!
IT WAS MY MYSTERY AND YOU GAVE IT AWAY!
BUHBUT CAIN, IT'S NOT ONE OF THE BIG SECRETS. IT'S NOT IMPORTANT.
THAT'S NOT THE POINT!
I KEEP TELLING YOU: IT'S THE MYSTERY THAT ENDURES. NOT THE EXPLANATION.
A GOOD MYSTERY CAN LAST FOR EVER.
THE MYSTERIOUS CORPSE HAS A MAGIC ALL ITS OWN.
NOBODY REALLY CARES WHO-DONE-IT. THEY'LL PECK YOU TO PIECES IF YOU TELL THEM, LITTLE BROTHER...
IT'S FOR YOUR OWN GOOD...
I'LL...
I'LL SEE YOU TOMORROW, THEN. IT'S YOUR TURN TO MAKE DINNER.
TAKE CARE OF YOURSELF.

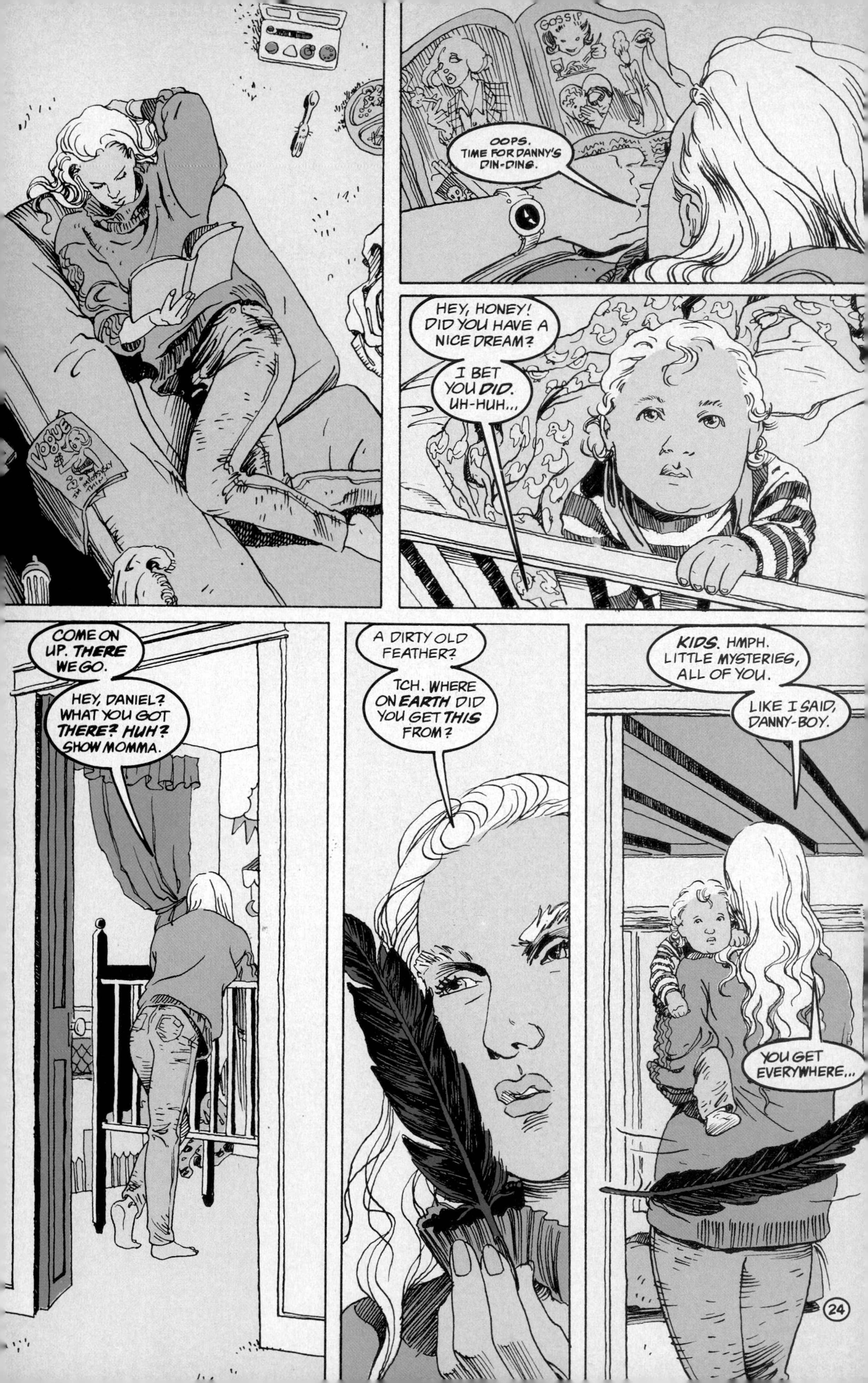
GOSSIP
OOPS. TIME FOR DANNY'S DIN-DING.
HEY, HONEY! DID YOU HAVE A NICE DREAM?
I BET YOU DID. UH-HUH...
COME ON UP. THERE WE GO.
HEY, DANIEL? WHAT YOU GOT THERE? HUH? SHOW MOMMA.
A DIRTY OLD FEATHER?
TCH. WHERE ON EARTH DID YOU GET THIS FROM?
KIDS. HMPH. LITTLE MYSTERIES, ALL OF YOU.
LIKE I SAID, DANNY-BOY.
YOU GET EVERYWHERE...

fables

reflections

Famadan

In the
name of Allah,
the compassionate,
the all-merciful,
I tell my tale.
For there is no
God but Allah,
and Mohammed
is his Prophet.

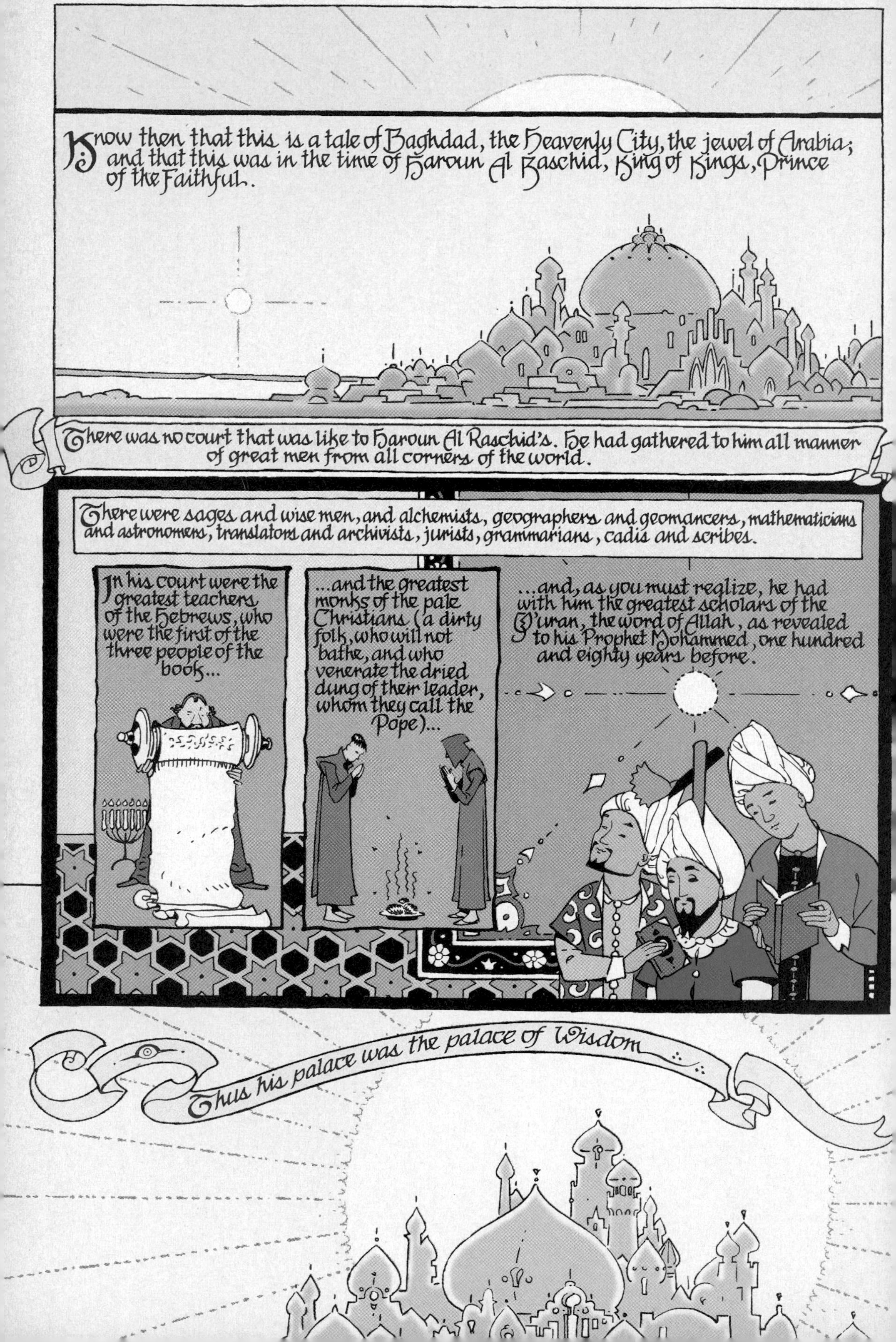
Know then that this is a tale of Baghdad, the Heavenly City, the jewel of Arabia; and that this was in the time of Haroun Al Raschid, King of Kings, Prince of the Faithful.
There was no court that was like to Haroun Al Raschid's. He had gathered to him all manner of great men from all corners of the world.
There were sages and wise men, and alchemists, geographers and geomancers, mathematicians and astronomers, translators and archivists, jurists, grammarians, cadis and scribes.
In his court were the greatest teachers of the Hebrews, who were the first of the three people of the book...
...and the greatest monks of the pale Christians (a dirty folk, who will not bathe, and who venerate the dried dung of their leader, whom they call the Pope)...
...and, as you must realize, he had with him the greatest scholars of the Q'uran, the word of Allah, as revealed to his Prophet Mohammed, one hundred and eighty years before.
Thus his palace was the palace of Wisdom

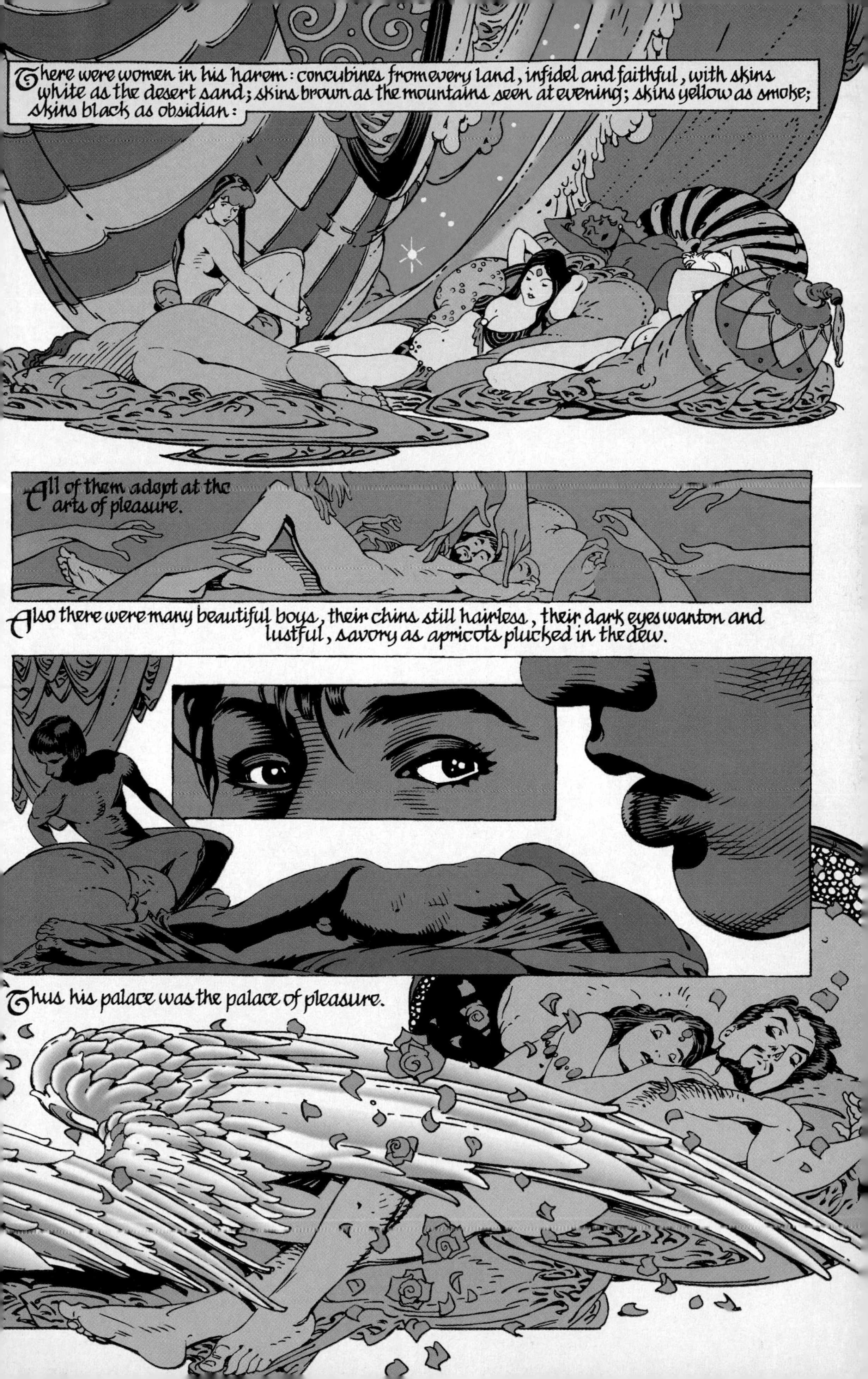
There were women in his harem: concubines from every land, infidel and faithful, with skins white as the desert sand; skins brown as the mountains seen at evening; skins yellow as smoke; skins black as obsidian:
All of them adept at the arts of pleasure.
Also there were many beautiful boys, their chins still hairless, their dark eyes wanton and lustful, savory as apricots plucked in the dew.
Thus his palace was the palace of pleasure.

There were magicians in his palace: astrologers, who could interpret the will of Allah from the high dances of the distant stars;

Enchanters from China and the Mongol lands, with high fur hats and long sleeves full of secrets;

Ascetic Bedouin sorcerers, who knew the secrets of angels and of djinn and of men.

And there were poets and musicians, and men of high wit and perfect taste.

And there were strange prodigies in that place--men with the heads of animals,

And animals that spoke like men,

And marvelous mechanical wonders that counterfeited life, and sang, or moved, when they were spoken to.

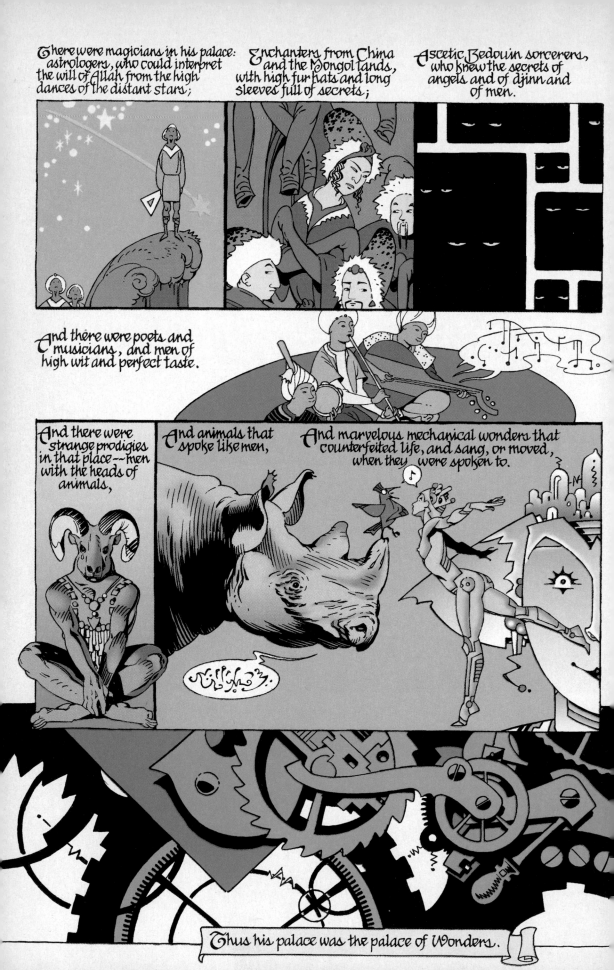

Thus his palace was the palace of Wonders.

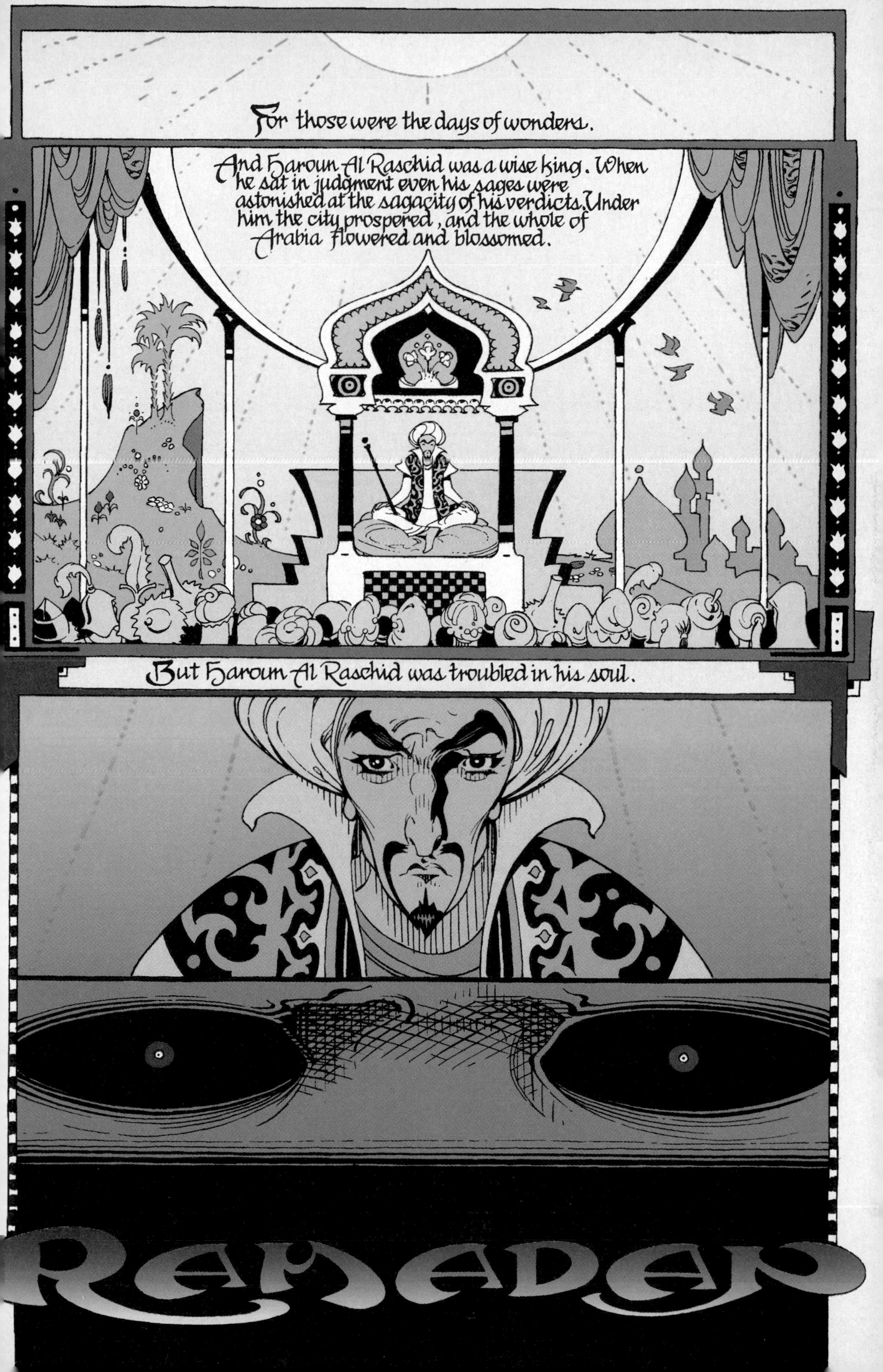
For those were the days of wonders.
And Haroun Al Raschid was a wise king. When he sat in judgment even his sages were astonished at the sagacity of his verdicts. Under him the city prospered, and the whole of Arabia flowered and blossomed.
But Haroun Al Raschid was troubled in his soul.
RAMADAN

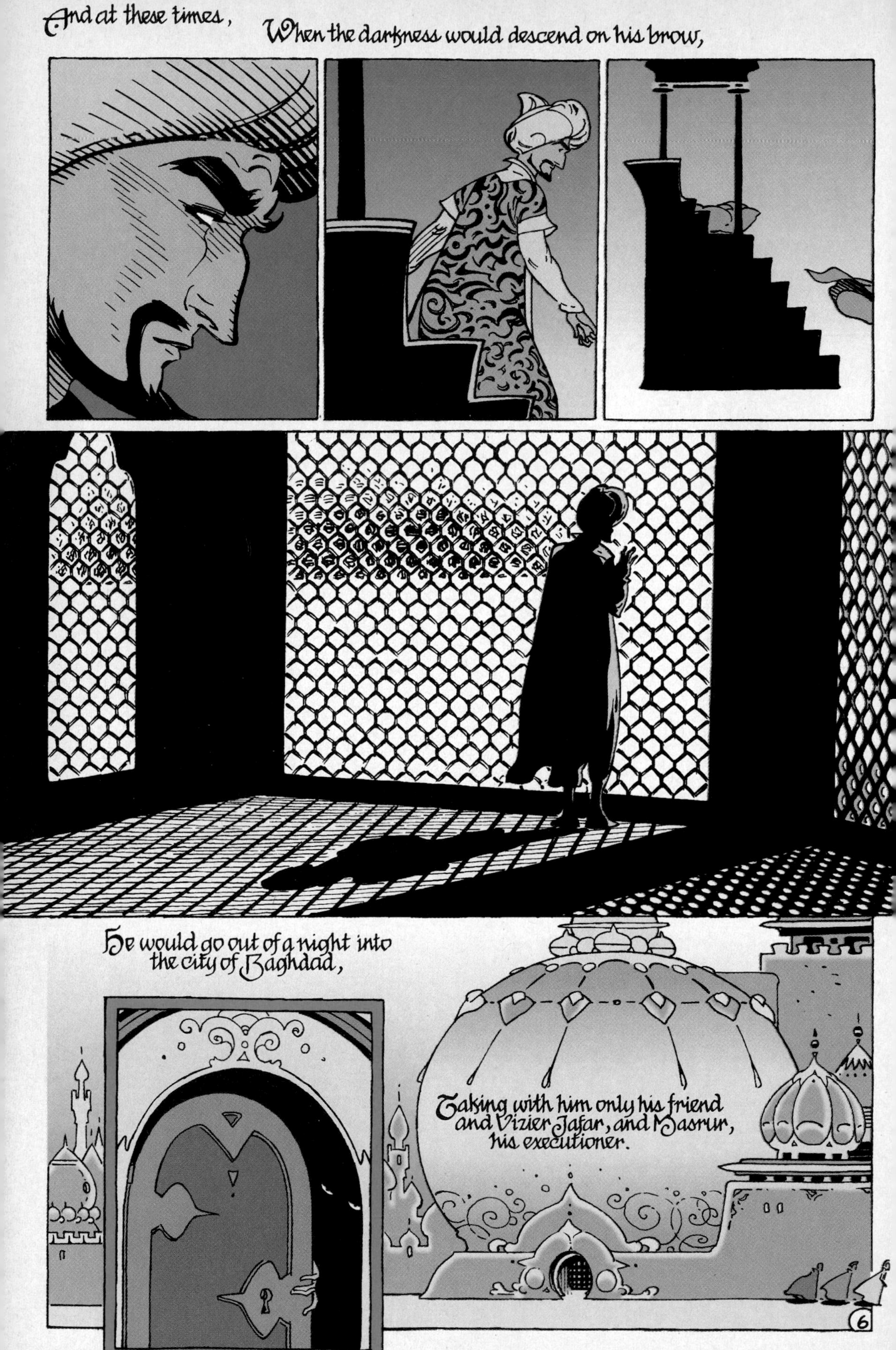
And at these times,
When the darkness would descend on his brow,
He would go out of a night into the city of Baghdad,
Taking with him only his friend and Vizier Jafar, and Masrur, his executioner.
6

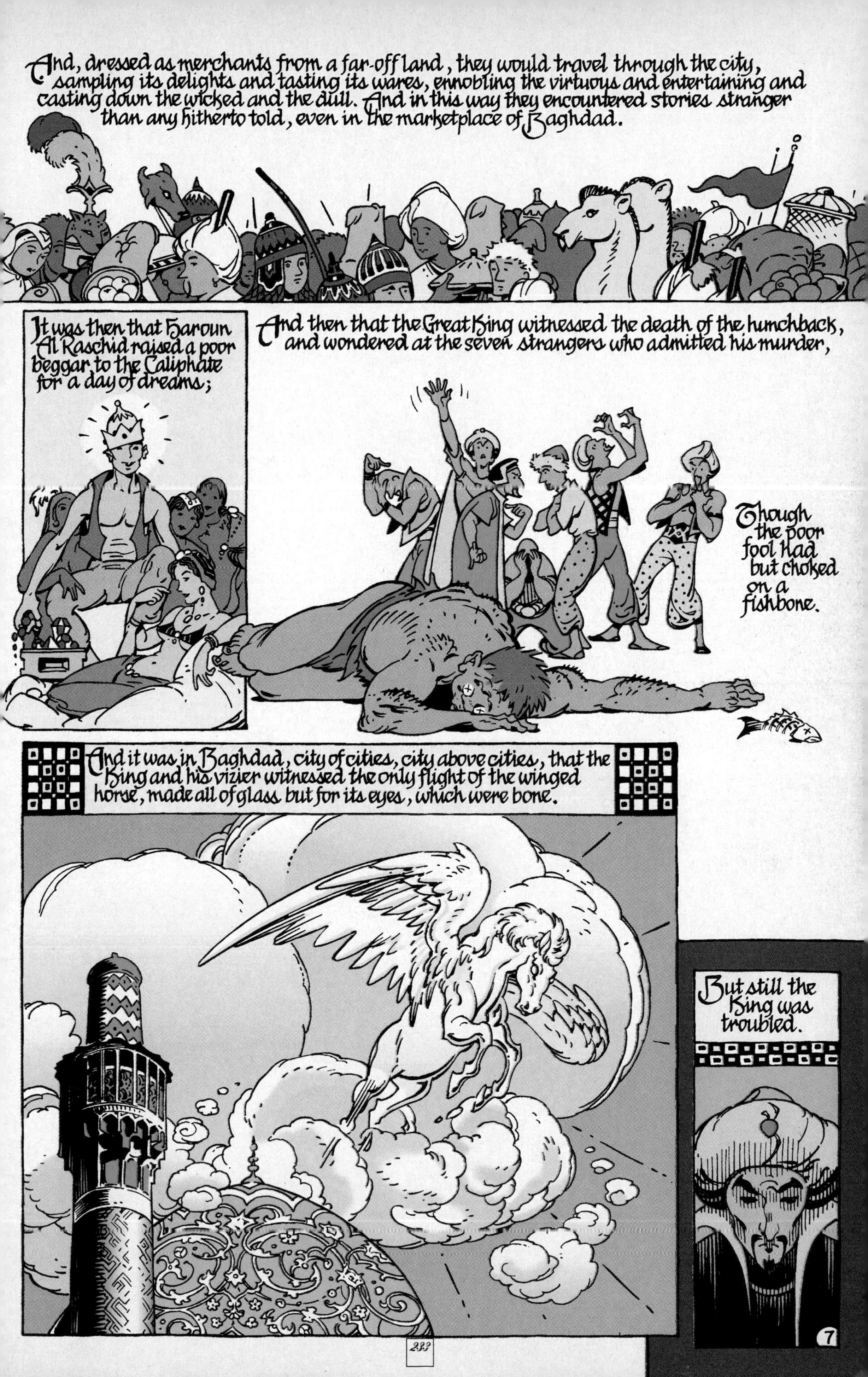

And, dressed as merchants from a far-off land, they would travel through the city, sampling its delights and tasting its wares, ennobling the virtuous and entertaining and casting down the wicked and the dull. And in this way they encountered stories stranger than any hitherto told, even in the marketplace of Baghdad.
It was then that Haroun Al Raschid raised a poor beggar to the Caliphate for a day of dreams;
And then that the Great King witnessed the death of the hunchback, and wondered at the seven strangers who admitted his murder,
Though the poor fool had but choked on a fishbone.
And it was in Baghdad, city of cities, city above cities, that the King and his vizier witnessed the only flight of the winged horse, made all of glass but for its eyes, which were bone.
But still the King was troubled.
7

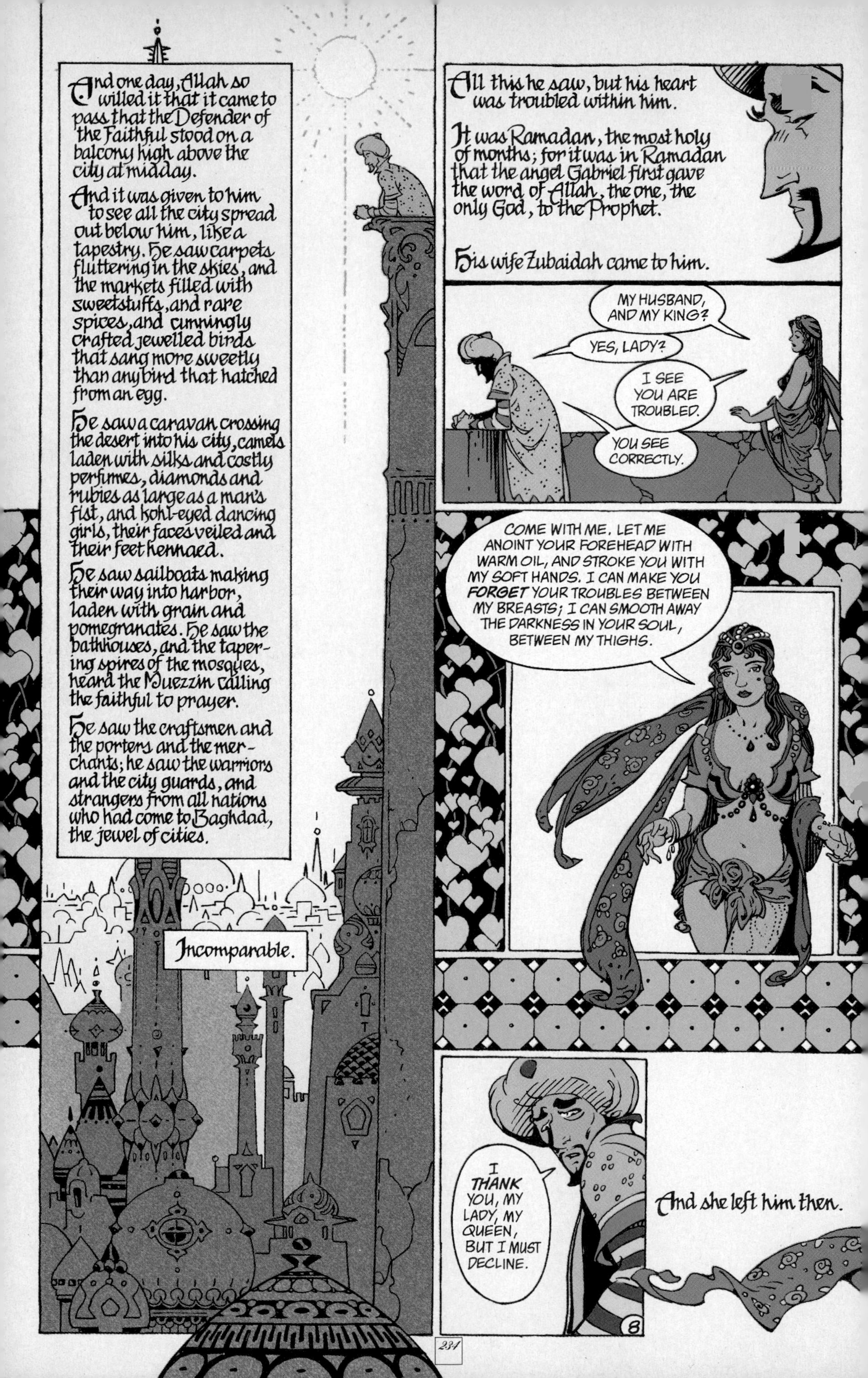
And one day, Allah so willed it that it came to pass that the Defender of the Faithful stood on a balcony high above the city at midday.
And it was given to him to see all the city spread out below him, like a tapestry. He saw carpets fluttering in the skies, and the markets filled with sweetstuffs, and rare spices, and cunningly crafted jewelled birds that sang more sweetly than any bird that hatched from an egg.
He saw a caravan crossing the desert into his city, camels laden with silks and costly perfumes, diamonds and rubies as large as a man's fist, and kohl-eyed dancing girls, their faces veiled and their feet hennaed.
He saw sailboats making their way into harbor, laden with grain and pomegranates. He saw the bathhouses, and the tapering spires of the mosques, heard the Muezzin calling the faithful to prayer.
He saw the craftsmen and the porters and the merchants; he saw the warriors and the city guards, and strangers from all nations who had come to Baghdad, the jewel of cities.
Incomparable.
All this he saw, but his heart was troubled within him.
It was Ramadan, the most holy of months; for it was in Ramadan that the angel Gabriel first gave the word of Allah, the one, the only God, to the Prophet.
His wife Zubaidah came to him.
MY HUSBAND, AND MY KING?
YES, LADY?
I SEE YOU ARE TROUBLED.
YOU SEE CORRECTLY.
COME WITH ME. LET ME ANOINT YOUR FOREHEAD WITH WARM OIL, AND STROKE YOU WITH MY SOFT HANDS. I CAN MAKE YOU FORGET YOUR TROUBLES BETWEEN MY BREASTS; I CAN SMOOTH AWAY THE DARKNESS IN YOUR SOUL, BETWEEN MY THIGHS.
I THANK YOU, MY LADY, MY QUEEN, BUT I MUST DECLINE.
And she left him then.
8

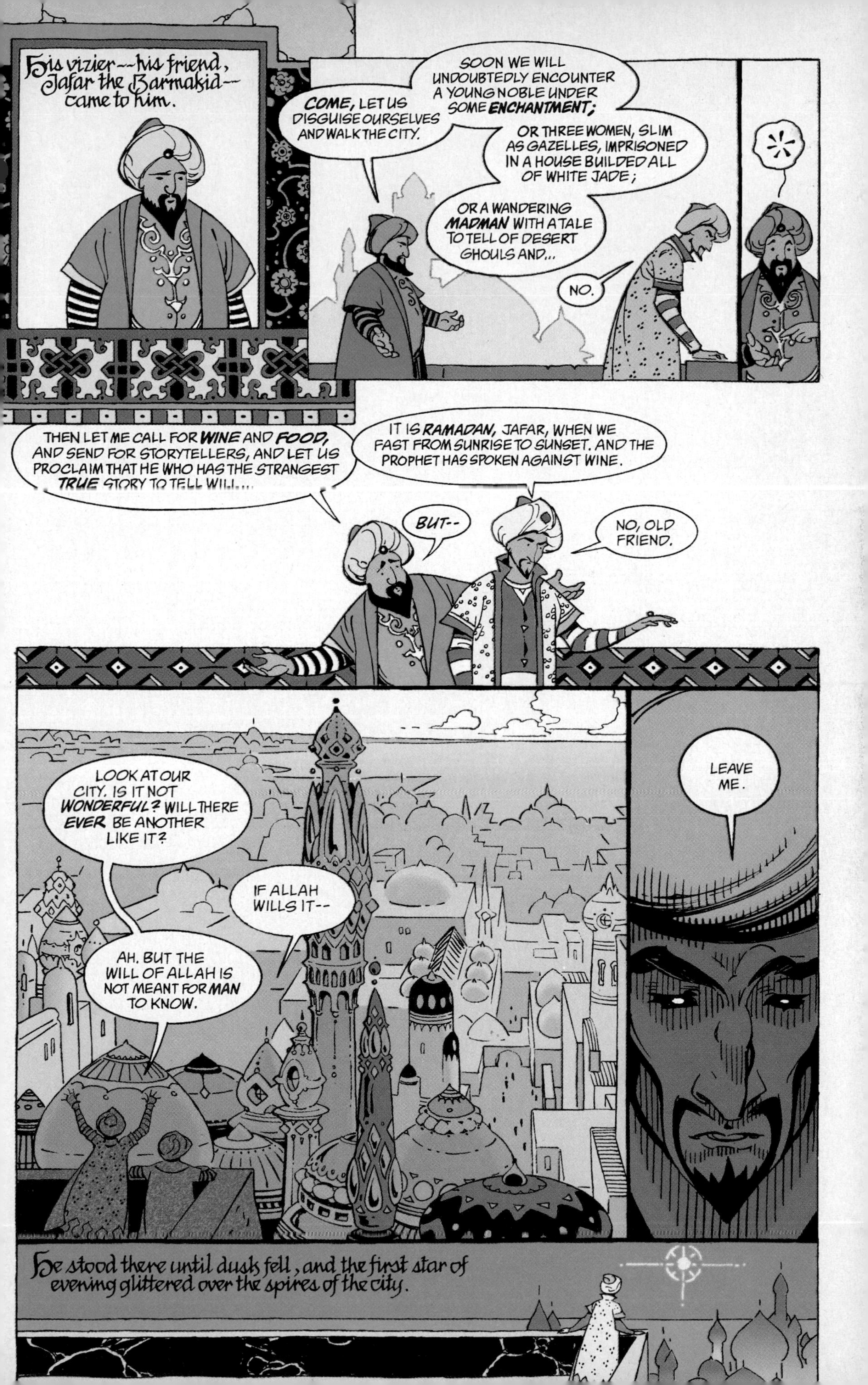
His vizier--his friend, Jafar the Barmakid--came to him.
COME, LET US DISGUISE OURSELVES AND WALK THE CITY.
SOON WE WILL UNDOUBTEDLY ENCOUNTER A YOUNG NOBLE UNDER SOME ENCHANTMENT;
OR THREE WOMEN, SLIM AS GAZELLES, IMPRISONED IN A HOUSE BUILDED ALL OF WHITE JADE;
OR A WANDERING MADMAN WITH A TALE TO TELL OF DESERT GHOULS AND...
NO.
!
THEN LET ME CALL FOR WINE AND FOOD, AND SEND FOR STORYTELLERS, AND LET US PROCLAIM THAT HE WHO HAS THE STRANGEST TRUE STORY TO TELL WILL...
IT IS RAMADAN, JAFAR, WHEN WE FAST FROM SUNRISE TO SUNSET. AND THE PROPHET HAS SPOKEN AGAINST WINE.
BUT--
NO, OLD FRIEND.
LOOK AT OUR CITY. IS IT NOT WONDERFUL? WILL THERE EVER BE ANOTHER LIKE IT?
IF ALLAH WILLS IT--
AH. BUT THE WILL OF ALLAH IS NOT MEANT FOR MAN TO KNOW.
LEAVE ME.
He stood there until dusk fell, and the first star of evening glittered over the spires of the city.

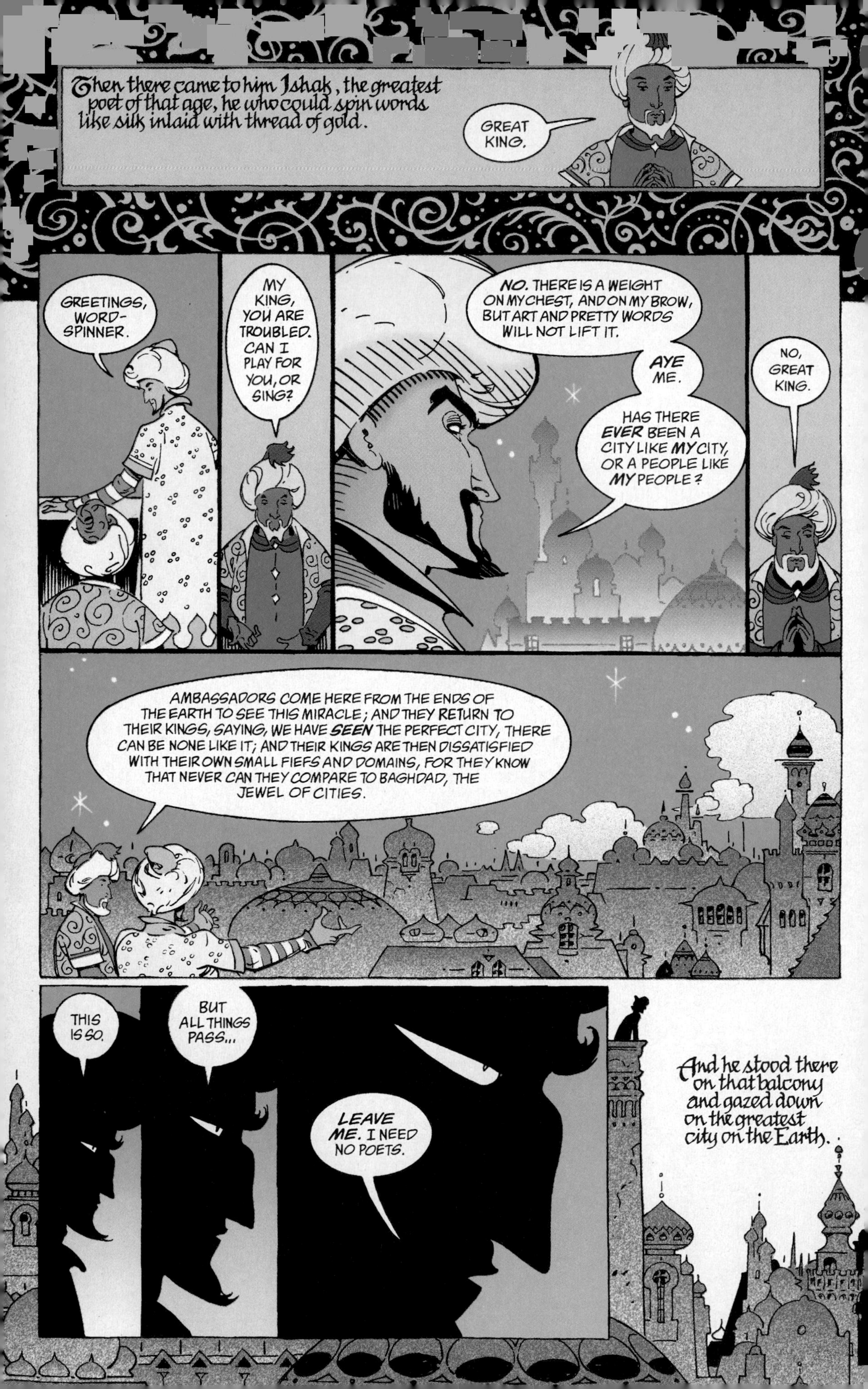
Then there came to him Ishak, the greatest poet of that age, he who could spin words like silk inlaid with thread of gold.
GREAT KING.
GREETINGS, WORD-SPINNER.
MY KING, YOU ARE TROUBLED. CAN I PLAY FOR YOU, OR SING?
NO. THERE IS A WEIGHT ON MY CHEST, AND ON MY BROW, BUT ART AND PRETTY WORDS WILL NOT LIFT IT.
AYE ME.
HAS THERE EVER BEEN A CITY LIKE MY CITY, OR A PEOPLE LIKE MY PEOPLE?
NO, GREAT KING.
AMBASSADORS COME HERE FROM THE ENDS OF THE EARTH TO SEE THIS MIRACLE; AND THEY RETURN TO THEIR KINGS, SAYING, WE HAVE SEEN THE PERFECT CITY, THERE CAN BE NONE LIKE IT; AND THEIR KINGS ARE THEN DISSATISFIED WITH THEIR OWN SMALL FIEFS AND DOMAINS, FOR THEY KNOW THAT NEVER CAN THEY COMPARE TO BAGHDAD, THE JEWEL OF CITIES.
THIS IS SO.
BUT ALL THINGS PASS...
LEAVE ME. I NEED NO POETS.
And he stood there on that balcony and gazed down on the greatest city on the Earth.

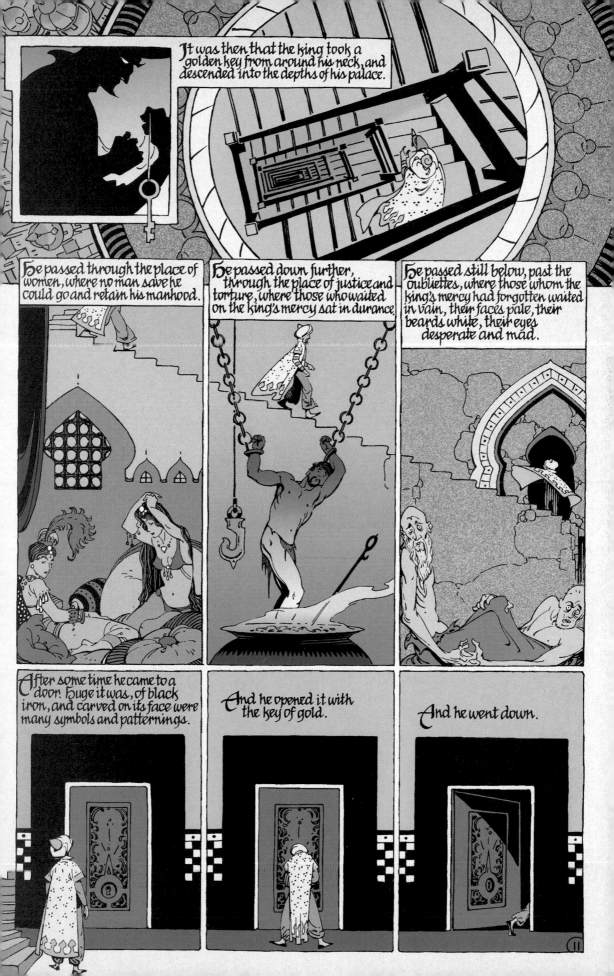

It was then that the king took a golden key from around his neck, and descended into the depths of his palace.

He passed through the place of women, where no man save he could go and retain his manhood.

He passed down further, through the place of justice and torture, where those who waited on the king's mercy sat in durance.

He passed still below, past the oubliettes, where those whom the king's mercy had forgotten waited in vain, their faces pale, their beards white, their eyes desperate and mad.

After some time he came to a door. Huge it was, of black iron, and carved on its face were many symbols and patternings.

And he opened it with the key of gold.

And he went down.

11

Now the steps were narrow and damp, and the air swam with half-seen figures and faces.

And the king thought he heard the voices of those he had loved and had killed, over the years: the pale girl from the northland with hair like spun silver;

The boy from the desert who had brought him a rose carved from palest pinkest quartz, and had stayed in the palace for a year and a day;

The captain of the palace guard, who, save for only the king, was the finest bowman, and swordsman, and spear, in the city, but who had, perhaps, coveted the throne...

Voices he heard.

But he paid them no mind.

Haroun Al Raschid came to the door of bronze, banded with green copper, and inset with mother of pearl.

And he opened it with the key of gold.

And he went down.

He threaded his way through the labyrinth then, eyes hard closed, counting steps and half steps, and rights in his head.

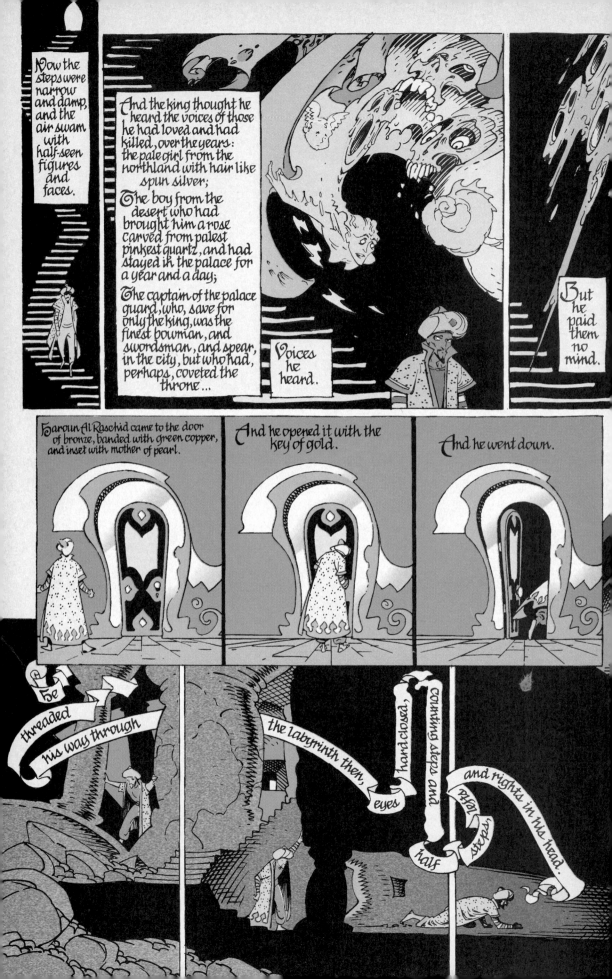

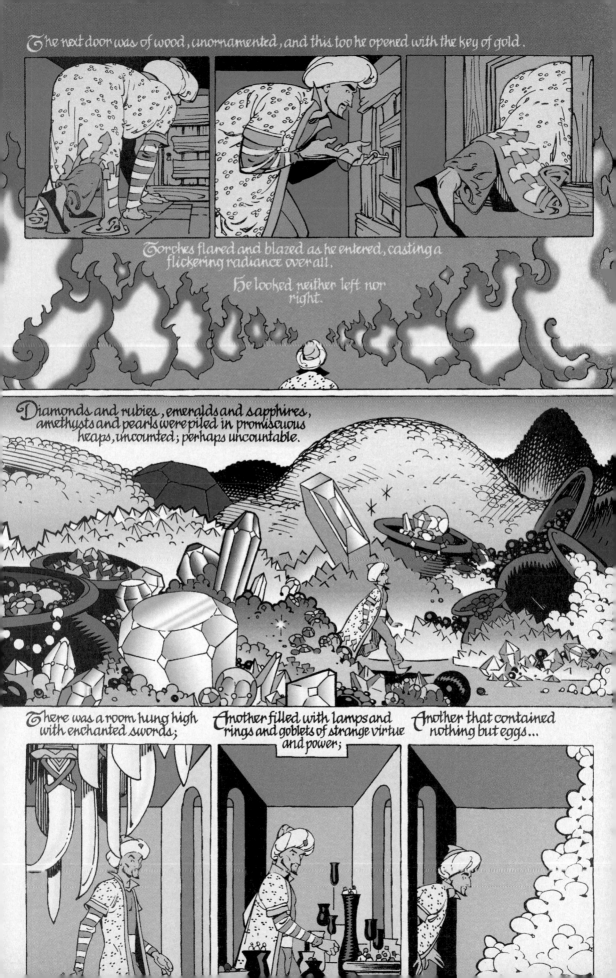

The next door was of wood, unornamented, and this too he opened with the key of gold.

Torches flared and blazed as he entered, casting a flickering radiance over all.

He looked neither left nor right.

Diamonds and rubies, emeralds and sapphires, amethysts and pearls were piled in promiscuous heaps, uncounted; perhaps uncountable.

There was a room hung high with enchanted swords;

Another filled with lamps and rings and goblets of strange virtue and power;

Another that contained nothing but eggs...

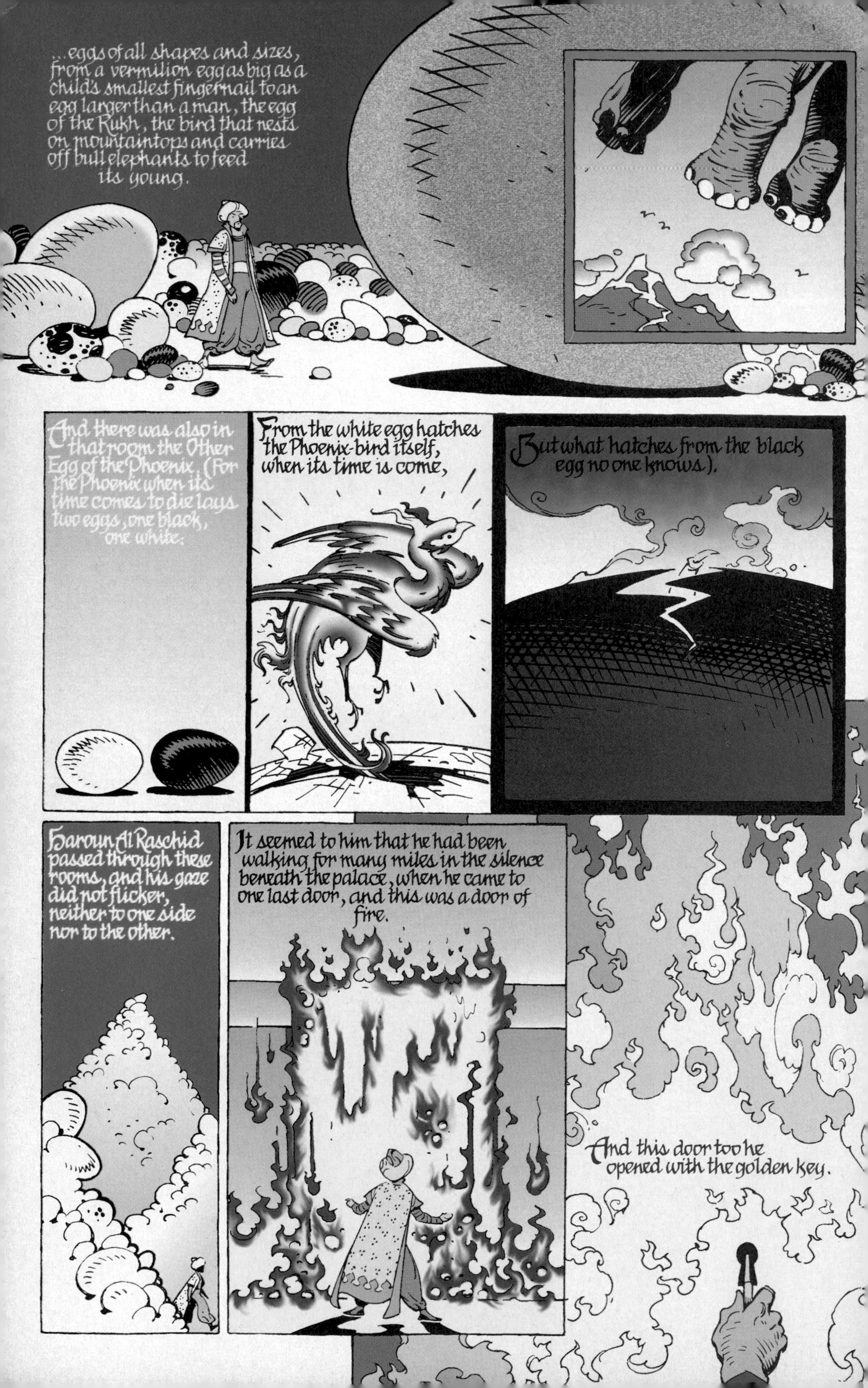
...eggs of all shapes and sizes, from a vermilion egg as big as a child's smallest fingernail to an egg larger than a man, the egg of the Rukh, the bird that nests on mountaintops and carries off bull elephants to feed its young.
And there was also in that room the Other Egg of the Phoenix. (For the Phoenix when its time comes to die lays two eggs, one black, one white.
From the white egg hatches the Phoenix-bird itself, when its time is come,
But what hatches from the black egg no one knows).
Haroun Al Raschid passed through these rooms, and his gaze did not flicker, neither to one side nor to the other.
It seemed to him that he had been walking for many miles in the silence beneath the palace, when he came to one last door, and this was a door of fire.
And this door too he opened with the golden key.

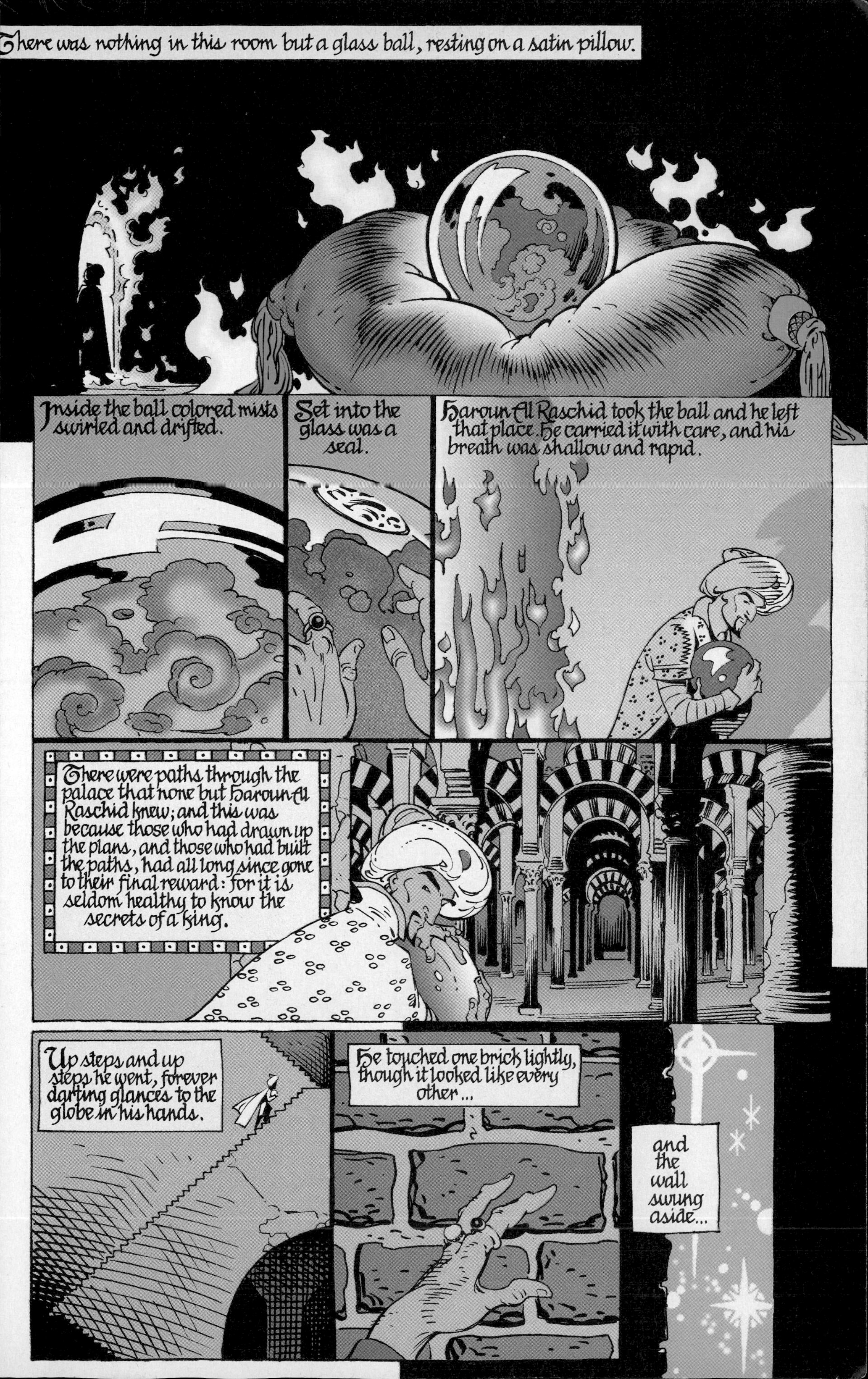
There was nothing in this room but a glass ball, resting on a satin pillow.
Inside the ball colored mists swirled and drifted.
Set into the glass was a seal.
Haroun Al Raschid took the ball and he left that place. He carried it with care, and his breath was shallow and rapid.
There were paths through the palace that none but Haroun Al Raschid knew; and this was because those who had drawn up the plans, and those who had built the paths, had all long since gone to their final reward: for it is seldom healthy to know the secrets of a king.
Up steps and up steps he went, forever darting glances to the globe in his hands.
He touched one brick lightly, though it looked like every other...
and the wall swung aside...

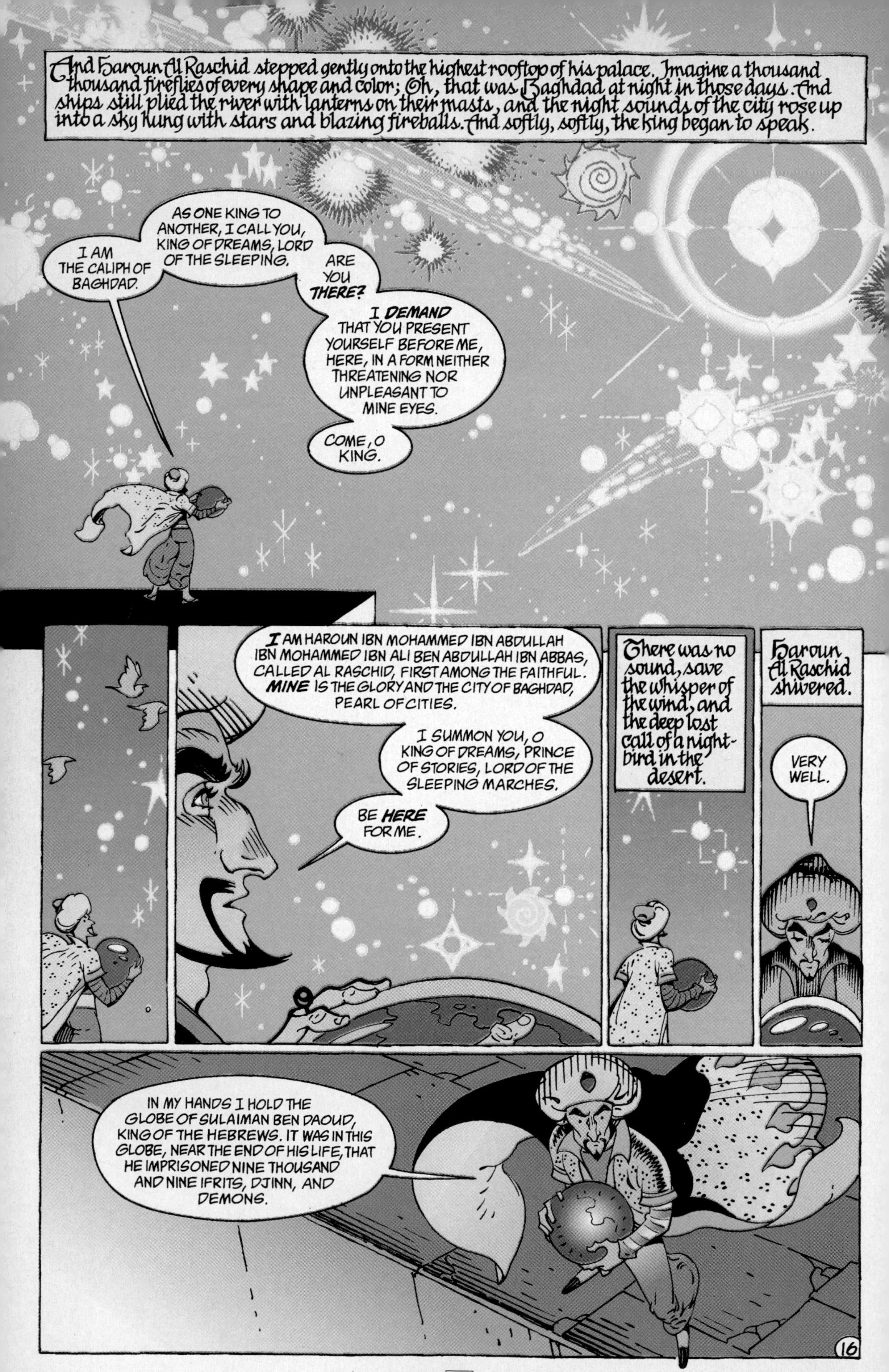
And Haroun Al Raschid stepped gently onto the highest rooftop of his palace. Imagine a thousand thousand fireflies of every shape and color; Oh, that was Baghdad at night in those days. And ships still plied the river with lanterns on their masts, and the night sounds of the city rose up into a sky hung with stars and blazing fireballs. And softly, softly, the king began to speak.
I AM THE CALIPH OF BAGHDAD.
AS ONE KING TO ANOTHER, I CALL YOU, KING OF DREAMS, LORD OF THE SLEEPING.
ARE YOU THERE?
I DEMAND THAT YOU PRESENT YOURSELF BEFORE ME, HERE, IN A FORM NEITHER THREATENING NOR UNPLEASANT TO MINE EYES.
COME, O KING.
I AM HAROUN IBN MOHAMMED IBN ABDULLAH IBN MOHAMMED IBN ALI BEN ABDULLAH IBN ABBAS, CALLED AL RASCHID, FIRST AMONG THE FAITHFUL. MINE IS THE GLORY AND THE CITY OF BAGHDAD, PEARL OF CITIES.
I SUMMON YOU, O KING OF DREAMS, PRINCE OF STORIES, LORD OF THE SLEEPING MARCHES.
BE HERE FOR ME.
There was no sound, save the whisper of the wind, and the deep lost call of a night-bird in the desert.
Haroun Al Raschid shivered.
VERY WELL.
IN MY HANDS I HOLD THE GLOBE OF SULAIMAN BEN DAOUD, KING OF THE HEBREWS. IT WAS IN THIS GLOBE, NEAR THE END OF HIS LIFE, THAT HE IMPRISONED NINE THOUSAND AND NINE IFRITS, DJINN, AND DEMONS.
16

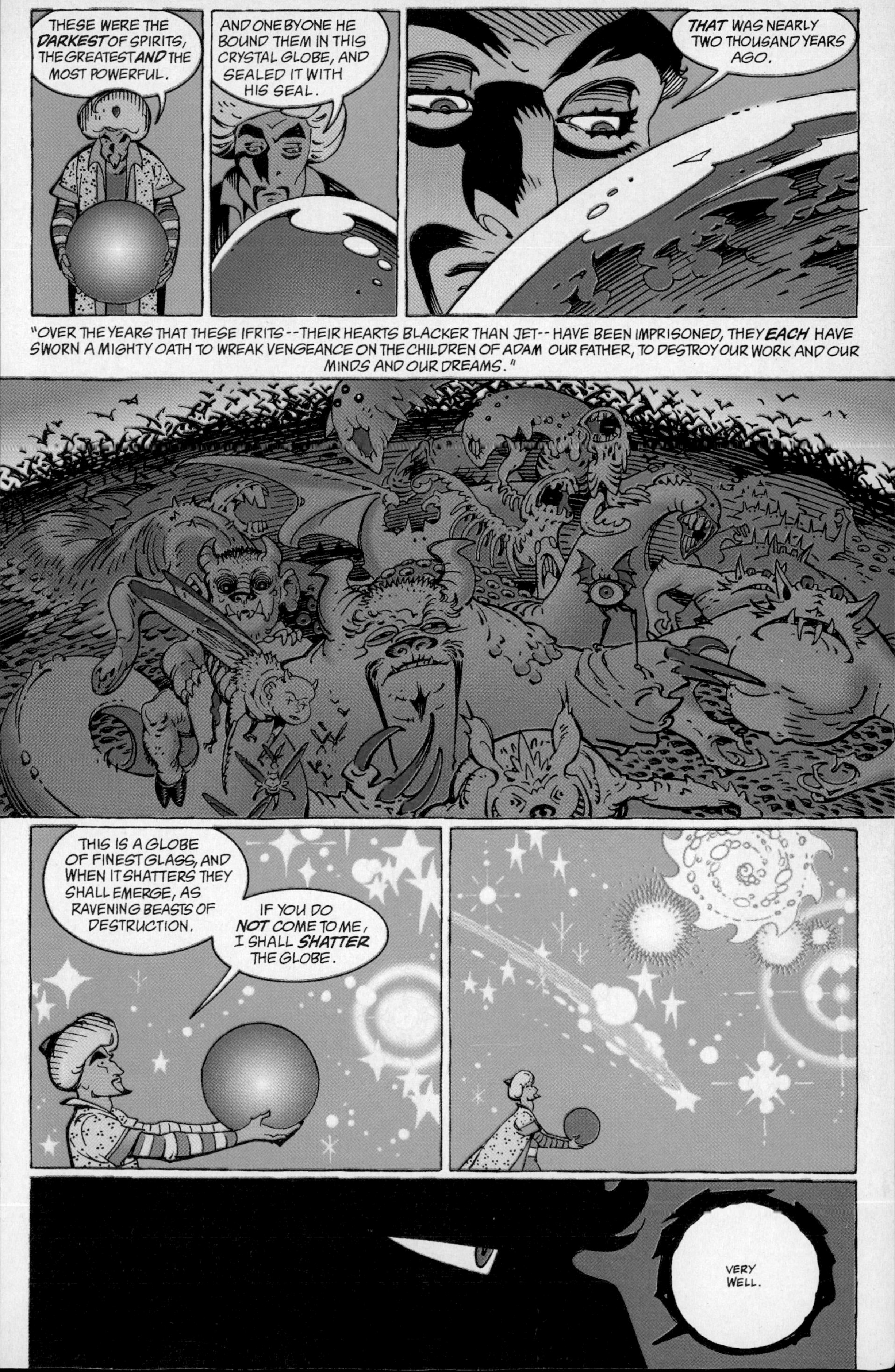
THESE WERE THE DARKEST OF SPIRITS, THE GREATEST AND THE MOST POWERFUL.
AND ONE BY ONE HE BOUND THEM IN THIS CRYSTAL GLOBE, AND SEALED IT WITH HIS SEAL.
THAT WAS NEARLY TWO THOUSAND YEARS AGO.
"OVER THE YEARS THAT THESE IFRITS--THEIR HEARTS BLACKER THAN JET--HAVE BEEN IMPRISONED, THEY EACH HAVE SWORN A MIGHTY OATH TO WREAK VENGEANCE ON THE CHILDREN OF ADAM OUR FATHER, TO DESTROY OUR WORK AND OUR MINDS AND OUR DREAMS."
THIS IS A GLOBE OF FINEST GLASS, AND WHEN IT SHATTERS THEY SHALL EMERGE, AS RAVENING BEASTS OF DESTRUCTION.
IF YOU DO NOT COME TO ME, I SHALL SHATTER THE GLOBE.
VERY WELL.

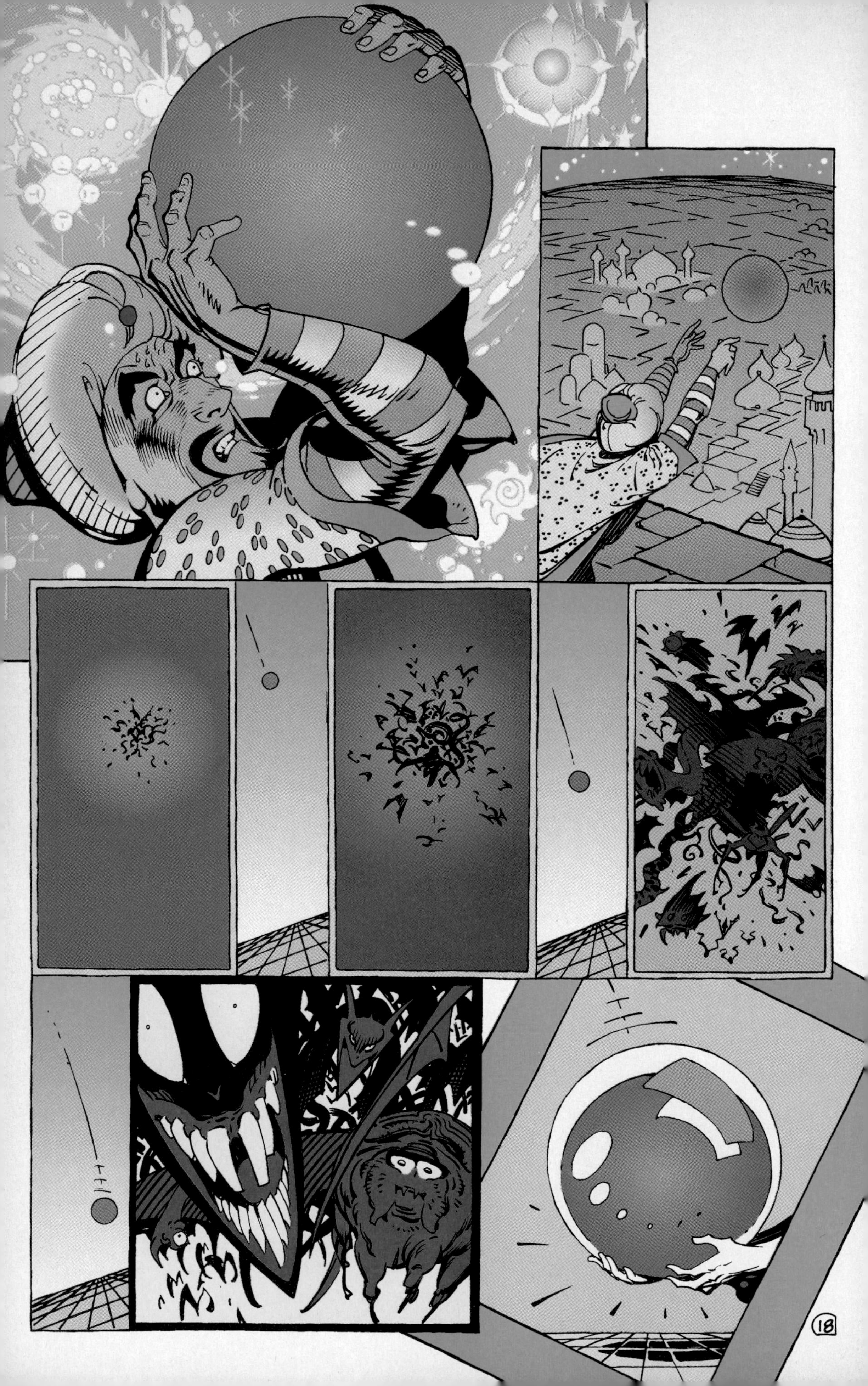

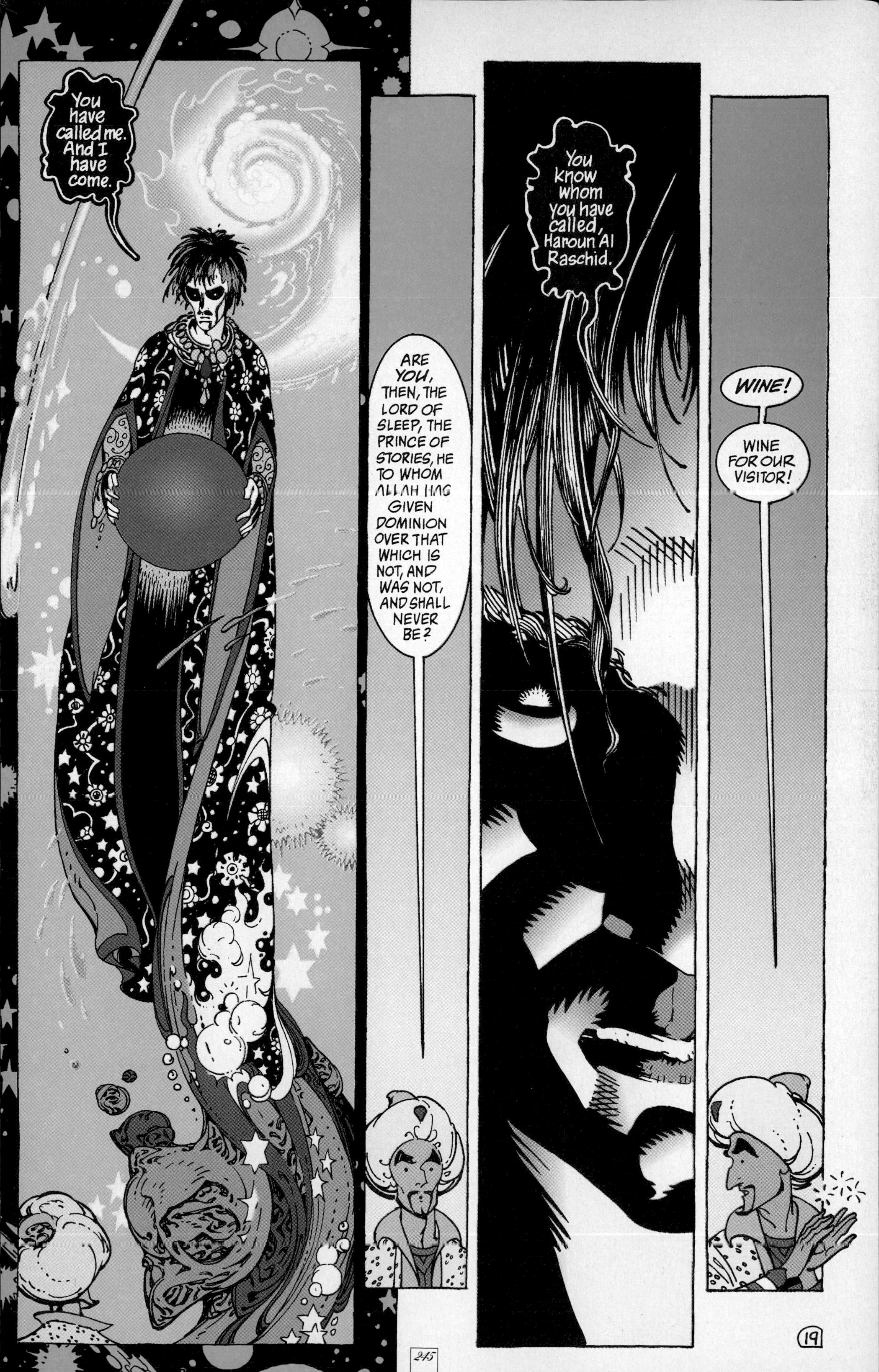
You have called me. And I have come.
ARE *YOU*, THEN, THE LORD OF SLEEP, THE PRINCE OF STORIES, HE TO WHOM ALLAH HAS GIVEN DOMINION OVER THAT WHICH IS NOT, AND WAS NOT, AND SHALL NEVER BE?
You know whom you have called, Haroun Al Raschid.
WINE!
WINE FOR OUR VISITOR!
19

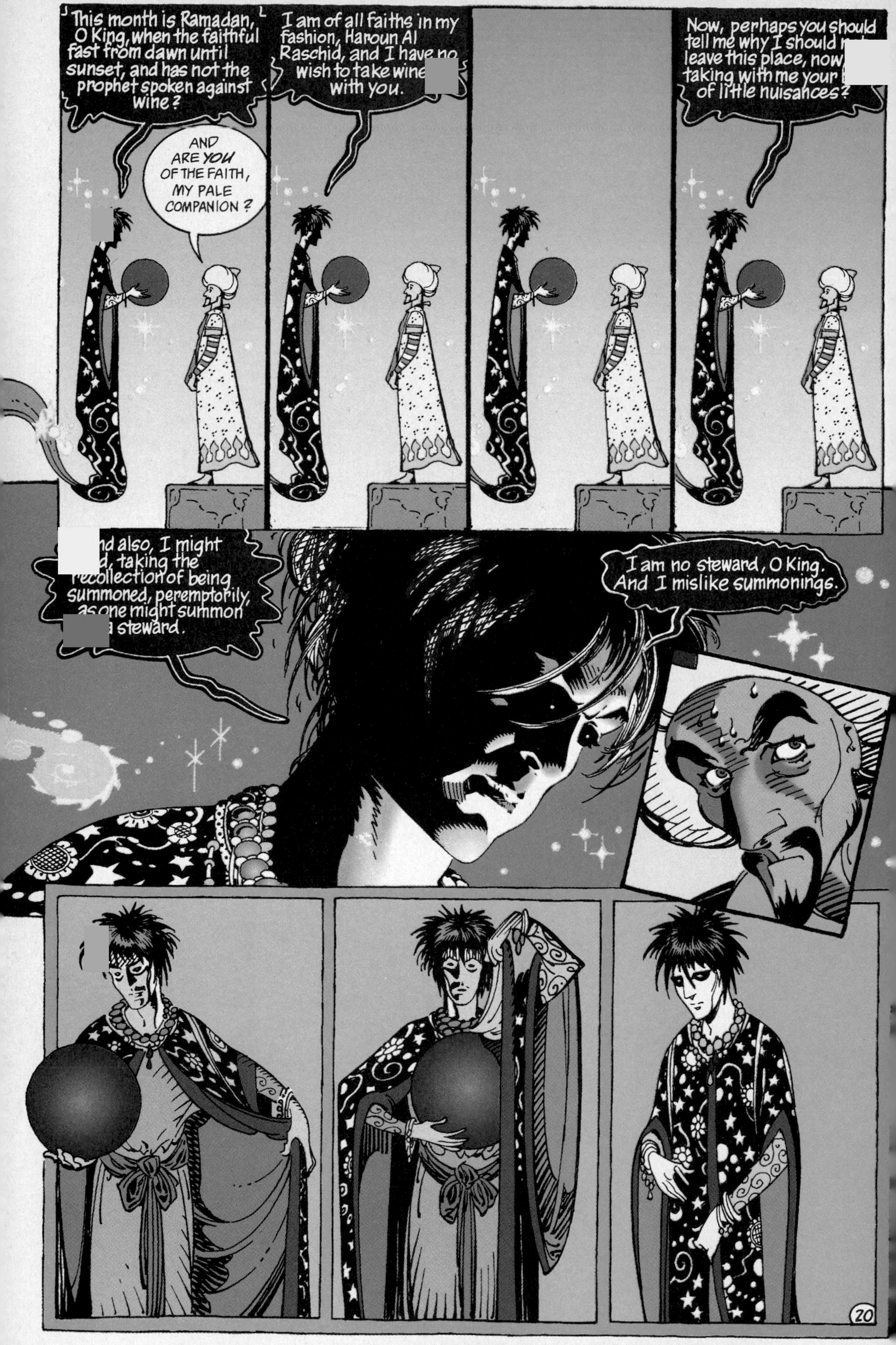
This month is Ramadan, O King, when the faithful fast from dawn until sunset, and has not the prophet spoken against wine?
AND ARE YOU OF THE FAITH, MY PALE COMPANION?
I am of all faiths in my fashion, Haroun Al Raschid, and I have no wish to take wine with you.
Now, perhaps you should tell me why I should n leave this place, now, taking with me your of little nuisances?
nd also, I might d, taking the recollection of being summoned, peremptorily, as one might summon a steward.
I am no steward, O King. And I mislike summonings.
20

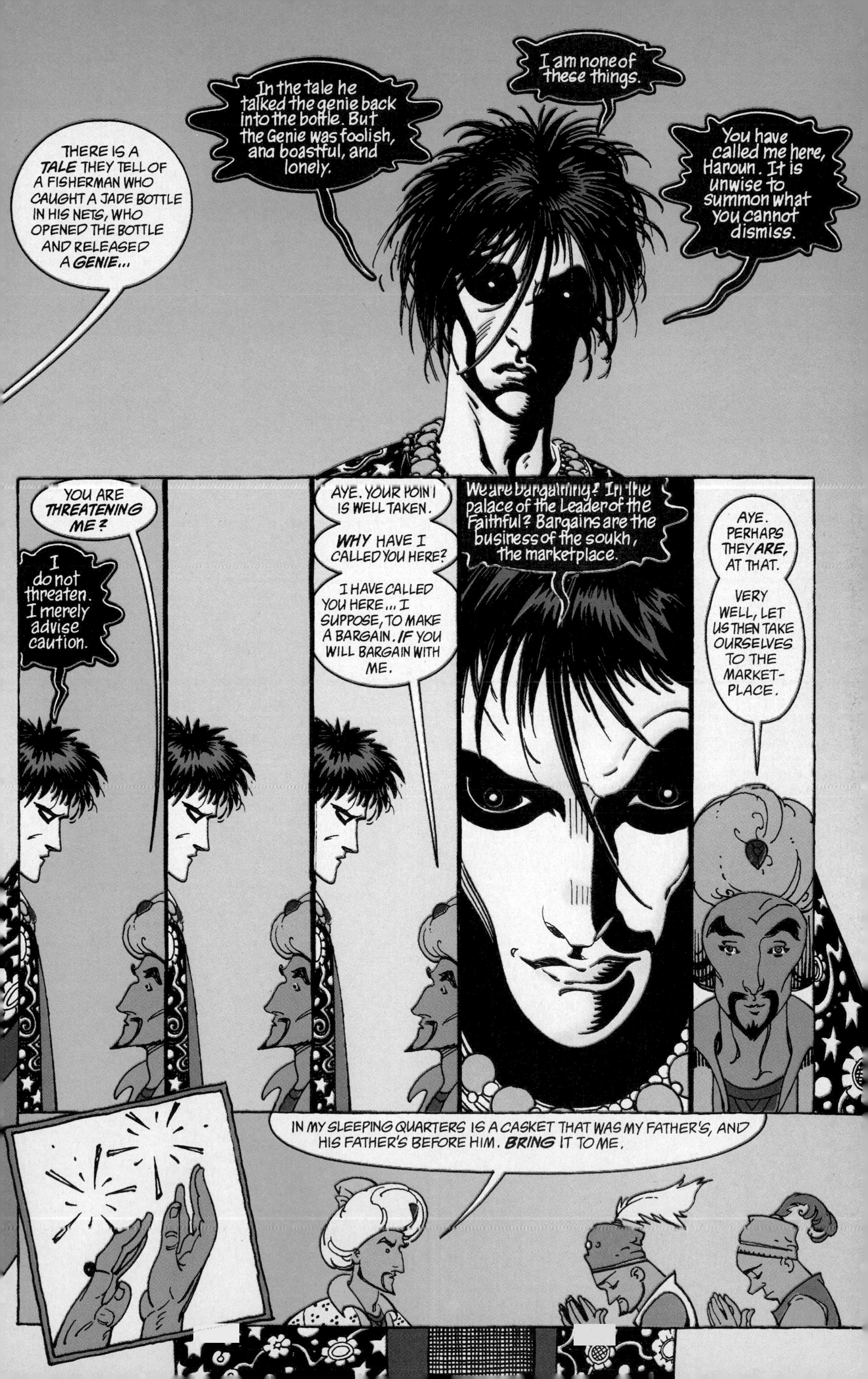

THERE IS A TALE THEY TELL OF A FISHERMAN WHO CAUGHT A JADE BOTTLE IN HIS NETS, WHO OPENED THE BOTTLE AND RELEASED A GENIE...
In the tale he talked the genie back into the bottle. But the Genie was foolish, ana boastful, and lonely.
I am none of these things.
You have called me here, Haroun. It is unwise to summon what you cannot dismiss.
YOU ARE THREATENING ME?
I do not threaten. I merely advise caution.
AYE. YOUR POINT IS WELL TAKEN.
WHY HAVE I CALLED YOU HERE?
I HAVE CALLED YOU HERE... I SUPPOSE, TO MAKE A BARGAIN. IF YOU WILL BARGAIN WITH ME.
We are bargaining? In the palace of the Leader of the Faithful? Bargains are the business of the soukh, the marketplace.
AYE. PERHAPS THEY ARE, AT THAT.
VERY WELL, LET US THEN TAKE OURSELVES TO THE MARKET-PLACE.
IN MY SLEEPING QUARTERS IS A CASKET THAT WAS MY FATHER'S, AND HIS FATHER'S BEFORE HIM. BRING IT TO ME.

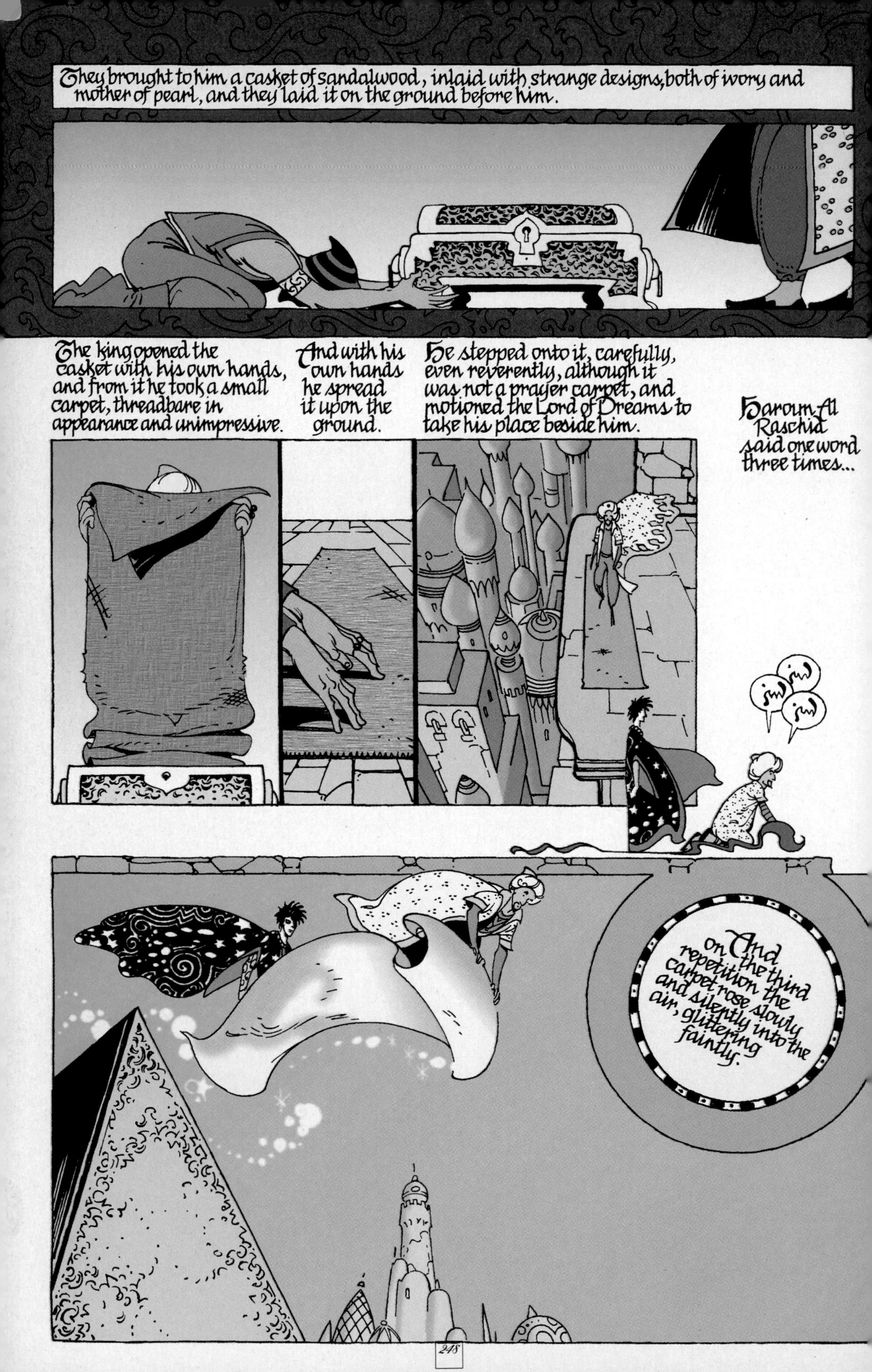
They brought to him a casket of sandalwood, inlaid with strange designs, both of ivory and mother of pearl, and they laid it on the ground before him.
The king opened the casket with his own hands, and from it he took a small carpet, threadbare in appearance and unimpressive.
And with his own hands he spread it upon the ground.
He stepped onto it, carefully, even reverently, although it was not a prayer carpet, and motioned the Lord of Dreams to take his place beside him.
Haroun Al Raschid said one word three times...
And on the third repetition the carpet rose slowly and silently into the air, glittering faintly.

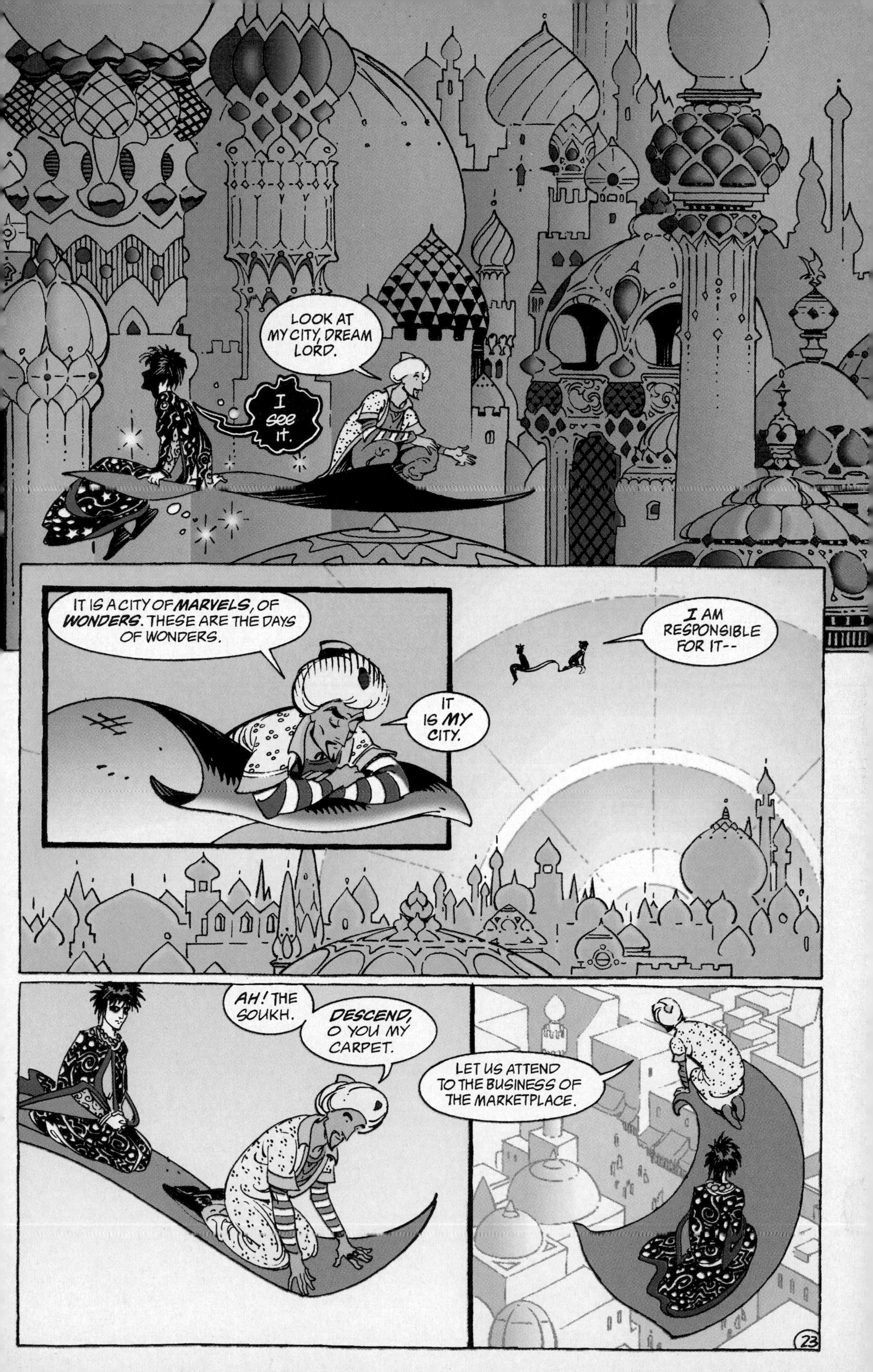
LOOK AT MY CITY, DREAM LORD.
I see it.
IT IS A CITY OF **MARVELS**, OF **WONDERS**. THESE ARE THE DAYS OF WONDERS.
IT IS **MY** CITY.
I AM RESPONSIBLE FOR IT--
AH! THE SOUKH.
DESCEND, O YOU MY CARPET.
LET US ATTEND TO THE BUSINESS OF THE MARKETPLACE.
23

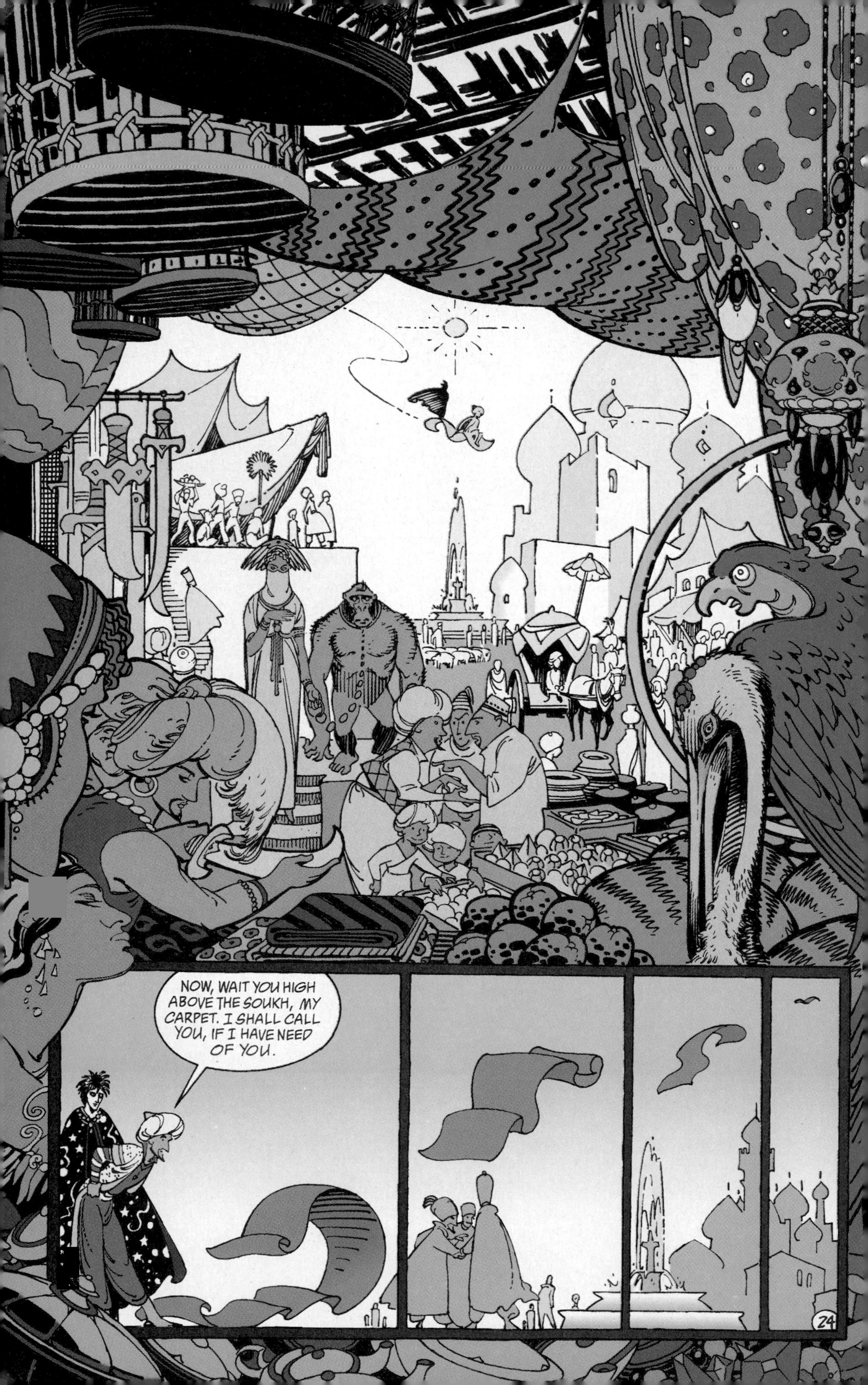
NOW, WAIT YOU HIGH ABOVE THE SOUKH, MY CARPET. I SHALL CALL YOU, IF I HAVE NEED OF YOU.

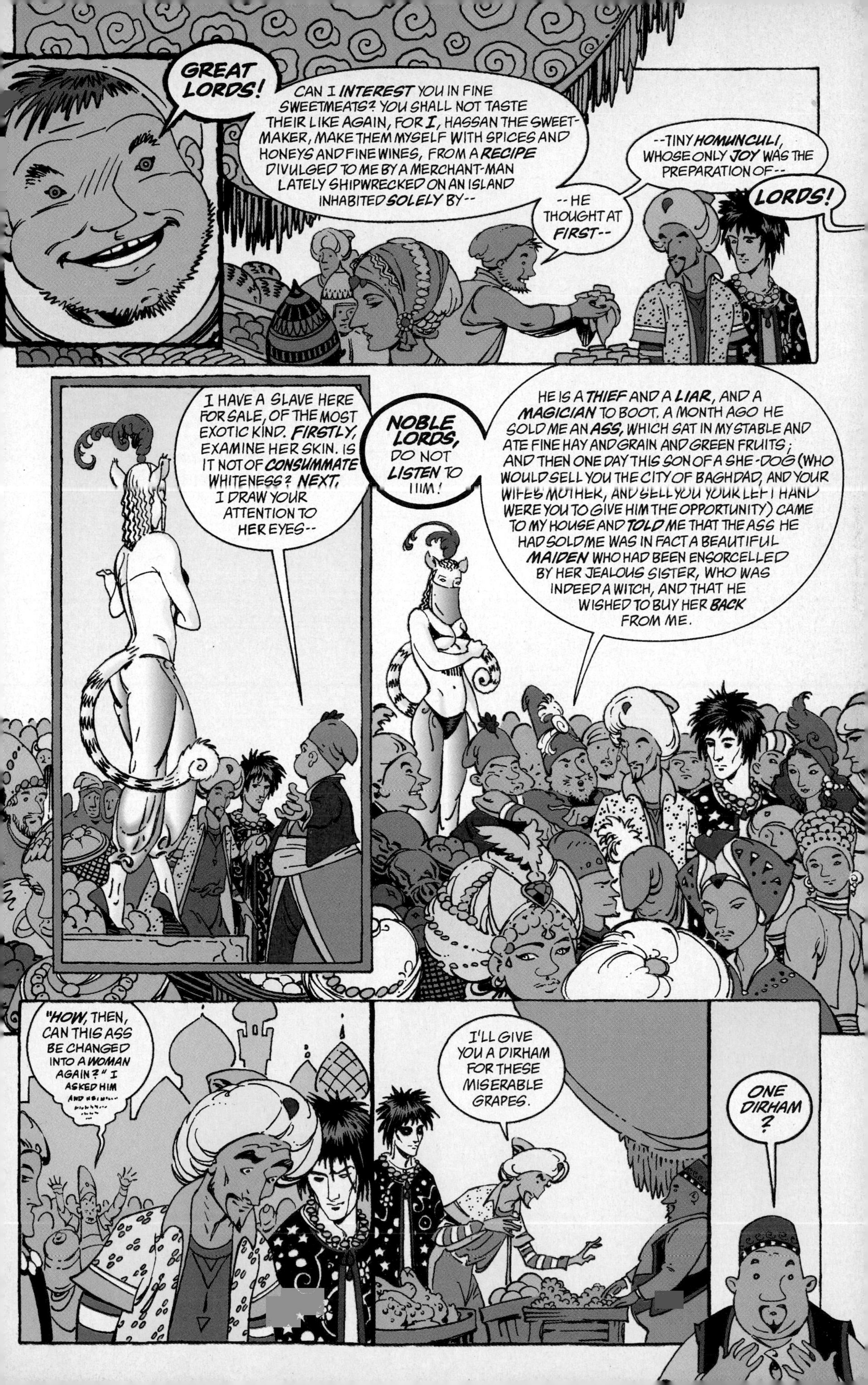

GREAT LORDS!
CAN I INTEREST YOU IN FINE SWEETMEATS? YOU SHALL NOT TASTE THEIR LIKE AGAIN, FOR I, HASSAN THE SWEET-MAKER, MAKE THEM MYSELF WITH SPICES AND HONEYS AND FINE WINES, FROM A RECIPE DIVULGED TO ME BY A MERCHANT-MAN LATELY SHIPWRECKED ON AN ISLAND INHABITED SOLELY BY--
--HE THOUGHT AT FIRST--
--TINY HOMUNCULI, WHOSE ONLY JOY WAS THE PREPARATION OF--
LORDS!
I HAVE A SLAVE HERE FOR SALE, OF THE MOST EXOTIC KIND. FIRSTLY, EXAMINE HER SKIN. IS IT NOT OF CONSUMMATE WHITENESS? NEXT, I DRAW YOUR ATTENTION TO HER EYES--
NOBLE LORDS, DO NOT LISTEN TO HIM!
HE IS A THIEF AND A LIAR, AND A MAGICIAN TO BOOT. A MONTH AGO HE SOLD ME AN ASS, WHICH SAT IN MY STABLE AND ATE FINE HAY AND GRAIN AND GREEN FRUITS; AND THEN ONE DAY THIS SON OF A SHE-DOG (WHO WOULD SELL YOU THE CITY OF BAGHDAD, AND YOUR WIFE'S MOTHER, AND SELL YOU YOUR LEFT HAND WERE YOU TO GIVE HIM THE OPPORTUNITY) CAME TO MY HOUSE AND TOLD ME THAT THE ASS HE HAD SOLD ME WAS IN FACT A BEAUTIFUL MAIDEN WHO HAD BEEN ENSORCELLED BY HER JEALOUS SISTER, WHO WAS INDEED A WITCH, AND THAT HE WISHED TO BUY HER BACK FROM ME.
"HOW, THEN, CAN THIS ASS BE CHANGED INTO A WOMAN AGAIN?" I ASKED HIM
I'LL GIVE YOU A DIRHAM FOR THESE MISERABLE GRAPES.
ONE DIRHAM?

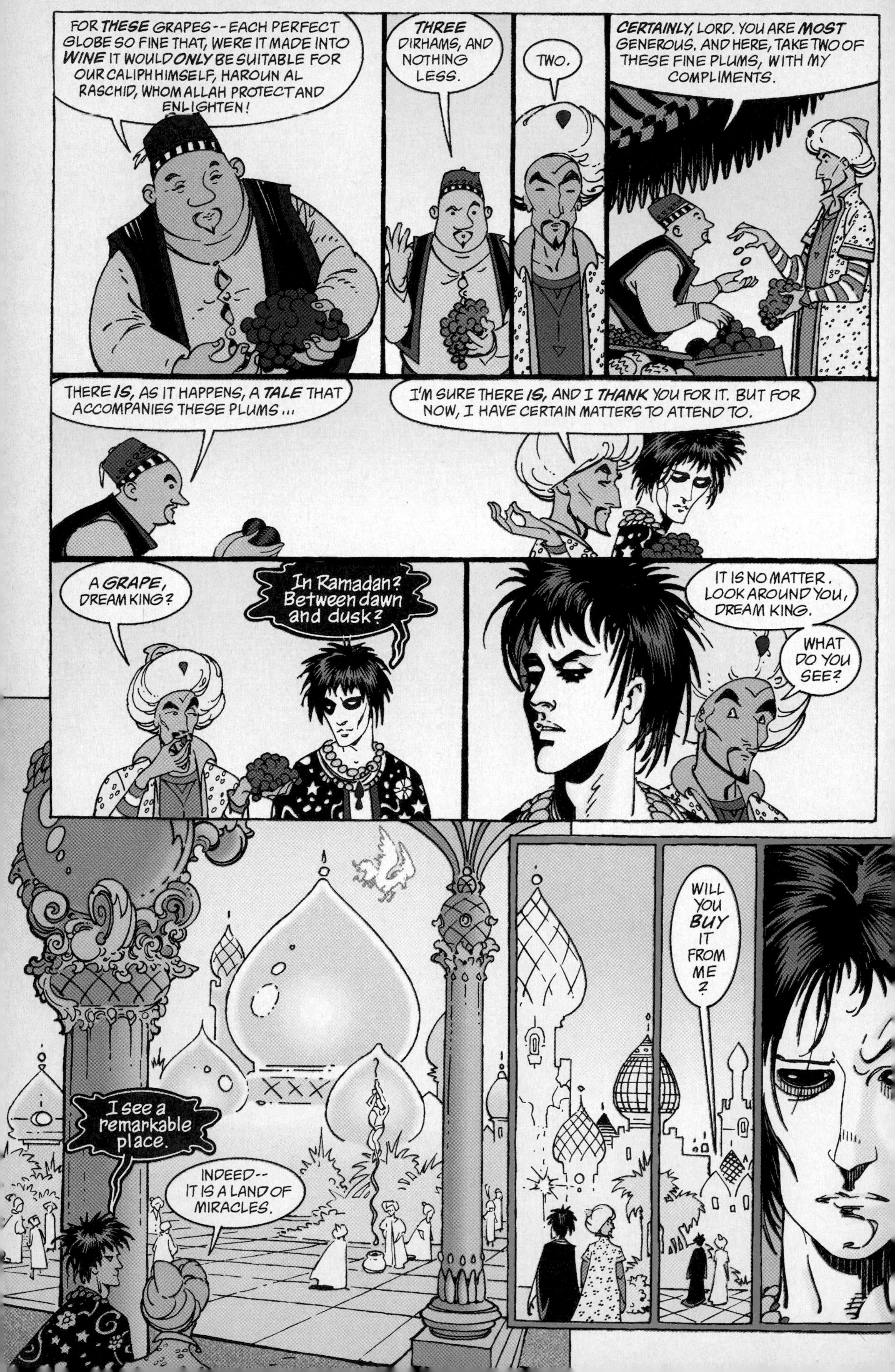

FOR THESE GRAPES -- EACH PERFECT GLOBE SO FINE THAT, WERE IT MADE INTO WINE IT WOULD ONLY BE SUITABLE FOR OUR CALIPH HIMSELF, HAROUN AL RASCHID, WHOM ALLAH PROTECT AND ENLIGHTEN!
THREE DIRHAMS, AND NOTHING LESS.
TWO.
CERTAINLY, LORD. YOU ARE MOST GENEROUS. AND HERE, TAKE TWO OF THESE FINE PLUMS, WITH MY COMPLIMENTS.
THERE IS, AS IT HAPPENS, A TALE THAT ACCOMPANIES THESE PLUMS...
I'M SURE THERE IS, AND I THANK YOU FOR IT. BUT FOR NOW, I HAVE CERTAIN MATTERS TO ATTEND TO.
A GRAPE, DREAM KING?
In Ramadan? Between dawn and dusk?
IT IS NO MATTER. LOOK AROUND YOU, DREAM KING.
WHAT DO YOU SEE?
I see a remarkable place.
INDEED-- IT IS A LAND OF MIRACLES.
WILL YOU BUY IT FROM ME?

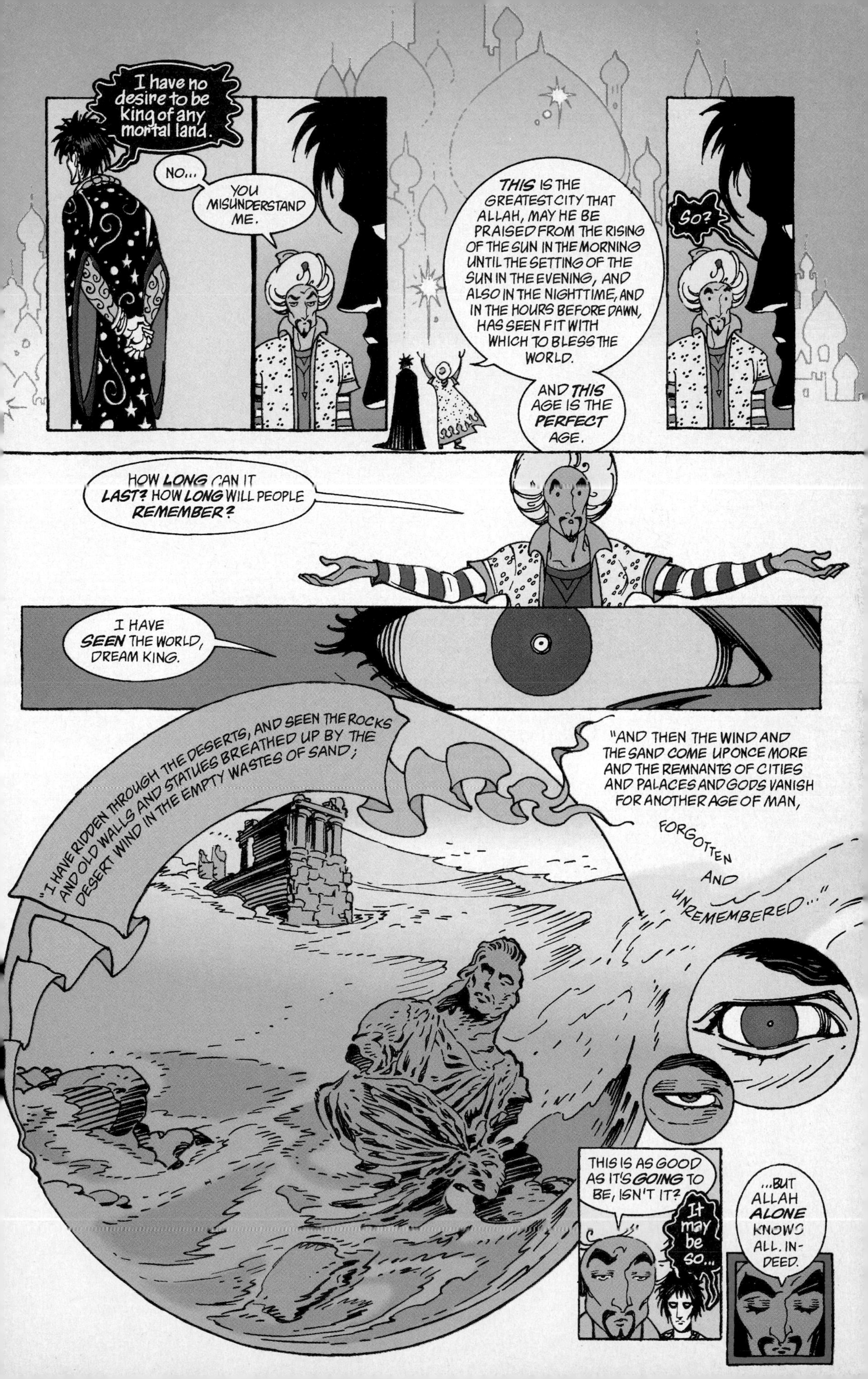
I have no desire to be king of any mortal land.
NO...
YOU MISUNDERSTAND ME.
THIS IS THE GREATEST CITY THAT ALLAH, MAY HE BE PRAISED FROM THE RISING OF THE SUN IN THE MORNING UNTIL THE SETTING OF THE SUN IN THE EVENING, AND ALSO IN THE NIGHTTIME, AND IN THE HOURS BEFORE DAWN, HAS SEEN FIT WITH WHICH TO BLESS THE WORLD.
AND THIS AGE IS THE PERFECT AGE.
So?
HOW LONG CAN IT LAST? HOW LONG WILL PEOPLE REMEMBER?
I HAVE SEEN THE WORLD, DREAM KING.
"I HAVE RIDDEN THROUGH THE DESERTS, AND SEEN THE ROCKS AND OLD WALLS AND STATUES BREATHED UP BY THE DESERT WIND IN THE EMPTY WASTES OF SAND;
"AND THEN THE WIND AND THE SAND COME UP ONCE MORE AND THE REMNANTS OF CITIES AND PALACES AND GODS VANISH FOR ANOTHER AGE OF MAN,
FORGOTTEN AND UNREMEMBERED..."
THIS IS AS GOOD AS IT'S GOING TO BE, ISN'T IT?
It may be so...
...BUT ALLAH ALONE KNOWS ALL. INDEED.

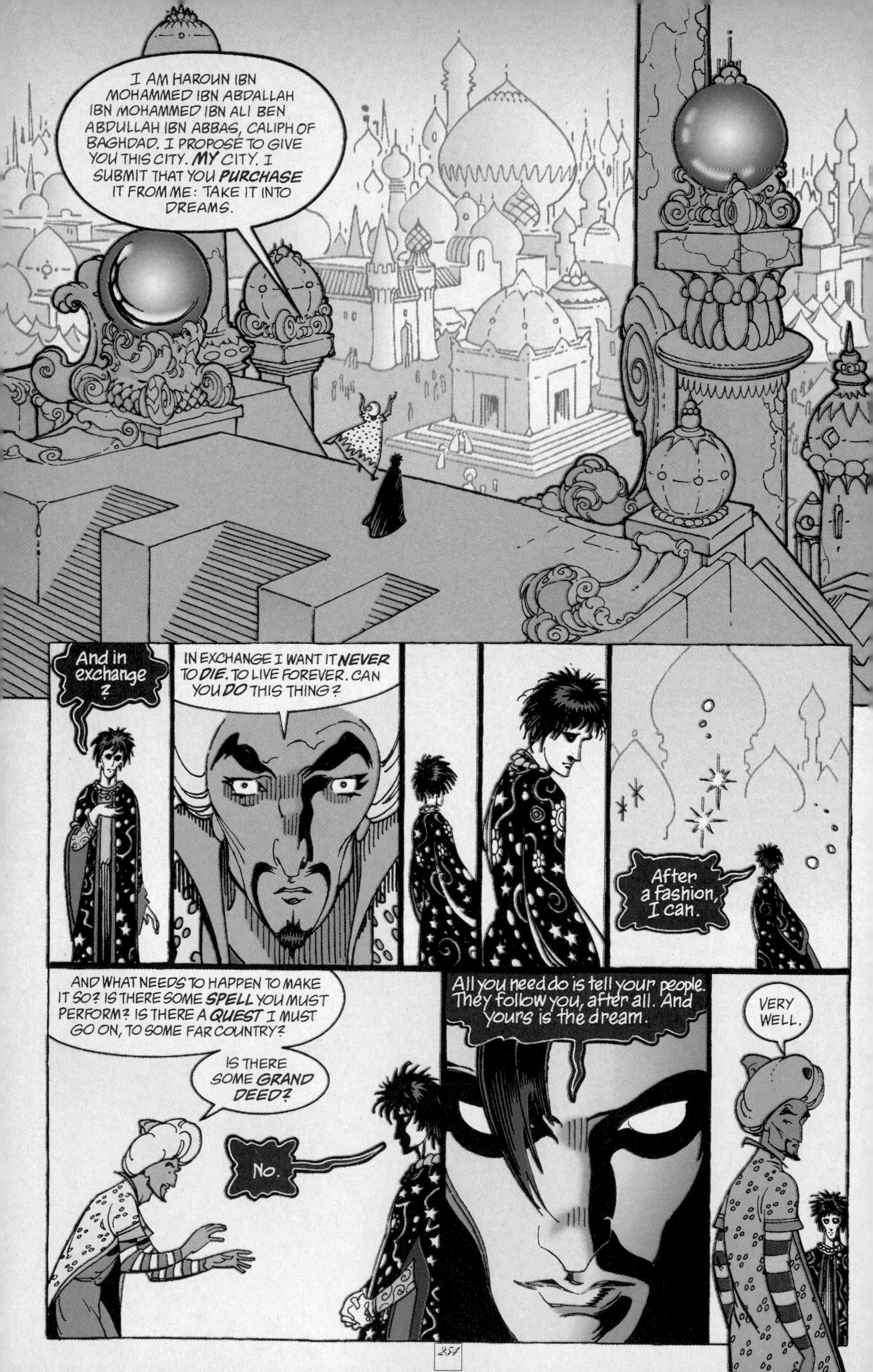
I AM HAROUN IBN MOHAMMED IBN ABDALLAH IBN MOHAMMED IBN ALI BEN ABDULLAH IBN ABBAS, CALIPH OF BAGHDAD. I PROPOSE TO GIVE YOU THIS CITY. MY CITY. I SUBMIT THAT YOU PURCHASE IT FROM ME: TAKE IT INTO DREAMS.
And in exchange?
IN EXCHANGE I WANT IT NEVER TO DIE. TO LIVE FOREVER. CAN YOU DO THIS THING?
After a fashion, I can.
AND WHAT NEEDS TO HAPPEN TO MAKE IT SO? IS THERE SOME SPELL YOU MUST PERFORM? IS THERE A QUEST I MUST GO ON, TO SOME FAR COUNTRY?
IS THERE SOME GRAND DEED?
No.
All you need do is tell your people. They follow you, after all. And yours is the dream.
VERY WELL.

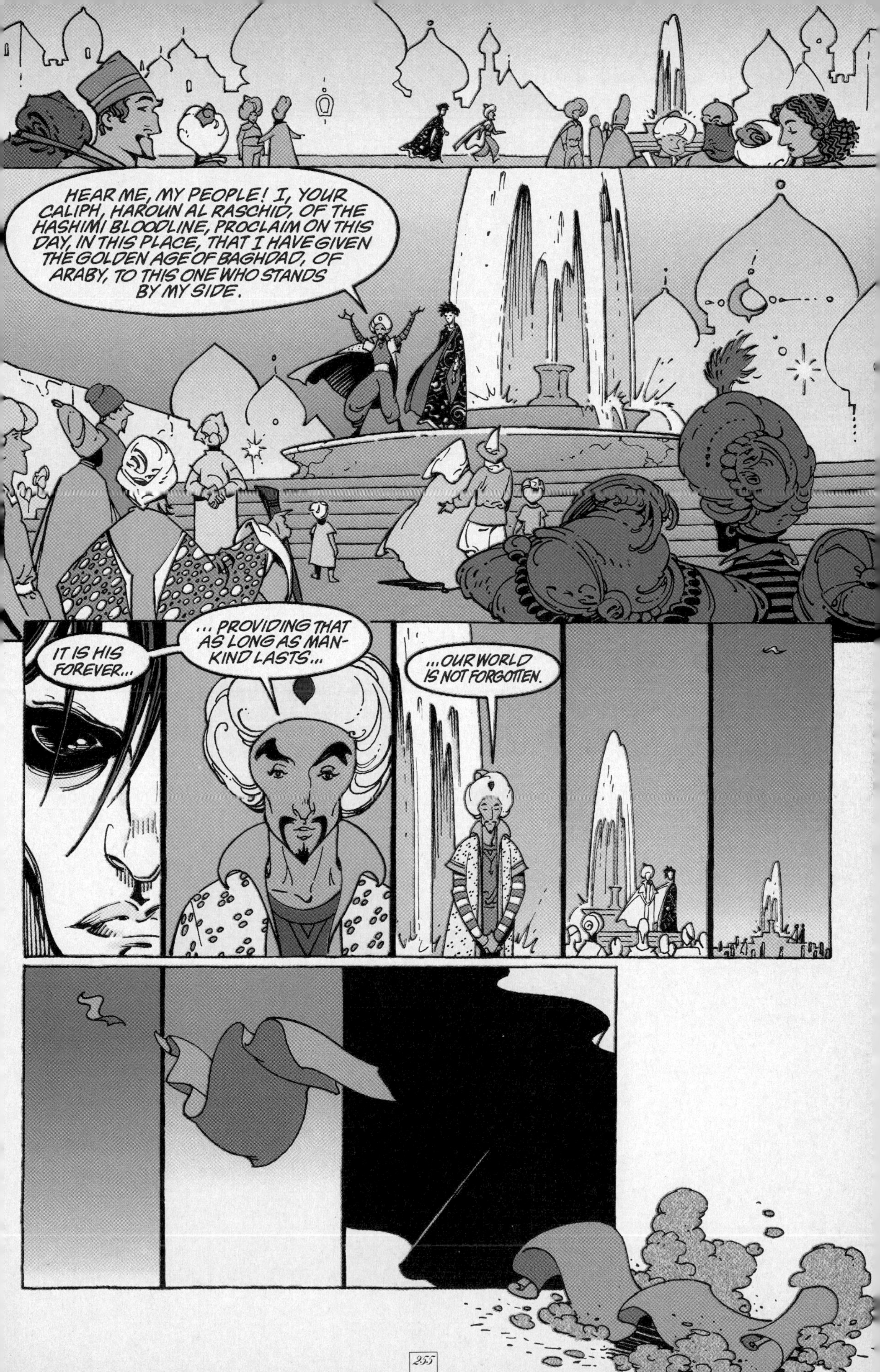
HEAR ME, MY PEOPLE! I, YOUR CALIPH, HAROUN AL RASCHID, OF THE HASHIMI BLOODLINE, PROCLAIM ON THIS DAY, IN THIS PLACE, THAT I HAVE GIVEN THE GOLDEN AGE OF BAGHDAD, OF ARABY, TO THIS ONE WHO STANDS BY MY SIDE.
IT IS HIS FOREVER...
... PROVIDING THAT AS LONG AS MAN-KIND LASTS...
...OUR WORLD IS NOT FORGOTTEN.

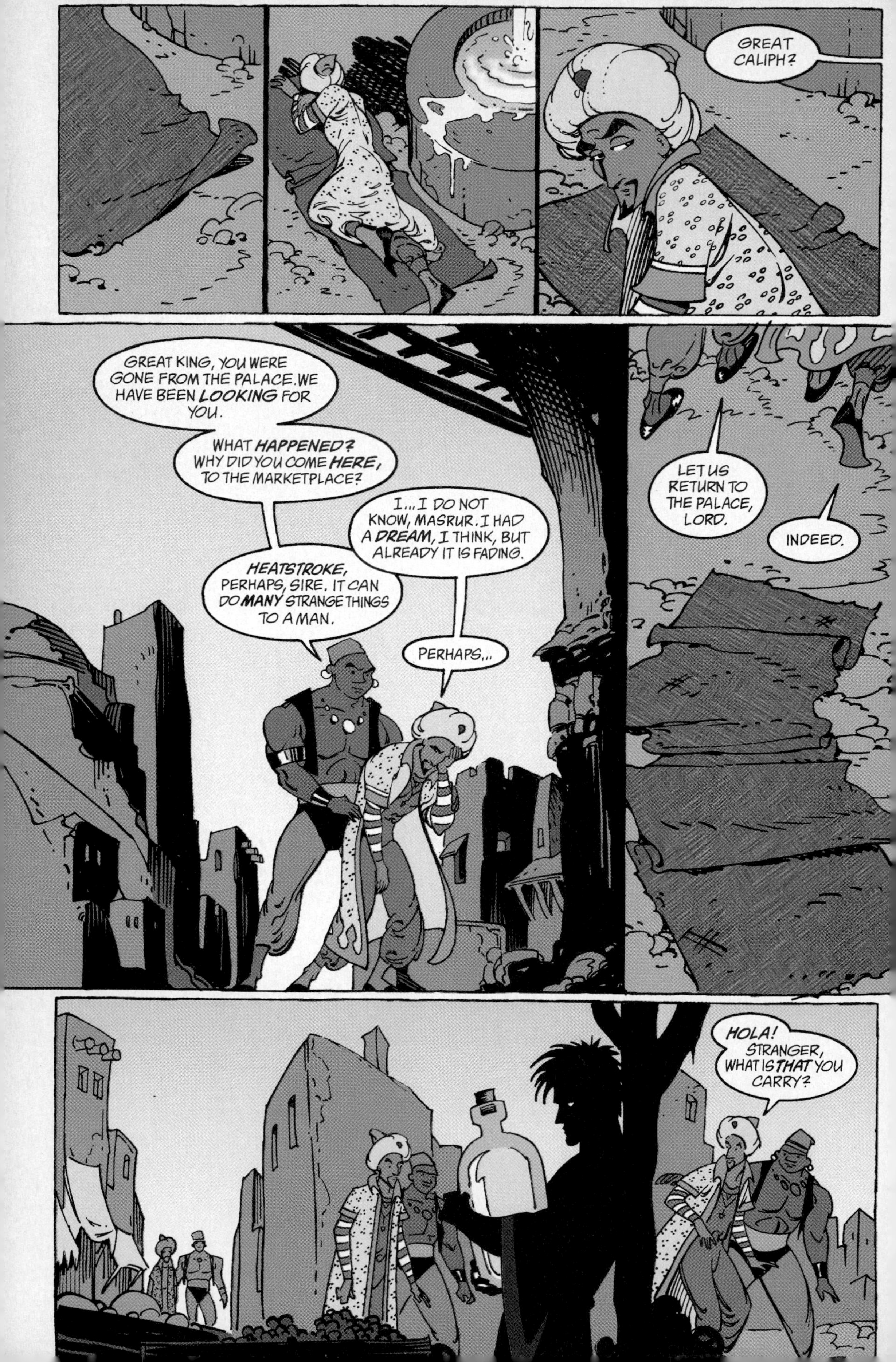
GREAT CALIPH?
GREAT KING, YOU WERE GONE FROM THE PALACE. WE HAVE BEEN LOOKING FOR YOU.
WHAT HAPPENED? WHY DID YOU COME HERE, TO THE MARKETPLACE?
I... I DO NOT KNOW, MASRUR. I HAD A DREAM, I THINK, BUT ALREADY IT IS FADING.
HEATSTROKE, PERHAPS, SIRE. IT CAN DO MANY STRANGE THINGS TO A MAN.
PERHAPS...
LET US RETURN TO THE PALACE, LORD.
INDEED.
HOLA! STRANGER, WHAT IS THAT YOU CARRY?

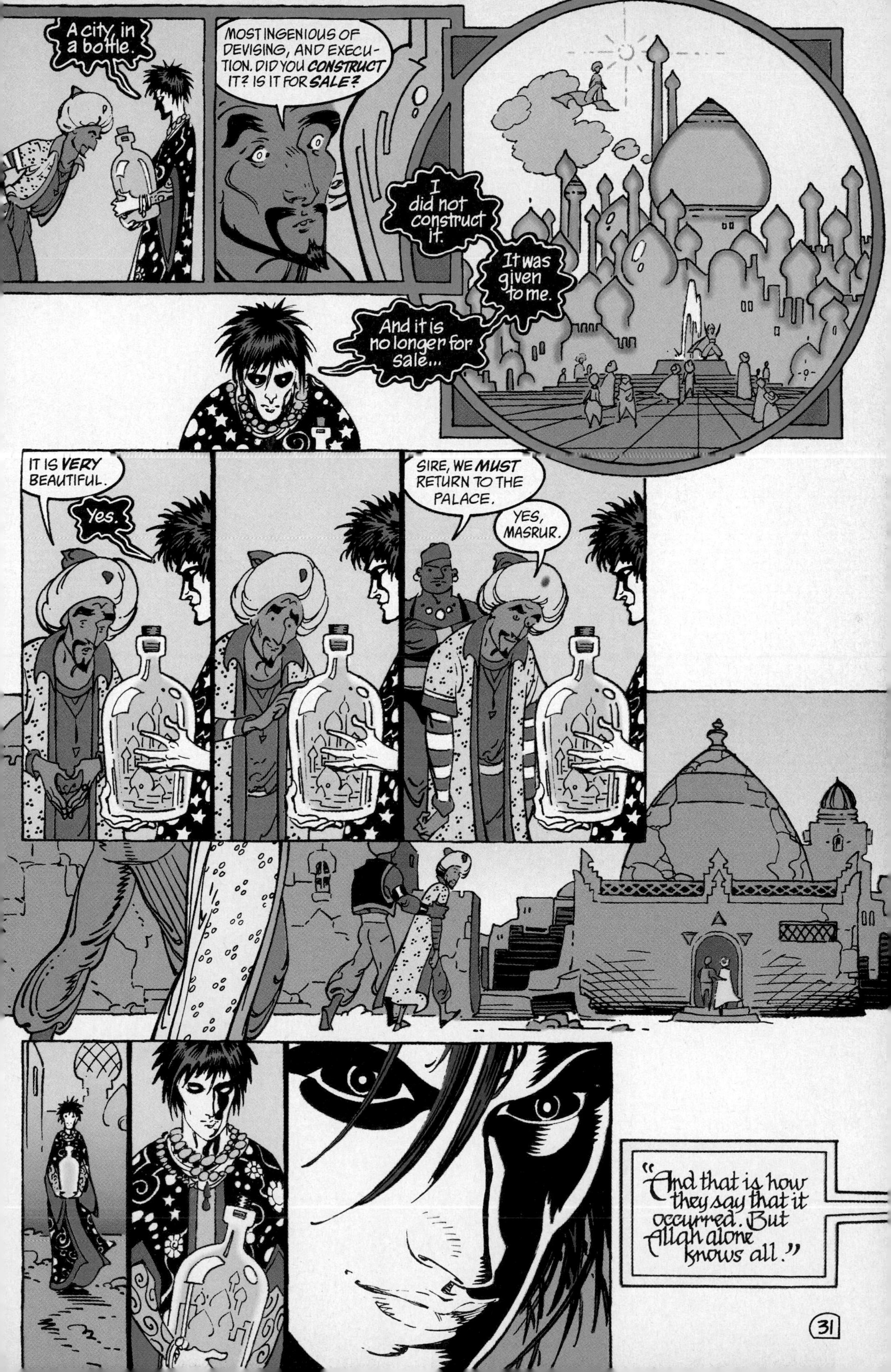
A city, in a bottle.
MOST INGENIOUS OF DEVISING, AND EXECUTION. DID YOU CONSTRUCT IT? IS IT FOR SALE?
I did not construct it.
It was given to me.
And it is no longer for sale...
IT IS VERY BEAUTIFUL.
Yes.
SIRE, WE MUST RETURN TO THE PALACE.
YES, MASRUR.
"And that is how they say that it occurred. But Allah alone knows all."
31

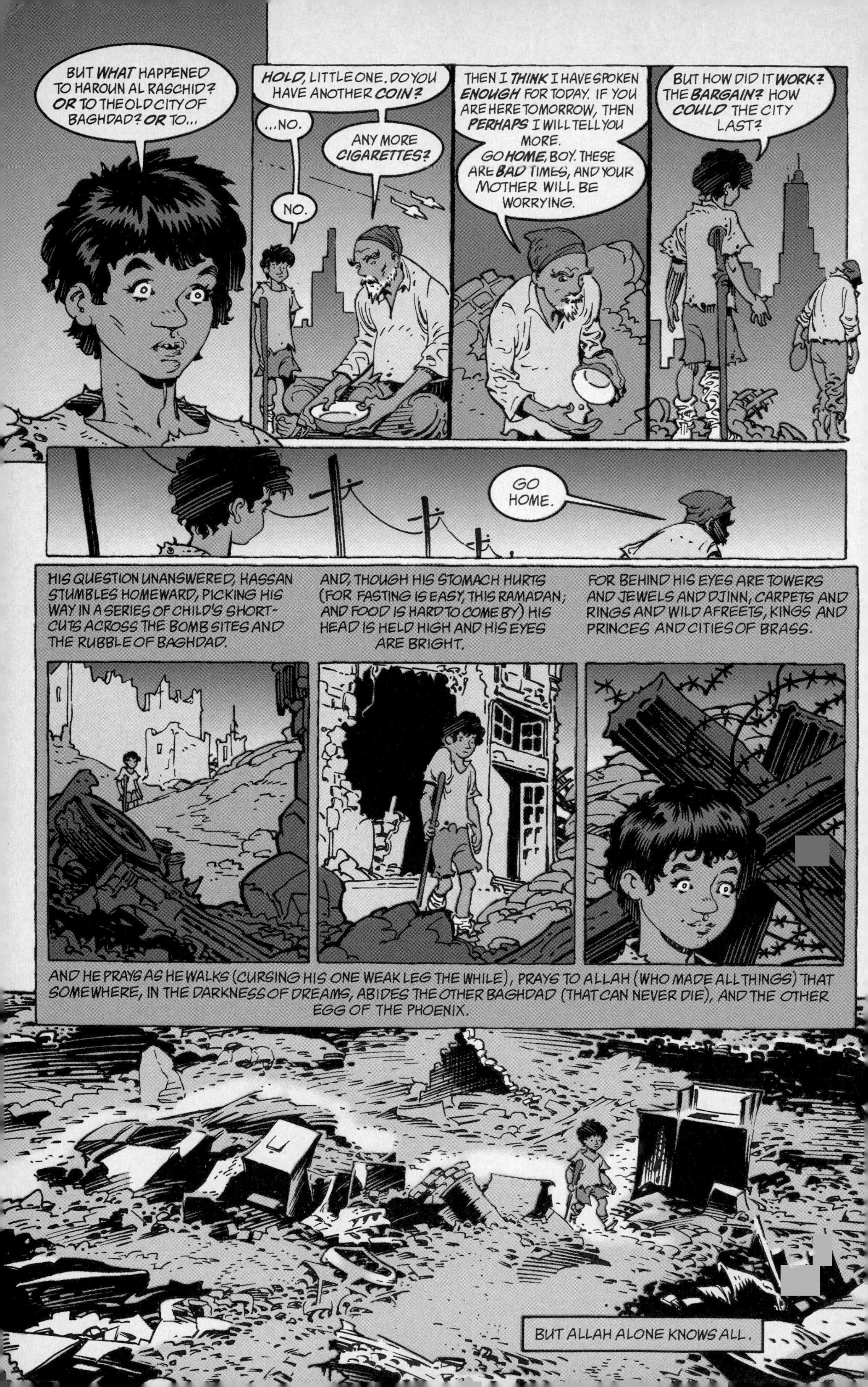
BUT WHAT HAPPENED TO HAROUN AL RASCHID? OR TO THE OLD CITY OF BAGHDAD? OR TO...
HOLD, LITTLE ONE. DO YOU HAVE ANOTHER COIN?
...NO.
ANY MORE CIGARETTES?
NO.
THEN I THINK I HAVE SPOKEN ENOUGH FOR TODAY. IF YOU ARE HERE TOMORROW, THEN PERHAPS I WILL TELL YOU MORE.
GO HOME, BOY. THESE ARE BAD TIMES, AND YOUR MOTHER WILL BE WORRYING.
BUT HOW DID IT WORK? THE BARGAIN? HOW COULD THE CITY LAST?
GO HOME.
HIS QUESTION UNANSWERED, HASSAN STUMBLES HOMEWARD, PICKING HIS WAY IN A SERIES OF CHILD'S SHORT-CUTS ACROSS THE BOMB SITES AND THE RUBBLE OF BAGHDAD.
AND, THOUGH HIS STOMACH HURTS (FOR FASTING IS EASY, THIS RAMADAN; AND FOOD IS HARD TO COME BY) HIS HEAD IS HELD HIGH AND HIS EYES ARE BRIGHT.
FOR BEHIND HIS EYES ARE TOWERS AND JEWELS AND DJINN, CARPETS AND RINGS AND WILD AFREETS, KINGS AND PRINCES AND CITIES OF BRASS.
AND HE PRAYS AS HE WALKS (CURSING HIS ONE WEAK LEG THE WHILE), PRAYS TO ALLAH (WHO MADE ALL THINGS) THAT SOMEWHERE, IN THE DARKNESS OF DREAMS, ABIDES THE OTHER BAGHDAD (THAT CAN NEVER DIE), AND THE OTHER EGG OF THE PHOENIX.
BUT ALLAH ALONE KNOWS ALL.

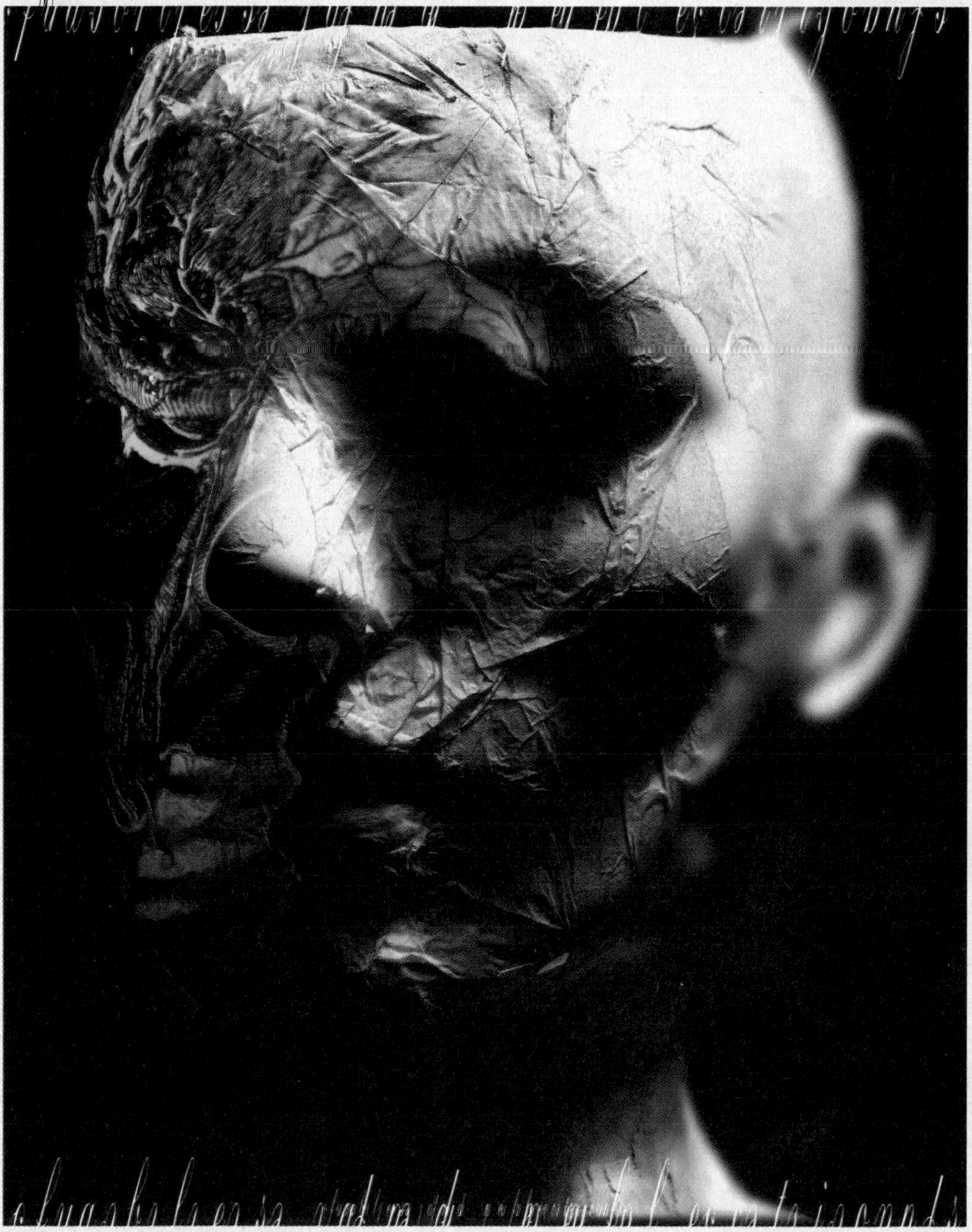

Biographies

This is Neil Gaiman. You shouldn't believe a word he says.

This is Gene Wolfe, lover, explorer, gourmet.

Kent Williams. Don't bother introducing me. I'm not that interesting.

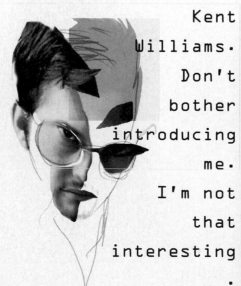

Sherilyn van Valkenburgh

And I'm married to him.

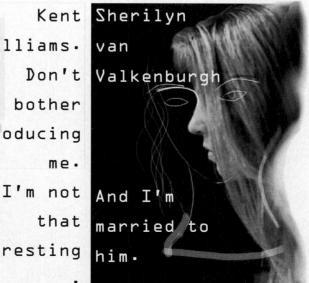

Shawn McManus

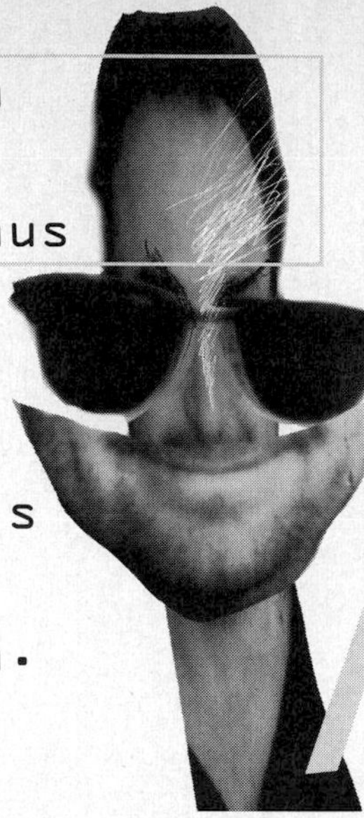

Here's Shawn.

This is Stan Woch. He only **looks** like Charles Manson.

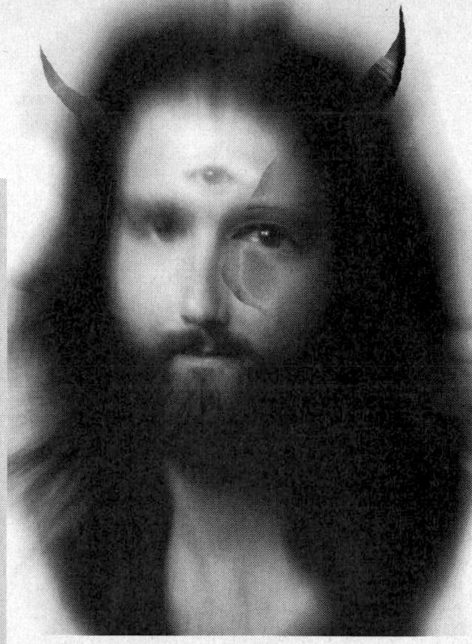

Hi, (insert woman's name here)... I'd like you to meet this really great guy, Dick Giordano! He's charming, generous **and** a great lover--(for an old guy!)

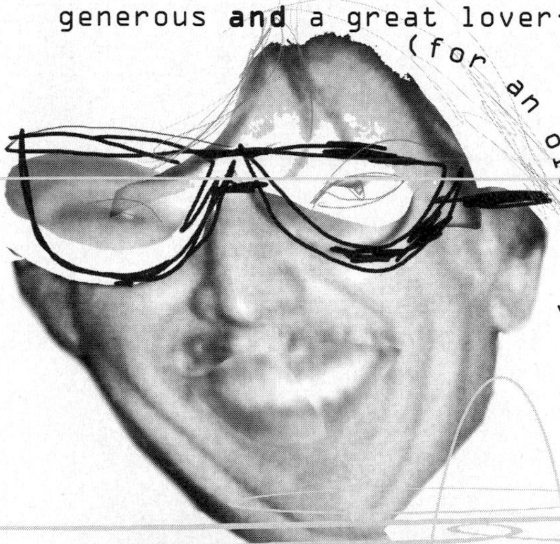

Hi, I'm Duncan. Let me take your coat. If you'd like to wait in the bar, I'll come get you when your table's ready.

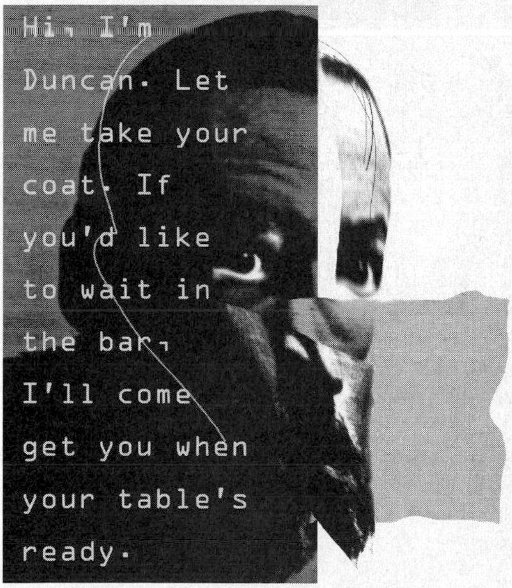

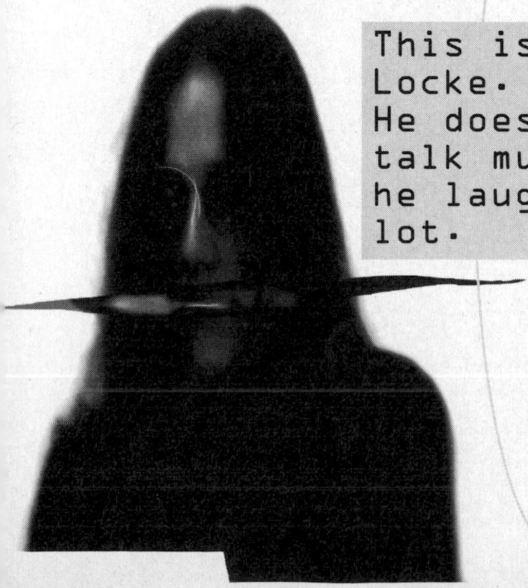

This is Vince Locke. He doesn't talk much but he laughs a lot.

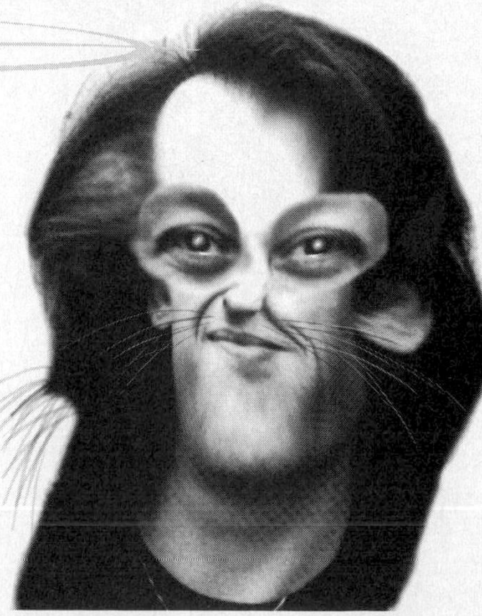

This is Bryan Talbot. He herds rats for fun and profit.

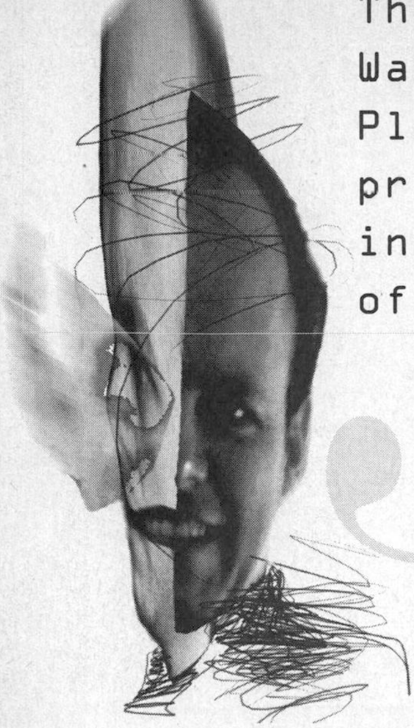

This is John Watkiss. Platonist, private investigator of the past.

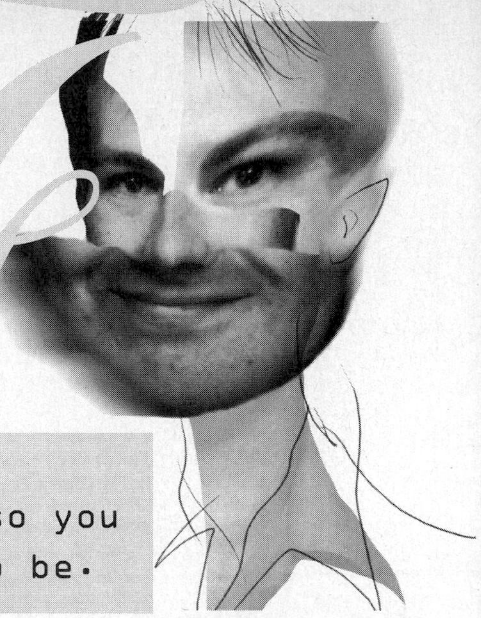

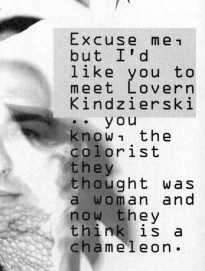

This is Mark Buckingham, so you don't have to be.

This is Jill Thompson, a fantastic artist, actress and comedienne, who in her spare time is working on the Universal Field Theory with Stephen Hawking.

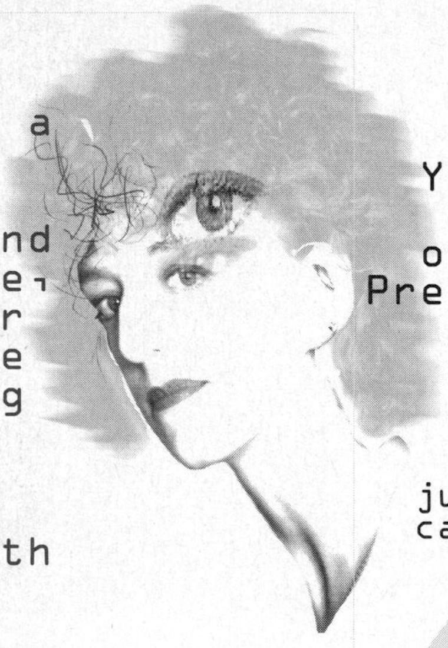

I'm P. Craig Russell.

You can call me an opera-loving Pre-Raphaelite ...

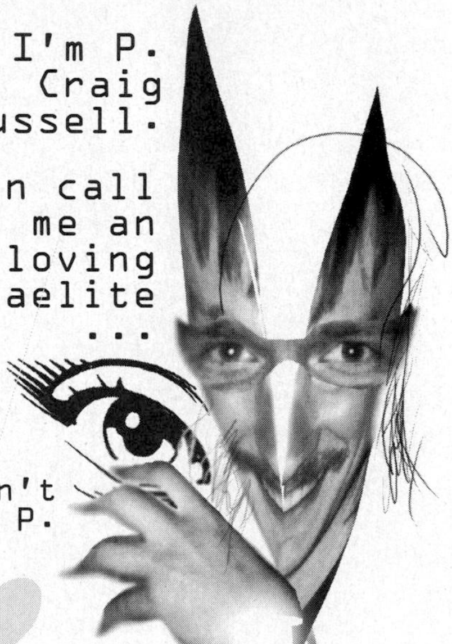

just don't call me P.

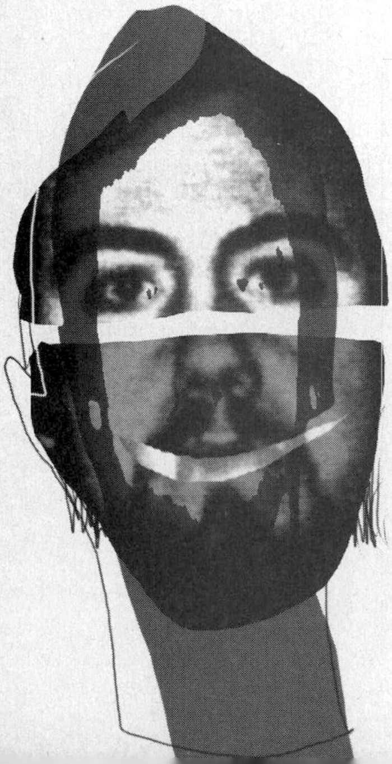

This is Danny Vozzo. He's the guy who hand-paints all the Ms on the green M&Ms.

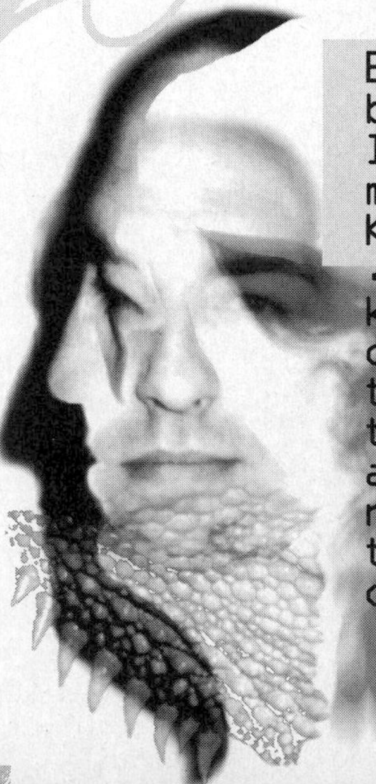

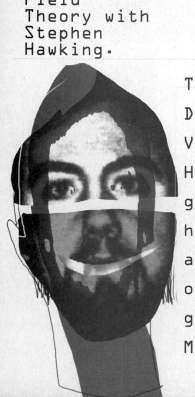

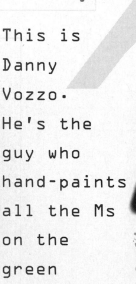

Excuse me, but I'd like you to meet Lovern Kindzierski .. you know, the colorist they thought was a woman and now they think is a chameleon.

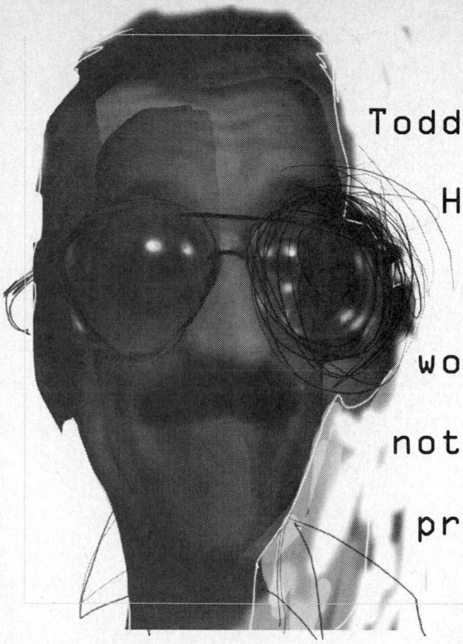

This is Todd Klein. He knows the big words but not how to pronounce them.

This is Karen Berger, who can see into the souls of the unwary.

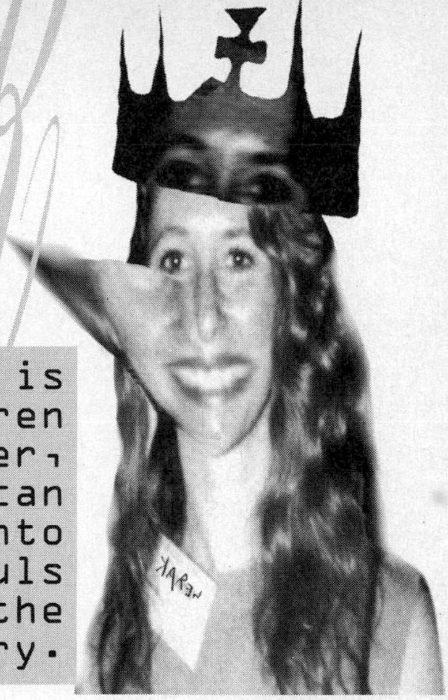

This is Alisa Kwitney, and the rest is all lies.

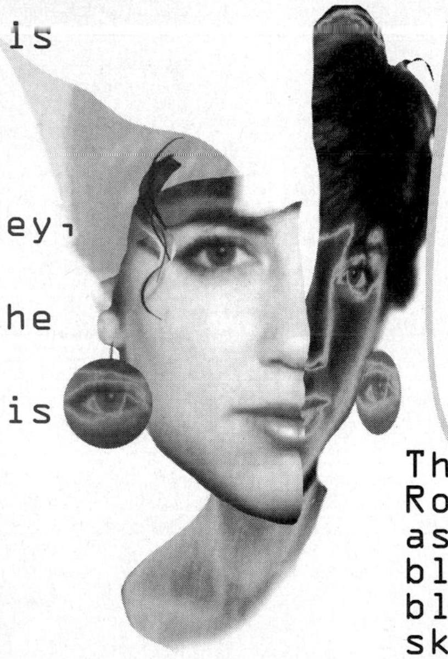

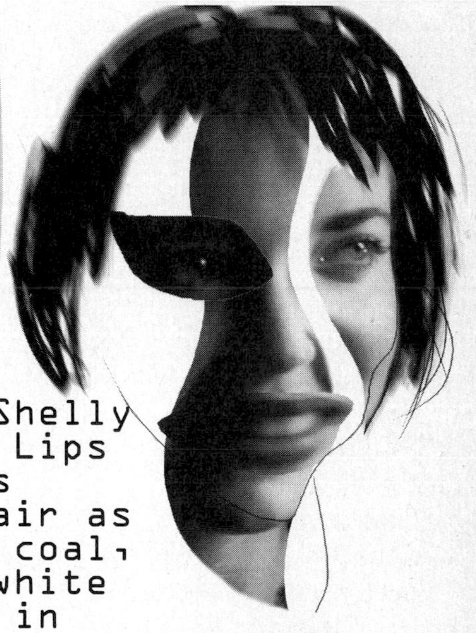

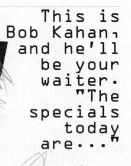

This is Shelly Roeberg. Lips as red as blood, hair as black as coal, skin as white as snow, in bells and plats.

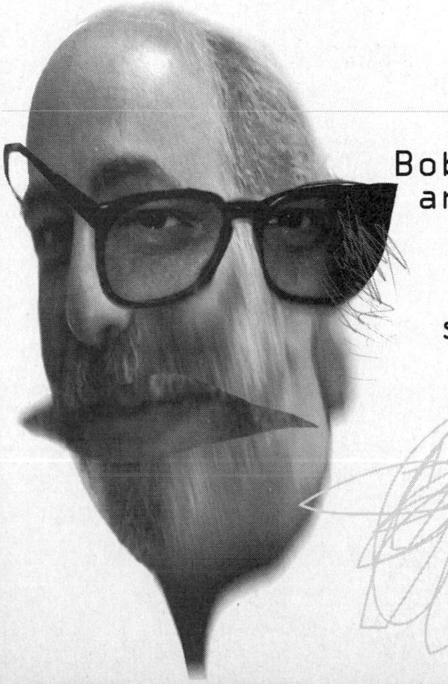

This is Bob Kahan, and he'll be your waiter. "The specials today are..."

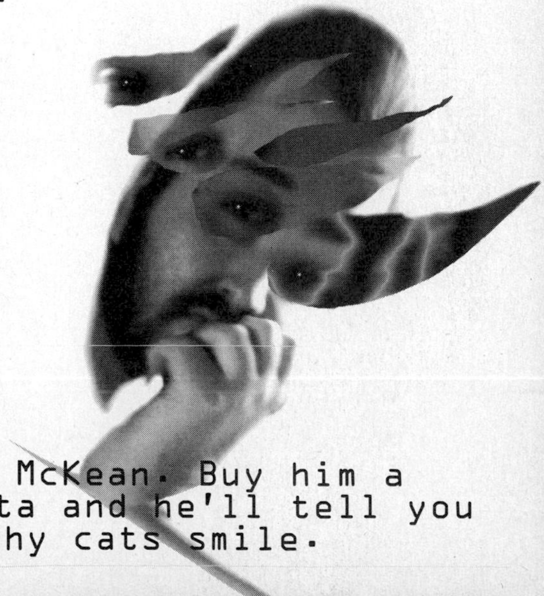

Dave McKean. Buy him a Margarita and he'll tell you why cats smile.

SANDMAN
fables and reflections

Published by DC Comics.

DC Comics
1700 Broadway
New York, NY 10019

A Warner Bros. Entertainment Company

Printed in Canada.

Eighth Printing.

ISBN: 1-56389-105-0

dave mckean
COVER & PUBLICATION DESIGN